# Toad Data Point v5.0 for End Users Course Guide

By Dan Hotka

Dan Hotka
Author/Instructor/Oracle Expert
CEO
www.DanHotka.com
Dan@DanHotka.com

From the Desk of Dan Hotka:

Thank you for attending this course on Toad Data Point. I have trained thousands of IT and power users on the various aspects of the popular Toad and Toad Data Point tools. I offer Toad in many of my courses including Intro to SQL, Intro to PL/SQL and my SQL Statement and Advanced Oracle Tuning courses.

I am sure you will find many of the tips and techniques learned in this course to be useful in your day-to-day work with business analysis needs.

Dan Hotka
Author/Instructor/Oracle Expert
www.DanHotka.com
Dan@DanHotka.com

Dan Hotka is a Training Specialist and an Oracle ACE Director Alumni (recognized Oracle Expert by Oracle Corp) who has over 40 years in the computer industry, over 35 years of experience with Oracle products. His experience with the Oracle RDBMS dates back to the Oracle V4.0 days. Dan enjoys sharing his knowledge of the Oracle RDBMS. Dan is well-published with 12 Oracle books and well over 200 published articles. He is frequently published in Oracle trade journals, regularly blogs, and speaks at Oracle conferences and user groups around the world.

Last Updated: 6/2018

## Table of Contents

# Toad Data Point Introduction and Setup

## Introduction

Toad was originally developed to run in early Windows environments as a click and shoot SQL processing environment. Features and short cuts were added as needed and as requested by the shareware user base. Toad grew thru the 1990's and was adapted to just data analysis/data extracts and this tool became Toad Data Point. Toad Data Point has many of the same easy coding features as Toad but has been adapted to about any data store. Items created in Toad Data Point can easily be shared with others using Toad Intelligence Central.

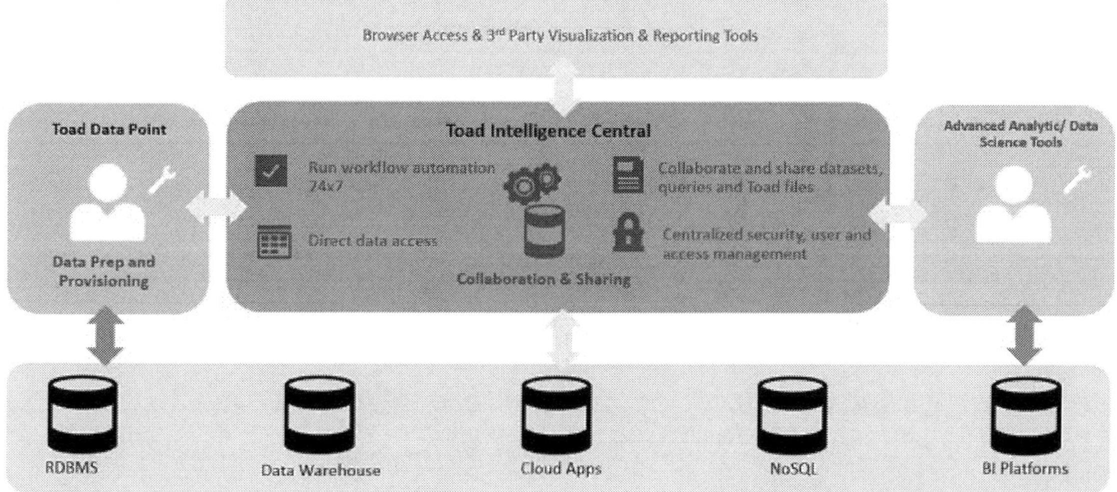


Toad™ Intelligence Central enables enterprise users to be far more productive with their tools including Toad Data Point by centralizing automation workflows, accessing data directly, collaborating and sharing on datasets, queries and Toad files and providing a secure and established way to manage your data sprawl.

- AUTOMATE - Toad users can schedule the regular automated execution of Toad Data Point automation scripts on Toad Intelligence Central.
- ACCESS - Toad users can access Toad files and basic data files published to Toad Intelligence Central that have been shared with them. An additional data connectivity license extends Toad Intelligence Central to work across a wide range of data stores including relational database models, data warehouses, No SQL and Business Intelligence data sources like OBIEE and SAP®.
- SHARE - Objects can be shared amongst users and groups and organized collectively in a familiar folder structure, assigned tags and given a description for easy search retrieval. Administration of users and groups can be managed locally or users and groups can be imported from Active Directory®.
- SECURE - Toad Intelligence Central provides a centrally managed, secure, stable and accessible system.

Distributions of Toad Intelligence Central include a Web Server and Admin Console for administrative and general user access. In addition, Toad Data Point and other collaborative Toad products can directly access Toad Intelligence Central (TIC). Data on Toad Intelligence Central can be accessed via a third party product such as Tableau for further data processing and visualization. The Toad Data Point Advanced Features 1-day hands on work shop covers how to configure and administrate this sharing environment.

## Installation and initial setup

Installation is easy. Download the product and answer the simple question if you are running in a 32 bit or 64 bit computing environment. Windows 10 is a 64 bit environment.

***Tip*** The instructor is running 32bit Toad DP on Windows 10 vmware environment against 32bit Office 2007 and Oracle12.2. He has to use Toad DP 32bit to access the MS Office products from within Toad DP.

### Supported Platforms

- **Toad Data Point**
  - Windows Server® 2008 (32-bit or 64-bit)
  - Windows Server® 2012
  - Windows Server® 2012 R2
  - Windows® 7 (32-bit or 64-bit)
  - Windows® 8 (32-bit and 64-bit)
  - Windows® 8.1 (32-bit and 64-bit)
  - Windows® 10
  - .Net 4.5
  - Oracle Client
  - DB2 Client
  - Terradata .net
- **Toad Intelligence Central**
  - Windows 10
  - Windows 8.1
  - Windows 7 SP2
  - Windows Server 2012
  - Windows Server 2008 r2

**See release notes for complete list and versions** www.*DanHotka*.com

See page 166 of the Toad DP v5 Release and Installation Notes (Appendix 1) for more supported platforms.

## Supported Databases

- Toad Data Point
  - Oracle 9i+
  - DB2 9+
  - SQL Server 2005+
  - MySQL 4.5+
  - SAP (see release notes)
  - Teradata 12+
  - Access 2003+
  - Excel 2003+
  - ODBC v3.0 to many, including Ingress, Postgress, NoSQL
- Toad Intelligence Central
  - ODBC compliant databases
  - DB2
  - MySQL
  - Oracle
  - SQL Azure
  - SQL Server
  - Sybase
  - Teradata

**See release notes for complete list and versions** www.*DanHotka*.com

## Supported Data Sources

- Toad Data Point
  - SAP
  - Oracle BI Extended Edition
  - Sales Force
  - SQL Server Analysis Services
  - Google Analytics
  - Azure DataMart
  - Share Point
  - NoSQL
  - Apache Hbase
  - Apache Hive
  - MongoDB
- Toad Intelligence Central
  - Dell Boomi
  - Azure DataMarket
  - Google Analytics
  - Oracle BI Extended Edition
  - SAP
  - Sales Force
  - Share Point
  - Hive

**See release notes for complete list and versions** www.*DanHotka*.com

# Toad Data Point Versions

- **Toad DP V4.1**
  - Works best with Intelligence Central v3.2
- **Toad DP V4.2 – Toad DP 4.3**
  - Works best with Intelligence Central v3.3
- **Toad DP 4.3+ release #s sync with TIC now**
- **Toad DP Viewer**
  - Used to view Toad DP files
  - No editing of anything is allowed

- **Intelligence Central**
  - Supports Automation
  - Supports data sharing
  - Supports automation
  - Supports publishing
    - Downloadable via web
- **Intelligence Central Community Edition**
  - Free
    - Select 'no' to license request on install
  - Sharing of Toad DP files
  - Supports Automation

Click Here **to review Product Matrix** www.*DanHotka*.com

You can always download the current release of Data Point and Intelligence Central and there will be an upgrade feature. This feature allows you to maintain all of your connections and work history and licensing.

There is a Data Point viewer that just allows for reports to be viewed but nothing to be created or changed.

Depending on you save your documents, you may not need any Toad DP products at all!

Toad DP v4.3+ synchronized release numbers with the associated Toad Intelligence Central. This makes life easier for everyone.

The author considers Intelligence Central a key component of Data Point and it should be installed in either of its versions. The purchased version allows for considerable additional sharing of items and ease of download from any web browser. The free (community edition) allows for some sharing. Both allow for automation which is key for your workflows.

## Toad DP Intro & Setup Topics

- **Featured Content/Community News**
- **Built in Web Browser**
- **Toad DP Interface**
  - Menu bars
  - Ribbon bars
  - Key strokes
  - Right mouse click

www.DanHotka.com

## Toad Data Point

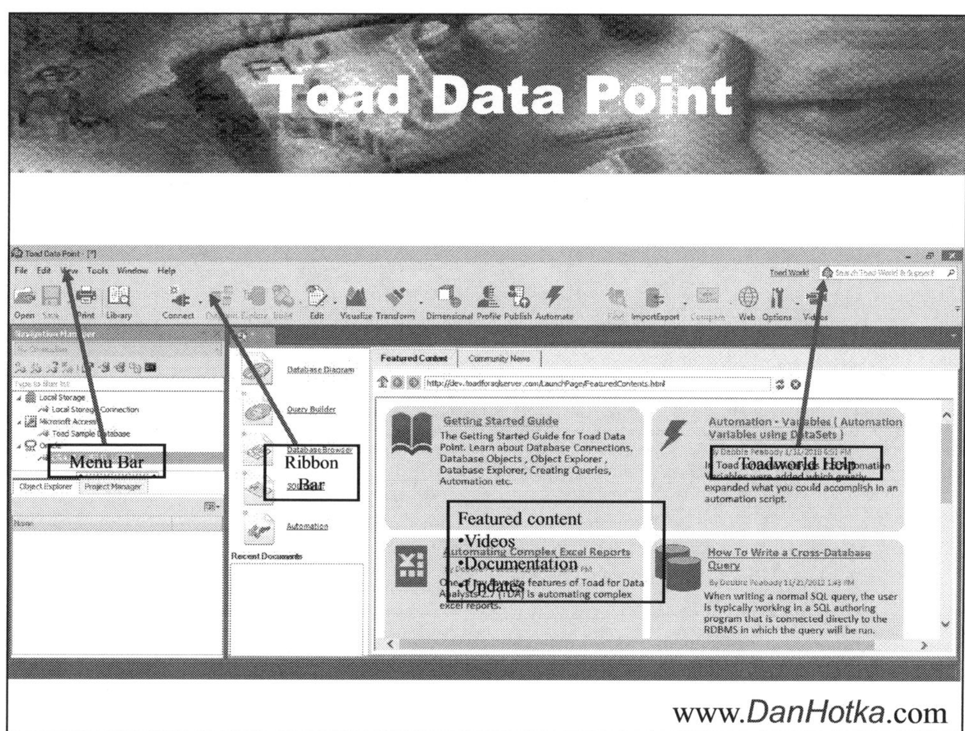


www.DanHotka.com

When Toad DP starts up, the featured content, useful items featured on Toadworld will appear. You can search for specific Toad DP articles using the Toad world box in the upper right hand corner. This featured area will disappear automatically once you are connected to a data source.

The Community News tab is a running forum of Toad DP users…the questions and answers as they appear in Toadworld.

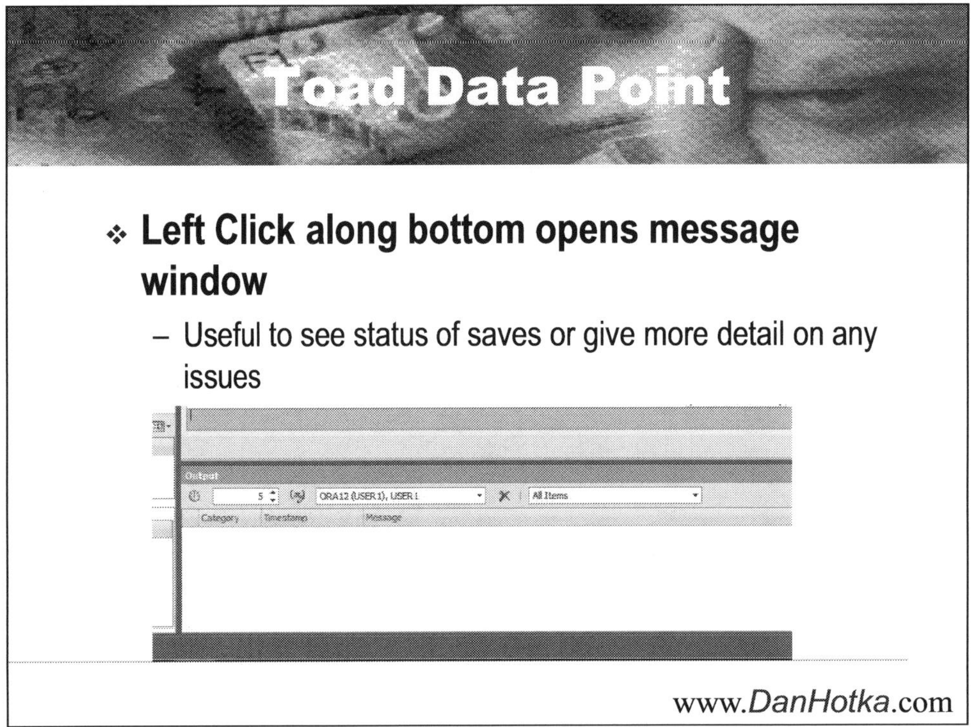


There are about 3 ways to do about anything in Toad DP:

- Menu Bar
- Ribbon Bar
- Keystroke

Then there are all kinds of options with the right-mouse click. Right click on about anything for additional options for that particular feature.

## Getting Connected

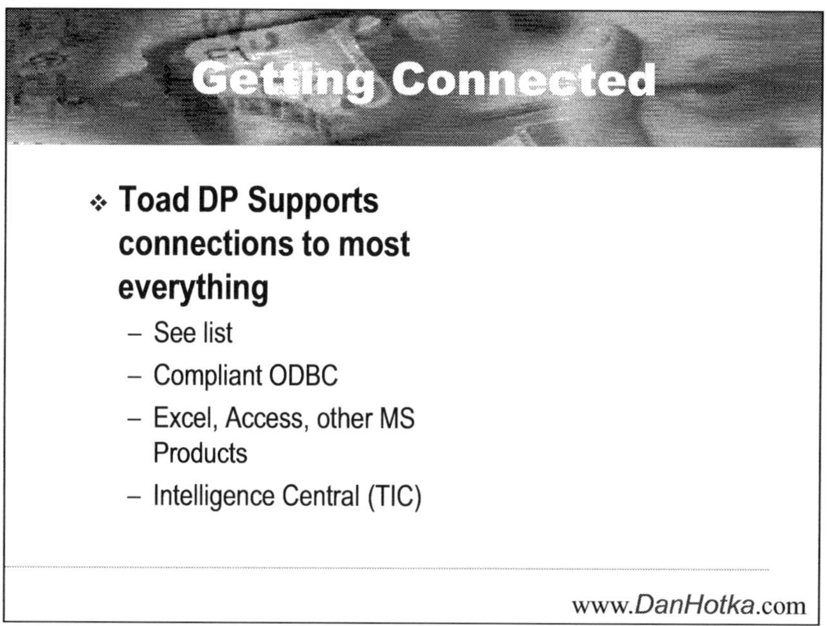


Toad DP allows connections to most any data store.

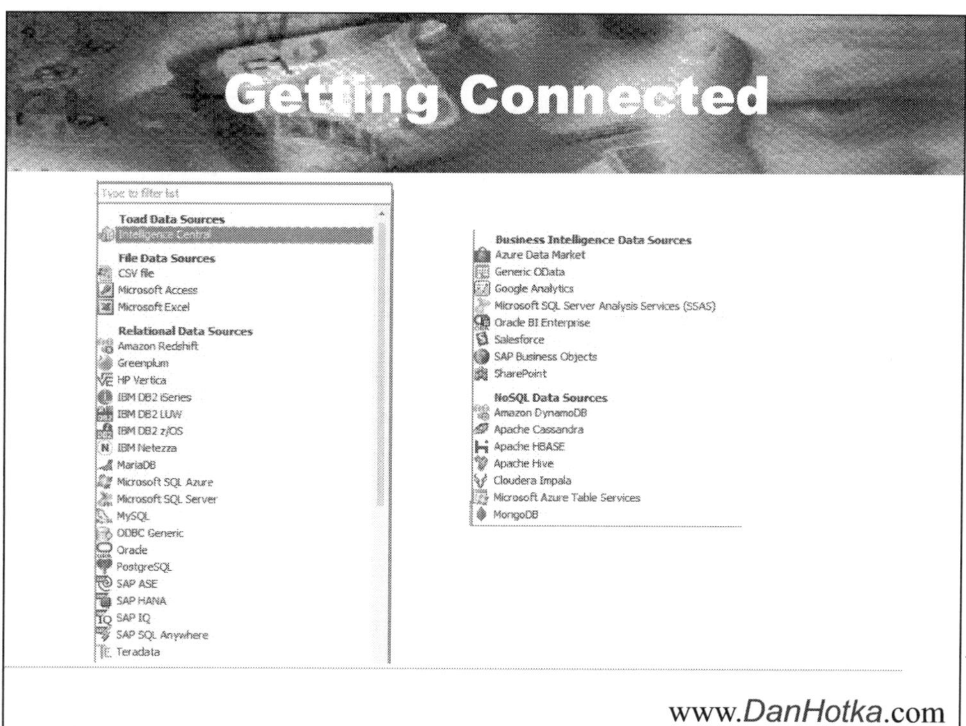

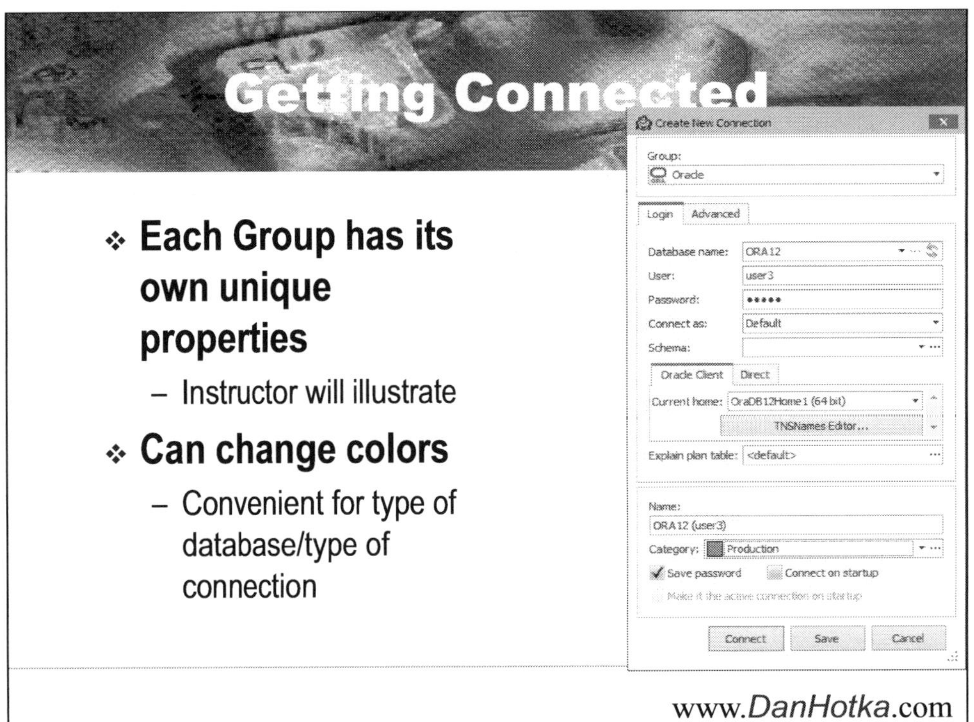


Each type of data store has its own unique properties. The instructor will show some of the other data stores perhaps.

***Note*** being an Oracle Expert, the Instructor tends to run the course using Oracle database connections. Once we get connected, the remainder of the tool has little to do with the database. This is one of the real powers that Toad DP brings to your data world, the ability to hide the complexities of each database type.

The Login connection information is rather straight forward for each database type. Check with your support staff, or, another person in your group if you need the correct connection information.

***Tip*** Many shops/departments have an existing list of the connections you might need. Simply copy from Toad Intelligence Central, or import from a shared folder on your lan.

Near the bottom, you can choose to save your passwords. They will be stored in an encrypted form.

The category part you might find of high interest! This will associate a color with your connection. Notice the red dot below on the User3 connection. You can also add more categories associated with more colors.

*****Tip***** The instructor uses red when using system type connections. You can use blue for production, green for test/QA, etc.

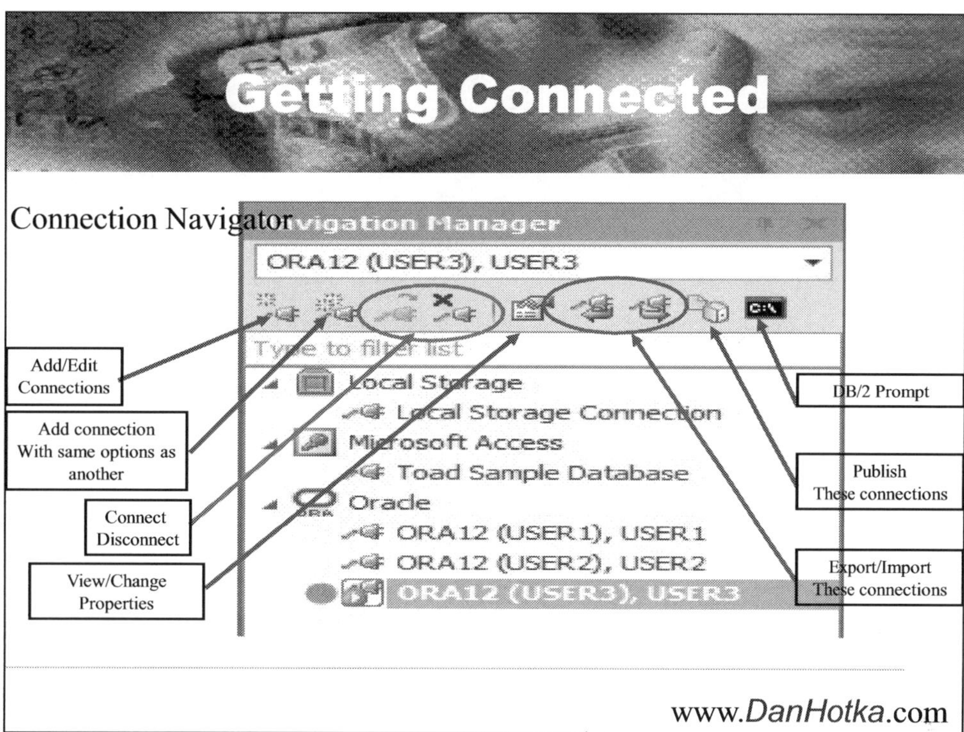
Getting Connected
Connection Navigator
Navigation Manager
ORA12 (USER3), USER3
Type to filter list
Local Storage
Local Storage Connection
Microsoft Access
Toad Sample Database
Oracle
ORA12 (USER1), USER1
ORA12 (USER2), USER2
ORA12 (USER3), USER3
Add/Edit Connections
Add connection With same options as another
Connect Disconnect
View/Change Properties
DB/2 Prompt
Publish These connections
Export/Import These connections
www.DanHotka.com

The Navigation Manager allows for the management of your connections. The first button allows you to create a new connection, brings up the above-mentioned dialog box. The next button is of HIGH interest to you! It allows you to make a connection and use the defaults/options already defined for another. This means you don't have to change file paths and other options you have already customized for your use of Toad DP and your data needs.

The next two buttons allows for you to connect/disconnect from the connection with the focus. You can also double-click on any connection to connect to the data store.

The connection properties button brings up the same panel but for an existing connection. This allows you to change the login attributes of an existing connection, say to change the category perhaps. This is also where you might change the password if it were to have changed.

The import/export buttons brings in/saves to…connections from a file on your system or on the shared lan. Passwords are maintained but are stored encrypted.

You can publish these connections to Toad Intelligence Central (TIC) for easy sharing with others in your work group.

The final button brings up a DB2 prompt for people connecting to an IBM DB2 data store.

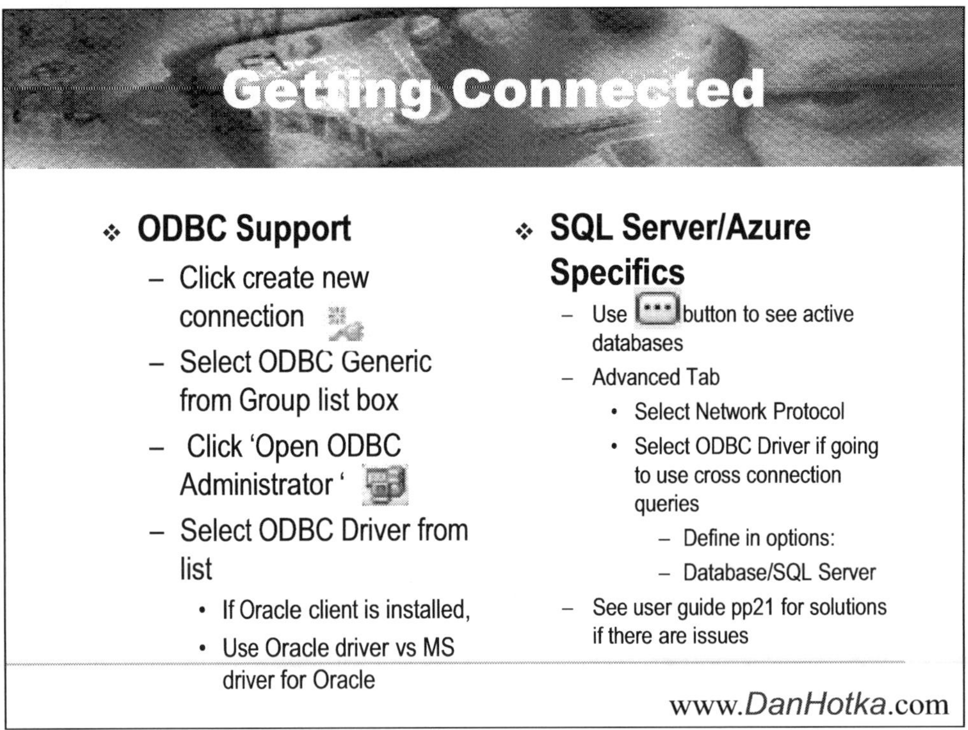
Getting Connected
ODBC Support
– Click create new connection
– Select ODBC Generic from Group list box
– Click 'Open ODBC Administrator'
– Select ODBC Driver from list
• If Oracle client is installed,
• Use Oracle driver vs MS driver for Oracle
SQL Server/Azure Specifics
– Use button to see active databases
– Advanced Tab
• Select Network Protocol
• Select ODBC Driver if going to use cross connection queries
– Define in options:
– Database/SQL Server
– See user guide pp21 for solutions if there are issues
www.DanHotka.com

## Getting Connected

- **Oracle using Oracle Client Software**
  - Can use LDAP
  - Uses TNS (host strings) to connect
    - Appears nicely in dropdown list
  - Supports more data types
  - Oracle9i+

- **Oracle not using Oracle Client Software**
  - Cannot use LDAP
  - Connects directly to DB using TCP/IP
  - Supports basic data types
  - Use for Oracle8i databases
  - Cannot use in cross connection query

www.DanHotka.com

## Getting Connected

- **Additional Help**
  - See Connect section of the user guide – pp 11
  - The user guide is accessible from the Help menu item

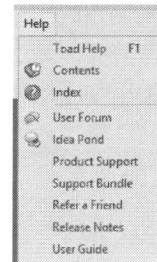

Help
Toad Help F1
Contents
Index
User Forum
Idea Pond
Product Support
Support Bundle
Refer a Friend
Release Notes
User Guide

www.DanHotka.com

# Getting Connected

- **Connection Manager**
  - Top drop down box shows all connections
  - Can color code your connections using the Category settings
    - Instructor uses 'Red' for system management type connections
    - Convenient as tabs pick up the color too
    - Helps greatly when doing multi connection data work
  - Drag to undock, use pin to auto hide

www.*DanHotka*.com

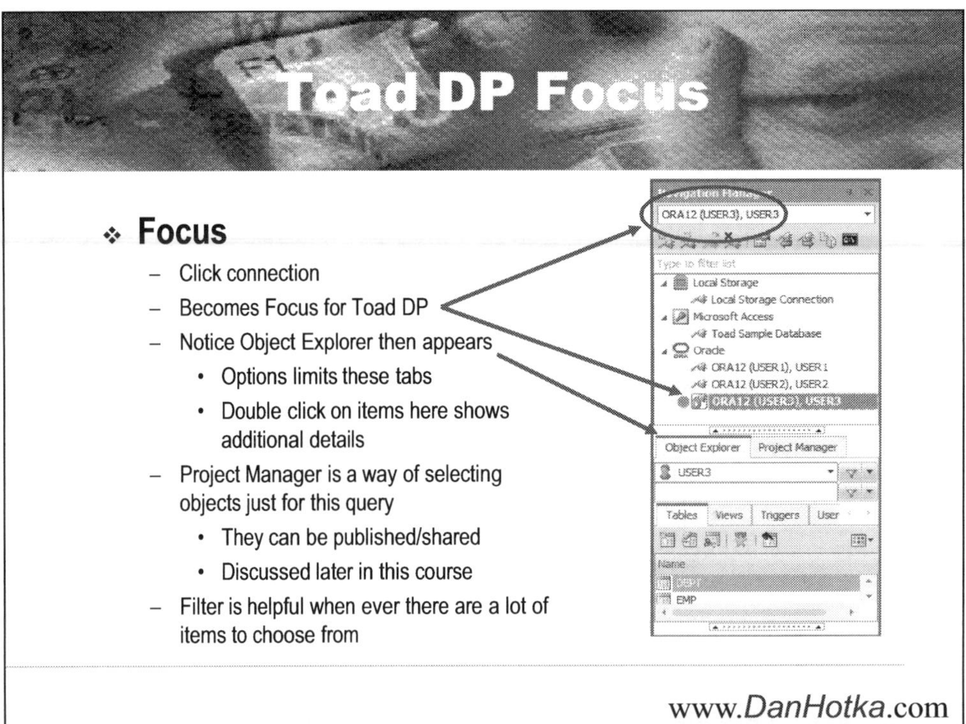
Toad DP Focus
Focus
Click connection
Becomes Focus for Toad DP
Notice Object Explorer then appears
Options limits these tabs
Double click on items here shows additional details
Project Manager is a way of selecting objects just for this query
They can be published/shared
Discussed later in this course
Filter is helpful when ever there are a lot of items to choose from
ORA12 (USER3), USER3
Local Storage
Local Storage Connection
Microsoft Access
Toad Sample Database
Oracle
ORA12 (USER1), USER1
ORA12 (USER2), USER2
ORA12 (USER3), USER3
Object Explorer
Project Manager
USER3
Tables
Views
Triggers
User
Name
DEPT
EMP
www.DanHotka.com

This is a term we will use throughout the course.

Single Click: moves/sets focus
Double Click: shows objects associated with the focus

Focus is the data store/connection that is currently highlighted in the Navigation Manager, and appears in the very top dropdown bar as well. You can change the focus of Toad DP by selecting one of these connections from the drop down bar or by single-clicking on the connection, highlighting it.

When you select a data store, the Object Explorer/Project Manager part of the Navigation Manager will appear. This will give you quick access to the objects you have permissions to use. When we get to Query Builder, you simply drag and drop these objects to the canvas… Also, you can double click on the objects and more information will appear about them, including the columns, 1000 rows of data, and other useful information (including the create script for those in the IT world perhaps).

The Local Storage is just that, a place to save queries, data, connections, and more to your computer. Anything saved will then be visible in the Object Explorer. There is an option to control the folder these items are stored in.

## Filtering

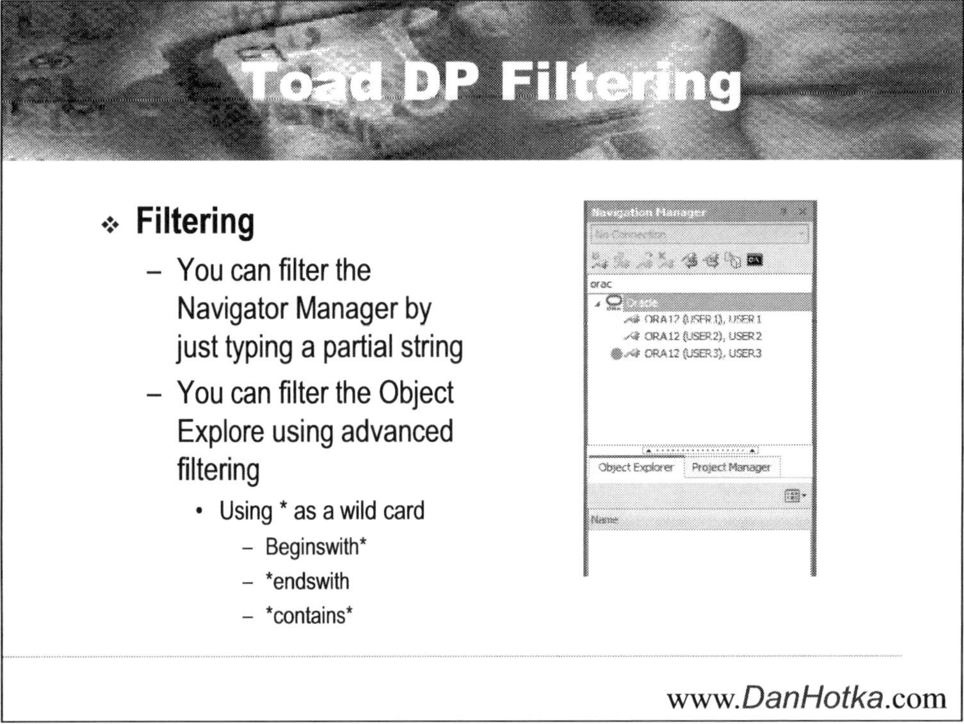

Toad DP Filtering
Filtering
– You can filter the Navigator Manager by just typing a partial string
– You can filter the Object Explore using advanced filtering
• Using * as a wild card
– Beginswith*
– *endswith
– *contains*
Navigation Manager
orac
Oracle
ORA12 (USER2), USER2
ORA12 (USER3), USER3
Object Explorer
Project Manager
Name
www.DanHotka.com


Filtering is a useful technique to limit the number of items visible. Filtering just doesn't display the items, they are not removed or altered in any way, simply not displayed.

The Navigation Manager has a filter box. It is just a simple text search. You can use it to help find/display certain connections or connection groups. The above examples shows a search on 'orac'…showing the Oracle group.

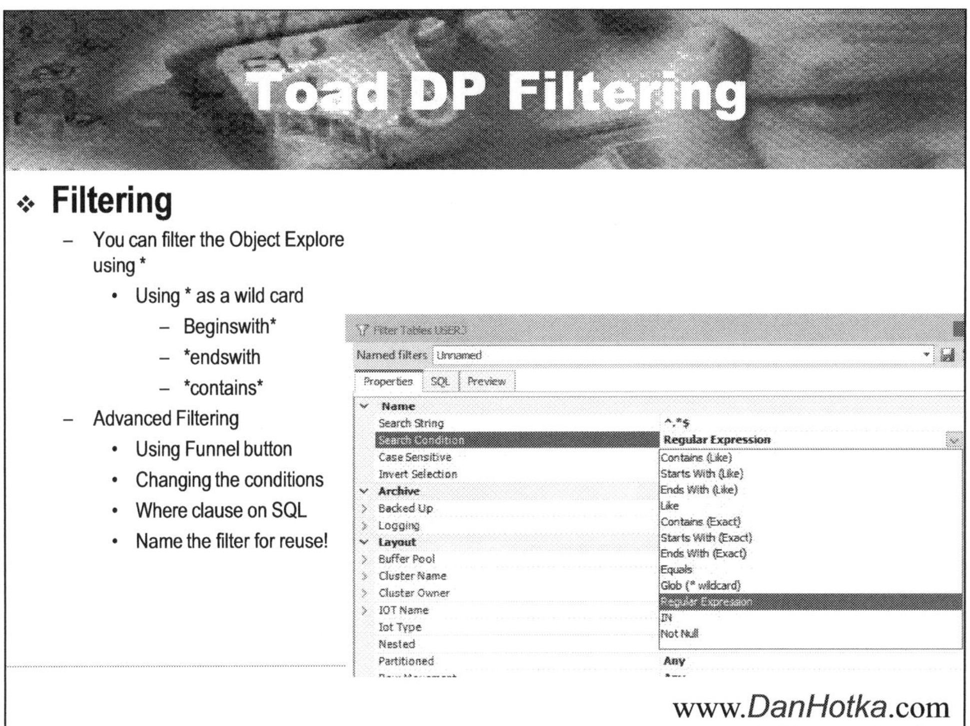


The Object Navigator has filtering too. This filtering can simply use '*' as a global search character. The above example shows where to place the asterisk and what you get back.

Advanced filtering is accessed by clicking the funnel button. This button allows for the search criteria to be changed and named. The named searches can easily be enabled using the drop down box next to the funnel.

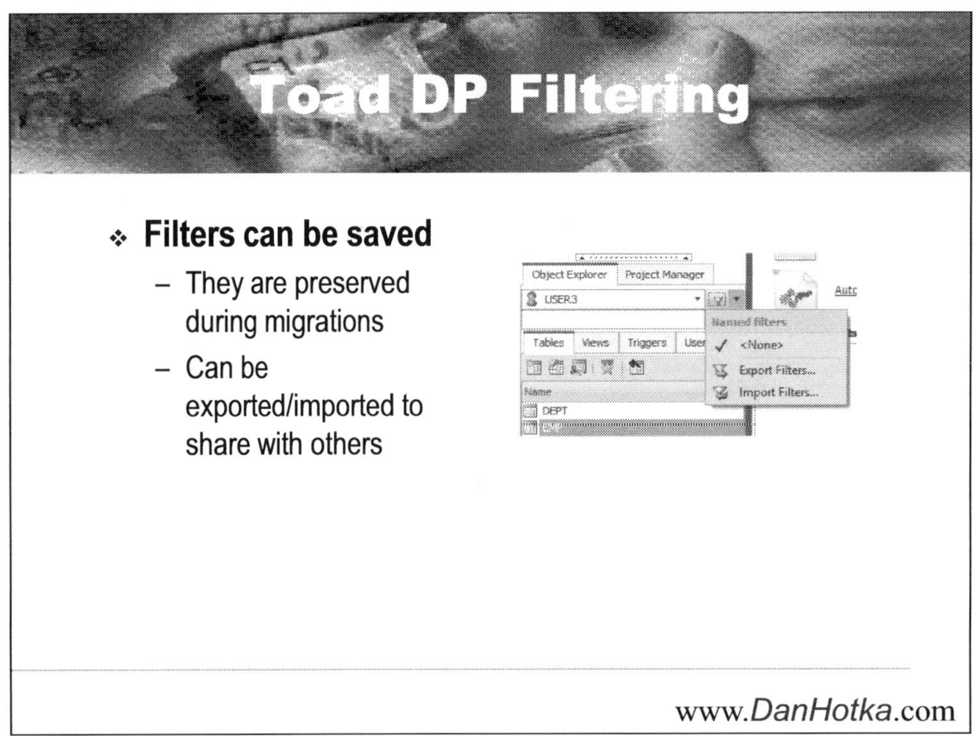
Toad DP Filtering
Filters can be saved
– They are preserved during migrations
– Can be exported/imported to share with others
Object Explorer
Project Manager
USER3
Named filters
<None>
Export Filters...
Import Filters...
Tables
Views
Triggers
Name
DEPT
www.DanHotka.com

You can also export these filters to be shared with others in your group. You can import filters created by others for your data analysis needs. These filters are preserved during Toad DP upgrades but to be safe, it's always best to export about anything you might want to use again (such as these filters, your connections, etc).

## Focus

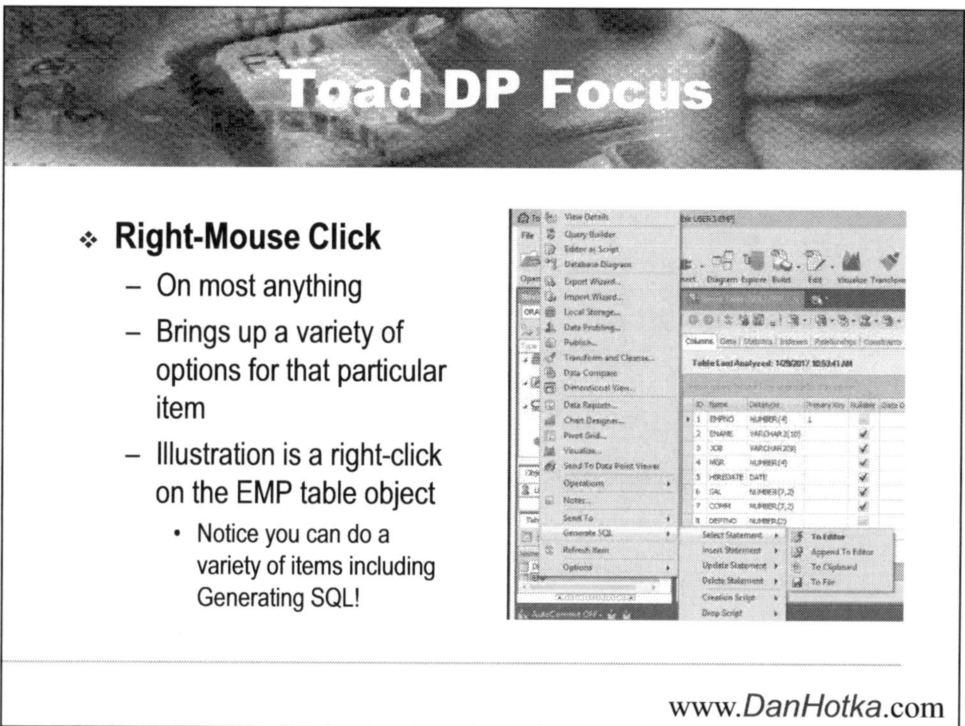


You can right-click on about anything in Toad DP. As previously discussed, there are 3 or more ways to do about anything including Menu items, ribbon buttons, function keys/key strokes, and now right-mouse click.

This illustration shows a right-click on the EMP table object. Notice you can do about anything from this right-mouse click…including generating a variety of useful SQL syntax related to this particular object.

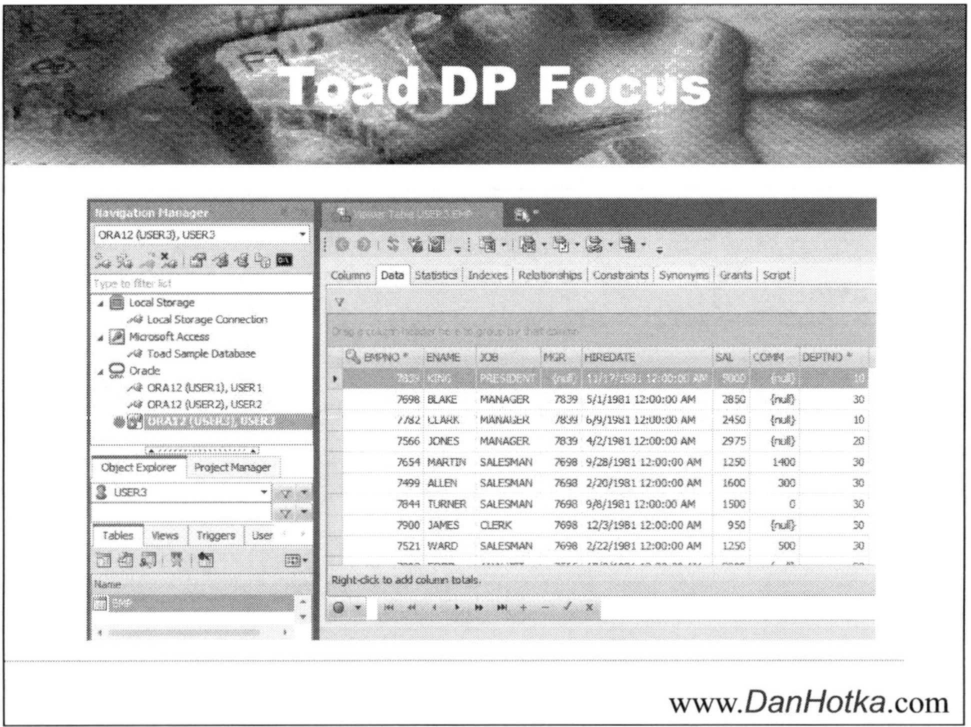


The instructor double-clicked on the EMP table object. Notice the Viewer opened up useful information about this data store and used the category color on the tab! IF you use these colors, will make it very easy to see the various data stores/connections you are working with and when your focus has changed from one connection type to another.

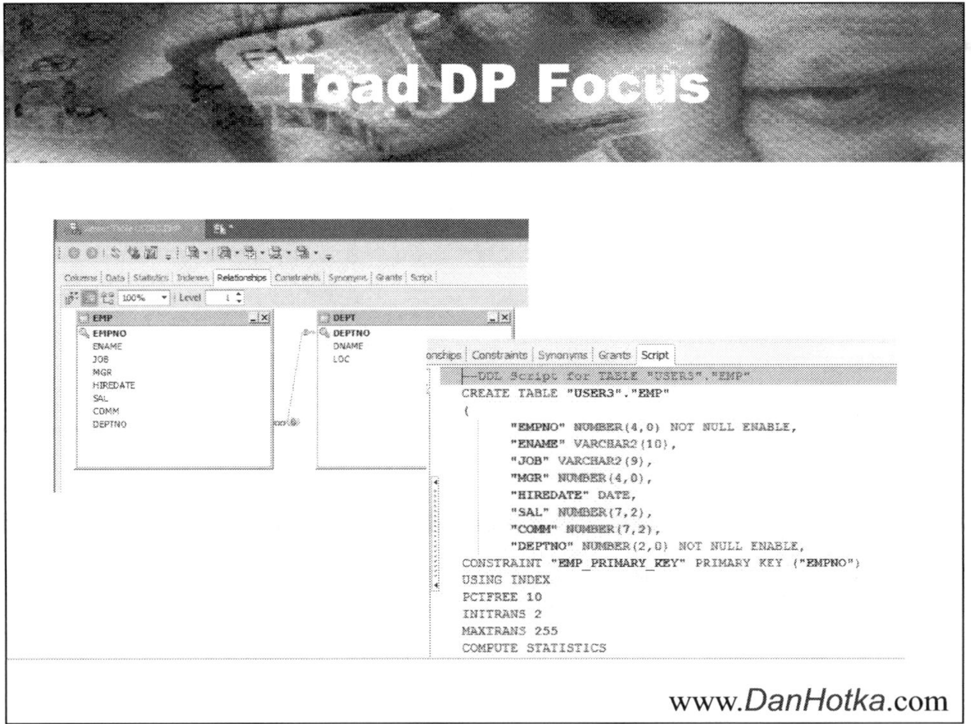

The relationship tab shows you the keys used when selecting data from two or more data stores. This course will show you how to use these to your advantage.

The script tab shows the actual code used to create this particular object. This is probably not useful information to the novice and this same information is also visible and more useful in the columns tab.

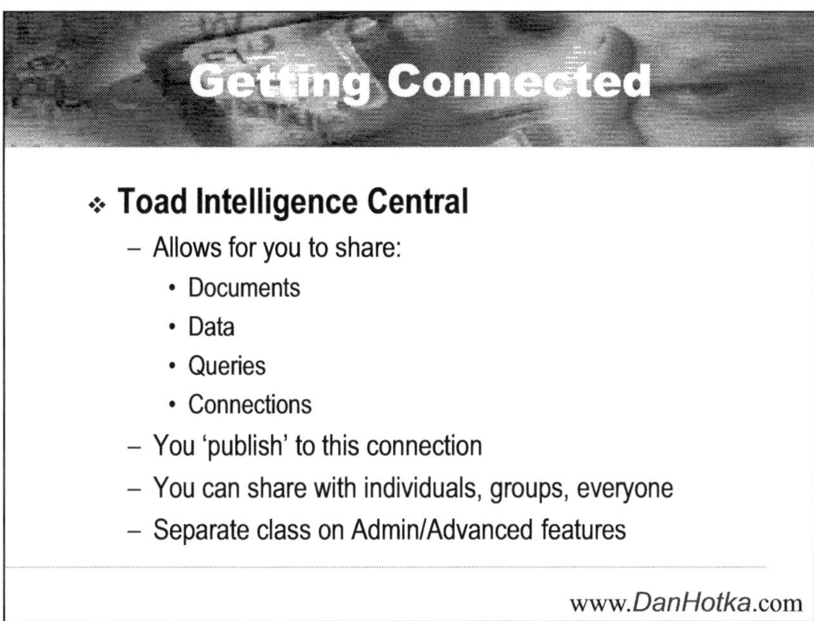
Getting Connected
Toad Intelligence Central
– Allows for you to share:
• Documents
• Data
• Queries
• Connections
– You 'publish' to this connection
– You can share with individuals, groups, everyone
– Separate class on Admin/Advanced features
www.DanHotka.com

Toad Intelligence Central (TIC) is a central repository where you can easily store and share data/documents/queries/files with others. The repository can be located anywhere in your network.

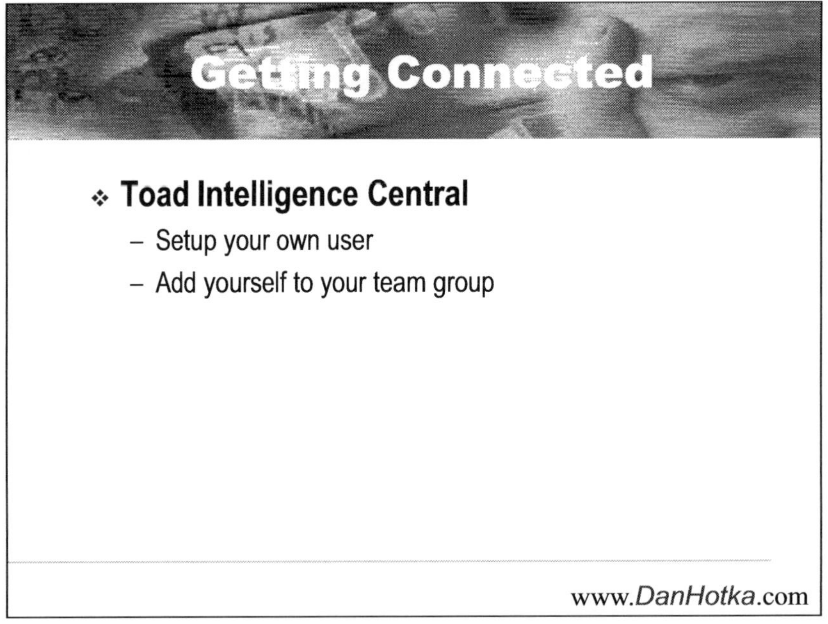


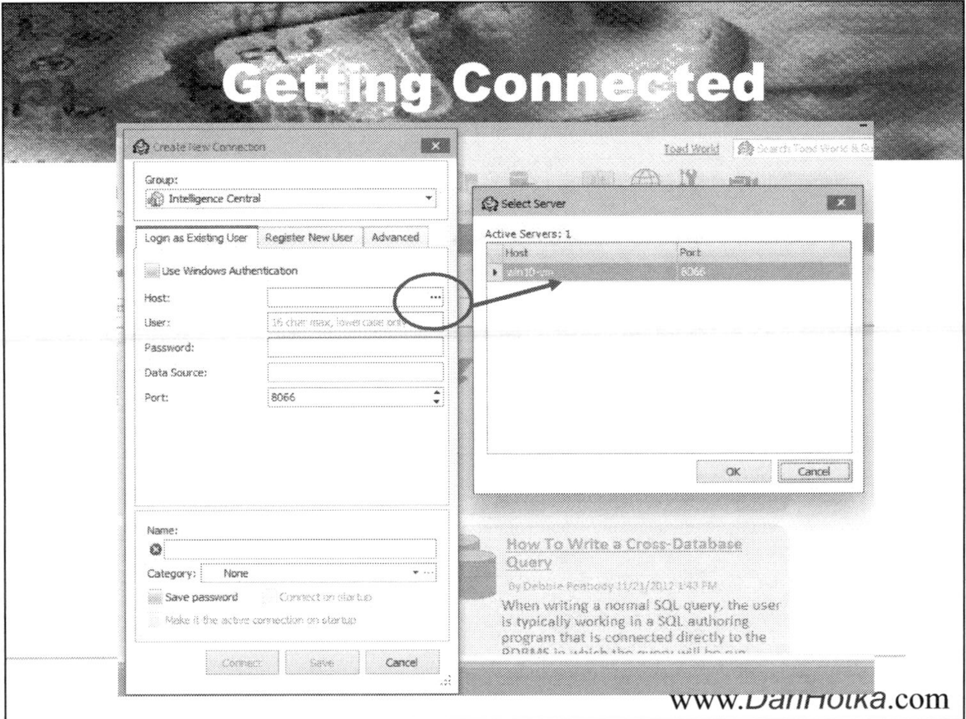


You simply use the 'New Connection' and create a new connection. You can also establish yourself as a new TIC user. Both of these tabs (Login and Register) have the 'Select Server', the three dots in the Host box. This will show all the TIC servers your Toad DP found.

Check with your group or local administrator on which TIC to connect to best fit your business needs.

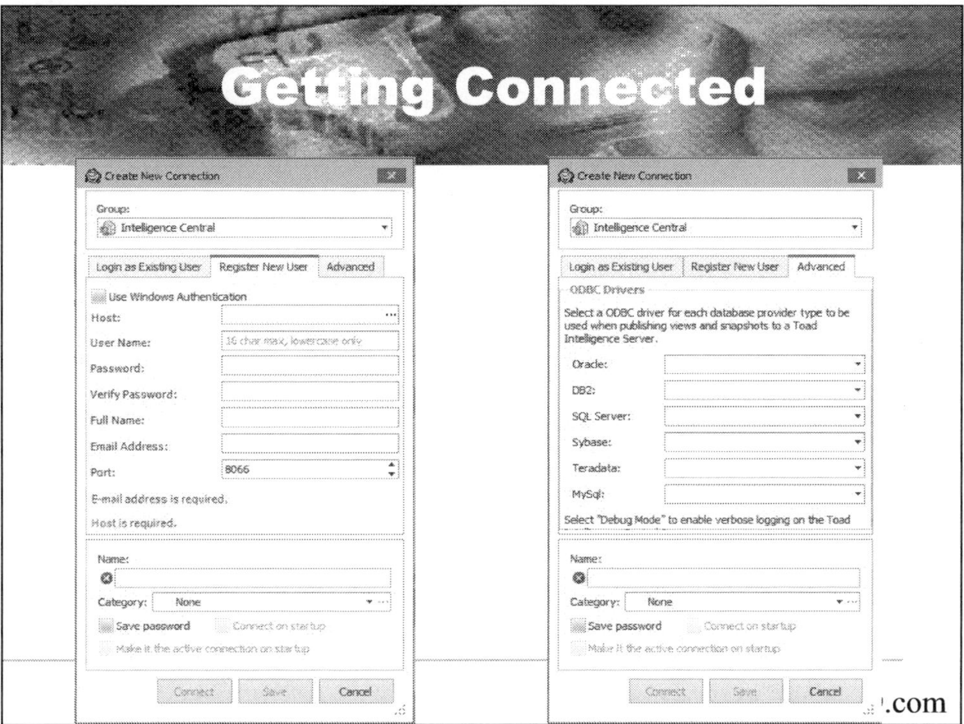


TIC works closely with Active Directory. The administrators can automatically set you up with an account based on your Active Directory authentication credentials. Be sure to check first with your team or TIC administrator to make sure you don't already have an account.

Notice in the Advanced Tab that the TIC repository can reside in existing database types.

***FYI*** TIC resides in a MySQL database unless the administrator sets it up in another database environment.

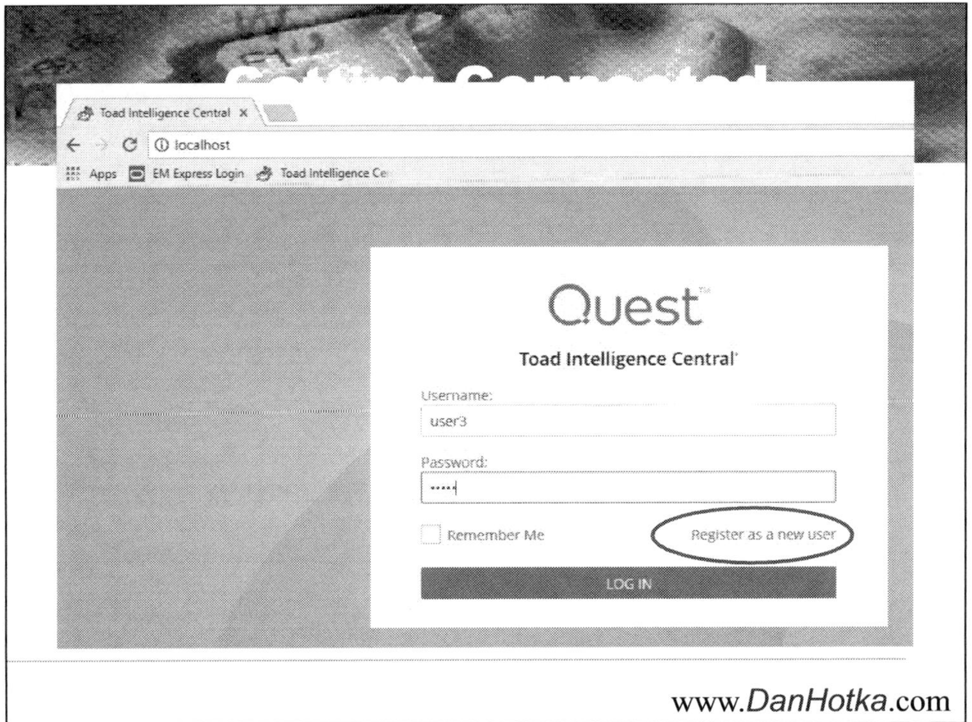


You can also use this web interface to register and see your TIC messages and documents being shared along with other information. You access this by just typing in the host name. The instructors machine…you can access it 2 ways:

1. http://localhost …probably locked out…this can be a security risk…
2. Win10-vm …the host name

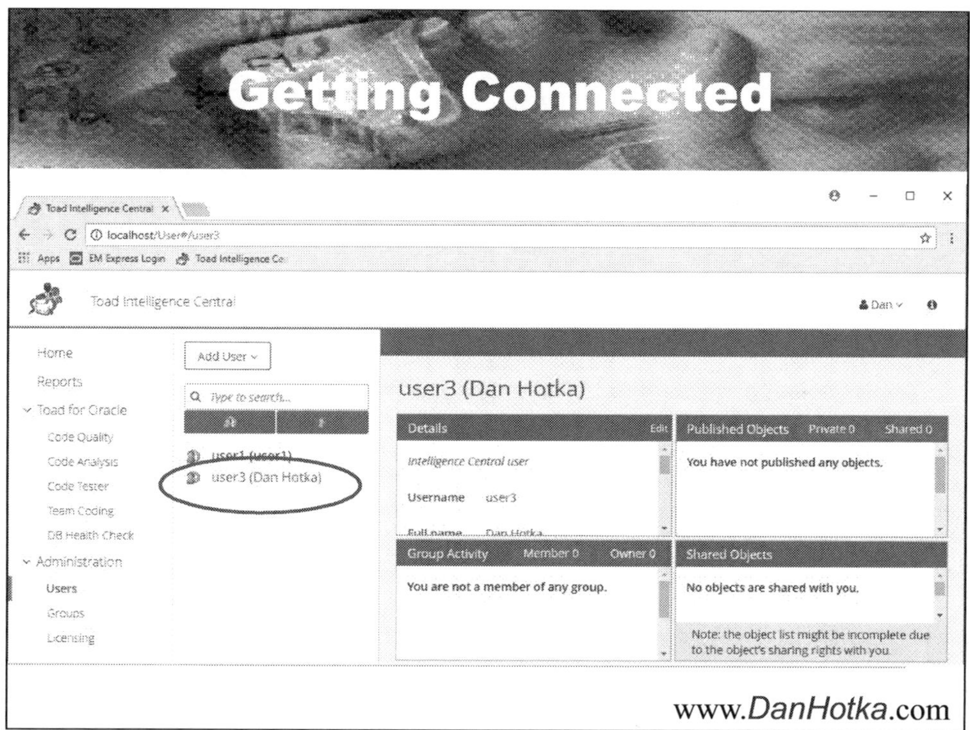


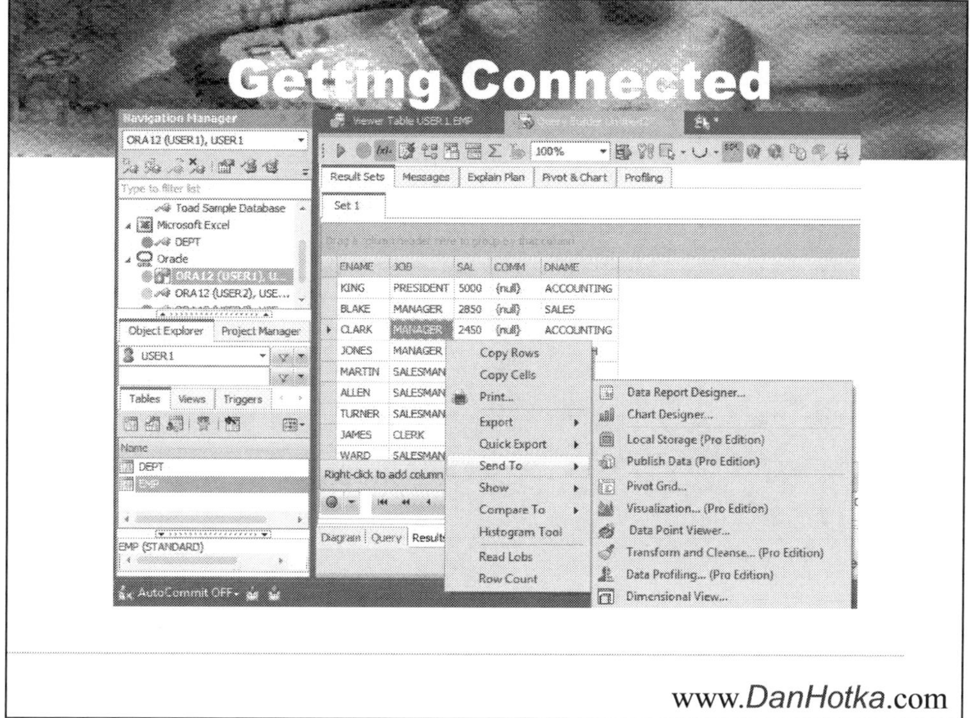


With TIC users setup, you can publish to them via right mouse click on any data grid.

## Getting Connected Lab

Getting Connected Lab

- **Getting Connected Lab**
  - If using your own computer/laptop:
    - Get connected to the data stores that will be used in this class
      - IF the connection already exists
        - » Change your category color
        - » Review your login properties
    - Setup a connection to Local Storage
    - IF your company is using TIC…and you do not have a TIC account
      - Set one up
      - Follow your companies policy on using Active Directory
  - **If using the Instructor-provided cloud solution**:
    - Follow his/her instructions on remote desktop connection
    - Start Toad Data Point
    - Setup the user "User1" with the password being the same ('user1') for the Oracle database ORA12.
      - Set your category color to something of your choosing

www.DanHotka.com

## Getting Connected Lab Answers

### Database Connection

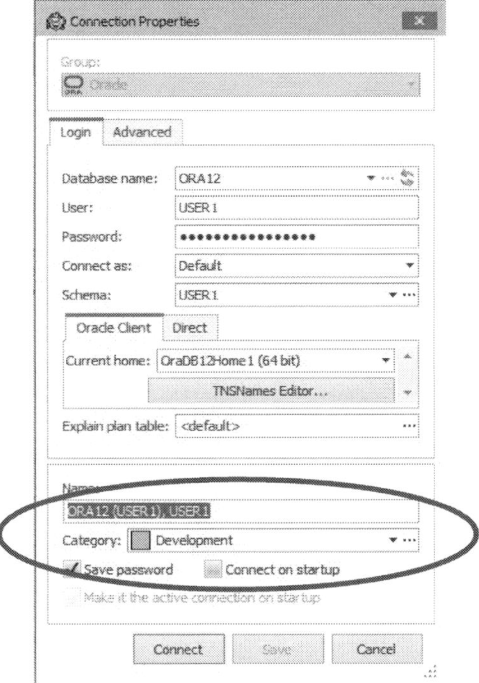


This is a connection setup for an Oracle Account. Notice the database can be selected from a drop down list. At the bottom, notice this user selected a ‘development’ category and to save the passwords. The password is stored encrypted. Do follow your company policy on password setup/storage/sharing. These connections can be exported and published to share with your entire group perhaps.

### Local Storage Connection

To connect to local storage, click on the Local Storage Connection and make sure its screen is filled out properly. It should be. You can right click and change its category (connection color).

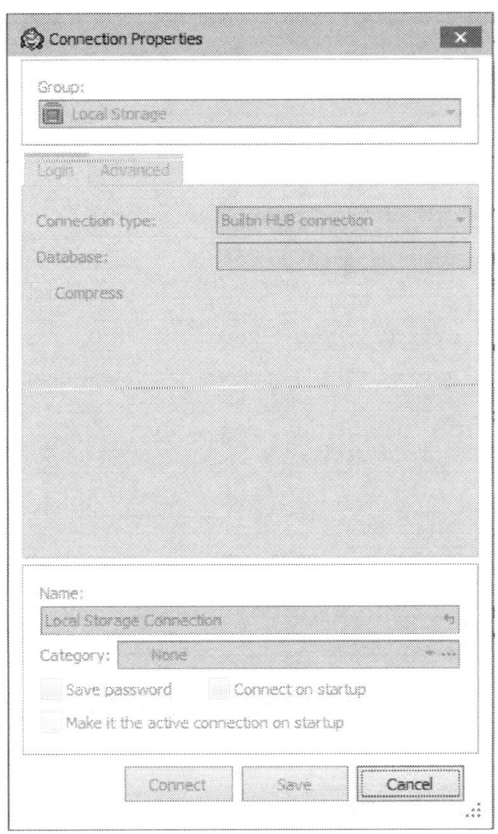


**Intelligence Central Login**

Click on 'Create New Connection'

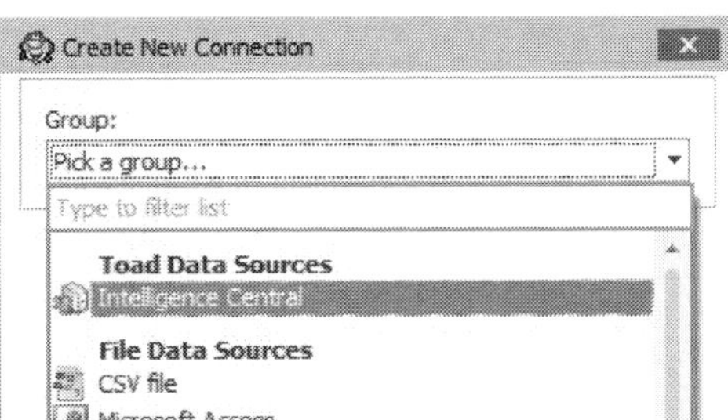


And select Intelligence Central as the group.

You can finish the connection to Intelligence Central if you already have an ID in TIC, otherwise go to the Register New User and set yourself up. Again, following your companies user id and password policies.

Notice near the bottom you can automatically connect at startup and set your connection color (category). You can also choose to save the passwords.

*****Note***** The instructor always saves passwords but he/she is in a self-contained class training environment.

New User Intelligence Central Setup Example

# Toad Quick Start

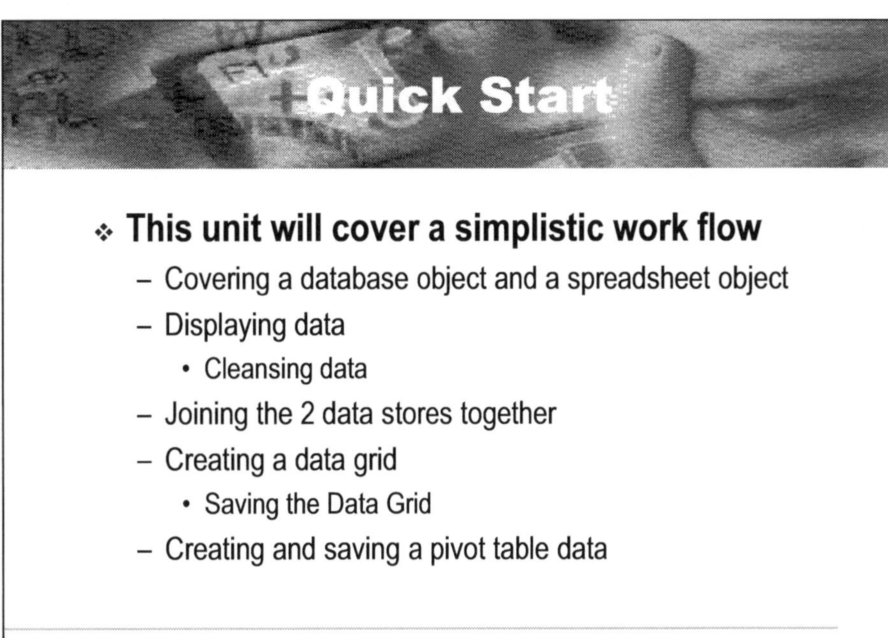
Quick Start
This unit will cover a simplistic work flow
– Covering a database object and a spreadsheet object
– Displaying data
• Cleansing data
– Joining the 2 data stores together
– Creating a data grid
• Saving the Data Grid
– Creating and saving a pivot table data
www.DanHotka.com

This unit will be a group exercise and the intent is to walk the class attendees through a data load/data analysis/data cleansing/creating spreadsheets/saving data for future use…

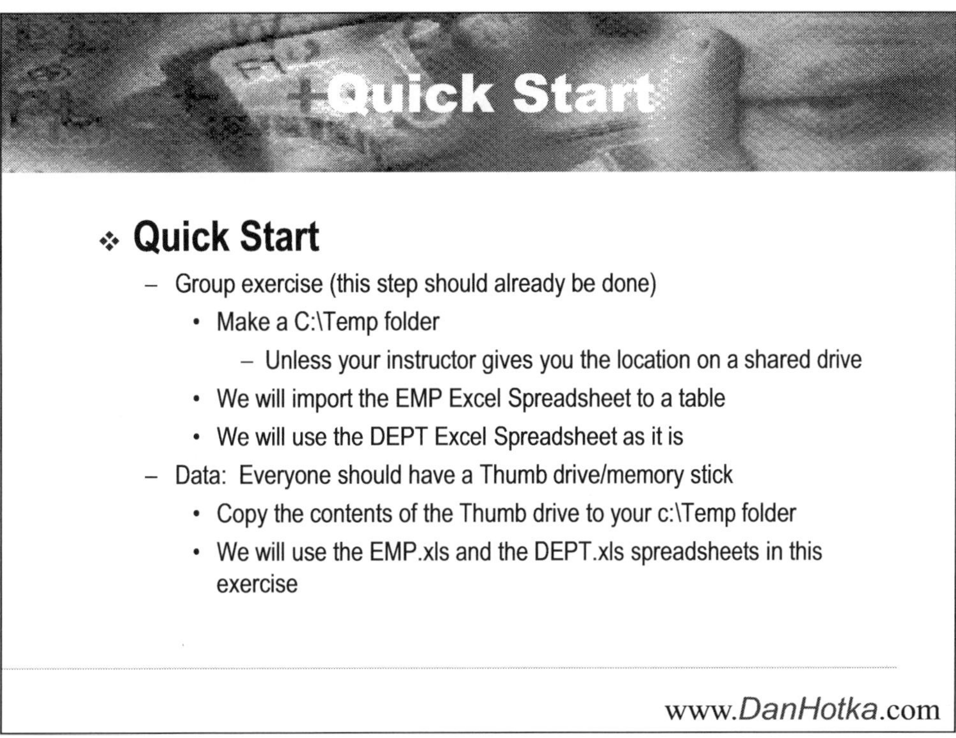
Quick Start
Quick Start
– Group exercise (this step should already be done)
• Make a C:\Temp folder
– Unless your instructor gives you the location on a shared drive
• We will import the EMP Excel Spreadsheet to a table
• We will use the DEPT Excel Spreadsheet as it is
– Data: Everyone should have a Thumb drive/memory stick
• Copy the contents of the Thumb drive to your c:\Temp folder
• We will use the EMP.xls and the DEPT.xls spreadsheets in this exercise
www.DanHotka.com

Each attendee should have a connection to a database (really doesn't matter which one) and possibly (but not overly important) a connection to Toad Intelligence Central.

## Import Data

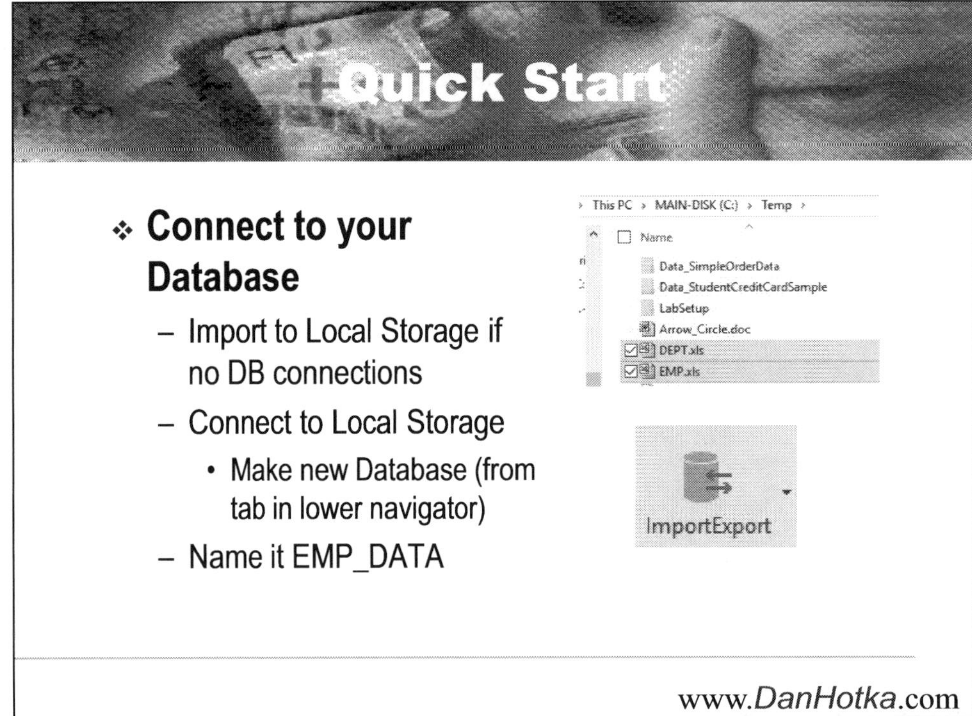


Most classes use this option. Most users do not have the ability to create anything or to change the data.

If you are importing to your Local Storage connection, make sure you have a 'database' setup for your table/data. In Local Storage, these databases are like folders and you can think of them as this. This is simply a way of organizing your saved data on your work station. You can create and clean up these folders/databases from the Navigation Manager.

You will need at least one of these.

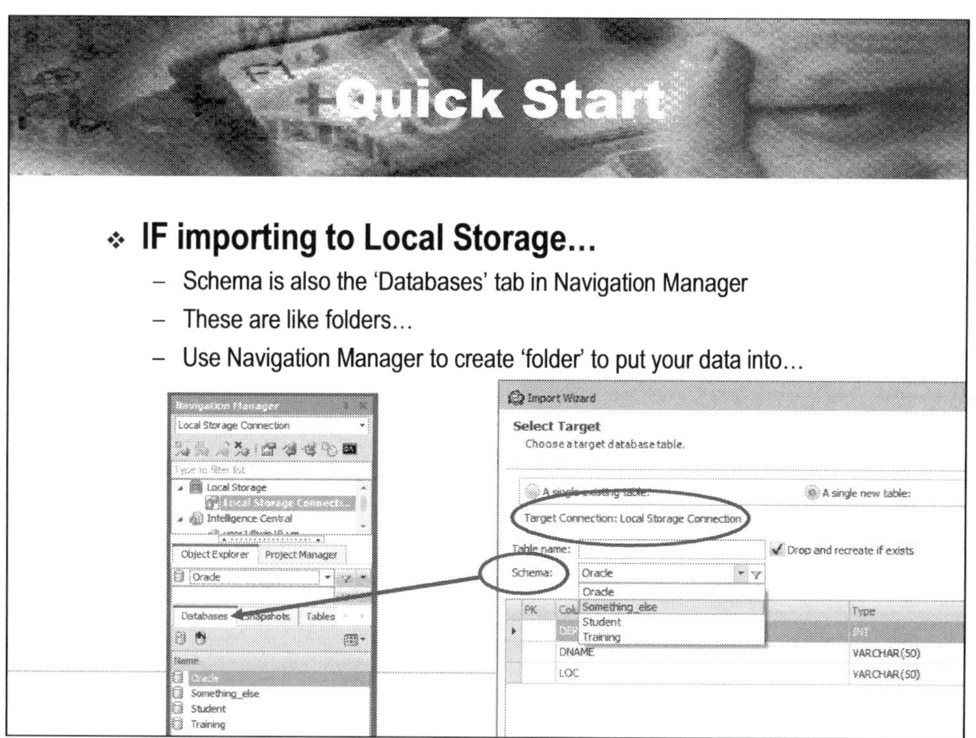
Quick Start
IF importing to Local Storage…
– Schema is also the 'Databases' tab in Navigation Manager
– These are like folders…
– Use Navigation Manager to create 'folder' to put your data into…
Navigation Manager
Local Storage Connection
Local Storage
Intelligence Central
Object Explorer
Project Manager
Oracle
Databases
Snapshots
Tables
Name
Oracle
Something_else
Student
Training
Import Wizard
Select Target
Choose a target database table.
A single new table:
Target Connection: Local Storage Connection
Table name:
Drop and recreate if exists
Schema:
Oracle
Oracle
Something_else
Student
Training
PK
Type
INT
DNAME
VARCHAR(50)
LOC
VARCHAR(50)

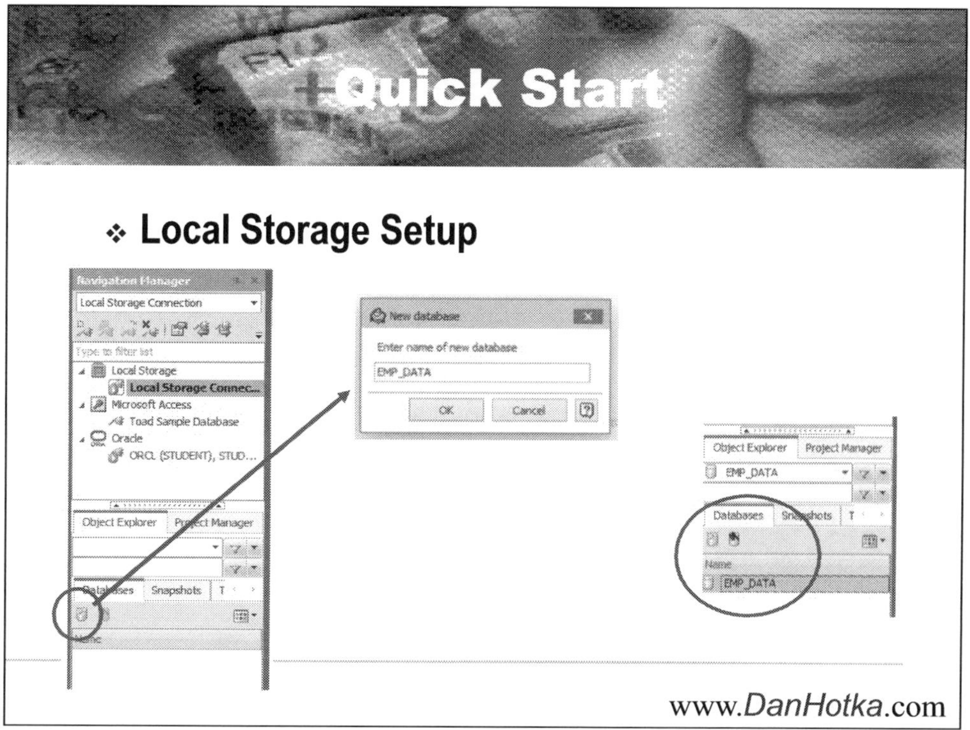
Quick Start
Local Storage Setup
Navigation Manager
Local Storage Connection
Local Storage
Local Storage Connec...
Microsoft Access
Toad Sample Database
Oracle
ORCL (STUDENT), STUD...
Object Explorer
Project Manager
Databases
Snapshots
New database
Enter name of new database
EMP_DATA
OK
Cancel
Object Explorer
Project Manager
EMP_DATA
Databases
Snapshots
Name
EMP_DATA
www.DanHotka.com

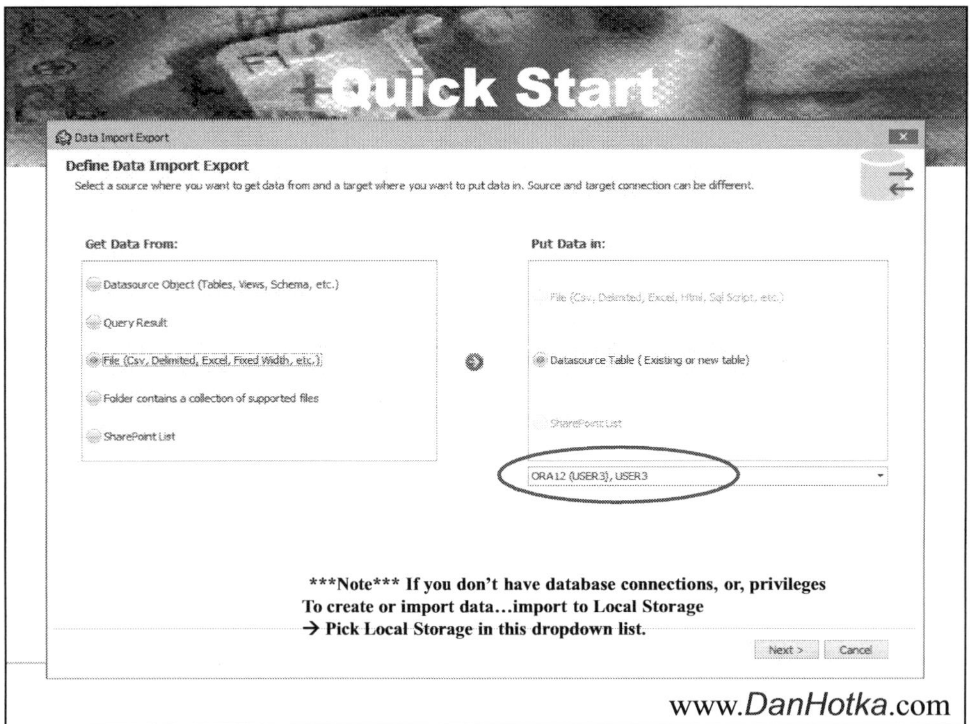


Select File on the left and Database Table on the right.

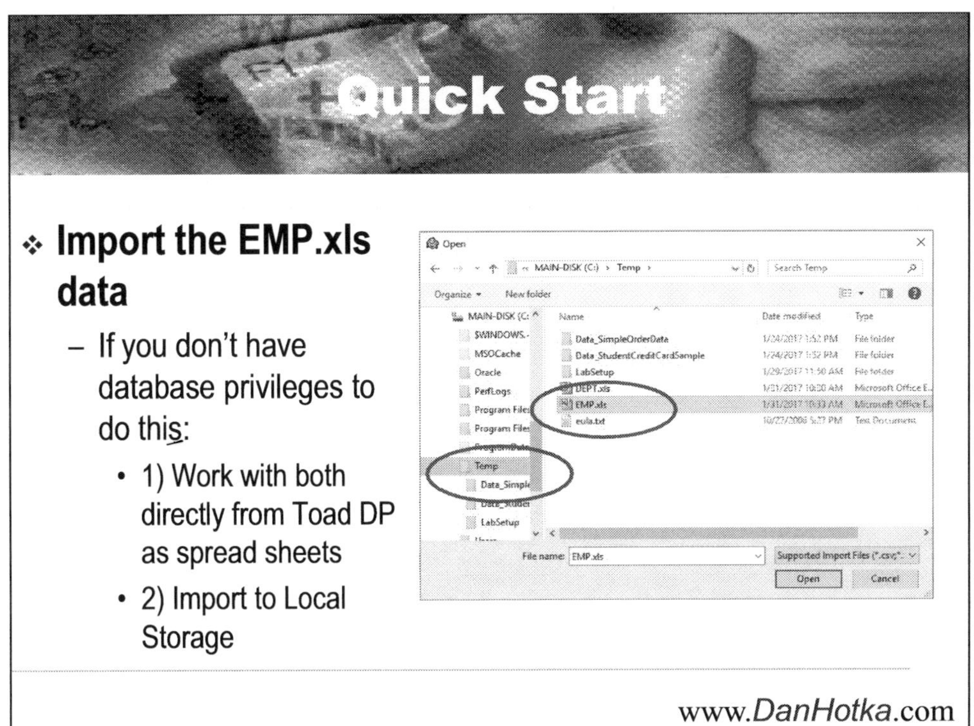
Quick Start
Import the EMP.xls data
– If you don't have database privileges to do this:
• 1) Work with both directly from Toad DP as spread sheets
• 2) Import to Local Storage
Open
MAIN-DISK (C:) › Temp ›
Organize
New folder
Name
Date modified
Type
Data_SimpleOrderData
Data_StudentCreditCardSample
LabSetup
DEPT.xls
EMP.xls
eula.txt
Temp
File name: EMP.xls
Open
Cancel
www.DanHotka.com

***Note*** you will need database permissions to do this step. IF this does not work, not a problem! Import to Local Storage or use the Microsoft Excel connection for both spreadsheets. Skip to Excel Connection…

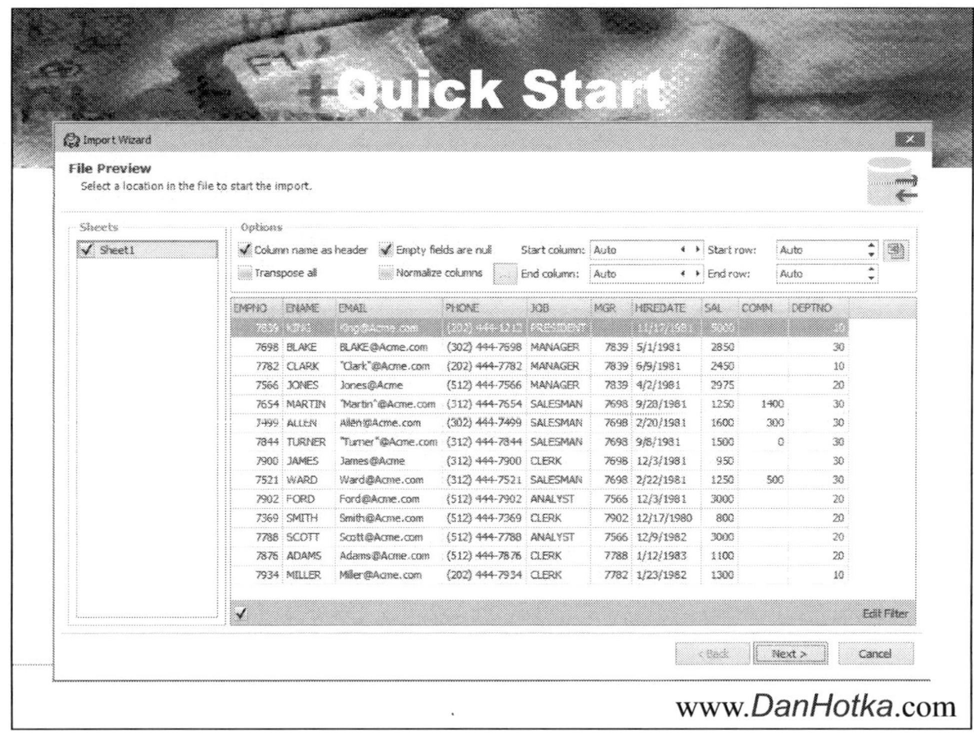
Quick Start
Import Wizard
File Preview
Select a location in the file to start the import.
Sheets
Sheet1
Options
Column name as header
Empty fields are null
Start column: Auto
Start row: Auto
Transpose all
Normalize columns
End column: Auto
End row: Auto
EMPNO ENAME EMAIL PHONE JOB MGR HIREDATE SAL COMM DEPTNO
7839 KING King@Acme.com (202) 444-1212 PRESIDENT 11/17/1981 5000 10
7698 BLAKE BLAKE@Acme.com (302) 444-7698 MANAGER 7839 5/1/1981 2850 30
7782 CLARK "Clark"@Acme.com (202) 444-7782 MANAGER 7839 6/9/1981 2450 10
7566 JONES Jones@Acme (512) 444-7566 MANAGER 7839 4/2/1981 2975 20
7654 MARTIN "Martin"@Acme.com (312) 444-7654 SALESMAN 7698 9/28/1981 1250 1400 30
7499 ALLEN Allen@Acme.com (302) 444-7499 SALESMAN 7698 2/20/1981 1600 300 30
7844 TURNER "Turner"@Acme.com (312) 444-7844 SALESMAN 7698 9/8/1981 1500 0 30
7900 JAMES James@Acme (312) 444-7900 CLERK 7698 12/3/1981 950 30
7521 WARD Ward@Acme.com (312) 444-7521 SALESMAN 7698 2/22/1981 1250 500 30
7902 FORD Ford@Acme.com (512) 444-7902 ANALYST 7566 12/3/1981 3000 20
7369 SMITH Smith@Acme.com (512) 444-7369 CLERK 7902 12/17/1980 800 20
7788 SCOTT Scott@Acme.com (512) 444-7788 ANALYST 7566 12/9/1982 3000 20
7876 ADAMS Adams@Acme.com (512) 444-7876 CLERK 7788 1/12/1983 1100 20
7934 MILLER Miller@Acme.com (202) 444-7934 CLERK 7782 1/23/1982 1300 10
Edit Filter
< Back
Next >
Cancel
www.DanHotka.com

Quick Start
Import Wizard
Define Columns
Select and edit the columns to include in the import.
Column Name Sample Data
EMPNO 7839
ENAME KING
EMAIL King@Acme.com
PHONE (202) 444-1212
JOB PRESIDENT
MGR
HIREDATE 11/17/1981 12:00:00 AM
SAL 5000
COMM
DEPTNO 10
Add
Remove
Reset
< Back
Next >
Cancel

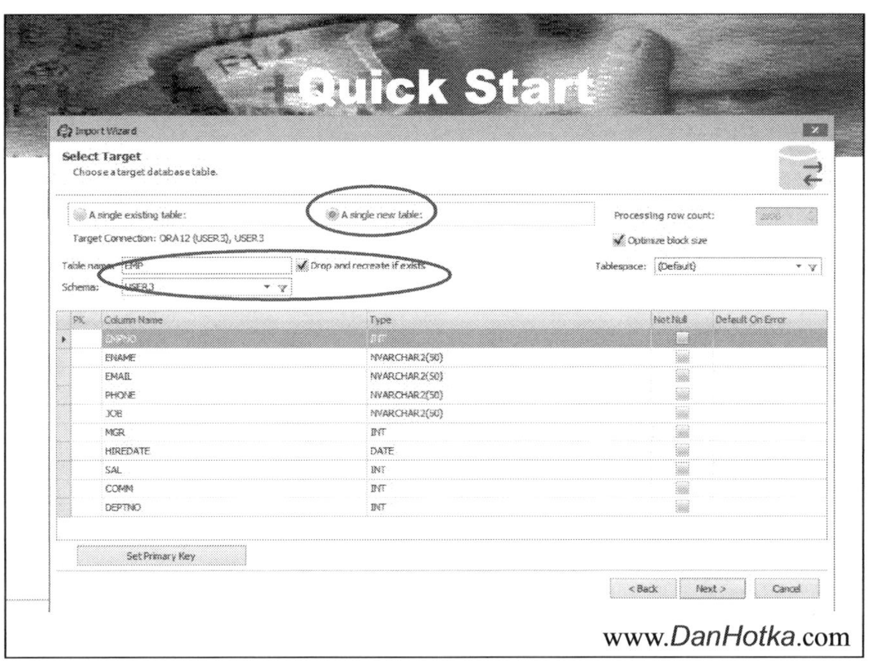
Quick Start
Import Wizard
Select Target
Choose a target database table.
A single existing table:
A single new table:
Processing row count:
Target Connection: ORA12 (USER3), USER3
Optimize block size
Table name: EMP
Drop and recreate if exists
Tablespace: (Default)
Schema: USER3
PK
Column Name
Type
Not Null
Default On Error
EMPNO
INT
ENAME
NVARCHAR2(50)
EMAIL
NVARCHAR2(50)
PHONE
NVARCHAR2(50)
JOB
NVARCHAR2(50)
MGR
INT
HIREDATE
DATE
SAL
INT
COMM
INT
DEPTNO
INT
Set Primary Key
< Back
Next >
Cancel
www.DanHotka.com

Quick Start
Import Wizard
Add Import Source
Add an import source from a file, a folder, a SQL query, a table, or a list from SharePoint. Add additional objects or click next to summary page.
Import objects list:
"EMP.xls" into a new table USER3.EMP
Add File...
Add Folder
Add Query
Add Table
SharePoint
Edit
Remove
< Back
Next >
Cancel
www.DanHotka.com

Quick Start
Import Wizard
Save Settings as Template
Select a location and file name for the template.
Import Data Now
Import Data Later
Send to Automation
Save template
If error occurs, save unimported rows to a discard file (csv)
SaveLog
< Back
Finish
Cancel
www.DanHotka.com

Quick Start
Import Wizard
Save Settings as Template
Select a location and file name for the template.
Import Data Now
Import Data Later
Send to Automation
Save template
If error occurs, save unimported rows to a discard file (csv)
SaveLog
< Back
Finish
Cancel
www.DanHotka.com

Quick Start
Success!
Import Finished
Import data summary results:
Description
Read Rows
Imported Rows
Status
File Name
Finished
14
14
Do not prompt me again
OK
www.DanHotka.com

## Navigating Toad DP

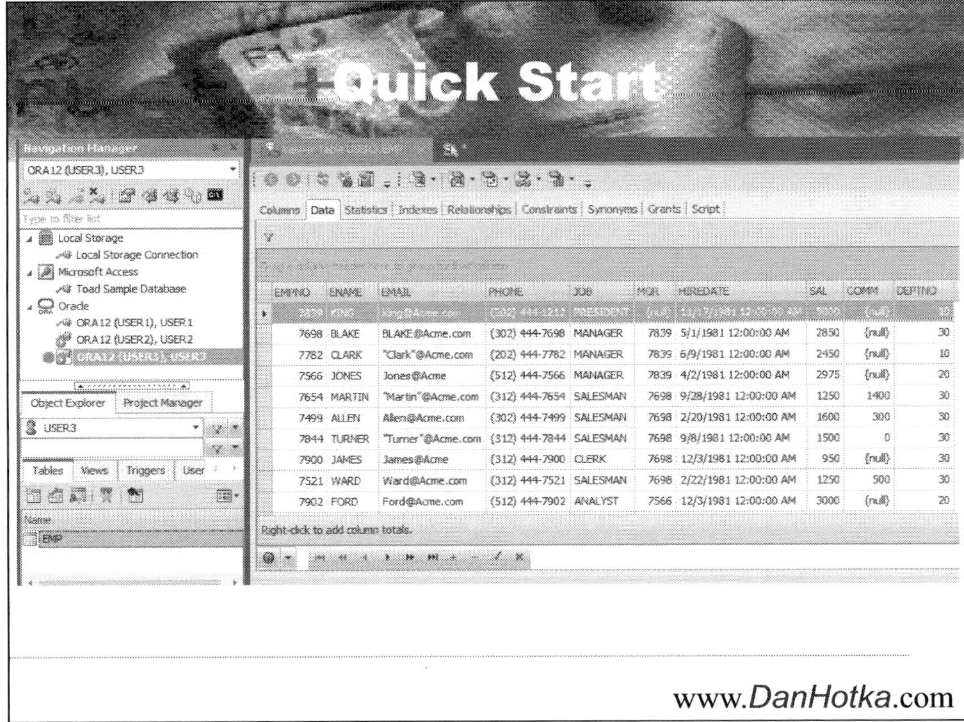
Quick Start
Navigation Manager
ORA12 (USER3), USER3
Type to filter list
Local Storage
Local Storage Connection
Microsoft Access
Toad Sample Database
Oracle
ORA12 (USER1), USER1
ORA12 (USER2), USER2
ORA12 (USER3), USER3
Object Explorer
Project Manager
USER3
Tables
Views
Triggers
User
Name
EMP
Columns
Data
Statistics
Indexes
Relationships
Constraints
Synonyms
Grants
Script
EMPNO ENAME EMAIL PHONE JOB MGR HIREDATE SAL COMM DEPTNO
7698 BLAKE BLAKE@Acme.com (302) 444-7698 MANAGER 7839 5/1/1981 12:00:00 AM 2850 {null} 30
7782 CLARK "Clark"@Acme.com (202) 444-7782 MANAGER 7839 6/9/1981 12:00:00 AM 2450 {null} 10
7566 JONES Jones@Acme (512) 444-7566 MANAGER 7839 4/2/1981 12:00:00 AM 2975 {null} 20
7654 MARTIN "Martin"@Acme.com (312) 444-7654 SALESMAN 7698 9/28/1981 12:00:00 AM 1250 1400 30
7499 ALLEN Allen@Acme.com (302) 444-7499 SALESMAN 7698 2/20/1981 12:00:00 AM 1600 300 30
7844 TURNER "Turner"@Acme.com (312) 444-7844 SALESMAN 7698 9/8/1981 12:00:00 AM 1500 0 30
7900 JAMES James@Acme (312) 444-7900 CLERK 7698 12/3/1981 12:00:00 AM 950 {null} 30
7521 WARD Ward@Acme.com (312) 444-7521 SALESMAN 7698 2/22/1981 12:00:00 AM 1250 500 30
7902 FORD Ford@Acme.com (512) 444-7902 ANALYST 7566 12/3/1981 12:00:00 AM 3000 {null} 20
Right-click to add column totals.
www.DanHotka.com

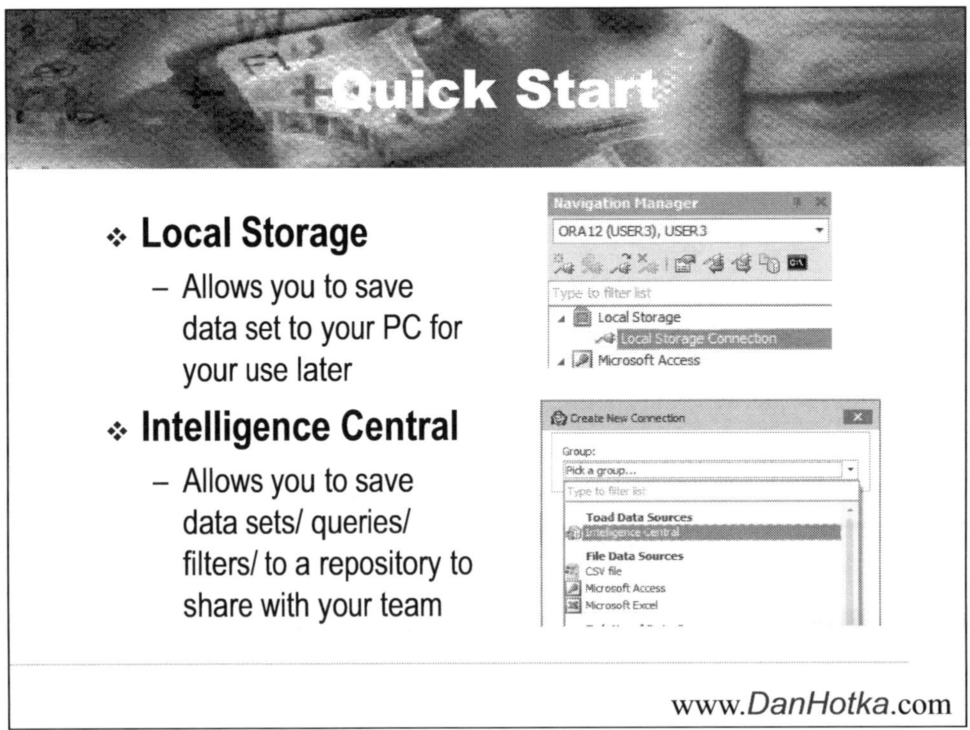
Quick Start
❖ Local Storage
– Allows you to save data set to your PC for your use later
❖ Intelligence Central
– Allows you to save data sets/ queries/ filters/ to a repository to share with your team
Navigation Manager
ORA12 (USER3), USER3
Type to filter list
Local Storage
Local Storage Connection
Microsoft Access
Create New Connection
Group:
Pick a group...
Type to filter list
Toad Data Sources
Intelligence Central
File Data Sources
CSV file
Microsoft Access
Microsoft Excel
www.DanHotka.com

## Excel Connection

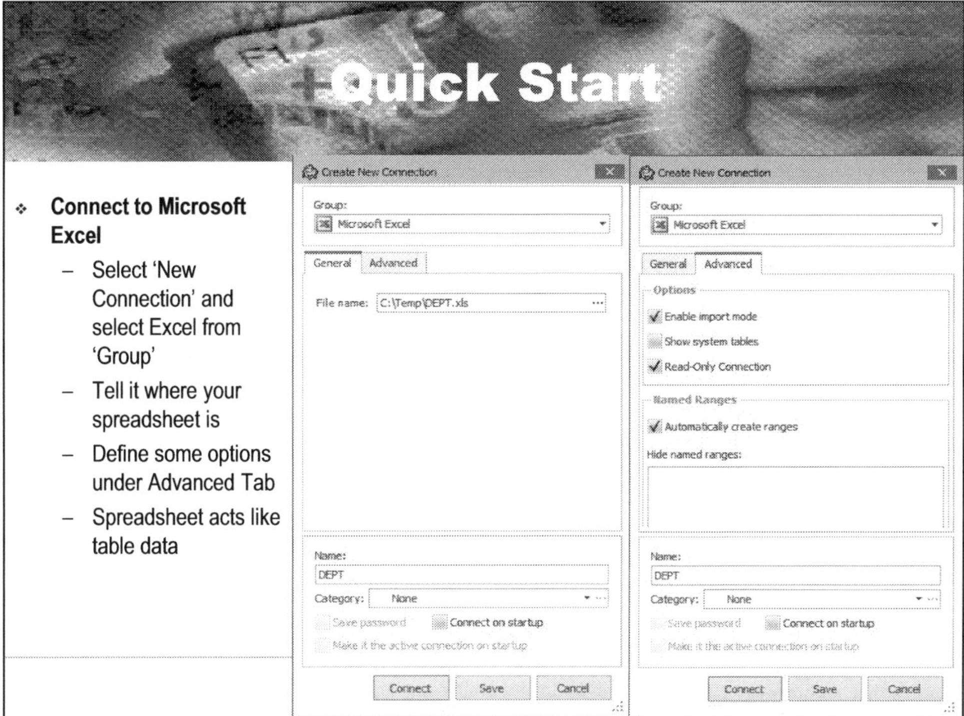


## Accessing Data with Query Builder

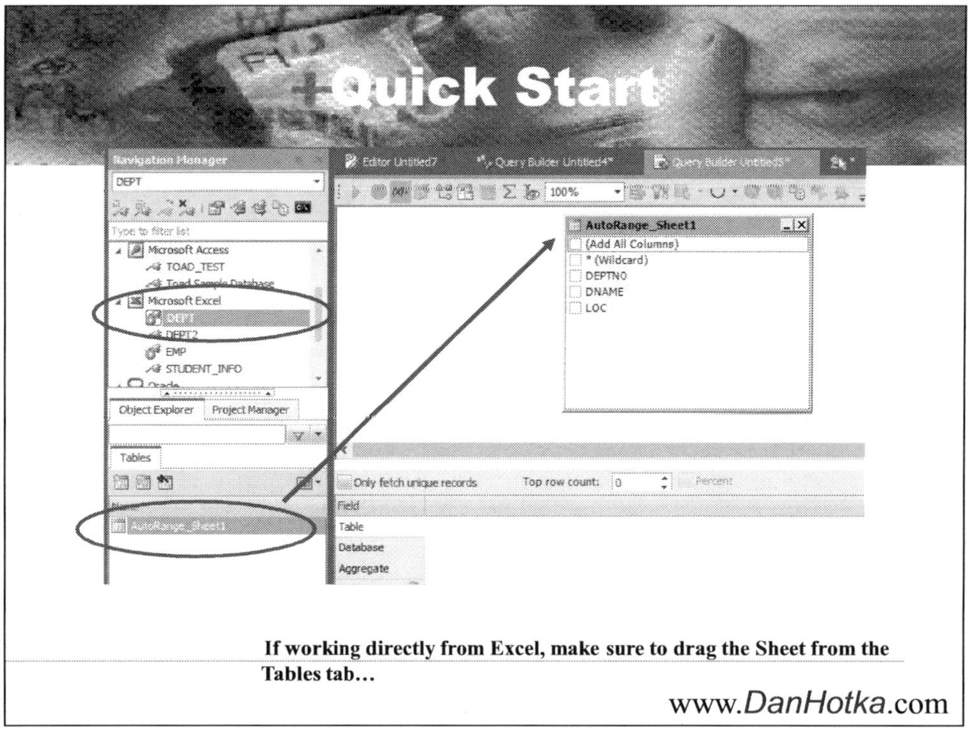
Quick Start
If working directly from Excel, make sure to drag the Sheet from the Tables tab…
www.DanHotka.com

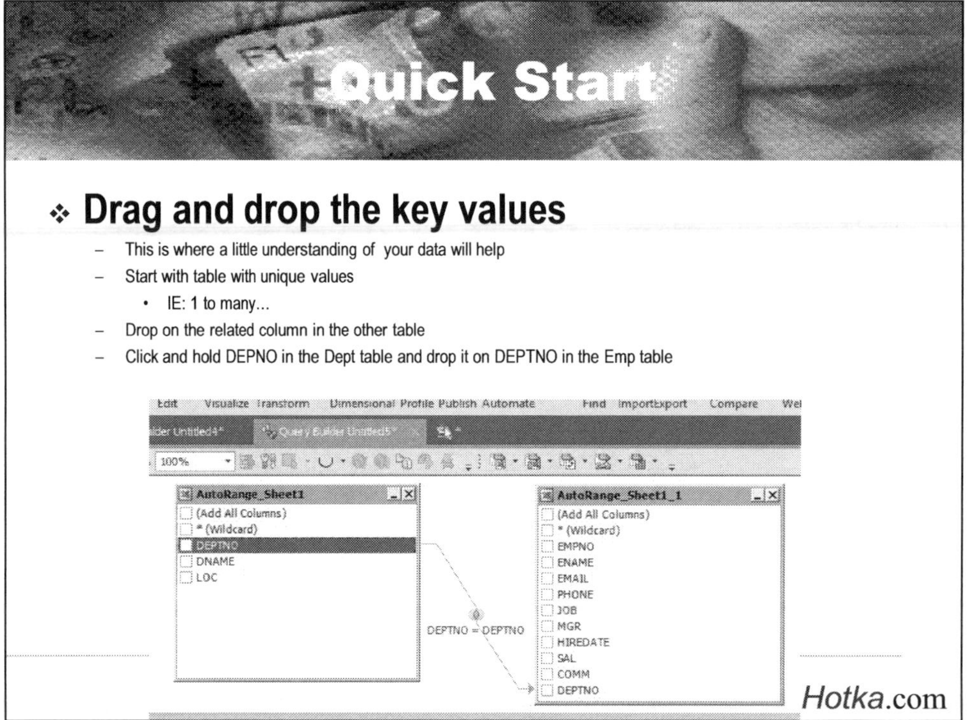
Quick Start
Drag and drop the key values
This is where a little understanding of your data will help
Start with table with unique values
IE: 1 to many…
Drop on the related column in the other table
Click and hold DEPNO in the Dept table and drop it on DEPTNO in the Emp table
AutoRange_Sheet1
AutoRange_Sheet1_1
DEPTNO = DEPTNO
Hotka.com

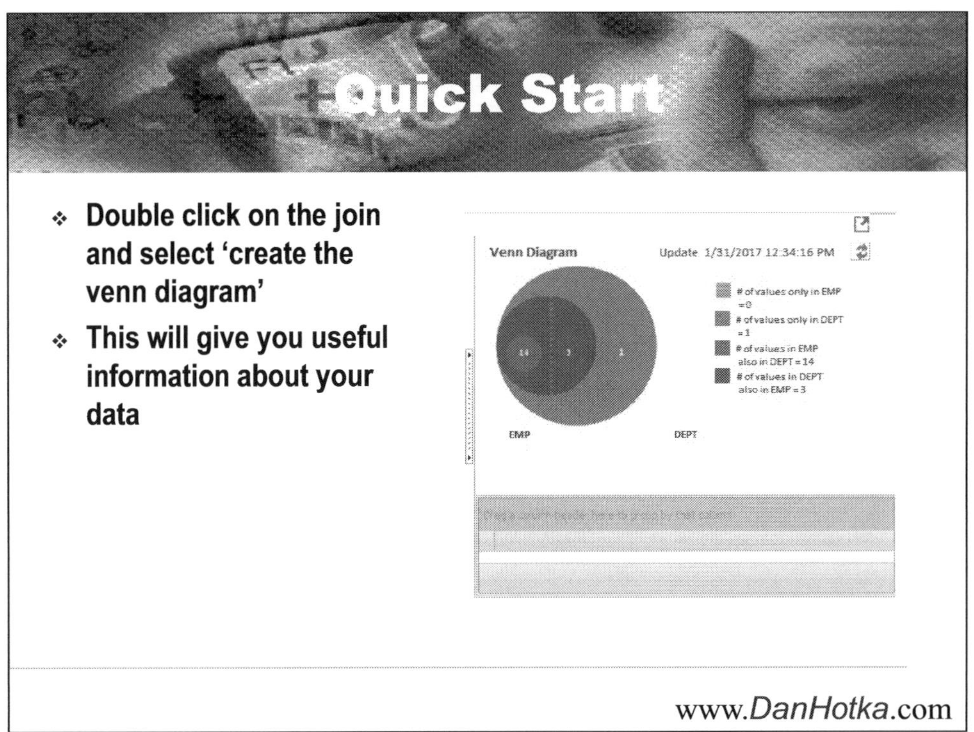
Quick Start
Double click on the join and select 'create the venn diagram'
This will give you useful information about your data
Venn Diagram
Update 1/31/2017 12:34:16 PM
# of values only in EMP =0
# of values only in DEPT =1
# of values in EMP also in DEPT = 14
# of values in DEPT also in EMP = 3
EMP
DEPT
www.DanHotka.com

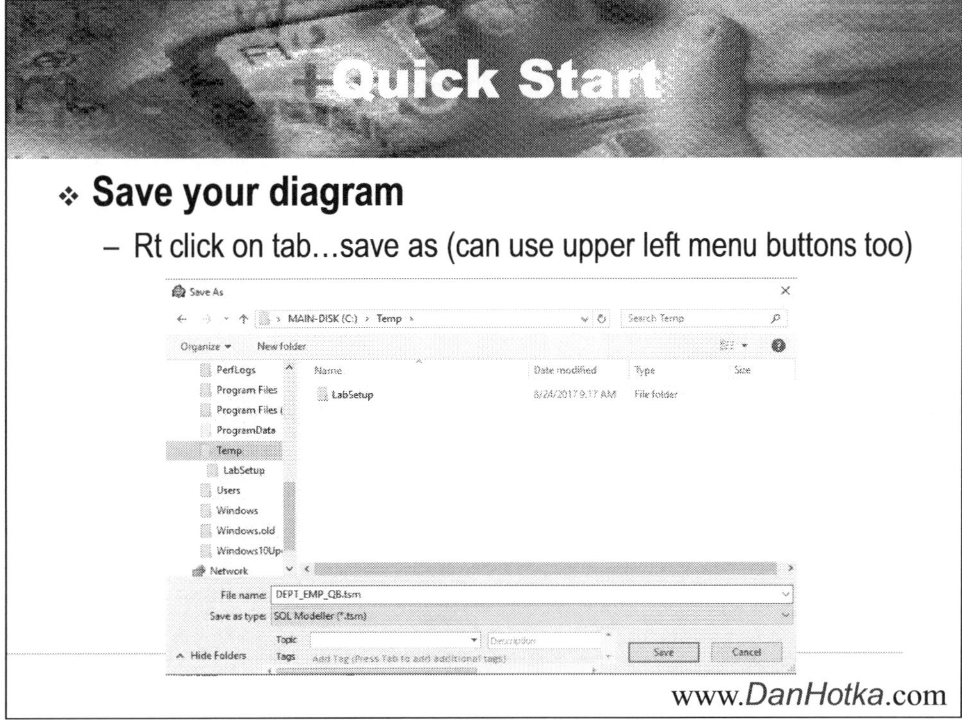
Quick Start
Save your diagram
– Rt click on tab…save as (can use upper left menu buttons too)
Save As
MAIN-DISK (C:) › Temp ›
Search Temp
Organize
New folder
Name
Date modified
Type
Size
LabSetup
8/24/2017 9:17 AM
File folder
PerfLogs
Program Files
ProgramData
Temp
LabSetup
Users
Windows
Windows.old
Network
File name: DEPT_EMP_QB.tsm
Save as type: SQL Modeller (*.tsm)
Topic
Tags
Hide Folders
Save
Cancel
www.DanHotka.com

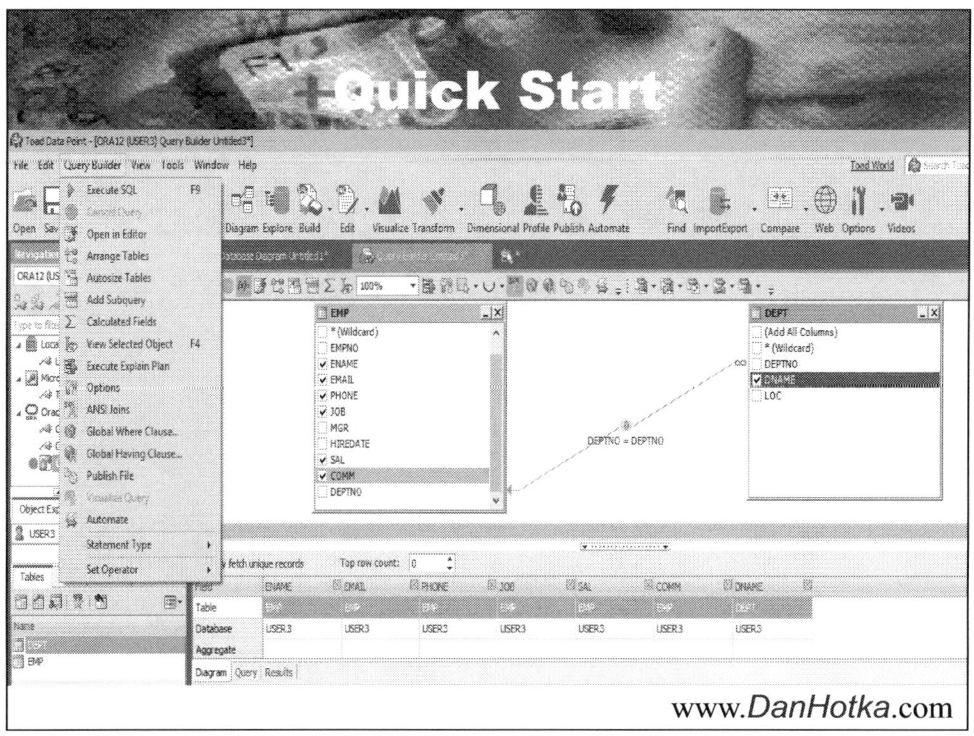
Quick Start
Toad Data Point - [ORA12 (USER3) Query Builder Untitled3*]
File Edit Query Builder View Tools Window Help
Execute SQL F9
Open in Editor
Arrange Tables
Autosize Tables
Add Subquery
Calculated Fields
View Selected Object F4
Execute Explain Plan
Options
ANSI Joins
Global Where Clause...
Global Having Clause...
Publish File
Automate
Statement Type
Set Operator
Diagram Explore Build Edit Visualize Transform Dimensional Profile Publish Automate Find Import/Export Compare Web Options Videos
EMP
* (Wildcard)
EMPNO
ENAME
EMAIL
PHONE
JOB
MGR
HIREDATE
SAL
COMM
DEPTNO
DEPT
(Add All Columns)
* (Wildcard)
DEPTNO
DNAME
LOC
DEPTNO = DEPTNO
Top row count:
Field Table Database Aggregate
ENAME EMAIL PHONE JOB SAL COMM DNAME
USER3
Diagram Query Results
www.DanHotka.com

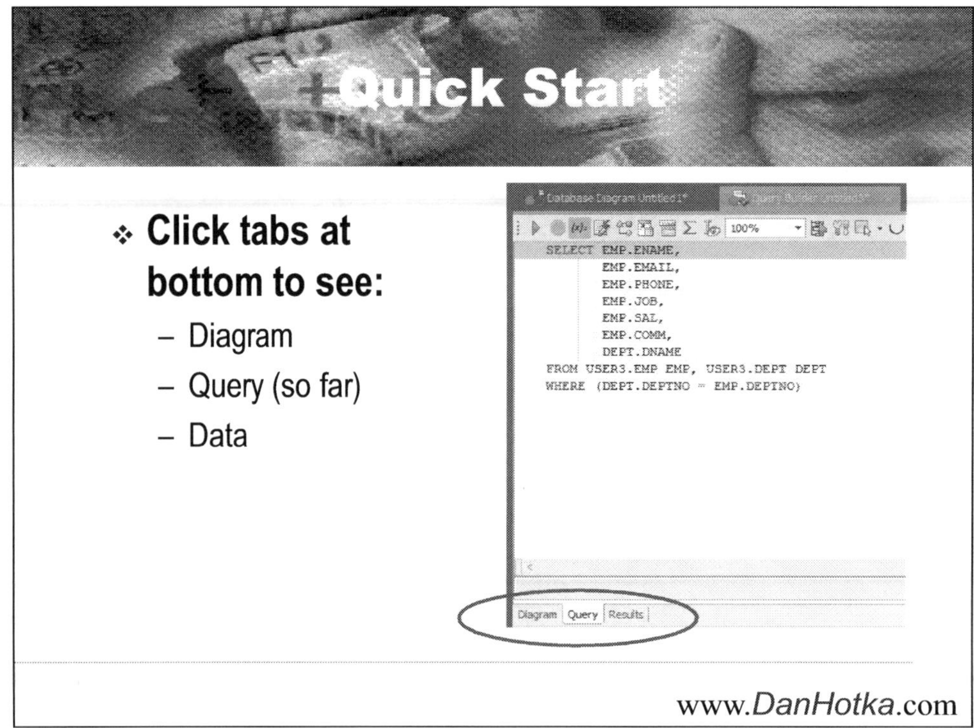
Quick Start
Click tabs at bottom to see:
– Diagram
– Query (so far)
– Data
SELECT EMP.ENAME,
EMP.EMAIL,
EMP.PHONE,
EMP.JOB,
EMP.SAL,
EMP.COMM,
DEPT.DNAME
FROM USER3.EMP EMP, USER3.DEPT DEPT
WHERE (DEPT.DEPTNO = EMP.DEPTNO)
Diagram Query Results
www.DanHotka.com

Quick Start
Results Tab
Database Diagram Untitled1*
100%
Result Sets
Messages
Explain Plan
Pivot & Chart
Profiling
Set 1
ENAME EMAIL PHONE JOB SAL COMM DNAME
BLAKE BLAKE@Acme.com (302) 444-7698 MANAGER 2850 {null} SALES
CLARK "Clark"@Acme.com (202) 444-7782 MANAGER 2450 {null} ACCOUNTING
JONES Jones@Acme (512) 444-7566 MANAGER 2975 {null} RESEARCH
MARTIN "Martin"@Acme.com (312) 444-7654 SALESMAN 1250 1400 SALES
ALLEN Allen@Acme.com (302) 444-7499 SALESMAN 1600 300 SALES
TURNER "Turner"@Acme.com (312) 444-7844 SALESMAN 1500 0 SALES
JAMES James@Acme (312) 444-7900 CLERK 950 {null} SALES
WARD Ward@Acme.com (312) 444-7521 SALESMAN 1250 500 SALES
Right-click to add column totals.
Duration: 0:00:00.109
Diagram
Query
Results
www.DanHotka.com

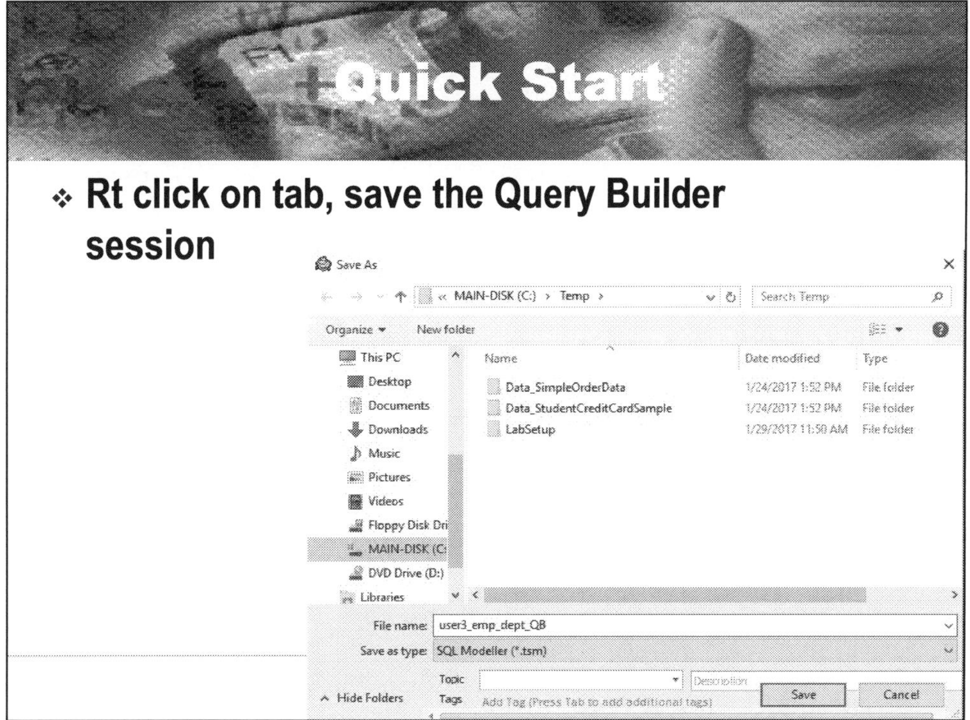
Quick Start
Rt click on tab, save the Query Builder session
Save As
« MAIN-DISK (C:) › Temp ›
Search Temp
Organize
New folder
This PC
Desktop
Documents
Downloads
Music
Pictures
Videos
Floppy Disk Dri
MAIN-DISK (C:
DVD Drive (D:)
Libraries
Name
Date modified
Type
Data_SimpleOrderData 1/24/2017 1:52 PM File folder
Data_StudentCreditCardSample 1/24/2017 1:52 PM File folder
LabSetup 1/29/2017 11:50 AM File folder
File name: user3_emp_dept_QB
Save as type: SQL Modeller (*.tsm)
Topic
Tags
Add Tag (Press Tab to add additional tags)
Hide Folders
Save
Cancel

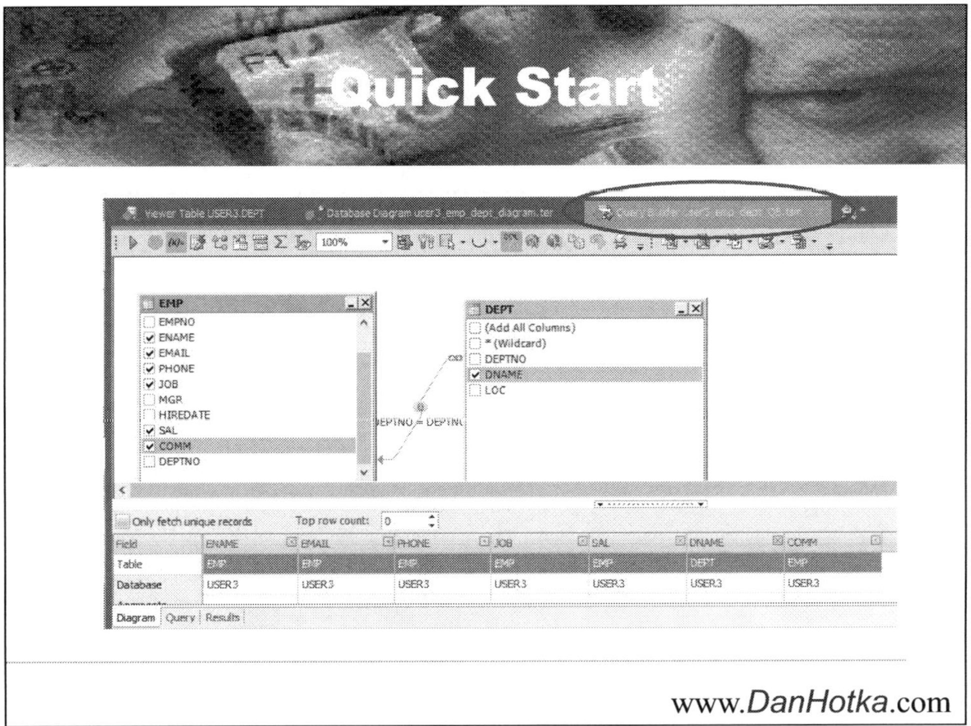


## Working with Data

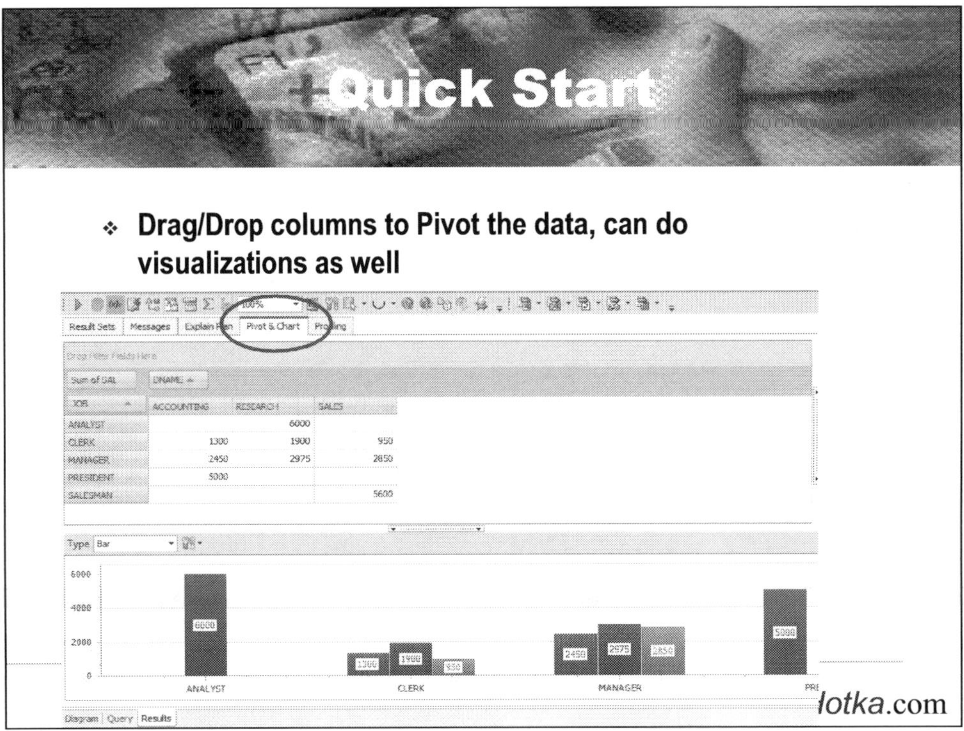

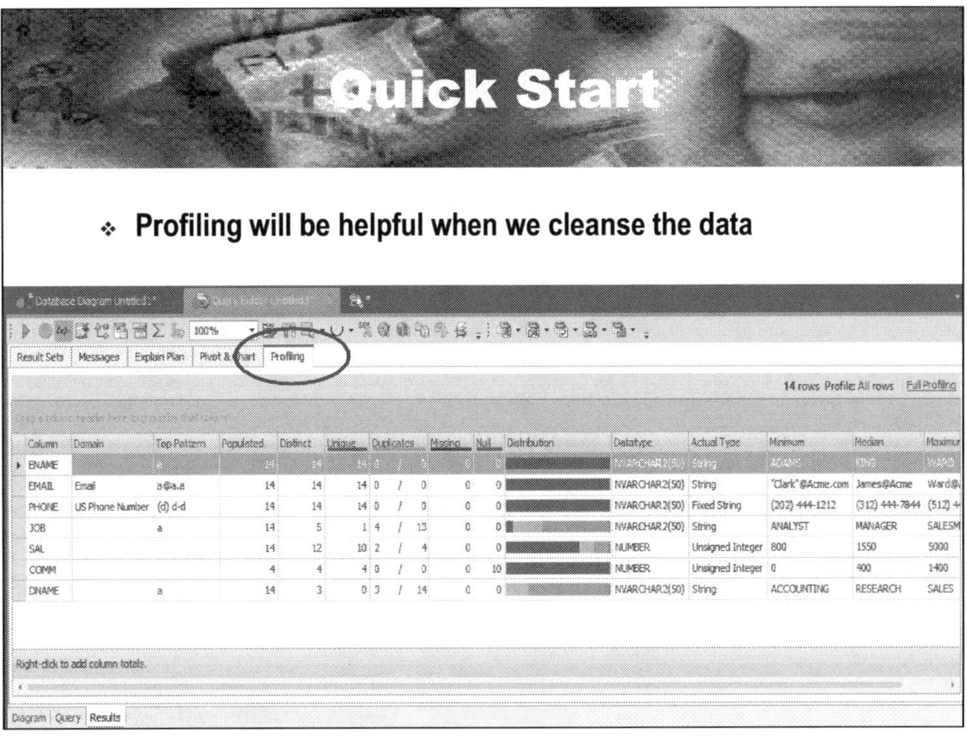


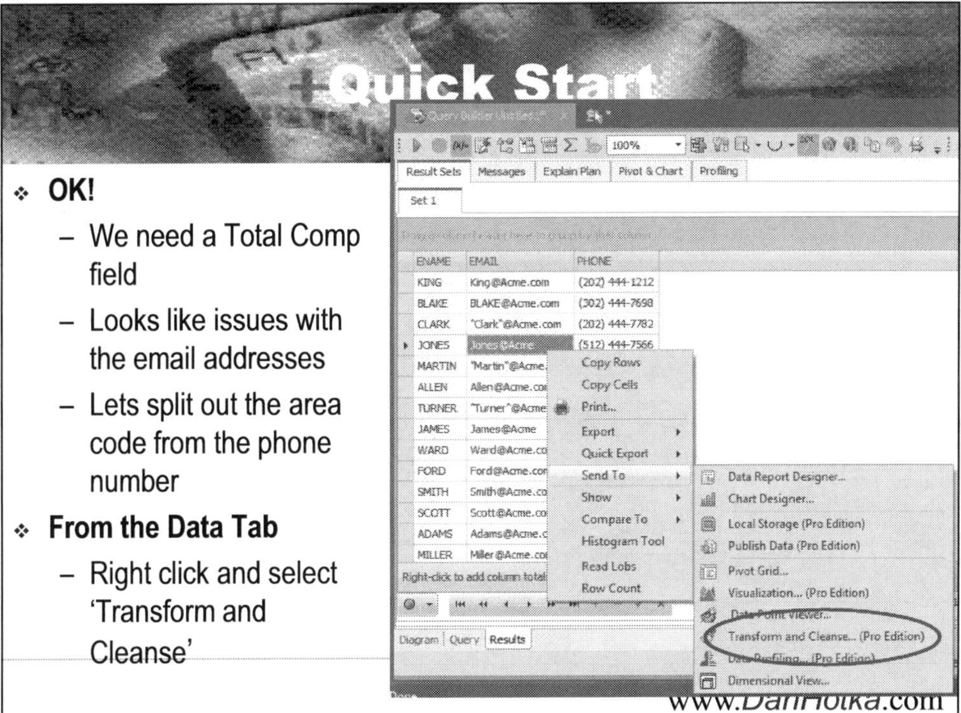


Notice above that we have email addresses that do not have a .com suffix and some include quotes. Right click selecting 'Send To' then 'Transform and Cleanse…'.

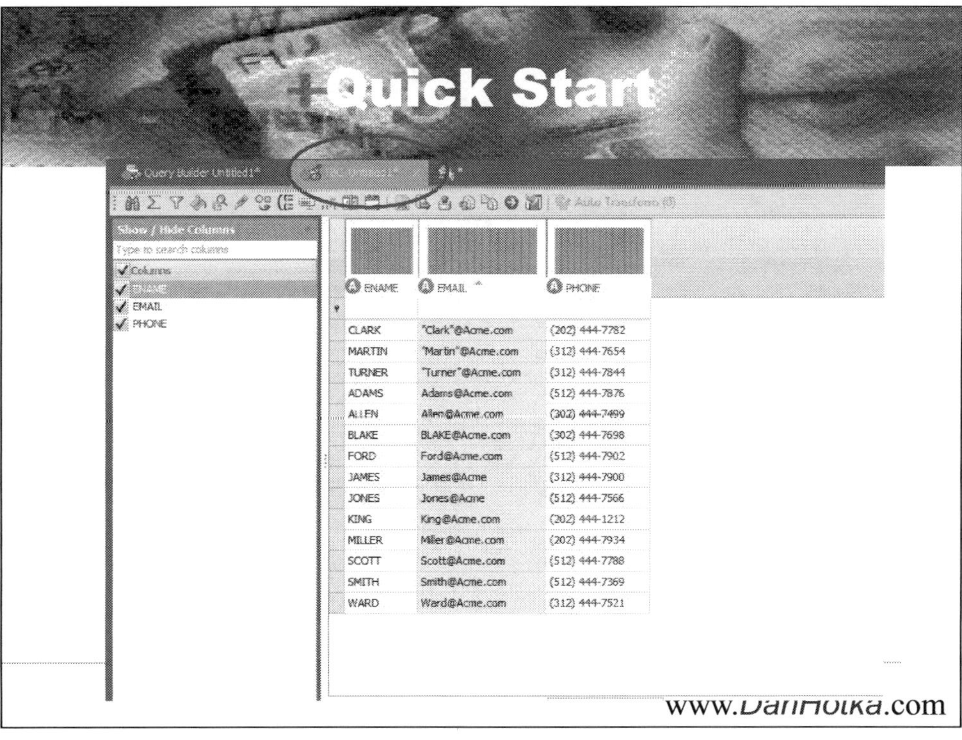
Quick Start
Query Builder Untitled1*
Show / Hide Columns
Type to search columns
Columns
ENAME
EMAIL
PHONE
ENAME
EMAIL
PHONE
CLARK "Clark"@Acme.com (202) 444-7782
MARTIN "Martin"@Acme.com (312) 444-7654
TURNER "Turner"@Acme.com (312) 444-7844
ADAMS Adams@Acme.com (512) 444-7876
ALLEN Allen@Acme.com (302) 444-7499
BLAKE BLAKE@Acme.com (302) 444-7698
FORD Ford@Acme.com (512) 444-7902
JAMES James@Acme (312) 444-7900
JONES Jones@Acme (512) 444-7566
KING King@Acme.com (202) 444-1212
MILLER Miller@Acme.com (202) 444-7934
SCOTT Scott@Acme.com (512) 444-7788
SMITH Smith@Acme.com (512) 444-7369
WARD Ward@Acme.com (312) 444-7521

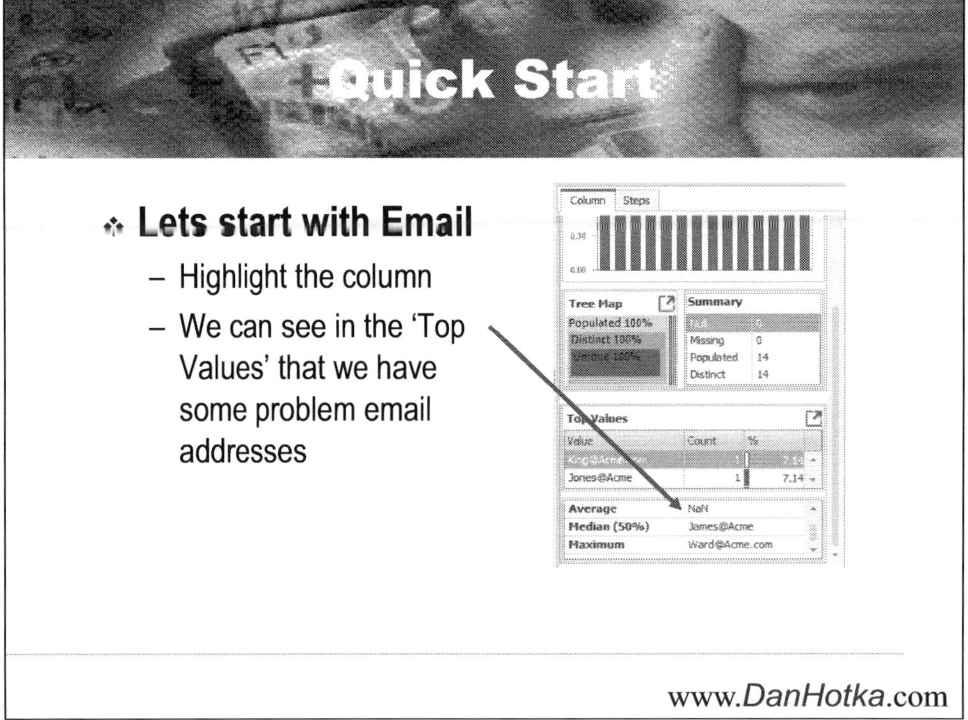
Quick Start
Lets start with Email
– Highlight the column
– We can see in the 'Top Values' that we have some problem email addresses
Column
Steps
Tree Map
Populated 100%
Distinct 100%
Summary
Missing 0
Populated 14
Distinct 14
Top Values
Value
Count
%
Jones@Acme 1 7.14
Average NaN
Median (50%) James@Acme
Maximum Ward@Acme.com
www.DanHotka.com

There are some features along the right side to help us find the issues.

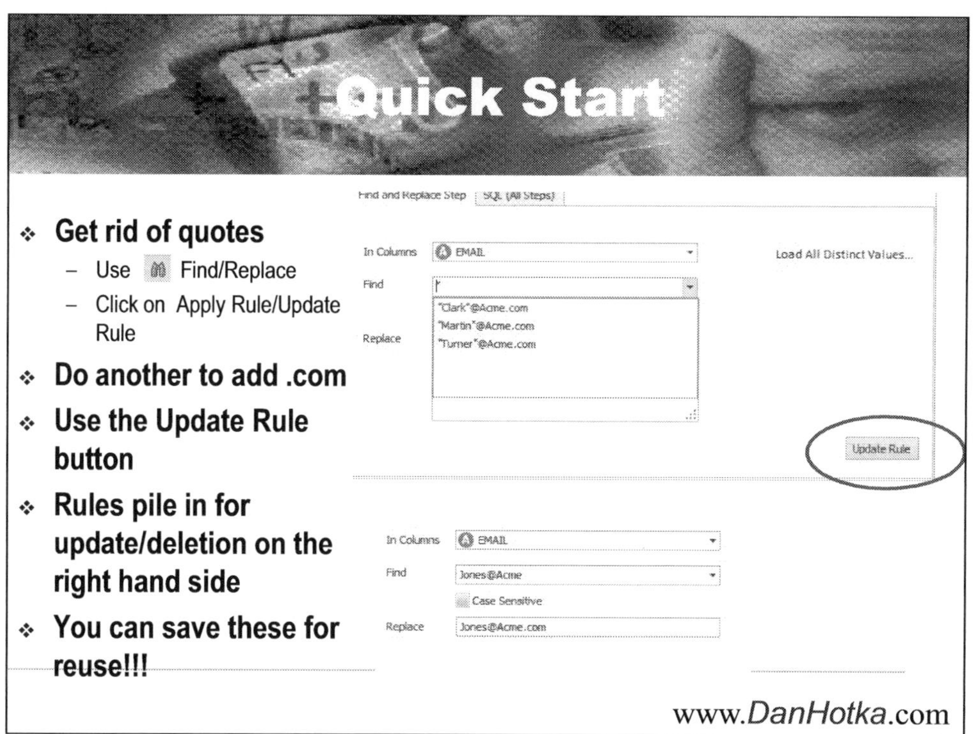
Quick Start
Get rid of quotes
– Use Find/Replace
– Click on Apply Rule/Update Rule
Do another to add .com
Use the Update Rule button
Rules pile in for update/deletion on the right hand side
You can save these for reuse!!!
In Columns
EMAIL
Find
Replace
Load All Distinct Values...
"Clark"@Acme.com
"Martin"@Acme.com
"Turner"@Acme.com
Update Rule
Jones@Acme
Case Sensitive
Jones@Acme.com
www.DanHotka.com

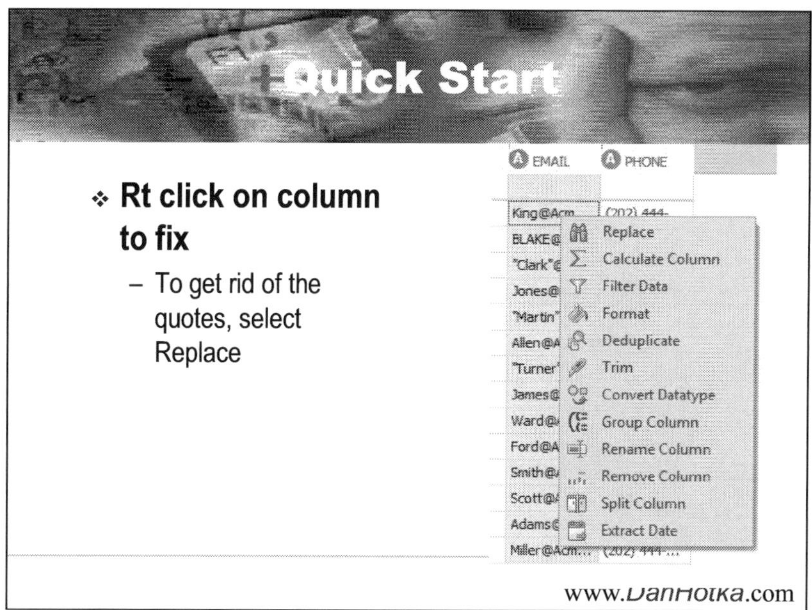
Quick Start
Rt click on column to fix
– To get rid of the quotes, select Replace
EMAIL
PHONE
Replace
Calculate Column
Filter Data
Format
Deduplicate
Trim
Convert Datatype
Group Column
Rename Column
Remove Column
Split Column
Extract Date
www.DanHotka.com

We will use the Replace feature to fix our problems. Notice there are many other things you can do…including Split the column. This feature is useful for say phone numbers to make the area code and the phone number separate columns. You can filter, rename, and add columns (using the Calculate Column selection).

Right Click and select 'Replace'.

Quick Start
Find and Replace Step
SQL (All Steps)
In Columns
EMAIL
Load All Distinct Values...
Find
"
Found in 3 rows
"Clark"@Acme.com
"Martin"@Acme.com
"Turner"@Acme.com
Replace
Apply Rule
www.DanHotka.com


Let's start with the double quotes. Fill out the grid for the find but leave the replace blank. Click on Apply rule. Notice the rule appears in the 'Steps' tab on the right hand side. You can save these, drag them up/down (change the order of the steps), delete them, edit them.

## Quick Start

| ENAME | EMAIL | PHONE |
|---|---|---|
| KING | King@Acme.com | (202) 444-1212 |
| BLAKE | BLAKE@Acme.com | (302) 444-7698 |
| CLARK | Clark@Acme.com | (202) 444-7782 |
| JONES | Jones@Acme | (512) 444-7566 |

Find and Replace Step | SQL (All Steps)

In Columns: EMAIL

Find: James@Acme

Replace: James@Acme.com

Load All Distinct Values...

Update Rule

Column | Steps (2)

Step

EMAIL Find '',Replace

EMAIL Find James@Acme,Replace James@Acme.com

Transforms Repository

Type to filter rule list

Transforms

Notes

www.DanHotka.com

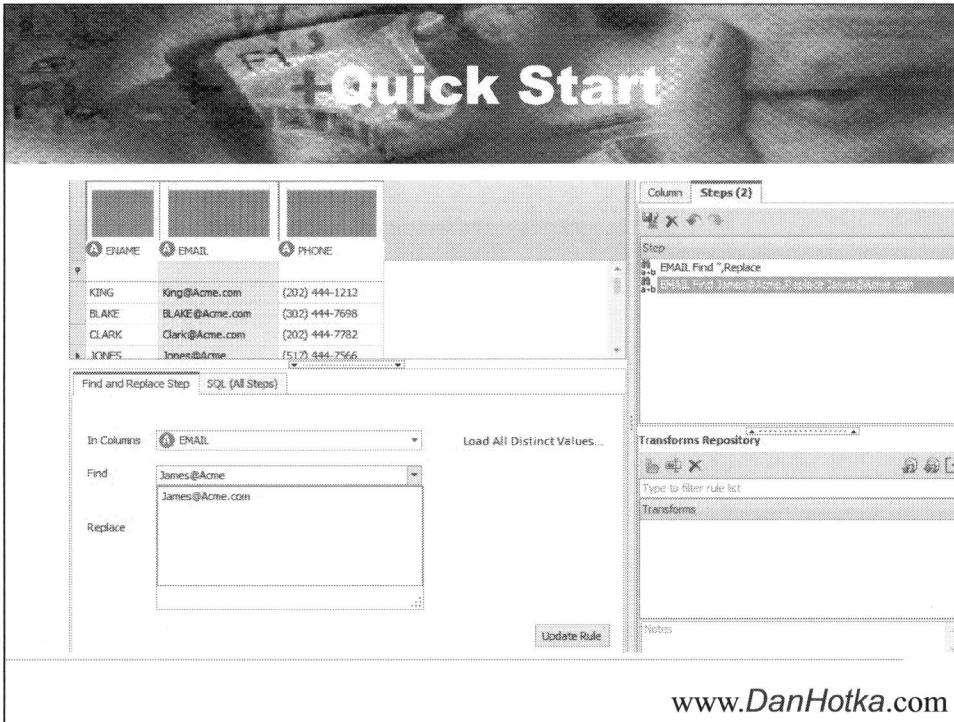

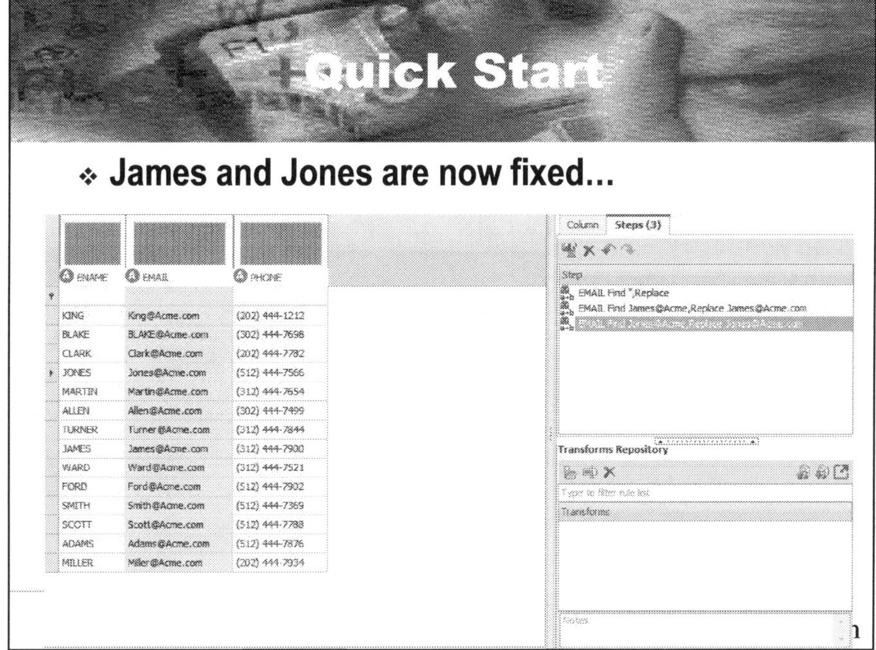

Quick Start
James and Jones are now fixed...
Column
Steps (3)
Step
EMAIL Find '',Replace
EMAIL Find James@Acme,Replace James@Acme.com
Transforms Repository
ENAME
EMAIL
PHONE
KING King@Acme.com (202) 444-1212
BLAKE BLAKE@Acme.com (302) 444-7698
CLARK Clark@Acme.com (202) 444-7782
JONES Jones@Acme.com (512) 444-7566
MARTIN Martin@Acme.com (312) 444-7654
ALLEN Allen@Acme.com (302) 444-7499
TURNER Turner@Acme.com (312) 444-7844
JAMES James@Acme.com (312) 444-7900
WARD Ward@Acme.com (312) 444-7521
FORD Ford@Acme.com (512) 444-7902
SMITH Smith@Acme.com (512) 444-7369
SCOTT Scott@Acme.com (512) 444-7788
ADAMS Adams@Acme.com (512) 444-7876
MILLER Miller@Acme.com (202) 444-7934


The missing suffix is a bit more messy. If we simply replace all of the above email addresses using the replace, we have to do them one at a time. In the future, what if there are more mistakes.

There are a couple of options here.

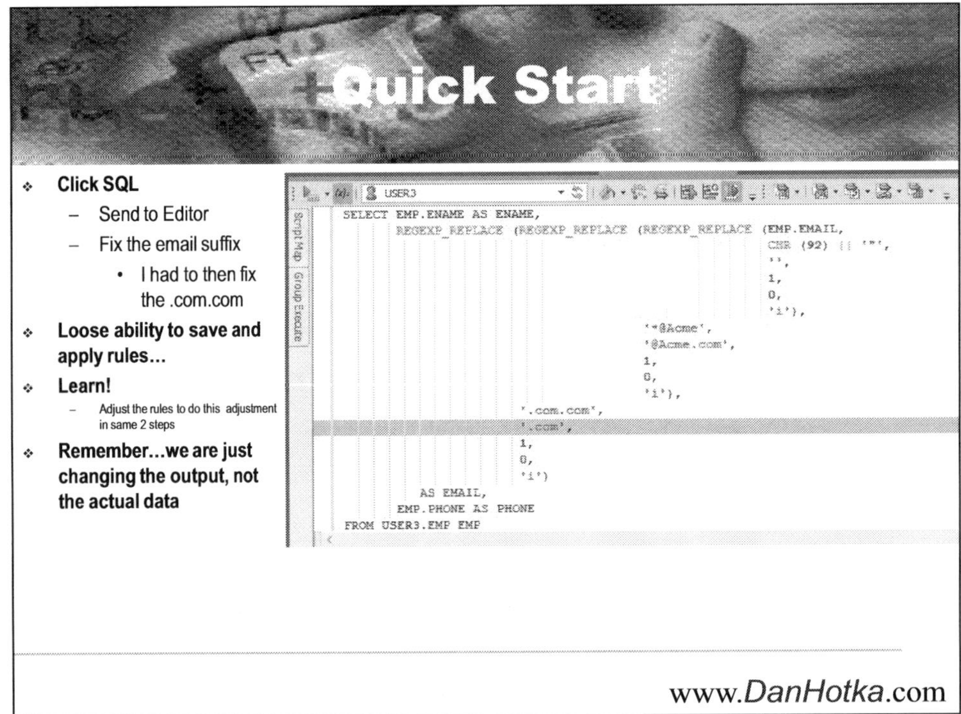
Quick Start
Click SQL
Send to Editor
Fix the email suffix
I had to then fix the .com.com
Loose ability to save and apply rules…
Learn!
Adjust the rules to do this adjustment in same 2 steps
Remember…we are just changing the output, not the actual data
SELECT EMP.ENAME AS ENAME,
FROM USER3.EMP EMP
www.DanHotka.com

You can click the SQL button along the bottom, transferring the SQL to the Editor where, if you have the knowledge, you can adjust the SQL to fix the issues across the entire data set.

I got this to work in the SQL by making some simple changes to the syntax. But…this type of fix will just fix things for this 1 data pull, the rules cannot be saved and used for another.

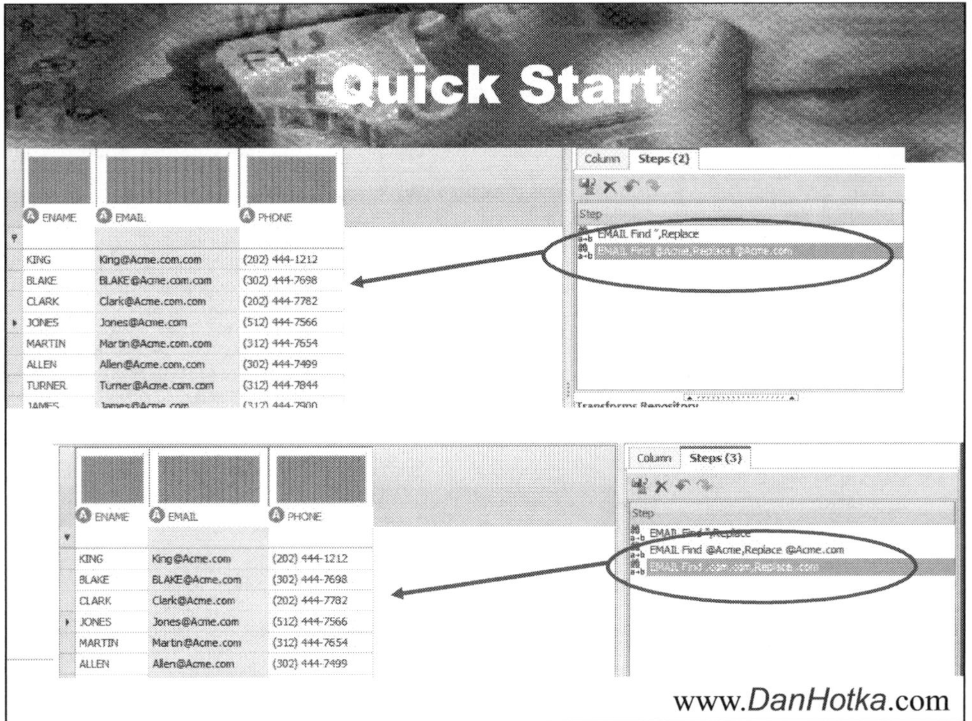
Quick Start
Column
Steps (2)
Step
EMAIL Find ",Replace
ENAME
EMAIL
PHONE
KING
King@Acme.com.com
(202) 444-1212
BLAKE
BLAKE@Acme.com.com
(302) 444-7698
CLARK
Clark@Acme.com.com
(202) 444-7782
JONES
Jones@Acme.com
(512) 444-7566
MARTIN
Martin@Acme.com.com
(312) 444-7654
ALLEN
Allen@Acme.com.com
(302) 444-7499
TURNER
Turner@Acme.com.com
(312) 444-7844
Column
Steps (3)
Step
EMAIL Find @Acme,Replace @Acme.com
ENAME
EMAIL
PHONE
KING
King@Acme.com
(202) 444-1212
BLAKE
BLAKE@Acme.com
(302) 444-7698
CLARK
Clark@Acme.com
(202) 444-7782
JONES
Jones@Acme.com
(512) 444-7566
MARTIN
Martin@Acme.com
(312) 444-7654
ALLEN
Allen@Acme.com
(302) 444-7499
www.DanHotka.com

I take the above knowledge and make 2 rules…one to fix the missing .com but this fix makes a mess of the addresses that already had a .com…hmmmmm.

*****Note***** Watch for this behavior to change in future releases of Toad DP. The instructor works closely with the Toad and Toad DP teams and has recommended that this be changed to use global characters, much like how the filtering works in other parts of Toad DP.

So I add another rule for .com.com back to a single .com. You can drag and drop these rules to be performed in any order. They are performed top-down.

Save your rules, give them a name. Next time you need to cleanse an email column, just open this file and it will pick up these rules. You can publish the rules to the repository for others to use, you can include them in Automation…so…that when data is being prepared for use, these rules are automatically applied before the analyst/end user gets the final result. You can then store the final result as a table data (several ways to do this too) so analysts/end users use the cleansed data for their reporting needs, no need for everyone to do the same transformation steps. This can all be setup ahead of time and automated for everyone's gained productivity

## Adding Calculations

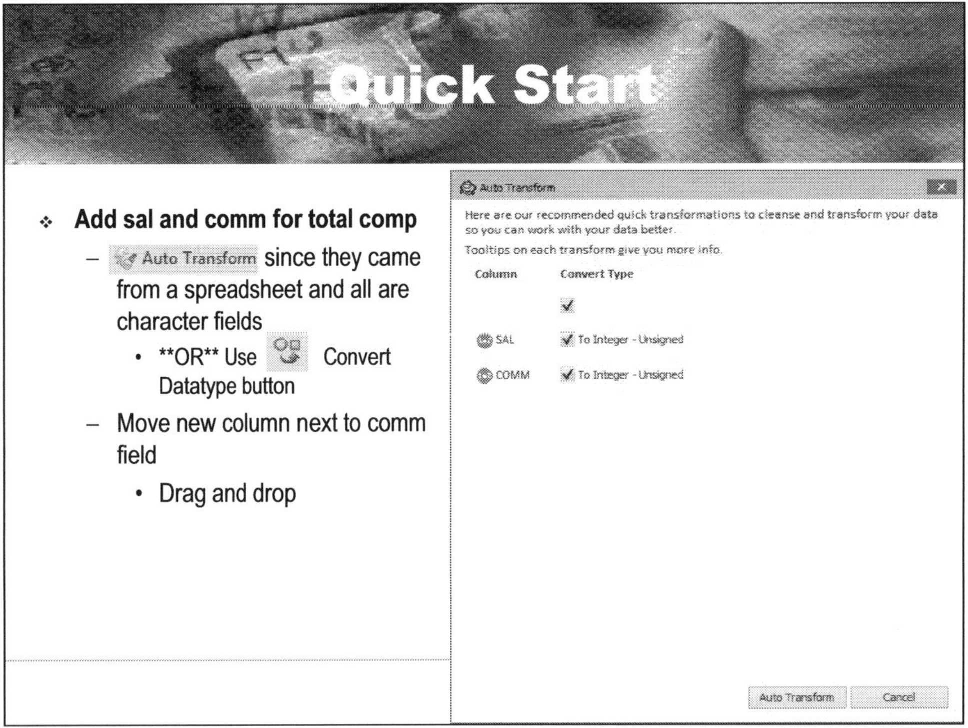
Quick Start
Add sal and comm for total comp
– Auto Transform since they came from a spreadsheet and all are character fields
• **OR** Use Convert Datatype button
– Move new column next to comm field
• Drag and drop
Auto Transform
Here are our recommended quick transformations to cleanse and transform your data so you can work with your data better.
Tooltips on each transform give you more info.
Column
Convert Type
SAL
To Integer - Unsigned
COMM
To Integer - Unsigned
Auto Transform
Cancel

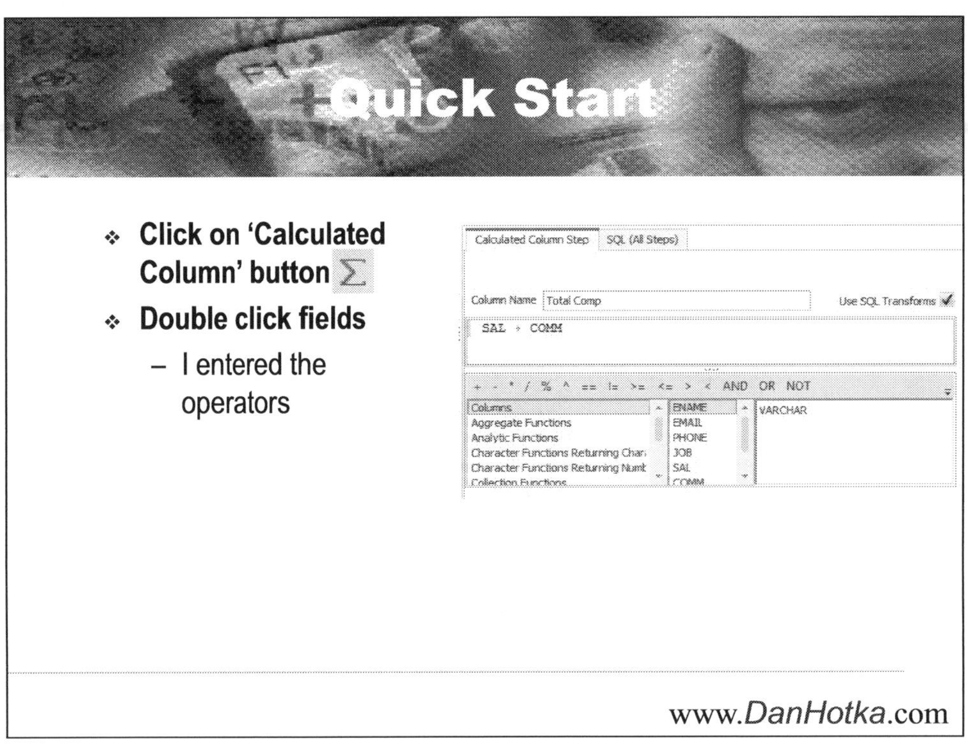
Quick Start
Click on 'Calculated Column' button
Double click fields
– I entered the operators
Calculated Column Step
SQL (All Steps)
Column Name
Total Comp
Use SQL Transforms
SAL + COMM
AND OR NOT
Columns
Aggregate Functions
Analytic Functions
ENAME
EMAIL
PHONE
JOB
SAL
VARCHAR
www.DanHotka.com

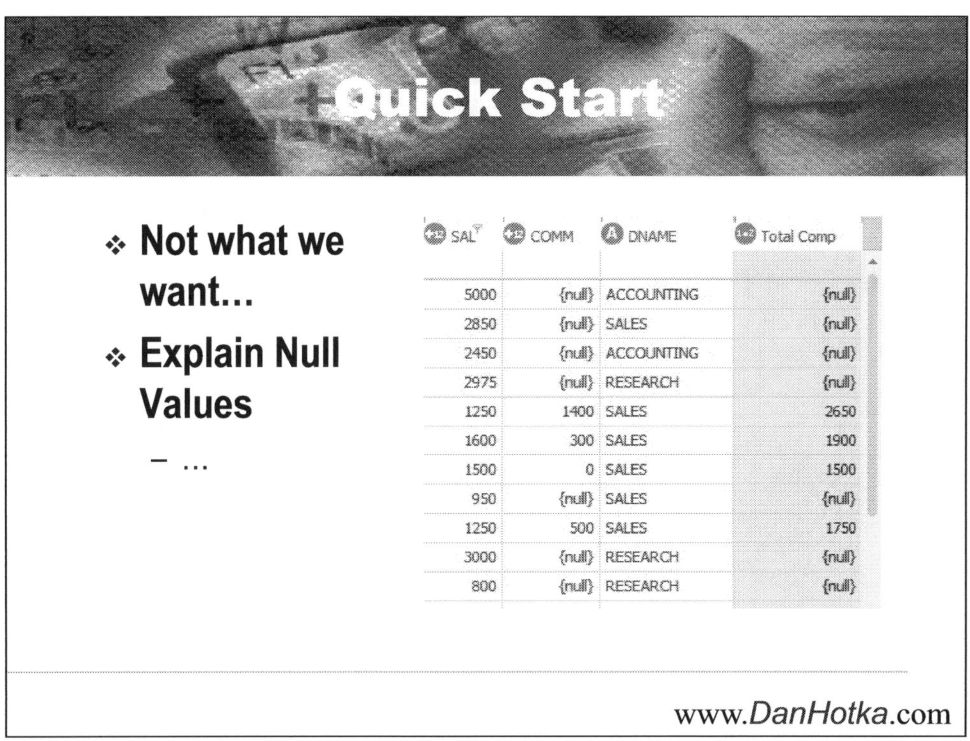
Quick Start
Not what we want…
Explain Null Values
– …
SAL
COMM
DNAME
Total Comp
5000 {null} ACCOUNTING {null}
2850 {null} SALES {null}
2450 {null} ACCOUNTING {null}
2975 {null} RESEARCH {null}
1250 1400 SALES 2650
1600 300 SALES 1900
1500 0 SALES 1500
950 {null} SALES {null}
1250 500 SALES 1750
3000 {null} RESEARCH {null}
800 {null} RESEARCH {null}
www.DanHotka.com

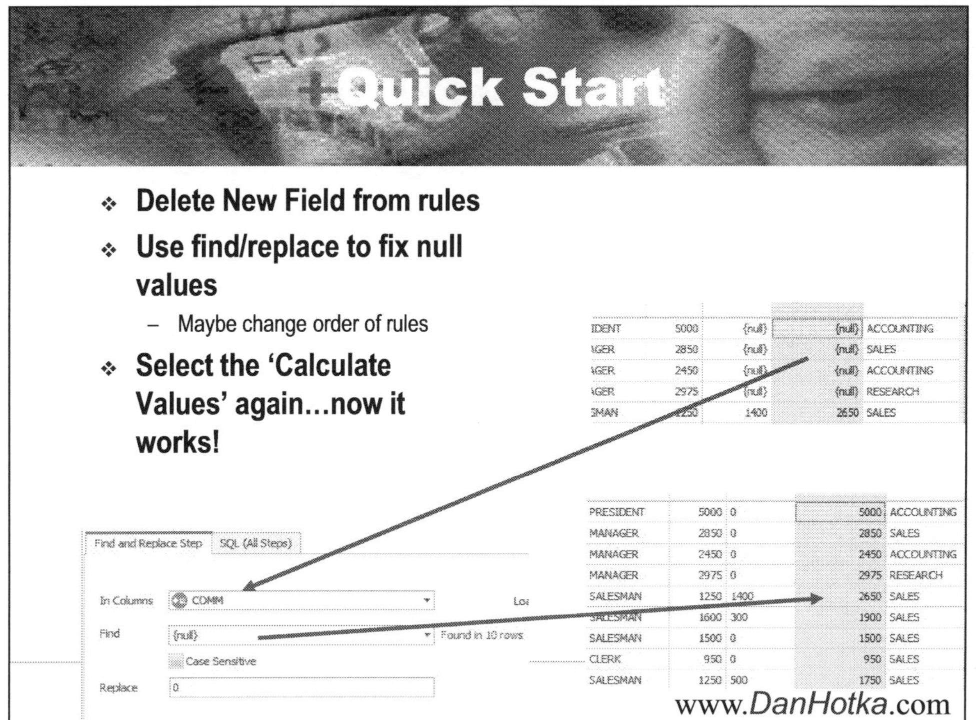
Quick Start
Delete New Field from rules
Use find/replace to fix null values
– Maybe change order of rules
Select the 'Calculate Values' again…now it works!
Find and Replace Step
SQL (All Steps)
In Columns
COMM
Find
{null}
Found in 10 rows
Case Sensitive
Replace
0
PRESIDENT 5000 0 5000 ACCOUNTING
MANAGER 2850 0 2850 SALES
MANAGER 2450 0 2450 ACCOUNTING
MANAGER 2975 0 2975 RESEARCH
SALESMAN 1250 1400 2650 SALES
1600 300 1900 SALES
SALESMAN 1500 0 1500 SALES
CLERK 950 0 950 SALES
SALESMAN 1250 500 1750 SALES
www.DanHotka.com

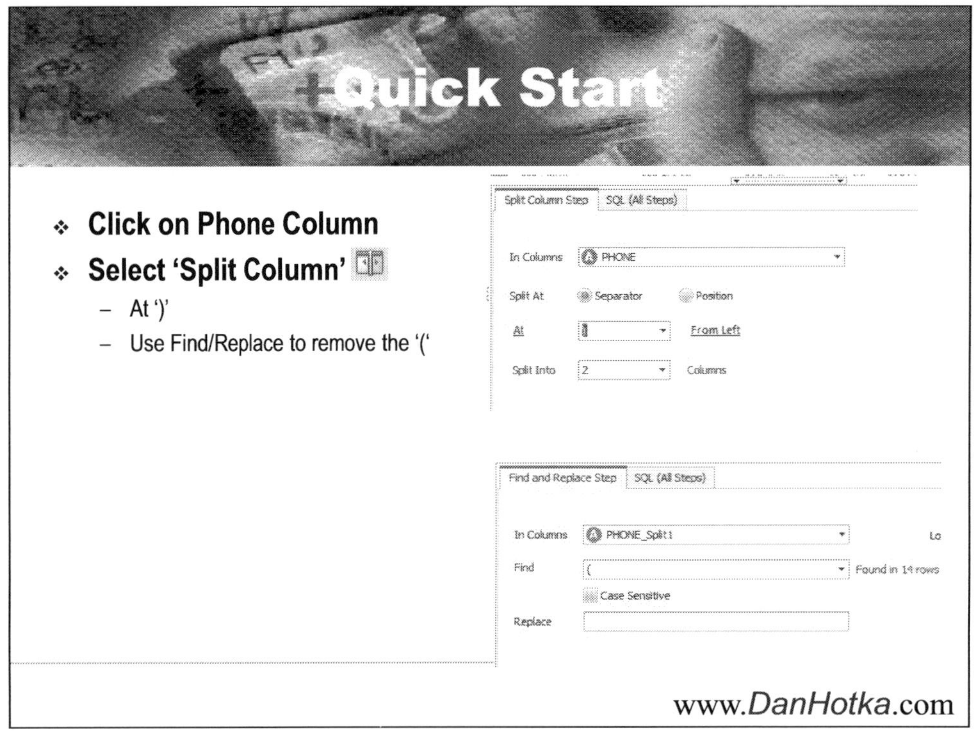
Quick Start
Click on Phone Column
Select 'Split Column'
At ')'
Use Find/Replace to remove the '('
Split Column Step
SQL (All Steps)
In Columns
PHONE
Split At
Separator
Position
At
From Left
Split Into
2
Columns
Find and Replace Step
SQL (All Steps)
In Columns
PHONE_Split1
Find
(
Found in 14 rows
Case Sensitive
Replace
www.DanHotka.com

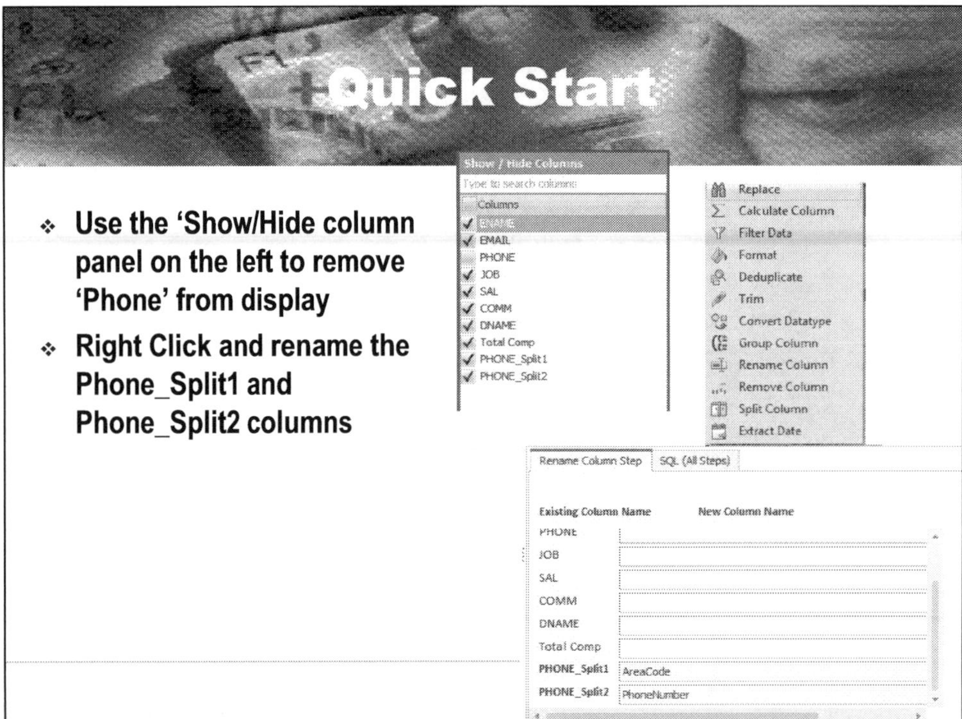
Quick Start
Use the 'Show/Hide column panel on the left to remove 'Phone' from display
Right Click and rename the Phone_Split1 and Phone_Split2 columns
Show / Hide Columns
Columns
ENAME
EMAIL
PHONE
JOB
SAL
COMM
DNAME
Total Comp
PHONE_Split1
PHONE_Split2
Replace
Calculate Column
Filter Data
Format
Deduplicate
Trim
Convert Datatype
Group Column
Rename Column
Remove Column
Split Column
Extract Date
Rename Column Step
SQL (All Steps)
Existing Column Name
New Column Name
PHONE
JOB
SAL
COMM
DNAME
Total Comp
PHONE_Split1
AreaCode
PHONE_Split2
PhoneNumber

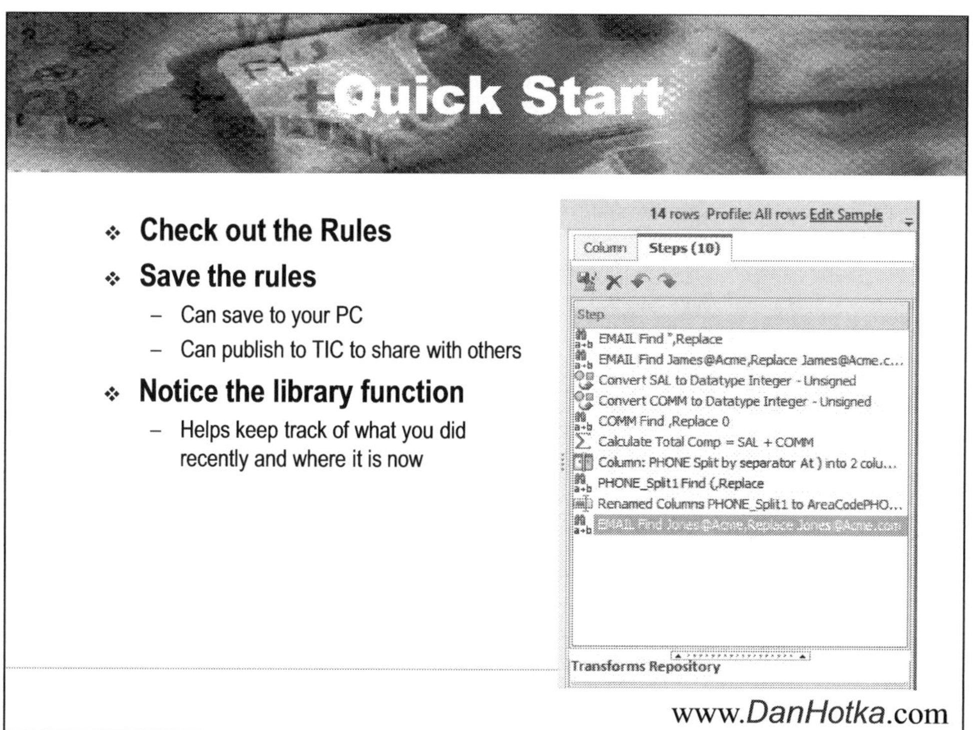
Quick Start
Check out the Rules
Save the rules
– Can save to your PC
– Can publish to TIC to share with others
Notice the library function
– Helps keep track of what you did recently and where it is now
14 rows Profile: All rows Edit Sample
Column
Steps (10)
Step
EMAIL Find ",Replace
EMAIL Find James@Acme,Replace James@Acme.c...
Convert SAL to Datatype Integer - Unsigned
Convert COMM to Datatype Integer - Unsigned
COMM Find ,Replace 0
Calculate Total Comp = SAL + COMM
Column: PHONE Split by separator At ) into 2 colu...
PHONE_Split1 Find (,Replace
Renamed Columns PHONE_Split1 to AreaCodePHO...
EMAIL Find Jones@Acme,Replace Jones@Acme.com
Transforms Repository
www.DanHotka.com

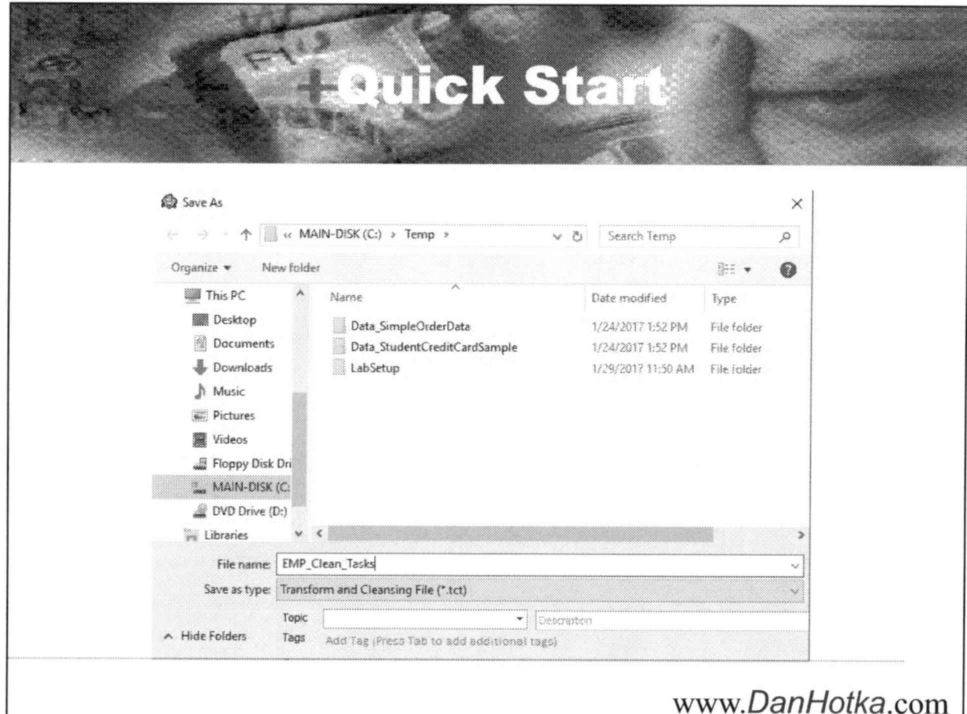
Quick Start
Save As
MAIN-DISK (C:) › Temp ›
Search Temp
Organize
New folder
This PC
Desktop
Documents
Downloads
Music
Pictures
Videos
Floppy Disk Dri
MAIN-DISK (C:
DVD Drive (D:)
Libraries
Name
Date modified
Type
Data_SimpleOrderData
1/24/2017 1:52 PM
File folder
Data_StudentCreditCardSample
1/24/2017 1:52 PM
File folder
LabSetup
1/29/2017 11:50 AM
File folder
File name: EMP_Clean_Tasks
Save as type: Transform and Cleansing File (*.tct)
Topic
Description
Tags
Add Tag (Press Tab to add additional tags)
Hide Folders
www.DanHotka.com

## Saving Data

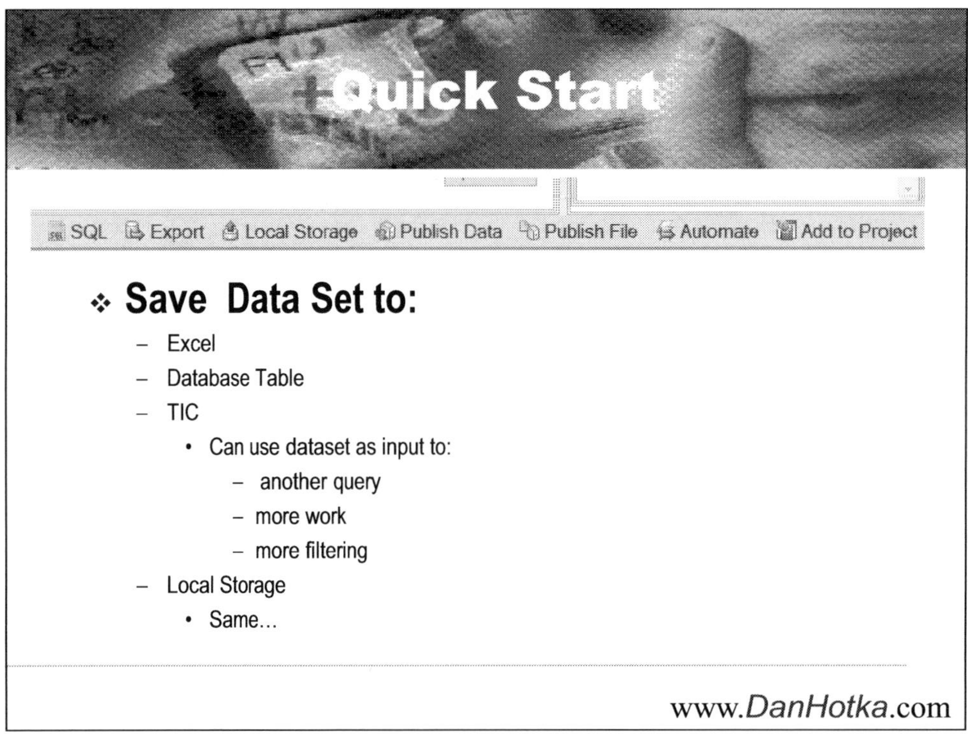
Quick Start
SQL
Export
Local Storage
Publish Data
Publish File
Automate
Add to Project
Save Data Set to:
– Excel
– Database Table
– TIC
• Can use dataset as input to:
– another query
– more work
– more filtering
– Local Storage
• Same…
www.DanHotka.com

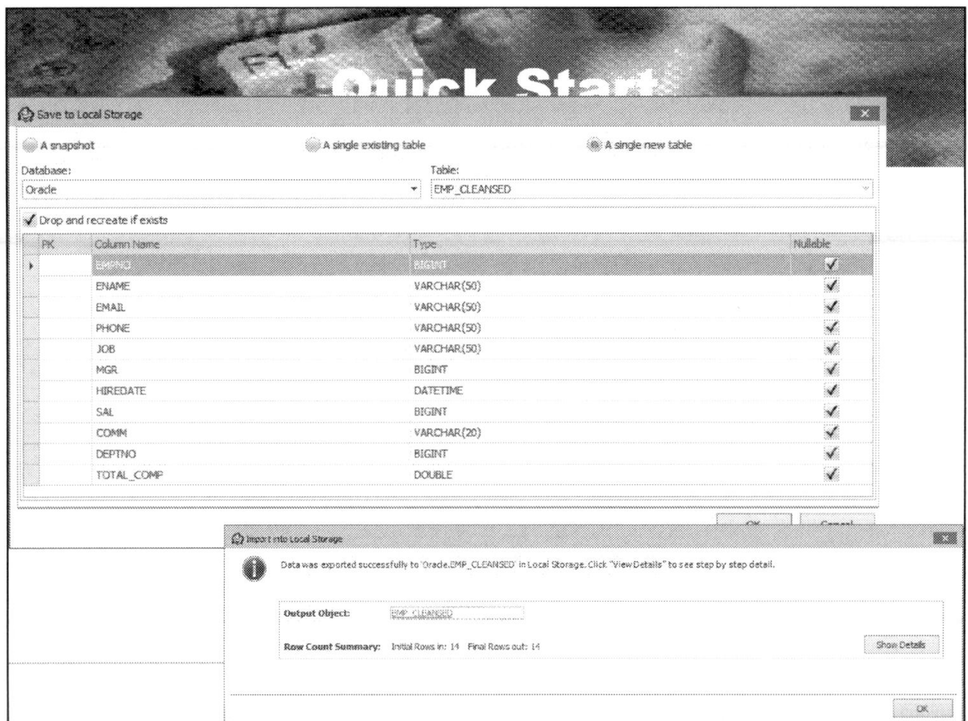
Save to Local Storage
A snapshot
A single existing table
A single new table
Database:
Oracle
Table:
EMP_CLEANSED
Drop and recreate if exists
PK
Column Name
Type
Nullable
EMPNO
BIGINT
ENAME
VARCHAR(50)
EMAIL
VARCHAR(50)
PHONE
VARCHAR(50)
JOB
VARCHAR(50)
MGR
BIGINT
HIREDATE
DATETIME
SAL
BIGINT
COMM
VARCHAR(20)
DEPTNO
BIGINT
TOTAL_COMP
DOUBLE
Import into Local Storage
Data was exported successfully to 'Oracle.EMP_CLEANSED' in Local Storage. Click "View Details" to see step by step detail.
Output Object:
EMP_CLEANSED
Row Count Summary:
Initial Rows in: 14 Final Rows out: 14
Show Details
OK

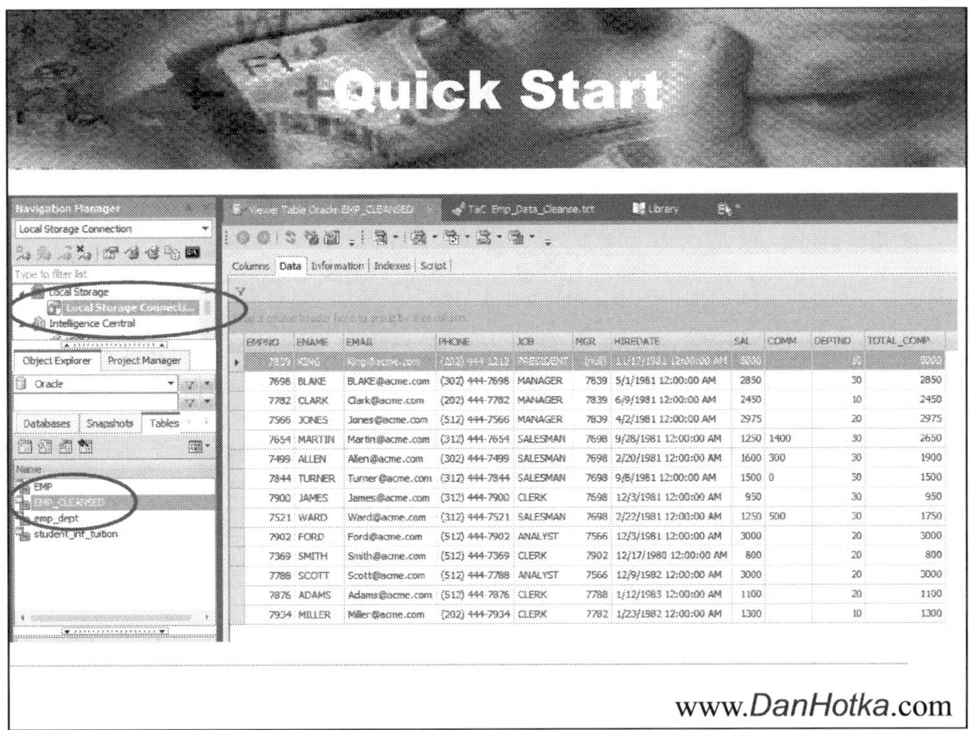


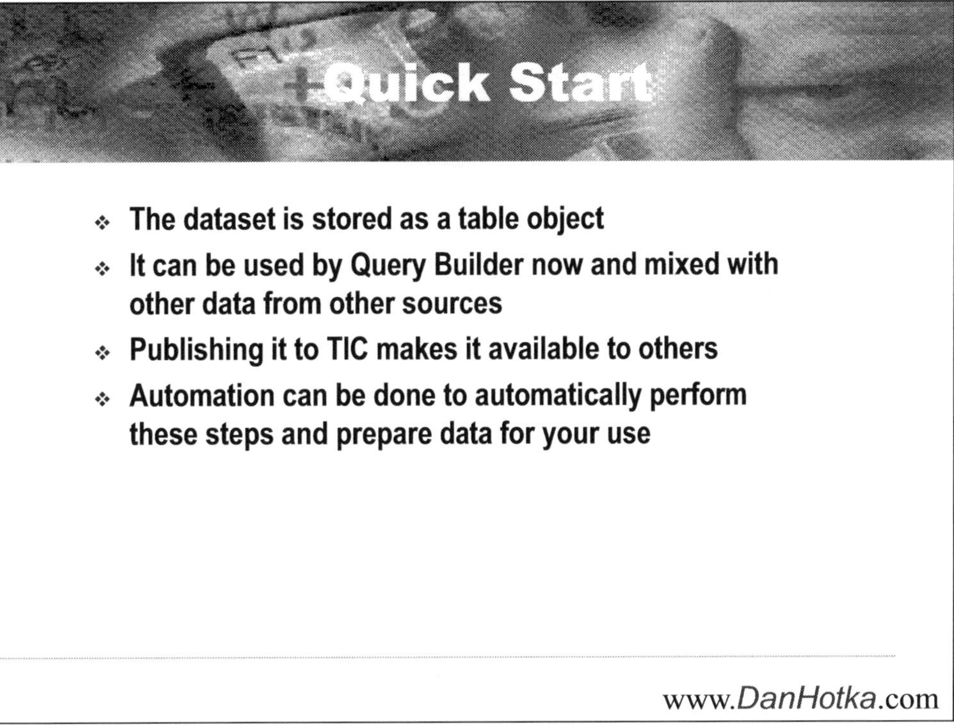


## Pivot Tables

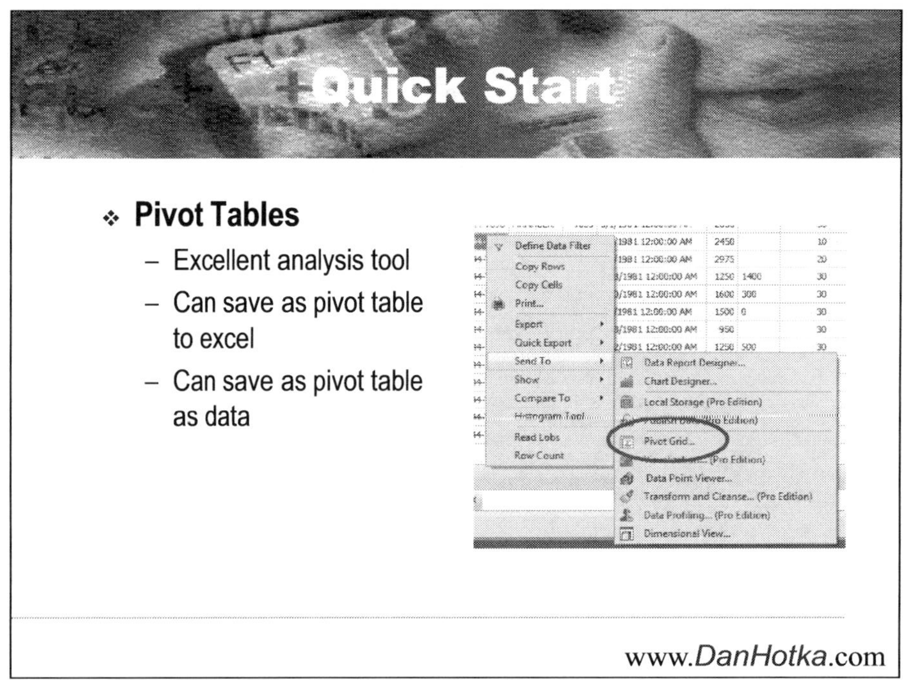
Quick Start
Pivot Tables
Excellent analysis tool
Can save as pivot table to excel
Can save as pivot table as data
Define Data Filter
Copy Rows
Copy Cells
Print...
Export
Quick Export
Send To
Show
Compare To
Histogram Tool
Read Lobs
Row Count
Data Report Designer...
Chart Designer...
Local Storage (Pro Edition)
Pivot Grid...
Data Point Viewer...
Transform and Cleanse... (Pro Edition)
Data Profiling... (Pro Edition)
Dimensional View...
www.DanHotka.com

Toad 4.3 has enhanced the Pivot Grid reporting. You can now build pivot grids easier and save them as pivot tables to Excel. Of course, the data can be saved locally, in the database, or published to share with others.

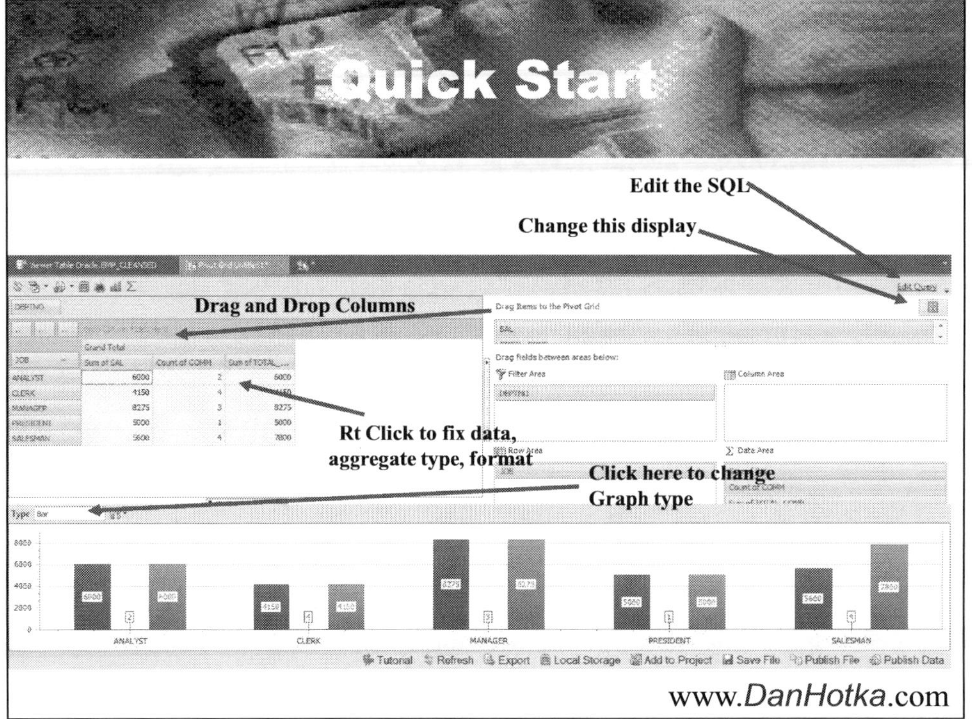
Quick Start
Edit the SQL
Change this display
Drag and Drop Columns
Rt Click to fix data, aggregate type, format
Click here to change Graph type
ANALYST
CLERK
MANAGER
PRESIDENT
SALESMAN
Tutorial
Refresh
Export
Local Storage
Add to Project
Save File
Publish File
Publish Data
www.DanHotka.com

Building the pivot grid is easy using a drag n drop mouse operation from the columns area (upper right). Notice you can change the layout of the display. You can change the graph layout. You can edit the SQL used to pull the columns. You can add filters, etc.

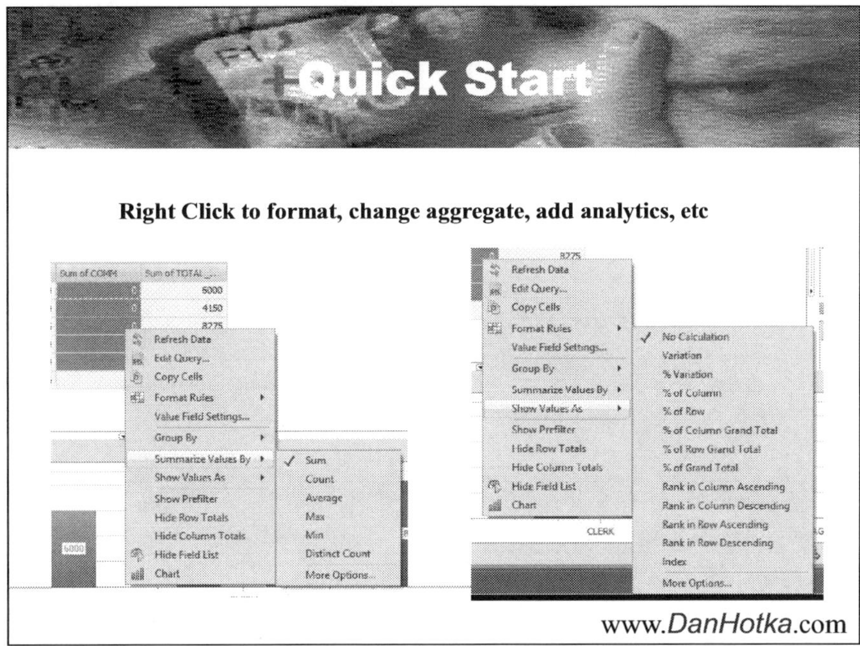


Right click on the columns allows you to change the aggregate type, the format, the column headings, and even utilize additional analytic functions.

Use the Export Pivot button to export as a pivot table to Excel. This starts the Export wizard where you can decide how to name and where to locate the spread sheet.

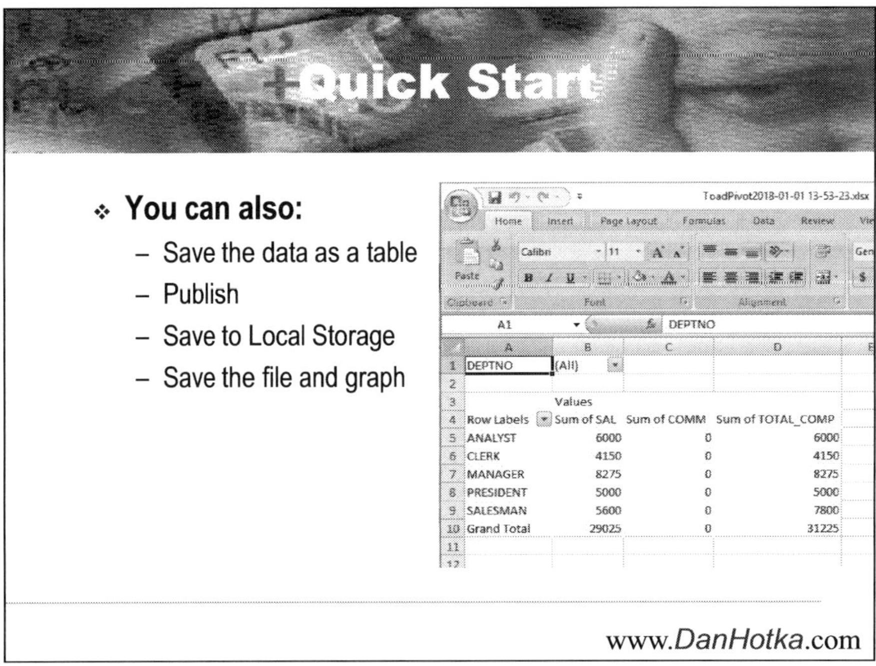


Yes, you can save the data, publish the data/spread sheet, save the data and graph, and this course will cover how to automate all of this into a job stream. If you are using TIC, you can then easily share the output to a group or list of users.

## Quick Start Summary

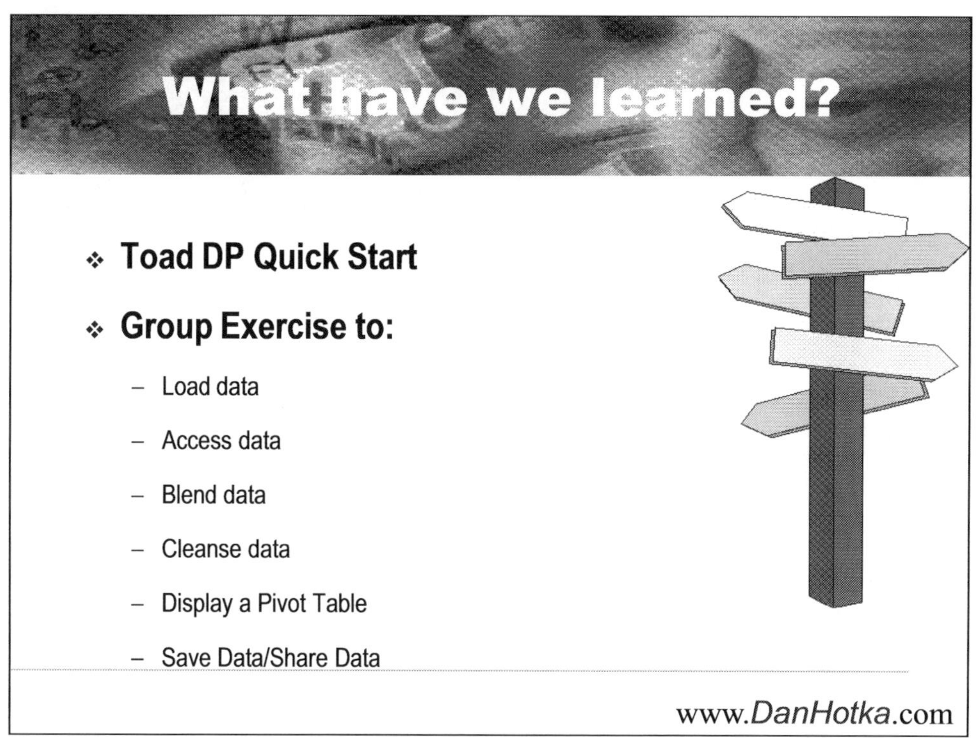
What have we learned?
Toad DP Quick Start
Group Exercise to:
– Load data
– Access data
– Blend data
– Cleanse data
– Display a Pivot Table
– Save Data/Share Data
www.DanHotka.com

This was a group exercise. No Lab, perhaps break time.

# Toad DP Options

This unit will illustrate various useful and important options of Toad DP. We will review some of these features again when we get to where they are used in this course. I'll be sure to refresh you and show you the option and how it works to your benefit.

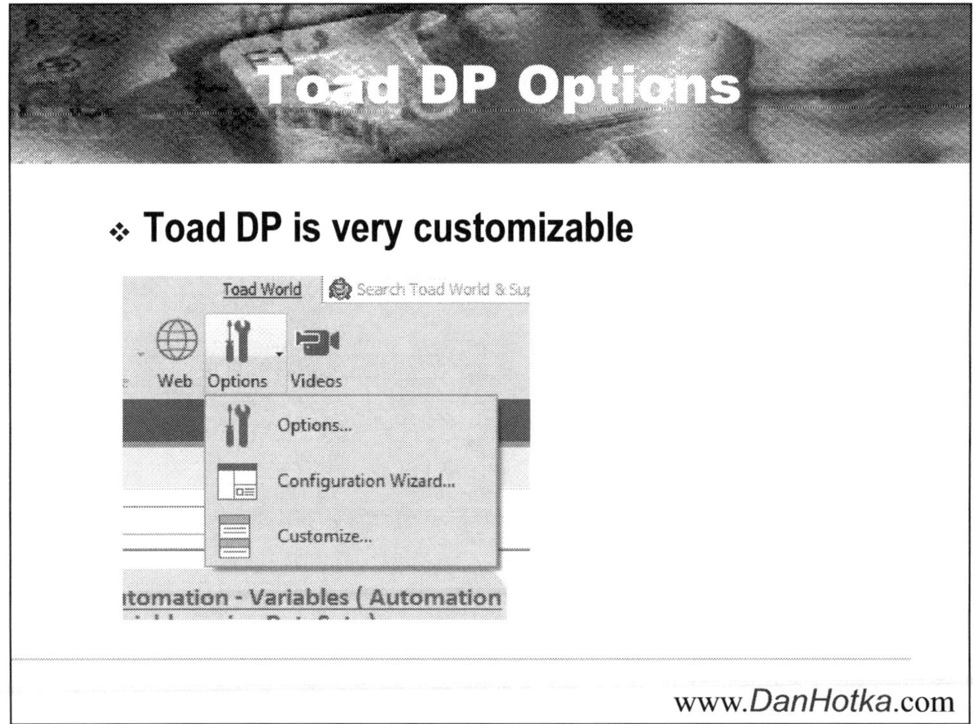


Toad DP is very customizable. You can change the buttons on the tool bars, remove buttons on the tool bar, make the whole tool look like a different tool, and adjust many of the features within the tool.

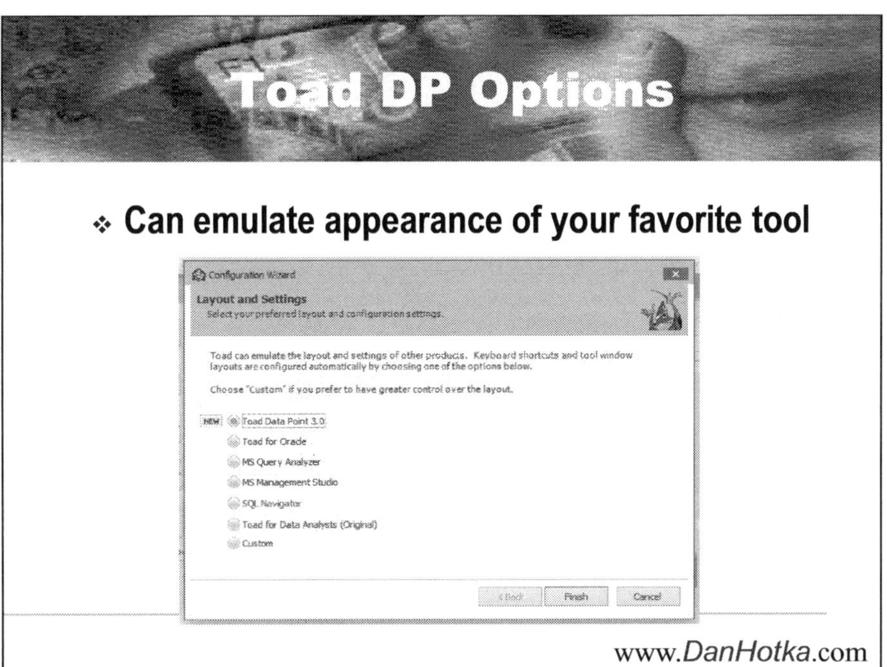


The Configuration Wizard can make the appearance/touch/feel of the tool emulate a tool you might be more familiar with perhaps.

Under the customize feature, you can adjust the content/buttons on the various tool bars. Select the item of interest and simply drag and drop it to the location on Toad DP you wish for it to appear.

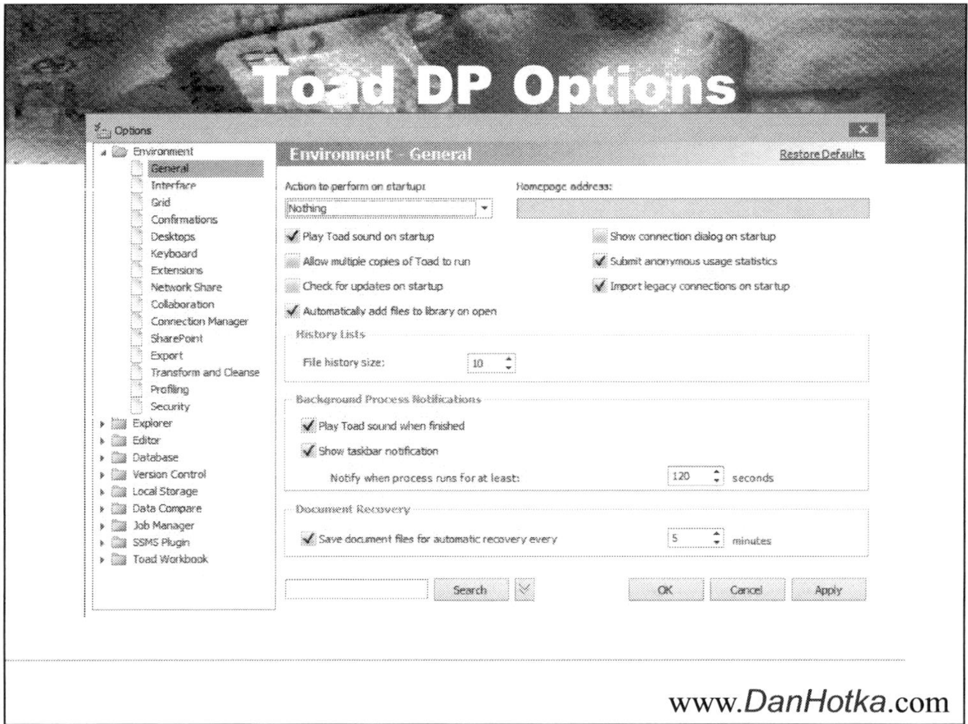


The Options part has many items of interest. We will walk thru these features and I'll re-discuss them as we see them in use within the tool.

***Tip*** You can restore most everything back to its original default settings. Notice the link in the upper right hand corner. I MIGHT have been responsible for this ability!

I like to disable the Toad croak. Other options include multiple versions of Toad running at the same time. For example, if you are both a Toad for Oracle user and work with data using Toad Data Point, you will need this selected in both tools to have both running at the same time.

It is probably a good idea to leave the updates feature on.

Toad DP Options

Options

Environment
General
Interface
Grid
Confirmations
Desktops
Keyboard
Extensions
Network Share
Collaboration
Connection Manager
SharePoint
Export
Transform and Cleanse
Security
Explorer
Editor
Database
Version Control
Local Storage
Data Compare
Job Manager

Environment - General
Restore Defaults
Action to perform on startup:
Nothing
Homepage address:
Play Toad sound on startup
Show connection dialog on startup
Allow multiple copies of Toad to run
Submit anonymous usage statistics
Check for updates on startup
Import legacy connections on startup
Automatically add files to library on open
History Lists
File history size: 10
Background Process Notifications
Play Toad sound when finished
Show taskbar notification
Notify when process runs for at least: 120 seconds
Document Recovery
Save document files for automatic recovery every 5 minutes
Search
OK
Cancel
Apply

www.DanHotka.com

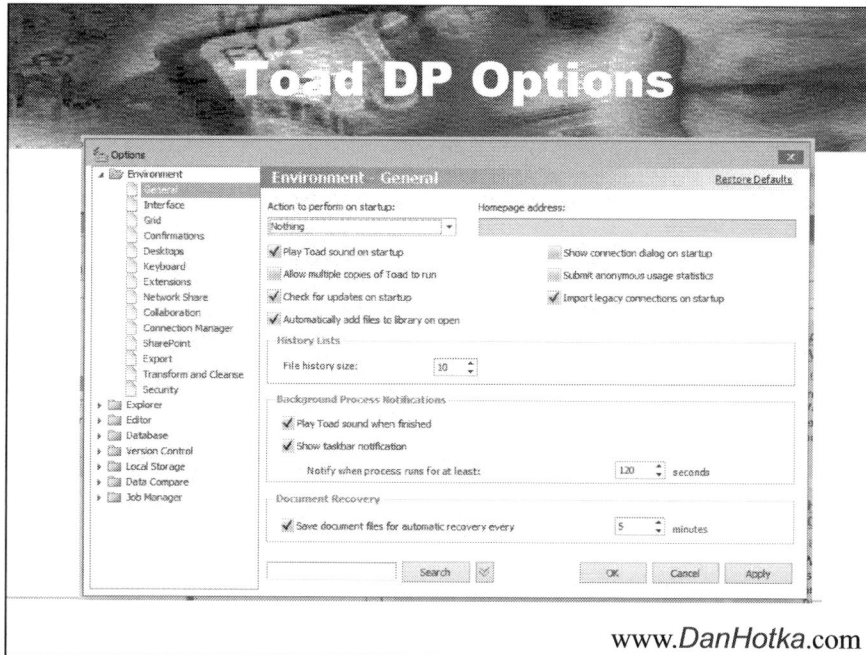

This panel allows you to save your output directly to a shared network folder!

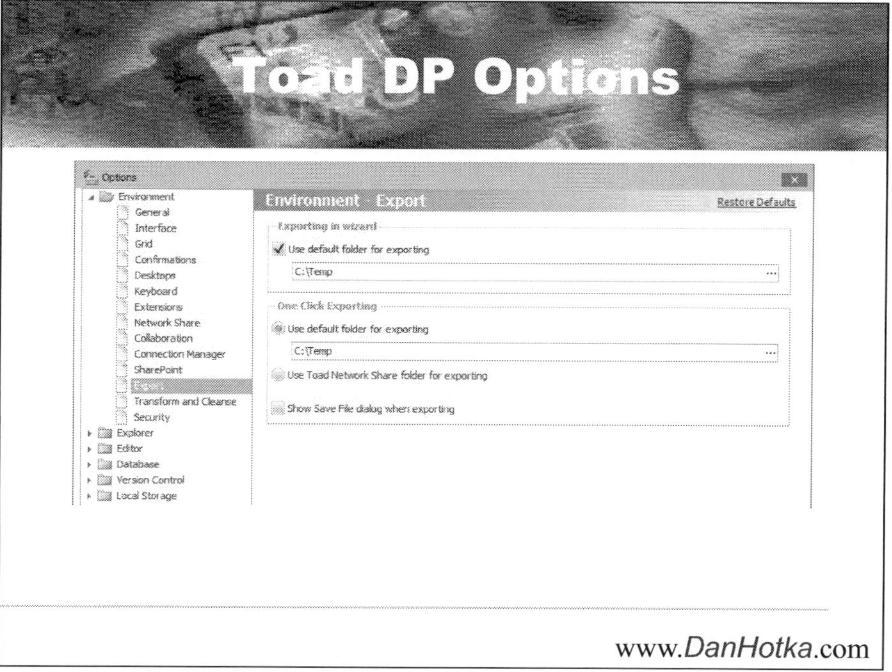


This screen allows you to change the folder that your exports will default to. Notice I changed mine to the c:\Temp folder. This makes these items easy for me to find. Also notice this default export folder can also be on a shared drive (based on prior panel).

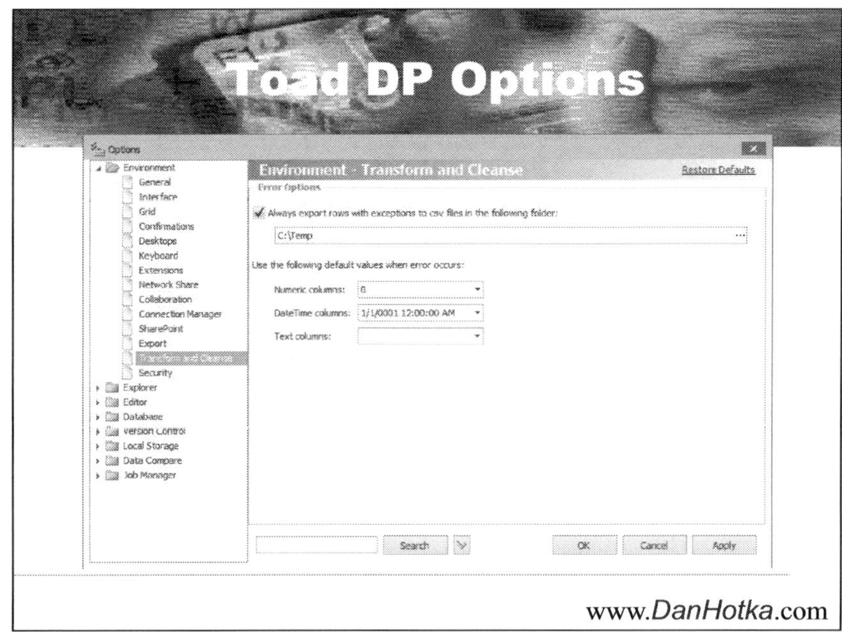


This screen allows you to set some common defaults for column data transformations. It also allows you to set the default location for the errors to be saved. I've set its default location to c:\Temp…again…to make the output easy for me to find.

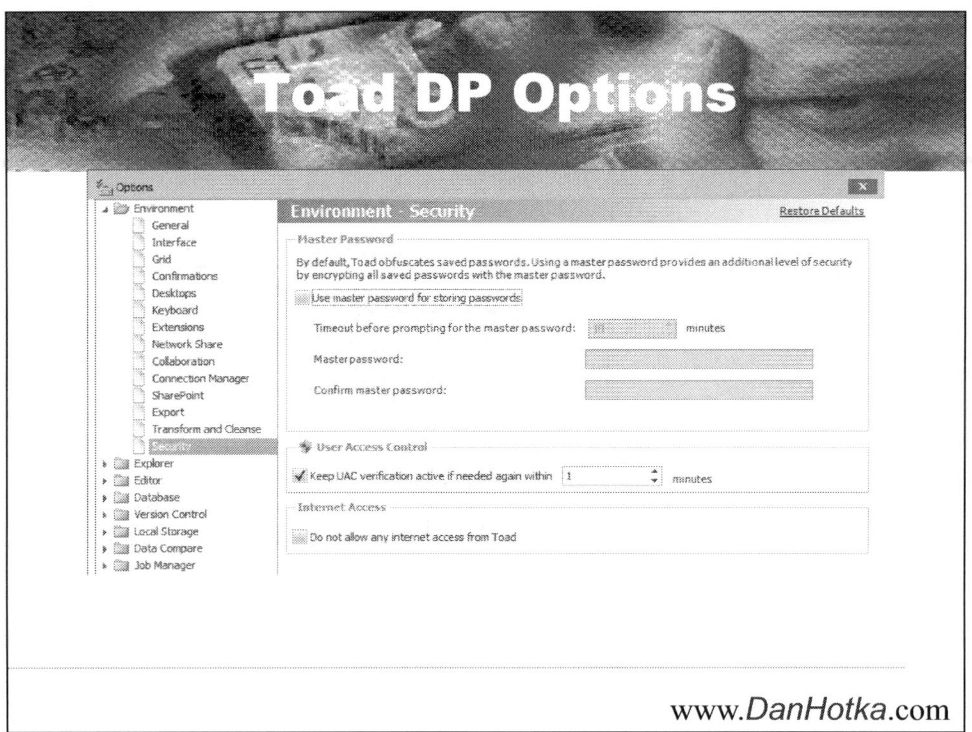

This screen gives you an extra layer of security when using the saved password feature. Also notice the very last item…I find it convenient to web browse from Toad…but you might not. Clicking this box does not allow for you to web browse from the Toad environment.

***** Tip ***** I use the web browser within Toad to both check my email without leaving the app or to work with ToadWorld on additional learning tips and techniques. You might find it useful if some of your data is available via a web page.

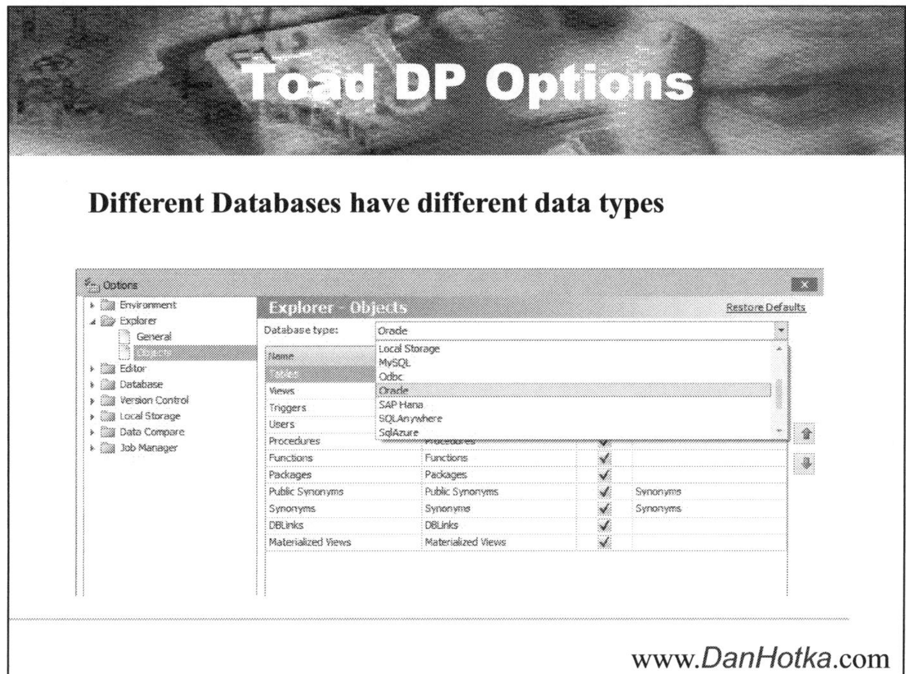


This screen is very handy when working with your various database connections. If you are just working with data in Oracle (for example), you can uncheck everything but objects and views. This will greatly clean up the drop down options in the Toad Navigator window. I'll remind you when we get to that part of the course. Each database has its own list of various object types you can select/deselect. Notice in the upper right hand corner that it is very easy to restore all the defaults for most all of these option screens.

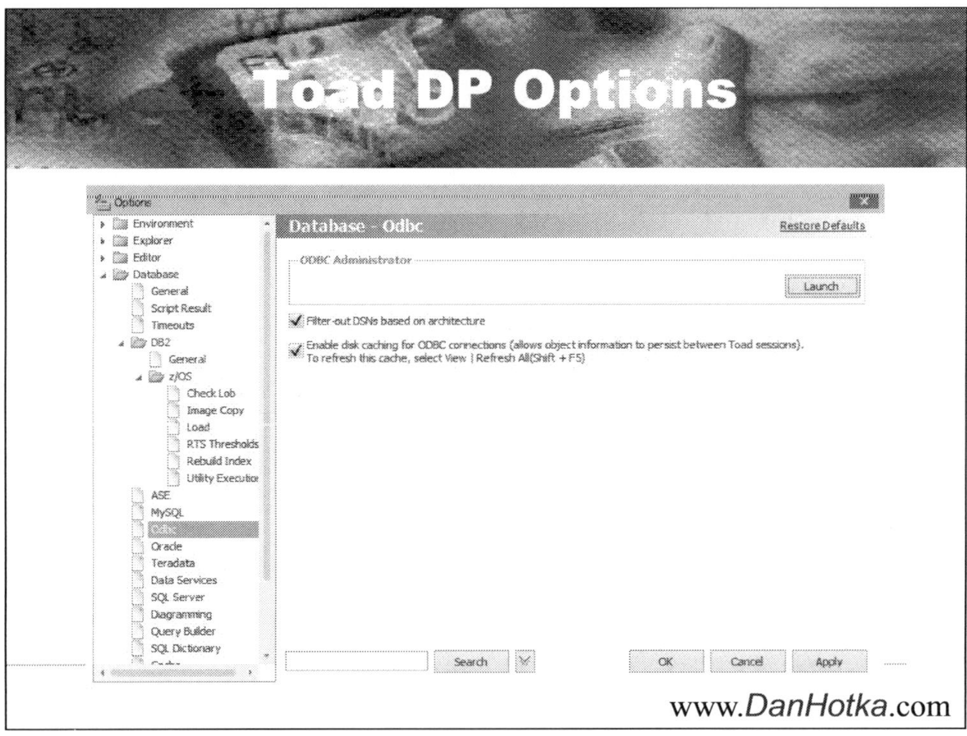
Toad DP Options
Options
Environment
Explorer
Editor
Database
General
Script Result
Timeouts
DB2
General
z/OS
Check Lob
Image Copy
Load
RTS Thresholds
Rebuild Index
ASE
MySQL
Odbc
Oracle
Teradata
Data Services
SQL Server
Diagramming
Query Builder
SQL Dictionary
Database - Odbc
Restore Defaults
ODBC Administrator
Launch
Filter-out DSNs based on architecture
Enable disk caching for ODBC connections (allows object information to persist between Toad sessions).
To refresh this cache, select View | Refresh All(Shift + F5)
Search
OK
Cancel
Apply
www.DanHotka.com

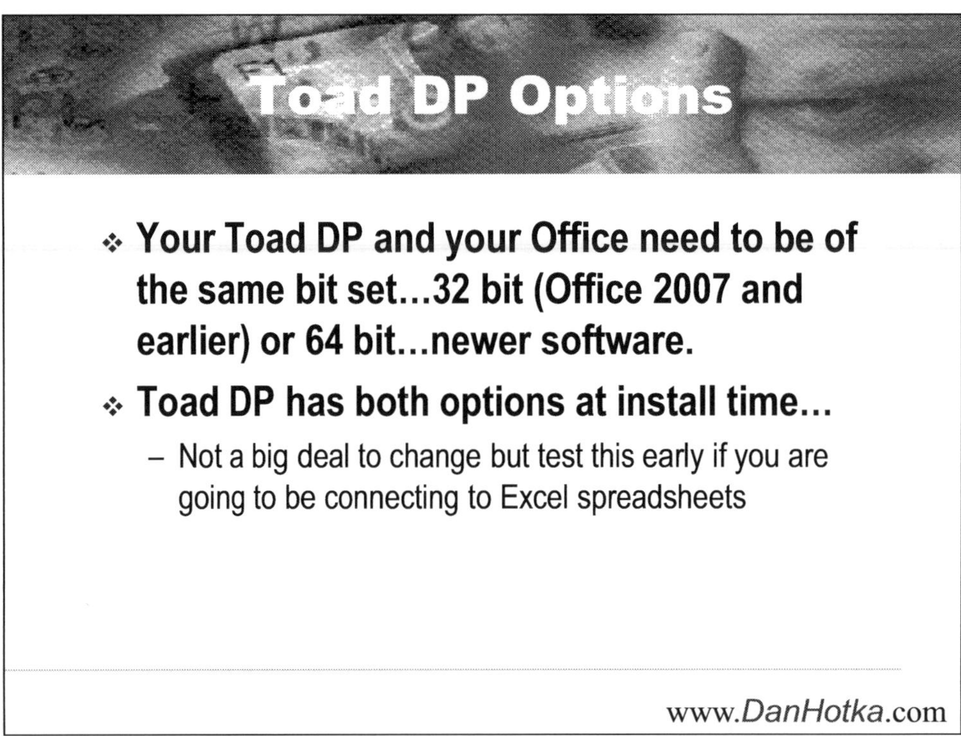
Toad DP Options
❖ Your Toad DP and your Office need to be of the same bit set…32 bit (Office 2007 and earlier) or 64 bit…newer software.
❖ Toad DP has both options at install time…
– Not a big deal to change but test this early if you are going to be connecting to Excel spreadsheets
www.DanHotka.com

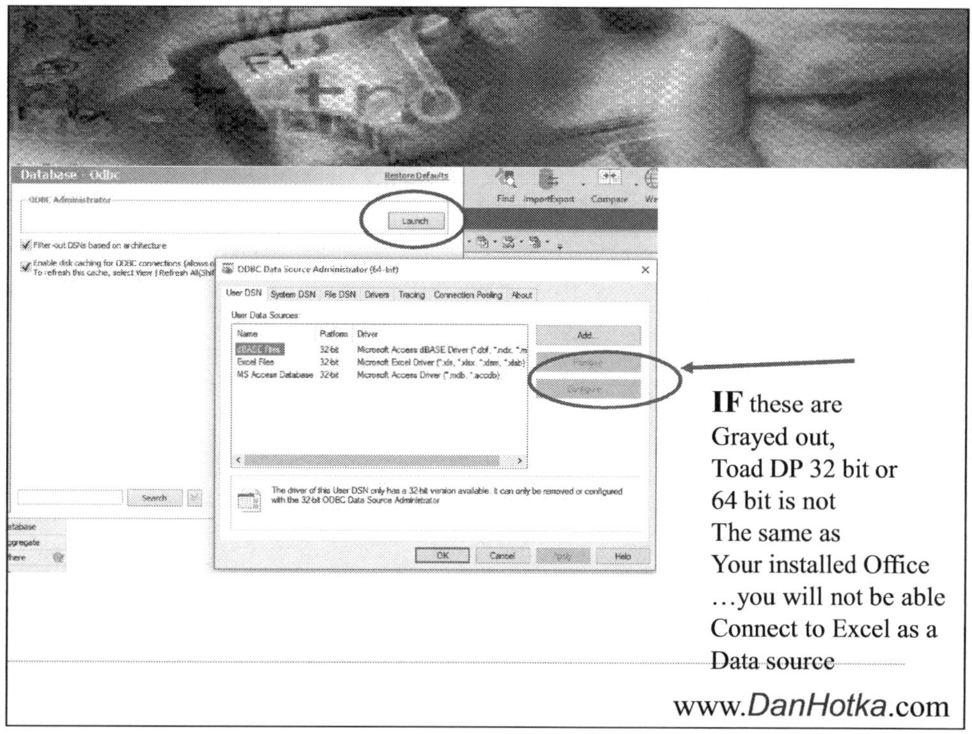
IF these are
Grayed out,
Toad DP 32 bit or
64 bit is not
The same as
Your installed Office
…you will not be able
Connect to Excel as a
Data source
www.DanHotka.com

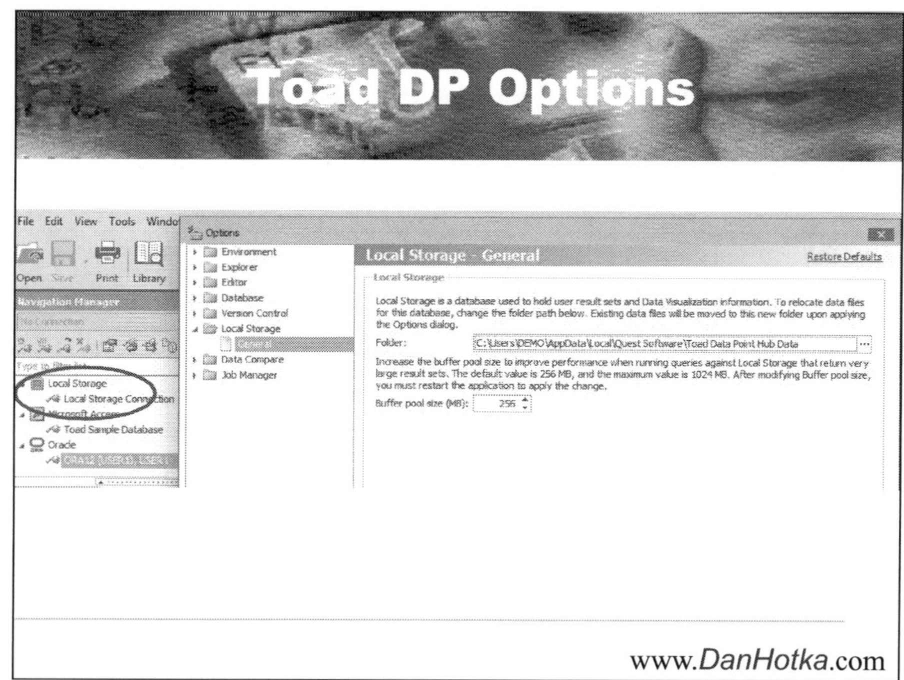
Toad DP Options
www.DanHotka.com

Local storage is an option to store retrieved data on your work station. This is the panel that allows you to define the location of the save. Once saved, this item will act as a data store to be used again in your queries or published to Intelligence Central.

## Database Explorer

# Database Explorer

- This section will Introduce/review
  - Navigation Manager
  - Viewing Objects
  - Viewing Data
  - Reverse Engineering Data to SQL

www.DanHotka.com

## Tool Bars

Toad DP is very configurable. It will remember your settings/docked navigator locations and more. To reset these, go to Options and select the 'Restore Defaults' in the very upper right hand corner. Be careful…this feature will return Toad DP to its initial fresh installed state.

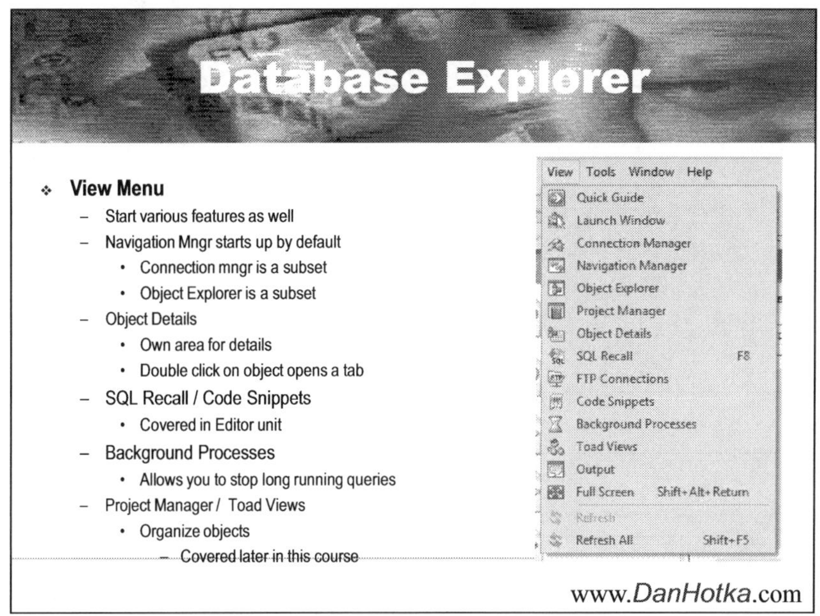

The Navigation Manager allows for connectivity and to select the 'focus' of Toad DP. It also displays object information with the click (shows info in the manager) or by double click (opens a tab and displays the information). The Connection Manager and Object Explorer are mere subsets of the Navigation Manager. Perhaps these are more useful if you have limited screen space.

The Background Processes allows you to stop or kill long running tasks you started (like SQL or an export) that you don't wish to wait for or is erroneous.

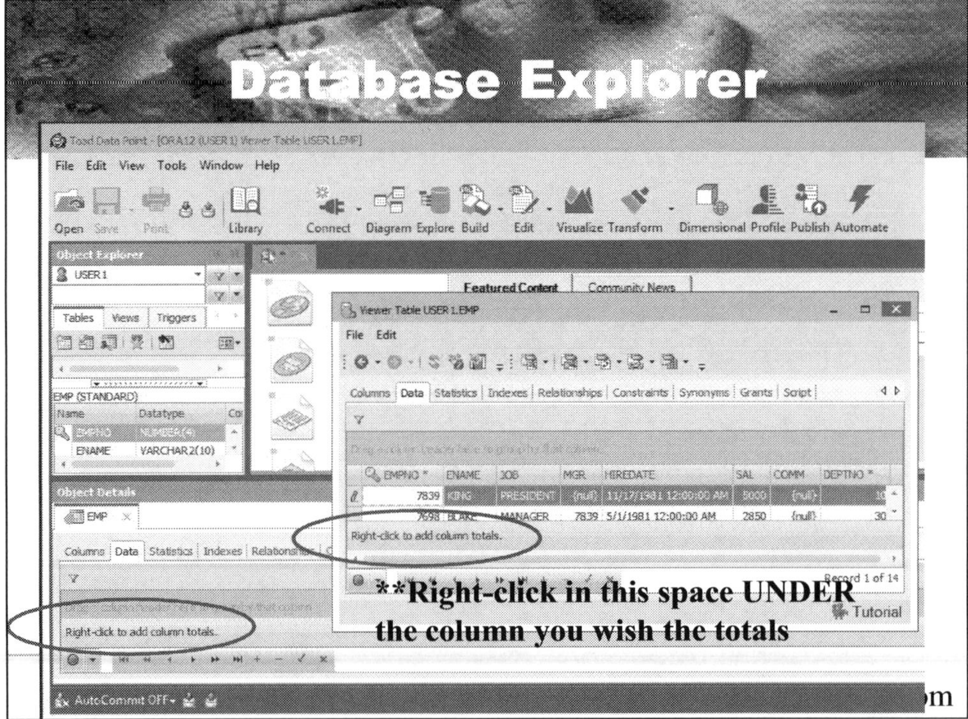


You open object details and drag/drop an object to the panel. You can double click on the object to gain the same information in an additional tab. You can use the object viewer to gain the same information as well.

## Finding Objects

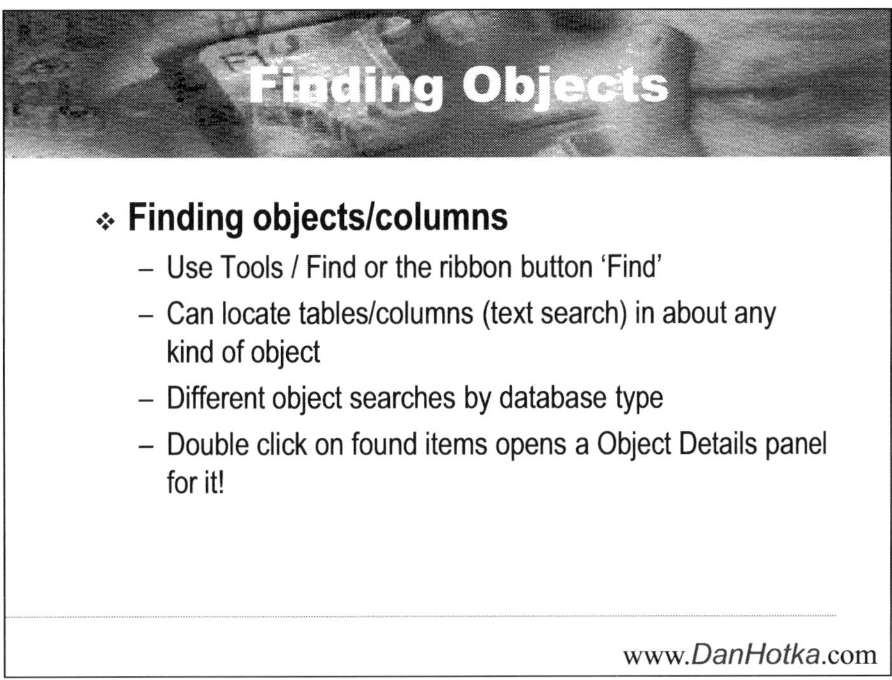
Finding Objects
Finding objects/columns
– Use Tools / Find or the ribbon button 'Find'
– Can locate tables/columns (text search) in about any kind of object
– Different object searches by database type
– Double click on found items opens a Object Details panel for it!
www.DanHotka.com

Use the menu item Tools → Find or the ribbon button 'Find' to find objects and columns in your schema, or schema's you have permissions to.

This is a quick and easy way to find related data and information you are looking for. Folks in the IT world, this gives a quick scope of a project size perhaps. Power users/analysts generally only need to search tables/views/materialized views. Programmers and IT professionals may need to search code. This Find does the code as well.

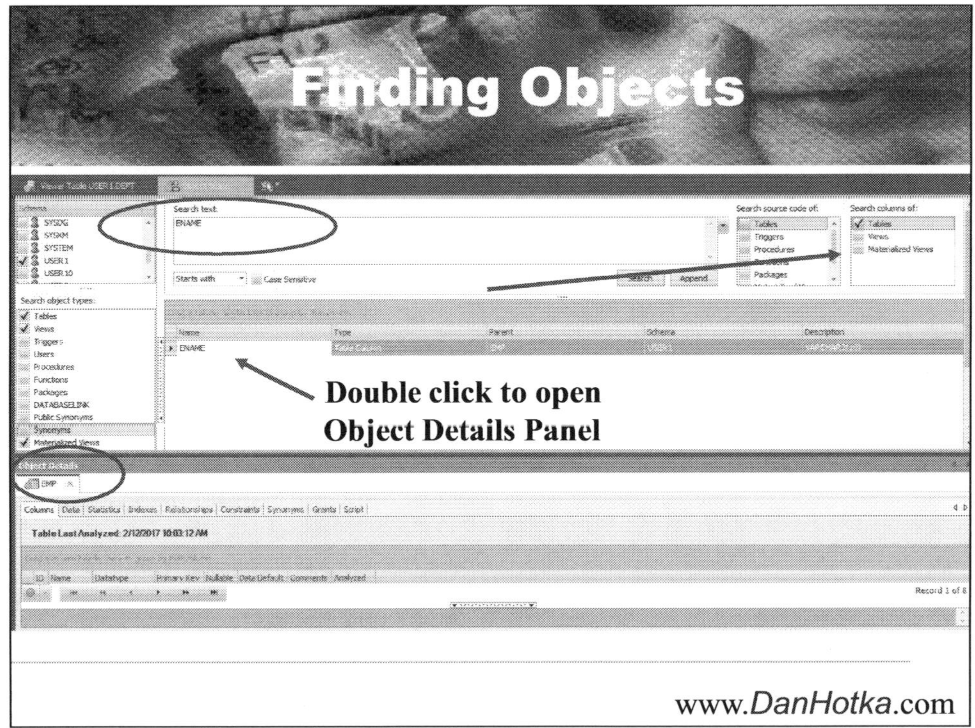
Finding Objects
Double click to open
Object Details Panel
www.DanHotka.com

You can use the drop down box to do: 'starts with', 'contains', 'ends with' type of searches. When you find something of interest, double click on it and Toad DP opens an Object Details panel for it.

## Navigation Manager

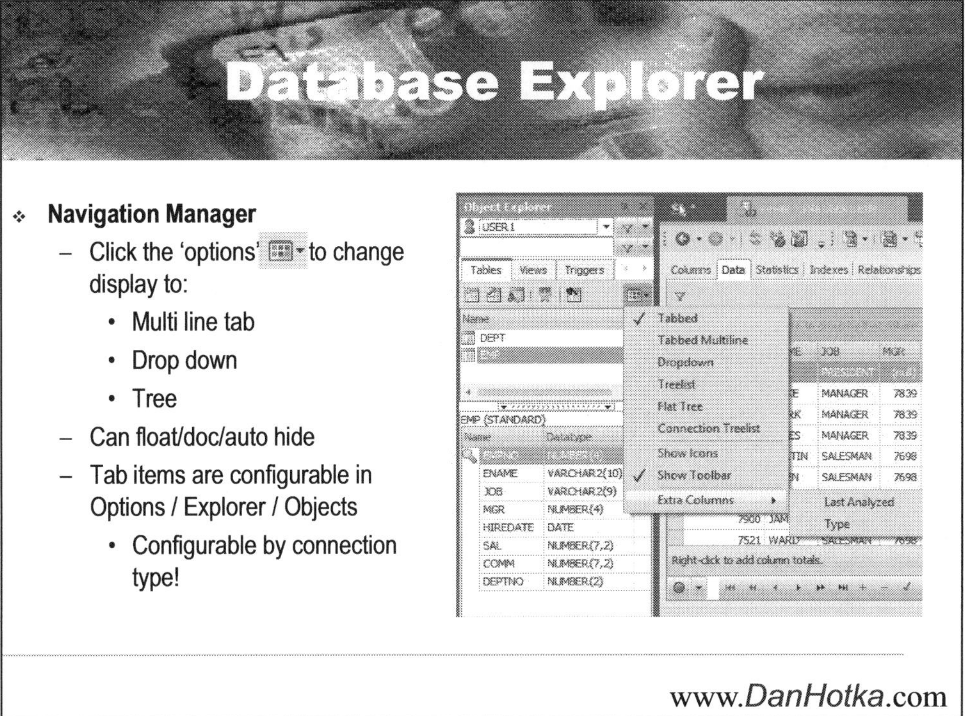


You can change the display type easily to a drop down, multi tab, or tree format. Click the options button indicated to get to these features. The number of options displayed is controlled by Options → Explorer → Objects. Turn off the ones you never use or don't have permissions to use anyway. This type of configuration will make Toad DP even easier for you to use. As discussed earlier, you can create a connection based off the options set for another by selecting 'create connection like another' button.

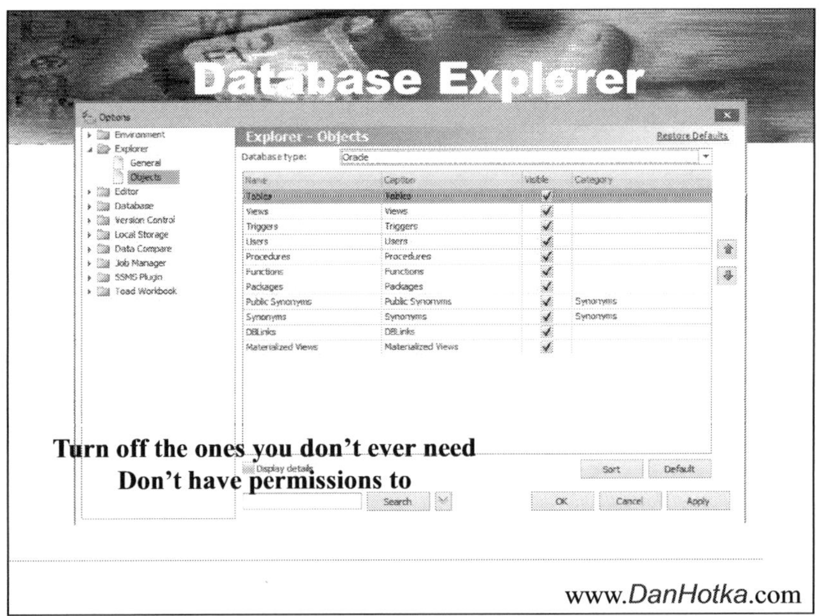
Database Explorer
Options
Environment
Explorer
General
Objects
Editor
Database
Version Control
Local Storage
Data Compare
Job Manager
SSMS Plugin
Toad Workbook
Explorer - Objects
Restore Defaults
Database type: Oracle
Name
Caption
Visible
Category
Tables
Views
Triggers
Users
Procedures
Functions
Packages
Public Synonyms
Synonyms
DBLinks
Materialized Views
Turn off the ones you don't ever need
Don't have permissions to
Display details
Sort
Default
Search
OK
Cancel
Apply
www.DanHotka.com

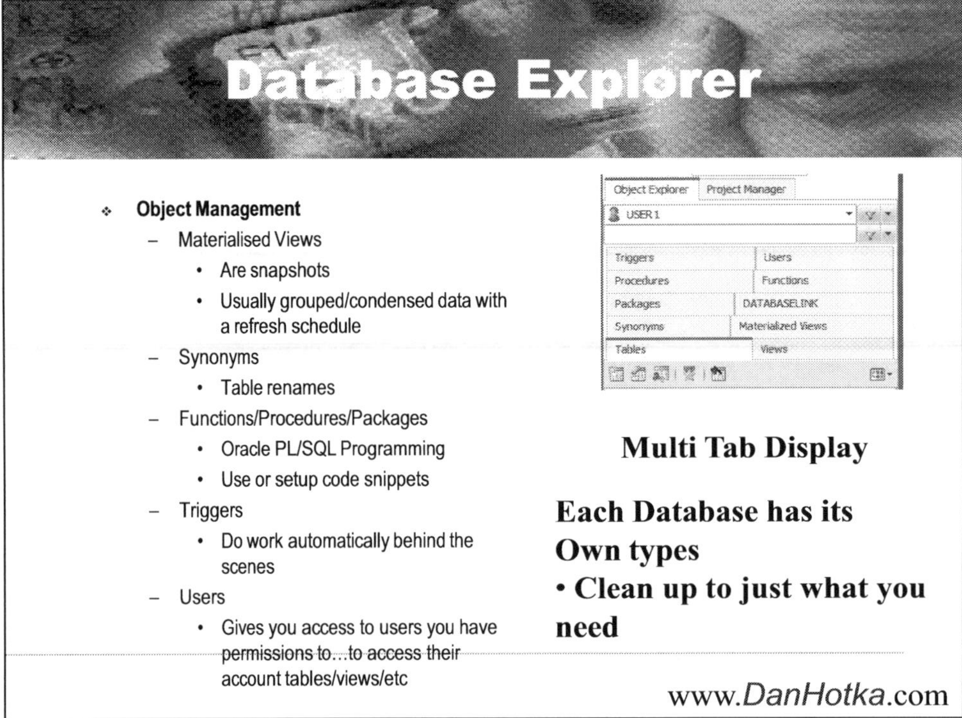
Database Explorer
Object Management
Materialised Views
Are snapshots
Usually grouped/condensed data with a refresh schedule
Synonyms
Table renames
Functions/Procedures/Packages
Oracle PL/SQL Programming
Use or setup code snippets
Triggers
Do work automatically behind the scenes
Users
Gives you access to users you have permissions to…to access their account tables/views/etc
Object Explorer
Project Manager
USER1
Triggers
Users
Procedures
Functions
Packages
DATABASELINK
Synonyms
Materialized Views
Tables
Views
Multi Tab Display
Each Database has its Own types
• Clean up to just what you need
www.DanHotka.com

This panel is organized using the multi-tab display. You click on the button in the lower right of this panel to change these features. Toad DP remembers the settings between uses.

Each database type has its own features. Most data analysts have no need for Synonyms, Procedures/Packages/Triggers. Sometimes it's nice to know what functions were specifically coded.

Most shops use specific objects for data and for specific reasons.

## Object Details

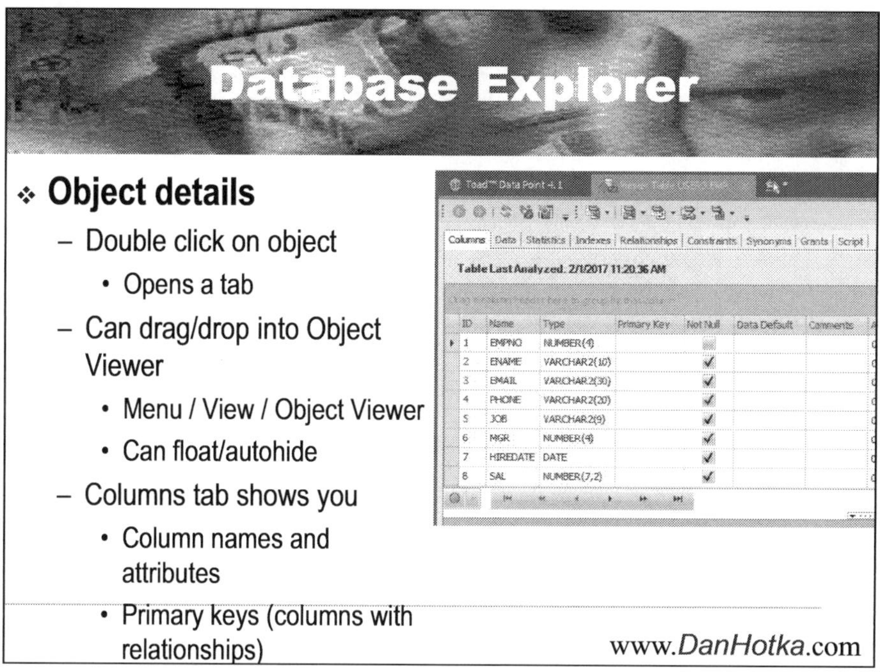
Database Explorer
Object details
– Double click on object
• Opens a tab
– Can drag/drop into Object Viewer
• Menu / View / Object Viewer
• Can float/autohide
– Columns tab shows you
• Column names and attributes
• Primary keys (columns with relationships)
www.DanHotka.com

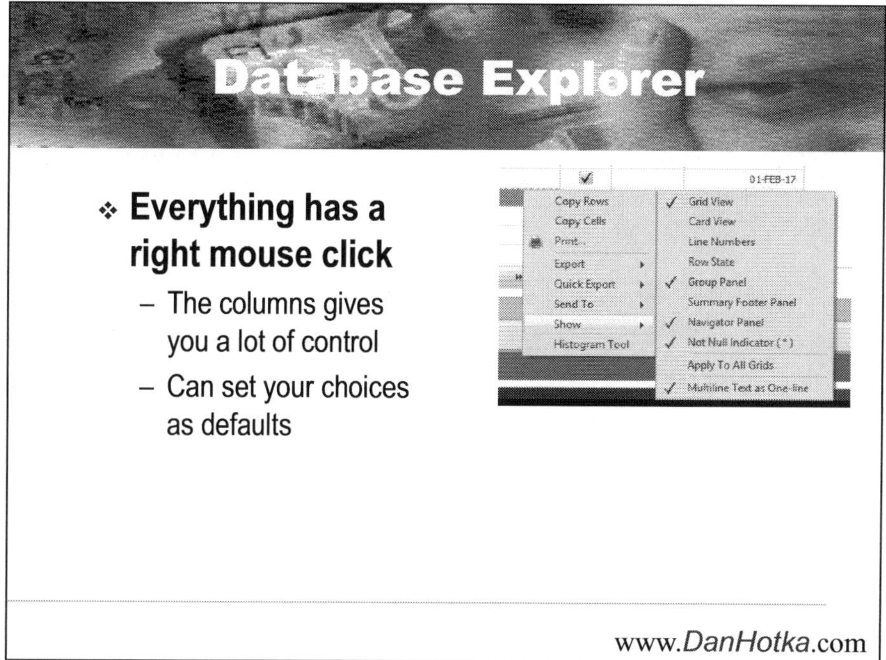
Database Explorer
Everything has a right mouse click
– The columns gives you a lot of control
– Can set your choices as defaults
www.DanHotka.com

The right mouse click from the columns header area allows you to turn on/off various features as well as save/export the data.

## Toad DP Options

Options

- Environment
- Explorer
  - General
  - Objects
- Editor
- Database
- Version Control
- Local Storage
- Data Compare
- Job Manager
- SSMS Plugin
- Toad Workbook

**Explorer - General** Restore Defaults

Prompt to filter list after: 2500 items Default Filter:

Subfolder location in list: (Including system objects)
- Top
- Bottom
- Merged to flat list

Double-click behavior:
- Open details
- Invoke default action

Default Filter:
- Last Selected
- Contains (Like)
- Starts With (Like)
- Ends With (Like)
- Like
- Contains (Exact)
- Starts With (Exact)
- Ends With (Exact)
- Glob (* Wildcard)
- Equals
- Regular Expression
- IN

- [ ] Use object details to display details
- [x] Sort list alphabetically when in drop-down mode
- [x] Allow editing of the schema or database list
- [ ] Display followed links in object details
- [ ] Automatically format generated SQL
- [ ] Separate schema or database by type (Only for non treeview)
- [ ] Use fully qualified object names when dragging objects
- [ ] Do not use case sensitive filtering in Object Explorer
- [x] Enable Horizontal Scrolling in Object Explorer

Search | OK | Cancel | Apply

www.DanHotka.com

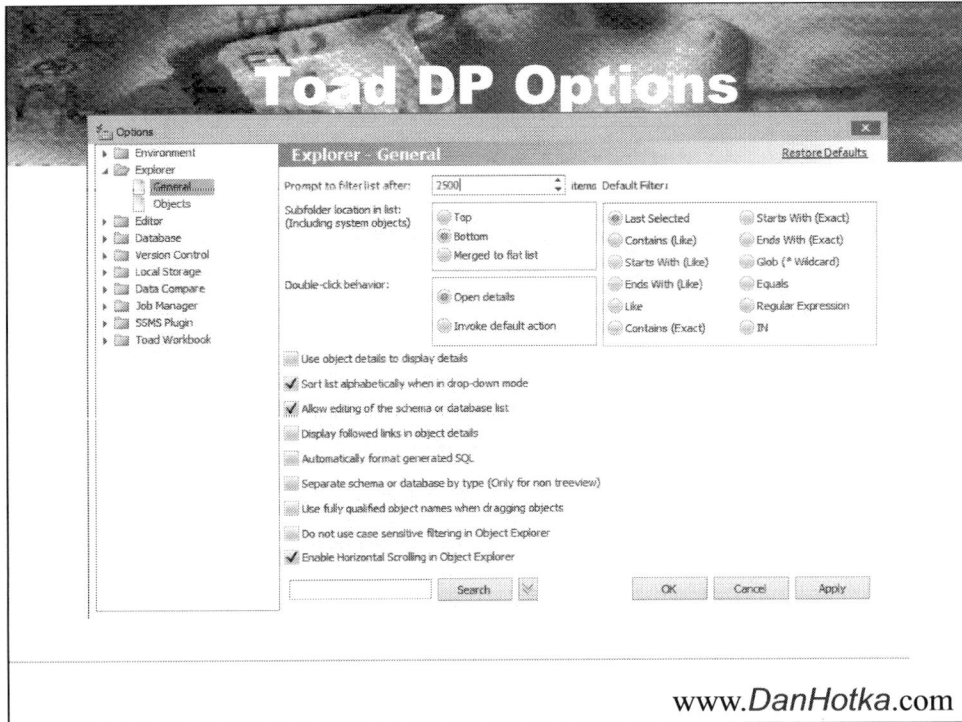

In Toad Options → Explorer → General, you have control over how many of these Explorer items appear.

## Working with Data

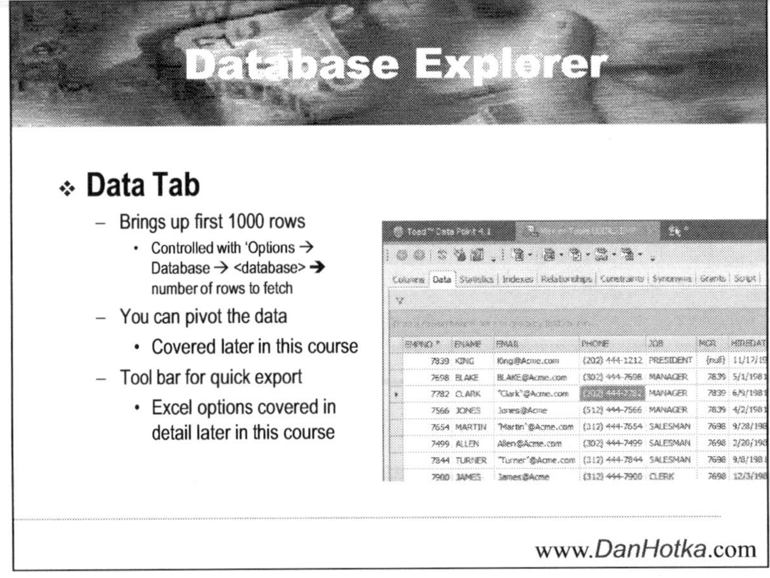

Database Explorer
Data Tab
– Brings up first 1000 rows
• Controlled with 'Options → Database → <database> → number of rows to fetch
– You can pivot the data
• Covered later in this course
– Tool bar for quick export
• Excel options covered in detail later in this course
www.DanHotka.com

The data tab is configurable using the Options → Database → General. This option allows you to define how many rows are brought back initially. The default is 1000 rows.

You can drag a column to the Group By section, creating a pivot table. You can then save to Excel as a pivot table. These topics are covered in detail later in this course.

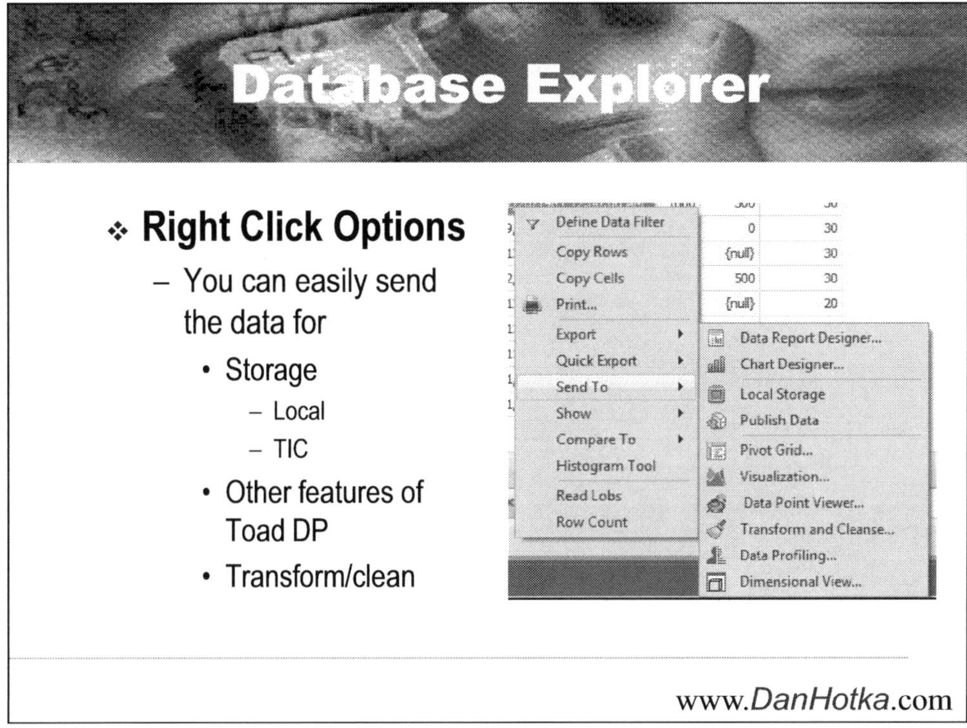

# Database Explorer

- **Statistics Tab**
  - Can see some behind-the-scenes info
  - Maybe its of use to you?
- **Index tab**
  - Your data extract/query will probably perform better if you include columns with indexes in your filtering
- **Constraints**
  - Shows you textually the data relationships

www.*DanHotka*.com

# Database Explorer

- **Right Click Options**
  - You can easily send the data for
    - Storage
      - Local
      - TIC
    - Other features of Toad DP
    - Transform/clean

Define Data Filter
Copy Rows
Copy Cells
Print...
Export
Quick Export
Send To
Show
Compare To
Histogram Tool
Read Lobs
Row Count
Data Report Designer...
Chart Designer...
Local Storage
Publish Data
Pivot Grid...
Visualization...
Data Point Viewer...
Transform and Cleanse...
Data Profiling...
Dimensional View...


www.*DanHotka*.com

## Database Explorer

- **Synonyms**
  - Any table/view rename shows up here
- **Grants**
  - The permissions on the object
- **Each database type will have some other options here perhaps**

www.*DanHotka*.com

### Creating SQL using a Mouse

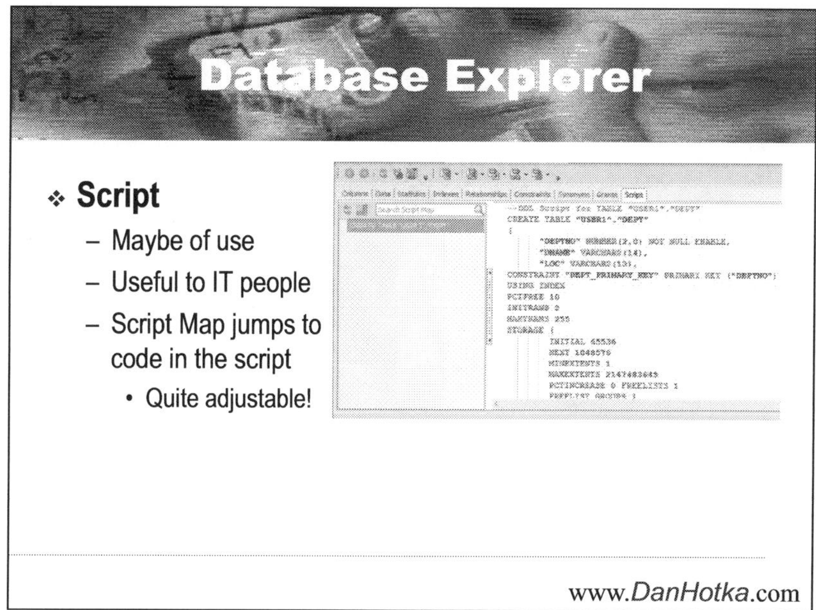

Database Explorer
Script
– Maybe of use
– Useful to IT people
– Script Map jumps to code in the script
• Quite adjustable!
www.DanHotka.com

*****Note***** The instructor uses the data tab quite a bit. The relationship part, he goes right to the Diagrammer because that does about the same thing (shows relationships) and quickly leads to developing the actual query.

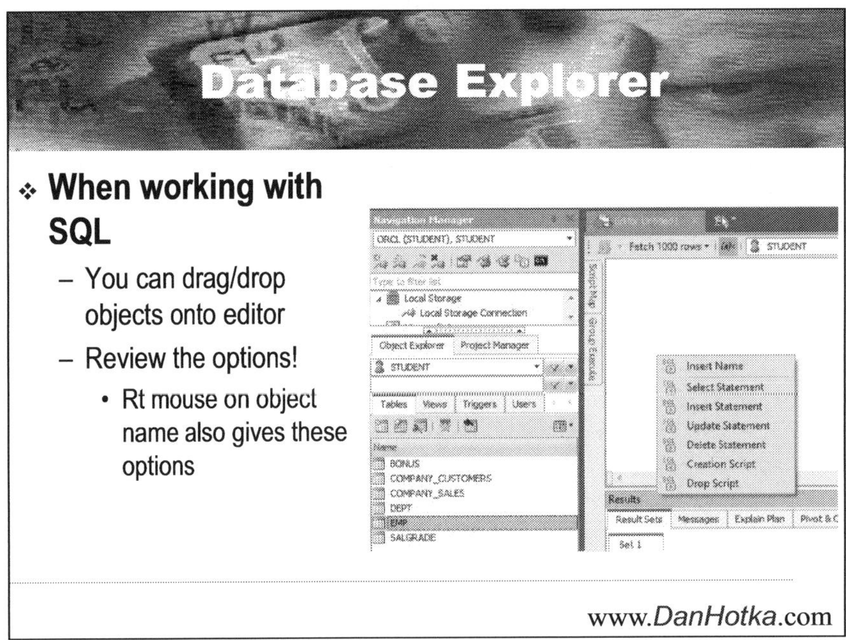


This is a REALLY slick way to create SQL quickly. Even the novice can quickly create a query without having to type in long column names. This section can then be used as input to Query Builder. If you can work with SQL, there is a whole section of this course devoted to this cool editor. The query builder is particularly useful when working with data from multiple connections (ie: multiple different databases, stored data, data from TIC).

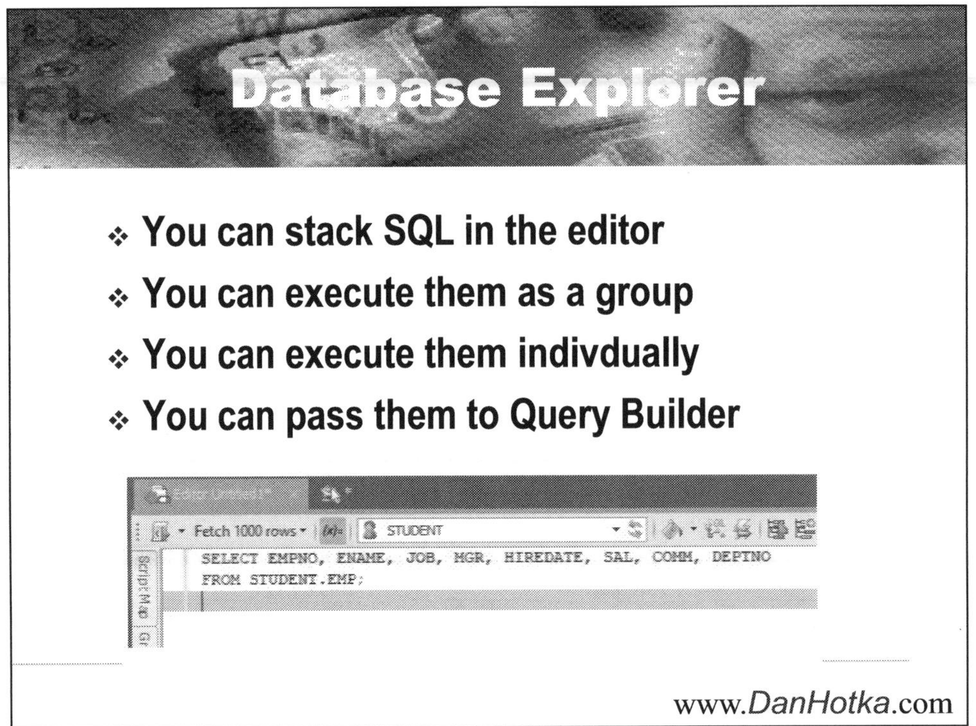

## Working with Data Grids

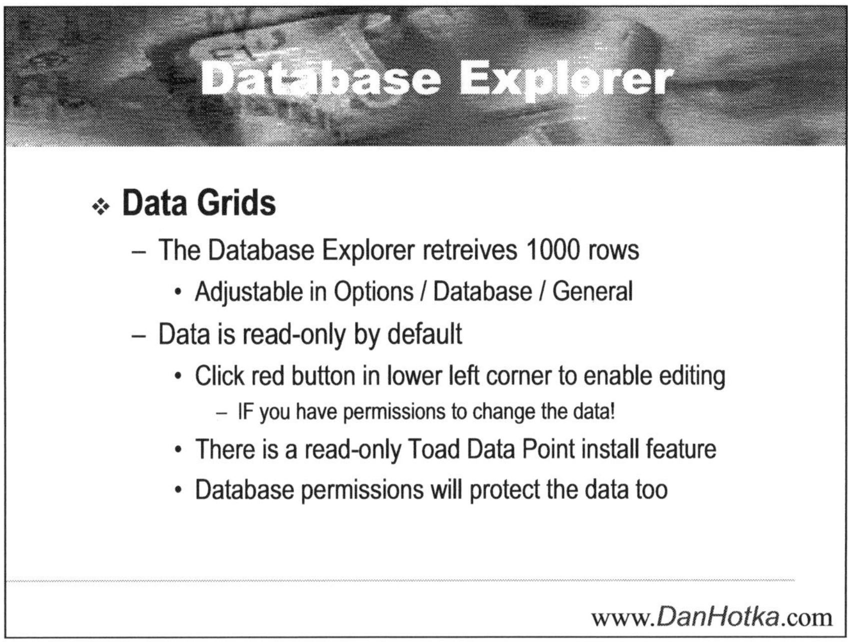
Database Explorer
Data Grids
– The Database Explorer retreives 1000 rows
• Adjustable in Options / Database / General
– Data is read-only by default
• Click red button in lower left corner to enable editing
– IF you have permissions to change the data!
• There is a read-only Toad Data Point install feature
• Database permissions will protect the data too
www.DanHotka.com

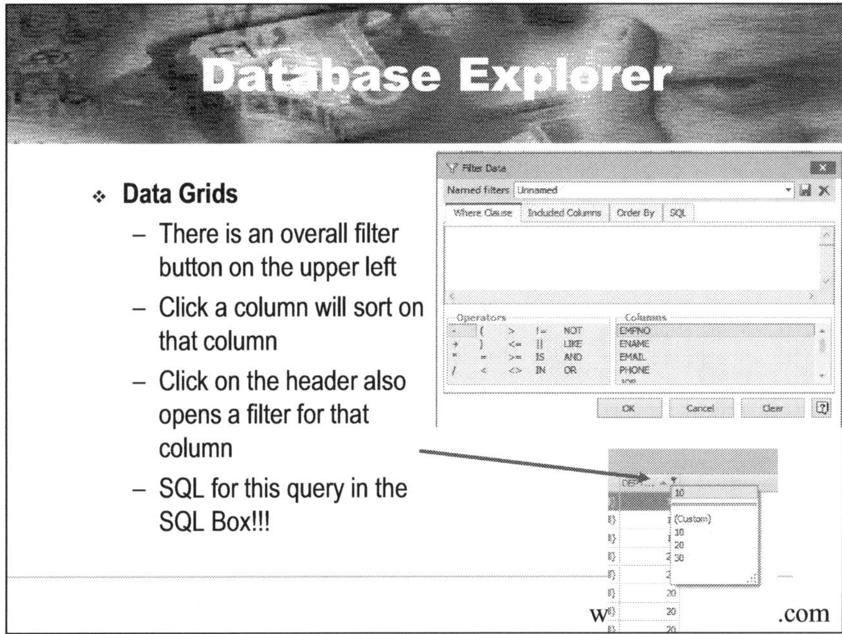
Database Explorer
Data Grids
– There is an overall filter button on the upper left
– Click a column will sort on that column
– Click on the header also opens a filter for that column
– SQL for this query in the SQL Box!!!
.com

Many people using Toad DP use this data grid to format the data the way they want/need, then simply export it to Excel. Done. Save the query used, save the data if others might use it, etc. The data grids allow for formatting and basic sorting of the data, filtering, etc.

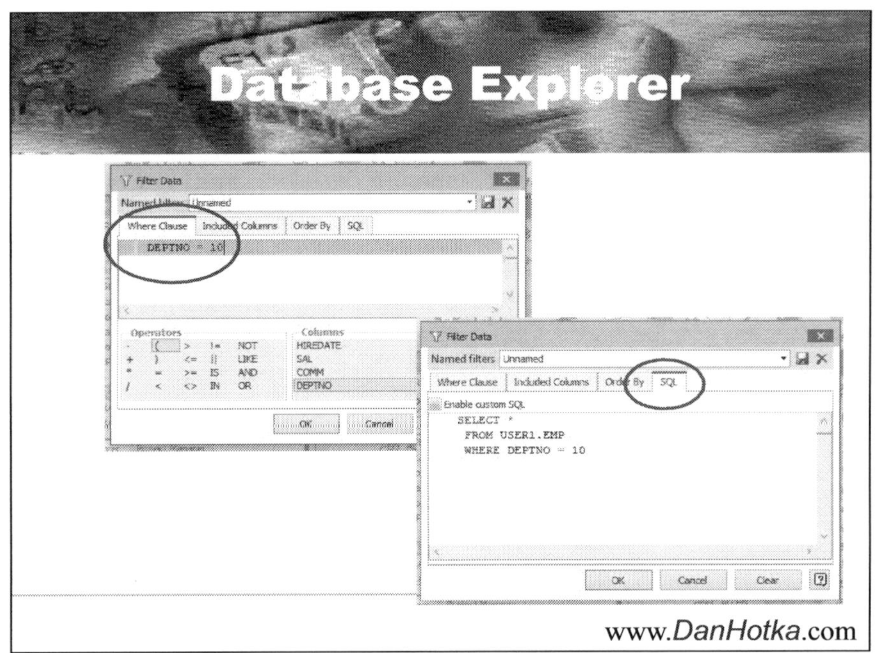


The filter box allows filtering, column selection, order by clause, and to view the SQL that populates the window!

*****Tip***** This is a VERY convenient SQL to move to the Editor and save.

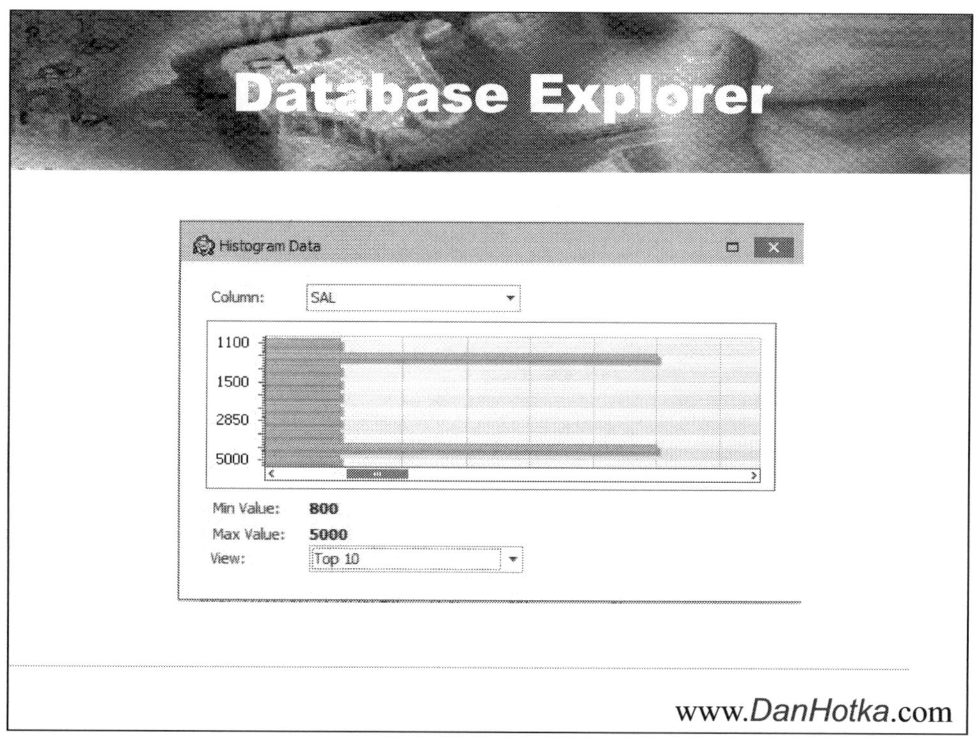
Database Explorer
Histogram Data
Column: SAL
1100
1500
2850
5000
Min Value: 800
Max Value: 5000
View: Top 10
www.DanHotka.com

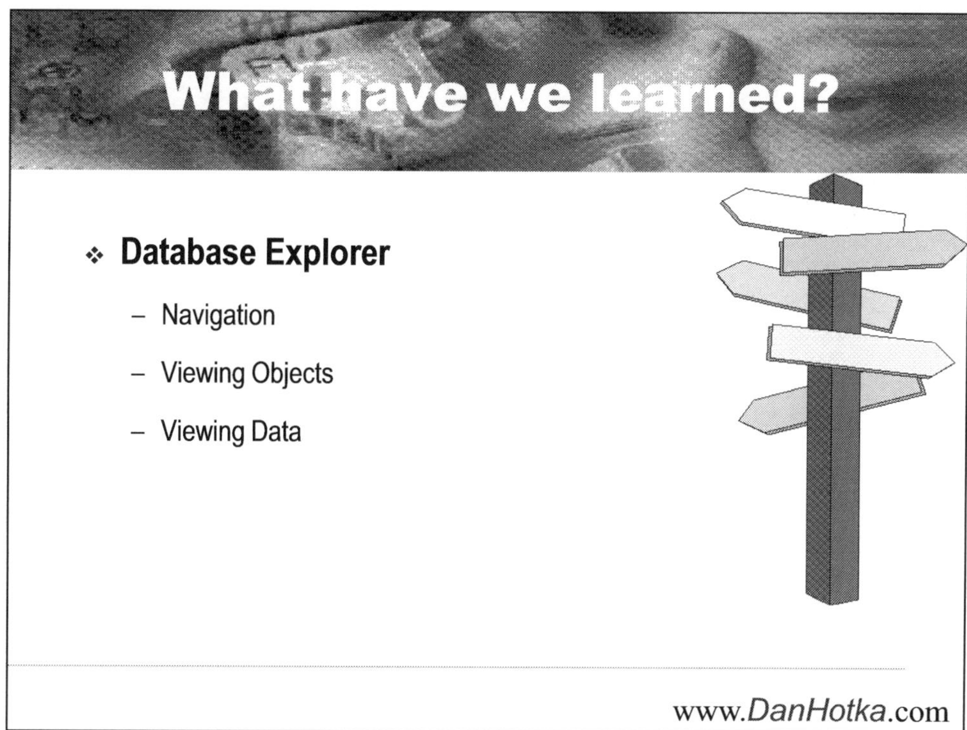
What have we learned?
Database Explorer
– Navigation
– Viewing Objects
– Viewing Data
www.DanHotka.com

## Database Explorer Lab

Database Explorer Lab

- **Database Explorer Lab**
  - Connect to your database
  - Using your xxxxxx table or the EMP table
    - Review the data using the Object Explorer/ or Data Explorer tab
    - Open the histogram feature at the column level. Review various column to see how granular the data is, the lowest/highest values.
    - Add a total to the SAL column
      - If using your data…to the xxxxxxxx column.
    - Review the Relationship tab
    - Review the script
    - Make a SELECT statement using just your mouse for the DEPT table or the xxxxxxxxxxxxxxx table

www.*DanHotka*.com

## Database Explorer Lab Answers

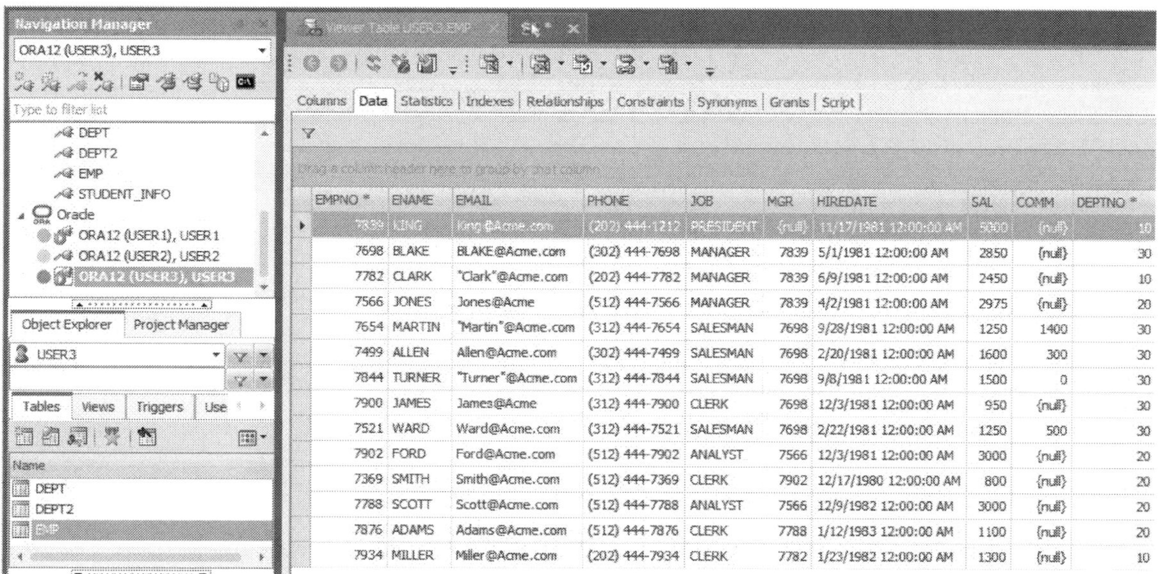

Click on the Table object in the Navigation Manager is the easiest way to get the Viewer screen up. From here, you can review the column data types, the data itself, and more.

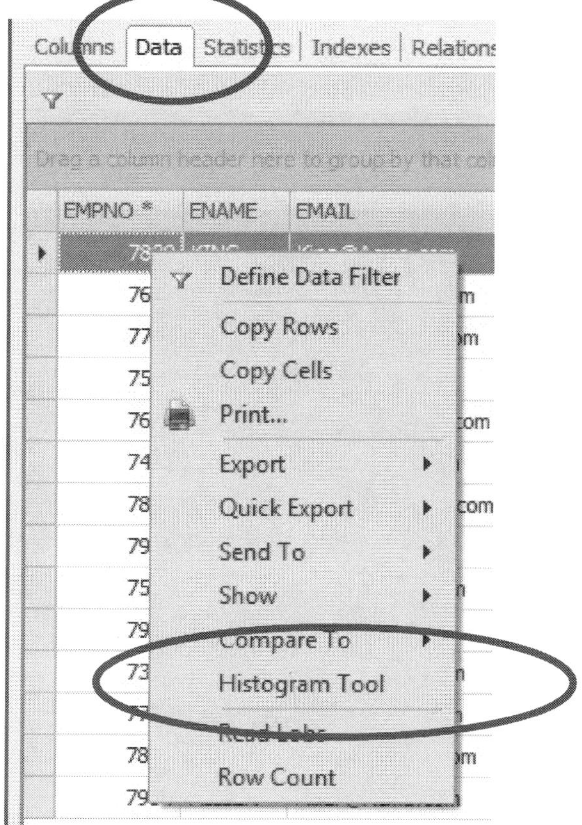

On the **data tab**, right click on a column name and bring up the Histogram Tool. Do this for the EMPNO then another column such as SAL.

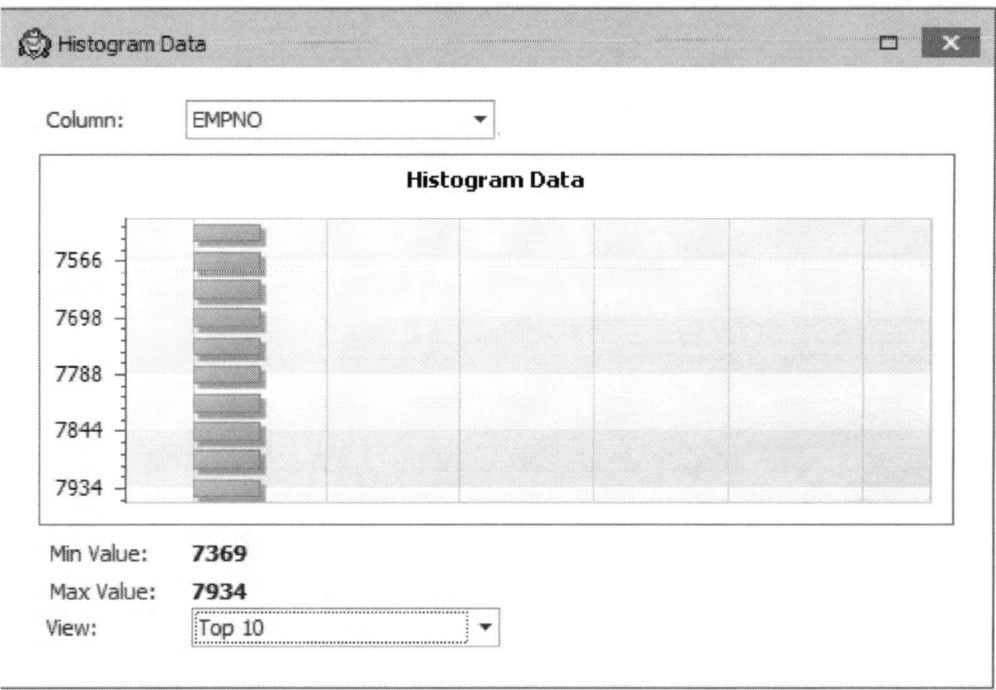


Even Data Distribution

Change the column to SAL then COMM…

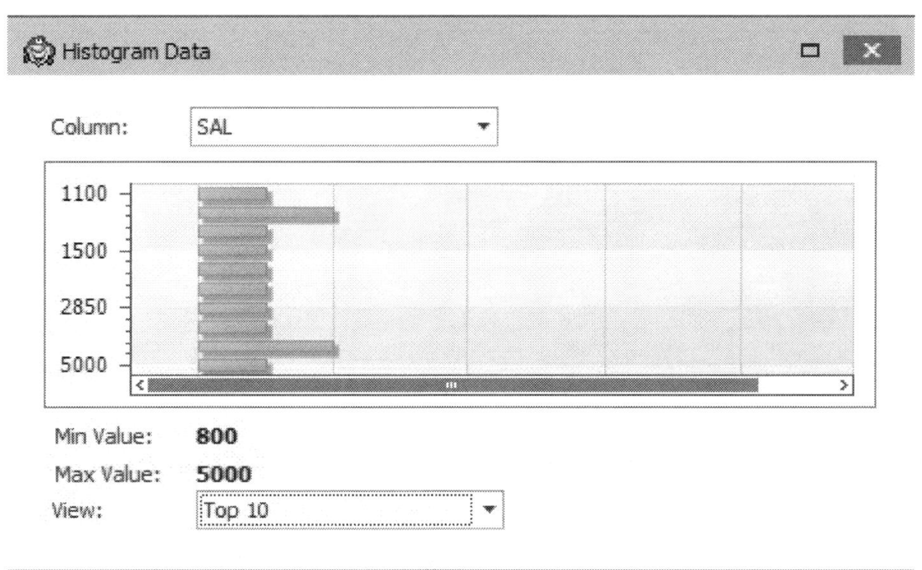


Sal is not so even

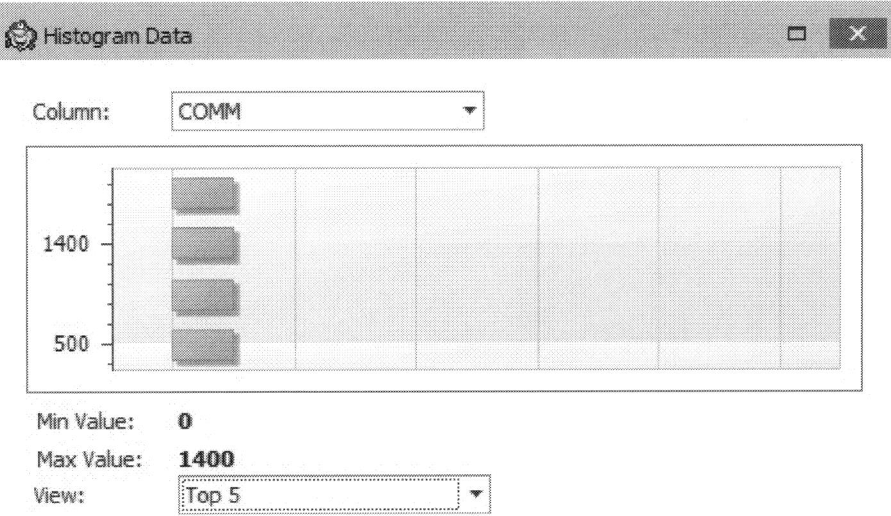


COMM only has 4 values…

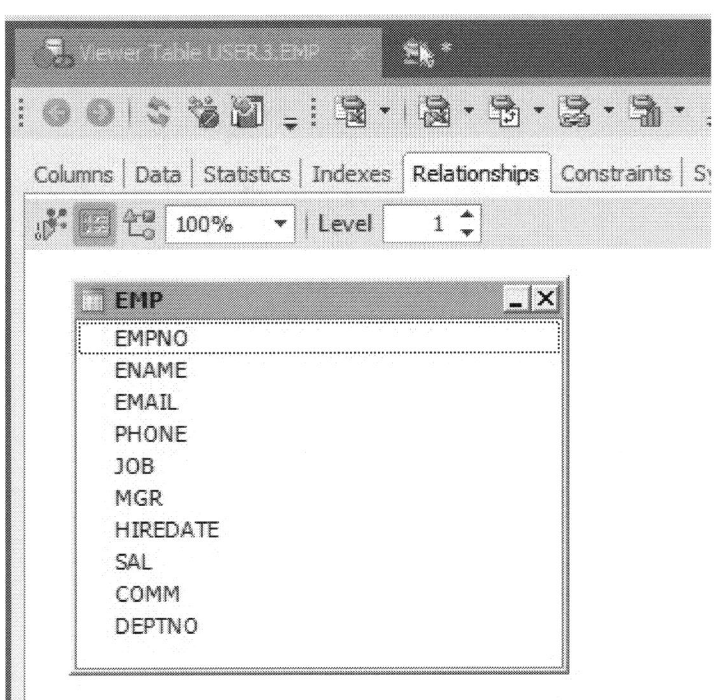


The Relationship Tab…this EMP object isn't related to anything else. IF I go to another schema where I have relationships, you would see this from the DEPT table's relationship tab:

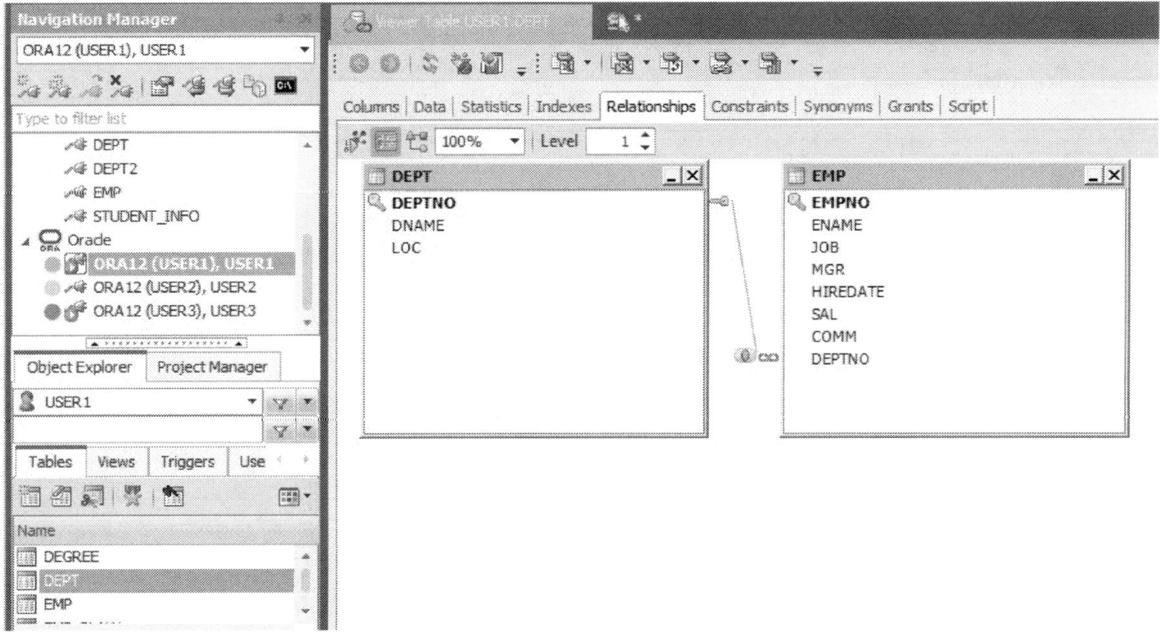


You can see the primary key fields and the relationship.

onships | Constraints | Synonyms | Grants | Script

```
--DDL Script for TABLE "USER1"."DEPT"
CREATE TABLE "USER1"."DEPT"
(
    "DEPTNO" NUMBER(2,0) NOT NULL ENABLE,
    "DNAME" VARCHAR2(14),
    "LOC" VARCHAR2(13),
CONSTRAINT "DEPT_PRIMARY_KEY" PRIMARY KEY ("DEPTNO")
USING INDEX
PCTFREE 10
INITRANS 2
MAXTRANS 255
COMPUTE STATISTICS
STORAGE (
```

The script tab might be useful for those of you who have worked with creating database objects in the past.

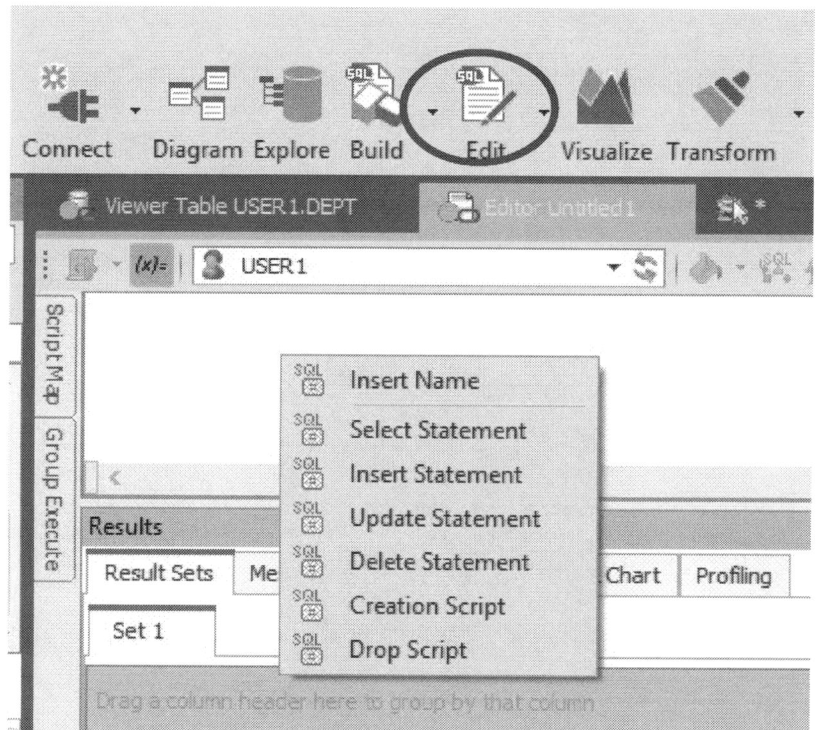


The easiest way to get a valid SQL statement without ANY typing is to open the SQL Editor window and select the type of SQL you would like.

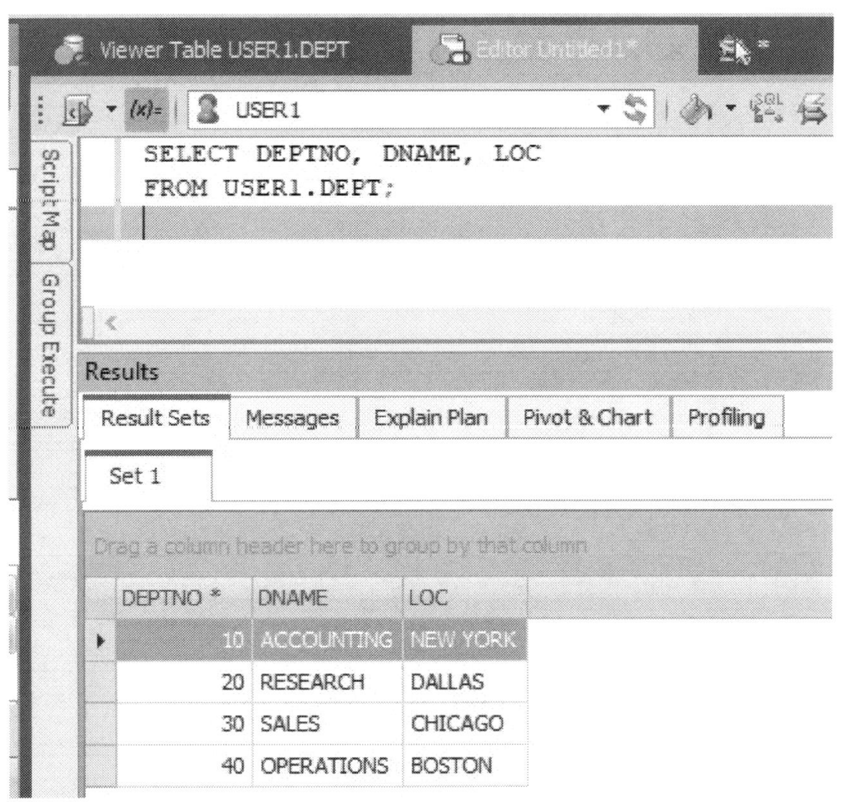
Viewer Table USER1.DEPT
Editor Untitled1*
USER1
SELECT DEPTNO, DNAME, LOC
FROM USER1.DEPT;
Script Map
Group Execute
Results
Result Sets
Messages
Explain Plan
Pivot & Chart
Profiling
Set 1
Drag a column header here to group by that column
DEPTNO *
DNAME
LOC
10 ACCOUNTING NEW YORK
20 RESEARCH DALLAS
30 SALES CHICAGO
40 OPERATIONS BOSTON

## Working with Results

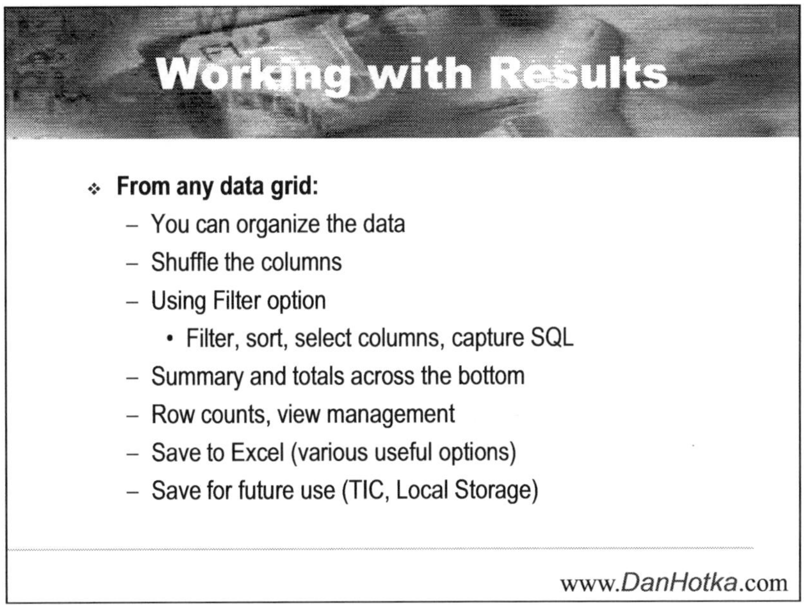
Working with Results
From any data grid:
– You can organize the data
– Shuffle the columns
– Using Filter option
• Filter, sort, select columns, capture SQL
– Summary and totals across the bottom
– Row counts, view management
– Save to Excel (various useful options)
– Save for future use (TIC, Local Storage)
www.DanHotka.com

A data grid is a data grid. Most, if not all of the functions listed here will work for any data grid…from this object info panel to query builder and editor windows.

### Organizing the Data

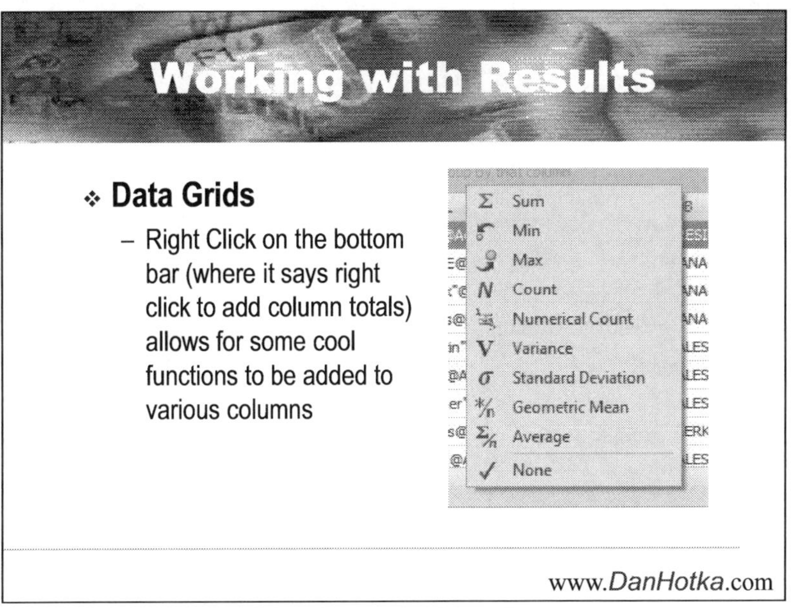
Working with Results
Data Grids
– Right Click on the bottom bar (where it says right click to add column totals) allows for some cool functions to be added to various columns
Sum
Min
Max
Count
Numerical Count
Variance
Standard Deviation
Geometric Mean
Average
None
www.DanHotka.com

Right click on the bottom of the data grids and you will get these options. Highlight a column and pick the option. Most of these are intended for numeric values.

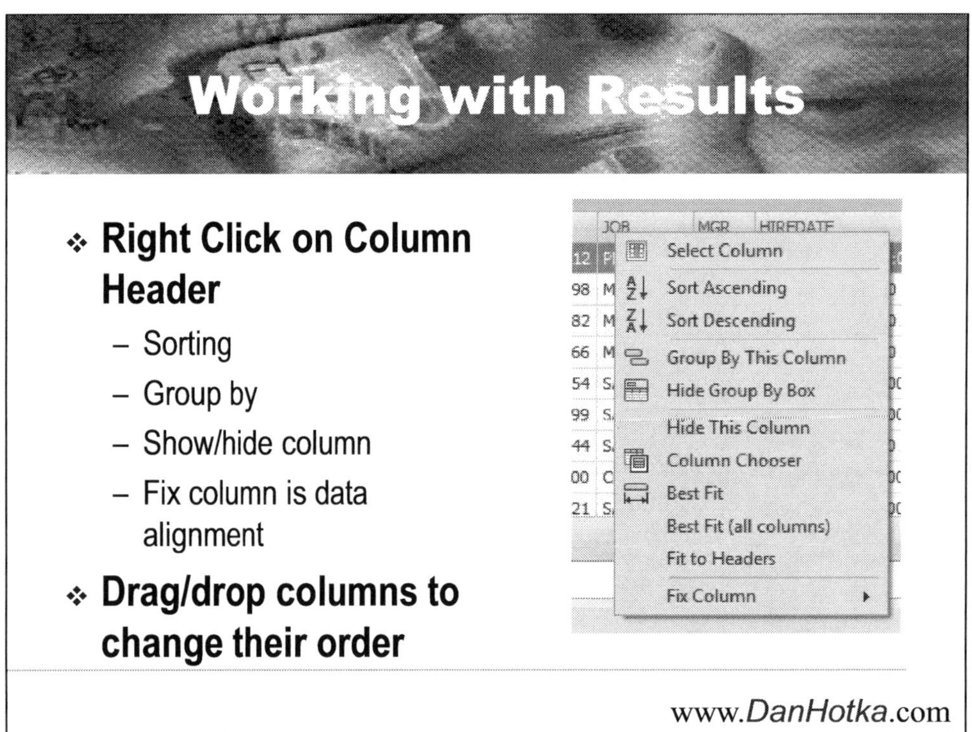
Working with Results
Right Click on Column Header
– Sorting
– Group by
– Show/hide column
– Fix column is data alignment
Drag/drop columns to change their order
Select Column
Sort Ascending
Sort Descending
Group By This Column
Hide Group By Box
Hide This Column
Column Chooser
Best Fit
Best Fit (all columns)
Fit to Headers
Fix Column
www.DanHotka.com

You can really massage the data and its appearance. Using a drag/drop operation, you can move the columns around buy dragging the column header to the location where you desire the field to be. Right mouse click on the column and you can hide it.

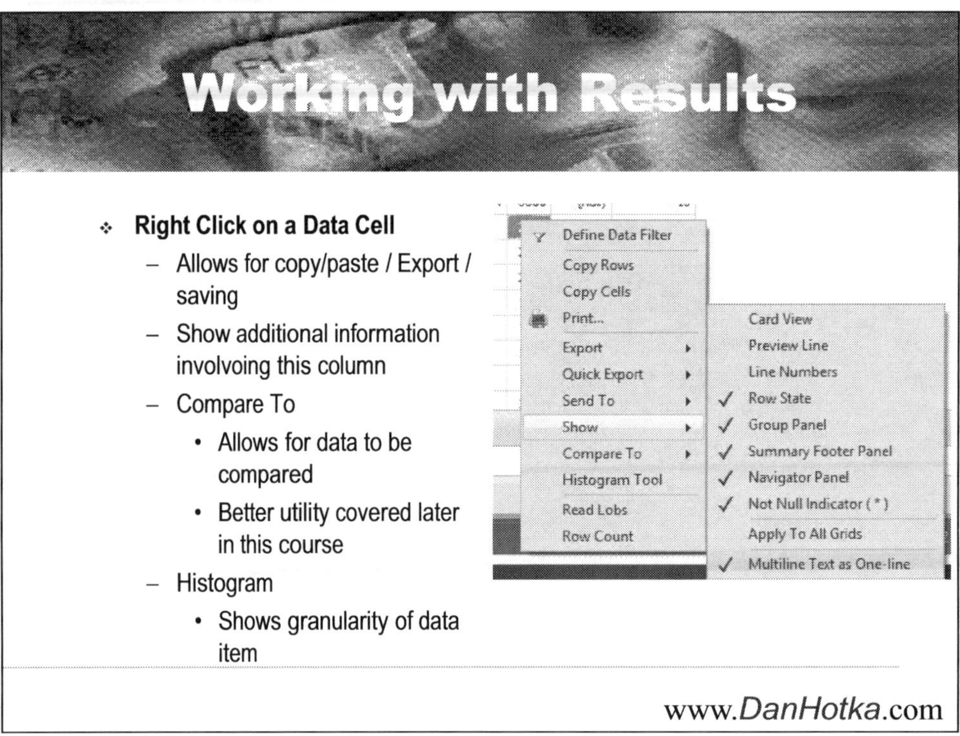
Working with Results
Right Click on a Data Cell
– Allows for copy/paste / Export / saving
– Show additional information involving this column
– Compare To
• Allows for data to be compared
• Better utility covered later in this course
– Histogram
• Shows granularity of data item
Define Data Filter
Copy Rows
Copy Cells
Print...
Export
Quick Export
Send To
Show
Compare To
Histogram Tool
Read Lobs
Row Count
Card View
Preview Line
Line Numbers
Row State
Group Panel
Summary Footer Panel
Navigator Panel
Not Null Indicator ( * )
Apply To All Grids
Multiline Text as One-line
www.DanHotka.com

Only the columns and data displayed, in the summary and/or order…will be saved.

## Exporting to Excel

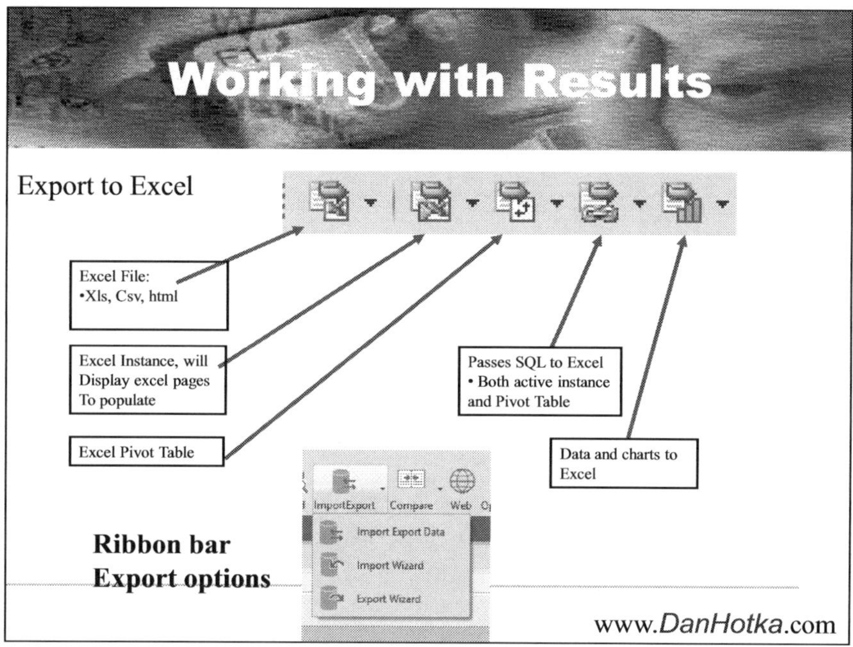


Toad DP works very well with Excel. You can use these buttons or right click and get the same options. You can also use the Import/Export button along the ribbon bar to export data to various Excel formats as well.

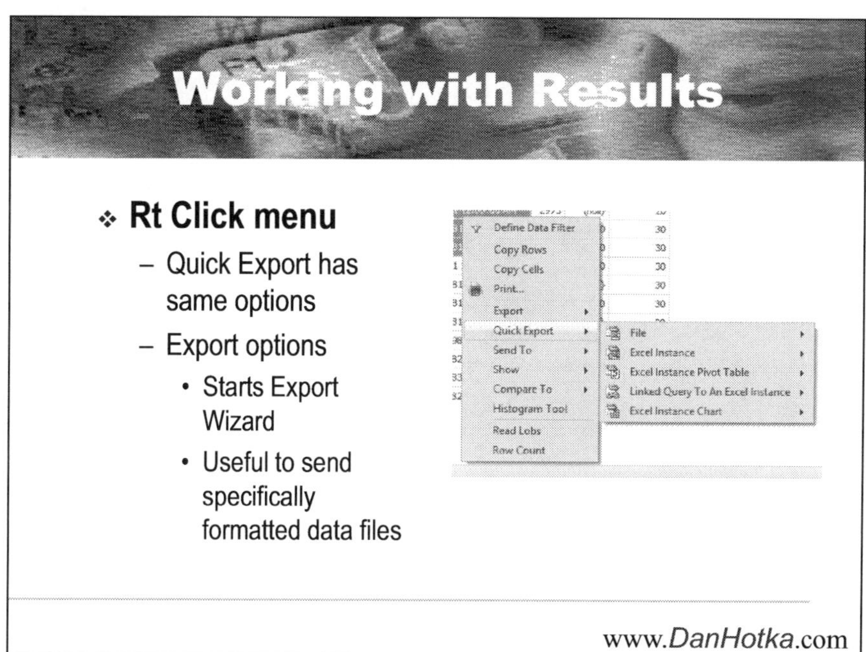

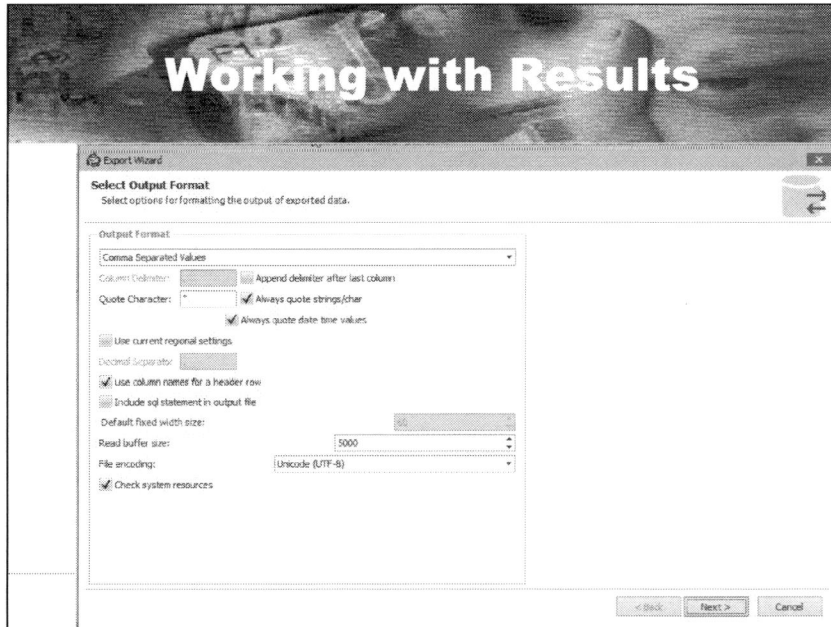

Working with Results

Export Wizard

Select Output Format

Select options for formatting the output of exported data.

Output Format

Comma Separated Values

Append delimiter after last column

Quote Character: "  Always quote strings/char

Always quote date time values

Use current regional settings

Use column names for a header row

Include sql statement in output file

Default fixed width size:

Read buffer size: 5000

File encoding: Unicode (UTF-8)

Check system resources

Next > Cancel

Notice all the options including how to present column names. You can even include the SQL used to generate this data load! Yet another way to generate SQL without typing.

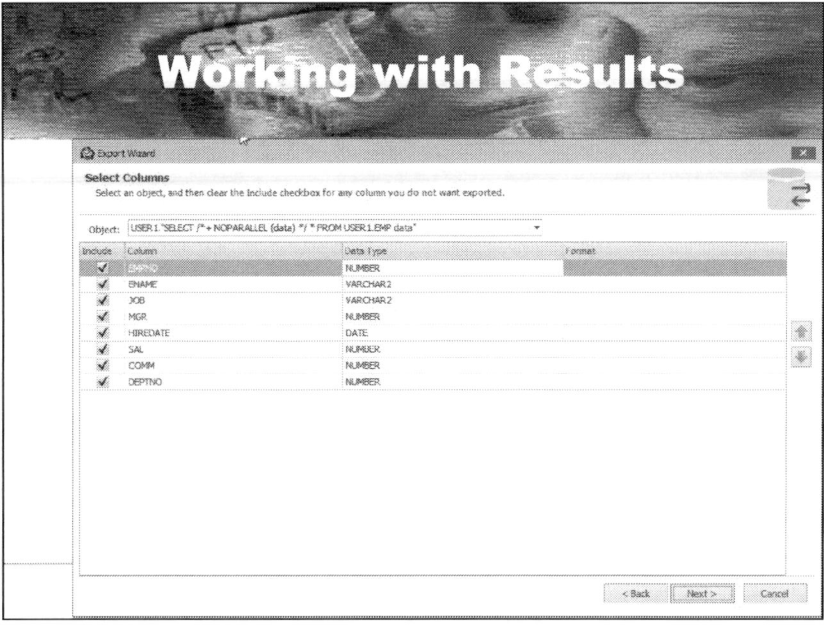


Select columns for the spreadsheet here.

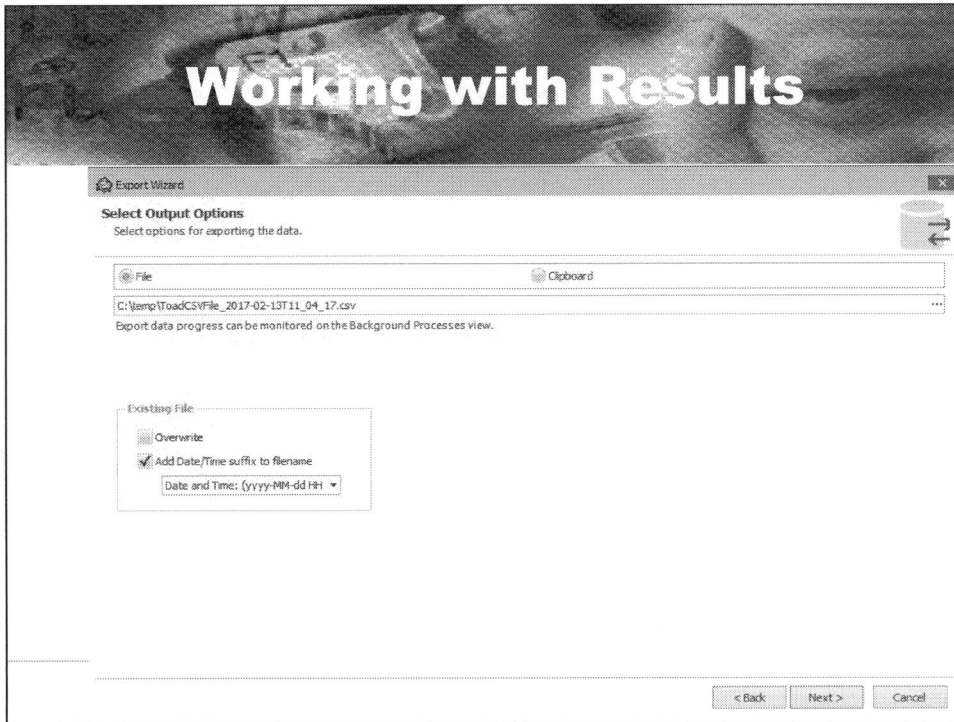

**Working with Results**

Export Wizard

**Select Output Options**

Select options for exporting the data.

File Clipboard

C:\temp\ToadCSVFile_2017-02-13T11_04_17.csv

Export data progress can be monitored on the Background Processes view.

Existing File

Overwrite

Add Date/Time suffix to filename

Date and Time: (yyyy-MM-dd HH

< Back Next > Cancel

Name and locate the output file.

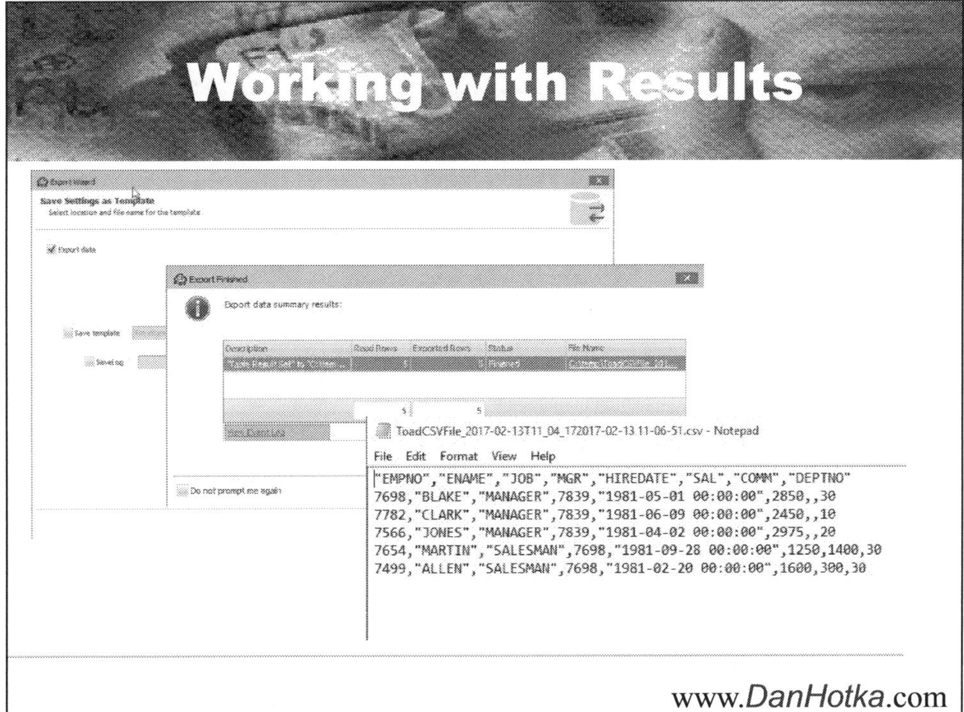


Let it rip! Toad DP will report back when the file has been created.

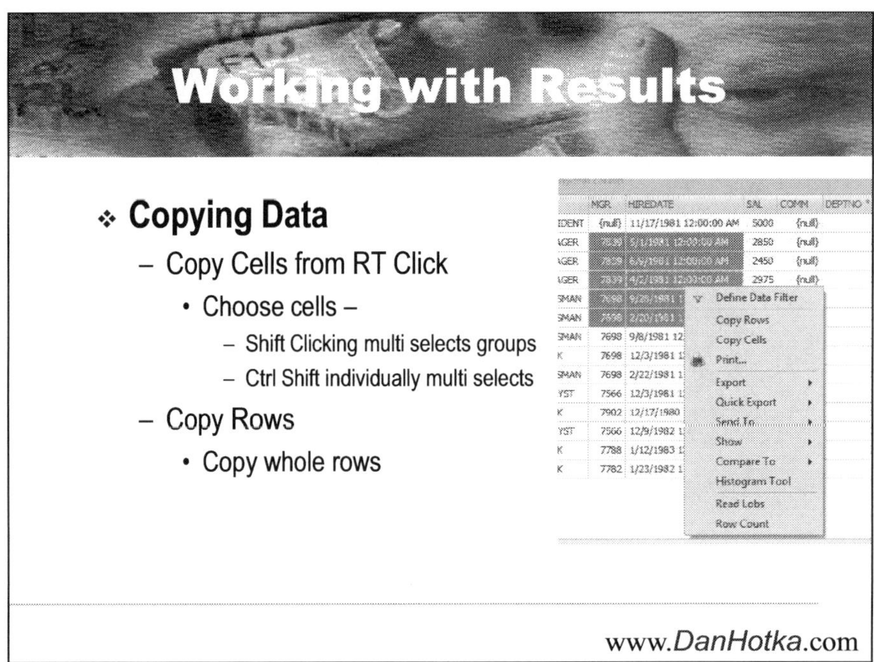
Working with Results
Copying Data
– Copy Cells from RT Click
• Choose cells –
– Shift Clicking multi selects groups
– Ctrl Shift individually multi selects
– Copy Rows
• Copy whole rows
Define Data Filter
Copy Rows
Copy Cells
Print...
Export
Quick Export
Send To
Show
Compare To
Histogram Tool
Read Lobs
Row Count
www.DanHotka.com

You can use the MS key strokes (actually these have been around all Ascii devices for a very long time)…select an item with a single left click…holding the shift key down allows you to select an area from where the cursor is to where you click again. Ctrl click allows for you to individually select/deselect items in the list. Ctrl+A selects all, Ctrl+C copies to the paste buffer and Ctrl+V pastes at the location of the cursor.

*****Tip***** Ask your instructor for a demonstration of these keyboarding techniques if you would like to use them.

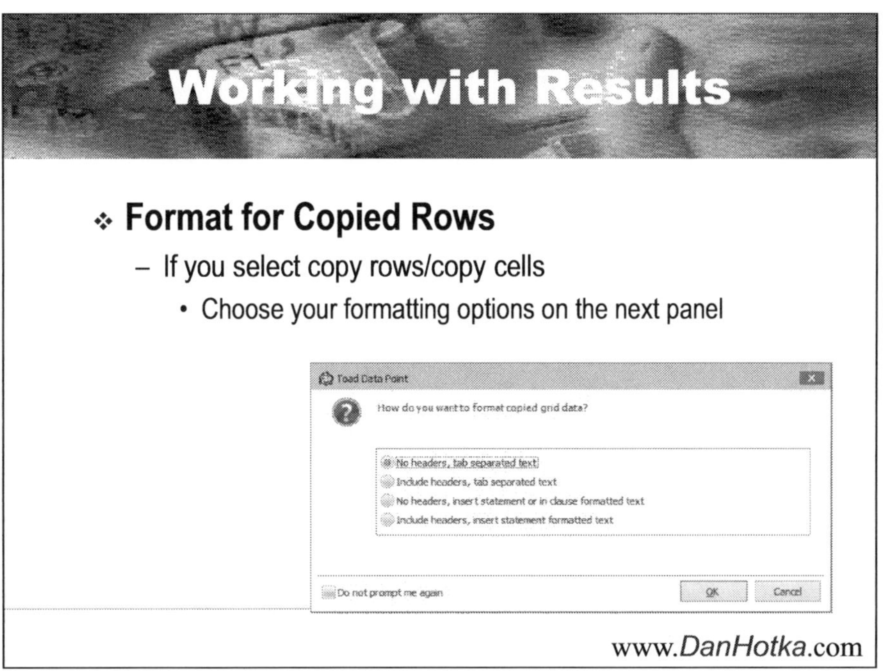
Working with Results
Format for Copied Rows
If you select copy rows/copy cells
Choose your formatting options on the next panel
Toad Data Point
How do you want to format copied grid data?
No headers, tab separated text
Include headers, tab separated text
No headers, insert statement or in clause formatted text
Include headers, insert statement formatted text
Do not prompt me again
OK
Cancel
www.DanHotka.com

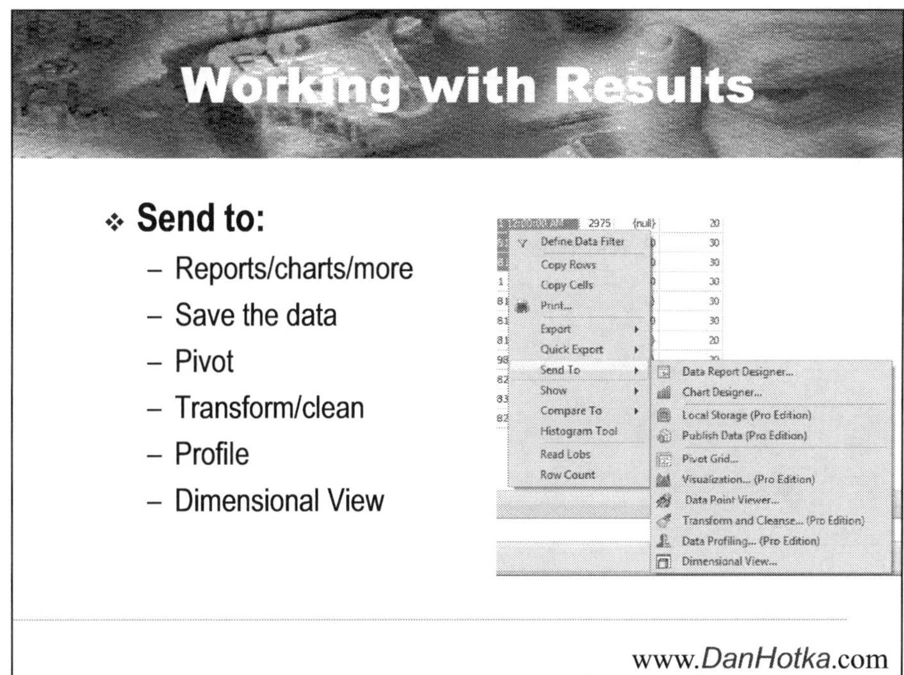
Working with Results
Send to:
Reports/charts/more
Save the data
Pivot
Transform/clean
Profile
Dimensional View
Define Data Filter
Copy Rows
Copy Cells
Print...
Export
Quick Export
Send To
Show
Compare To
Histogram Tool
Read Lobs
Row Count
Data Report Designer...
Chart Designer...
Local Storage (Pro Edition)
Publish Data (Pro Edition)
Pivot Grid...
Visualization... (Pro Edition)
Data Point Viewer...
Transform and Cleanse... (Pro Edition)
Data Profiling... (Pro Edition)
Dimensional View...
www.DanHotka.com

## Pivot Table Walk Through

**Working with Results**

- **Walk Thru Scenario:**
  - Need a pivot table with job salary doing down
  - Departments across the top
  - Saved to Excel as Pivot Table

www.*DanHotka*.com

The instructor will walk thru a workflow using simple data in a pivot format. He/she will demonstrate how this works and how to get this data into an Excel spreadsheet.

***Note*** The instructor is not an Excel expert. If you see a better way to do something, show him or her.

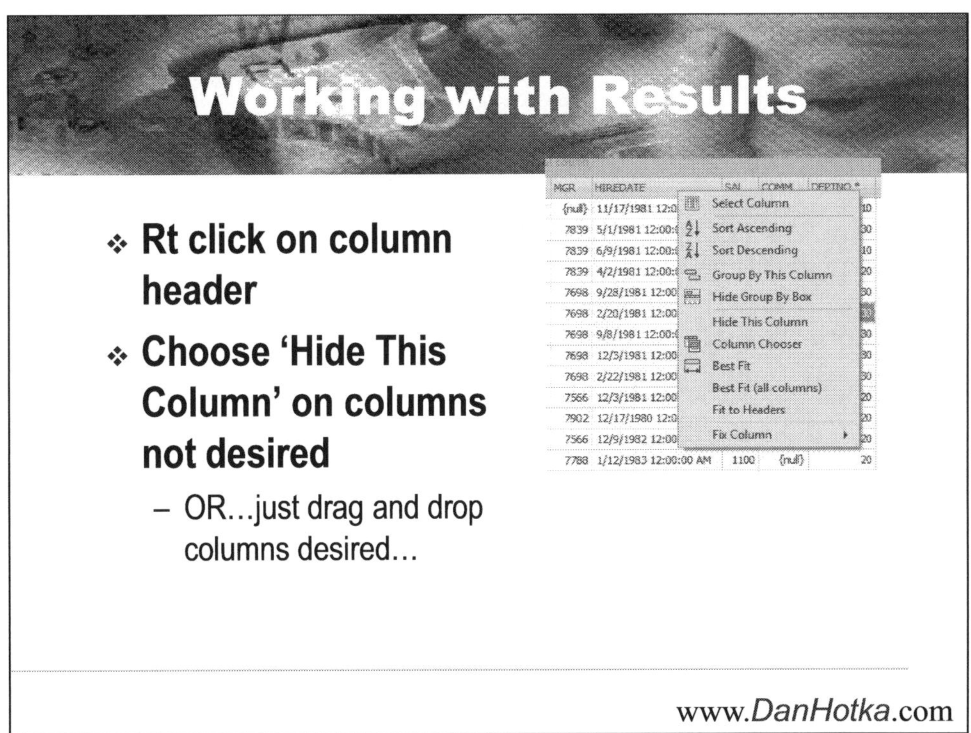
Working with Results
Rt click on column header
Choose 'Hide This Column' on columns not desired
– OR…just drag and drop columns desired…
Select Column
Sort Ascending
Sort Descending
Group By This Column
Hide Group By Box
Hide This Column
Column Chooser
Best Fit
Best Fit (all columns)
Fit to Headers
Fix Column
www.DanHotka.com

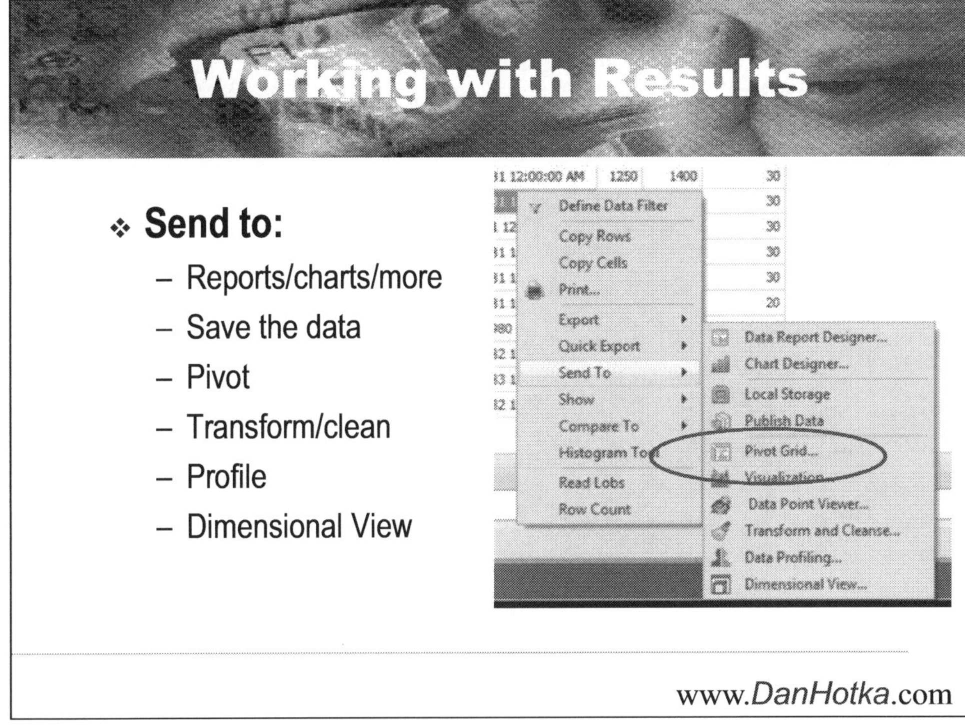
Working with Results
Send to:
– Reports/charts/more
– Save the data
– Pivot
– Transform/clean
– Profile
– Dimensional View
Define Data Filter
Copy Rows
Copy Cells
Print...
Export
Quick Export
Send To
Show
Compare To
Histogram Tool
Read Lobs
Row Count
Data Report Designer...
Chart Designer...
Local Storage
Publish Data
Pivot Grid...
Visualization
Data Point Viewer...
Transform and Cleanse...
Data Profiling...
Dimensional View...
www.DanHotka.com

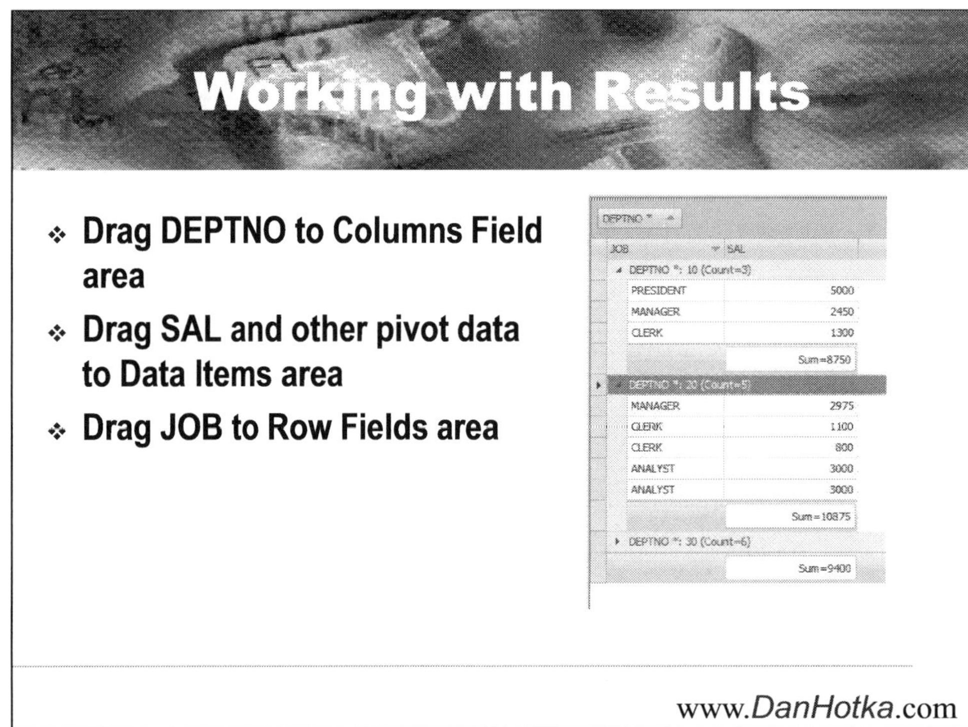
Working with Results
Drag DEPTNO to Columns Field area
Drag SAL and other pivot data to Data Items area
Drag JOB to Row Fields area
www.DanHotka.com

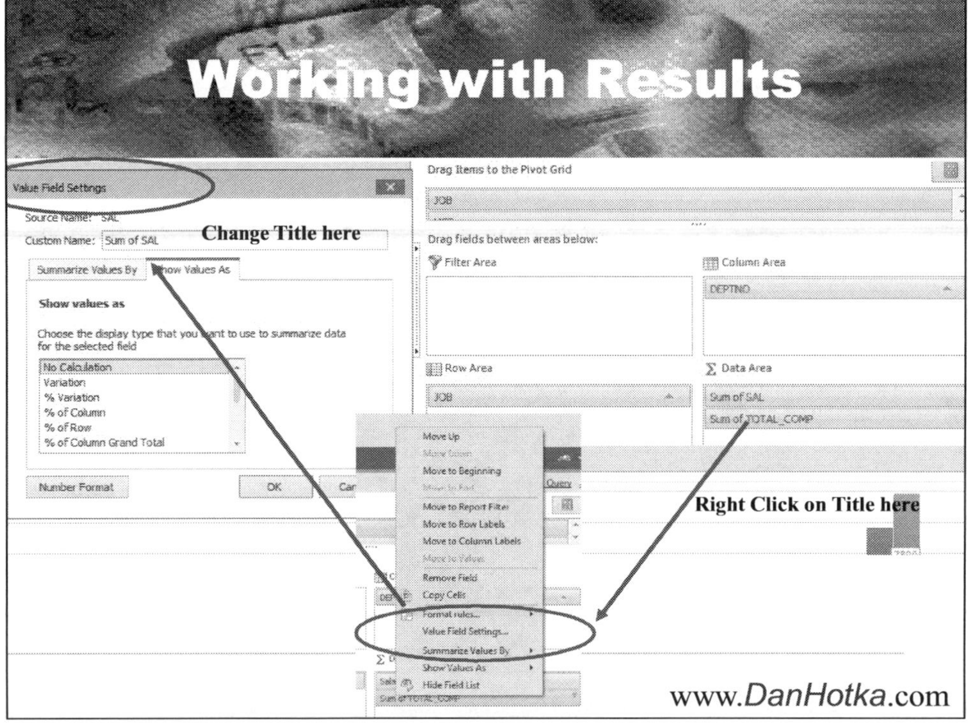
Working with Results
Change Title here
Right Click on Title here
www.DanHotka.com

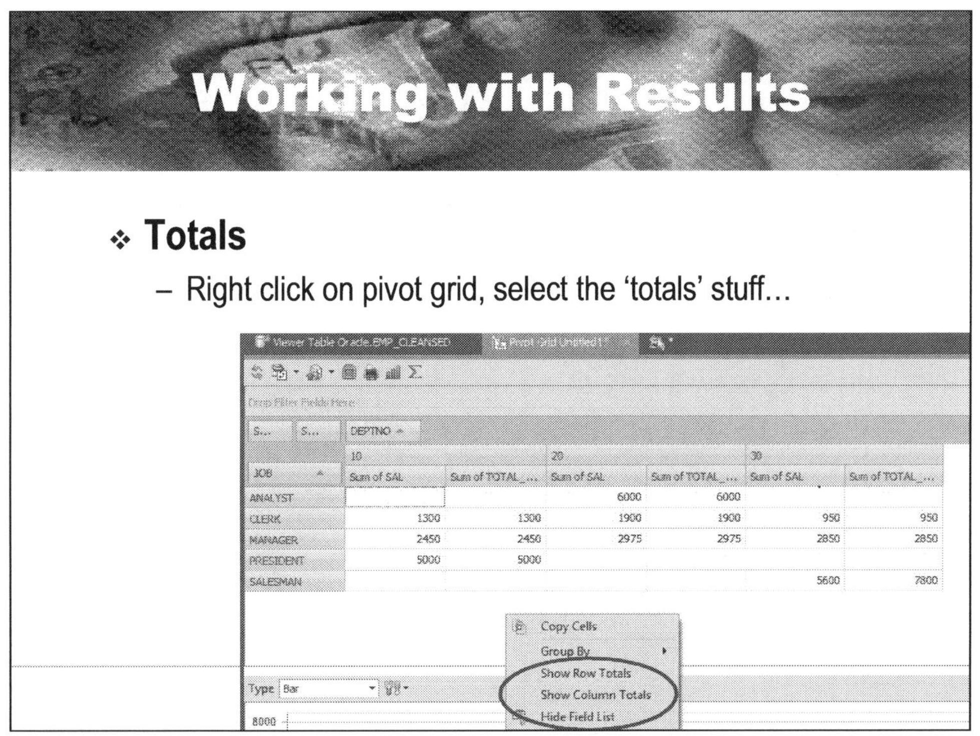


# Working with Results

Drop Filter Fields Here

| JOB | 10 Salary | 10 Total Salary | 20 Salary | 20 Total Salary | 30 Salary | 30 Total Salary | Grand Total Salary | T... |
|---|---|---|---|---|---|---|---|---|
| ANALYST | | | 6000 | 6000 | | | 6000 | |
| CLERK | 1300 | 1300 | 1900 | 1900 | 950 | 950 | 4150 | |
| MANAGER | 2450 | 2450 | 2975 | 2975 | 2850 | 2850 | 8275 | |
| PRESIDENT | 5000 | 5000 | | | | | 5000 | |
| SALESMAN | | | | | 5600 | 7800 | 5600 | |
| Grand Total | 8750 | 8750 | 10875 | 10875 | 9400 | 11600 | 29025 | |

www.*DanHotka*.com

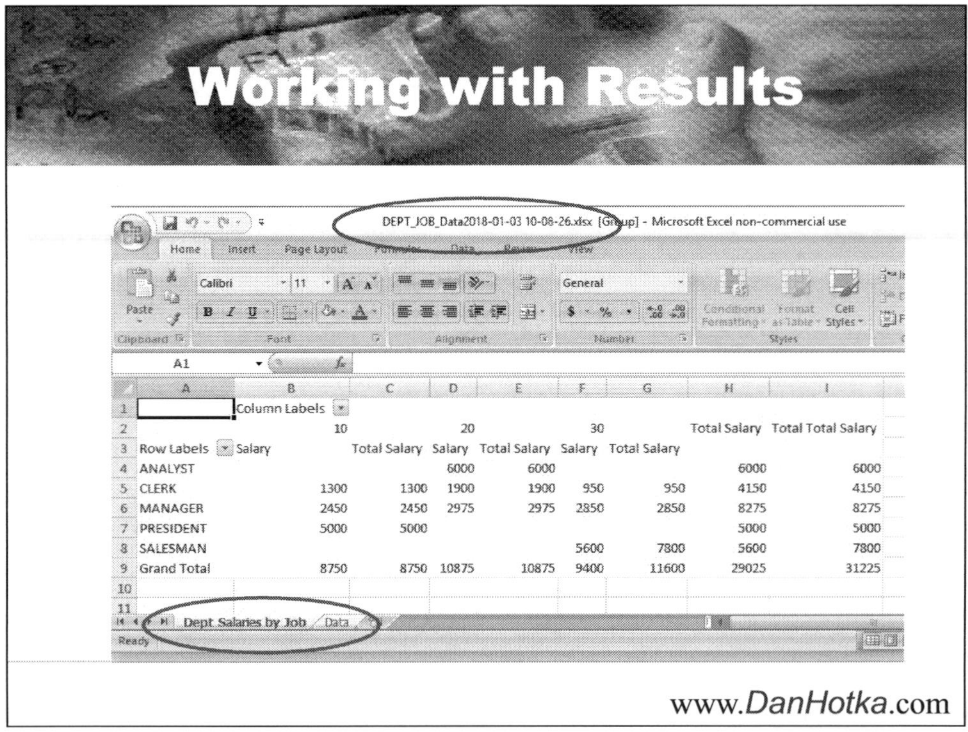


|  | Column Labels |  |  |  |  |  |  |  |
|---|---|---|---|---|---|---|---|---|
|  | 10 |  | 20 |  | 30 |  |  |  |
| Row Labels | Salary | Total Salary | Salary | Total Salary | Salary | Total Salary | Total Salary | Total Total Salary |
| ANALYST |  |  | 6000 | 6000 |  |  | 6000 | 6000 |
| CLERK | 1300 | 1300 | 1900 | 1900 | 950 | 950 | 4150 | 4150 |
| MANAGER | 2450 | 2450 | 2975 | 2975 | 2850 | 2850 | 8275 | 8275 |
| PRESIDENT | 5000 | 5000 |  |  |  |  | 5000 | 5000 |
| SALESMAN |  |  |  |  | 5600 | 7800 | 5600 | 7800 |
| Grand Total | 8750 | 8750 | 10875 | 10875 | 9400 | 11600 | 29025 | 31225 |

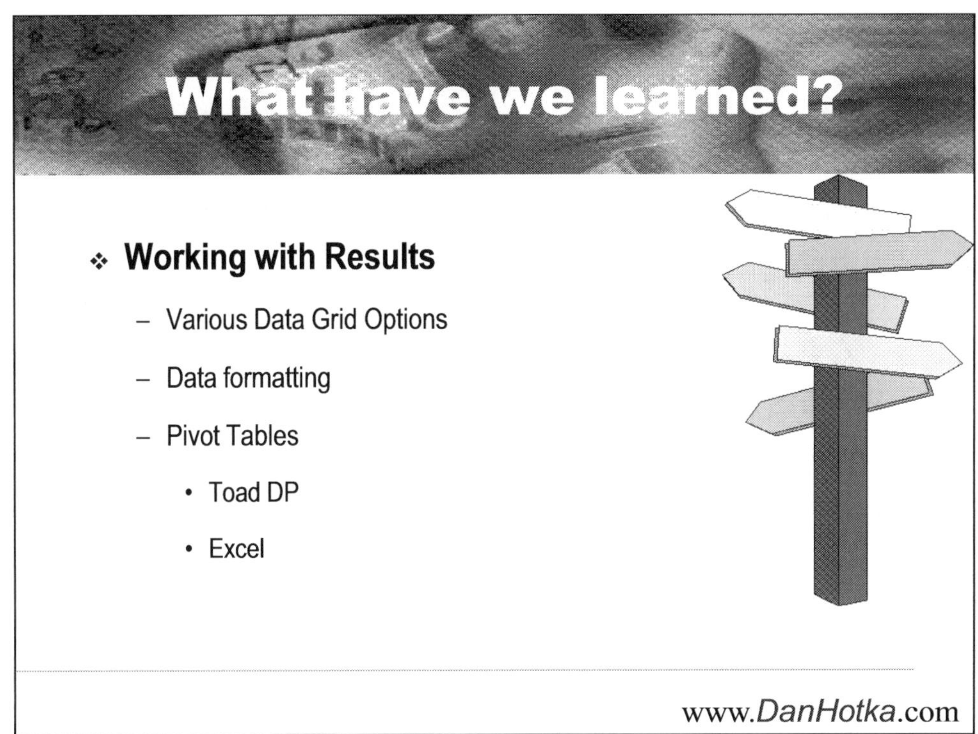
What have we learned?
Working with Results
– Various Data Grid Options
– Data formatting
– Pivot Tables
• Toad DP
• Excel
www.DanHotka.com

## Working with Results Lab

# Working with Results Lab

- Working with Results Lab
  - Using your xxxxxx table or the EMP table
    - Display the data
    - Add a total to the SAL column
      - If using your data…to the xxxxxxxx column.
    - Create a ':' delimited file
      - Give it a .txt suffix
      - Save to the Temp folder
      - Review your results
    - Create a pivot table
      - Select the pivot data
        - » EMP Table: Manager is the group by (top) column
        - » Side is the employee name
        - » Sum the SAL data
      - Save to Excel Pivot Table…Manager_Employee_Data

www.DanHotka.com

## Working with Results Lab Answers

- Using the EMP table
  - Display the data
  - Create a ':' delimited file
    - Give it a .txt suffix
    - Save to the Temp folder
    - Review your results

This example works from the EMP_CLEANSED created from the Quick Start part of this course. You can use any EMP table, or, your own data. You will need something to sum up and 2 axis data points. In this example, we will use JOB and DEPT, summing the SAL and TOTAL_COMP fields.

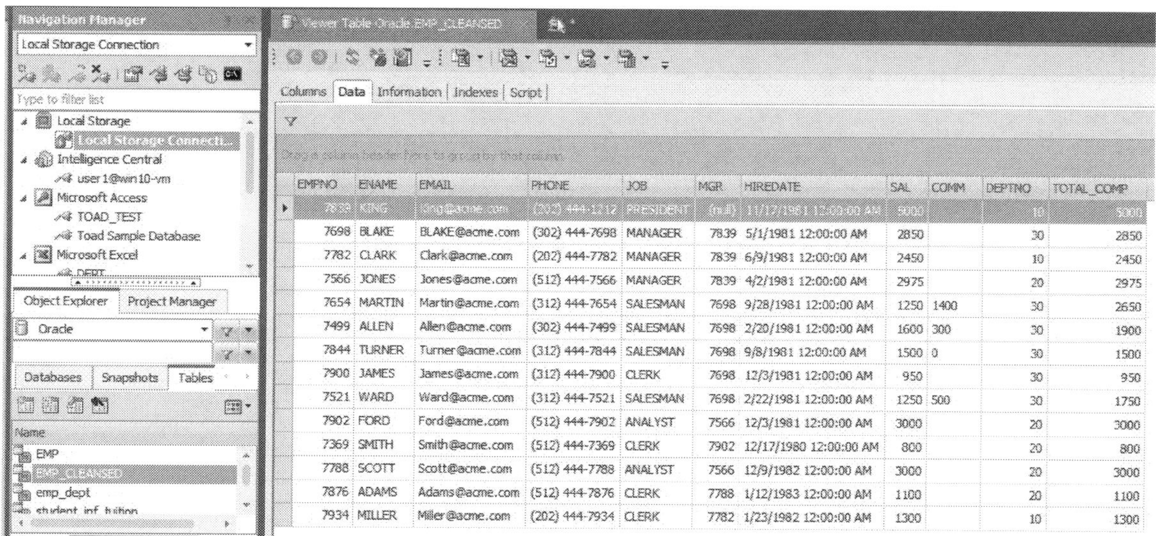

| EMPNO | ENAME | EMAIL | PHONE | JOB | MGR | HIREDATE | SAL | COMM | DEPTNO | TOTAL_COMP |
|---|---|---|---|---|---|---|---|---|---|---|
| 7839 | KING | king@acme.com | (202) 444-1212 | PRESIDENT | (null) | 11/17/1981 12:00:00 AM | 5000 | | 10 | 5000 |
| 7698 | BLAKE | BLAKE@acme.com | (302) 444-7698 | MANAGER | 7839 | 5/1/1981 12:00:00 AM | 2850 | | 30 | 2850 |
| 7782 | CLARK | Clark@acme.com | (202) 444-7782 | MANAGER | 7839 | 6/9/1981 12:00:00 AM | 2450 | | 10 | 2450 |
| 7566 | JONES | Jones@acme.com | (512) 444-7566 | MANAGER | 7839 | 4/2/1981 12:00:00 AM | 2975 | | 20 | 2975 |
| 7654 | MARTIN | Martin@acme.com | (312) 444-7654 | SALESMAN | 7698 | 9/28/1981 12:00:00 AM | 1250 | 1400 | 30 | 2650 |
| 7499 | ALLEN | Allen@acme.com | (302) 444-7499 | SALESMAN | 7698 | 2/20/1981 12:00:00 AM | 1600 | 300 | 30 | 1900 |
| 7844 | TURNER | Turner@acme.com | (312) 444-7844 | SALESMAN | 7698 | 9/8/1981 12:00:00 AM | 1500 | 0 | 30 | 1500 |
| 7900 | JAMES | James@acme.com | (312) 444-7900 | CLERK | 7698 | 12/3/1981 12:00:00 AM | 950 | | 30 | 950 |
| 7521 | WARD | Ward@acme.com | (312) 444-7521 | SALESMAN | 7698 | 2/22/1981 12:00:00 AM | 1250 | 500 | 30 | 1750 |
| 7902 | FORD | Ford@acme.com | (512) 444-7902 | ANALYST | 7566 | 12/3/1981 12:00:00 AM | 3000 | | 20 | 3000 |
| 7369 | SMITH | Smith@acme.com | (512) 444-7369 | CLERK | 7902 | 12/17/1980 12:00:00 AM | 800 | | 20 | 800 |
| 7788 | SCOTT | Scott@acme.com | (512) 444-7788 | ANALYST | 7566 | 12/9/1982 12:00:00 AM | 3000 | | 20 | 3000 |
| 7876 | ADAMS | Adams@acme.com | (512) 444-7876 | CLERK | 7788 | 1/12/1983 12:00:00 AM | 1100 | | 20 | 1100 |
| 7934 | MILLER | Miller@acme.com | (202) 444-7934 | CLERK | 7782 | 1/23/1982 12:00:00 AM | 1300 | | 10 | 1300 |

| | SAL | COMM | DEPTNO |
|---|---|---|---|
| ) AM | 800 | {null} | 20 |
| AM | 1600 | 300 | 30 |
| AM | 1250 | 500 | 30 |
| M | 2975 | {null} | 20 |
| AM | 1250 | 1400 | 30 |
| M | 2850 | | |
| M | 2450 | | |
| AM | 3000 | | |
| ) AM | 5000 | | |
| M | 1500 | | |
| AM | 1100 | | |
| AM | 950 | | |
| AM | 3000 | | |
| AM | 1300 | | |
| | Sum=29025 | Sum=2200 | |

Sum
Min
Max
Count
Numerical Count
Variance
Standard Deviation
Geometric Mean
Average
None

To add a total or a count of rows (or some other available analytic functions), right click on the bottom bar UNDER the column to get this popup menu.

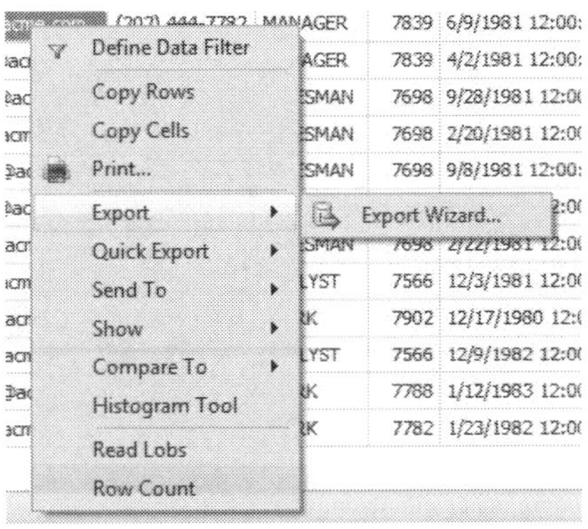

Define Data Filter
Copy Rows
Copy Cells
Print...
Export
Export Wizard...
Quick Export
Send To
Show
Compare To
Histogram Tool
Read Lobs
Row Count


Right click on the data grid, select Export → Export Wizard…

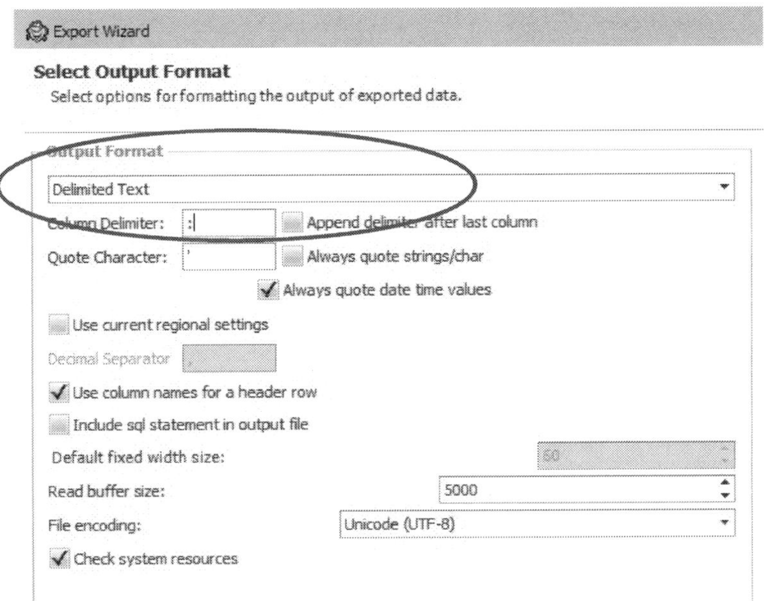


Pick your output type from the drop down menu and the column delimiter. Review the other options to see if you want those tool. Notice you can make SQL statements of the data as well. Click 'Next'.

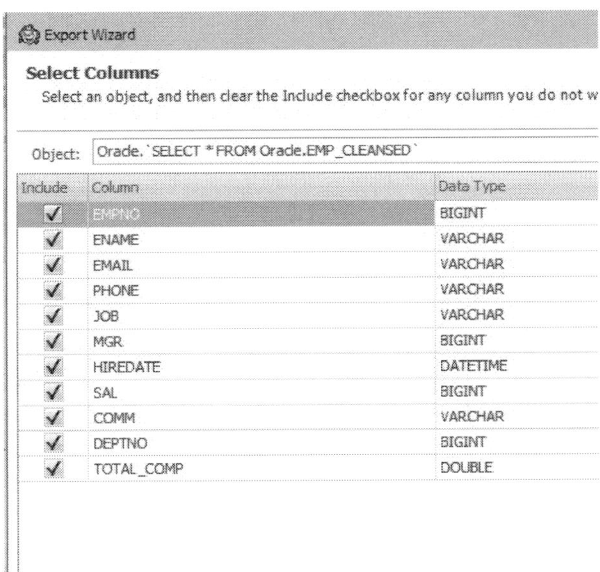


De-select any columns not desired, click 'Next'.

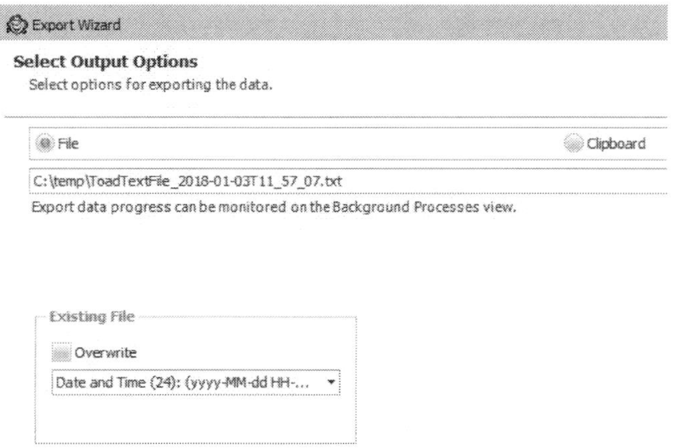
Export Wizard
Select Output Options
Select options for exporting the data.
File
Clipboard
C:\temp\ToadTextFile_2018-01-03T11_57_07.txt
Export data progress can be monitored on the Background Processes view.
Existing File
Overwrite
Date and Time (24): (yyyy-MM-dd HH-...

Name the output file and its location. Notice you can export to the clipboard…use Ctrl V to paste into any other app, or back into Toad DP's editor window.

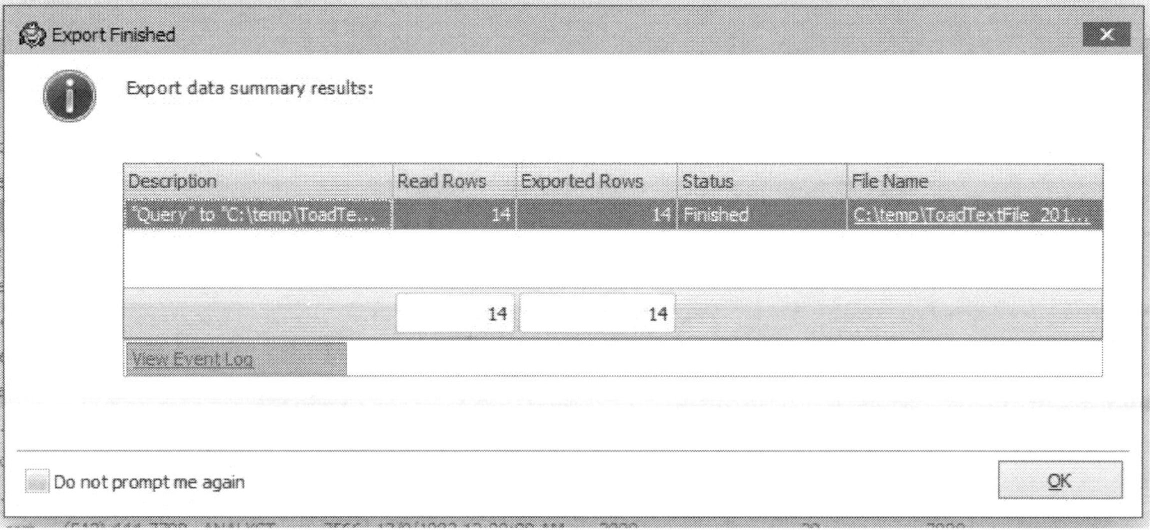
Export Finished
Export data summary results:
Description
Read Rows
Exported Rows
Status
File Name
"Query" to "C:\temp\ToadTe...
14
14
Finished
C:\temp\ToadTextFile_201...
14
14
View Event Log
Do not prompt me again
OK

Click Next thru the next couple of screens. When it is done, this pops up and allows you to see the output and the log that might have any errors if the row counts don't match.

```
ToadTextFile_2018-01-03T11_57_072018-01-03 11-58-44.txt - Notepad
File  Edit  Format  View  Help
EMPNO:ENAME:EMAIL:PHONE:JOB:MGR:HIREDATE:SAL:COMM:DEPTNO:TOTAL_COMP
7839:KING:King@acme.com:(202) 444-1212:PRESIDENT::'1981-11-17 00:00:00':5000::10:5000
7698:BLAKE:BLAKE@acme.com:(302) 444-7698:MANAGER:7839:'1981-05-01 00:00:00':2850::30:2850
7782:CLARK:Clark@acme.com:(202) 444-7782:MANAGER:7839:'1981-06-09 00:00:00':2450::10:2450
7566:JONES:Jones@acme.com:(512) 444-7566:MANAGER:7839:'1981-04-02 00:00:00':2975::20:2975
7654:MARTIN:Martin@acme.com:(312) 444-7654:SALESMAN:7698:'1981-09-28 00:00:00':1250:1400:30:265
7499:ALLEN:Allen@acme.com:(302) 444-7499:SALESMAN:7698:'1981-02-20 00:00:00':1600:300:30:1900
7844:TURNER:Turner@acme.com:(312) 444-7844:SALESMAN:7698:'1981-09-08 00:00:00':1500:0:30:1500
7900:JAMES:James@acme.com:(312) 444-7900:CLERK:7698:'1981-12-03 00:00:00':950::30:950
7521:WARD:Ward@acme.com:(312) 444-7521:SALESMAN:7698:'1981-02-22 00:00:00':1250:500:30:1750
7902:FORD:Ford@acme.com:(512) 444-7902:ANALYST:7566:'1981-12-03 00:00:00':3000::20:3000
7369:SMITH:Smith@acme.com:(512) 444-7369:CLERK:7902:'1980-12-17 00:00:00':800::20:800
7788:SCOTT:Scott@acme.com:(512) 444-7788:ANALYST:7566:'1982-12-09 00:00:00':3000::20:3000
7876:ADAMS:Adams@acme.com:(512) 444-7876:CLERK:7788:'1983-01-12 00:00:00':1100::20:1100
7934:MILLER:Miller@acme.com:(202) 444-7934:CLERK:7782:'1982-01-23 00:00:00':1300::10:1300
```

- Create a pivot table
    - Select the pivot data
        - EMP Table: Manager is the group by (top) column
        - Side is the employee name
        - Sum the SAL data

Save to Excel Pivot Table… save as Manager_Employee_Data

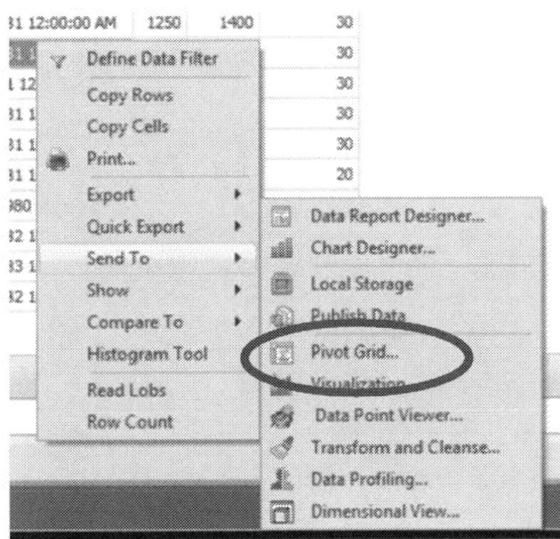


Drop the SAL field to the data items area. Drop the MNGR field to the row fields area. Drop the ENAME next to this MNGR field!

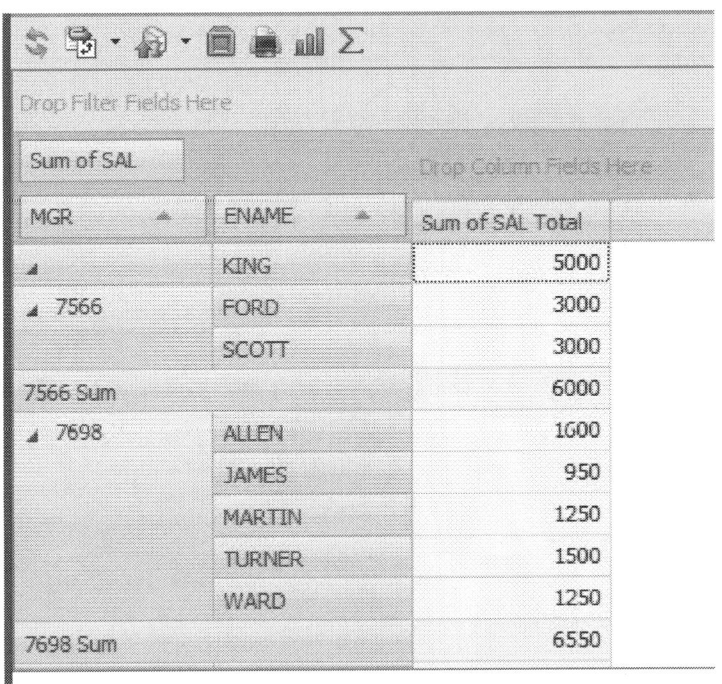

Drop Filter Fields Here

Sum of SAL

Drop Column Fields Here

| MGR | ENAME | Sum of SAL Total |
|---|---|---|
| | KING | 5000 |
| 7566 | FORD | 3000 |
| | SCOTT | 3000 |
| 7566 Sum | | 6000 |
| 7698 | ALLEN | 1600 |
| | JAMES | 950 |
| | MARTIN | 1250 |
| | TURNER | 1500 |
| | WARD | 1250 |
| 7698 Sum | | 6550 |

Check this out! You can drill and condense the data when more than one field appears in the row field area.

Click the Export Pivot button and save as MANAGER_EMPLOYEE_DATA

Export

Export As:

Excel

File Name and Path

C:\temp\Manager_Employee_Data.xlsx

Overwrite

Date and Time (24): (yyyy-MM-dd HH-mm-ss)

Worksheet name: Manager Employee Data

Append rows

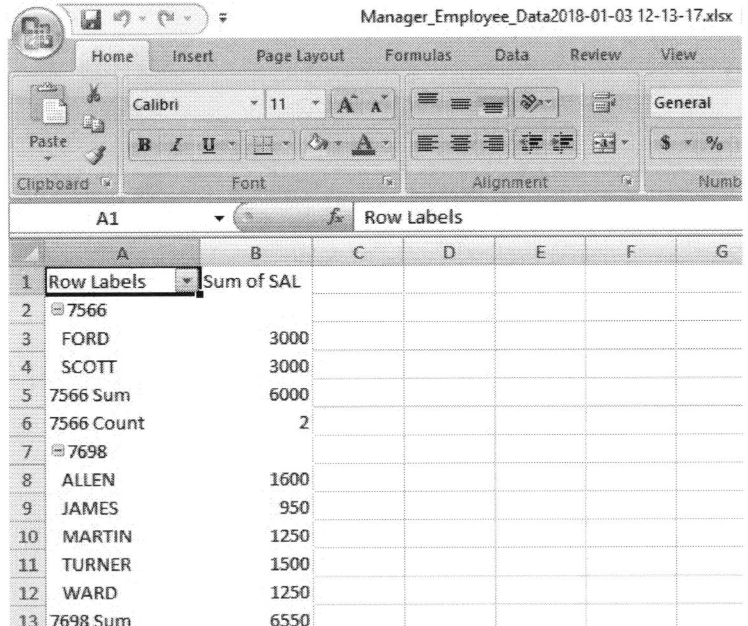

| | A | B |
|---|---|---|
| 1 | Row Labels | Sum of SAL |
| 2 | ⊟7566 | |
| 3 | FORD | 3000 |
| 4 | SCOTT | 3000 |
| 5 | 7566 Sum | 6000 |
| 6 | 7566 Count | 2 |
| 7 | ⊟7698 | |
| 8 | ALLEN | 1600 |
| 9 | JAMES | 950 |
| 10 | MARTIN | 1250 |
| 11 | TURNER | 1500 |
| 12 | WARD | 1250 |
| 13 | 7698 Sum | 6550 |

# Visualization Techniques

## Visualization Techniques

- This unit will cover:
  - Reports
  - Graphs and Charts

www.DanHotka.com

## Reports

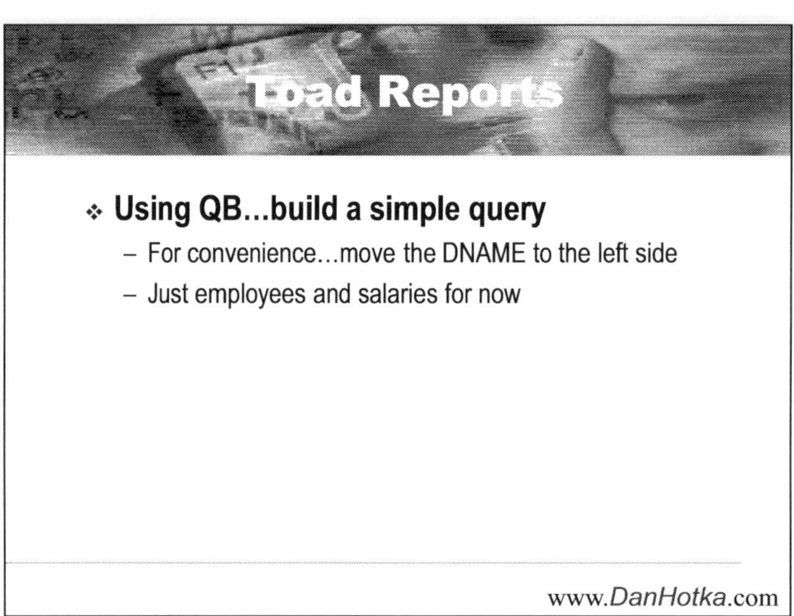
Toad Reports
Using QB…build a simple query
– For convenience…move the DNAME to the left side
– Just employees and salaries for now
www.DanHotka.com

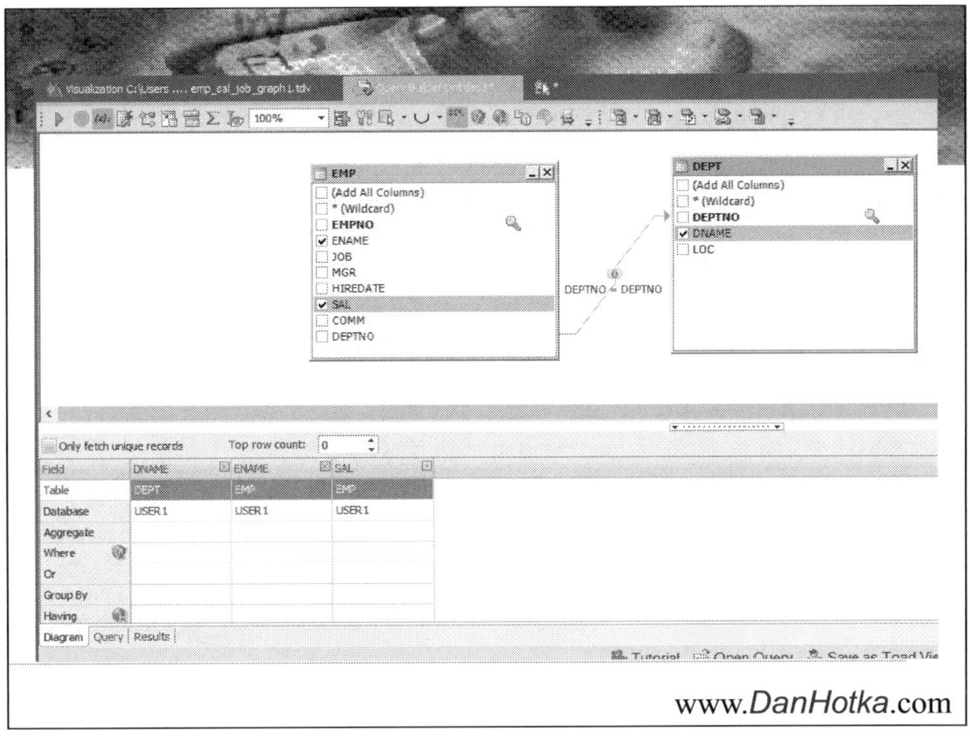
EMP
(Add All Columns)
* (Wildcard)
EMPNO
ENAME
JOB
MGR
HIREDATE
SAL
COMM
DEPTNO
DEPT
(Add All Columns)
* (Wildcard)
DEPTNO
DNAME
LOC
DEPTNO = DEPTNO
Only fetch unique records
Top row count:
Field
Table
Database
Aggregate
Where
Or
Group By
Having
DNAME
ENAME
SAL
DEPT
EMP
USER1
Diagram
Query
Results
www.DanHotka.com

Toad Reports
Run SQL
– right click on data grid
– Send To:
• Data Report Designer
Define Data Filter
Copy Rows
Copy Cells
Print...
Export
Quick Export
Send To
Show
Compare To
Histogram Tool
Read Lobs
Row Count
Data Report Designer...
Local Storage
Publish Data
Pivot Grid...
Visualization...
Data Point Viewer...
Transform and Cleanse...
Data Profiling...
Dimensional View...
www.DanHotka.com

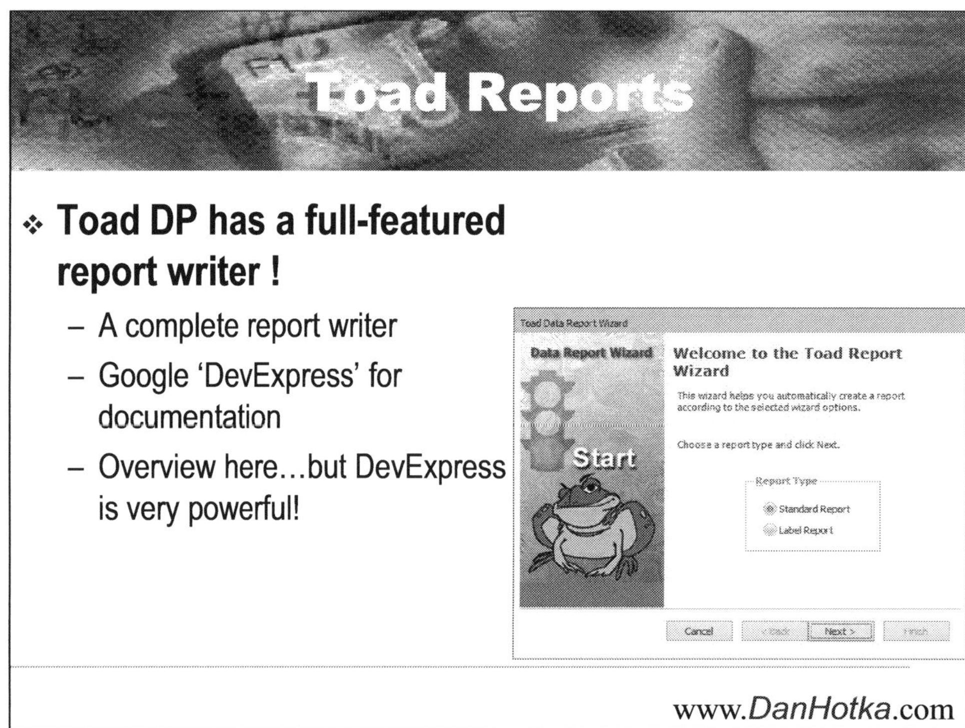
Toad Reports
Toad DP has a full-featured report writer !
– A complete report writer
– Google 'DevExpress' for documentation
– Overview here…but DevExpress is very powerful!
Toad Data Report Wizard
Data Report Wizard
Welcome to the Toad Report Wizard
This wizard helps you automatically create a report according to the selected wizard options.
Choose a report type and click Next.
Report Type
Standard Report
Label Report
Start
Cancel
Next >
www.DanHotka.com

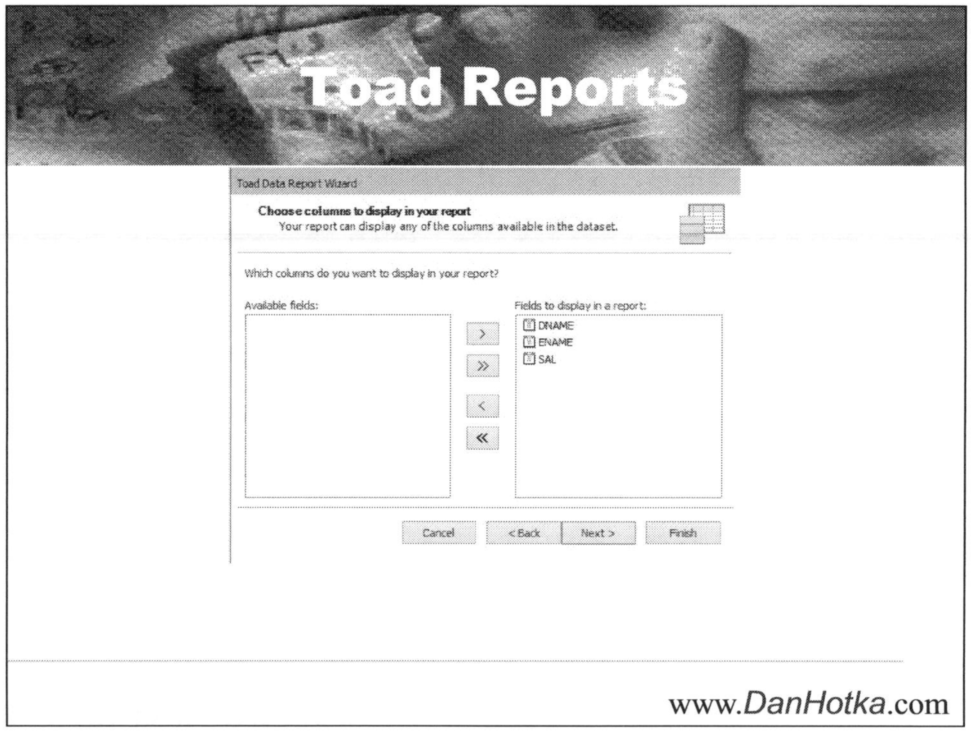
Toad Reports
Toad Data Report Wizard
Choose columns to display in your report
Your report can display any of the columns available in the dataset.
Which columns do you want to display in your report?
Available fields:
Fields to display in a report:
DNAME
ENAME
SAL
Cancel
< Back
Next >
Finish
www.DanHotka.com

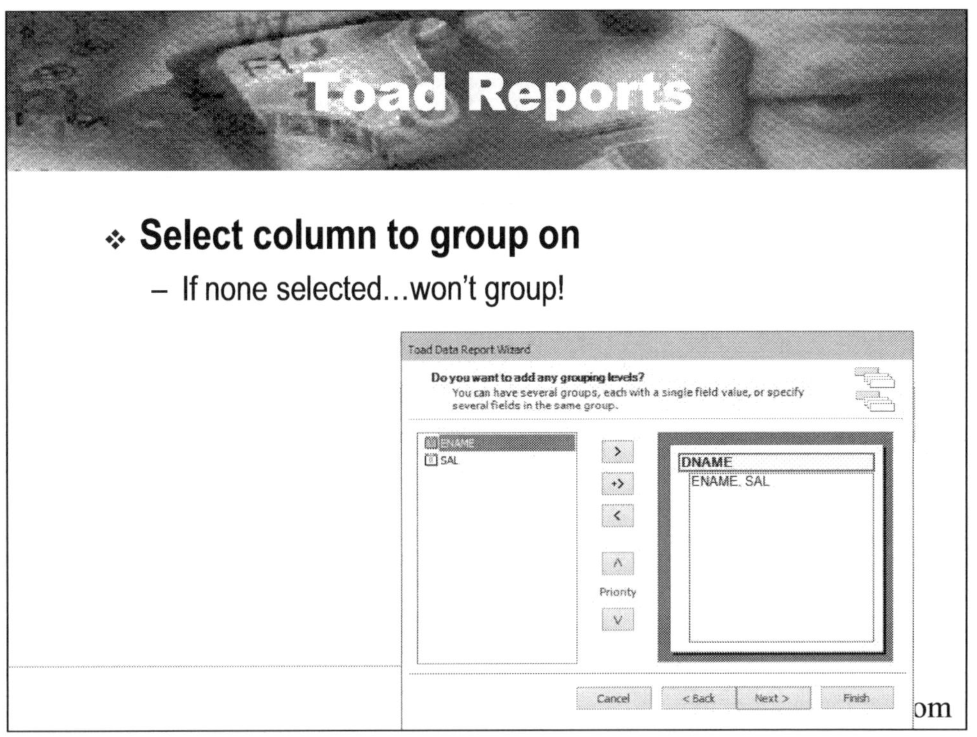
Toad Reports
Select column to group on
– If none selected…won't group!
Toad Data Report Wizard
Do you want to add any grouping levels?
You can have several groups, each with a single field value, or specify several fields in the same group.
ENAME
SAL
DNAME
ENAME, SAL
Priority
Cancel
< Back
Next >
Finish

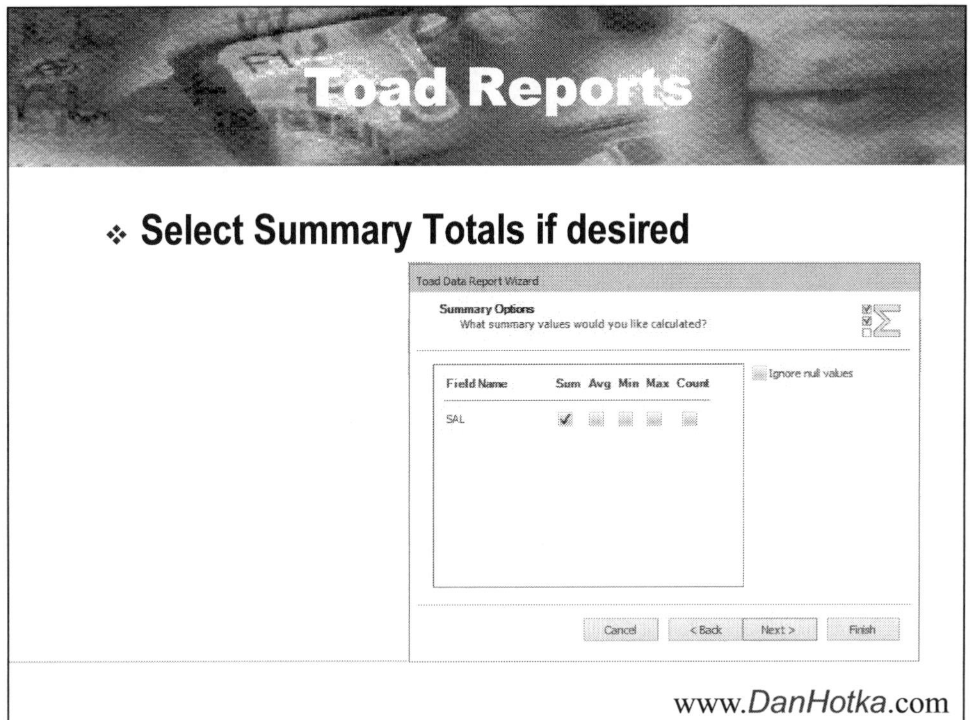
Toad Reports
Select Summary Totals if desired
Toad Data Report Wizard
Summary Options
What summary values would you like calculated?
Field Name
Sum
Avg
Min
Max
Count
SAL
Ignore null values
Cancel
< Back
Next >
Finish
www.DanHotka.com

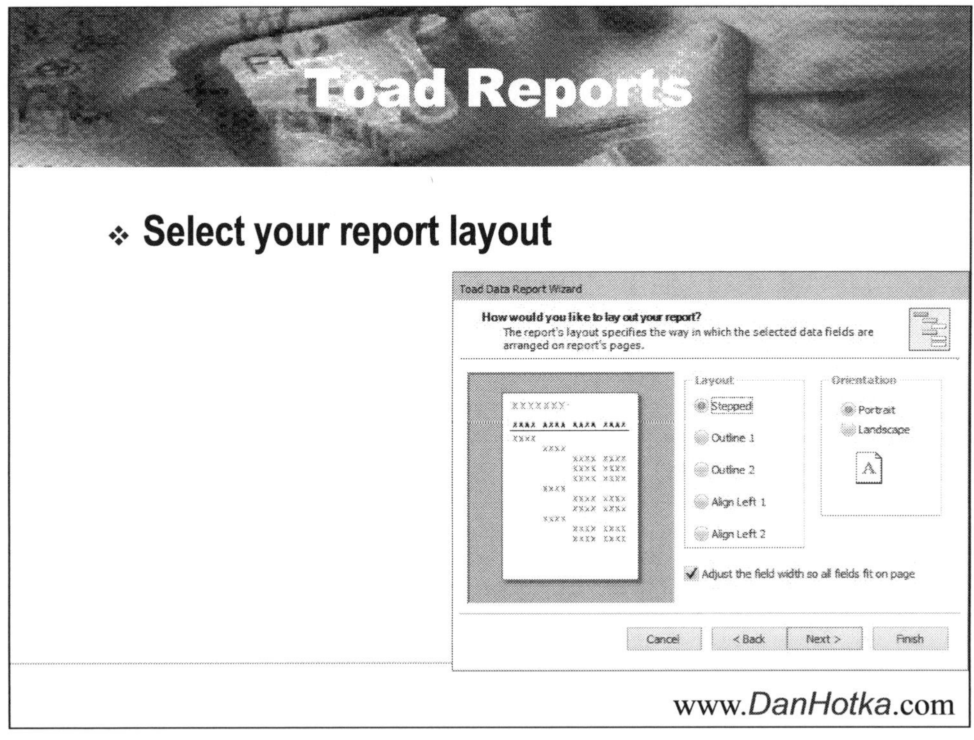
Toad Reports
Select your report layout
Toad Data Report Wizard
How would you like to lay out your report?
The report's layout specifies the way in which the selected data fields are arranged on report's pages.
Layout
Stepped
Outline 1
Outline 2
Align Left 1
Align Left 2
Orientation
Portrait
Landscape
Adjust the field width so all fields fit on page
Cancel
< Back
Next >
Finish
www.DanHotka.com

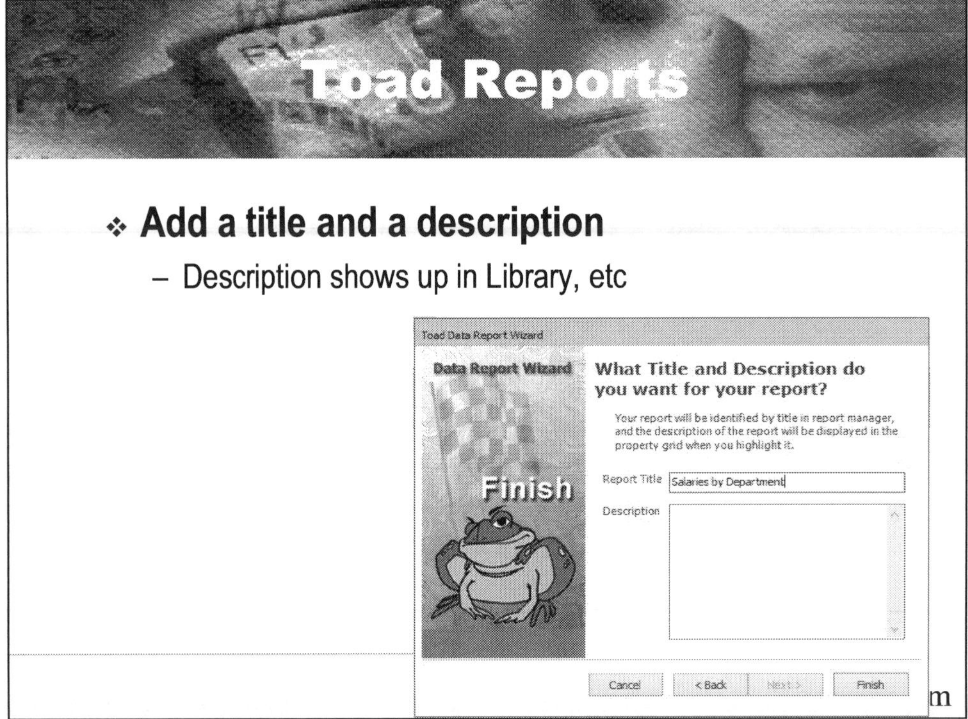
Toad Reports
Add a title and a description
– Description shows up in Library, etc
Toad Data Report Wizard
Data Report Wizard
Finish
What Title and Description do you want for your report?
Your report will be identified by title in report manager, and the description of the report will be displayed in the property grid when you highlight it.
Report Title
Salaries by Department
Description
Cancel
< Back
Next >
Finish

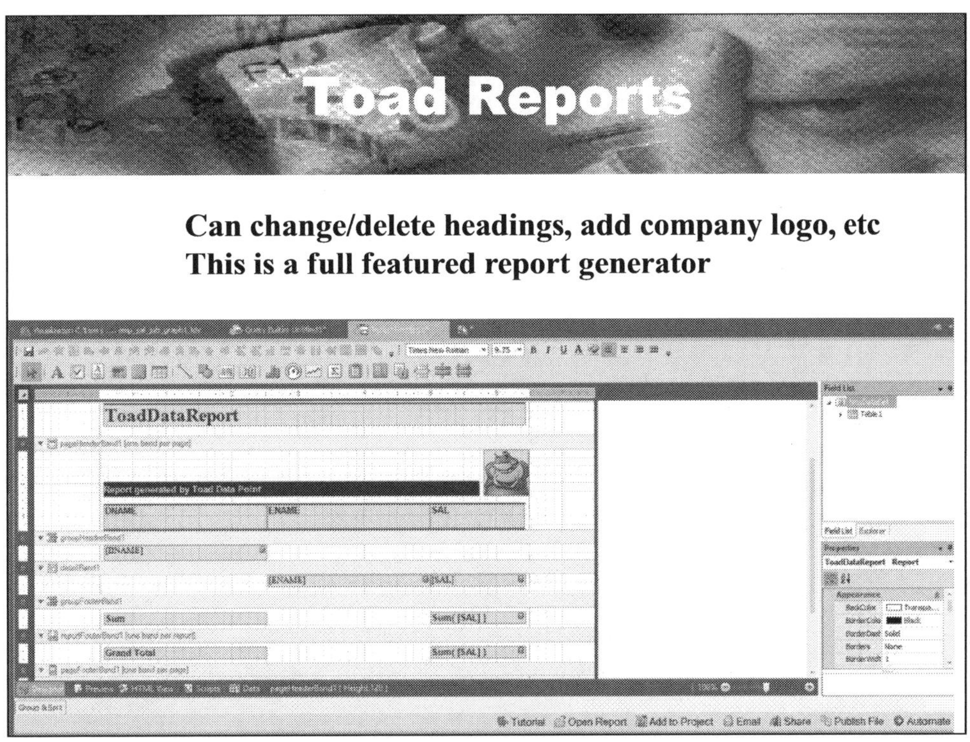
Toad Reports
Can change/delete headings, add company logo, etc
This is a full featured report generator
ToadDataReport
Report generated by Toad Data Point
DNAME
ENAME
SAL
[DNAME]
[ENAME]
[SAL]
Sum
Sum( [SAL] )
Grand Total
Sum( [SAL] )
Tutorial
Open Report
Add to Project
Email
Share
Publish File
Automate

Toad Reports
Save your report
Save As
Users › DEMO › Documents › Shared Toad
Search Shared Toad
Organize ▾
New folder
Quick access
Desktop
Downloads
Documents
Pictures
Desktop
OneDrive
DEMO
This PC
Libraries
Name
Date modified
Type
Size
emp_sal_rpt1.repx
9/14/2017 9:28 AM
REPX File
25 KB
File name:
Sal_by_Dept_rpt1
Save as type:
Report Designer Files (*.repx)
Hide Folders
Save
Cancel
www.DanHotka.com

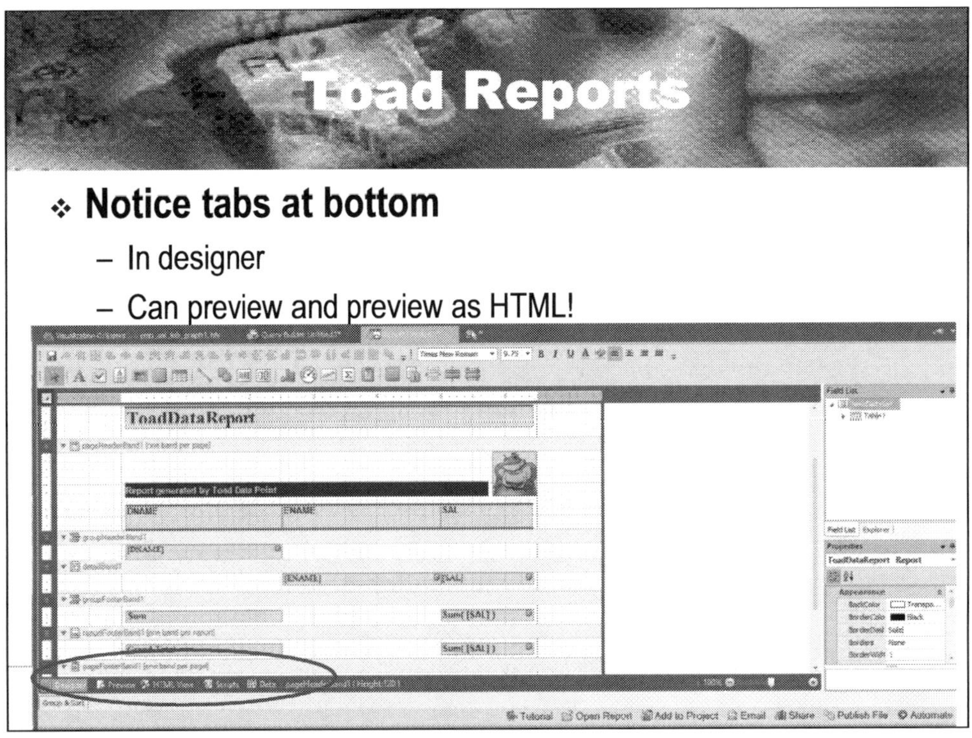


# Toad Reports

**ToadDataReport**

Report generated by Toad Data Point

| DNAME | ENAME | SAL |
|---|---|---|
| ACCOUNTING | | |
| | KING | 5000 |
| | CLARK | 2450 |
| | MILLER | 1300 |
| Sum | | $8,750.00 |
| RESEARCH | | |
| | ADAMS | 1100 |

www.*DanHotka*.com

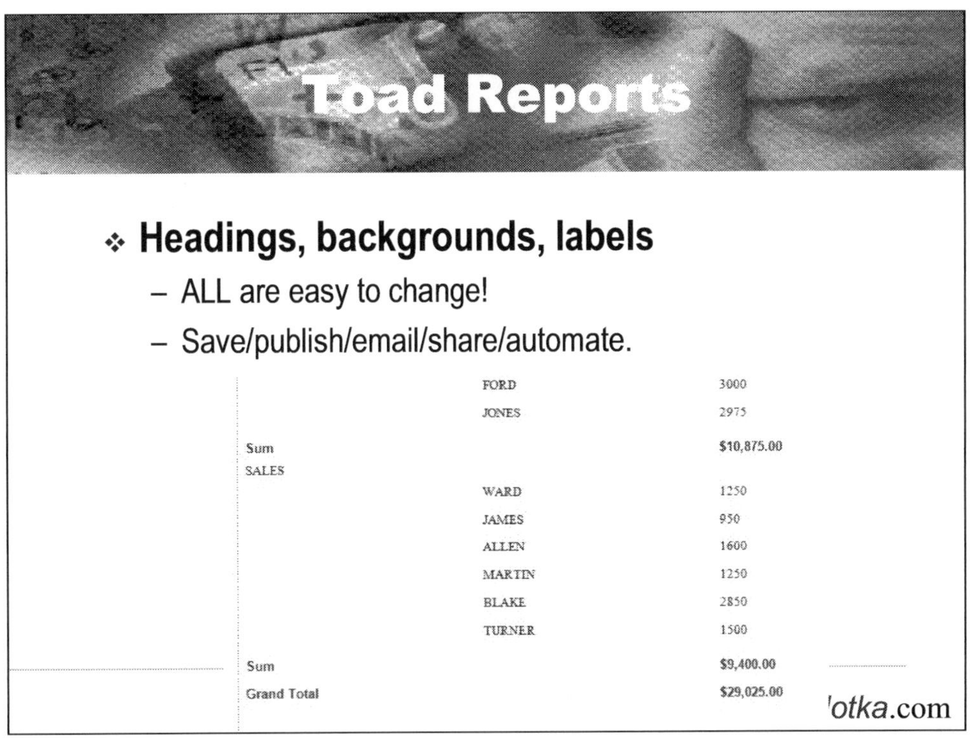
Toad Reports
Headings, backgrounds, labels
– ALL are easy to change!
– Save/publish/email/share/automate.
FORD 3000
JONES 2975
Sum $10,875.00
SALES
WARD 1250
JAMES 950
ALLEN 1600
MARTIN 1250
BLAKE 2850
TURNER 1500
Sum $9,400.00
Grand Total $29,025.00
'otka.com

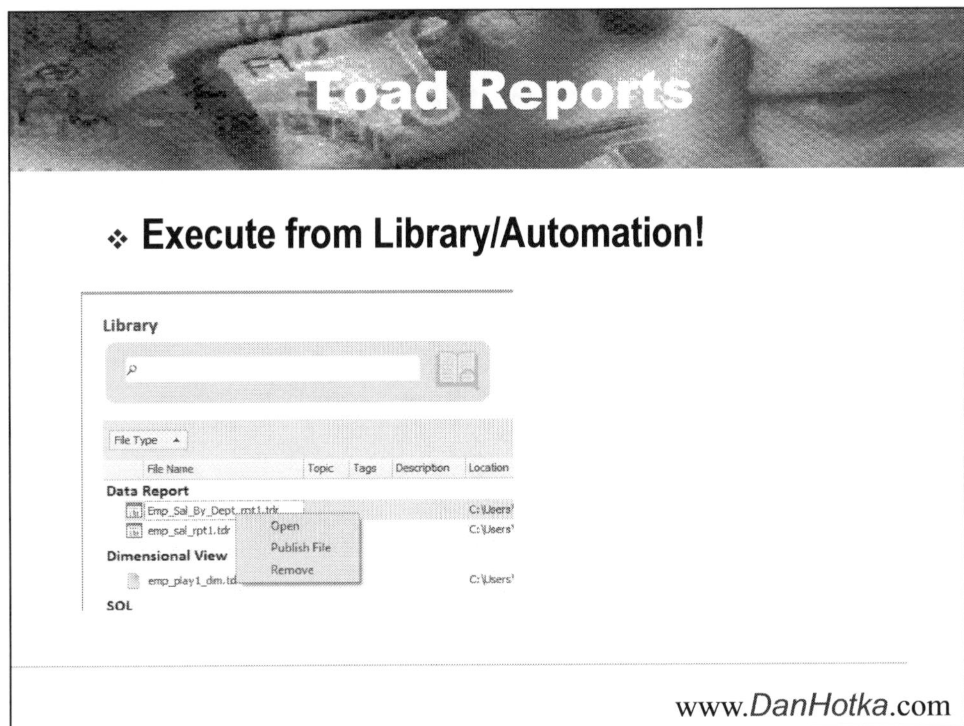
Toad Reports
Execute from Library/Automation!
Library
File Type
File Name
Topic
Tags
Description
Location
Data Report
Emp_Sal_By_Dept_rpt1.tdr
emp_sal_rpt1.tdr
Open
Publish File
Remove
Dimensional View
emp_play1_dim.td
SQL
www.DanHotka.com

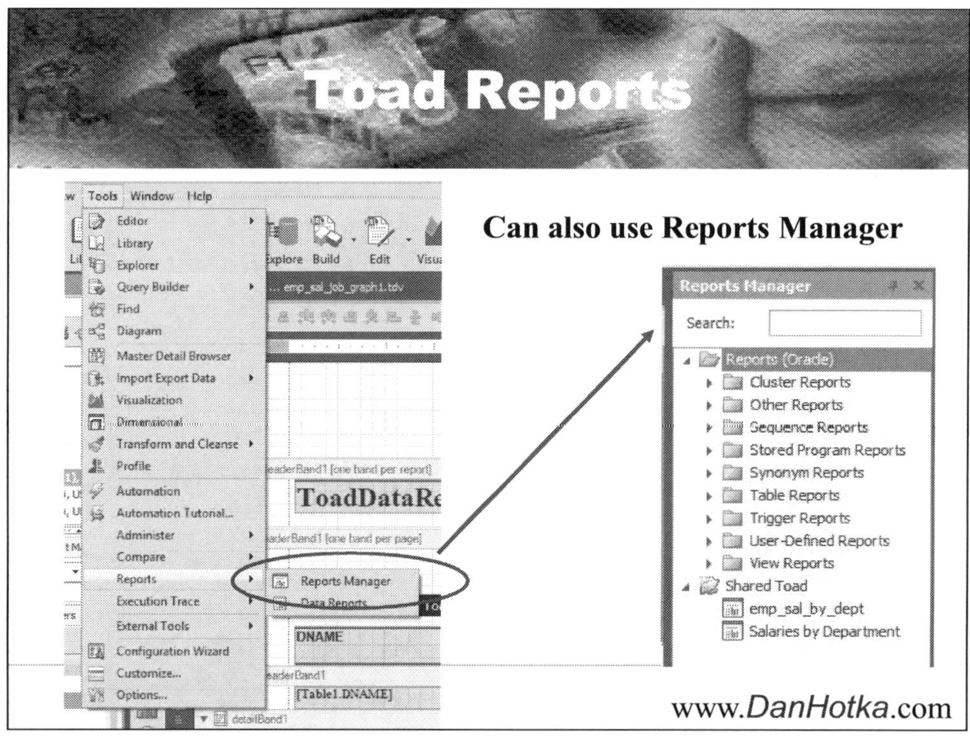
Toad Reports
Can also use Reports Manager
Tools Window Help
Editor
Library
Explorer
Query Builder
Find
Diagram
Master Detail Browser
Import Export Data
Visualization
Dimensional
Transform and Cleanse
Profile
Automation
Automation Tutorial...
Administer
Compare
Reports
Execution Trace
External Tools
Configuration Wizard
Customize...
Options...
Reports Manager
Data Reports
Reports Manager
Search:
Reports (Oracle)
Cluster Reports
Other Reports
Sequence Reports
Stored Program Reports
Synonym Reports
Table Reports
Trigger Reports
User-Defined Reports
View Reports
Shared Toad
emp_sal_by_dept
Salaries by Department
www.DanHotka.com

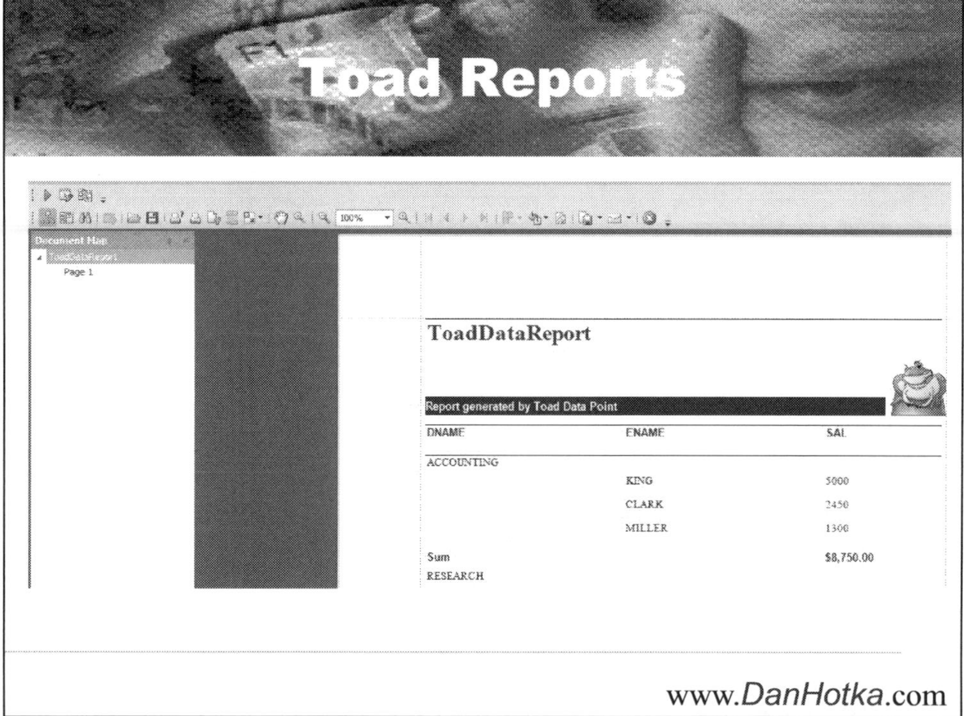
Toad Reports
ToadDataReport
Report generated by Toad Data Point
DNAME
ENAME
SAL
ACCOUNTING
KING 5000
CLARK 2450
MILLER 1300
Sum $8,750.00
RESEARCH
www.DanHotka.com

## Graphs and Charts

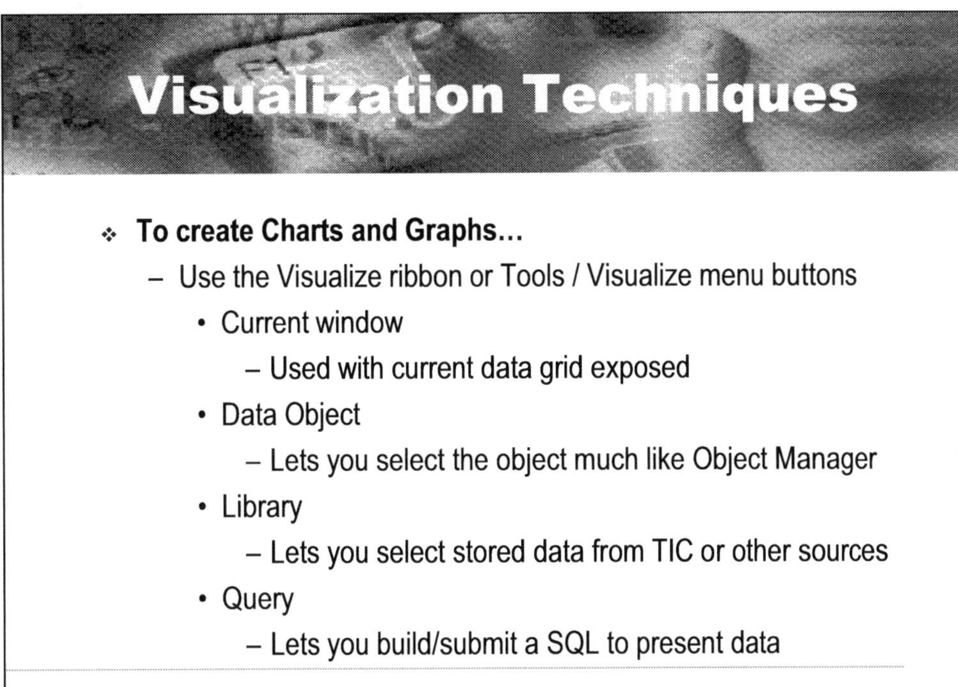
Visualization Techniques
To create Charts and Graphs…
– Use the Visualize ribbon or Tools / Visualize menu buttons
• Current window
– Used with current data grid exposed
• Data Object
– Lets you select the object much like Object Manager
• Library
– Lets you select stored data from TIC or other sources
• Query
– Lets you build/submit a SQL to present data
www.DanHotka.com

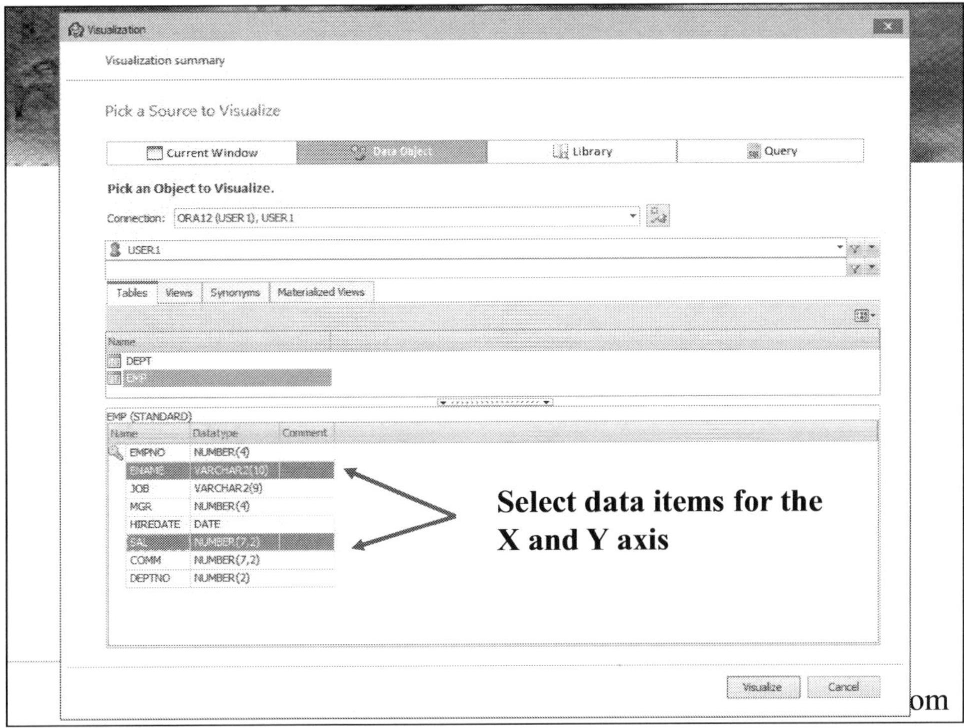
Visualization
Visualization summary
Pick a Source to Visualize
Current Window
Data Object
Library
Query
Pick an Object to Visualize.
Connection: ORA12 (USER 1), USER 1
USER1
Tables
Views
Synonyms
Materialized Views
Name
DEPT
EMP
EMP (STANDARD)
Name
Datatype
Comment
EMPNO NUMBER(4)
ENAME VARCHAR2(10)
JOB VARCHAR2(9)
MGR NUMBER(4)
HIREDATE DATE
SAL NUMBER(7,2)
COMM NUMBER(7,2)
DEPTNO NUMBER(2)
Select data items for the X and Y axis
Visualize
Cancel

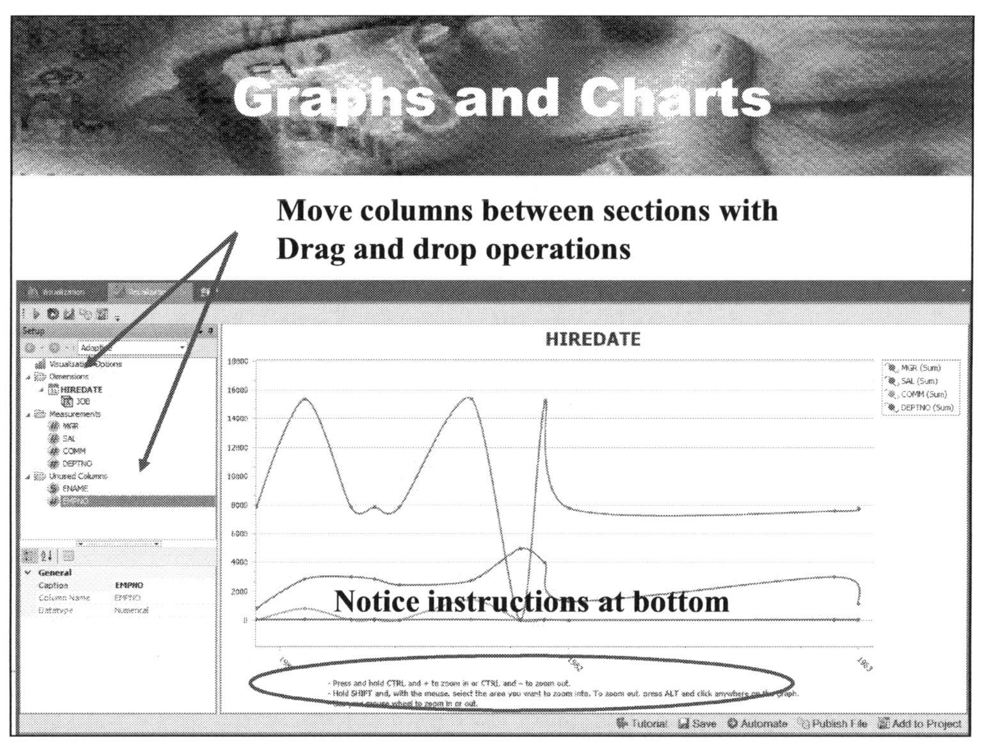
Graphs and Charts
Move columns between sections with
Drag and drop operations
HIREDATE
Notice instructions at bottom

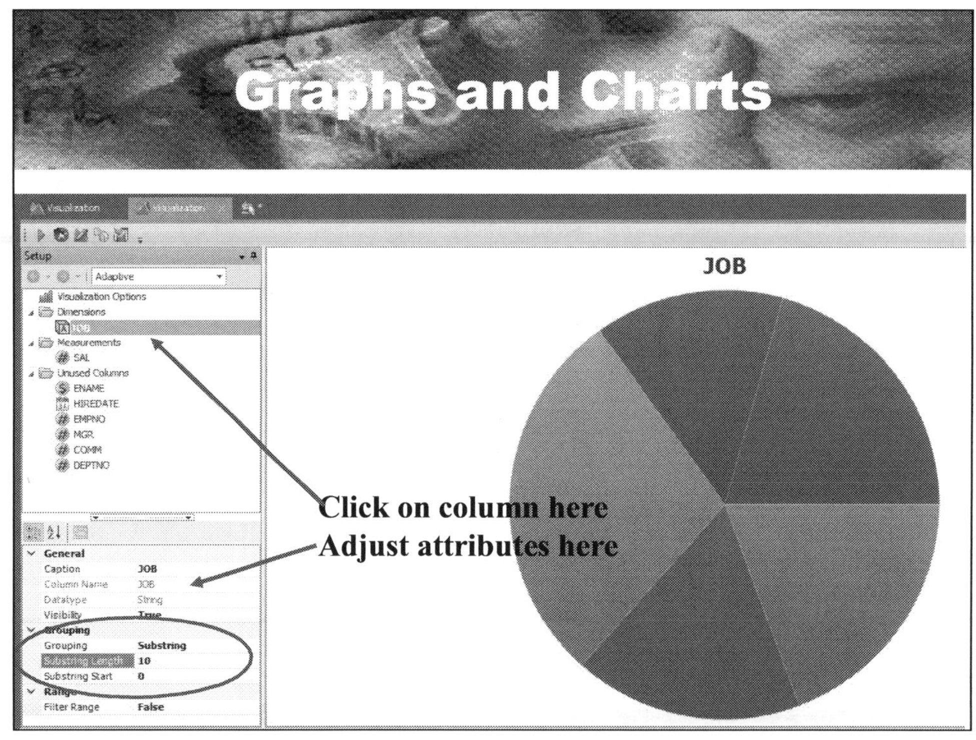
Graphs and Charts
JOB
Click on column here
Adjust attributes here

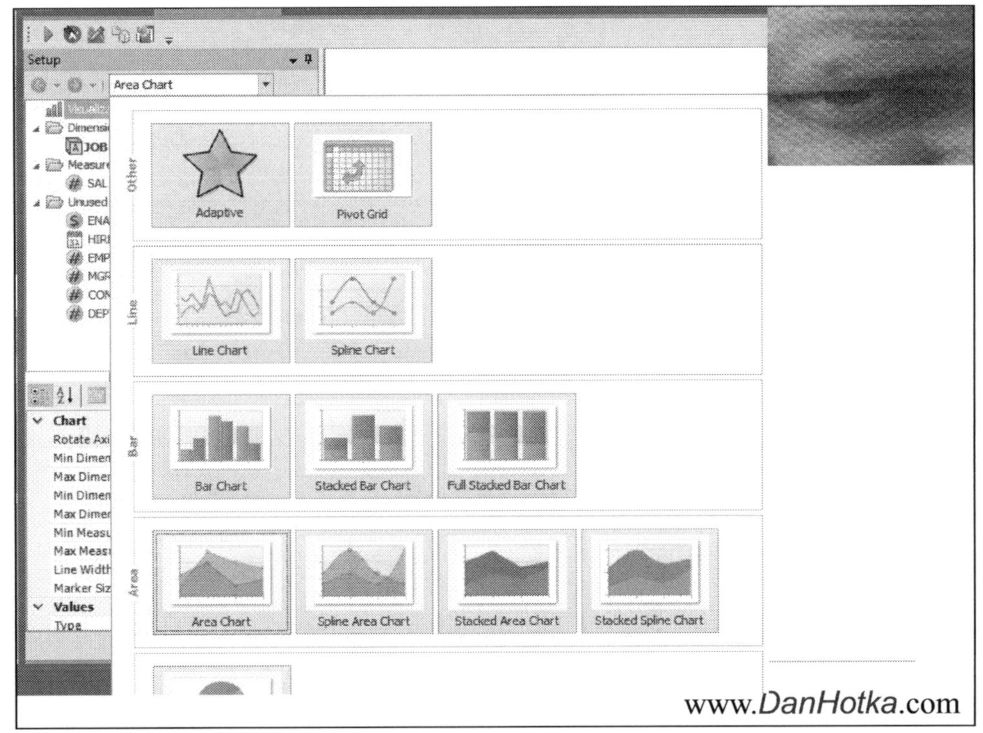
Setup
Area Chart
Other
Adaptive
Pivot Grid
Line
Line Chart
Spline Chart
Bar
Bar Chart
Stacked Bar Chart
Full Stacked Bar Chart
Area
Area Chart
Spline Area Chart
Stacked Area Chart
Stacked Spline Chart
Chart
Values
www.DanHotka.com

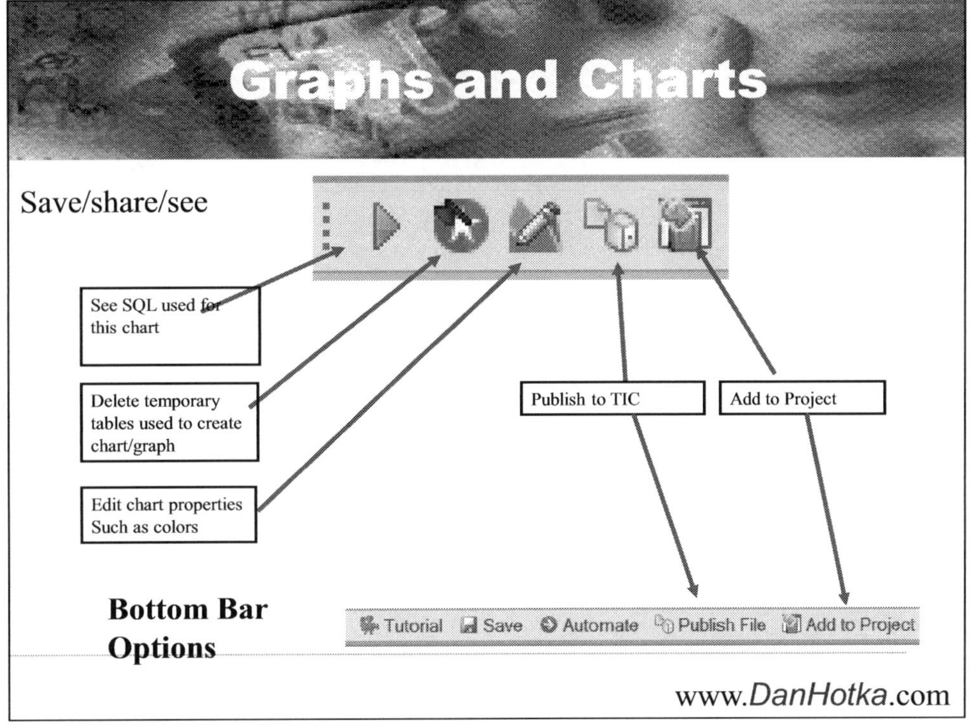
Graphs and Charts
Save/share/see
See SQL used for this chart
Delete temporary tables used to create chart/graph
Edit chart properties Such as colors
Publish to TIC
Add to Project
Bottom Bar Options
Tutorial
Save
Automate
Publish File
Add to Project
www.DanHotka.com

## Visualization Techniques

- Useful for quick graphs and charts
- Graphs/charts
  - Saved
  - Shared on TIC
  - Added to a Project
  - Included in Automation (covered in this course)
- For more information
  - Watch the Tutortial

www.*DanHotka*.com

## What have we learned?

- Toad DP Reports
- Toad DP Graphs and Charts

www.*DanHotka*.com

## Visualization Lab

# Visualization Techniques

- **Visualization Lab**
  - Build the report illustrated in this chapter
    - Save your report to your Temp Folder
  - Start the Visualization wizard
    - Using 2nd tab…select a table object
      - Select x and y axis data such as SAL and MANAGER
    - Change to a bar chart/line chart
      - Dimensions should be DEPTNO then JOB
      - Measurements should be SAL
    - Double click on the bar!

www.*DanHotka*.com

## Visualization Lab Answers

Report lab…Go to the Course Guide and find the Reports section under Visualization Techniques. Use the Table of Contents if you have not been following along in the course guide.

***Ask your instructor if you get stuck ***

- Start the Visualization wizard
  - Using 2nd tab…select a table object
    - Select x and y axis data such as SAL and MANAGER
  - Create a pie chart
    - Change the attributes so the entire title appears
  - Change to a bar chart/line chart

Save to your Temp folder

You can start building a graph from the Visualization wizard (Visualize button on the ribbon menu, as the lecture did) or you can right mouse click on a data grid and select Send To → Chart Designer.

The Visualization Wizard is a bit easier to build a graph or chart.

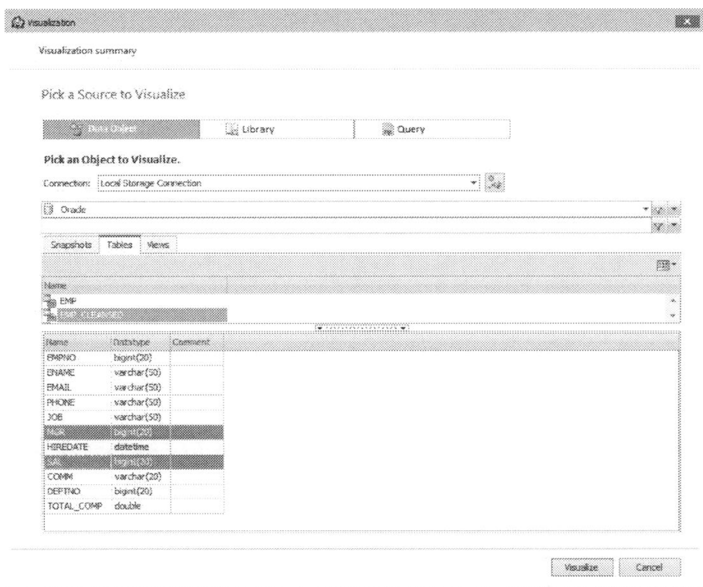

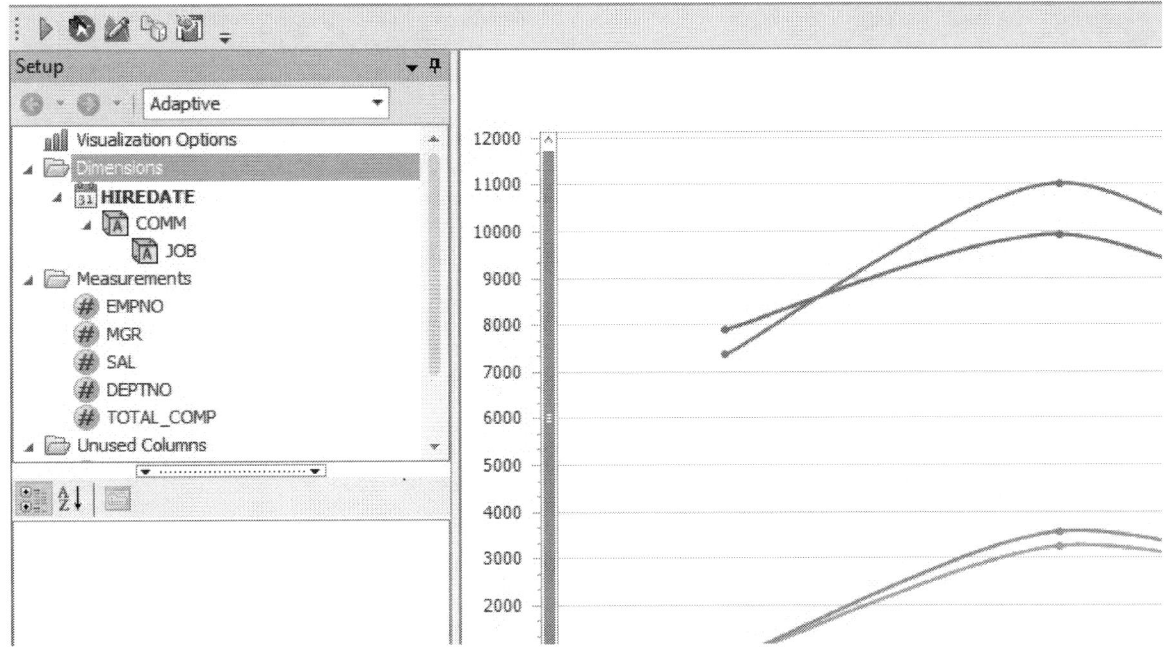


Change 'Adaptive' to a Bar chart.

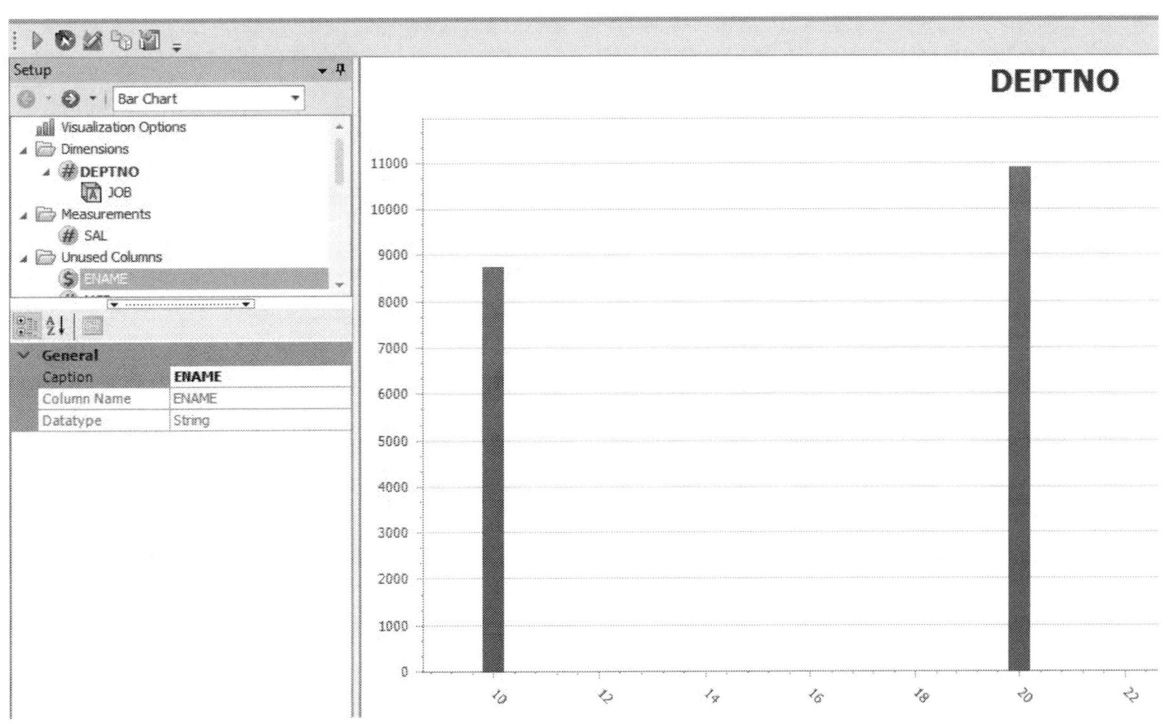


Drag and drop the Dimensions and the Measurements around. Drag all other columns to the Unused Columns area.

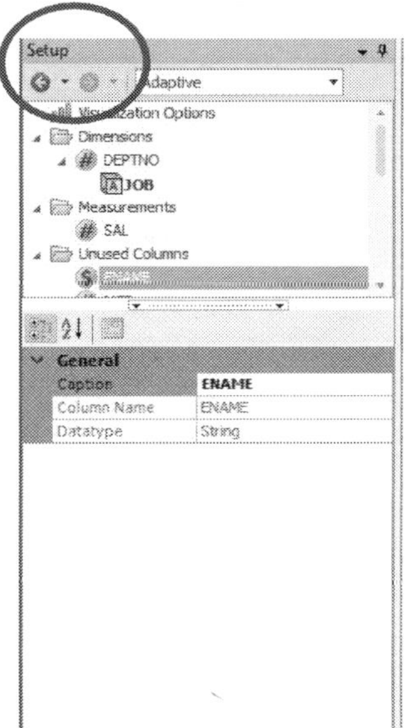

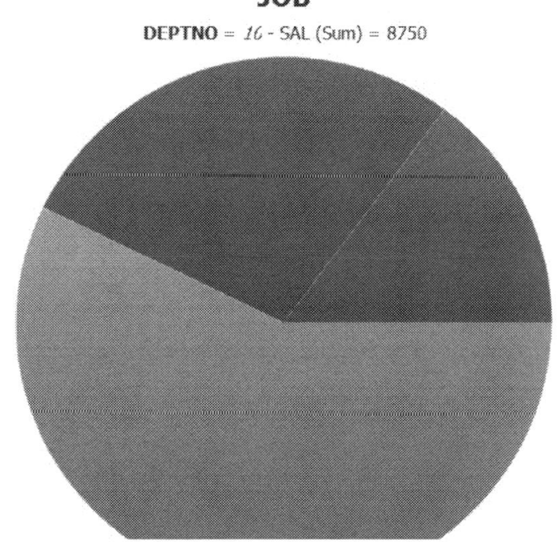


Now double click on the Bar and you get a pie chart drill down! Use the arrows (red circle) to go back and analyze another department.

Similar graph from the Chart Designer but uses the report designer to lay out the graph.

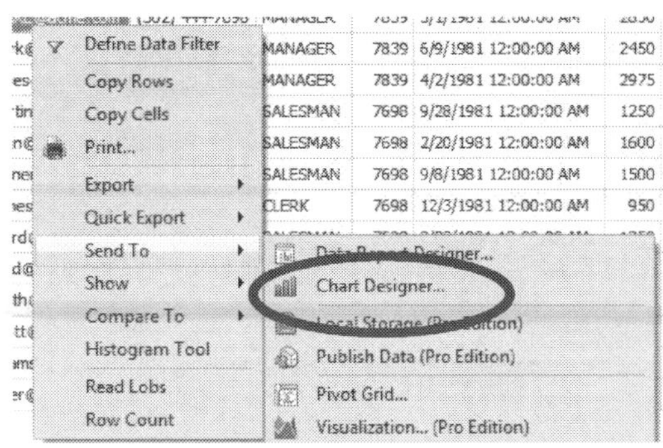

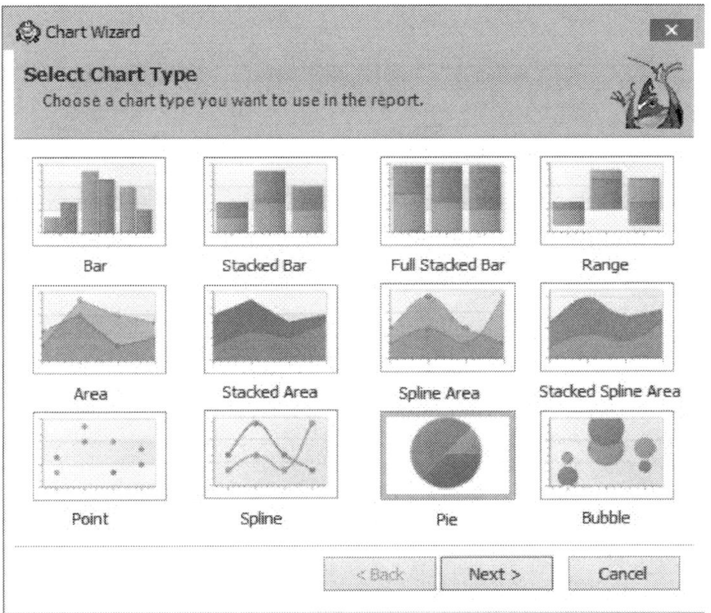


Select 'Pie' and click 'Next>'.

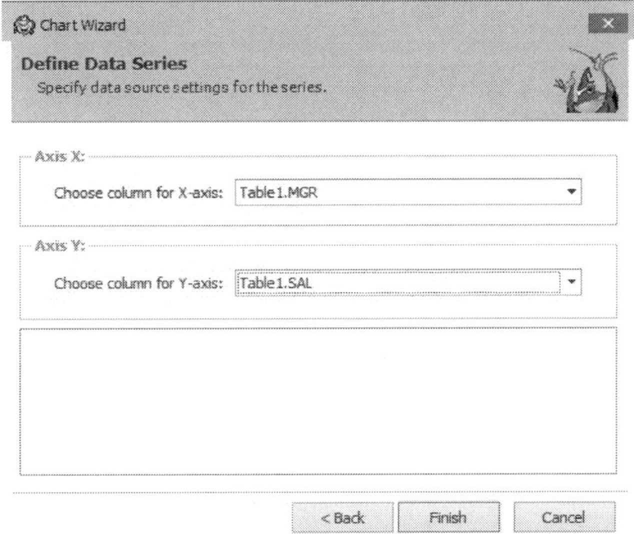


Using the drop down menus, select 'MGR' for the X axis and SAL for the Y axis. Click 'Finish' when ready.

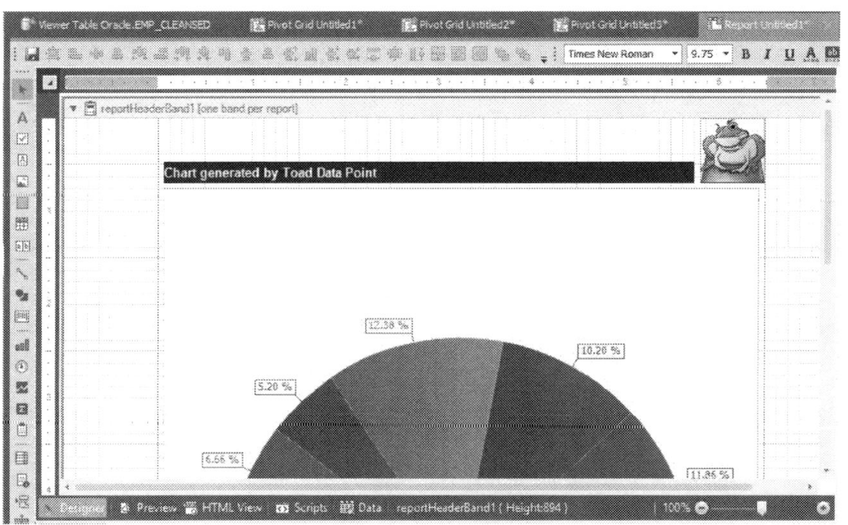
Viewer Table Oracle.EMP_CLEANSED
Pivot Grid Untitled1*
Pivot Grid Untitled2*
Pivot Grid Untitled3*
Report Untitled1*
Times New Roman
9.75
reportHeaderBand1 [one band per report]
Chart generated by Toad Data Point
12.38 %
10.20 %
5.20 %
6.66 %
11.86 %
Designer
Preview
HTML View
Scripts
Data
reportHeaderBand1 ( Height:894 )
100%

# Query Builder

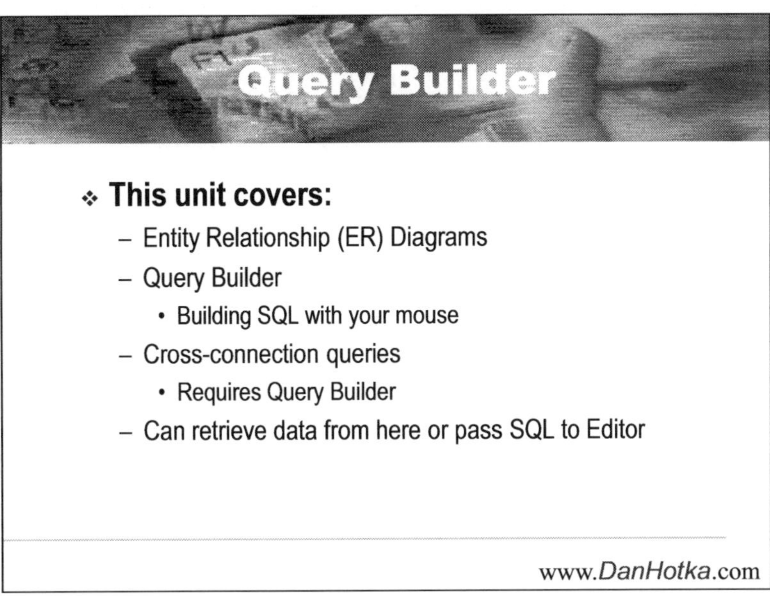
Query Builder
This unit covers:
– Entity Relationship (ER) Diagrams
– Query Builder
• Building SQL with your mouse
– Cross-connection queries
• Requires Query Builder
– Can retrieve data from here or pass SQL to Editor
www.DanHotka.com

Toad DP contains an Entity Relationship Diagrammer, a cool method of seeing data from related rows, and a query builder.

## Diagrammer

Toad has a Diagrammer used to visualize and establish the relationships between objects used in your data retrievals. Use the Diagram button, Diagram button on the ribbon menu to start the Diagrammer. This tool makes a nice ERD (entity relationship diagram) picture.

Diagrammer
Diagrammer
– The 'Add All Tables'
• Adds all related tables/objects to this canvas
• Paints in the relationships
– Can auto arrange/resize display
– Save to TIC, project, file
• Right click on tab
• Buttons across the bottom
www.DanHotka.com

This tool makes use of the Object Navigator as well. Drag and drop the table objects from this object palette and drop them into the main window.

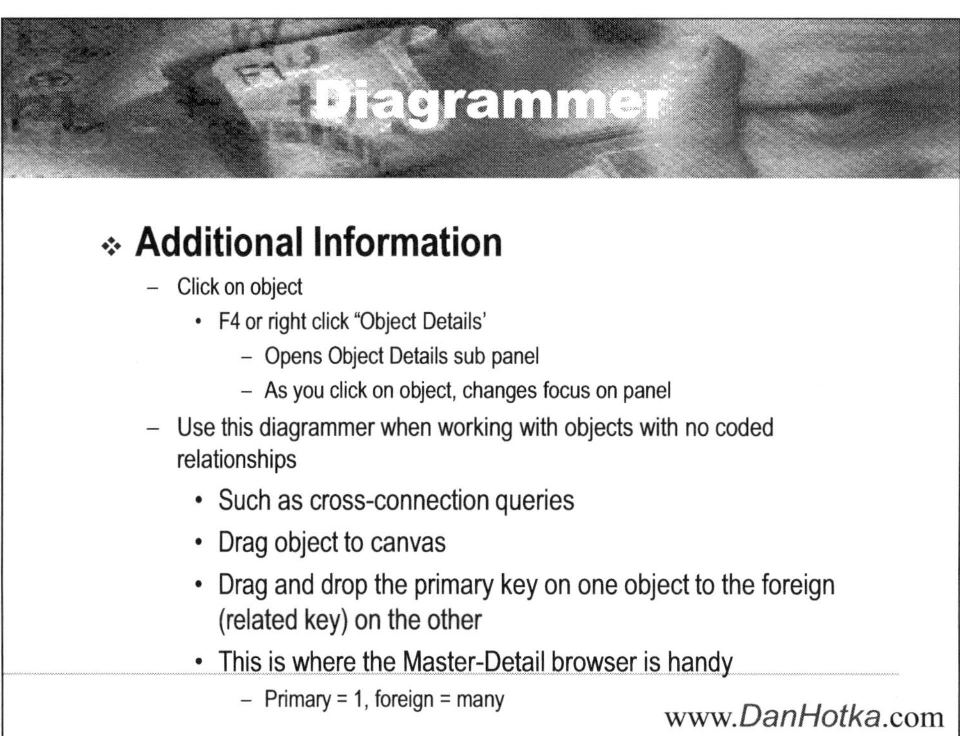
Diagrammer
Additional Information
– Click on object
• F4 or right click "Object Details'
– Opens Object Details sub panel
– As you click on object, changes focus on panel
– Use this diagrammer when working with objects with no coded relationships
• Such as cross-connection queries
• Drag object to canvas
• Drag and drop the primary key on one object to the foreign (related key) on the other
• This is where the Master-Detail browser is handy
– Primary = 1, foreign = many
www.DanHotka.com

Click on an object and press F4 (or right click and select 'Object Details') and the Object Details panel will appear.

Notice the relationships. The DEPT table has the primary key (gold key) that is related to a foreign key in the EMP table (blue key). This tells the user that the DEPT table should be the lead table in the Master/Detail Browser.

## Query Builder

The Query Builder is useful to build the data access to your data using a mouse. Toad DP uses SQL to access all your data. This Query Builder builds SQL that is then used to access your data.
The really nice thing about this tool is you don't need to know much about SQL at all.

You can access QB from the main ribbon menu Build, clicking Query Builder on the start canvas, from the Tools → Query Builder (or Cross-Connection Query), or can be passed from the Diagrammer using a button on the bottom of that tools canvas.

- **Allows for building and running of SQL**
- **Can start with QB and drag/drop objects onto its canvas**
- **Lots of functionality**
- **Useful for cross-connection queries**
  - You need Toad DP Pro to do these

www.*DanHotka*.com

You can drag/drop more objects onto the QB canvas as well. Establish any relationships in the data using drag and drop operations previously discussed.

QB is good enough for most of your data access needs. Spend some time here and get used to the interface and you will be amazed how well this tool can assemble data for you.

*** **Tip***** The cross-connection queries is a special item. I would always use it as the regular QB does not allow for objects from different database types.

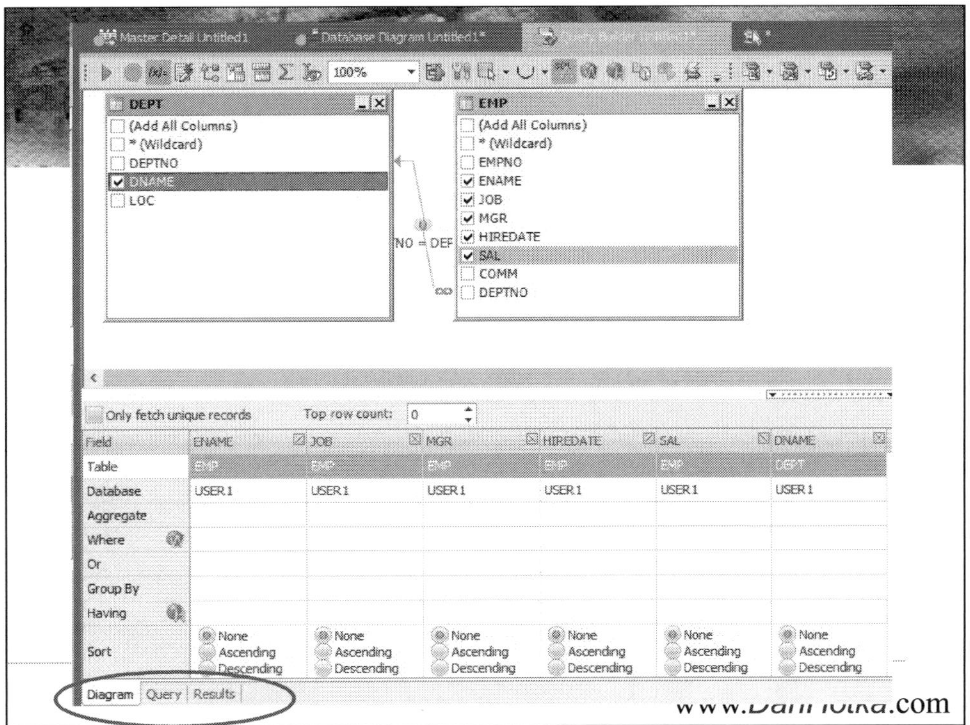


Notice as the columns are selected that the grid fills in on the left and the SQL builds in the bottom Query tab pane! Use the W and H buttons along the top tool bar to add global Where clause items and Having clause items to the SQL. Each selected column has a cell in the lower Diagram tab allowing for additional where clause/group by/and other items to be added. The query can be executed from here, saved (use right mouse click or buttons at the bottom), and even moved to the Editor (right mouse click menu)!

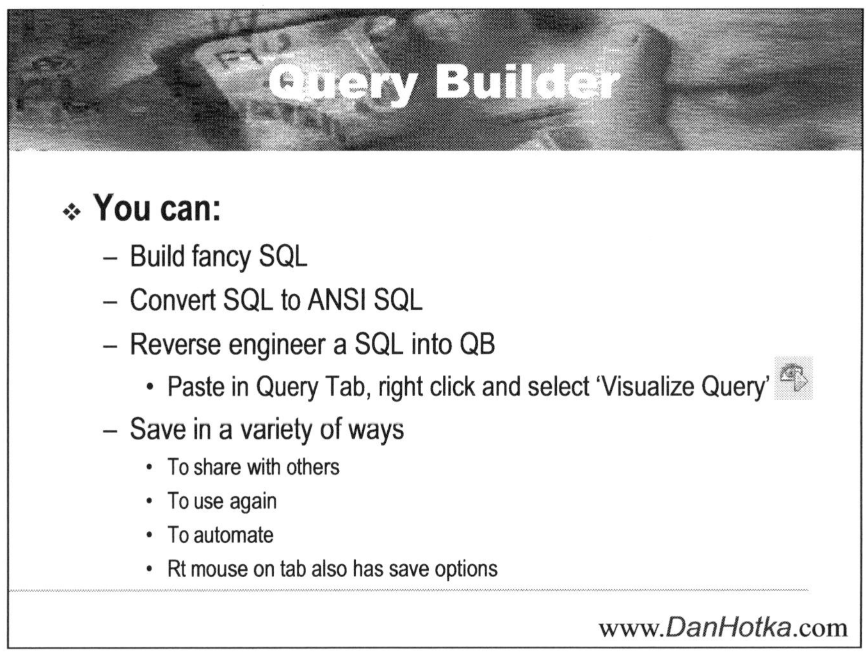

Query Builder
You can:
– Build fancy SQL
– Convert SQL to ANSI SQL
– Reverse engineer a SQL into QB
• Paste in Query Tab, right click and select 'Visualize Query'
– Save in a variety of ways
• To share with others
• To use again
• To automate
• Rt mouse on tab also has save options
www.DanHotka.com


Yes, paste your SQL into the Query Tab from other apps (such as Hyperion, Discoverer, etc) and right click/select Visualize Query. This will check your SQL with your connection and permissions, allowing you to tweek it up perhaps but mostly getting your existing SQL into Toad DP for use in your needs and work flows.

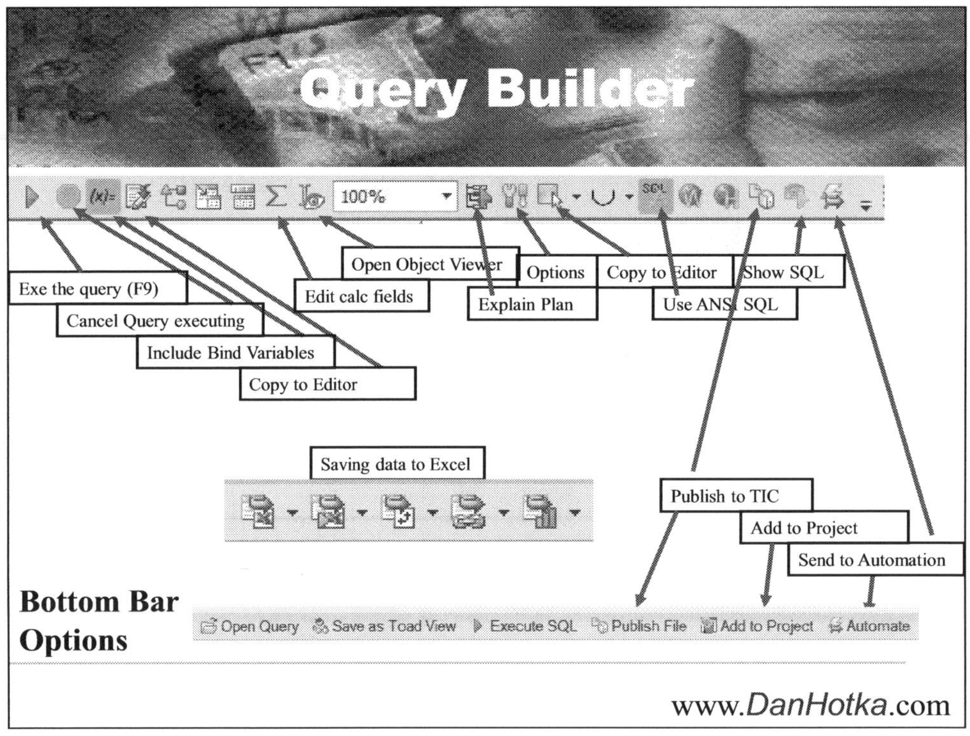

Query Builder
100%
Open Object Viewer
Options
Copy to Editor
Show SQL
Exe the query (F9)
Edit calc fields
Explain Plan
Use ANSI SQL
Cancel Query executing
Include Bind Variables
Copy to Editor
Saving data to Excel
Publish to TIC
Add to Project
Send to Automation
Bottom Bar Options
Open Query
Save as Toad View
Execute SQL
Publish File
Add to Project
Automate
www.DanHotka.com

Notice the various features of QB. Most of these are also available via a right mouse click menu.

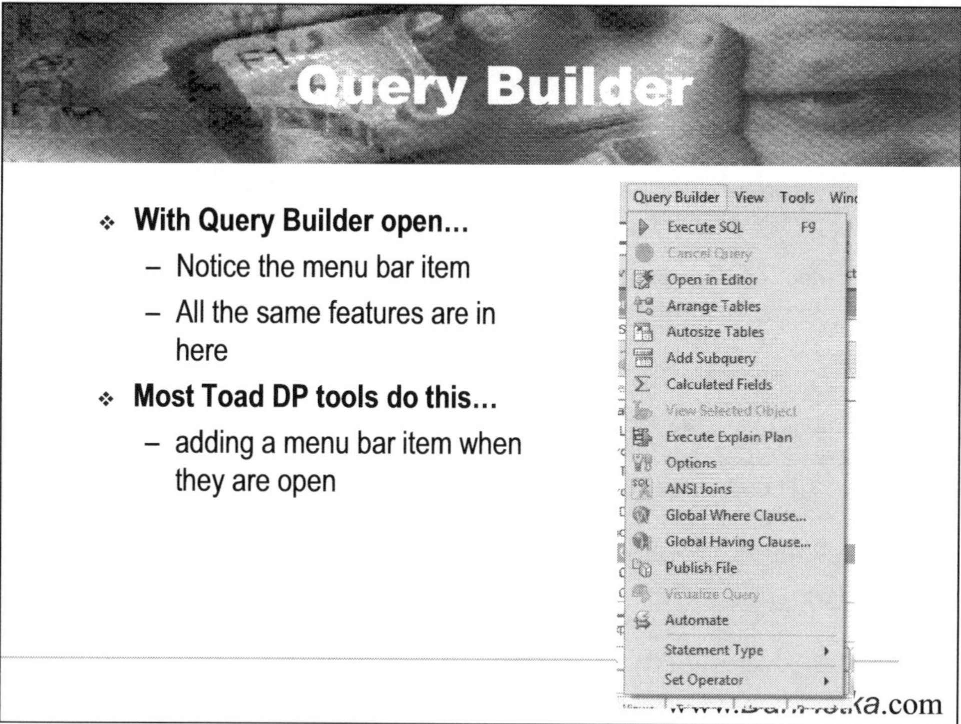


## Building SQL using your Mouse

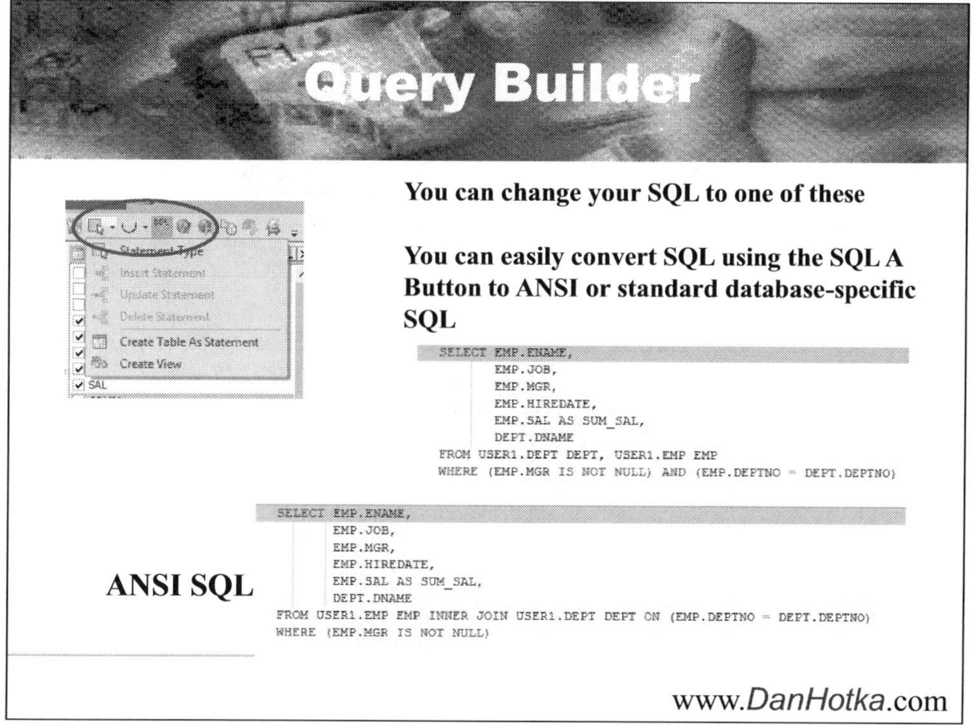

This SQL appears in the Query tab (along the lower left bottom).

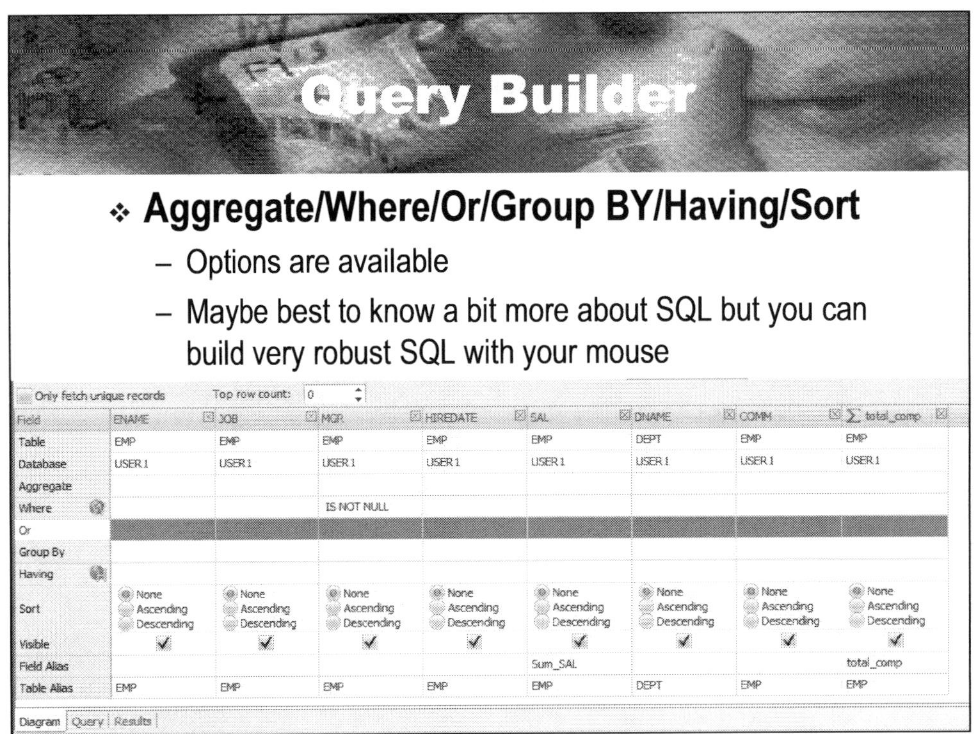

Query Builder
Aggregate/Where/Or/Group BY/Having/Sort
– Options are available
– Maybe best to know a bit more about SQL but you can build very robust SQL with your mouse
Only fetch unique records
Top row count: 0
Field
ENAME
JOB
MGR
HIREDATE
SAL
DNAME
COMM
total_comp
Table
Database
Aggregate
Where
IS NOT NULL
Or
Group By
Having
Sort
None
Ascending
Descending
Visible
Field Alias
Sum_SAL
Table Alias
EMP
DEPT
USER1
Diagram
Query
Results


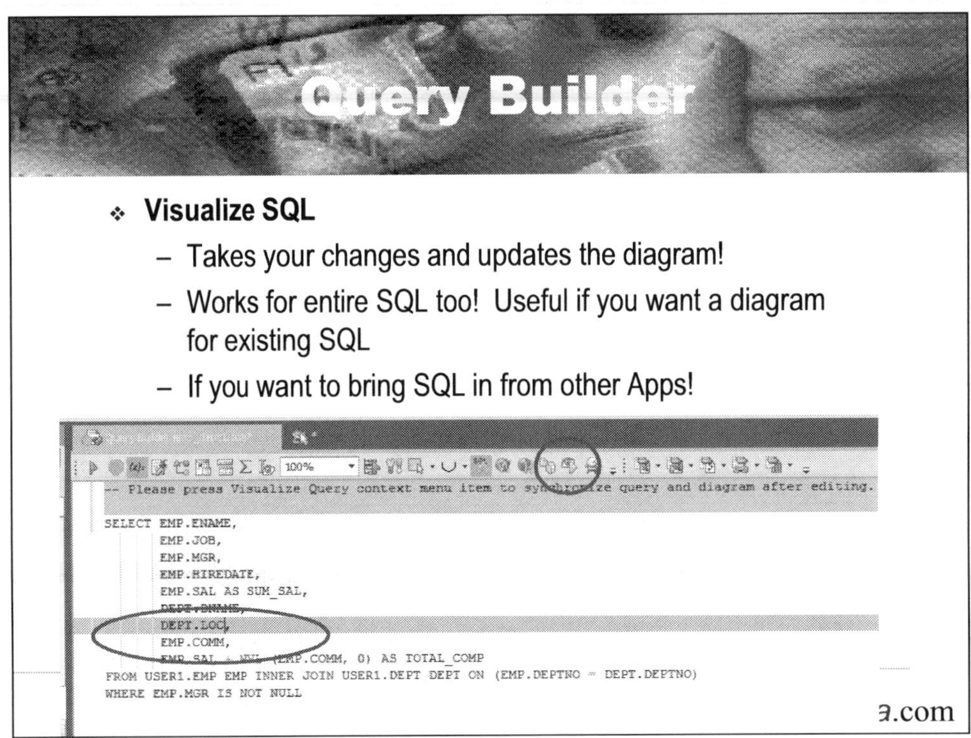

Query Builder
Visualize SQL
– Takes your changes and updates the diagram!
– Works for entire SQL too! Useful if you want a diagram for existing SQL
– If you want to bring SQL in from other Apps!
100%
-- Please press Visualize Query context menu item to synchronize query and diagram after editing.
SELECT EMP.ENAME,
EMP.JOB,
EMP.MGR,
EMP.HIREDATE,
EMP.SAL AS SUM_SAL,
DEPT.DNAME,
DEPT.LOC,
EMP.COMM,
(EMP.COMM, 0) AS TOTAL_COMP
FROM USER1.EMP EMP INNER JOIN USER1.DEPT DEPT ON (EMP.DEPTNO = DEPT.DEPTNO)
WHERE EMP.MGR IS NOT NULL

***Tip*** You can make changes to the SQL! When you type in this panel, another button will appear on the tool bar. This 'Visualize SQL' to push the changes back into the diagram panel.

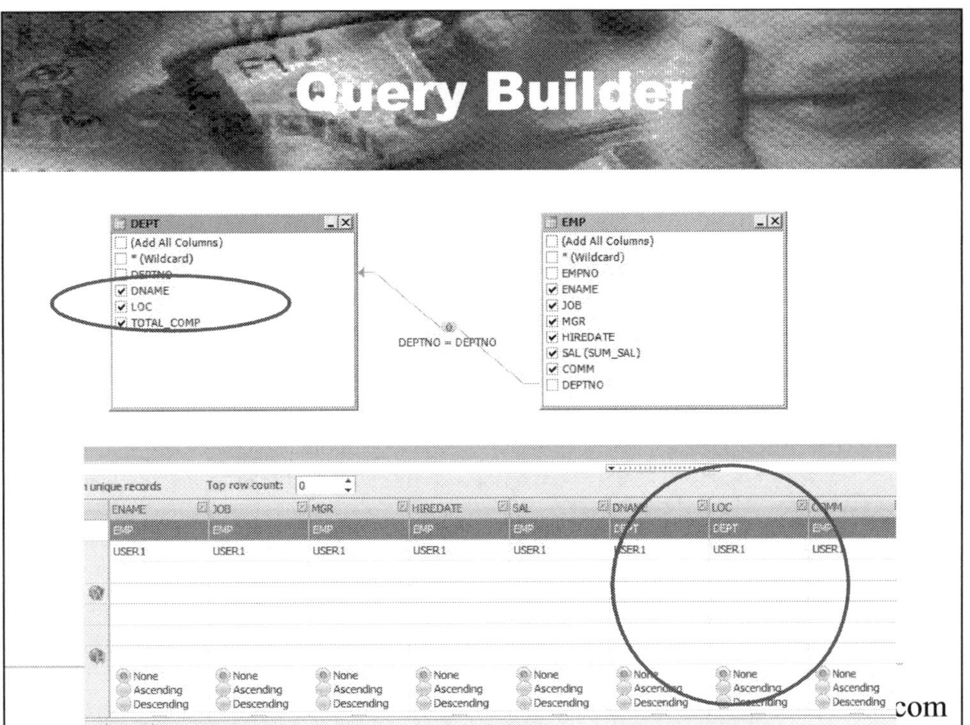

***Tip*** This trick works for entire SQL that you want a diagram for. Perhaps you are going to add some cross-connection information to an existing SQL, use this Query panel to paste the SQL then use 'Visualize SQL' to create a diagram from it. Ask the instructor to demonstrate this technique.

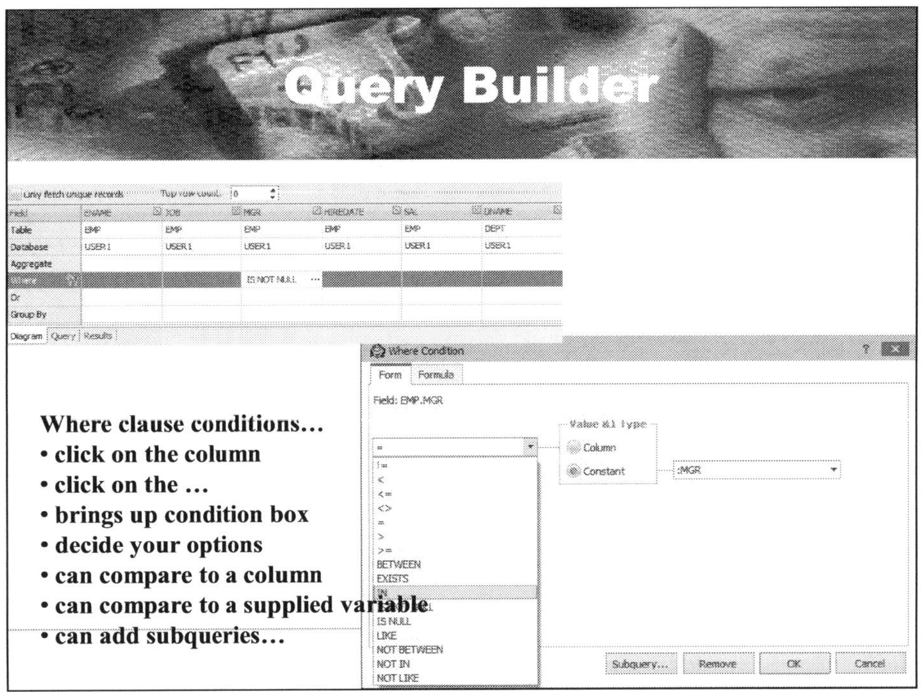
Query Builder
Where clause conditions…
• click on the column
• click on the …
• brings up condition box
• decide your options
• can compare to a column
• can compare to a supplied variable
• can add subqueries…

## Query Builder Output

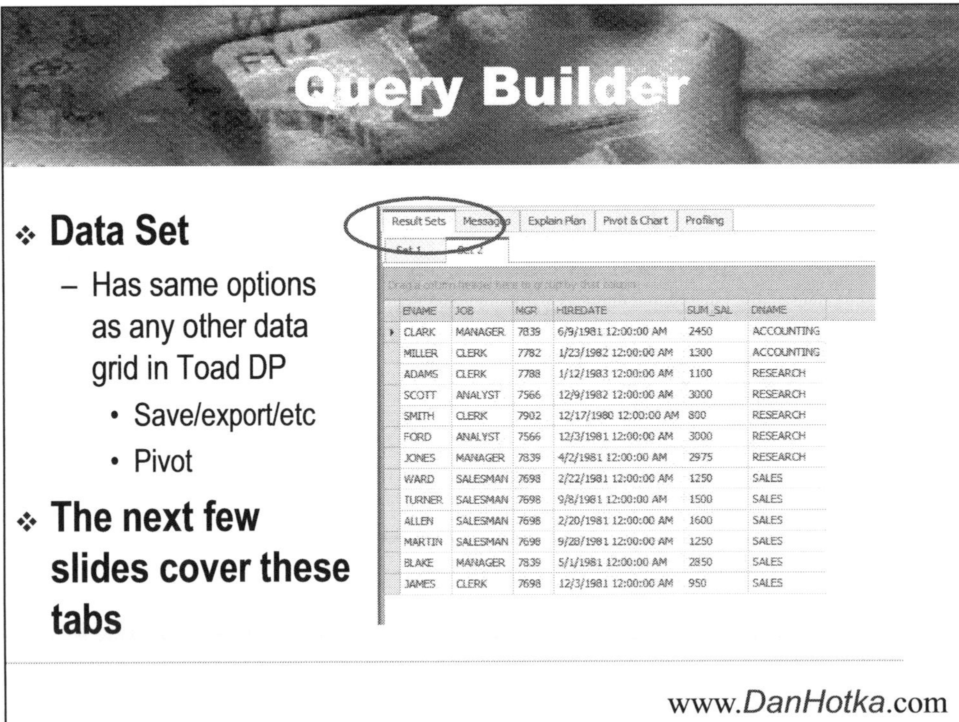
Query Builder
Data Set
– Has same options as any other data grid in Toad DP
• Save/export/etc
• Pivot
The next few slides cover these tabs
www.DanHotka.com

All data grids have about the same right mouse menu options. Saving the data and saving to Excel is a snap.

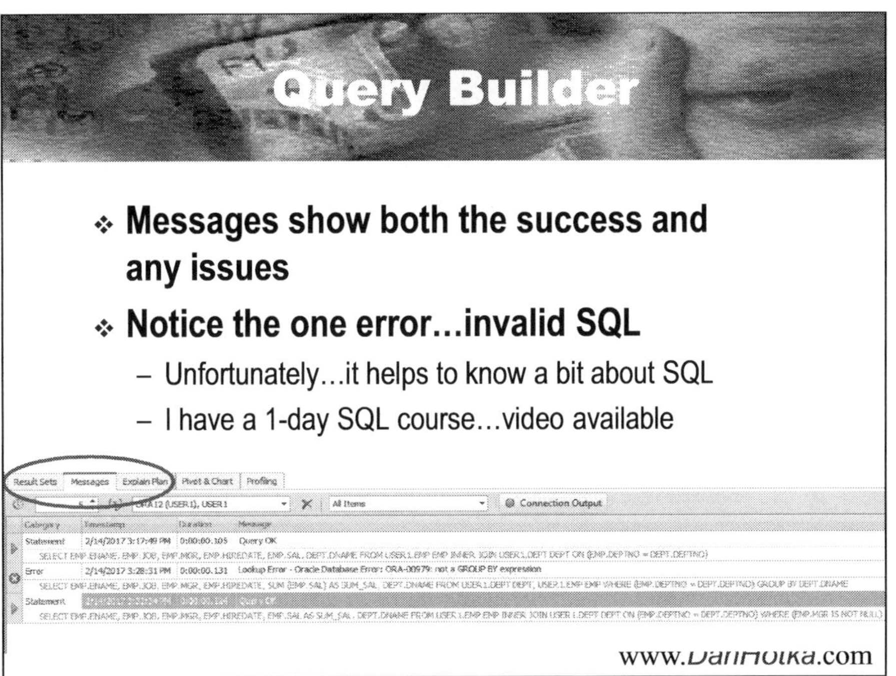


These errors are very useful when having problems retrieving data. They should give a pretty good indication as to what is wrong.

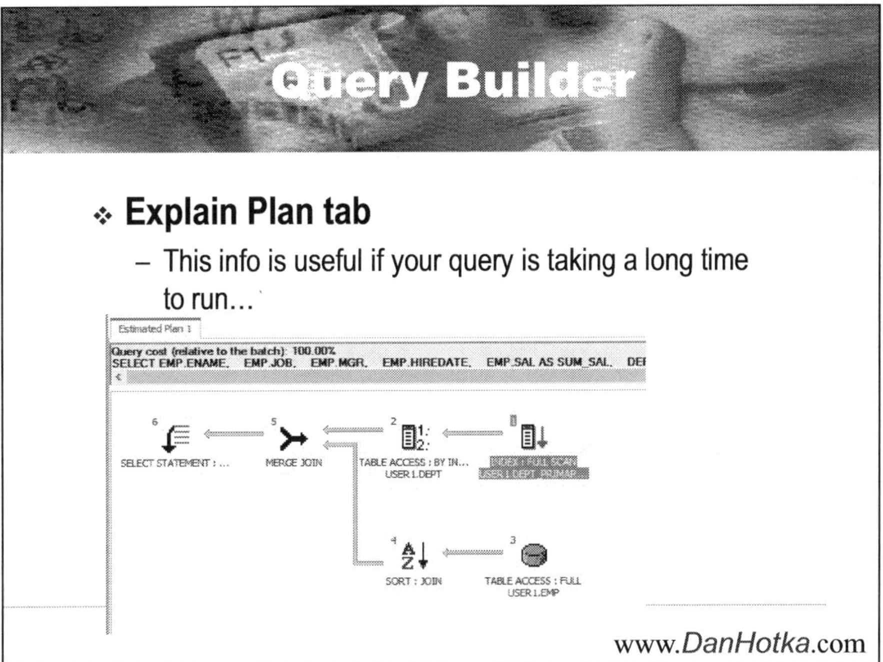


This is a performance tuning topic. For the novice or power user/analyst, this panel will be useful to the experts trying to assist you with a poorly performing data retrieval.

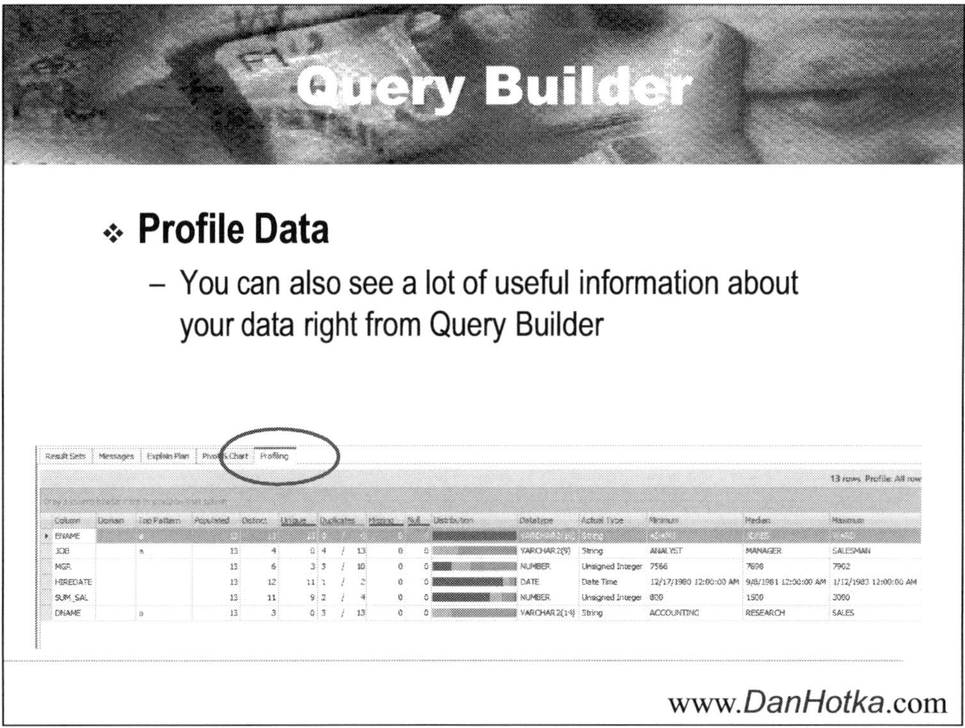


Profiling quickly shows you the dynamics of your data. This profiling is also useful to help spot problem data.

## Adding Calculations/Fields

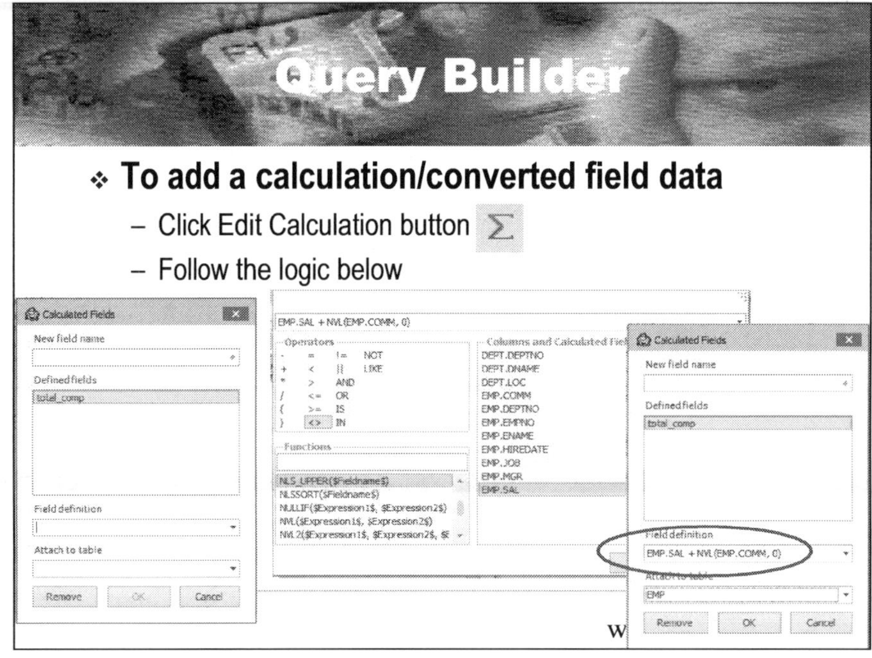

You can add calculations pretty easy. Use highlight and Ctrl+C to copy this calculation out to use in other SQL. You can also paste in valid syntax from other SQL as well.

This feature can also be used to format data for display. There are a few ways to do this but if you are comfortable with the database SQL features, such as functions (TO_DATE, DAYS_BETWEEN, NEXT_DAY, etc), you can add columns incorporating this syntax to format your columns right here in QB.

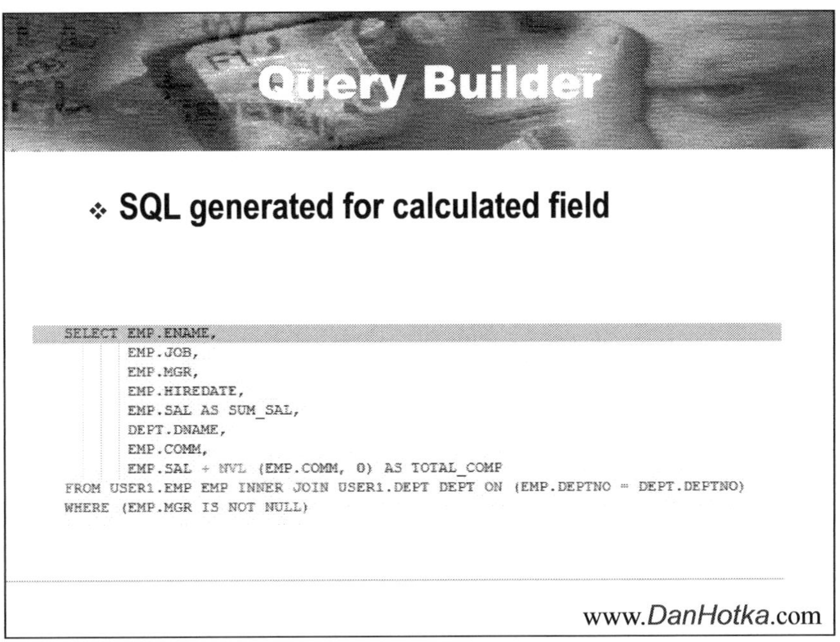
Query Builder
❖ SQL generated for calculated field
SELECT EMP.ENAME,
EMP.JOB,
EMP.MGR,
EMP.HIREDATE,
EMP.SAL AS SUM_SAL,
DEPT.DNAME,
EMP.COMM,
EMP.SAL + NVL (EMP.COMM, 0) AS TOTAL_COMP
FROM USER1.EMP EMP INNER JOIN USER1.DEPT DEPT ON (EMP.DEPTNO = DEPT.DEPTNO)
WHERE (EMP.MGR IS NOT NULL)
www.DanHotka.com

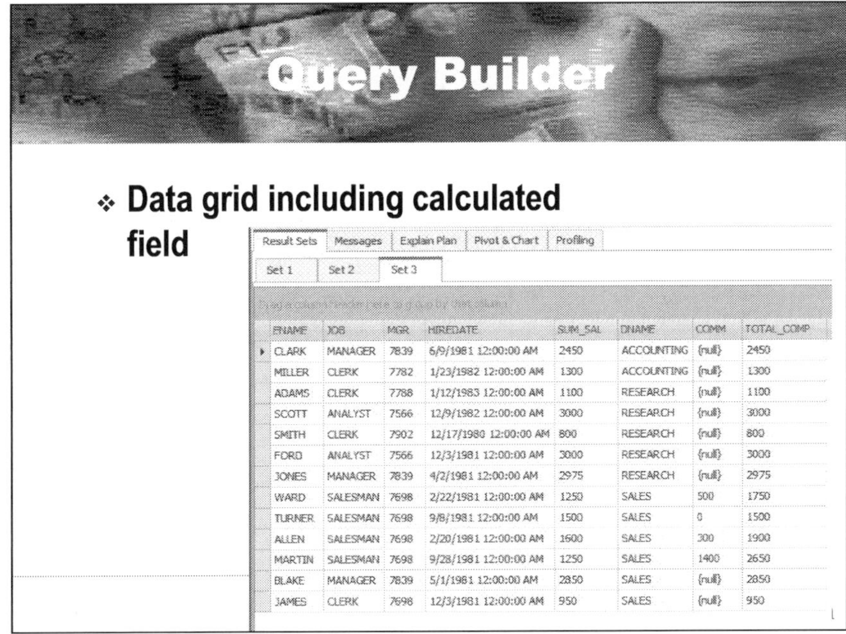
Query Builder
❖ Data grid including calculated field
Result Sets
Messages
Explain Plan
Pivot & Chart
Profiling
Set 1
Set 2
Set 3

| ENAME | JOB | MGR | HIREDATE | SUM_SAL | DNAME | COMM | TOTAL_COMP |
|---|---|---|---|---|---|---|---|
| CLARK | MANAGER | 7839 | 6/9/1981 12:00:00 AM | 2450 | ACCOUNTING | {null} | 2450 |
| MILLER | CLERK | 7782 | 1/23/1982 12:00:00 AM | 1300 | ACCOUNTING | {null} | 1300 |
| ADAMS | CLERK | 7788 | 1/12/1983 12:00:00 AM | 1100 | RESEARCH | {null} | 1100 |
| SCOTT | ANALYST | 7566 | 12/9/1982 12:00:00 AM | 3000 | RESEARCH | {null} | 3000 |
| SMITH | CLERK | 7902 | 12/17/1980 12:00:00 AM | 800 | RESEARCH | {null} | 800 |
| FORD | ANALYST | 7566 | 12/3/1981 12:00:00 AM | 3000 | RESEARCH | {null} | 3000 |
| JONES | MANAGER | 7839 | 4/2/1981 12:00:00 AM | 2975 | RESEARCH | {null} | 2975 |
| WARD | SALESMAN | 7698 | 2/22/1981 12:00:00 AM | 1250 | SALES | 500 | 1750 |
| TURNER | SALESMAN | 7698 | 9/8/1981 12:00:00 AM | 1500 | SALES | 0 | 1500 |
| ALLEN | SALESMAN | 7698 | 2/20/1981 12:00:00 AM | 1600 | SALES | 300 | 1900 |
| MARTIN | SALESMAN | 7698 | 9/28/1981 12:00:00 AM | 1250 | SALES | 1400 | 2650 |
| BLAKE | MANAGER | 7839 | 5/1/1981 12:00:00 AM | 2850 | SALES | {null} | 2850 |
| JAMES | CLERK | 7698 | 12/3/1981 12:00:00 AM | 950 | SALES | {null} | 950 |

## Query Builder Options

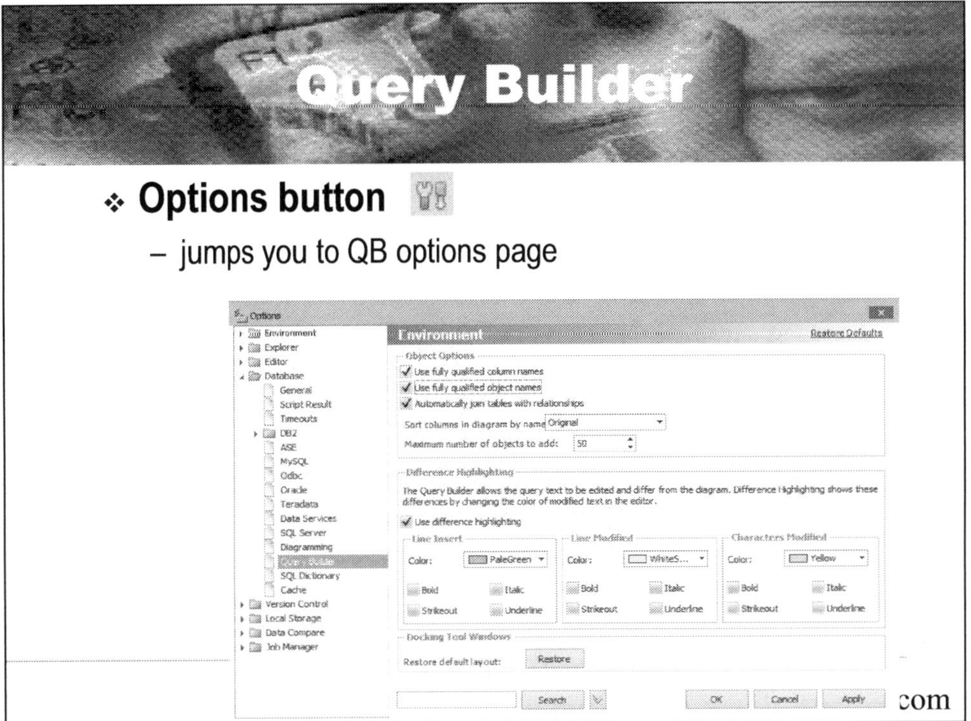


The top three items checked are very important. Using fully-qualified column and table names not only is good practice but very helpful to both the novice and someone new working with this query for the first time.

## Saving SQL and Data

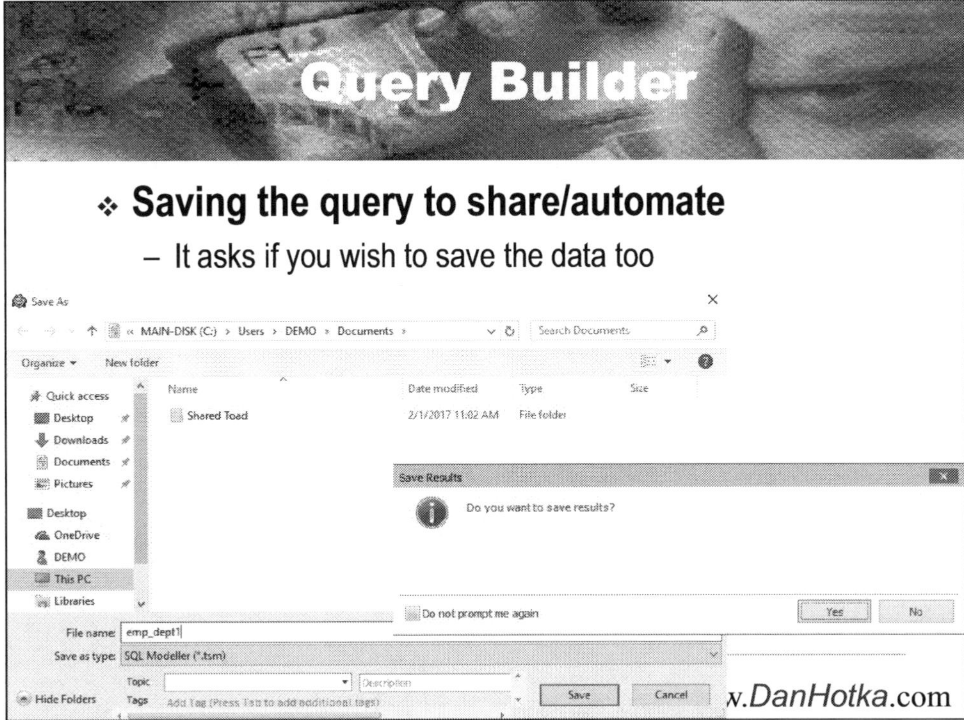


When data is saved, it can be accessed just like any other table object. You can save it locally to 'Local Storage' or you can publish it and share it with others in your group. This ability to share output can be used in a number of ways including but not limited to:

- Subsetting data for others to use
- Storing data for specific reporting needs
- Automating this same feature so the query you built and the data you saved happens automatically as per your business needs.

## Query Builder

```
SELECT EMP.ENAME,
       EMP.JOB,
       EMP.MGR,
       EMP.HIREDATE,
       EMP.SAL AS SUM_SAL,
       DEPT.DNAME,
       EMP.COMM,
       EMP.SAL + NVL (EMP.COMM, 0) AS TOTAL_COMP
FROM USER1.EMP EMP INNER JOIN USER1.DEPT DEPT ON (EMP.DEPTNO = DEPT.DEPTNO)
WHERE (EMP.MGR IS NOT NULL)
```

Save Toad View

Name of Toad View

emp_dept1

Open Toad View manager?

OK

Cancel

www.DanHotka.com

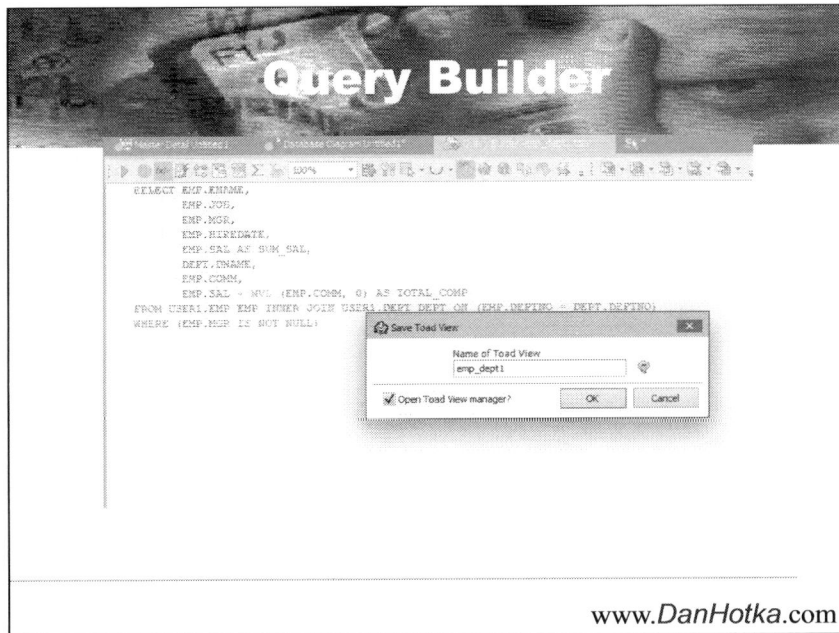

Toad Views are another way of saving the SQL for later use. Toad Views will be covered in detail later in this course.

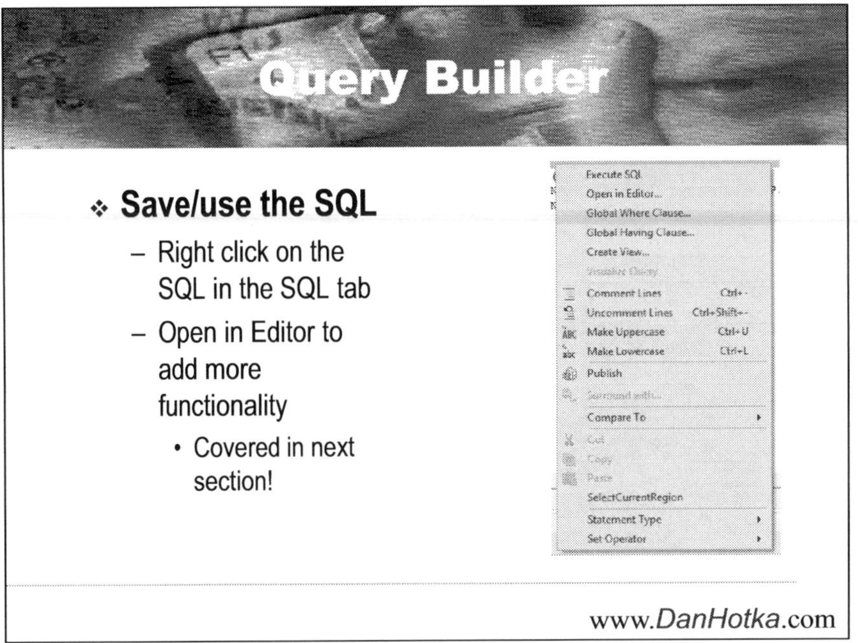


For those of you comfortable with working with the SQL code itself, QB can easily load what you have created here into the Editor for further tweeking and adjusting. The instructor illustrated earlier how you can put SQL back into QB for others to use that maybe are not familiar with SQL syntax.

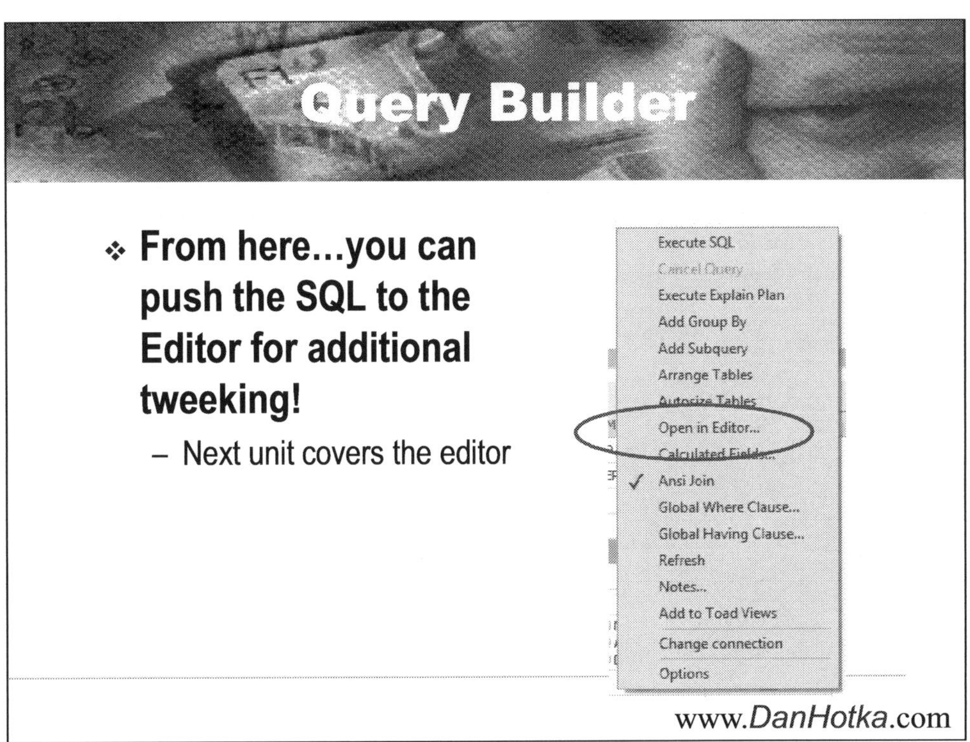
Query Builder
From here...you can push the SQL to the Editor for additional tweeking!
– Next unit covers the editor
Execute SQL
Cancel Query
Execute Explain Plan
Add Group By
Add Subquery
Arrange Tables
Autosize Tables
Open in Editor...
Calculated Fields...
Ansi Join
Global Where Clause...
Global Having Clause...
Refresh
Notes...
Add to Toad Views
Change connection
Options
www.DanHotka.com

**Sub Queries**

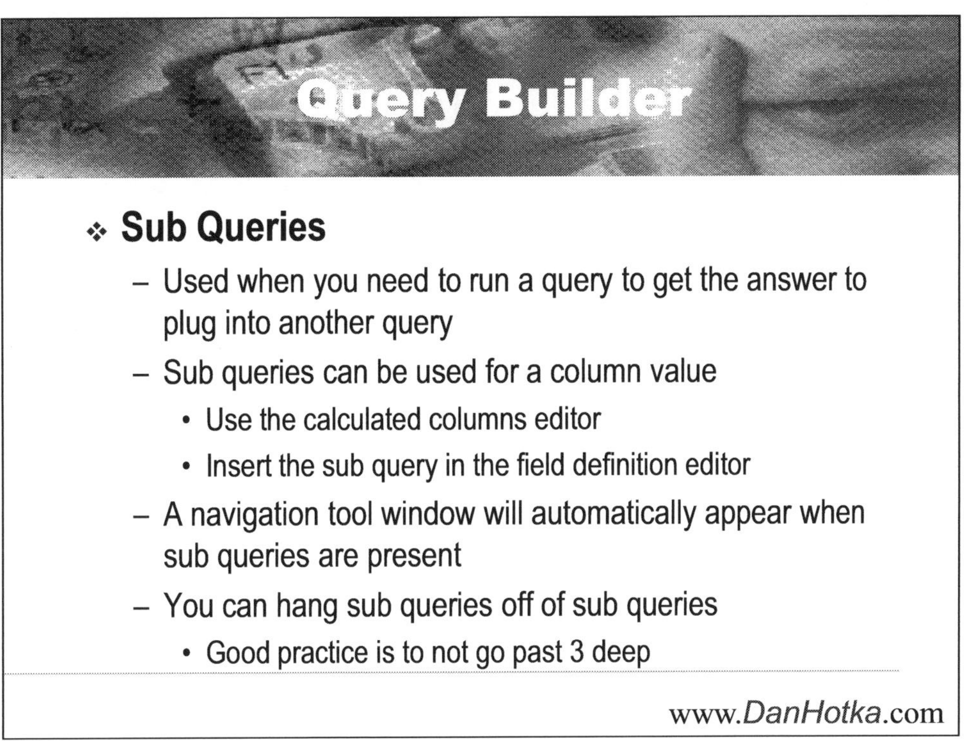
Query Builder
Sub Queries
– Used when you need to run a query to get the answer to plug into another query
– Sub queries can be used for a column value
• Use the calculated columns editor
• Insert the sub query in the field definition editor
– A navigation tool window will automatically appear when sub queries are present
– You can hang sub queries off of sub queries
• Good practice is to not go past 3 deep
www.DanHotka.com

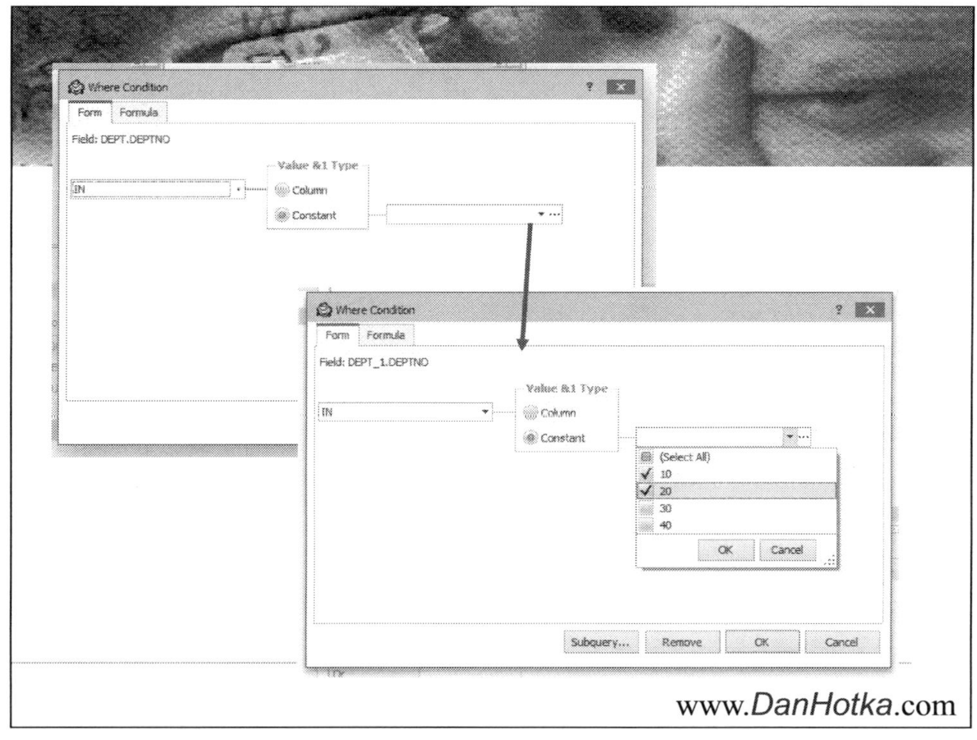
Where Condition
Form
Formula
Field: DEPT.DEPTNO
Value &1 Type
IN
Column
Constant
Field: DEPT_1.DEPTNO
(Select All)
10
20
30
40
OK
Cancel
Subquery...
Remove
www.DanHotka.com

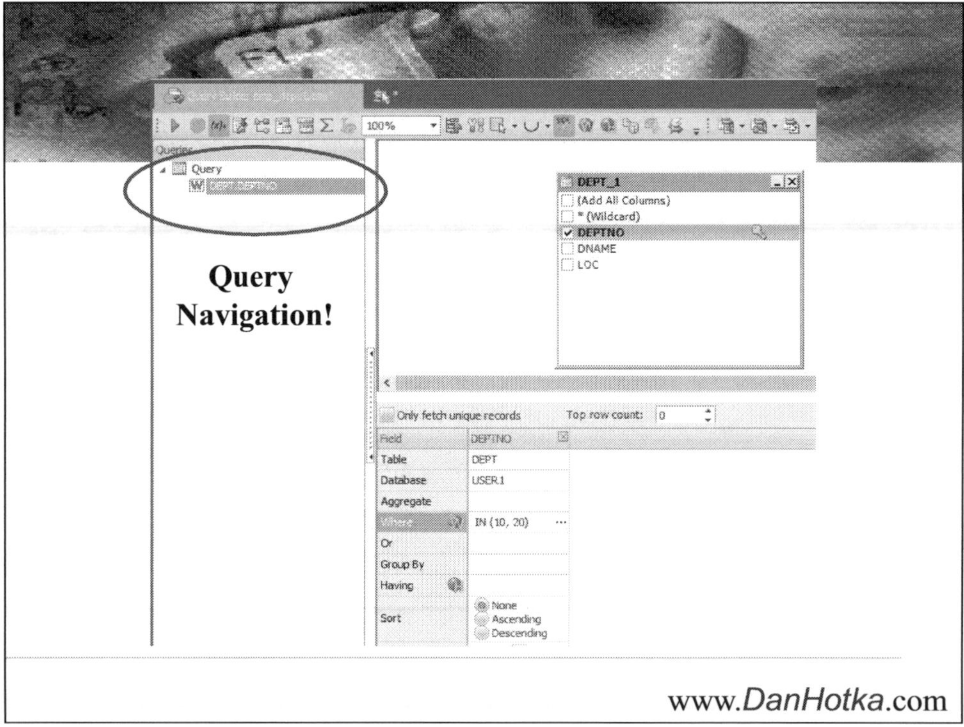
Query
Query
Navigation!
DEPT_1
(Add All Columns)
* (Wildcard)
DEPTNO
DNAME
LOC
Only fetch unique records
Top row count:
Field
DEPTNO
Table
DEPT
Database
USER1
Aggregate
Where
IN (10, 20)
Or
Group By
Having
Sort
None
Ascending
Descending
www.DanHotka.com

## Cross Connection Query

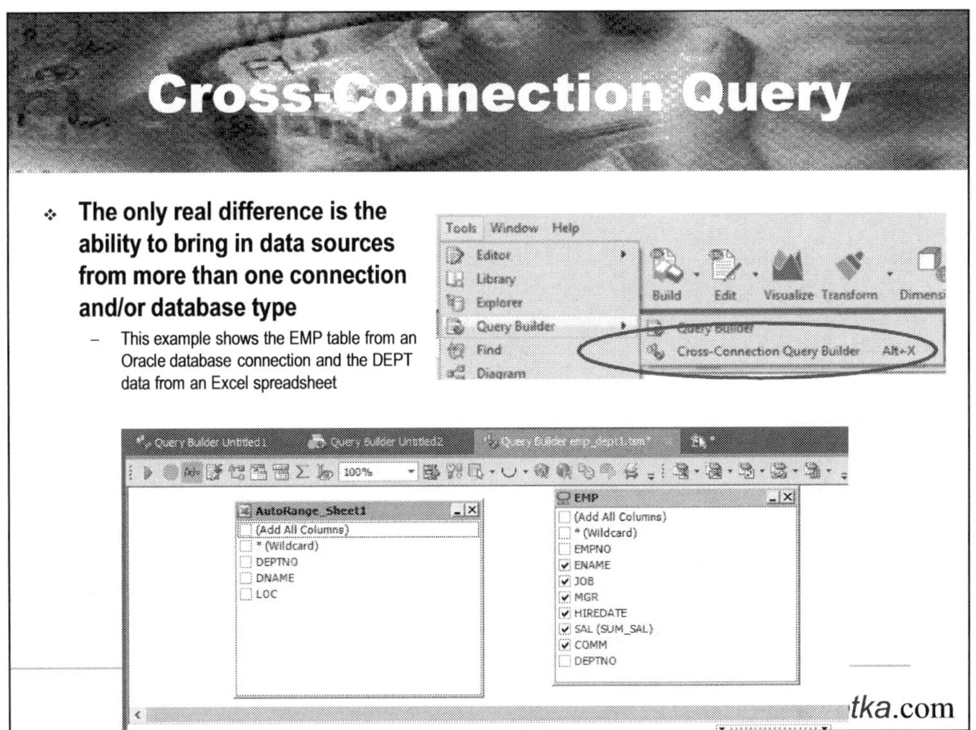

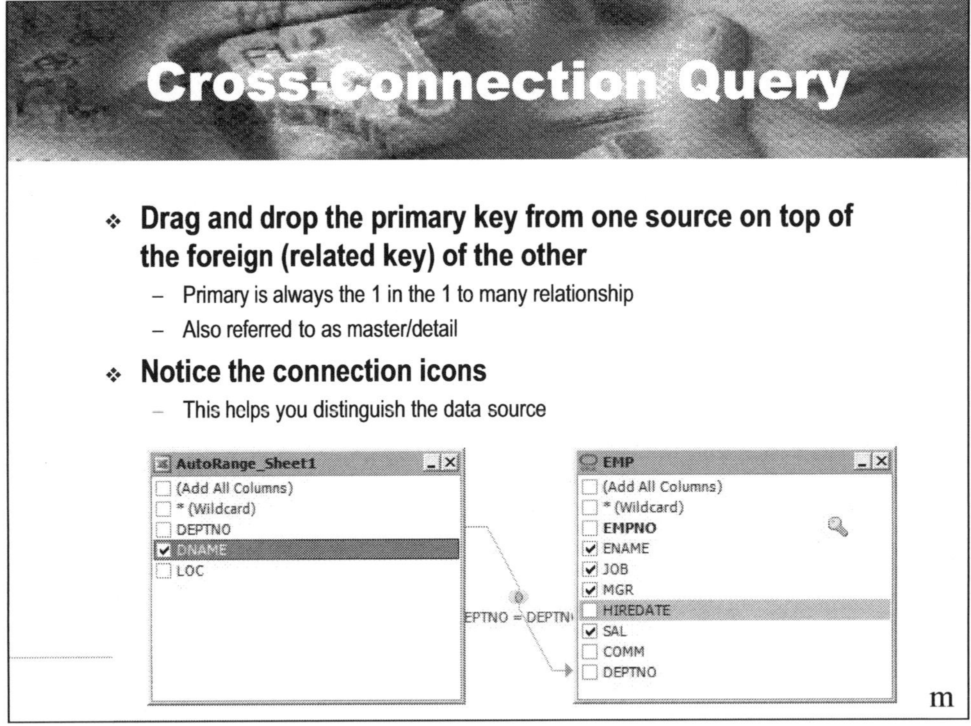
Cross-Connection Query
Drag and drop the primary key from one source on top of the foreign (related key) of the other
– Primary is always the 1 in the 1 to many relationship
– Also referred to as master/detail
Notice the connection icons
– This helps you distinguish the data source
AutoRange_Sheet1
(Add All Columns)
* (Wildcard)
DEPTNO
DNAME
LOC
EPTNO = DEPTN
EMP
(Add All Columns)
* (Wildcard)
EMPNO
ENAME
JOB
MGR
HIREDATE
SAL
COMM
DEPTNO
m

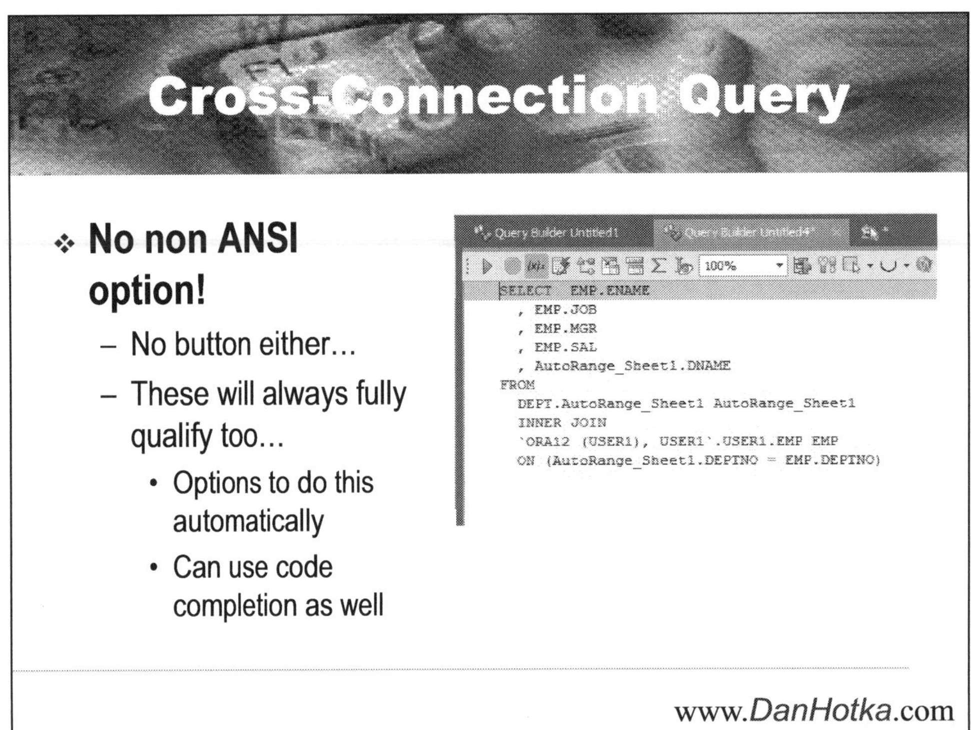
Cross-Connection Query
No non ANSI option!
– No button either…
– These will always fully qualify too…
• Options to do this automatically
• Can use code completion as well
Query Builder Untitled1
Query Builder Untitled4*
100%
SELECT EMP.ENAME
, EMP.JOB
, EMP.MGR
, EMP.SAL
, AutoRange_Sheet1.DNAME
FROM
DEPT.AutoRange_Sheet1 AutoRange_Sheet1
INNER JOIN
`ORA12 (USER1), USER1`.USER1.EMP EMP
ON (AutoRange_Sheet1.DEPTNO = EMP.DEPTNO)
www.DanHotka.com

## Query Builder Summary

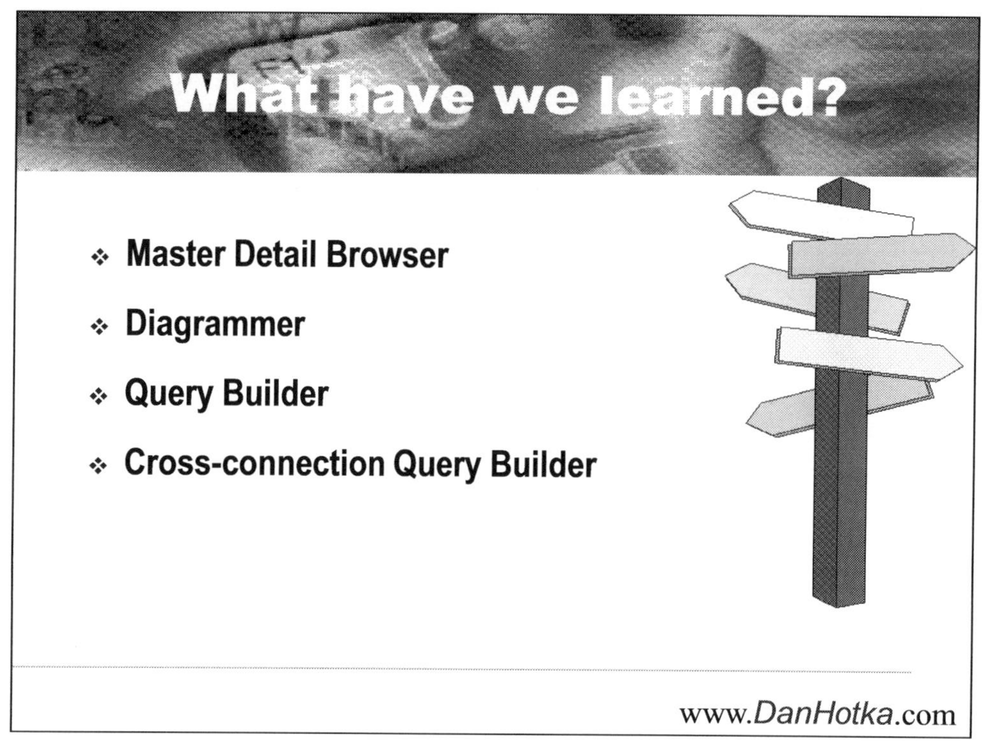
What have we learned?
Master Detail Browser
Diagrammer
Query Builder
Cross-connection Query Builder
www.DanHotka.com

## Query Builder Lab

Query Builder Lab

- **Follow the lecture scenario**
  - We will use the supplied EMP and DEPT tables for this lab
  - Use Diagram to build a diagram of the objects
    - Make sure to add the relationships
  - Pass this to Query Builder
    - Select several columns from both
      - ENAME, SAL, COMM, DNAME (from DEPT table)
    - Add a where clause where MGR is not null
    - Add a calculation, name it TOTAL_COMP
      - SAL + COMM
  - Save the diagram and save the query builder output
    - You do not have to save the data but you can if you like

www.*DanHotka*.com

## Query Builder Lab Answers

- Use Diagram to build a diagram of the objects
  - Make sure to add the relationships

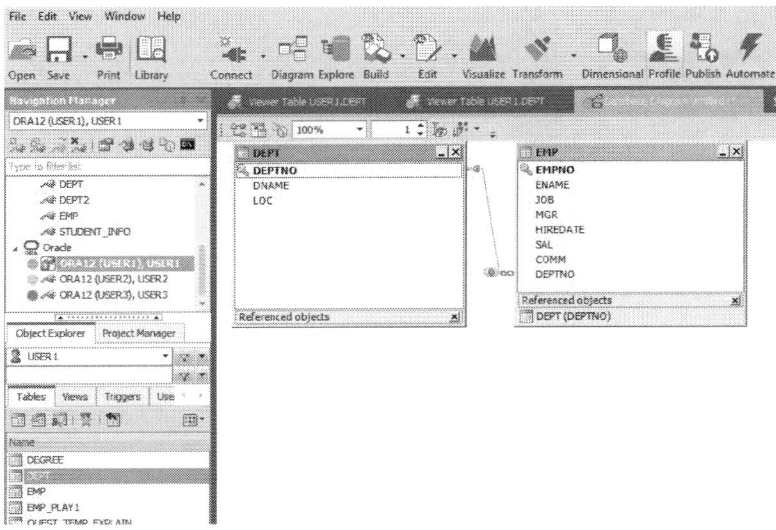

Using the supplied DEPT and EMP tables, start the Diagrammer and drag the DEPT table onto the canvas and drop it. IF there are related tables, they too will automatically appear.

IF the EMP table doesn't automatically appear, drag it to the canvas and then drag the DEPT DEPTNO column to the EMP DEPTNO column, creating the relationship.

In the lower right corner, click the 'Send to Query' button 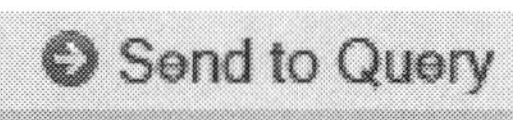


- Pass this to Query Builder
  - Select several columns from both
    - ENAME, SAL, COMM, DNAME (from DEPT table)
  - Add a where clause where MGR is not null
  - Add a calculation, name it TOTAL_COMP
    - SAL + COMM

Select the ENAME, SAL, COMM, DNAME, in this order from the check boxes in Query Builder. If you didn't select them in this order, you can shuffle the columns around using the mouse in the lower area so they are in this order.

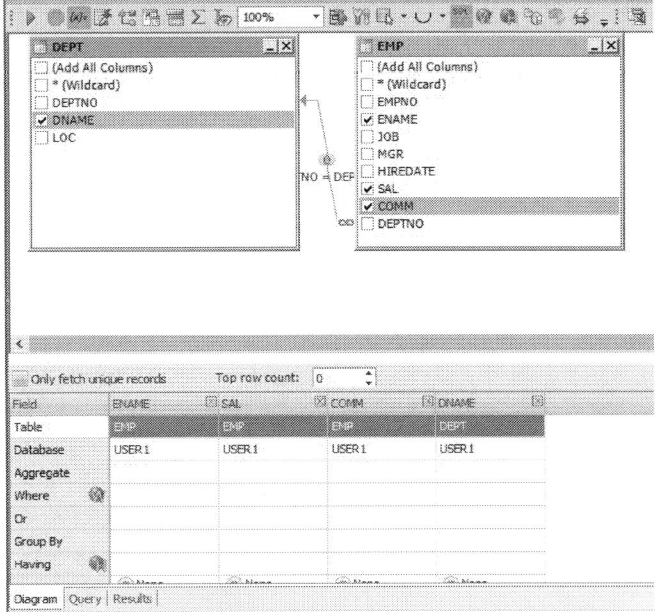

TO add the WHERE clause, click the global where clause button on the Query Builder Tool bar and using your mouse/keyboard…make it look like this:

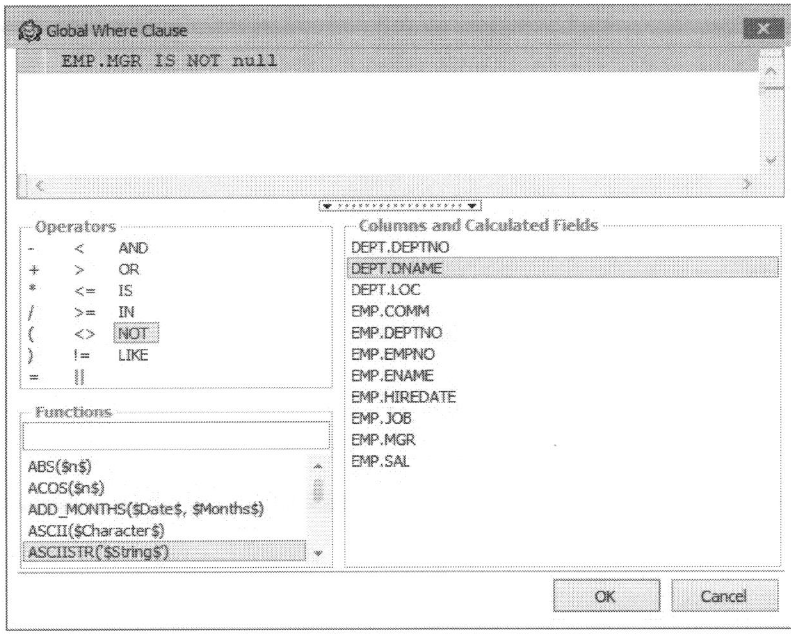

We also could have added the column to our output and adjusted the where clause in the lower section. Using the global where clause, the column doesn't need to appear in the query output.

Use the Calculated Field button Σ to add a calculation. In this case, its SAL + COMM.

Enter TOTAL_COMP in the New Field Name and click the + sign next to it. This then allows you to click the drop down menu for Field Definition. You also have to name the table to associate the data with.

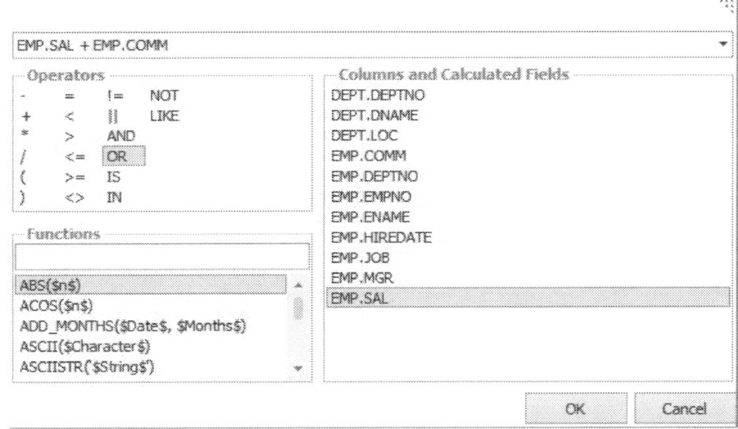


You can get fancy with the functions…add a NVL to the EMP.COMM field…so…it looks like this:

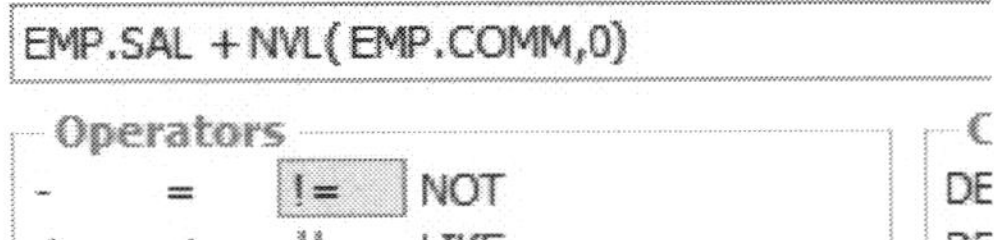
EMP.SAL + NVL( EMP.COMM,0)
Operators
-
=
!=
NOT
DE

Using the lower left tabs,

Review your SQL in the Query tab then run the SQL in the Results tab.

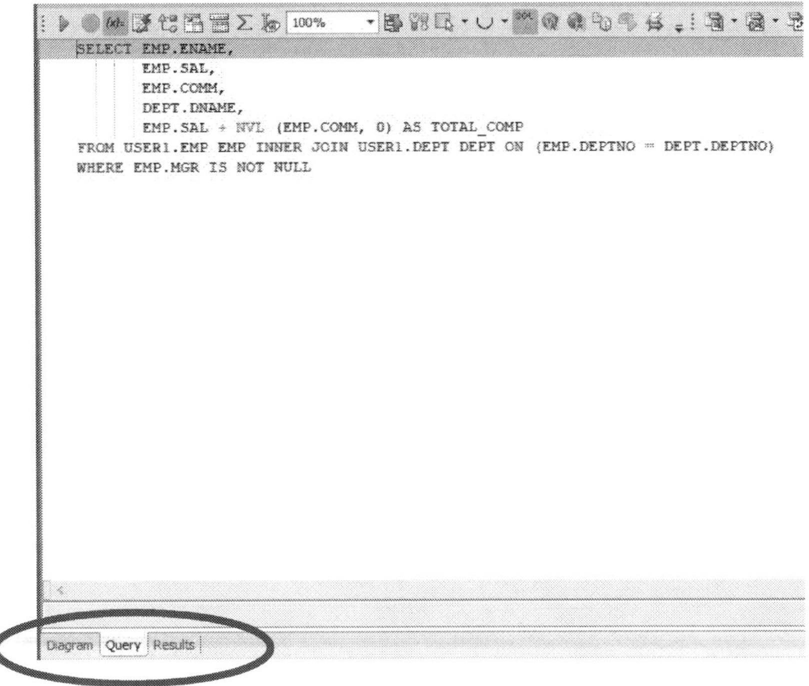
100%
SELECT EMP.ENAME,
EMP.SAL,
EMP.COMM,
DEPT.DNAME,
EMP.SAL + NVL (EMP.COMM, 0) AS TOTAL_COMP
FROM USER1.EMP EMP INNER JOIN USER1.DEPT DEPT ON (EMP.DEPTNO = DEPT.DEPTNO)
WHERE EMP.MGR IS NOT NULL
Diagram
Query
Results

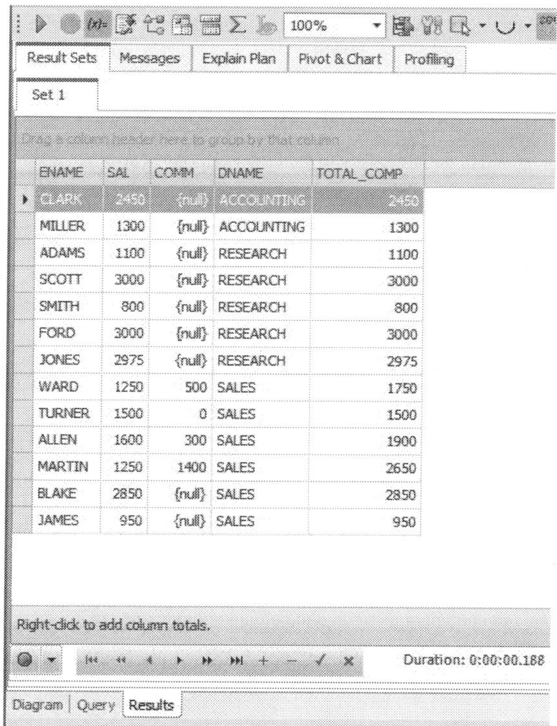


| ENAME | SAL | COMM | DNAME | TOTAL_COMP |
|---|---|---|---|---|
| CLARK | 2450 | {null} | ACCOUNTING | 2450 |
| MILLER | 1300 | {null} | ACCOUNTING | 1300 |
| ADAMS | 1100 | {null} | RESEARCH | 1100 |
| SCOTT | 3000 | {null} | RESEARCH | 3000 |
| SMITH | 800 | {null} | RESEARCH | 800 |
| FORD | 3000 | {null} | RESEARCH | 3000 |
| JONES | 2975 | {null} | RESEARCH | 2975 |
| WARD | 1250 | 500 | SALES | 1750 |
| TURNER | 1500 | 0 | SALES | 1500 |
| ALLEN | 1600 | 300 | SALES | 1900 |
| MARTIN | 1250 | 1400 | SALES | 2650 |
| BLAKE | 2850 | {null} | SALES | 2850 |
| JAMES | 950 | {null} | SALES | 950 |

– Save the diagram and save the query builder output

## Working with SQL

For those of you comfortable with the SQL language, the SQL Editor is quite powerful. Many of its features will be covered here. This editor allows for the execution of SQL, SQL Scripts, view data, save data into various formats and more. The SQL is saved in a history. There are a variety of ways that Toad DP saves on keystrokes. You can add your own keystroke shortcuts. This is easy to do and many people use this little-known feature. Toad DP can develop working SQL with a very minimal amount of entry.

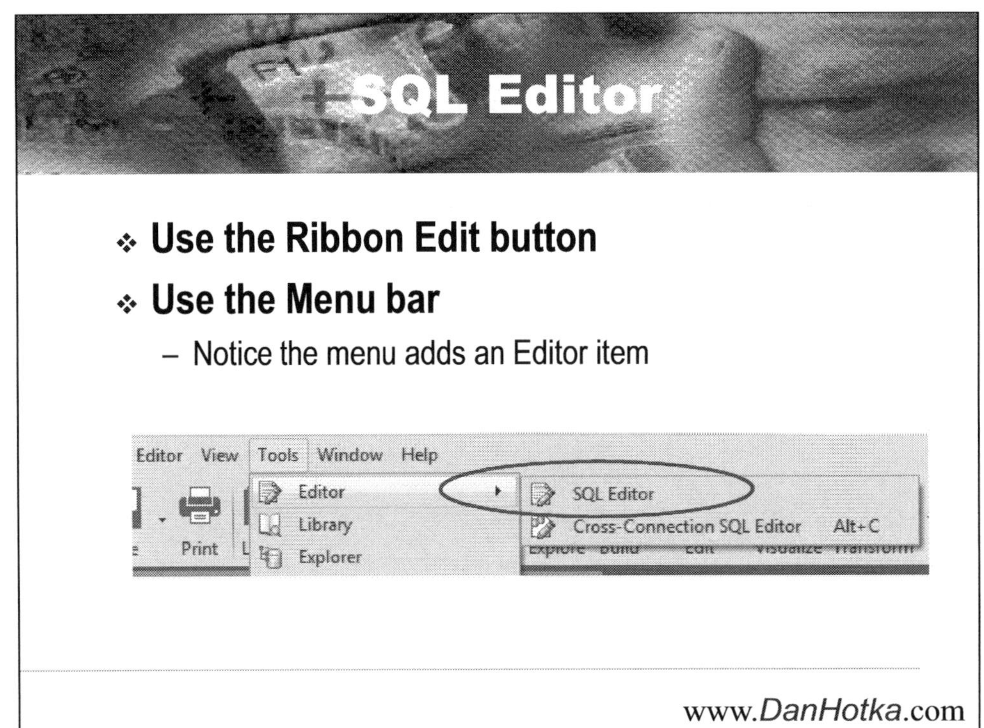
SQL Editor
Use the Ribbon Edit button
Use the Menu bar
– Notice the menu adds an Editor item
Editor
View
Tools
Window
Help
Print
Editor
Library
Explorer
SQL Editor
Cross-Connection SQL Editor
Alt+C
www.DanHotka.com

## Using the Interface

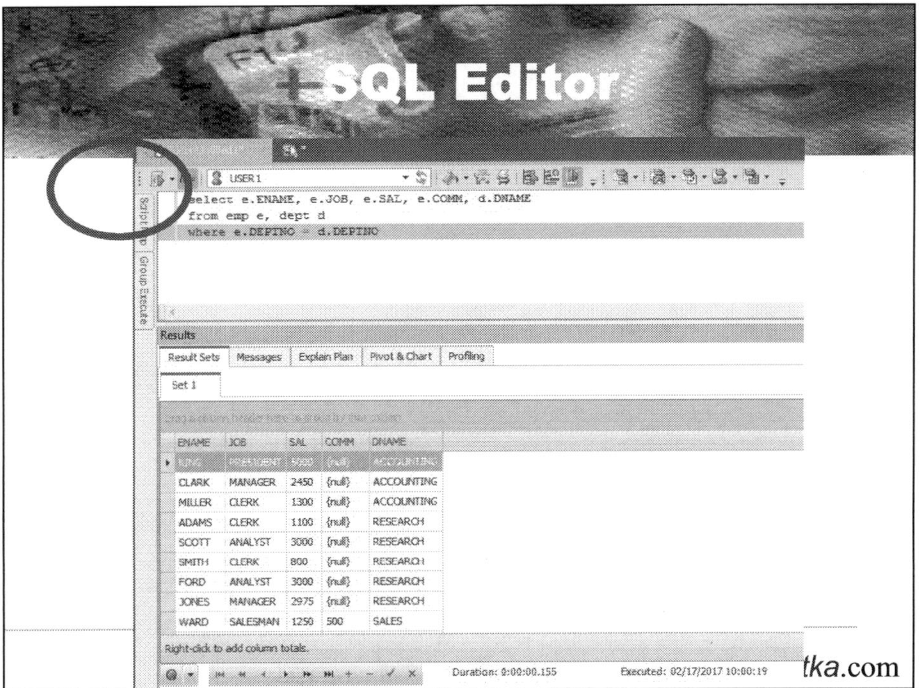


Simply enter a SQL statement and click the green triangle (in the red circle) and this will send the SQL the cursor is on (or the highlighted SQL) to the Oracle database. If the query was successful, then the data or success of the statement will be returned and displayed.

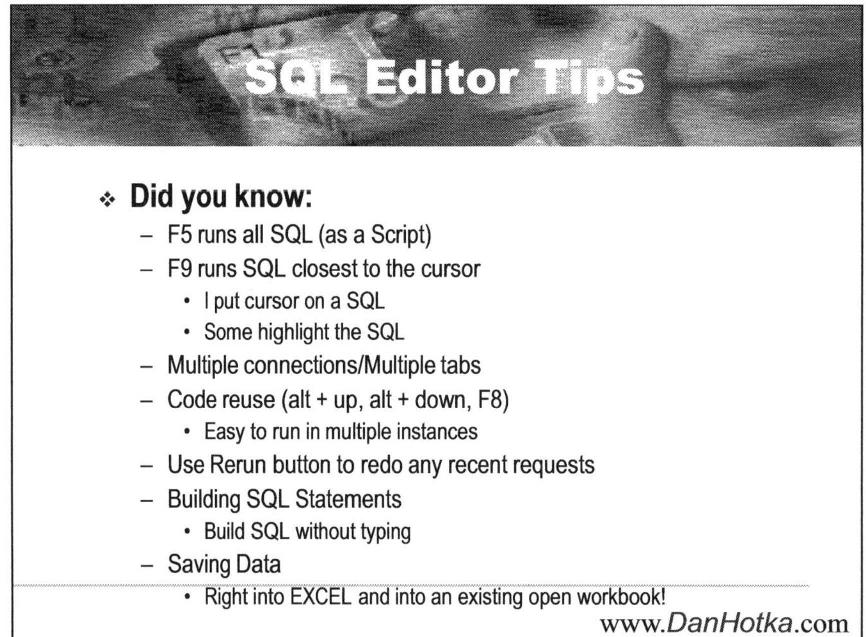
SQL Editor Tips
Did you know:
– F5 runs all SQL (as a Script)
– F9 runs SQL closest to the cursor
• I put cursor on a SQL
• Some highlight the SQL
– Multiple connections/Multiple tabs
– Code reuse (alt + up, alt + down, F8)
• Easy to run in multiple instances
– Use Rerun button to redo any recent requests
– Building SQL Statements
• Build SQL without typing
– Saving Data
• Right into EXCEL and into an existing open workbook!
www.DanHotka.com

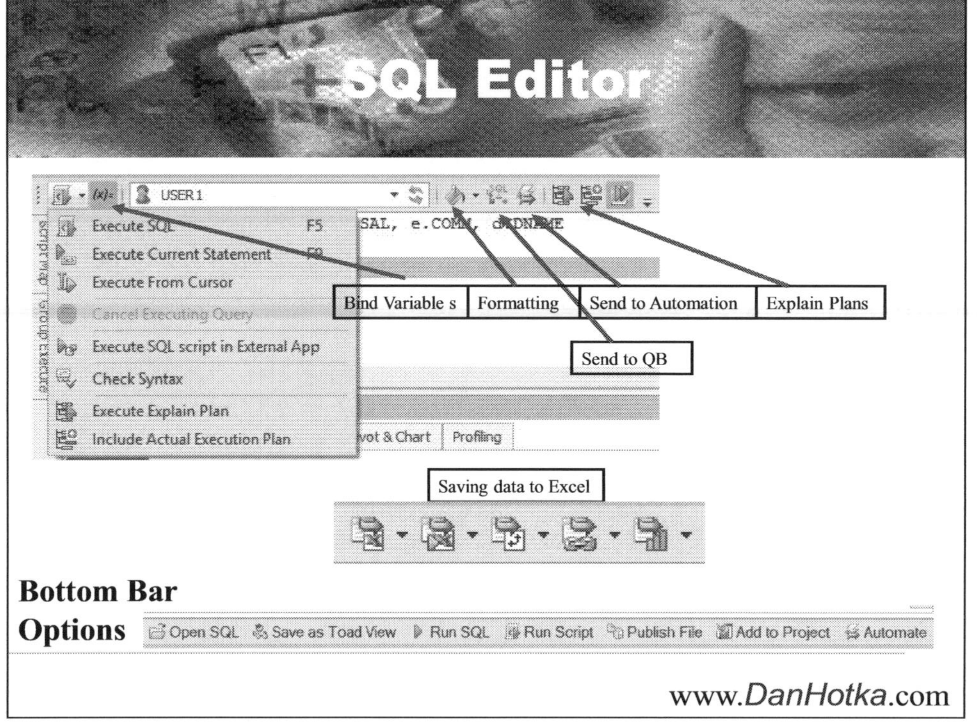
SQL Editor
USER1
Execute SQL F5
Execute Current Statement
Execute From Cursor
Cancel Executing Query
Execute SQL script in External App
Check Syntax
Execute Explain Plan
Include Actual Execution Plan
Bind Variable s
Formatting
Send to Automation
Explain Plans
Send to QB
Profiling
Saving data to Excel
Bottom Bar Options
Open SQL
Save as Toad View
Run SQL
Run Script
Publish File
Add to Project
Automate
www.DanHotka.com

*****Tip***** - Hover the mouse over any button and it will give a brief description of what it does!

There are several ways to execute your SQL. The F5 or Exe SQL is probably the most command and is used when only 1 SQL statement is in the editor. F9 or Current Statement executes with the SQL highlighted or the cursor is on/near a SQL Statement.

There is a syntax checker and you can see execution plans (whether your SQL will use an index or not…a performance tool).

You can format your SQL. The Options menu allows how the formatting will occur. You can send your SQL to the Query Builder! This works well for most SQL. You can send the SQL to Automation (covered later in this course). The explain plan buttons are useful and you can easily add any of these drop down menu buttons to this tool bar.

The saving to Excel buttons appear here as well. There are various options for opening and saving SQL across the bottom of the editor as well.

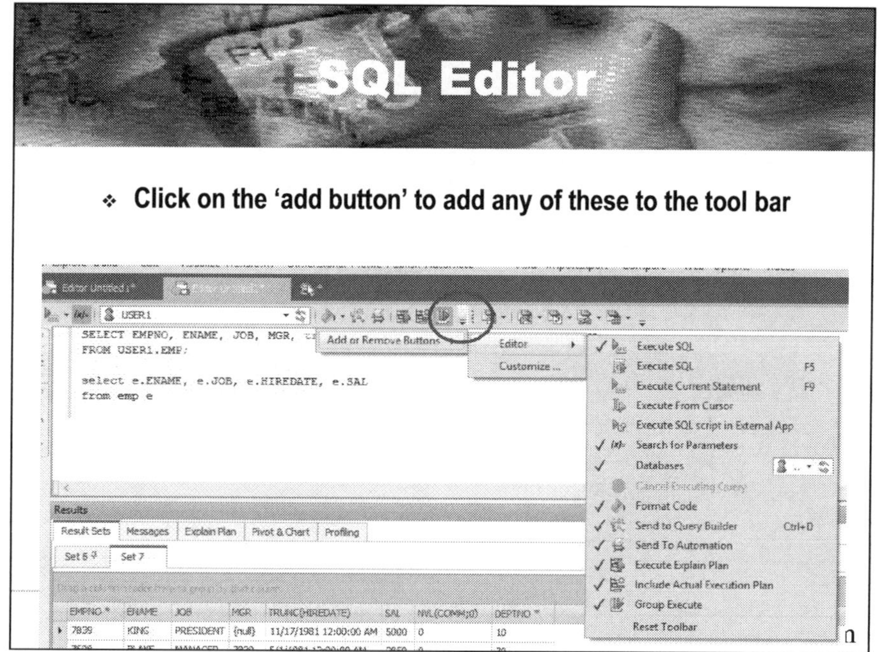


You can add any of these buttons to the tool bar by clicking on them.

Highlight a column of numbers and right click, select the Sum option and you will get totals at the bottom of the data grid.

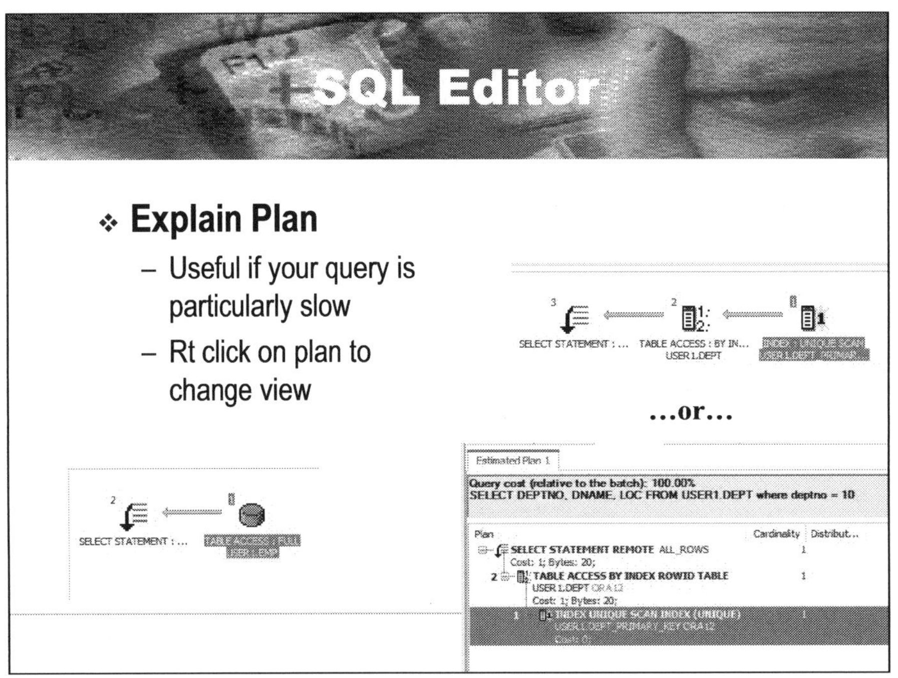


These Explain Plans are useful when your SQL is experiencing performance issues. Experienced IT professionals will need this information to help you with this particular SQL. You can use this to quickly see if your SQL is going to benefit from using an index.

## SQL without Typing

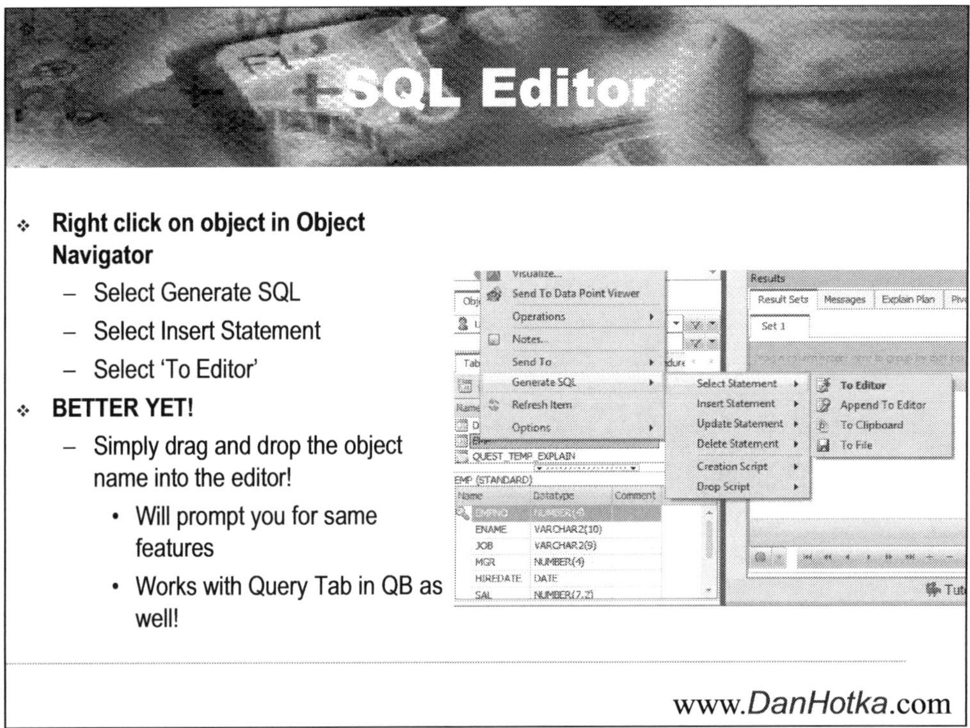
SQL Editor
Right click on object in Object Navigator
– Select Generate SQL
– Select Insert Statement
– Select 'To Editor'
BETTER YET!
– Simply drag and drop the object name into the editor!
• Will prompt you for same features
• Works with Query Tab in QB as well!
Send To Data Point Viewer
Operations
Notes...
Send To
Generate SQL
Refresh Item
Options
Select Statement
Insert Statement
Update Statement
Delete Statement
Creation Script
Drop Script
To Editor
Append To Editor
To Clipboard
To File
Results
Result Sets
Messages
Explain Plan
Set 1
QUEST_TEMP_EXPLAIN
EMP (STANDARD)
Name
Datatype
Comment
EMPNO
NUMBER(4)
ENAME
VARCHAR2(10)
JOB
VARCHAR2(9)
MGR
NUMBER(4)
HIREDATE
DATE
SAL
NUMBER(7,2)
www.DanHotka.com

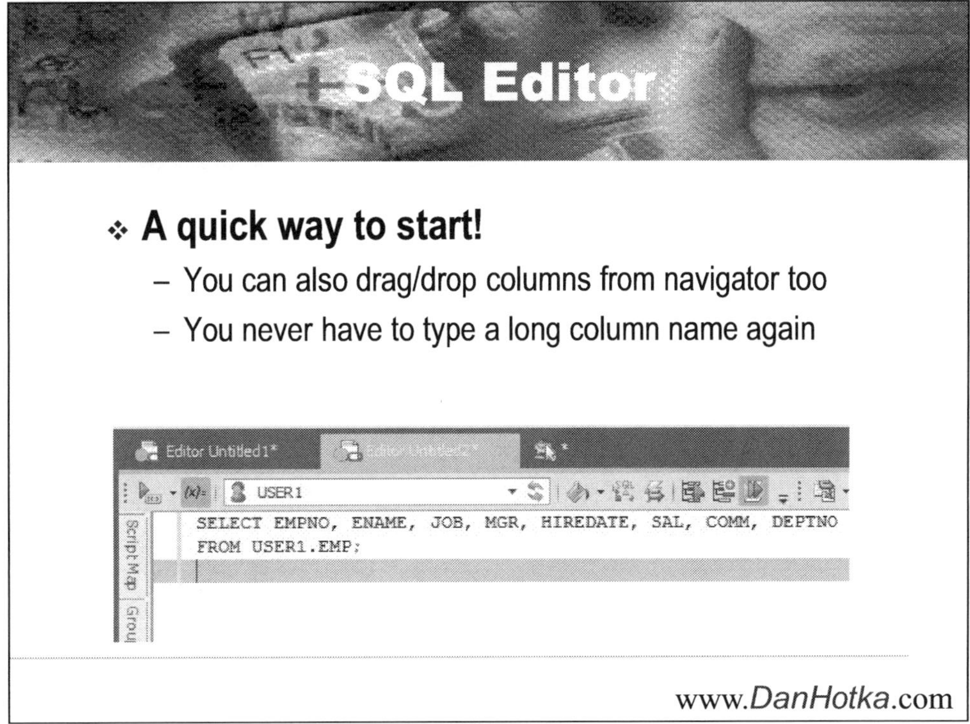
SQL Editor
A quick way to start!
– You can also drag/drop columns from navigator too
– You never have to type a long column name again
Editor Untitled1*
Editor Untitled2*
USER1
SELECT EMPNO, ENAME, JOB, MGR, HIREDATE, SAL, COMM, DEPTNO
FROM USER1.EMP;
Script Map
www.DanHotka.com

Probably the quickest way to get a working SQL statement, and maybe a good place to start, is to simply drag and drop a table object from the Navigator window and drop it onto the SQL Editor. It will ask you what kind of SQL statement you would like. It is just that easy. You get all the column names and the table name.

You can also right click on the table in the navigator. You can also drag and drop column names from the navigator as well.

There is just no reason you ever have to manually type in a long column name.

## Object Information

The F4, or Object Details button brings up the Object Details panel here too.. Simply put the cursor on a function and hit the F4 key and the function's code will be displayed.

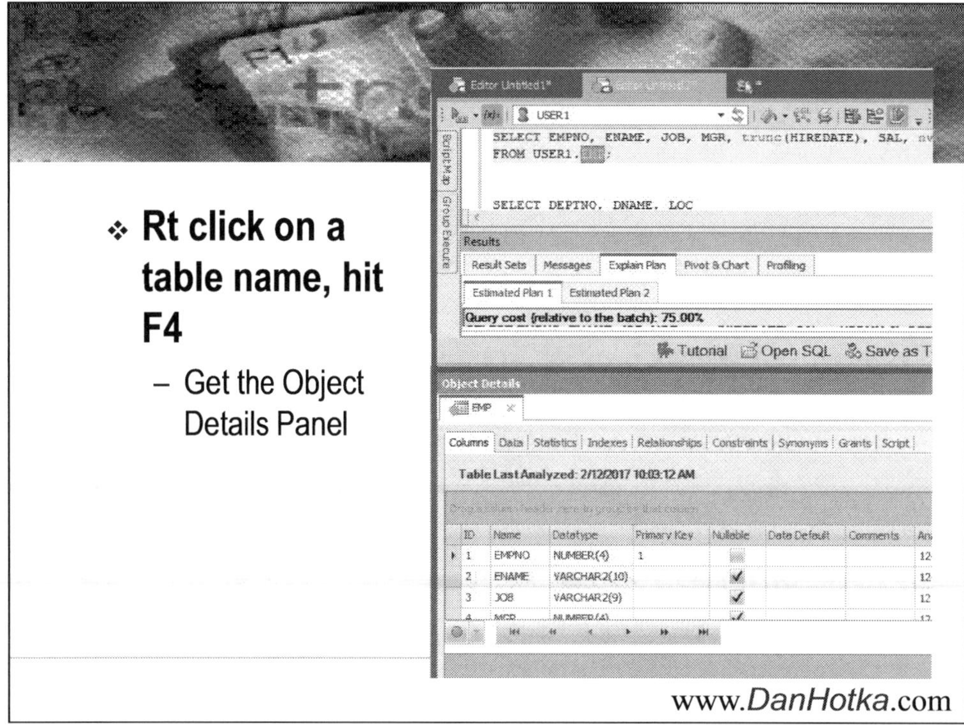


Notice the various tabs! These columns on the Columns tab can be dragged and dropped onto the SQL window. Other information such as available indexes, constraints, triggers, etc can be shown from this interface as well.

## More SQL without Typing (Code Completion)

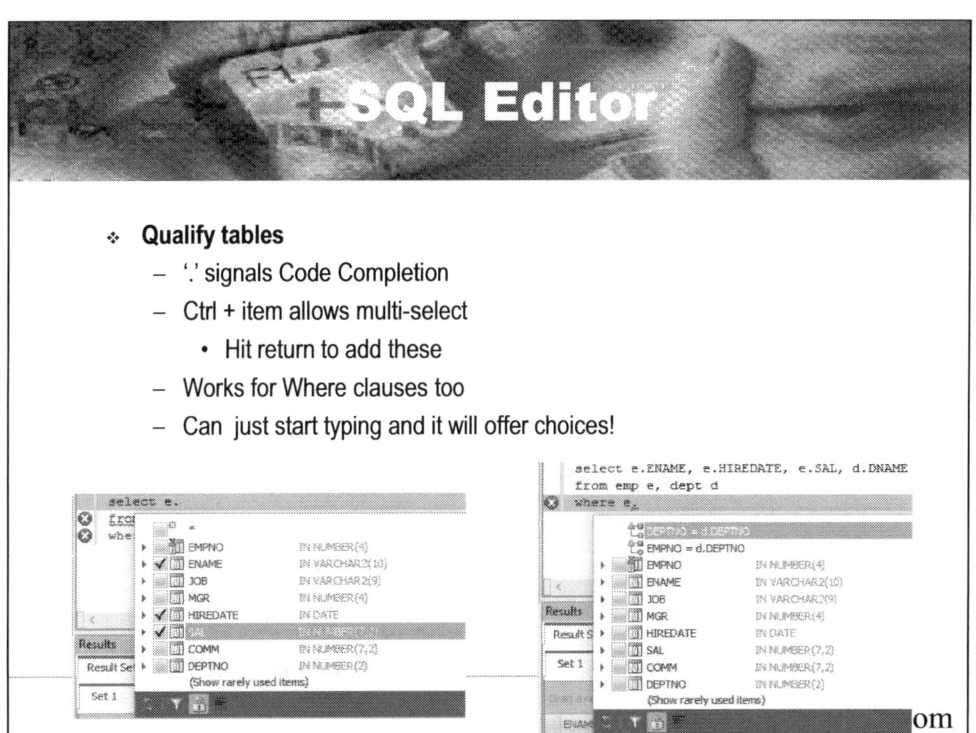
SQL Editor
Qualify tables
'.' signals Code Completion
Ctrl + item allows multi-select
Hit return to add these
Works for Where clauses too
Can just start typing and it will offer choices!
select e.ENAME, e.HIREDATE, e.SAL, d.DNAME
from emp e, dept d
where e.
select e.
EMPNO
ENAME
JOB
MGR
HIREDATE
SAL
COMM
DEPTNO
(Show rarely used items)
EMPNO = d.DEPTNO
Results
Set 1
om

Code Completion allow for object column names to be displayed following the entry of a '.'. Enter the table name followed by a '.' or a table alias followed by a '.'.

Double-click on a column name to automatically paste it into the Editor at the position of the cursor. Select multiple column names using the shift and click and ctrl and click keys, then hit return and all the selected columns are put into the Editor along with commas between the fields.

The Scripts tab will recreate a script that could be saved and used to re-create the object. Also, this script can be copied into a file and used when creating a test environment for your application. Most analysts have little need for this kind of information.

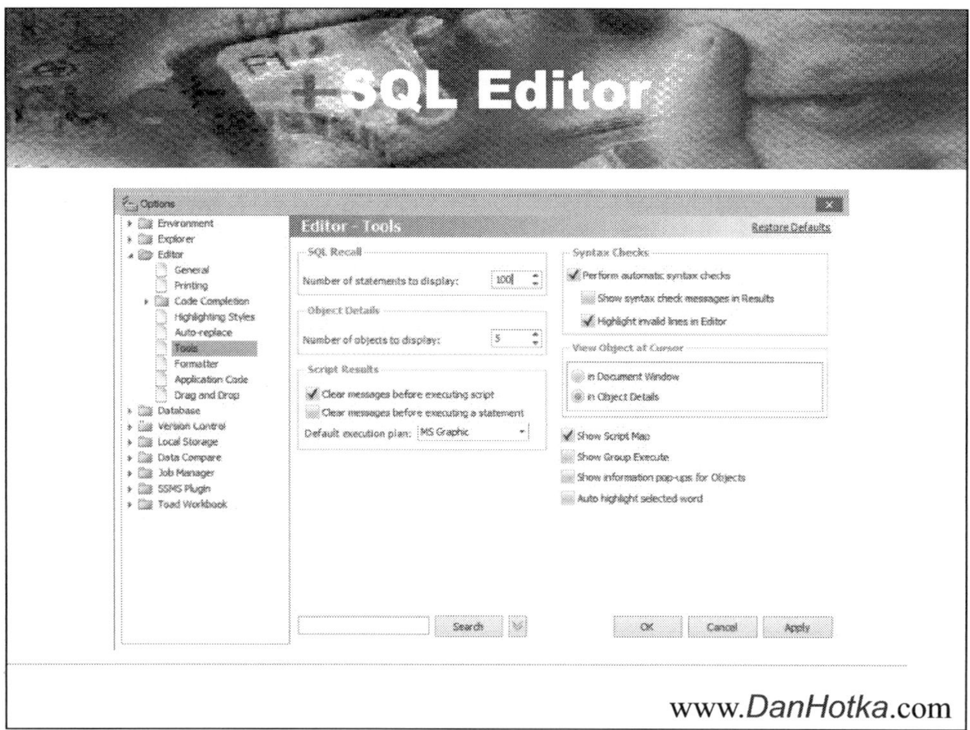
SQL Editor
Options
Environment
Explorer
Editor
General
Printing
Code Completion
Highlighting Styles
Auto-replace
Tools
Formatter
Application Code
Drag and Drop
Database
Version Control
Local Storage
Data Compare
Job Manager
SSMS Plugin
Toad Workbook
Editor - Tools
Restore Defaults
SQL Recall
Number of statements to display:
Object Details
Number of objects to display:
Script Results
Clear messages before executing script
Clear messages before executing a statement
Default execution plan: MS Graphic
Syntax Checks
Perform automatic syntax checks
Show syntax check messages in Results
Highlight invalid lines in Editor
View Object at Cursor
in Document Window
in Object Details
Show Script Map
Show Group Execute
Show information pop-ups for Objects
Auto highlight selected word
Search
OK
Cancel
Apply
www.DanHotka.com

The Options Code Completion General panel allows for control over how long it takes the panel to pop up, what kind of syntax it paints in, and more.

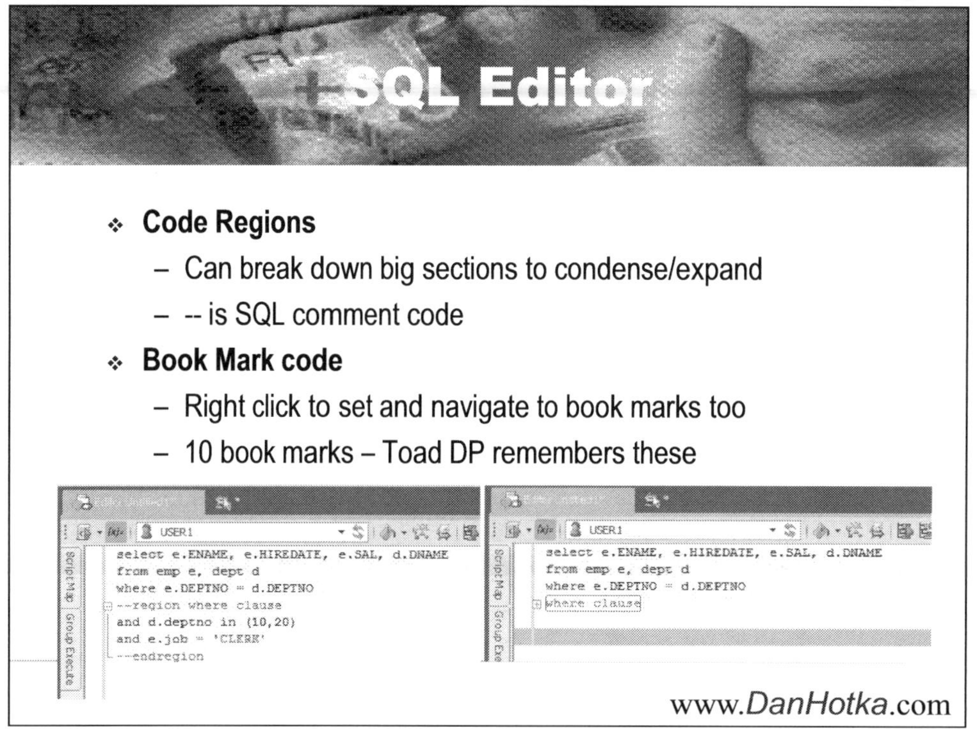
SQL Editor
Code Regions
– Can break down big sections to condense/expand
– -- is SQL comment code
Book Mark code
– Right click to set and navigate to book marks too
– 10 book marks – Toad DP remembers these
USER1
select e.ENAME, e.HIREDATE, e.SAL, d.DNAME
from emp e, dept d
where e.DEPTNO = d.DEPTNO
--region where clause
and d.deptno in (10,20)
and e.job = 'CLERK'
--endregion
Script Map
Group Execute
USER1
select e.ENAME, e.HIREDATE, e.SAL, d.DNAME
from emp e, dept d
where e.DEPTNO = d.DEPTNO
where clause
www.DanHotka.com

There are a couple of ways to make navigation around larger chunks of code easier. The first is using comments that Toad DP will interpret and allow for the code to be condensed or expanded as needed. The other are bookmarks. Right click and select a book mark for a position in the code. The right click also allows for navigation to these book marks. There are only 10 of these.

## SQL Recall (F8)

SQL Recall is the TOAD history of the SQL that was processed thru the SQL Editor window. F8 activates SQL Recall. SQL Recall can also be accessed via the View menu drop down.

****Note**** - The appendix of this book has a keystroke cross-reference.

The SQL Recall window is undockable…use the pushpin button to dock and undock this window.

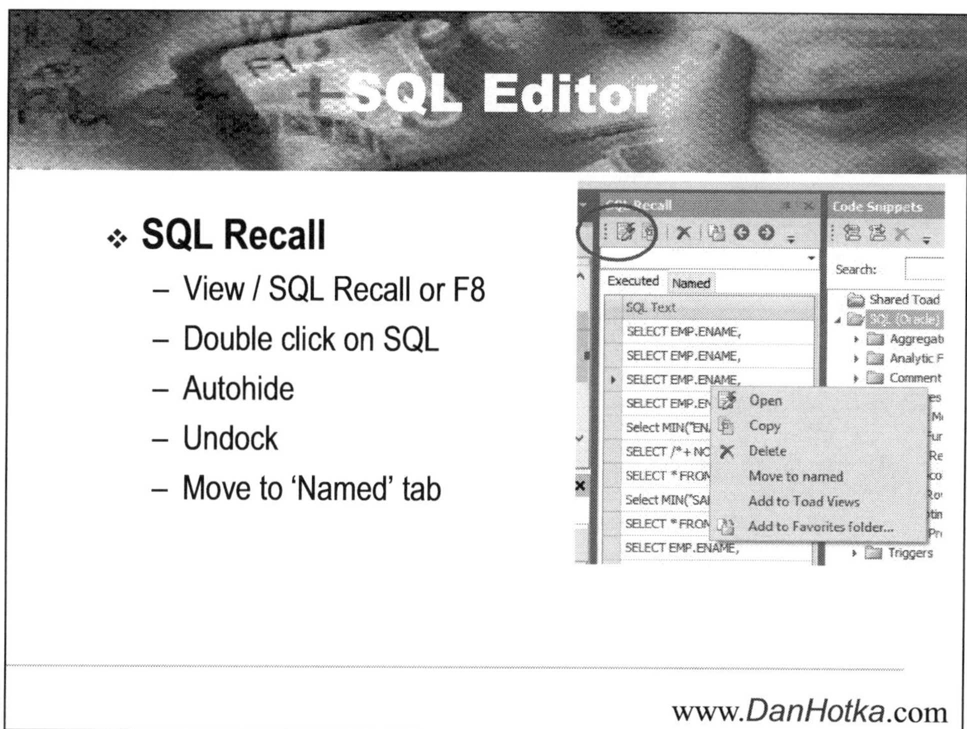


Find the SQL to work with and use the 'Open in SQL Editor' button (see circle above) to load into a new tab in the SQL Editor.

While in the SQL Editor, the key strokes ALT up-arrow and ALT-down-arrow also walks thru the SQL Recall history.

The Options Editor Tools panel gives control over how many SQL statements will be saved. This feature defaults to 100 and that should be more than enough.

***Note*** I have had to leave quickly…and was able to find my SQL in this history the very next day…saving me a ton of work.

***Tip*** Make sure you execute your SQL. This is when it is saved to the SQL Recall.

## Errors and Messages

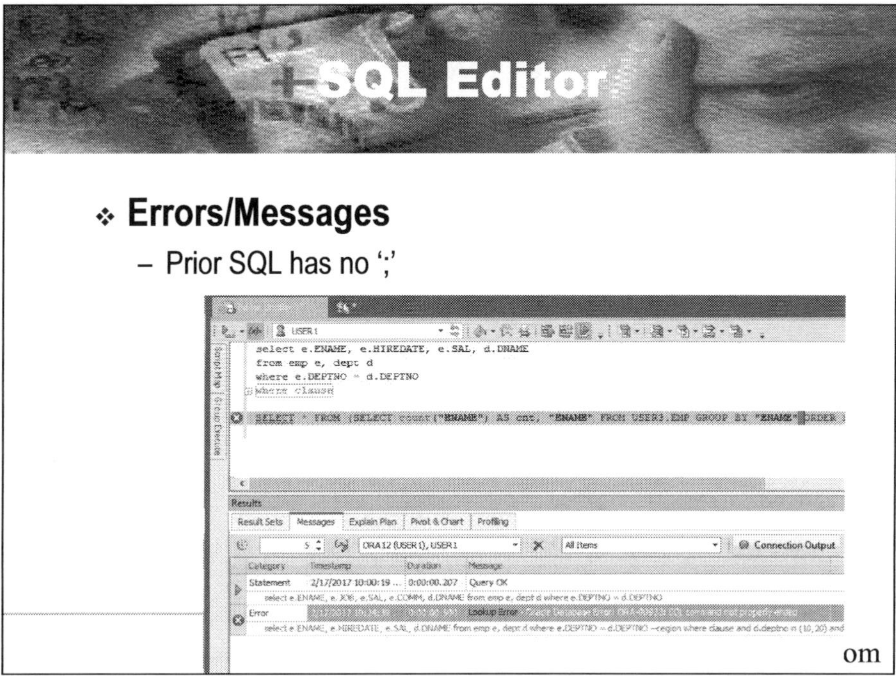


## Code Snippets

Toad DP contains bits of code called 'Code Snippets'. These snippets contain most of the SQL functions, date formats, hints, and other bits of SQL code that are of interest to the user. This panel also adapts to the focus of the database the editor is currently working with.

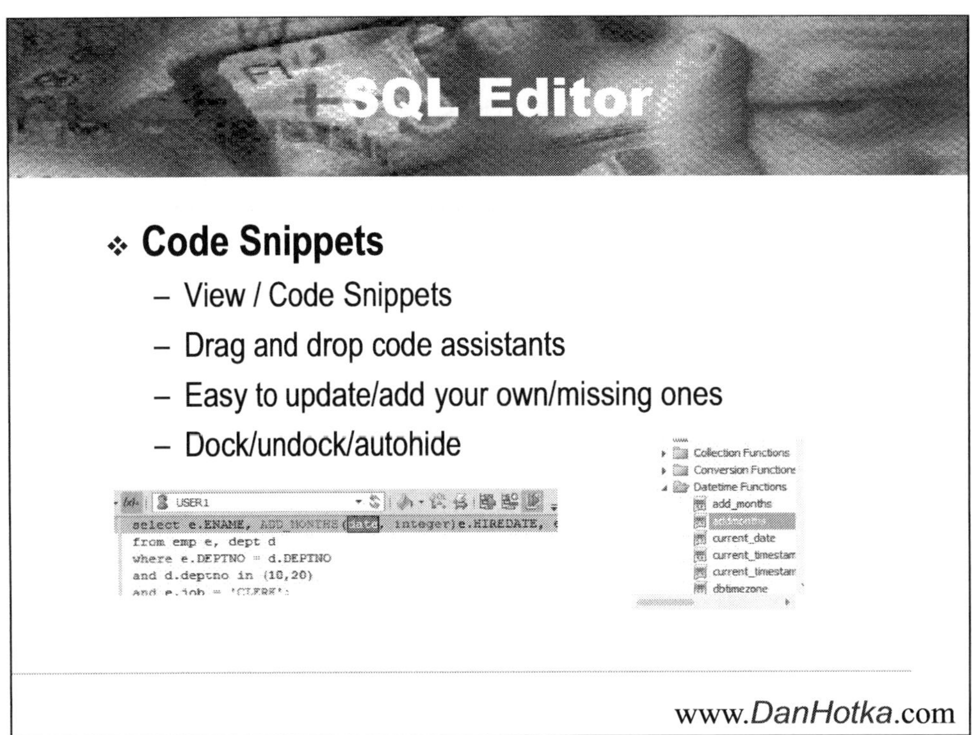
SQL Editor
Code Snippets
– View / Code Snippets
– Drag and drop code assistants
– Easy to update/add your own/missing ones
– Dock/undock/autohide
USER1
select e.ENAME, ADD_MONTHS(date, integer)e.HIREDATE,
from emp e, dept d
where e.DEPTNO = d.DEPTNO
and d.deptno in (10,20)
Collection Functions
Datetime Functions
add_months
current_date
dbtimezone
www.DanHotka.com

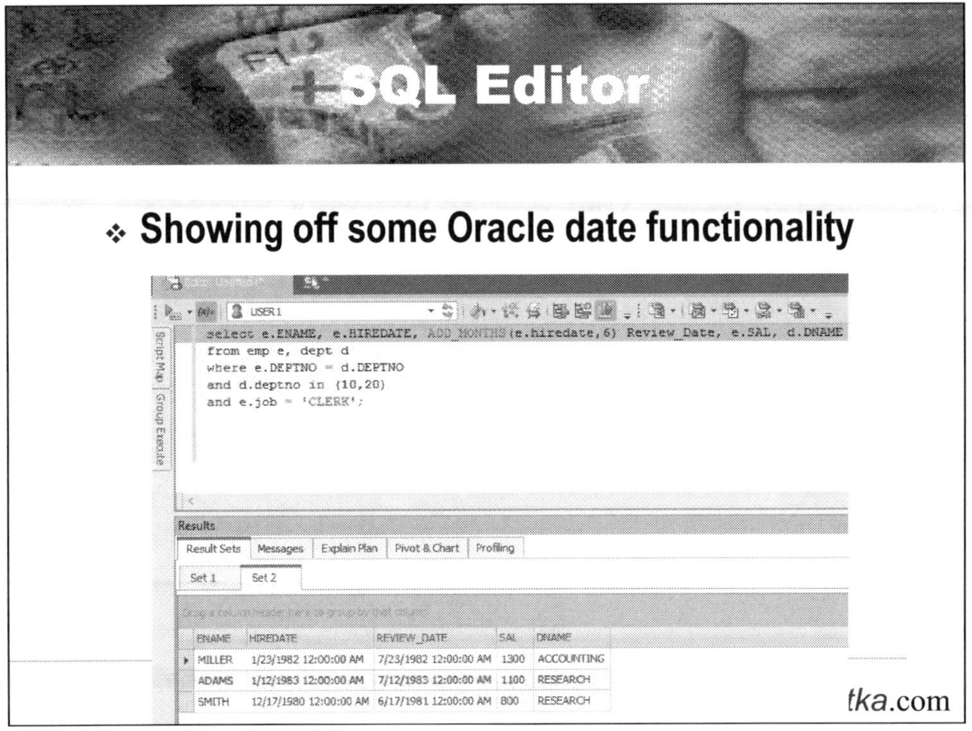
SQL Editor
Showing off some Oracle date functionality
USER1
select e.ENAME, e.HIREDATE, ADD_MONTHS(e.hiredate,6) Review_Date, e.SAL, d.DNAME
from emp e, dept d
where e.DEPTNO = d.DEPTNO
and d.deptno in (10,20)
and e.job = 'CLERK';
Results
Result Sets
Messages
Explain Plan
Pivot & Chart
Profiling
Set 1
Set 2
ENAME HIREDATE REVIEW_DATE SAL DNAME
MILLER 1/23/1982 12:00:00 AM 7/23/1982 12:00:00 AM 1300 ACCOUNTING
ADAMS 1/12/1983 12:00:00 AM 7/12/1983 12:00:00 AM 1100 RESEARCH
SMITH 12/17/1980 12:00:00 AM 6/17/1981 12:00:00 AM 800 RESEARCH
tka.com

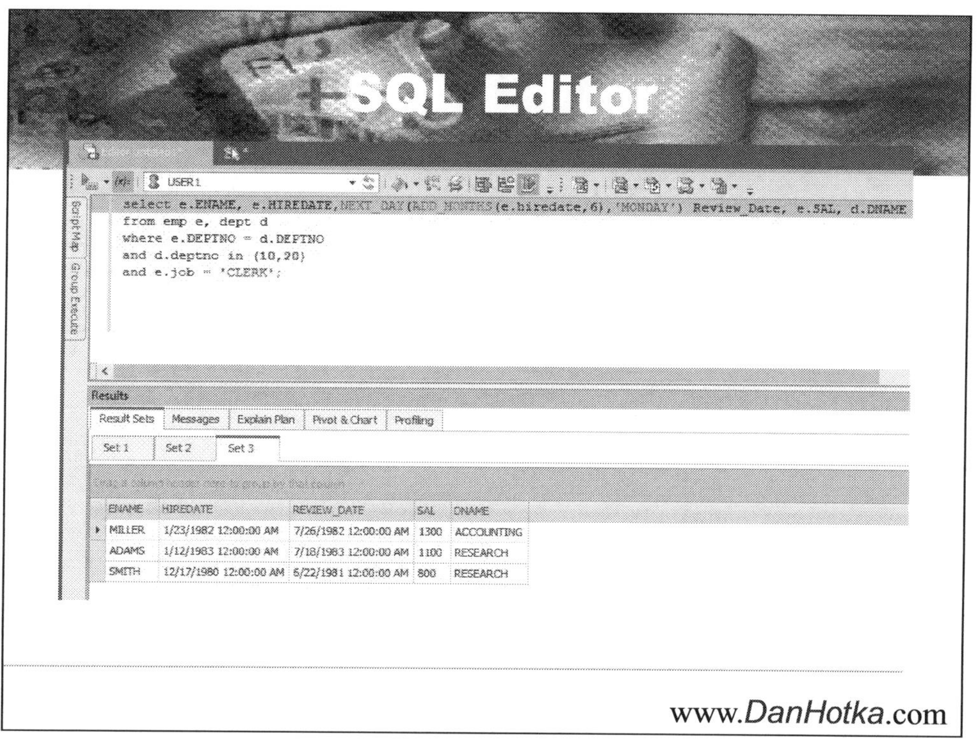
SQL Editor
select e.ENAME, e.HIREDATE,NEXT_DAY(ADD_MONTHS(e.hiredate,6),'MONDAY') Review_Date, e.SAL, d.DNAME
from emp e, dept d
where e.DEPTNO = d.DEPTNO
and d.deptno in (10,20)
and e.job = 'CLERK';
Results
Result Sets
Messages
Explain Plan
Pivot & Chart
Profiling
Set 1
Set 2
Set 3
ENAME HIREDATE REVIEW_DATE SAL DNAME
MILLER 1/23/1982 12:00:00 AM 7/26/1982 12:00:00 AM 1300 ACCOUNTING
ADAMS 1/12/1983 12:00:00 AM 7/18/1983 12:00:00 AM 1100 RESEARCH
SMITH 12/17/1980 12:00:00 AM 6/22/1981 12:00:00 AM 800 RESEARCH
www.DanHotka.com

SQL Editor
Code Snippets
– Rt click on new snippet to add to Code Snippets
Comment Lines
Uncomment Lines
Make Uppercase
Make Lowercase
Outlining
Set Numbered Bookmark
Go to Numbered Bookmark
Add to Toad Views
Publish
Advanced
Compare To
Add to Code Snippets...
Send To Query Builder
Add to Favorites folder
Snippet Name:
Null Value
Add to shared folder?
OK
Cancel
Connection Output
www.DanHotka.com

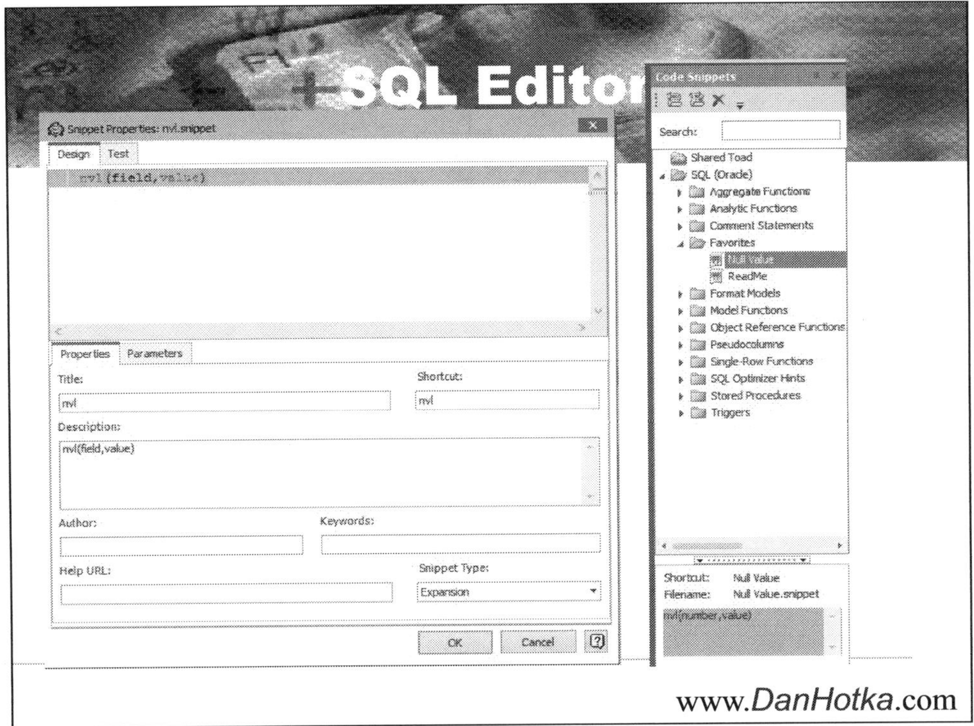
SQL Editor
Snippet Properties: nvl.snippet
Design
Test
nvl(field,value)
Properties
Parameters
Title:
nvl
Shortcut:
nvl
Description:
nvl(field,value)
Author:
Keywords:
Help URL:
Snippet Type:
Expansion
OK
Cancel
Code Snippets
Search:
Shared Toad
SQL (Oracle)
Aggregate Functions
Analytic Functions
Comment Statements
Favorites
Null Value
ReadMe
Format Models
Model Functions
Object Reference Functions
Pseudocolumns
Single-Row Functions
SQL Optimizer Hints
Stored Procedures
Triggers
Shortcut: Null Value
Filename: Null Value.snippet
nvl(number,value)
www.DanHotka.com

You can add a new function in the SQL, then right click and add it to Code Snippets. These will go into a Favorites folder. You can also add new snippets right in the Code Snippets panel. Add a folder, or right click on a folder to add a new snippet.

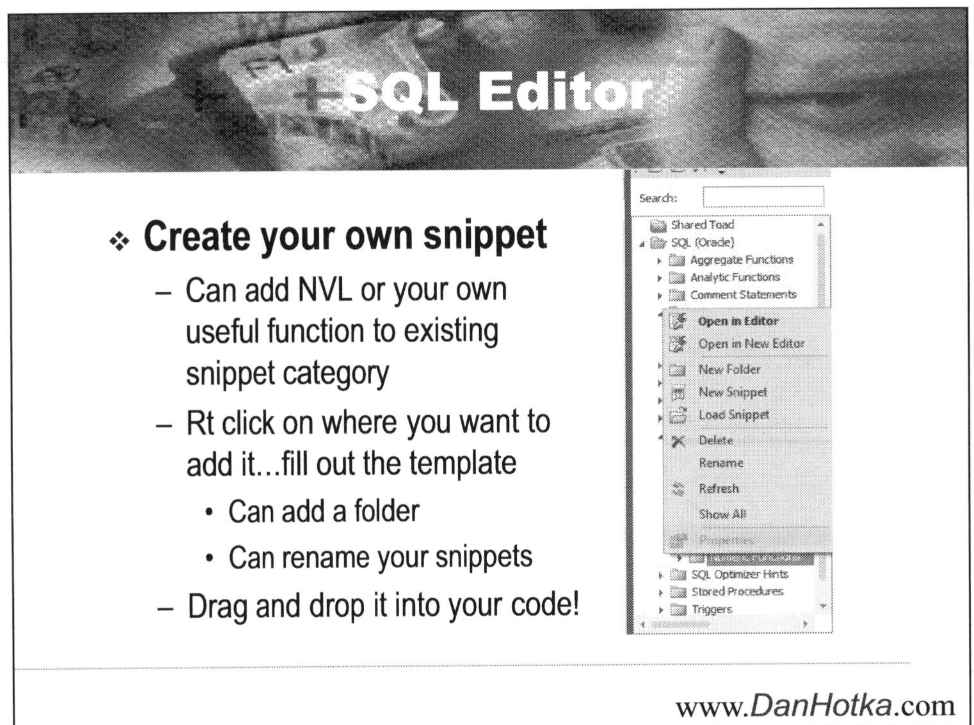
SQL Editor
Create your own snippet
– Can add NVL or your own useful function to existing snippet category
– Rt click on where you want to add it…fill out the template
• Can add a folder
• Can rename your snippets
– Drag and drop it into your code!
Search:
Shared Toad
SQL (Oracle)
Aggregate Functions
Analytic Functions
Comment Statements
Open in Editor
Open in New Editor
New Folder
New Snippet
Load Snippet
Delete
Rename
Refresh
Show All
Properties
SQL Optimizer Hints
Stored Procedures
Triggers
www.DanHotka.com

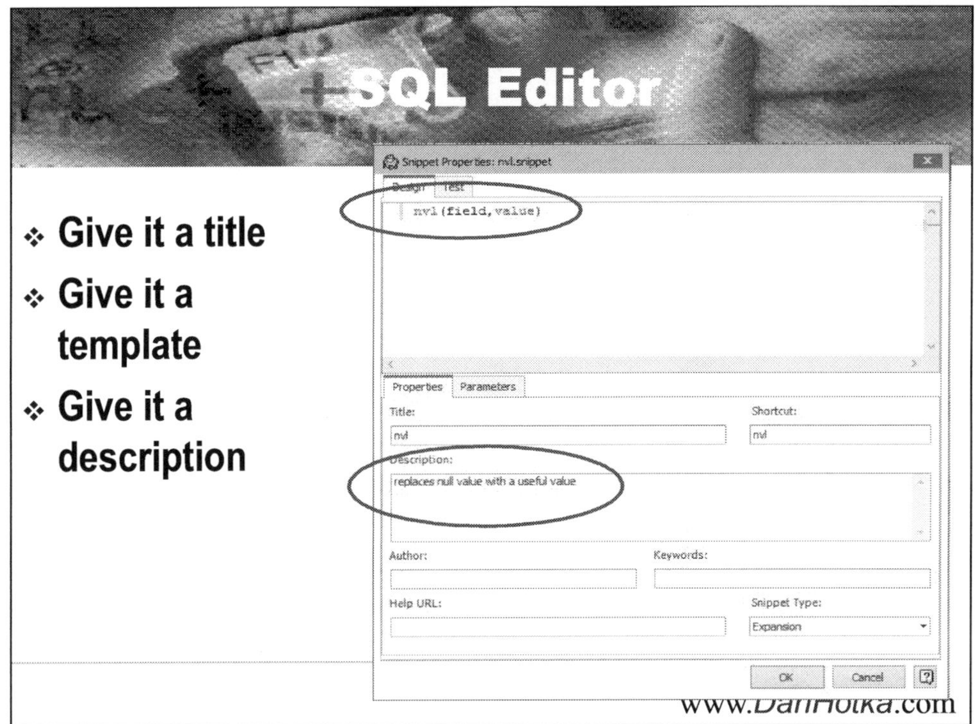
SQL Editor
Give it a title
Give it a template
Give it a description
Snippet Properties: nvl.snippet
Design
Test
nvl(field, value)
Properties
Parameters
Title:
nvl
Shortcut:
nvl
Description:
replaces null value with a useful value
Author:
Keywords:
Help URL:
Snippet Type:
Expansion
OK
Cancel
www.DanHotka.com

## Auto Replace

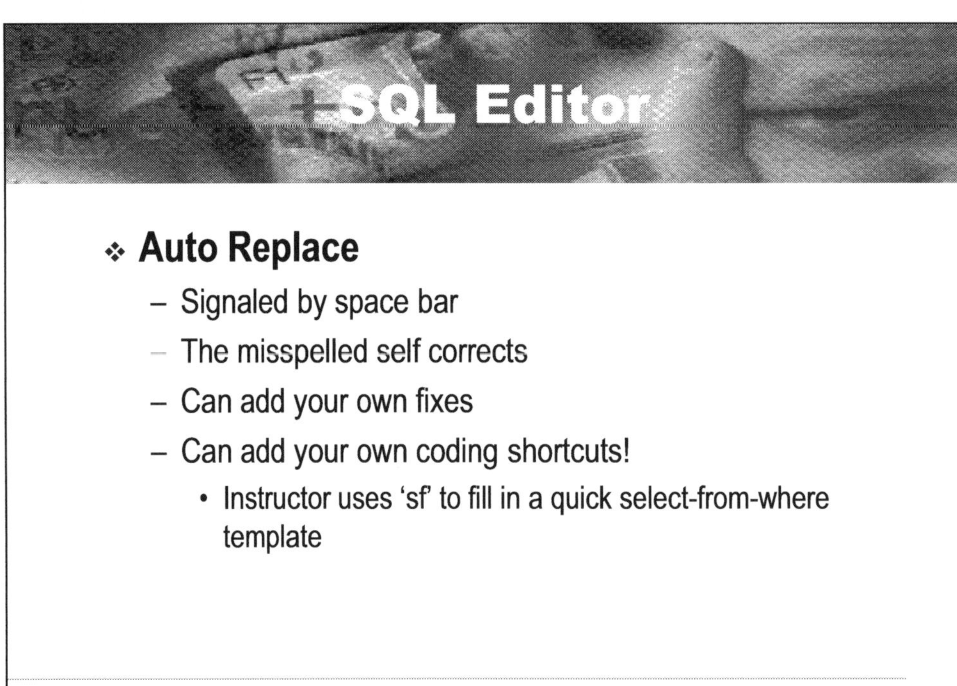
SQL Editor
Auto Replace
– Signaled by space bar
– The misspelled self corrects
– Can add your own fixes
– Can add your own coding shortcuts!
• Instructor uses 'sf' to fill in a quick select-from-where template
www.DanHotka.com

Auto replace is like a spell checker, in fact, this feature actually does correct some spelling errors, corrects obsolete code, etc. This feature is activated via the space bar. It takes the last item entered since the prior space bar and compares it to a list. If the text is found in the list, the auto replace item is automatically substituted.

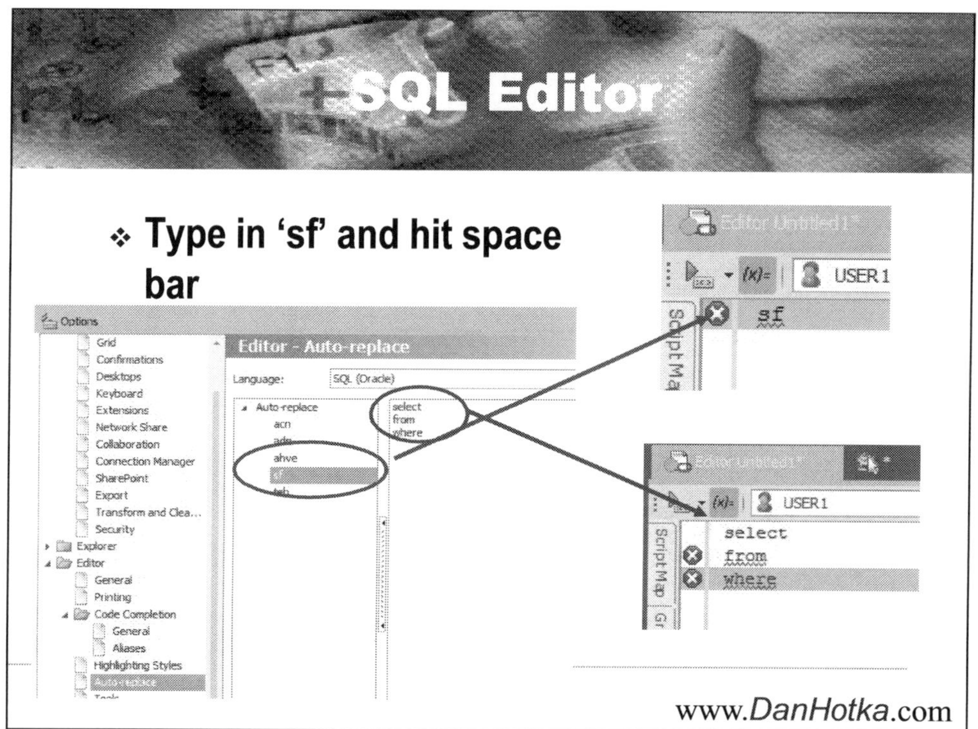
SQL Editor
Type in 'sf' and hit space bar
www.DanHotka.com

This feature is very nice for long column name perhaps but more for commonly entered items like 'sf' for 'SELECT * FROM' or 'pl' for 'DBMS_OUTPUT.PUTLINE( );'.

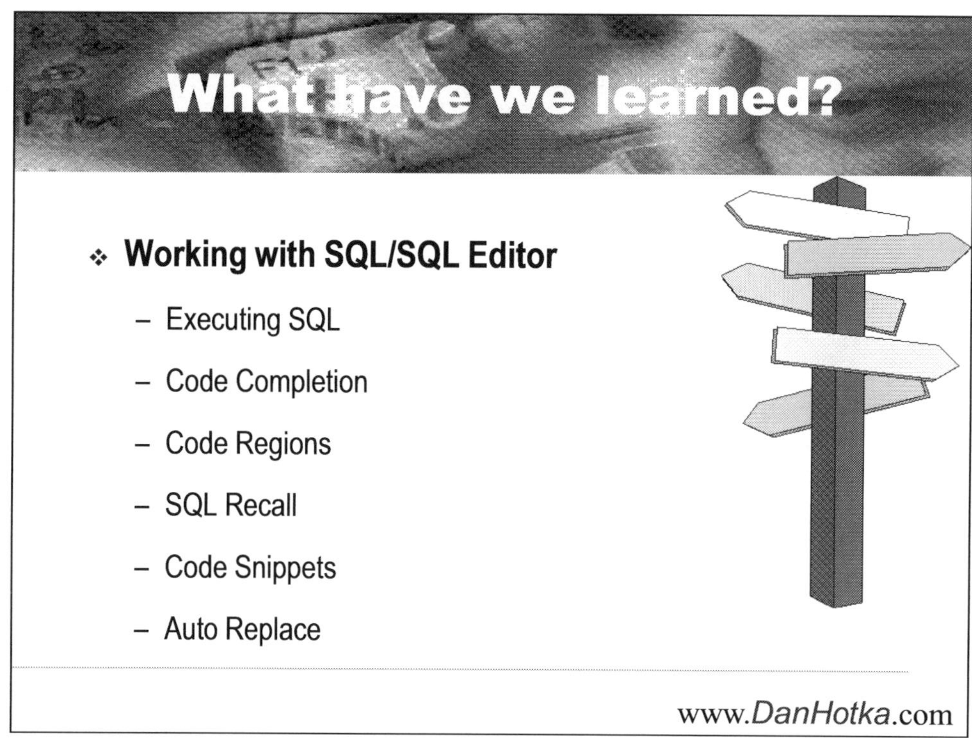
What have we learned?
Working with SQL/SQL Editor
– Executing SQL
– Code Completion
– Code Regions
– SQL Recall
– Code Snippets
– Auto Replace
www.DanHotka.com

## SQL Editor Summary

This unit has covered various aspects of the TOAD Editor. There are various ways to save keystrokes and various ways of having TOAD create SQL or contains SQL templates. Insights allows for easy access to object column names. This feature can save a lot of time when working with objects that have long column names. Column names can be dragged and dropped in via the Describe window and (not discussed yet) a Schema Browser window. The Editor even tracks all SQL entered and allows for it to be easily recalled.

## SQL Editor Lab

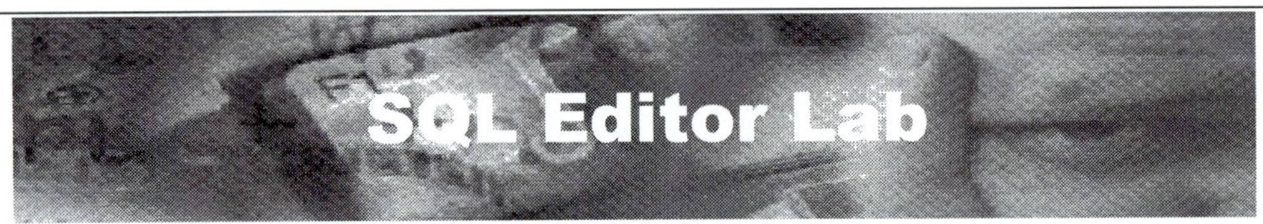


- **Working with SQL Lab**
  - Start the Editor
  - Create a SELECT statement from the EMP table
    - Or from one of your data tables
      - Pick a table with something we can add together
    - Execute your SQL
    - Show an explain plan
      - Did your SQL use an index?
  - Delete your SQL
  - Build a similar SQL using Code Completion
    - Ie: type in the select and from…then return to select and enter table name or table alias
    - Pick similar columns – can use multi select too…ctrl key then hit return
  - Check SQL Recall for your original SQL – pull it back in
  - Review code snippets for your chosen environment
    - If you have a date field…give a date for the following Monday
    - If you have
  - Add your own 'sf' template
    - Make sure it works

www.*DanHotka*.com

## SQL Editor Lab Answers

- Create a SELECT statement from the EMP table
  - Execute your SQL
  - Show an explain plan
    - Did your SQL use an index?
- Delete your SQL

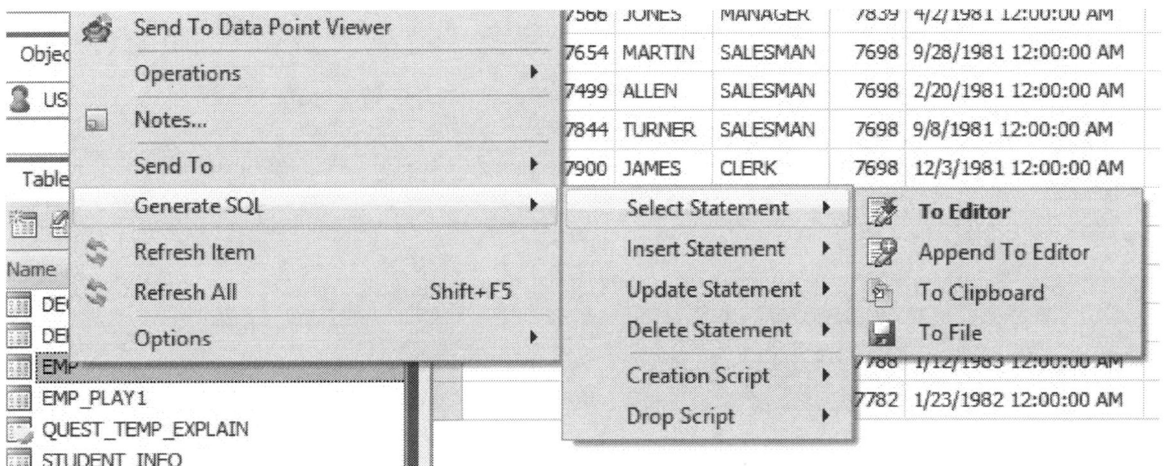


Right mouse click on your table (EMP in this case, follow the menus…

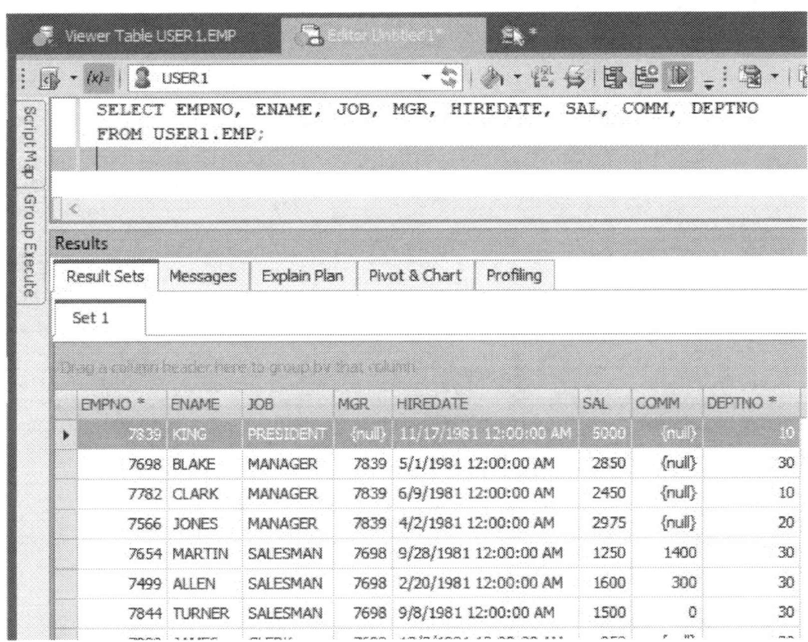

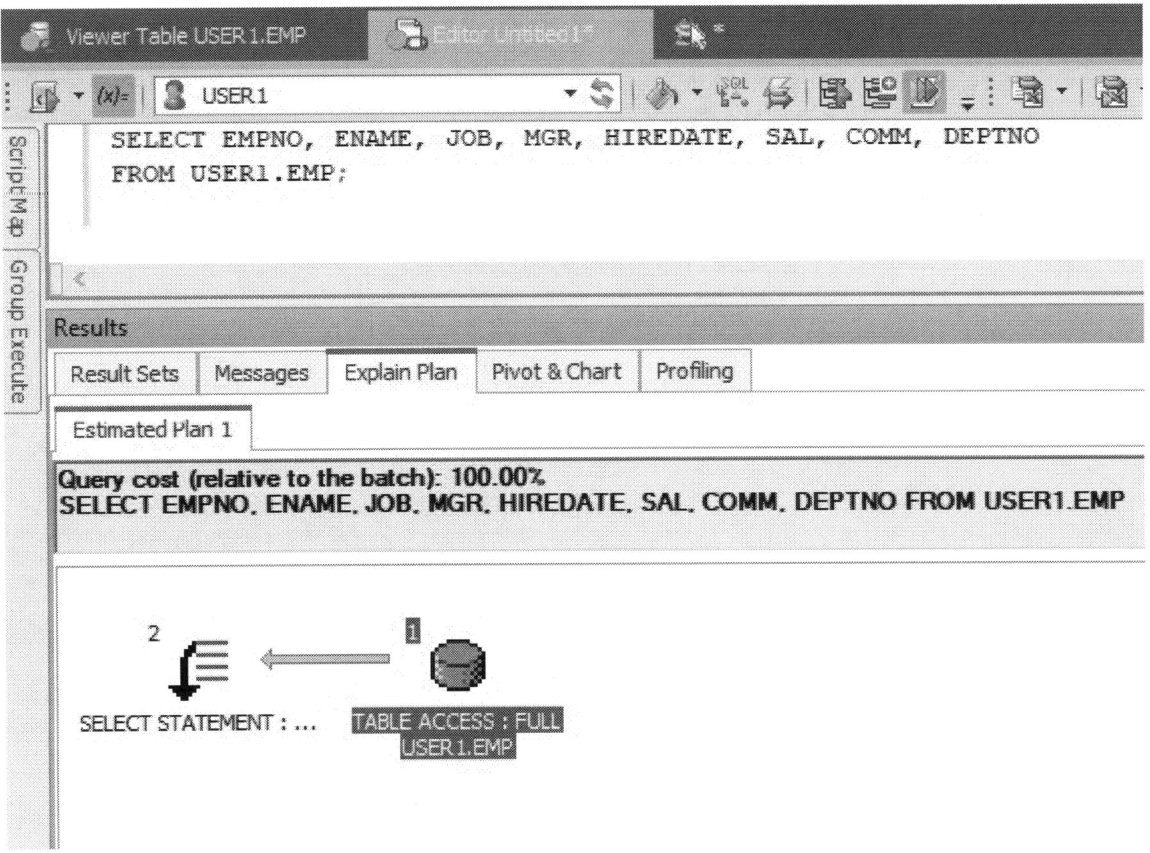


No indexes appear in this Explain Plan.

- Build a similar SQL using Code Completion
  - Ie: type in the select and from…then return to select and enter table name or table alias
  - Pick similar columns – can use multi select too…ctrl key then hit return

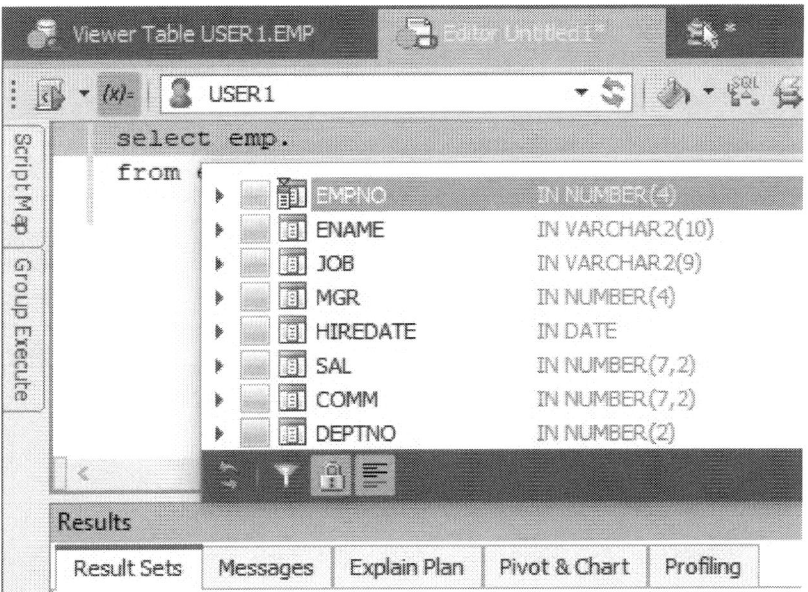


I start with a SELECT and on a new line FROM EMP…then you enter EMP. (or what ever table alias you may have used) and this popup comes up.

Select the columns one at a time by double clicking on them or select multiple (using the CTRL key held down) or select them all. These last 2 options…you use the Return key to get them into your SQL.

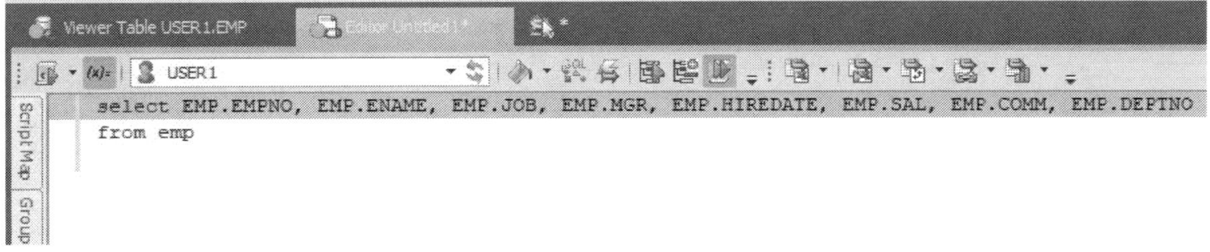


– Check SQL Recall for your original SQL – pull it back in

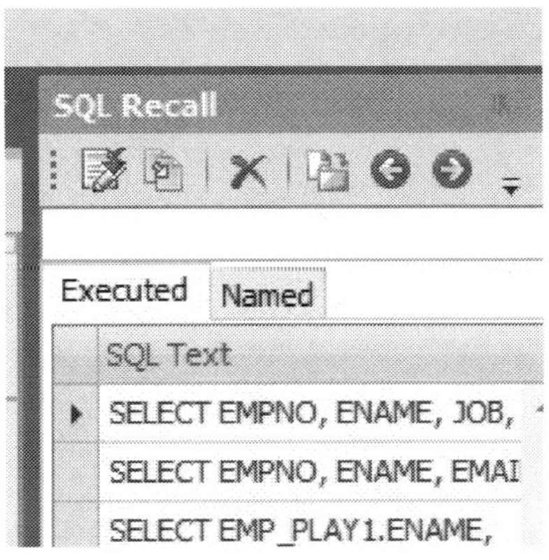


Press F8…your recent SQL should be near the top. You can right click on it to open it in an editor window, drag and drop it, or simply double click on it to move it to the current editor window.

- Review code snippets for your chosen environment
  - If you have a date field…give a date for the following Monday

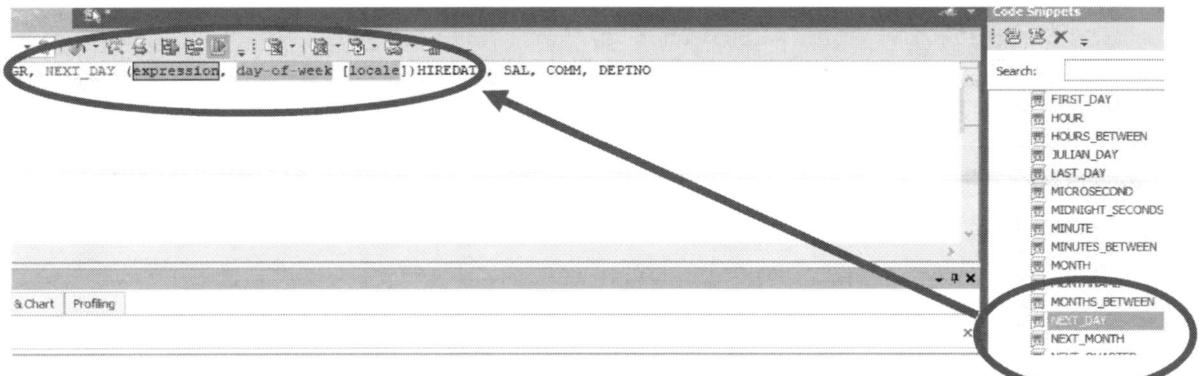


Find the code snippet of choice. Drag and drop it where you want it. We will be applying it to the HIREDATE field, but without any other input, this operation gives you all the syntax.

Clean it up, it looks like this:

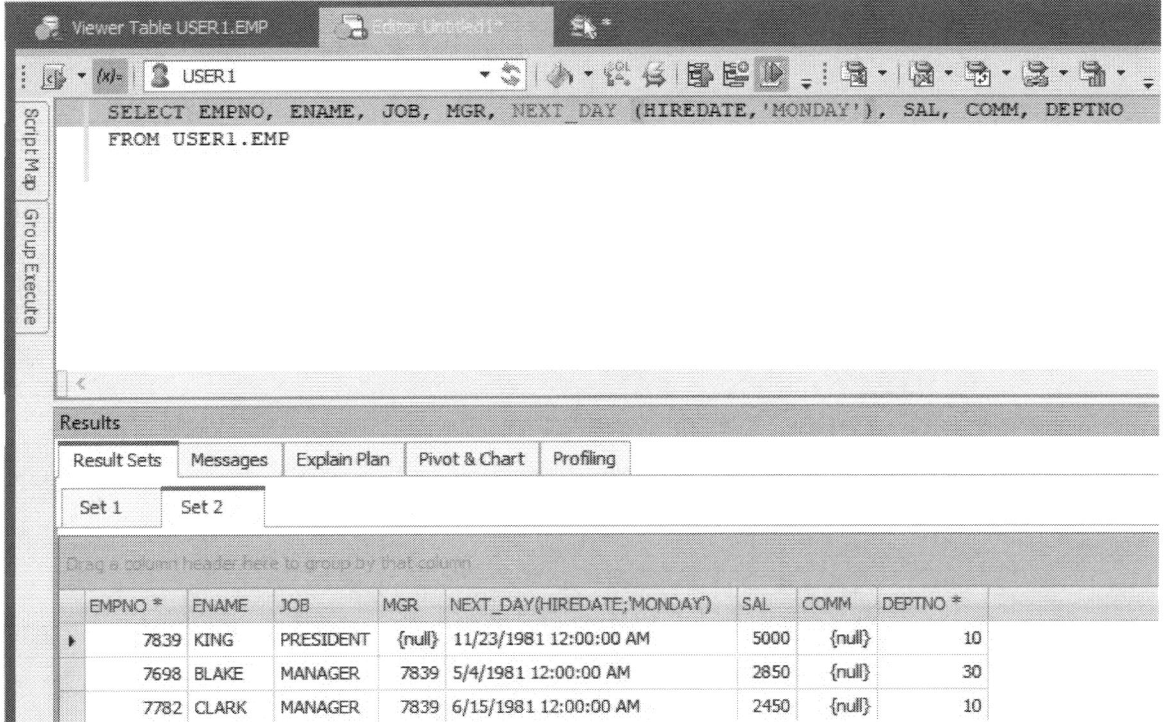

Adding your own shortcut is easy using Options → Editor → AutoReplace and adding it in there.

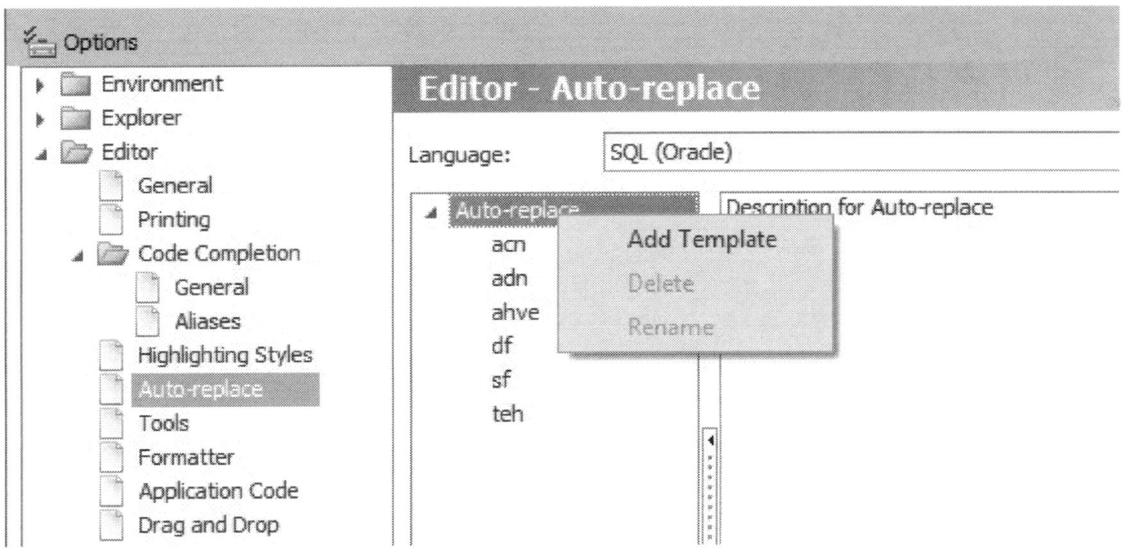

Right mouse click on the Auto Replace…(make sure to pick your database/language)…and select Add Template.

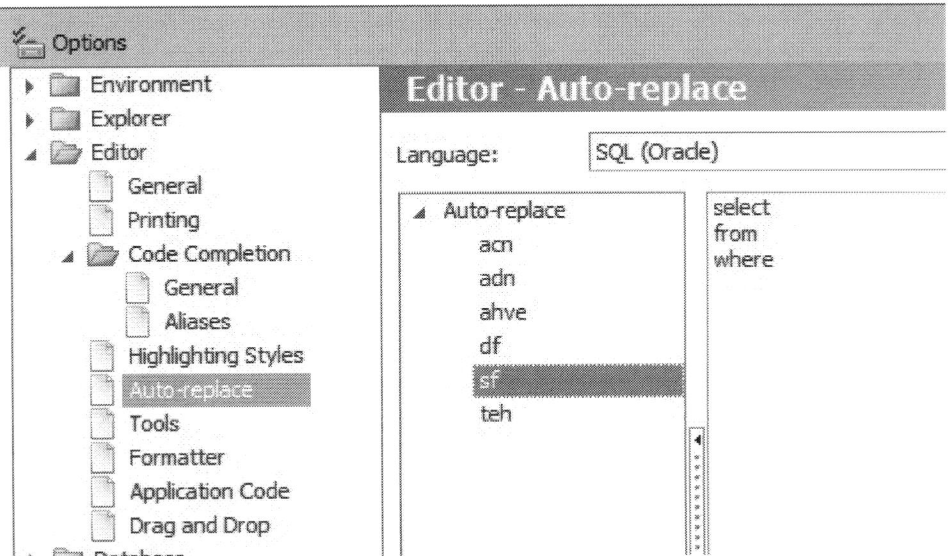


In the editor, when I type 'sf' and hit the space bar…I get this:

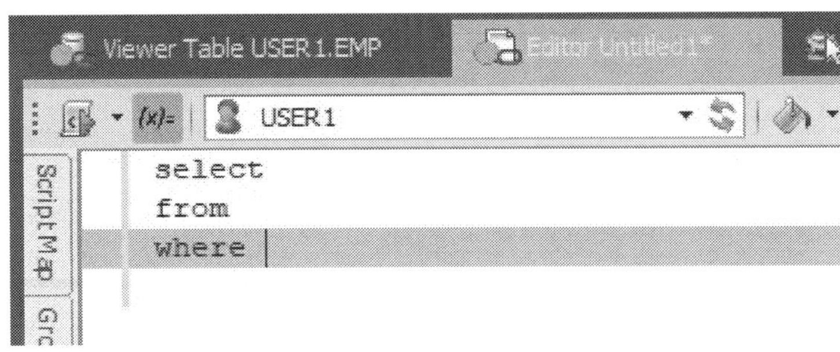

# Working with Toad Intelligence Central (TIC)

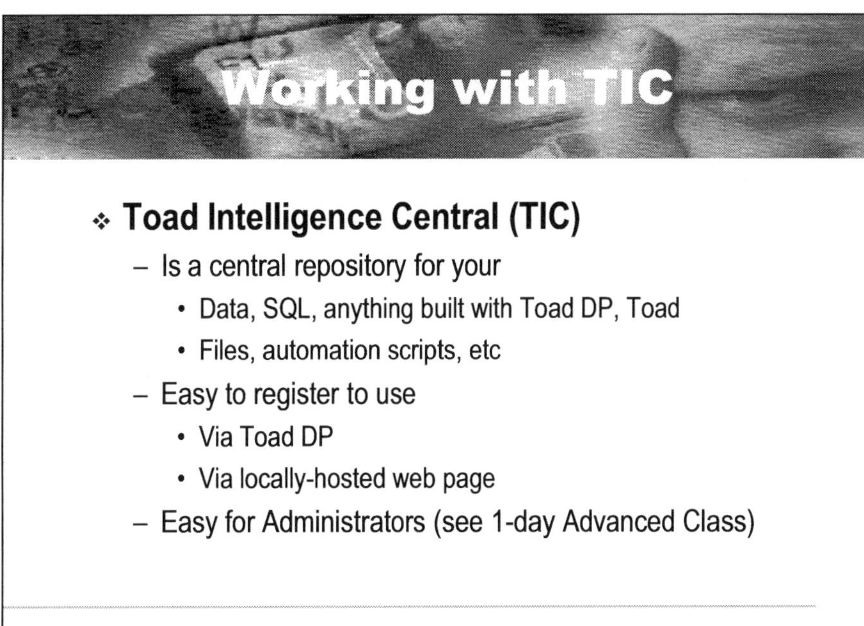
Working with TIC
Toad Intelligence Central (TIC)
– Is a central repository for your
• Data, SQL, anything built with Toad DP, Toad
• Files, automation scripts, etc
– Easy to register to use
• Via Toad DP
• Via locally-hosted web page
– Easy for Administrators (see 1-day Advanced Class)
www.DanHotka.com

## Register Users via Web Interface

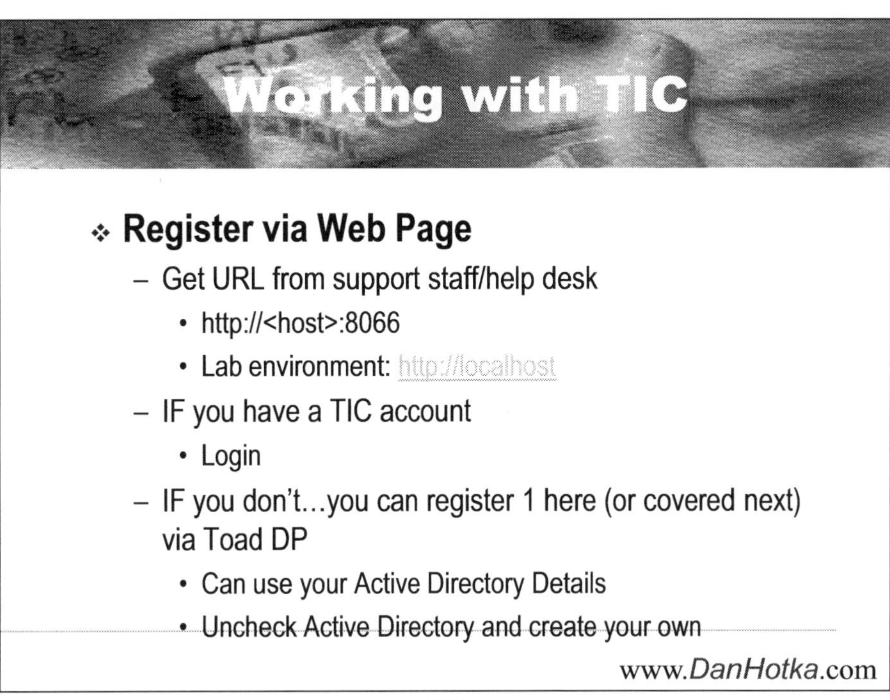
Working with TIC
Register via Web Page
– Get URL from support staff/help desk
• http://<host>:8066
• Lab environment: http://localhost
– IF you have a TIC account
• Login
– IF you don't…you can register 1 here (or covered next) via Toad DP
• Can use your Active Directory Details
• Uncheck Active Directory and create your own
www.DanHotka.com

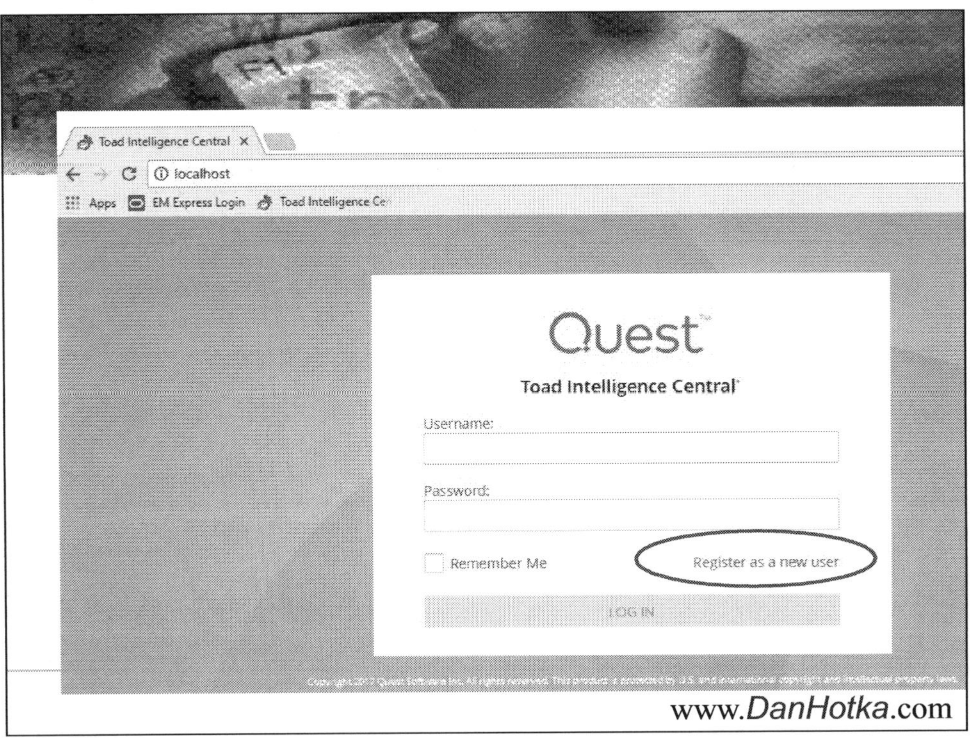


## Working with TIC

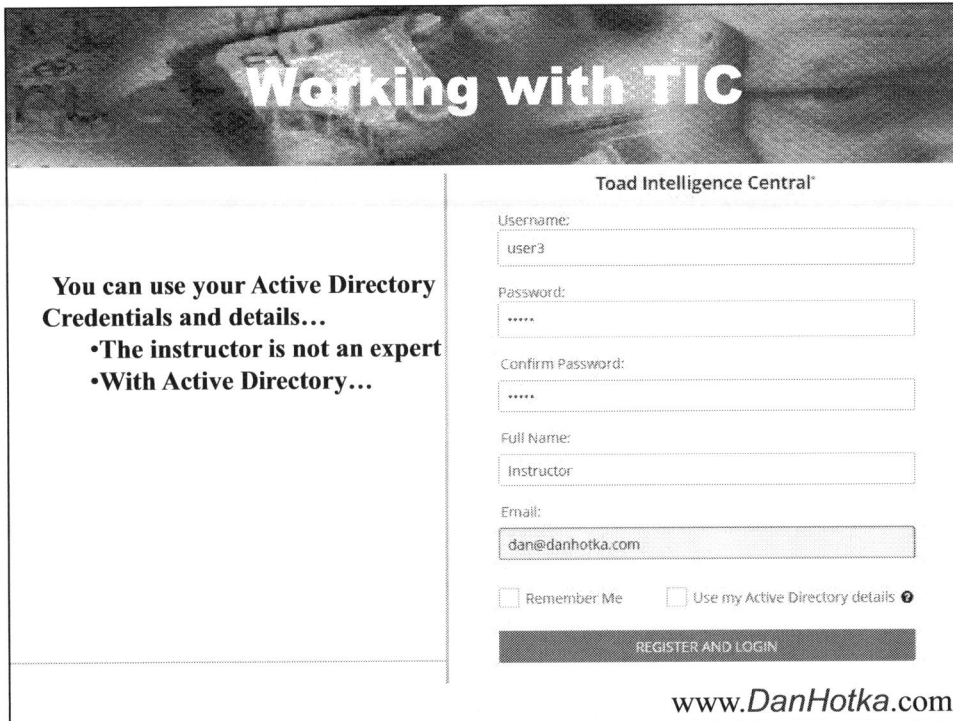

**You can use your Active Directory Credentials and details…**

- **The instructor is not an expert**
- **With Active Directory…**

Toad Intelligence Central

Username: user3

Password: •••••

Confirm Password: •••••

Full Name: Instructor

Email: dan@danhotka.com

Remember Me | Use my Active Directory details

REGISTER AND LOGIN

www.DanHotka.com

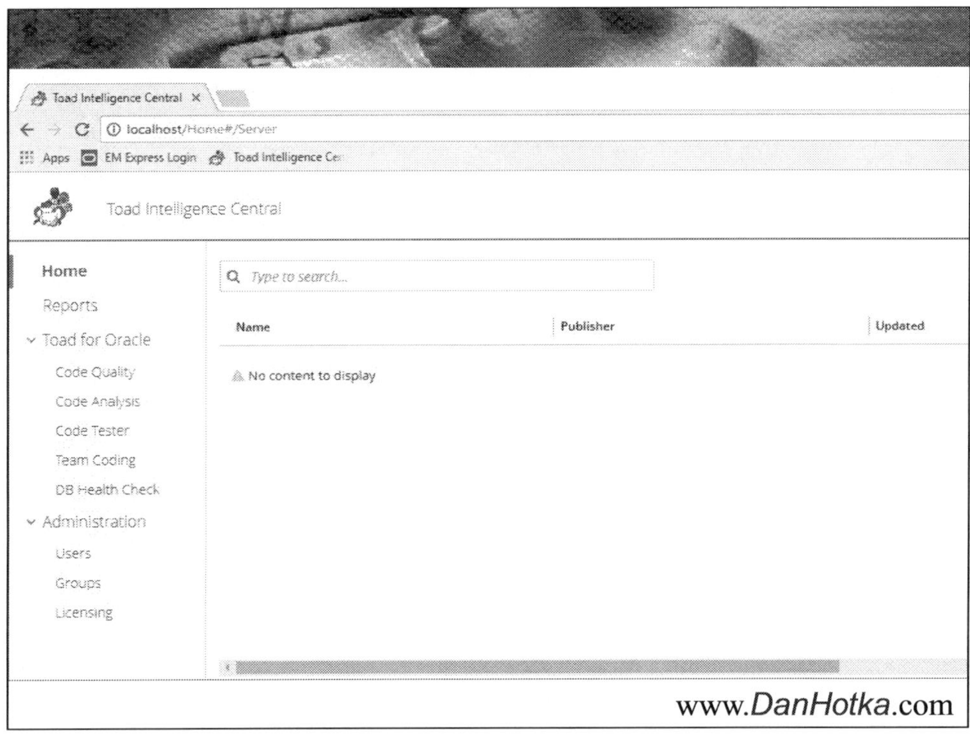


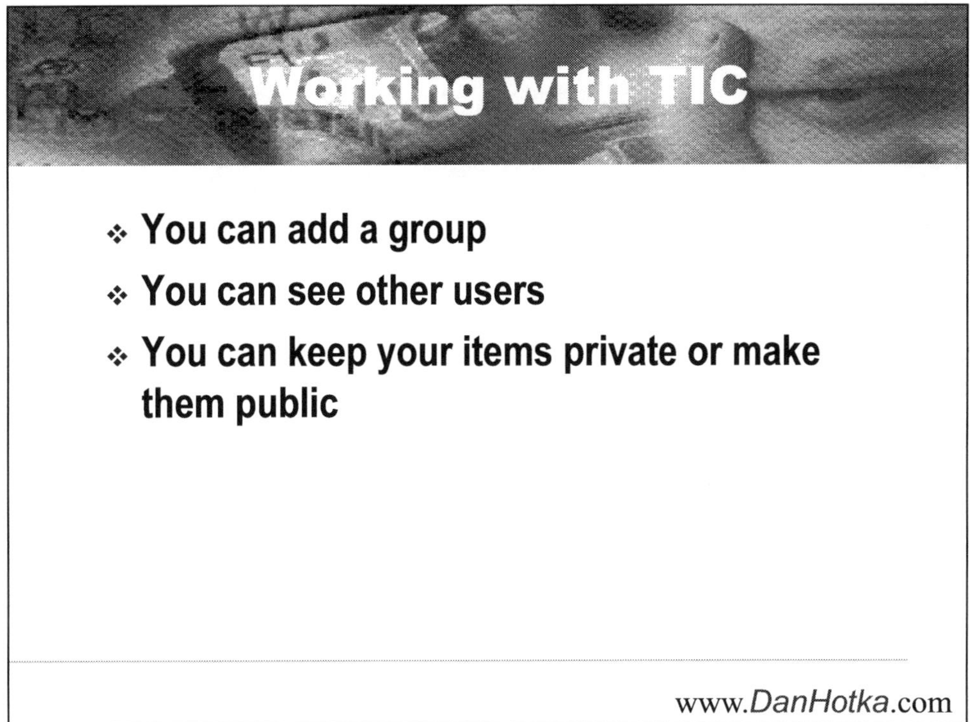


Intelligence Central is a repository for sharing information. You decide who can see it/use it/modify it.

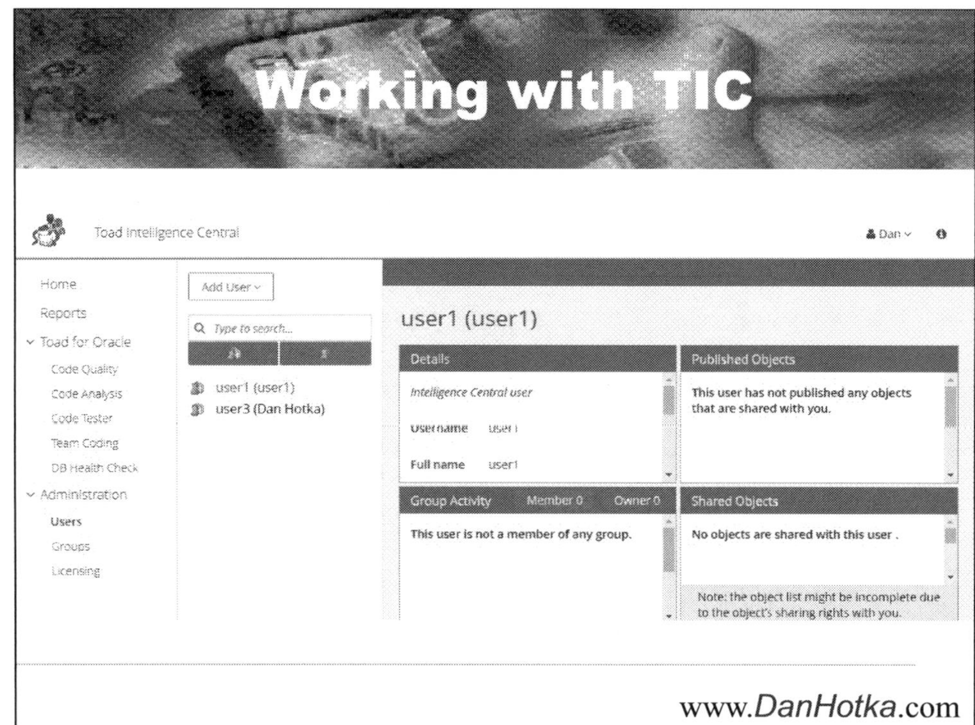
Working with TIC
Toad Intelligence Central
Dan
Home
Reports
Toad for Oracle
Code Quality
Code Analysis
Code Tester
Team Coding
DB Health Check
Administration
Users
Groups
Licensing
Add User
Type to search...
user1 (user1)
user3 (Dan Hotka)
user1 (user1)
Details
Intelligence Central user
Username user1
Full name user1
Published Objects
This user has not published any objects that are shared with you.
Group Activity Member 0 Owner 0
This user is not a member of any group.
Shared Objects
No objects are shared with this user .
Note: the object list might be incomplete due to the object's sharing rights with you.
www.DanHotka.com

TIC is pretty easy to use and to download any item to your work station. You can use the web interface at any time.

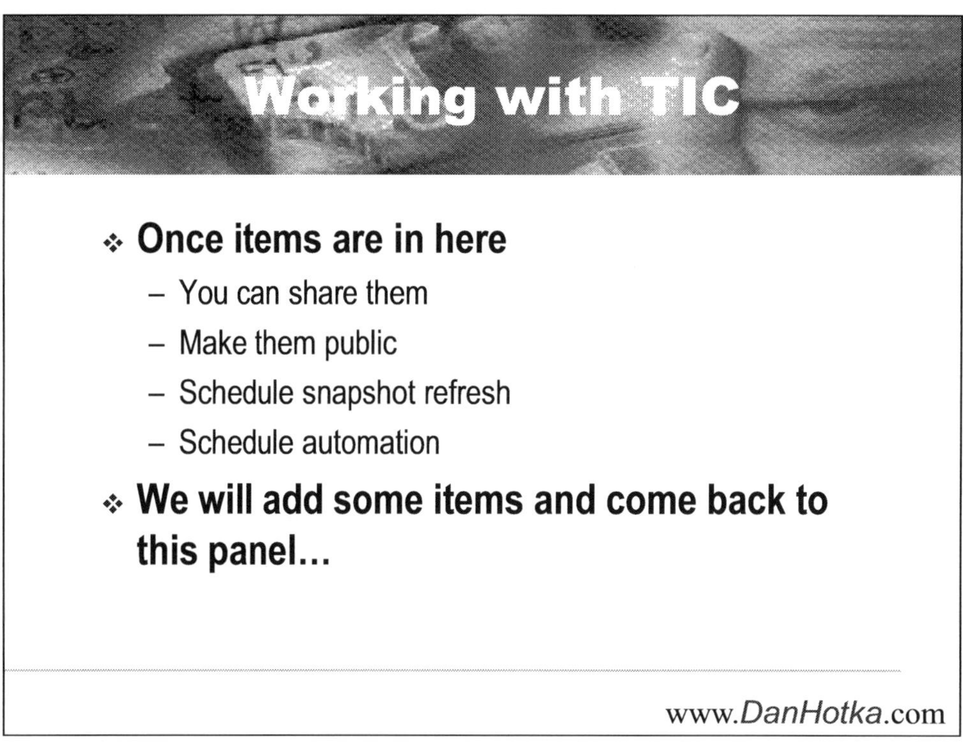
Working with TIC
Once items are in here
– You can share them
– Make them public
– Schedule snapshot refresh
– Schedule automation
We will add some items and come back to this panel…
www.DanHotka.com

## Registering Users via Toad DP

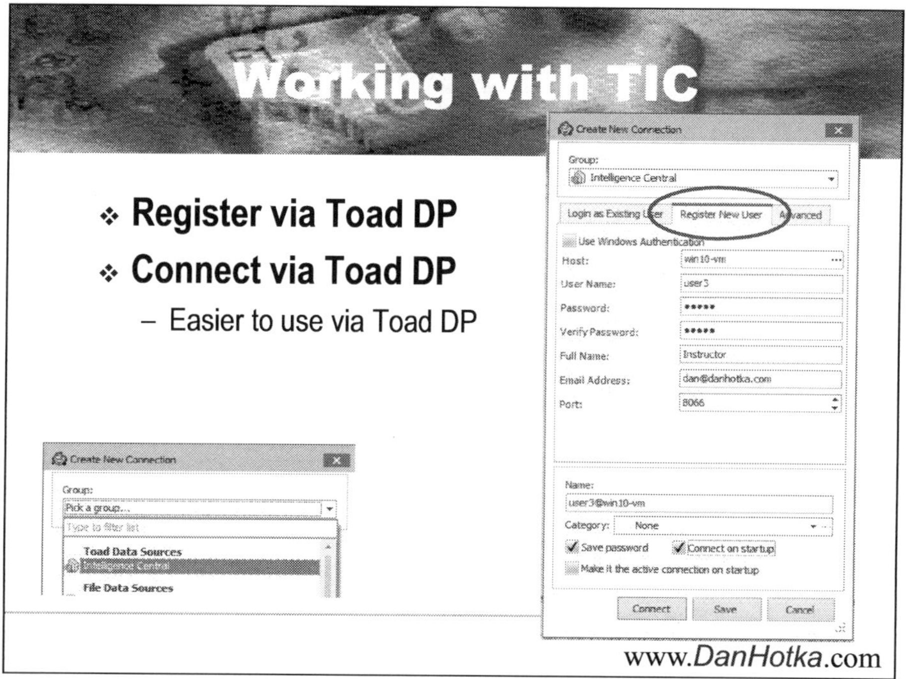


Toad DP has a nice interface to TIC. You can register yourself from Create New Connection.

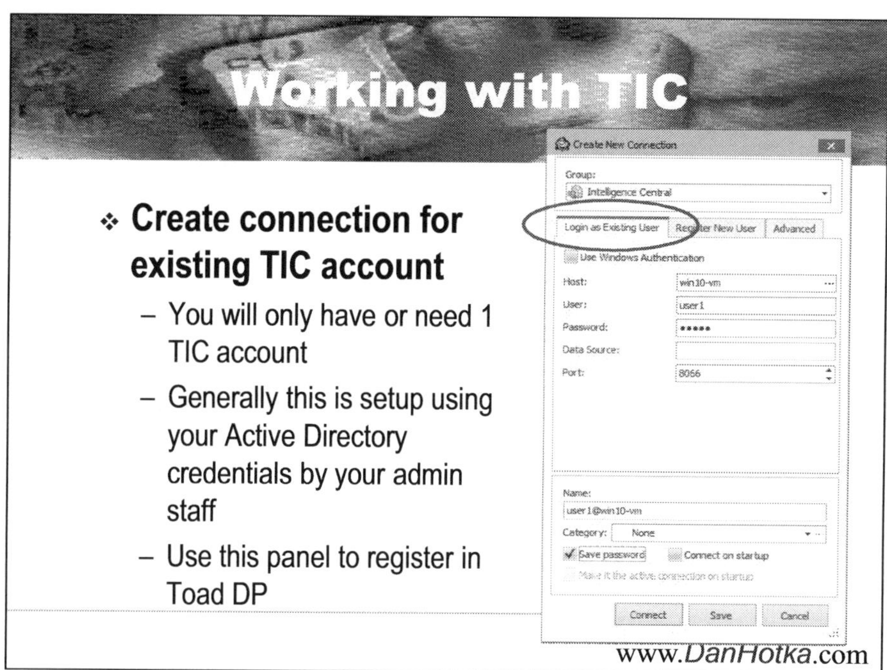

## Working with TIC

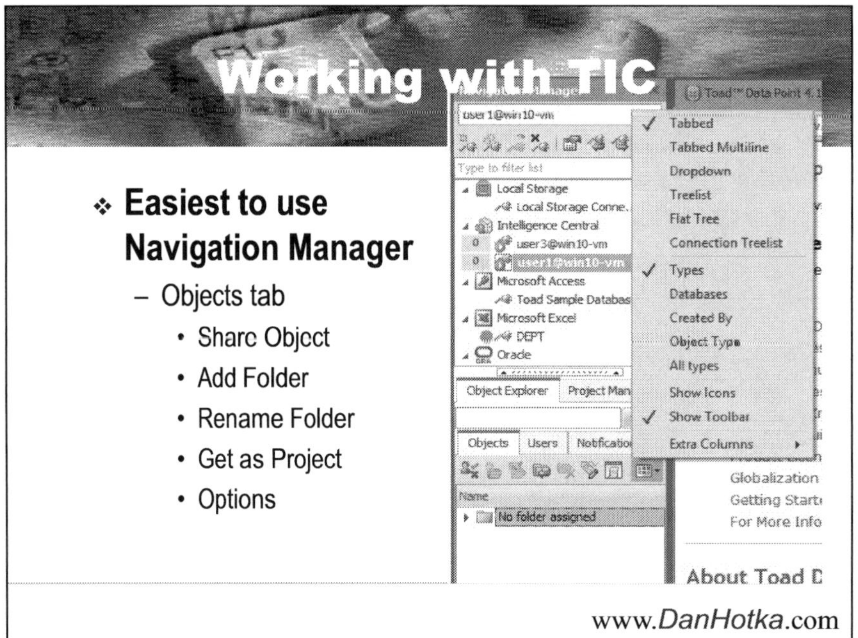


Navigating around in TIC from Toad DP is a snap using the Navigation Manager. It works roughly like any other data store in Toad DP. The right-mouse click items are appropriate for the item you are working with as well.

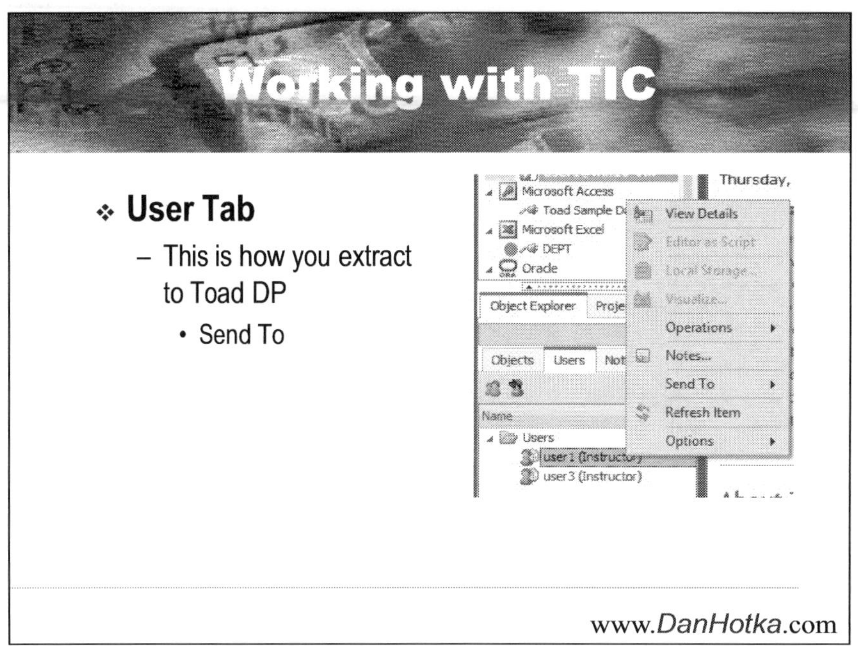

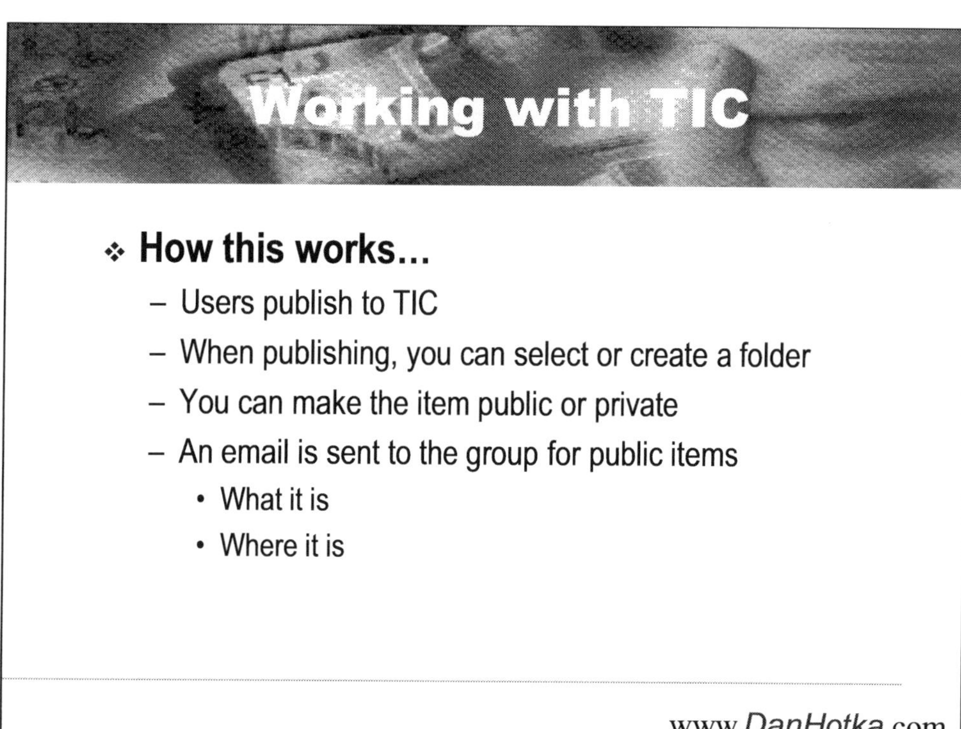
Working with TIC
How this works…
– Users publish to TIC
– When publishing, you can select or create a folder
– You can make the item public or private
– An email is sent to the group for public items
• What it is
• Where it is
www.DanHotka.com

**Publishing to TIC**

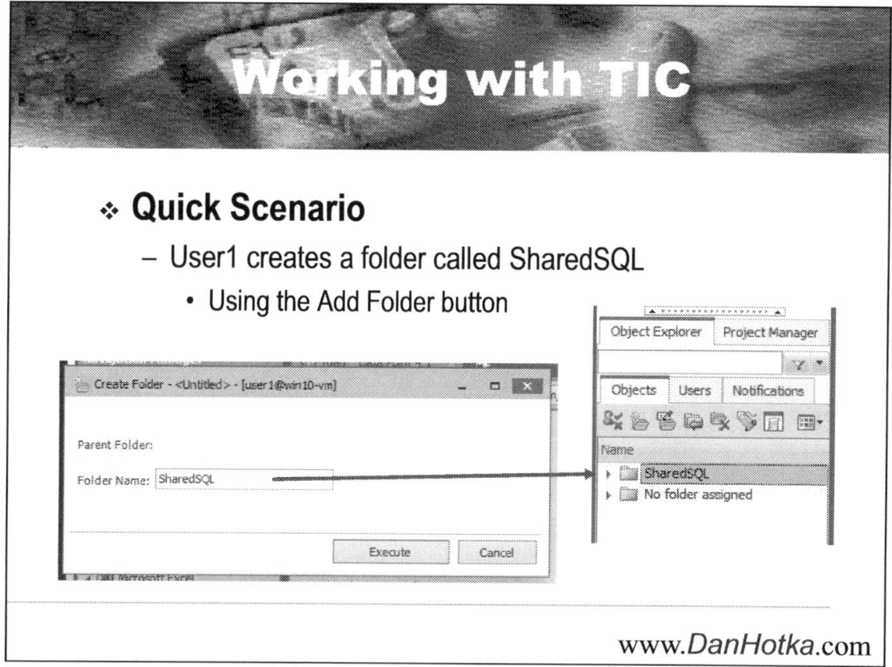
Working with TIC
Quick Scenario
– User1 creates a folder called SharedSQL
• Using the Add Folder button
Parent Folder:
Folder Name: SharedSQL
Execute
Cancel
Object Explorer
Project Manager
Objects
Users
Notifications
Name
SharedSQL
No folder assigned
www.DanHotka.com

When publishing, you can create a new folder or select an existing one. When announcing, you can have an email sent with the location and link of the item.

- **User1 creates some SQL and publishes to TIC**
  - You can publish the SQL
  - You can publish the data as a Snapshot

www.*DanHotka*.com

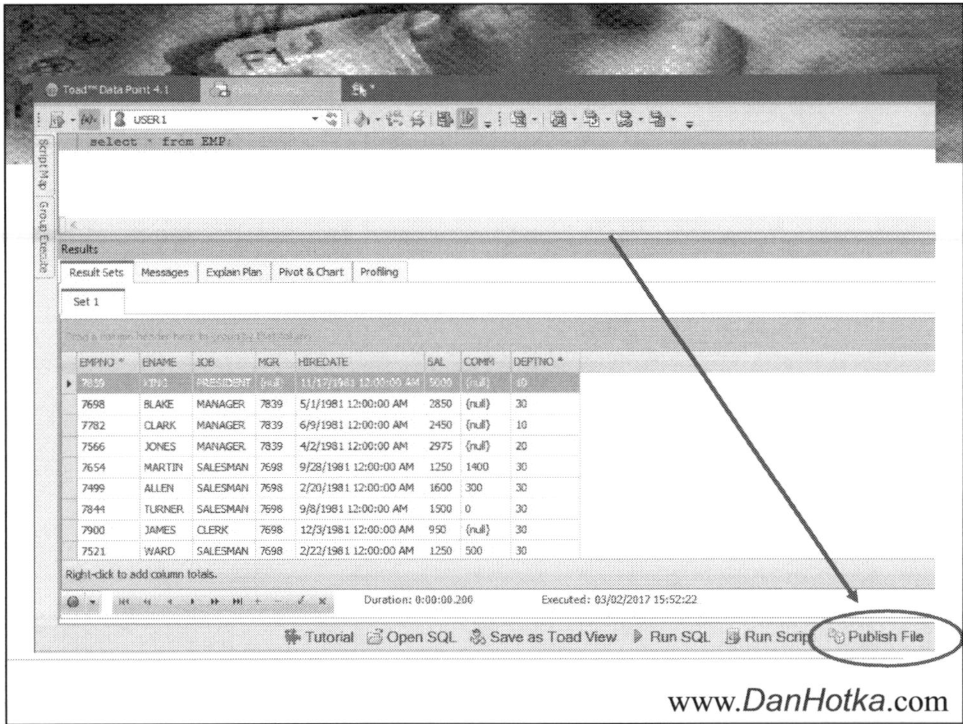


www.*DanHotka*.com

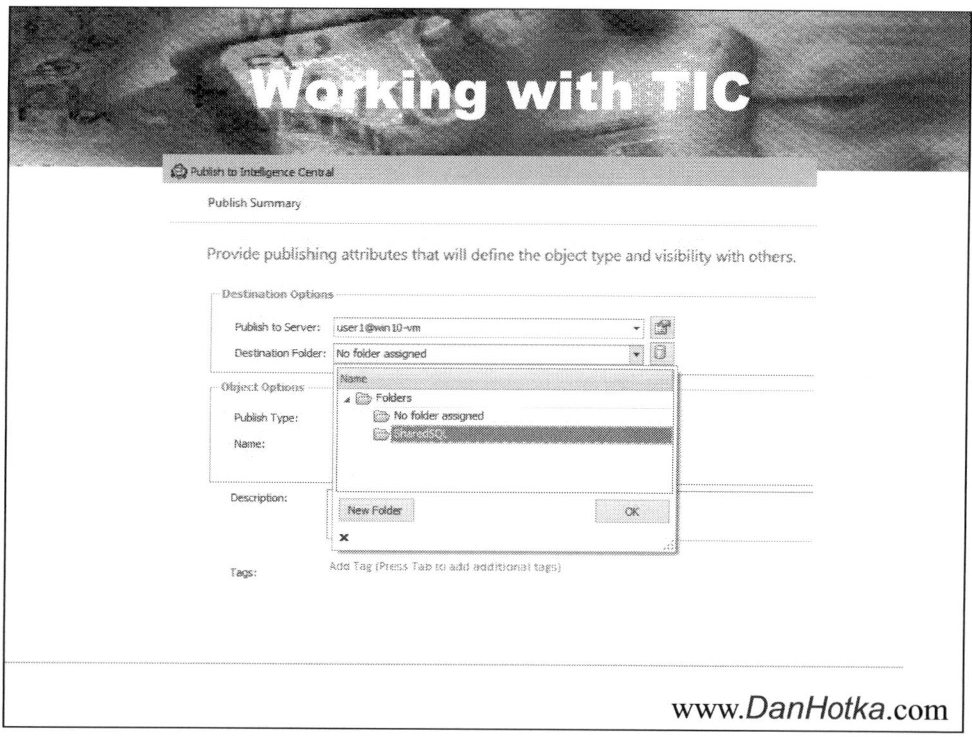
Working with TIC
Publish to Intelligence Central
Publish Summary
Provide publishing attributes that will define the object type and visibility with others.
Destination Options
Publish to Server:
user1@win10-vm
Destination Folder:
No folder assigned
Name
Folders
No folder assigned
SharedSQL
Object Options
Publish Type:
Name:
Description:
New Folder
OK
Tags:
Add Tag (Press Tab to add additional tags)
www.DanHotka.com

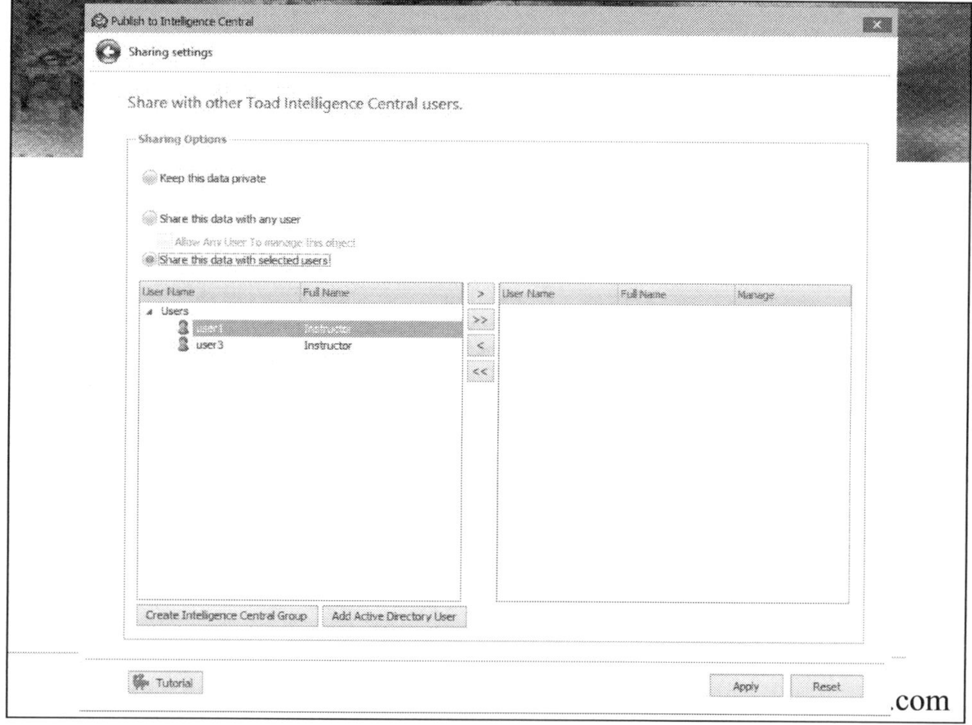
Publish to Intelligence Central
Sharing settings
Share with other Toad Intelligence Central users.
Sharing Options
Keep this data private
Share this data with any user
Allow Any User To manage this object
Share this data with selected users
User Name
Full Name
Users
user1
Instructor
user3
Instructor
User Name
Full Name
Manage
Create Intelligence Central Group
Add Active Directory User
Tutorial
Apply
Reset
.com

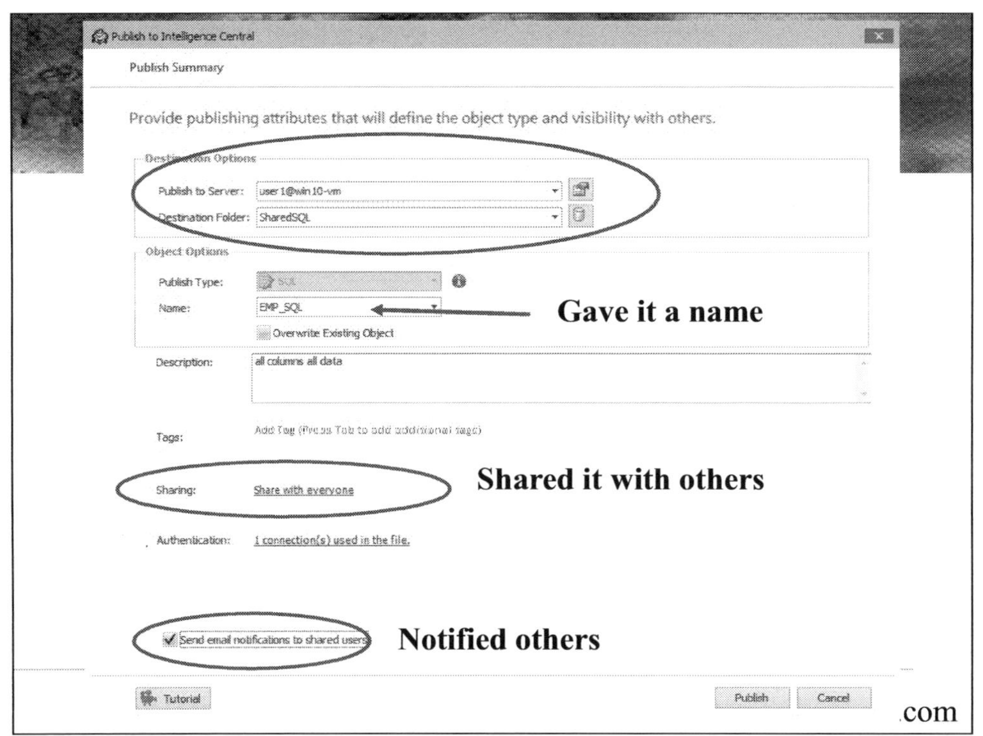
Publish to Intelligence Central
Publish Summary
Provide publishing attributes that will define the object type and visibility with others.
Destination Options
Publish to Server: user1@win10-vm
Destination Folder: SharedSQL
Object Options
Publish Type:
Name: EMP_SQL
Gave it a name
Overwrite Existing Object
Description: all columns all data
Tags:
Sharing: Share with everyone
Shared it with others
Authentication: 1 connection(s) used in the file.
Send email notifications to shared users
Notified others
Tutorial
Publish
Cancel
.com

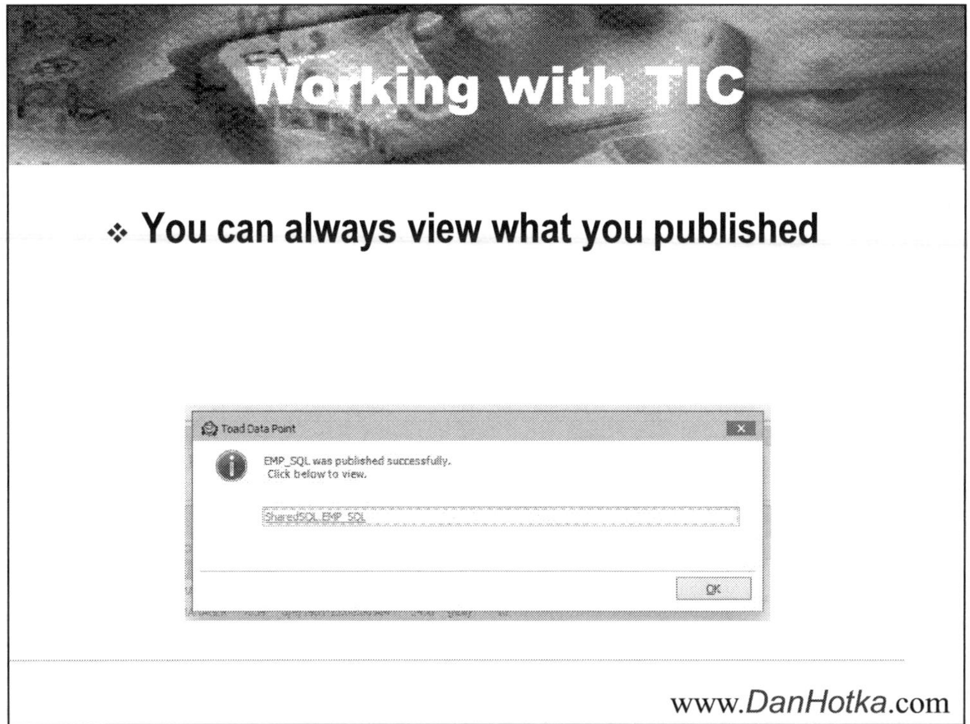
Working with TIC
You can always view what you published
Toad Data Point
EMP_SQL was published successfully.
Click below to view.
SharedSQL.EMP_SQL
OK
www.DanHotka.com

## Retrieving from TIC

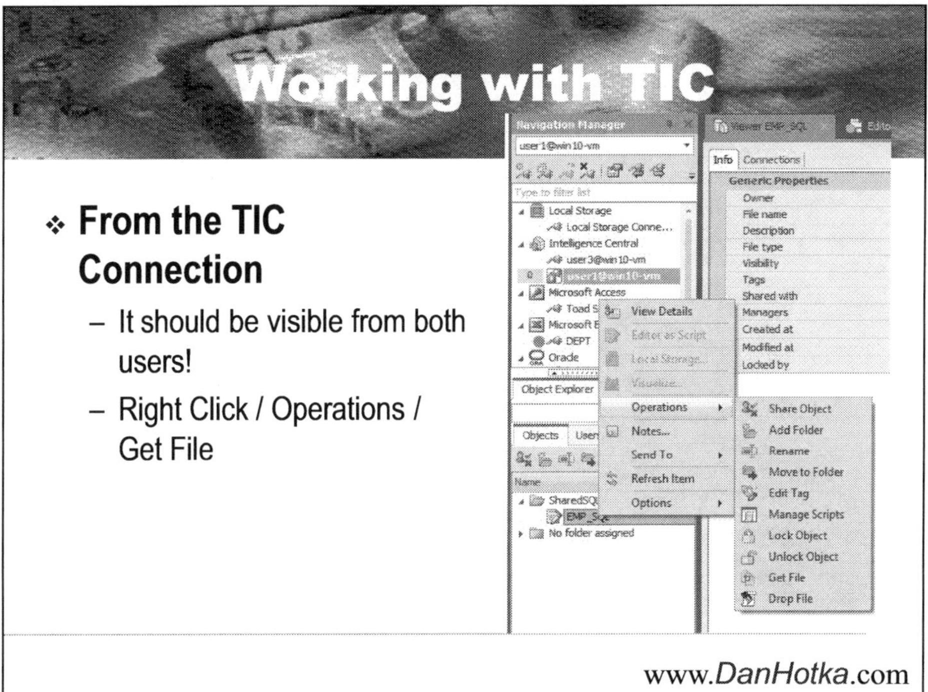

*****Tip***** copy and paste the SQL into the Editor…there are more options here than the window it opens in out of TIC. Remember…right-mouse click is your friend in Toad DP

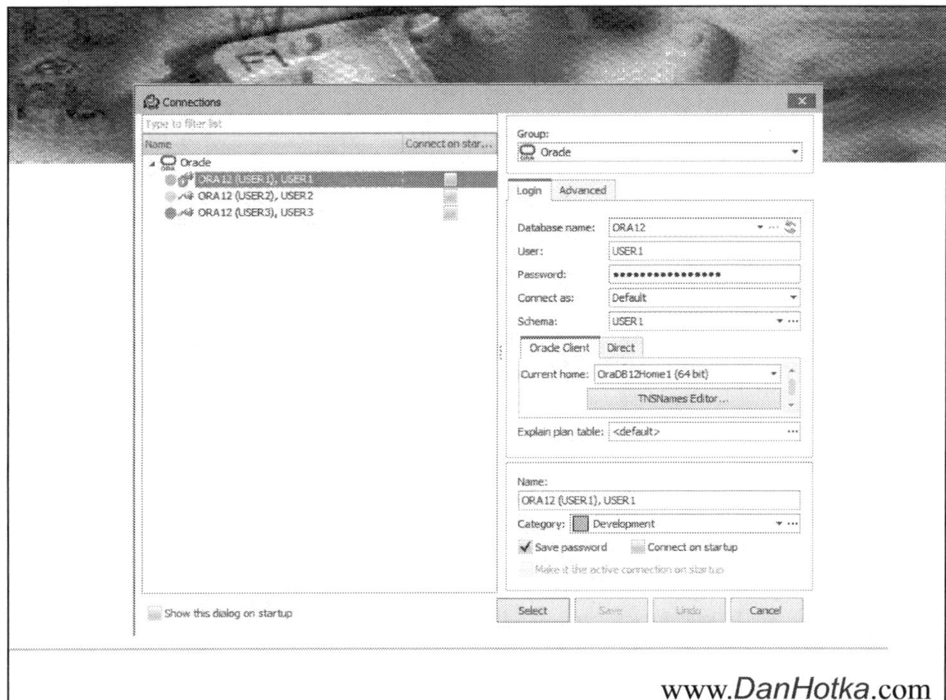

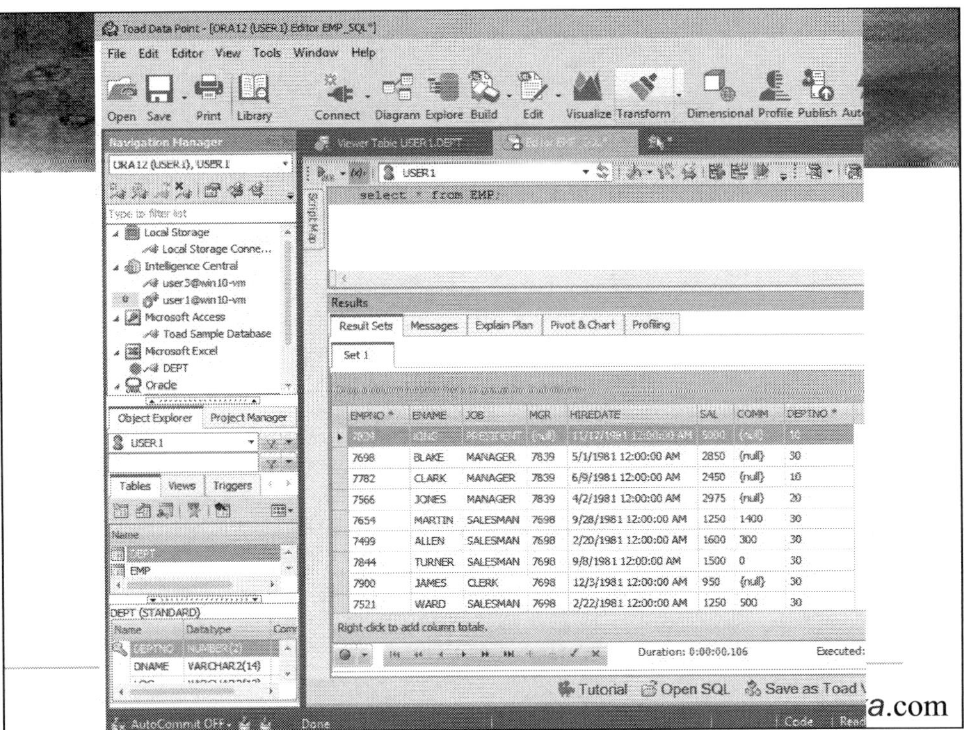

Toad Data Point - [ORA12 (USER1) Editor EMP_SQL*]
File Edit Editor View Tools Window Help
Open Save Print Library Connect Diagram Explore Build Edit Visualize Transform Dimensional Profile Publish
Navigation Manager
Local Storage
Intelligence Central
Microsoft Access
Toad Sample Database
Microsoft Excel
DEPT
Oracle
Object Explorer Project Manager
Tables Views Triggers
DEPT
EMP
select * from EMP;
Results
Result Sets Messages Explain Plan Pivot & Chart Profiling
Set 1
EMPNO ENAME JOB MGR HIREDATE SAL COMM DEPTNO
7698 BLAKE MANAGER 7839 5/1/1981 12:00:00 AM 2850 {null} 30
7782 CLARK MANAGER 7839 6/9/1981 12:00:00 AM 2450 {null} 10
7566 JONES MANAGER 7839 4/2/1981 12:00:00 AM 2975 {null} 20
7654 MARTIN SALESMAN 7698 9/28/1981 12:00:00 AM 1250 1400 30
7499 ALLEN SALESMAN 7698 2/20/1981 12:00:00 AM 1600 300 30
7844 TURNER SALESMAN 7698 9/8/1981 12:00:00 AM 1500 0 30
7900 JAMES CLERK 7698 12/3/1981 12:00:00 AM 950 {null} 30
7521 WARD SALESMAN 7698 2/22/1981 12:00:00 AM 1250 500 30
Right click to add column totals.
Tutorial Open SQL Save as Toad
a.com


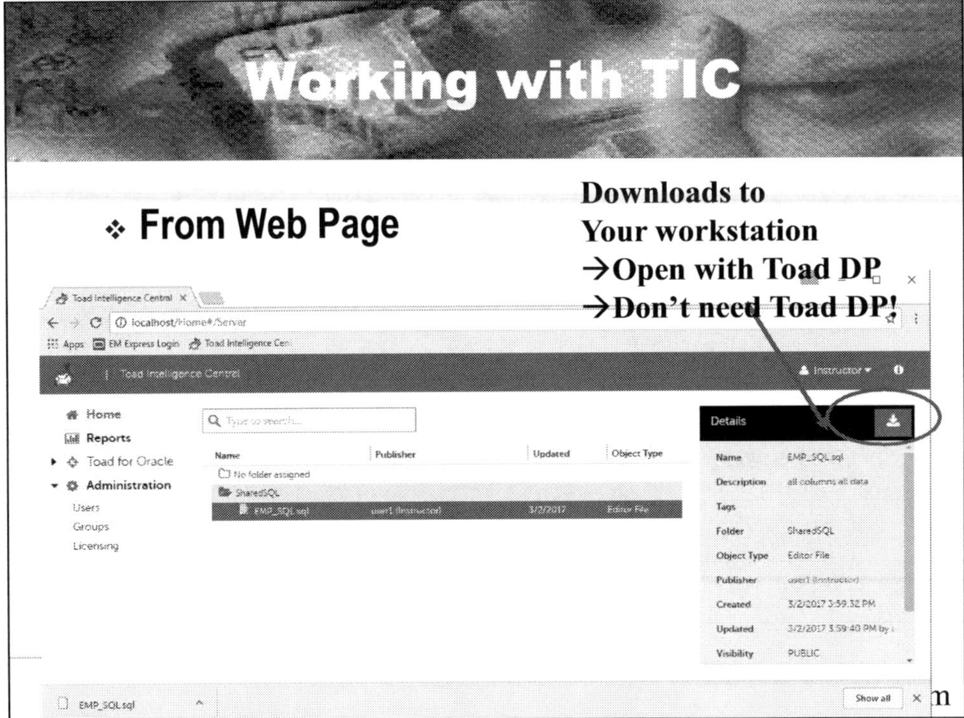

Working with TIC
From Web Page
Downloads to
Your workstation
→Open with Toad DP
→Don't need Toad DP!
Toad Intelligence Central
Home
Reports
Toad for Oracle
Administration
Users
Groups
Licensing
Details
Name EMP_SQL.sql
Folder SharedSQL
Object Type Editor File
Visibility PUBLIC
EMP_SQL.sql
Show all


You can use the TIC as a repository to share most anything with anyone! It's not just for Toad Data Point. You don't even need Toad DP! For example, you can open a saved Excel file using Excel.

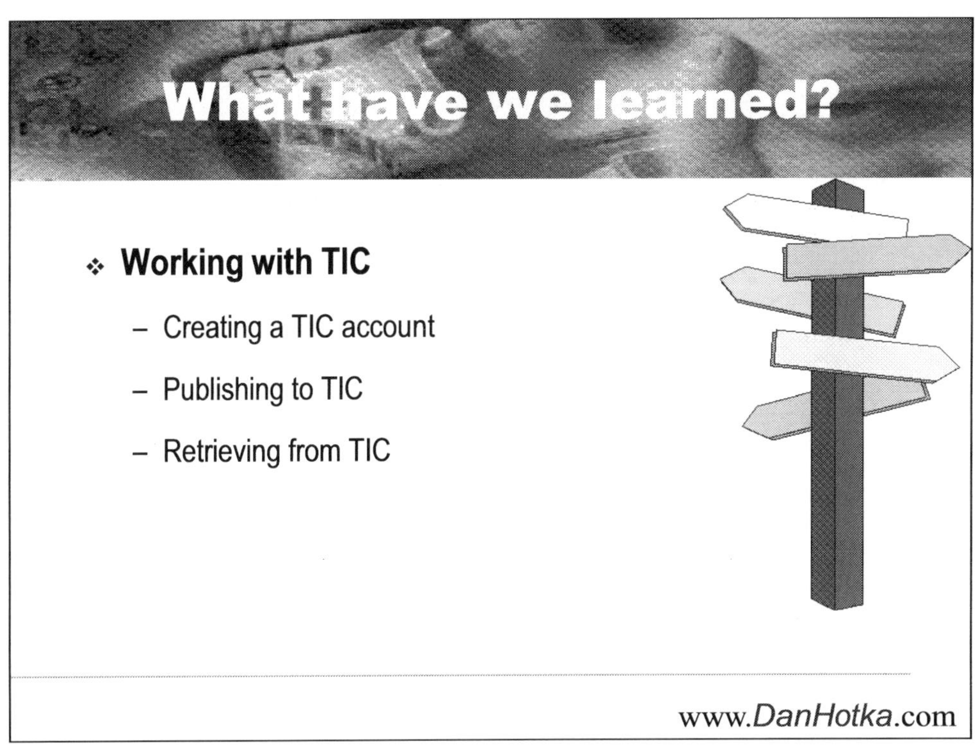
What have we learned?
Working with TIC
– Creating a TIC account
– Publishing to TIC
– Retrieving from TIC
www.DanHotka.com

## Working with TIC Lab

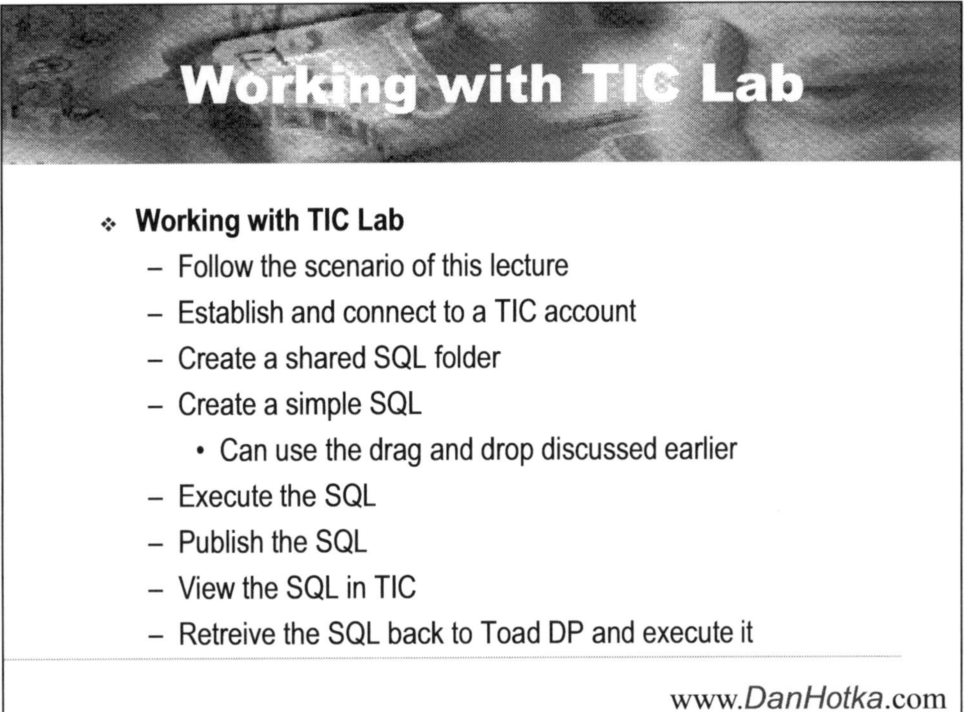
Working with TIC Lab
Working with TIC Lab
– Follow the scenario of this lecture
– Establish and connect to a TIC account
– Create a shared SQL folder
– Create a simple SQL
• Can use the drag and drop discussed earlier
– Execute the SQL
– Publish the SQL
– View the SQL in TIC
– Retreive the SQL back to Toad DP and execute it
www.DanHotka.com

## Working with TIC Lab Answers

Please open the course guide and navigate to 'Working with Toad Intelligence Central (TIC)'.

Please work the examples on each page. If you get stuck, please ask the instructor for help.

## Toad Workbook

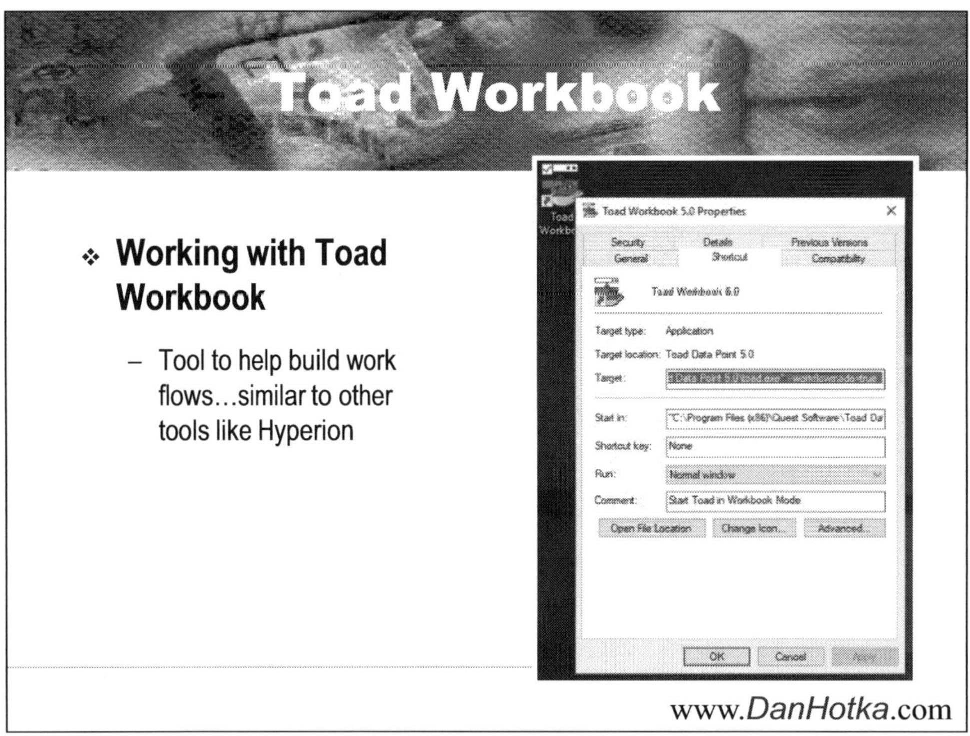


Toad Workbook is just a version of Toad Data Point. This feature allows you to build work flows easier than using the Automation tool and in a similar fashion that you might be used to using other BI tools such as Hyperion.

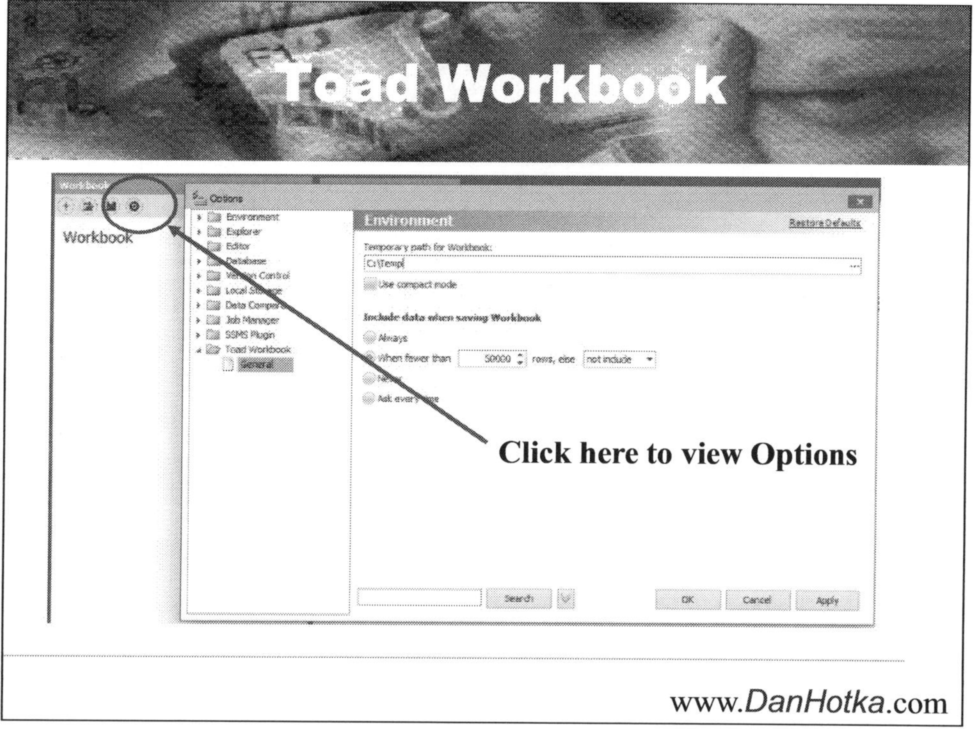


This is where the workbook will be built until you save it. The author usually changes these to the TEMP folder on his workstation.

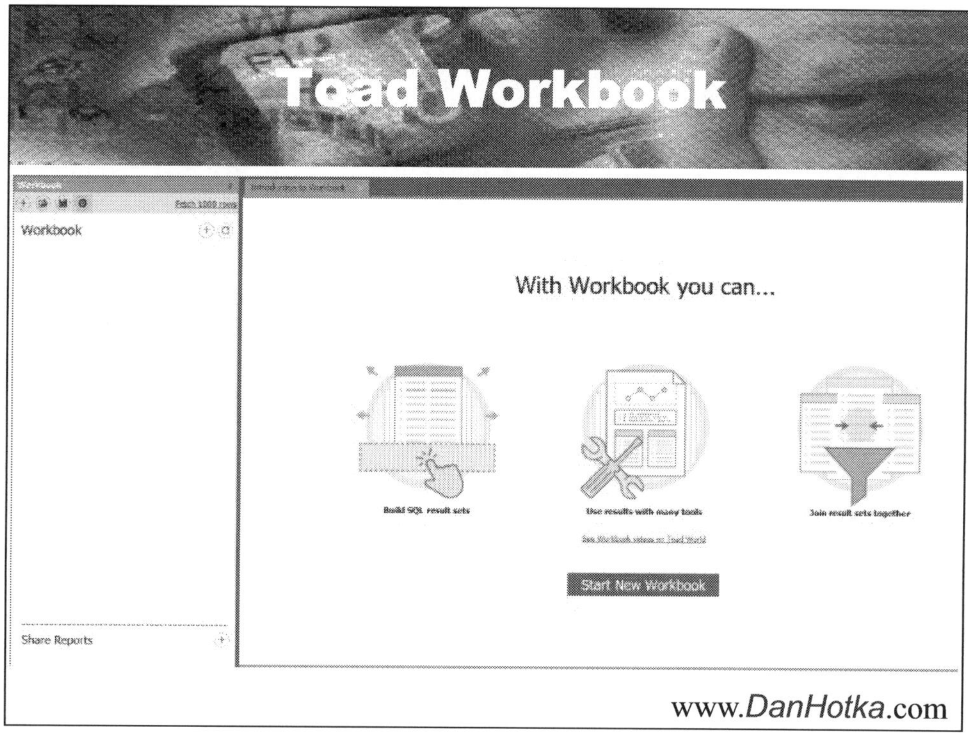


Lots of help…these are nice short video walk through's of each step of a workbook.

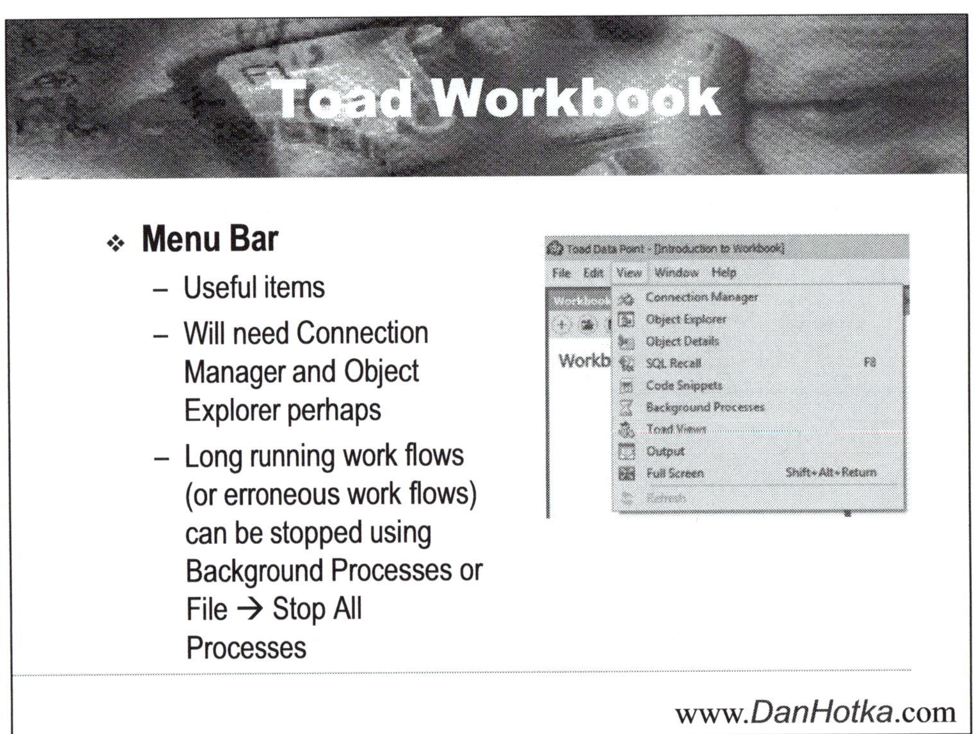
Toad Workbook
Menu Bar
– Useful items
– Will need Connection Manager and Object Explorer perhaps
– Long running work flows (or erroneous work flows) can be stopped using Background Processes or File → Stop All Processes
Toad Data Point - [Introduction to Workbook]
File Edit View Window Help
Connection Manager
Object Explorer
Object Details
SQL Recall F8
Code Snippets
Background Processes
Toad Views
Output
Full Screen Shift+Alt+Return
www.DanHotka.com

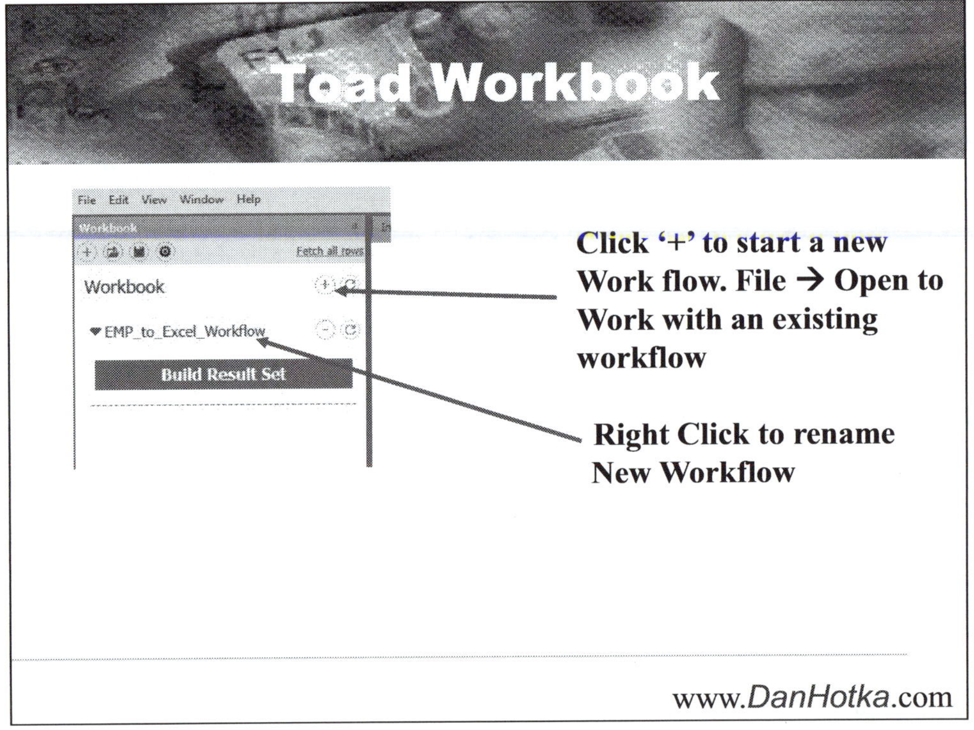
Toad Workbook
File Edit View Window Help
Workbook
Fetch all rows
Workbook
EMP_to_Excel_Workflow
Build Result Set
Click '+' to start a new Work flow. File → Open to Work with an existing workflow
Right Click to rename New Workflow
www.DanHotka.com

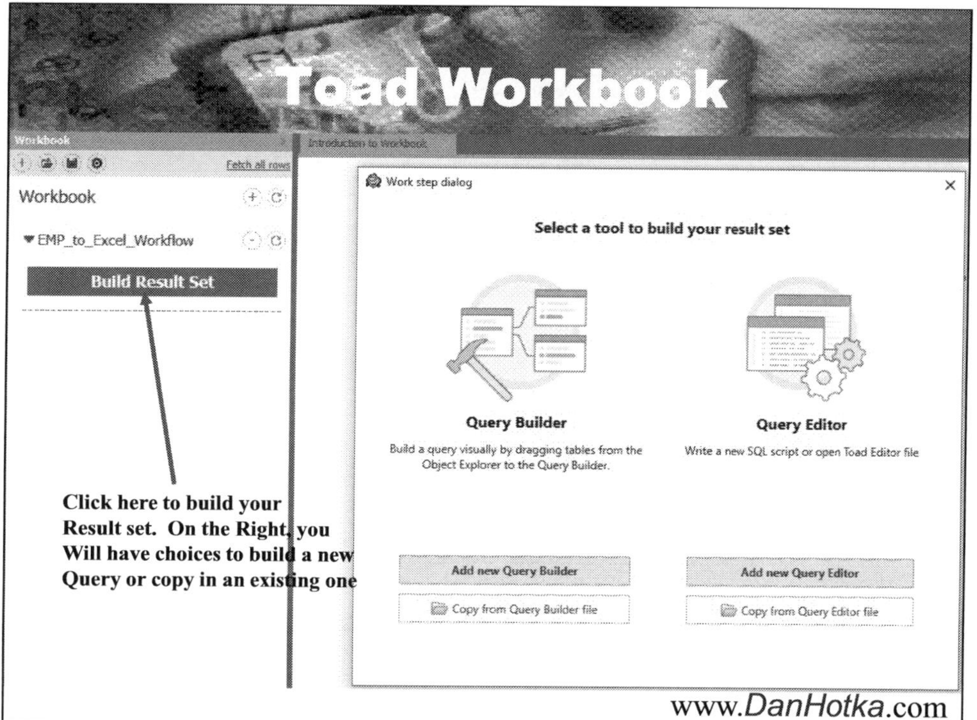


To start a new workflow, click the 'Build Result Set'. This brings up a panel that allows you to build the SQL using Query Builder or the Query Editor. In the Query Builder, you can paste in SQL from another application and build working SQL for this workflow easily. If you are SQL savvy…you can paste it into the Query Editor as well.

***Tip*** Make sure the SQL works!

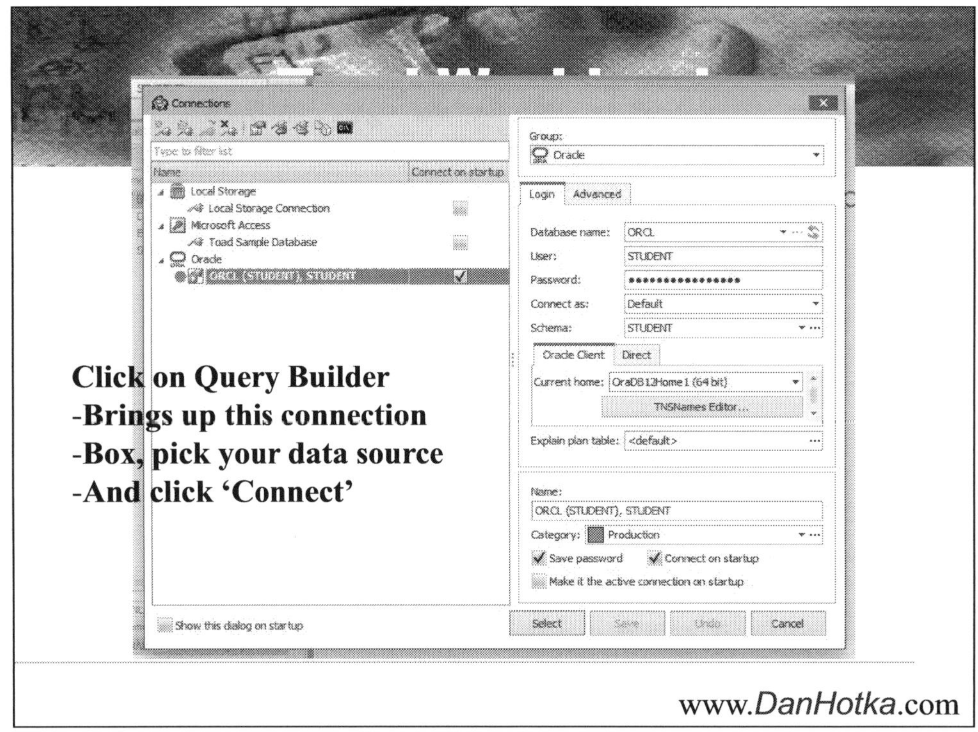
Connections
Group:
Oracle
Local Storage
Local Storage Connection
Microsoft Access
Toad Sample Database
Oracle
ORCL (STUDENT), STUDENT
Login
Advanced
Database name:
ORCL
User:
STUDENT
Password:
Connect as:
Default
Schema:
STUDENT
Oracle Client
Direct
Current home:
OraDB12Home1 (64 bit)
TNSNames Editor...
Explain plan table:
Name:
ORCL (STUDENT), STUDENT
Category:
Production
Save password
Connect on startup
Make it the active connection on startup
Show this dialog on startup
Select
Save
Undo
Cancel
Click on Query Builder
-Brings up this connection
-Box, pick your data source
-And click 'Connect'
www.DanHotka.com

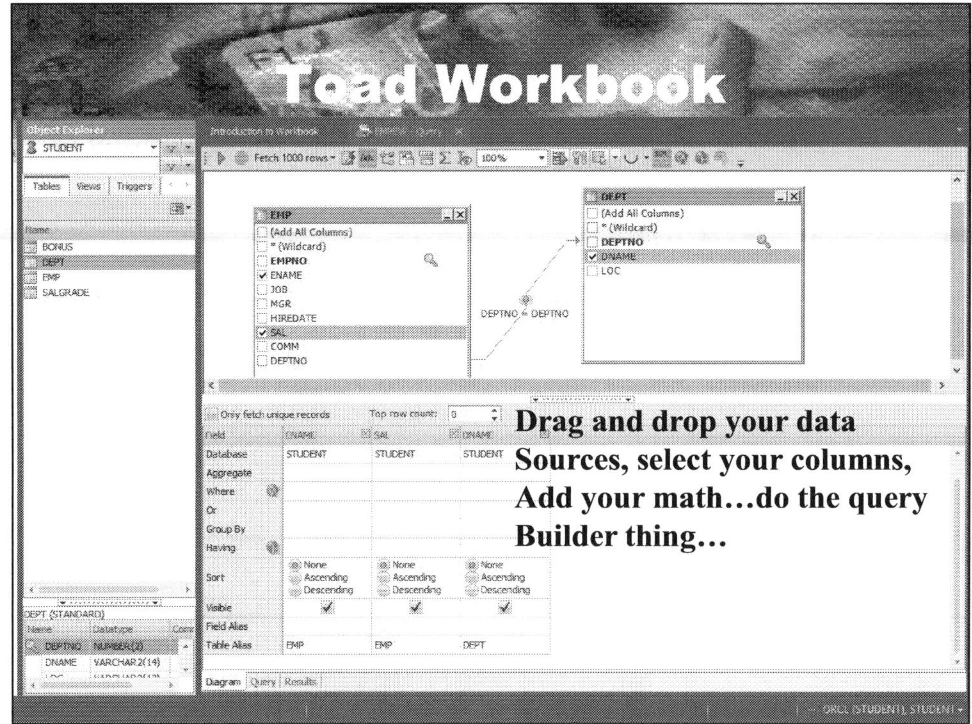
Toad Workbook
Object Explorer
STUDENT
Tables
Views
Triggers
BONUS
DEPT
EMP
SALGRADE
EMP
(Add All Columns)
* (Wildcard)
EMPNO
ENAME
JOB
MGR
HIREDATE
SAL
COMM
DEPTNO
DEPTNO = DEPTNO
DEPT
(Add All Columns)
* (Wildcard)
DEPTNO
DNAME
LOC
Only fetch unique records
Top row count:
Field
Database
Aggregate
Where
Or
Group By
Having
Sort
Visible
Field Alias
Table Alias
Diagram
Query
Results
Drag and drop your data
Sources, select your columns,
Add your math…do the query
Builder thing…

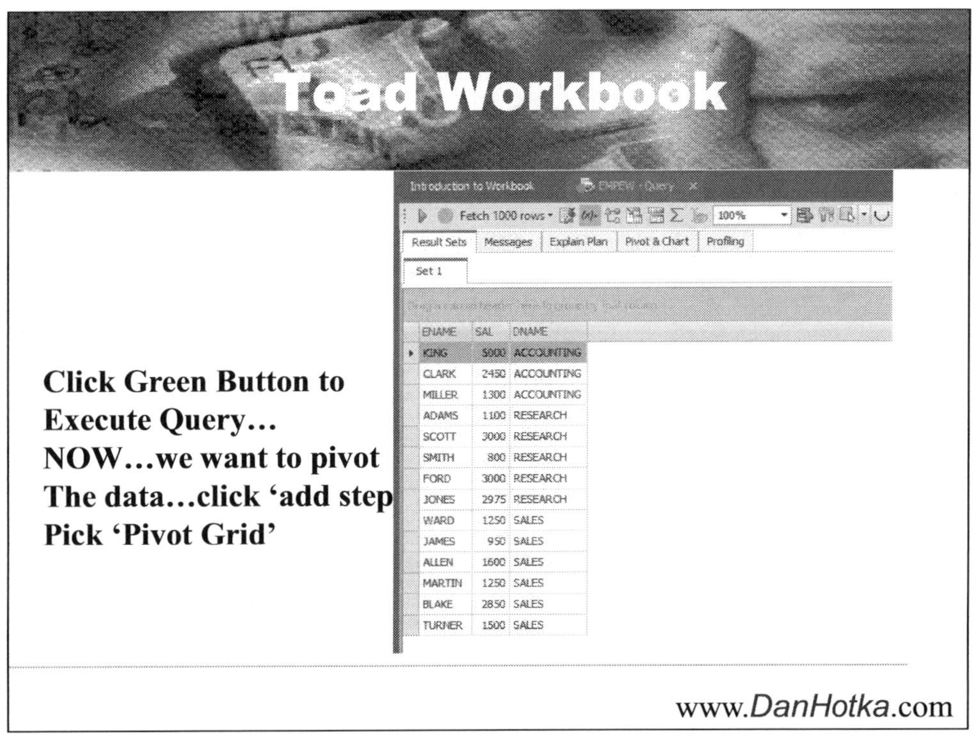
Toad Workbook
Click Green Button to
Execute Query…
NOW…we want to pivot
The data…click 'add step
Pick 'Pivot Grid'
Introduction to Workbook
Fetch 1000 rows
100%
Result Sets
Messages
Explain Plan
Pivot & Chart
Profiling
Set 1
ENAME
SAL
DNAME
KING 5000 ACCOUNTING
CLARK 2450 ACCOUNTING
MILLER 1300 ACCOUNTING
ADAMS 1100 RESEARCH
SCOTT 3000 RESEARCH
SMITH 800 RESEARCH
FORD 3000 RESEARCH
JONES 2975 RESEARCH
WARD 1250 SALES
JAMES 950 SALES
ALLEN 1600 SALES
MARTIN 1250 SALES
BLAKE 2850 SALES
TURNER 1500 SALES
www.DanHotka.com

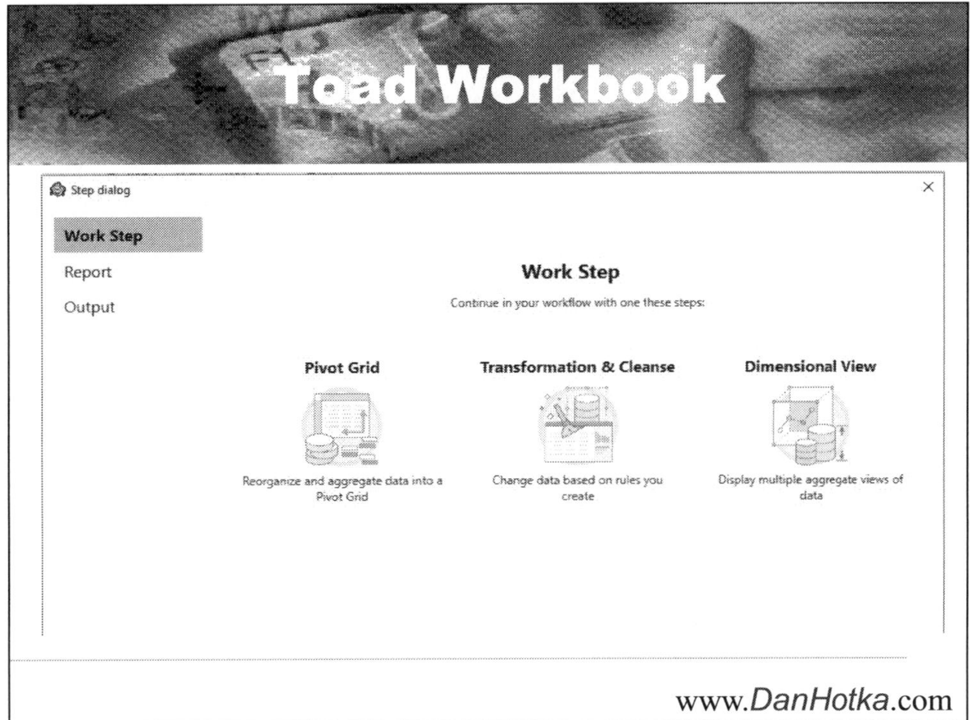
Toad Workbook
Step dialog
Work Step
Report
Output
Work Step
Continue in your workflow with one these steps:
Pivot Grid
Reorganize and aggregate data into a Pivot Grid
Transformation & Cleanse
Change data based on rules you create
Dimensional View
Display multiple aggregate views of data
www.DanHotka.com

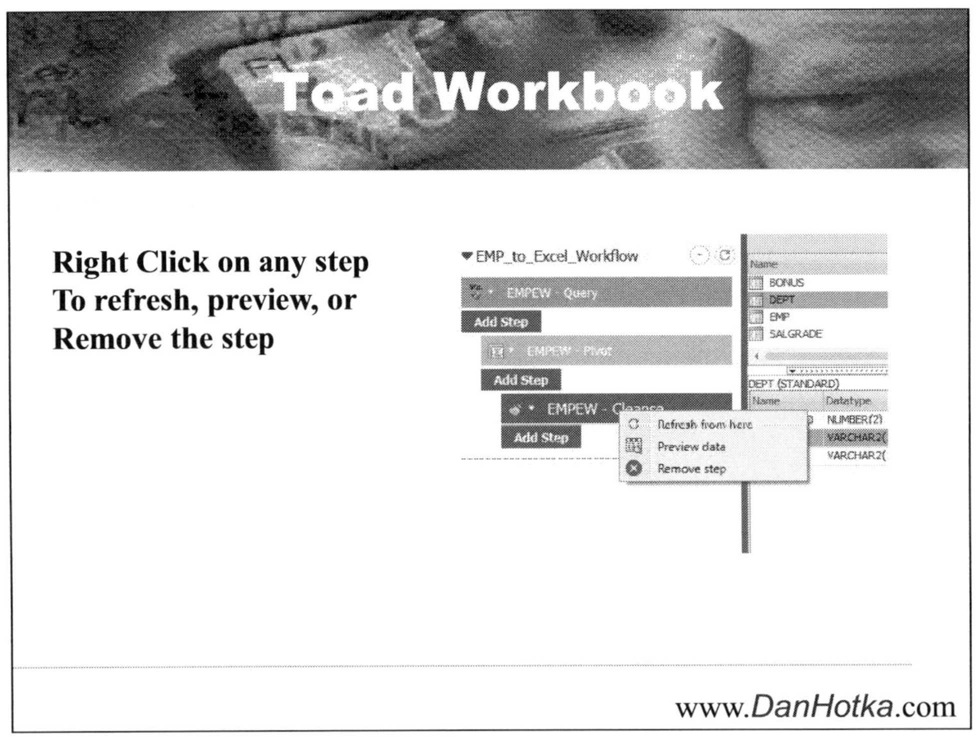
Toad Workbook
Right Click on any step
To refresh, preview, or
Remove the step
EMP_to_Excel_Workflow
EMPEW - Query
Add Step
EMPEW - Pivot
Add Step
EMPEW - Cleanse
Add Step
Refresh from here
Preview data
Remove step
Name
BONUS
DEPT
EMP
SALGRADE
DEPT (STANDARD)
Name
Datatype
NUMBER(2)
VARCHAR2(
VARCHAR2(
www.DanHotka.com

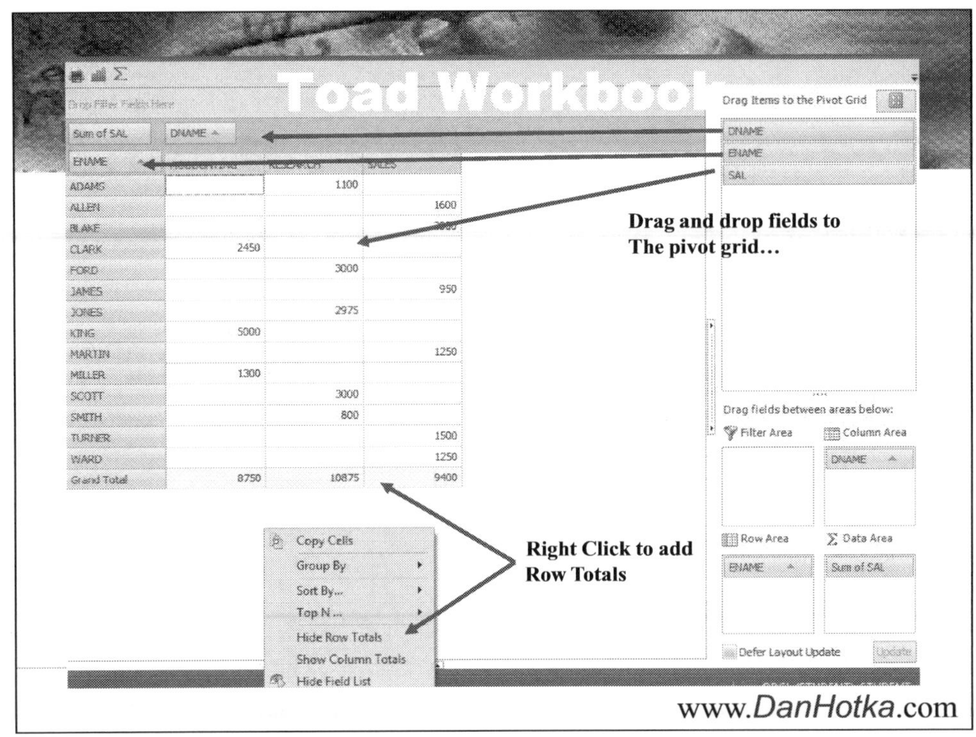
Toad Workbook
Sum of SAL
DNAME
ENAME
ADAMS 1100
ALLEN 1600
BLAKE
CLARK 2450
FORD 3000
JAMES 950
JONES 2975
KING 5000
MARTIN 1250
MILLER 1300
SCOTT 3000
SMITH 800
TURNER 1500
WARD 1250
Grand Total 8750 10875 9400
Drag Items to the Pivot Grid
DNAME
ENAME
SAL
Drag and drop fields to
The pivot grid…
Drag fields between areas below:
Filter Area
Column Area
DNAME
Row Area
Data Area
ENAME
Sum of SAL
Defer Layout Update
Update
Copy Cells
Group By
Sort By...
Top N ...
Hide Row Totals
Show Column Totals
Hide Field List
Right Click to add
Row Totals
www.DanHotka.com

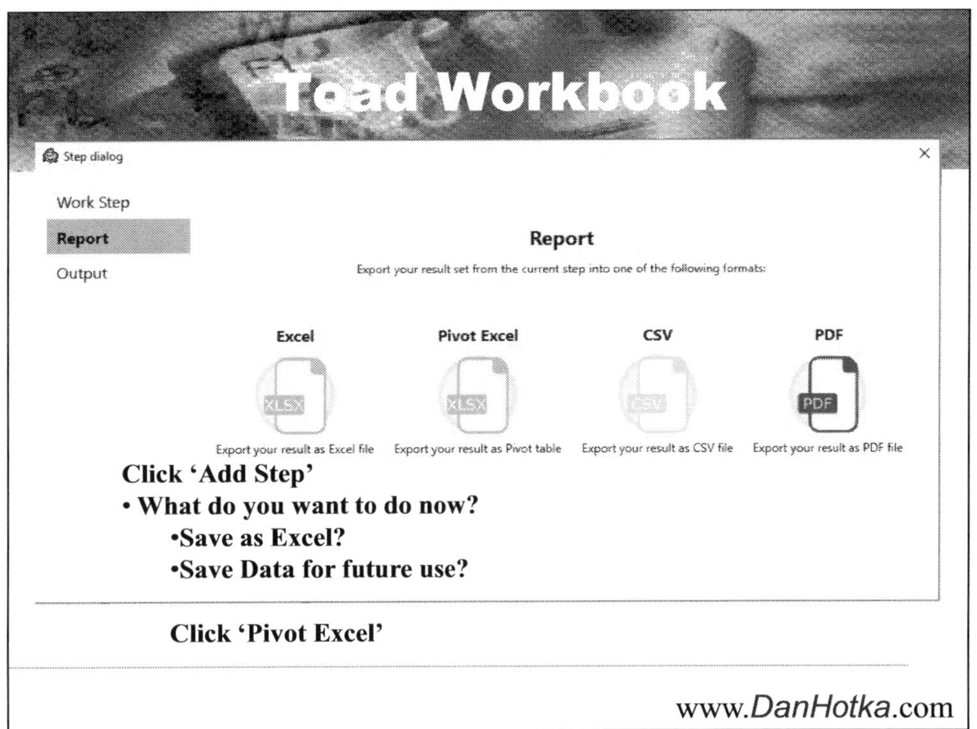
Toad Workbook
Step dialog
Work Step
Report
Output
Report
Export your result set from the current step into one of the following formats:
Excel
Pivot Excel
CSV
PDF
Export your result as Excel file
Export your result as Pivot table
Export your result as CSV file
Export your result as PDF file
Click 'Add Step'
• What do you want to do now?
•Save as Excel?
•Save Data for future use?
Click 'Pivot Excel'
www.DanHotka.com

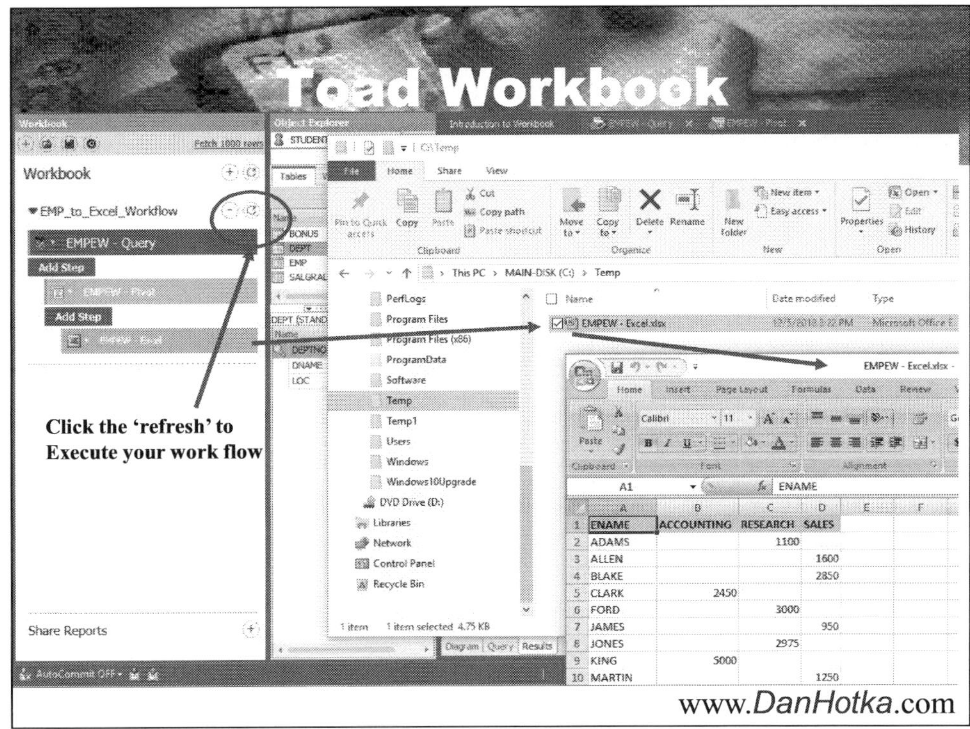
Toad Workbook
Workbook
EMP_to_Excel_Workflow
EMPEW - Query
Add Step
Add Step
Click the 'refresh' to
Execute your work flow
Share Reports
www.DanHotka.com

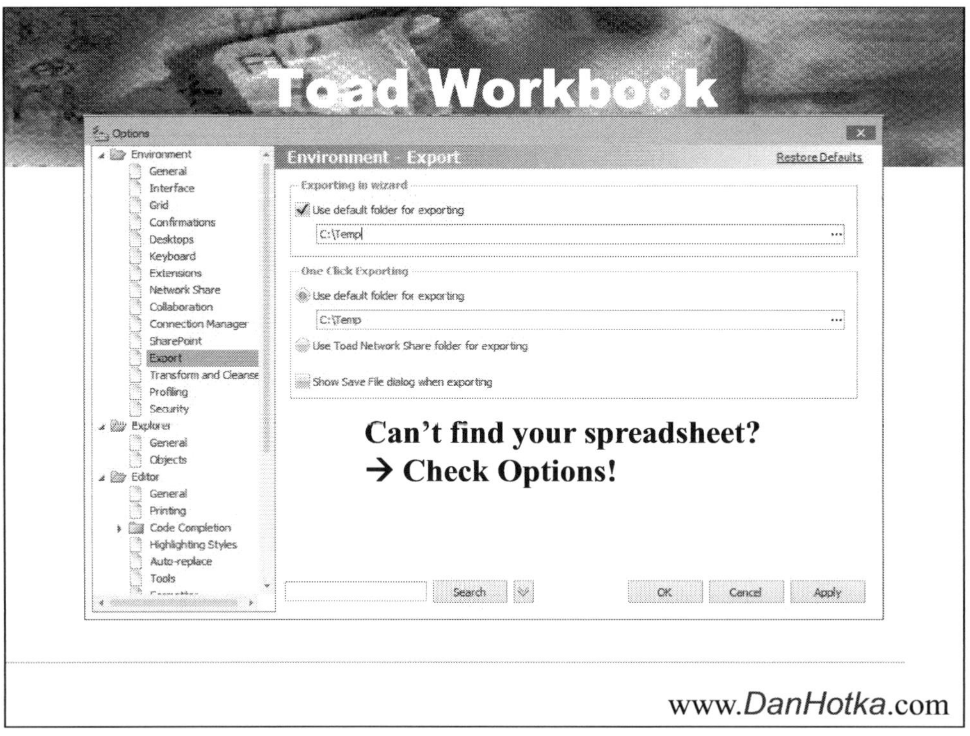
Toad Workbook
Options
Environment - Export
Restore Defaults
Exporting in wizard
Use default folder for exporting
C:\Temp
One Click Exporting
Use default folder for exporting
C:\Temp
Use Toad Network Share folder for exporting
Show Save File dialog when exporting
Can't find your spreadsheet?
→ Check Options!
Search
OK
Cancel
Apply
www.DanHotka.com

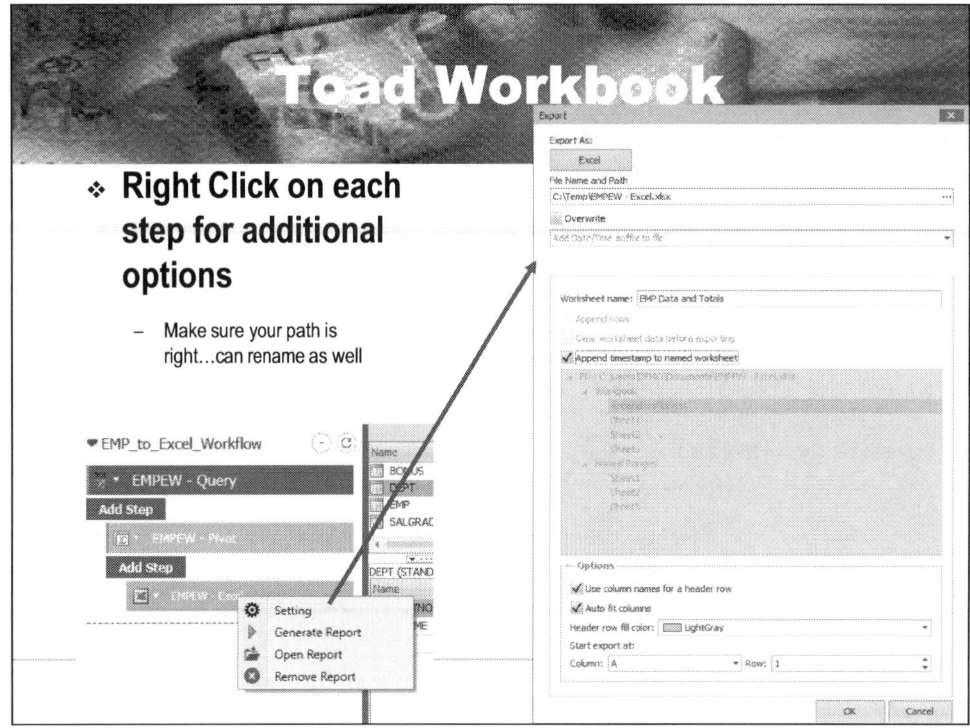
Toad Workbook
Right Click on each step for additional options
Make sure your path is right…can rename as well
EMP_to_Excel_Workflow
EMPEW - Query
Add Step
Add Step
Setting
Generate Report
Open Report
Remove Report
Export
Export As:
Excel
File Name and Path
C:\Temp\EMPEW - Excel.xlsx
Overwrite
Worksheet name: EMP Data and Totals
Append timestamp to named worksheet
Options
Use column names for a header row
Auto fit columns
Header row fill color: LightGray
Start export at:
Column: A
Row: 1
OK
Cancel

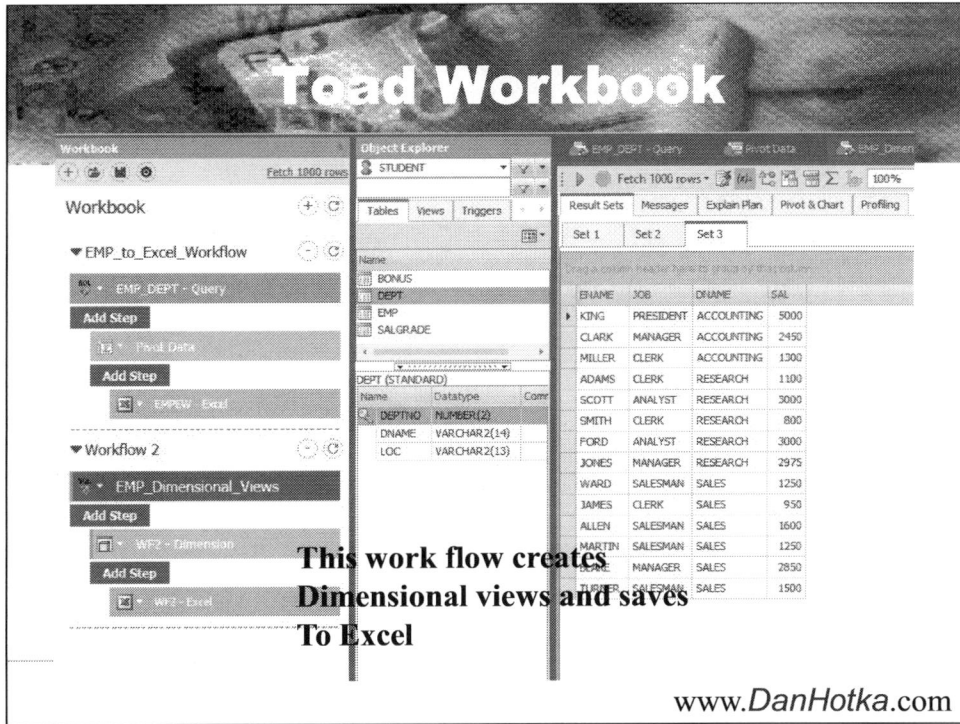

## Toad Workbook

This work flow creates
Dimensional views and saves
To Excel

www.DanHotka.com

This Workflow creates dimensional views and saves those to Excel!

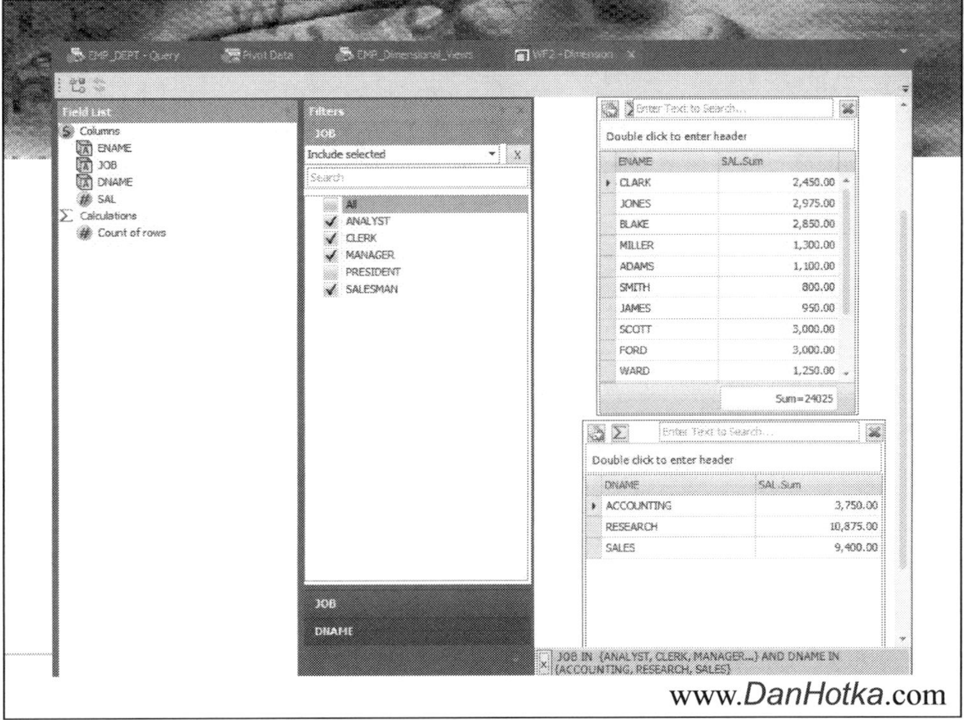

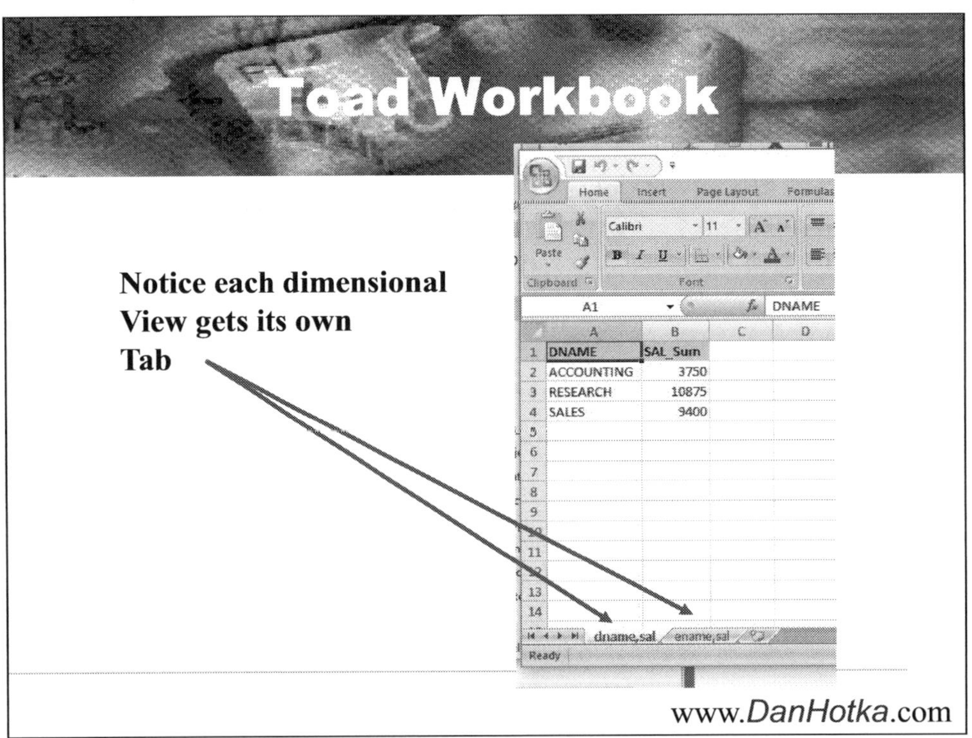


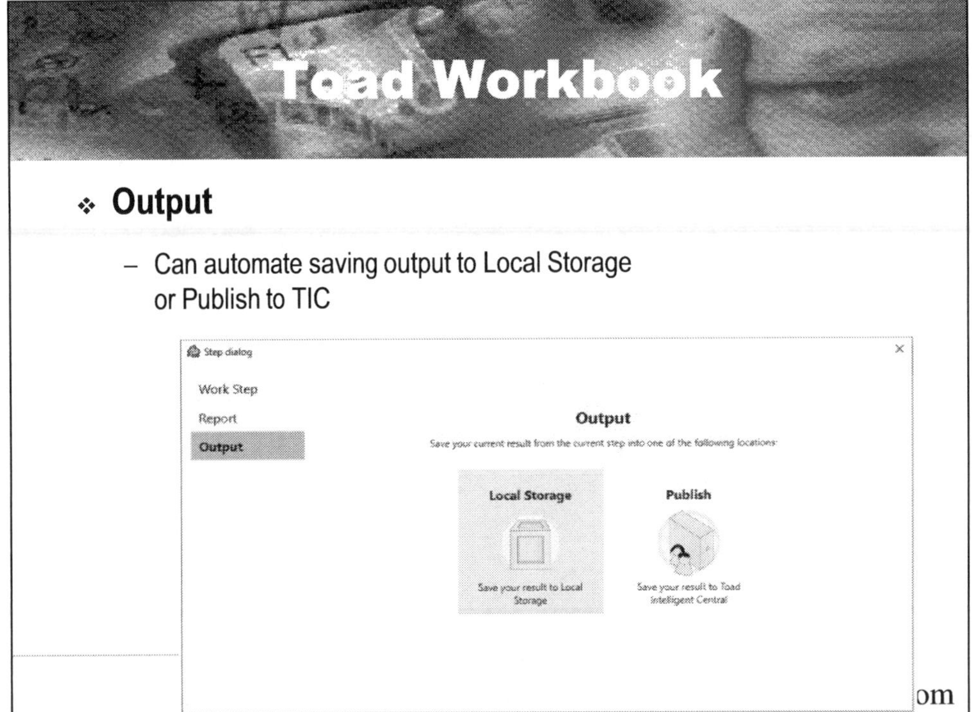


The 'Add Step' has one more feature that allows you to save the workflow output to either Local Storage or Publish to TIC.

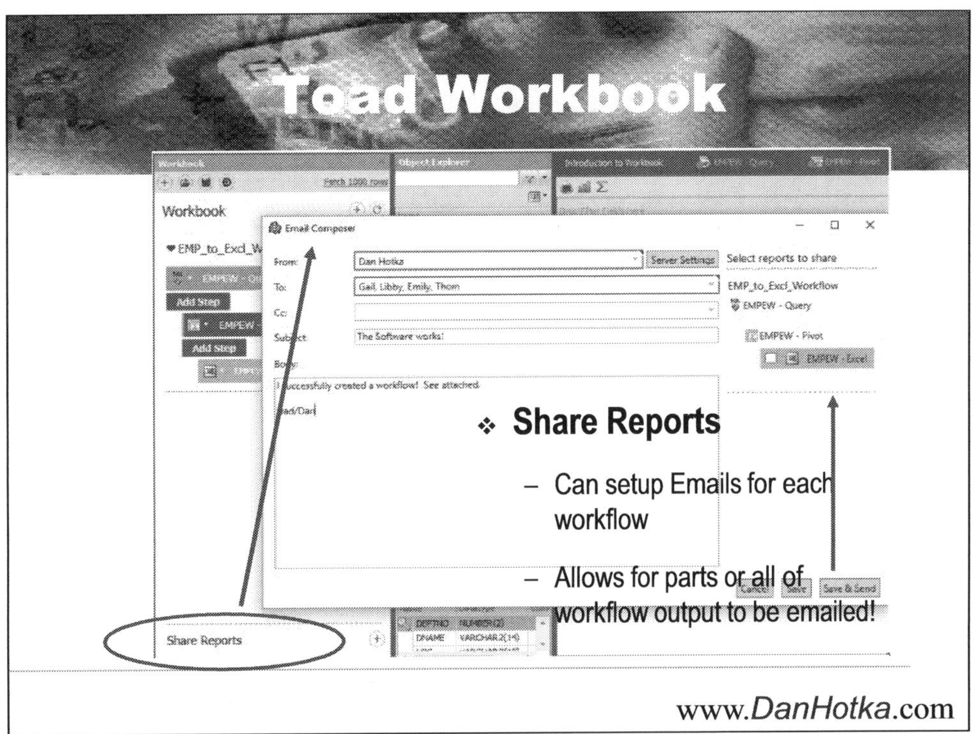
Toad Workbook
Workbook
Email Composer
From:
Dan Hotka
Server Settings
Select reports to share
To:
Gail, Libby, Emily, Thom
EMP_to_Excl_Workflow
EMPEW - Query
Cc:
Subject:
The Software works!
EMPEW - Pivot
EMPEW - Excel
Body:
Share Reports
Can setup Emails for each workflow
Allows for parts or all of workflow output to be emailed!
Cancel
Save
Save & Send
Share Reports
www.DanHotka.com

The 'Share Reports' allows you to email workflow output by individual output to anyone…using your email system.

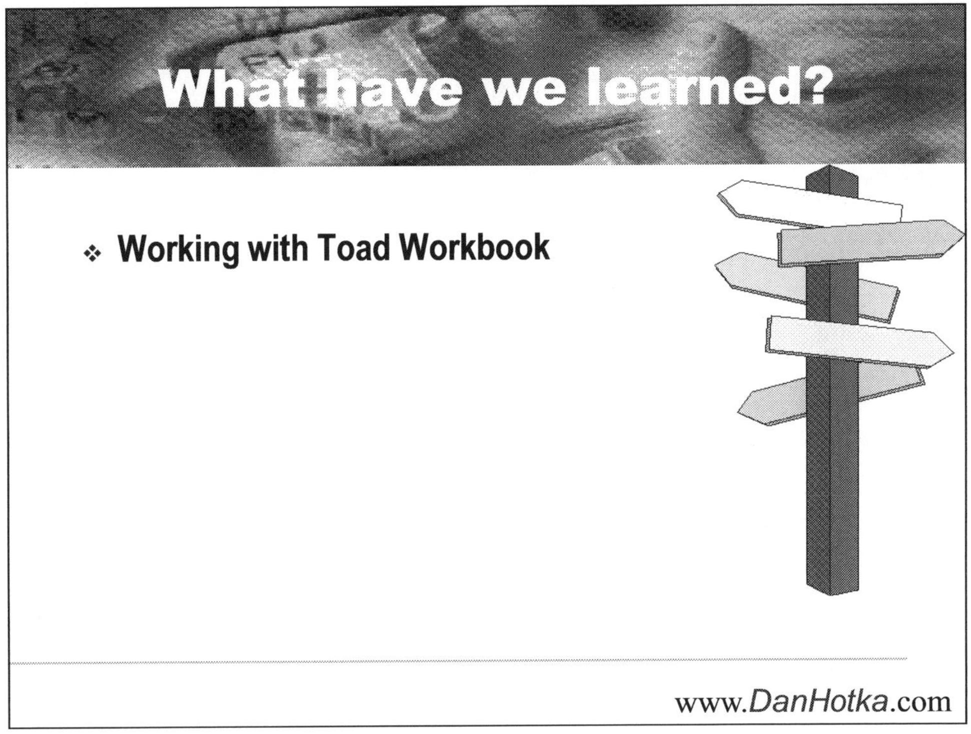
What have we learned?
Working with Toad Workbook
www.DanHotka.com

## Toad Workbook Lab

# Toad Workbook Lab

- **Working with Toad Workbook Lab**
  - Build the examples in this chapter
    - Unless we did them as a group exercise

www.DanHotka.com

## Automating Tasks

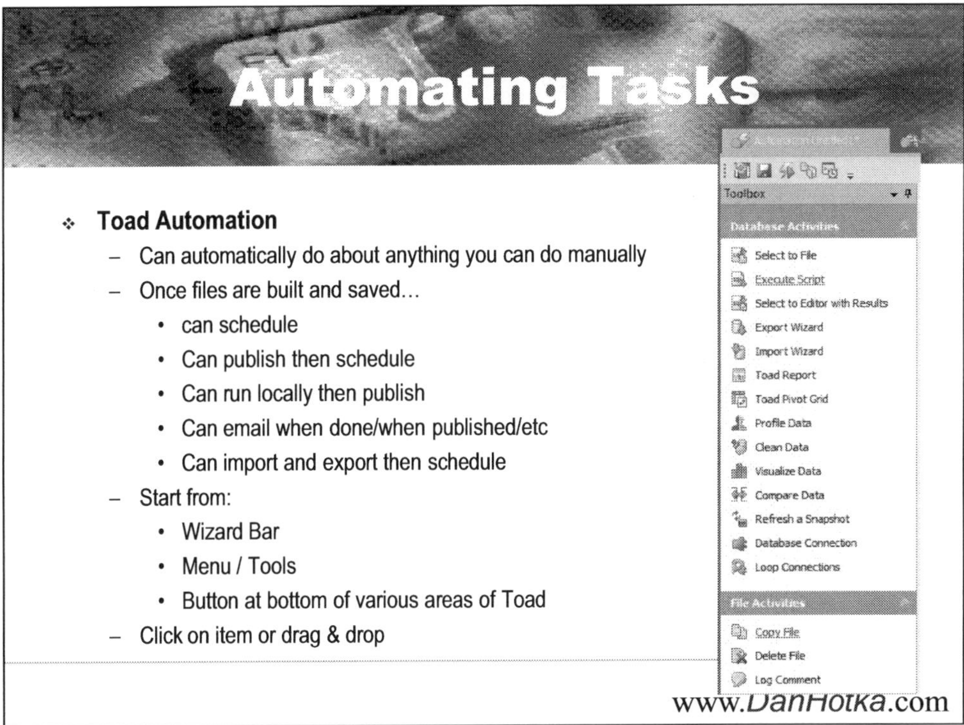


Toad DP can automate about any data prep/migration/report/chart that you want. It contains looping and conditional options as well. This automation is designed to elevate you of the repetitive task of running a job stream to produce the same type of output.

***Tip*** Hyperion Brio users use this to bring their work flows together!

The primary use of this tool is to formulate a series of tasks into a task or job itself then schedule it and automatically inform people that the data is ready or simply email them the created spreadsheet.

Once in the Automation Designer, you can click on the location you want a task then click on the task in the activities task bar. You can also drag and drop these tasks to the automation canvas.

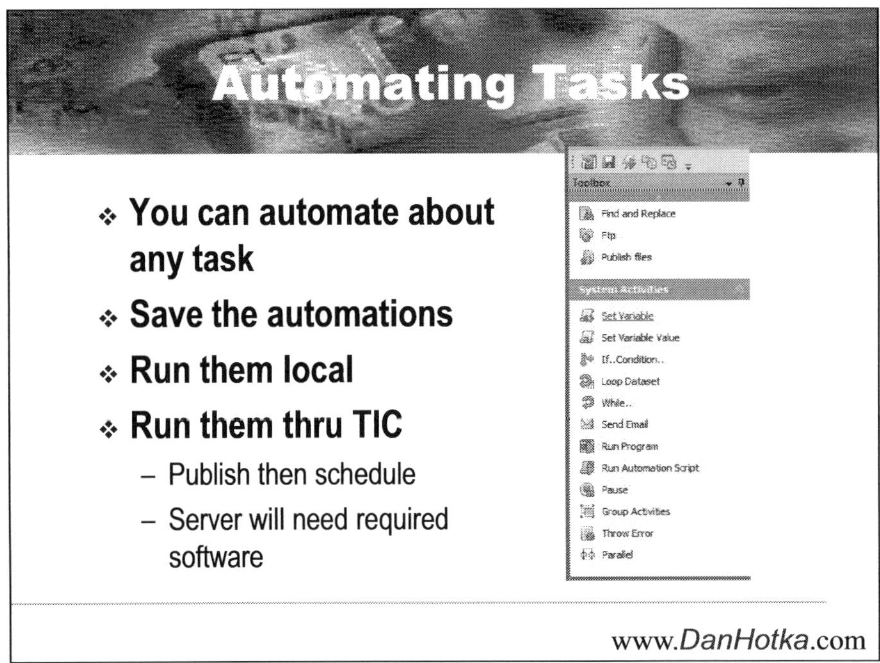

Automating Tasks
You can automate about any task
Save the automations
Run them local
Run them thru TIC
– Publish then schedule
– Server will need required software
Toolbox
Find and Replace
Ftp
Publish files
System Activities
Set Variable
Set Variable Value
If..Condition..
Loop Dataset
While..
Send Email
Run Program
Run Automation Script
Pause
Group Activities
Throw Error
Parallel
www.DanHotka.com


Once the automation script exists and has been tested, you can schedule it to run on your own workstation or publish to Toad Intelligence Central and schedule it there for execution and distribution. Where it runs depends on department protocol, whether the combined task is just for your benefit, etc.

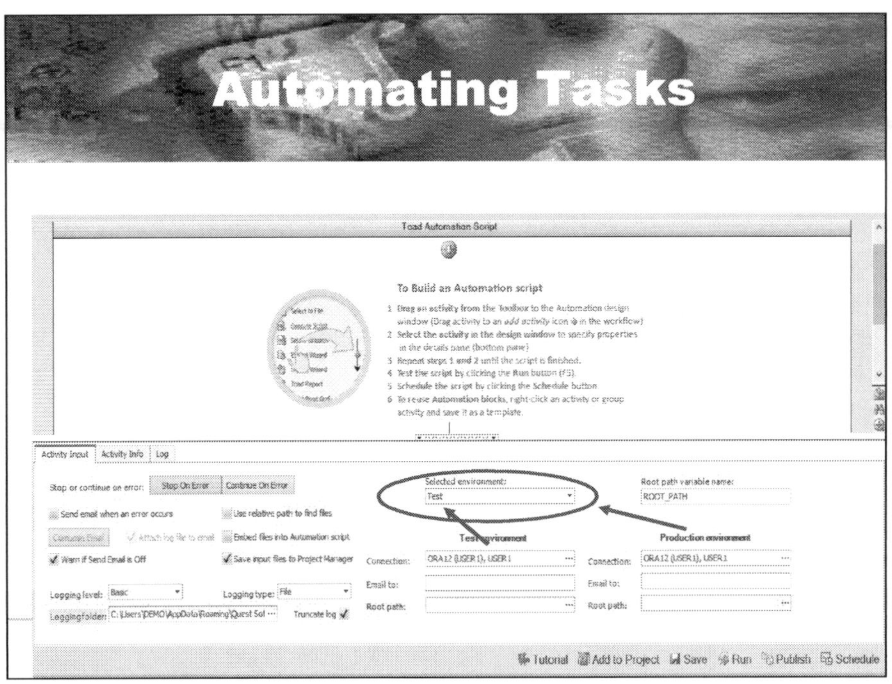

Automating Tasks
Toad Automation Script
To Build an Automation script
Activity Input
Activity Info
Log
Stop or continue on error:
Stop On Error
Continue On Error
Selected environment:
Test
Root path variable name:
ROOT_PATH
Test environment
Production environment
Connection:
Email to:
Root path:
Logging level:
Basic
Logging type:
File
Tutorial
Add to Project
Save
Run
Publish
Schedule


Toad DP sets up connections for both the test environment and the production environment.

***Note*** your connections must have saved passwords for any scheduled task to run unattended.

This is the Options part of the script. This task is always at the top. Any error handling listed here will be used throughout the script. You can override this behavior at the task level. This area also has the connection that will be used for both test and production. When done with your test, make sure to change the 'selected environment'.

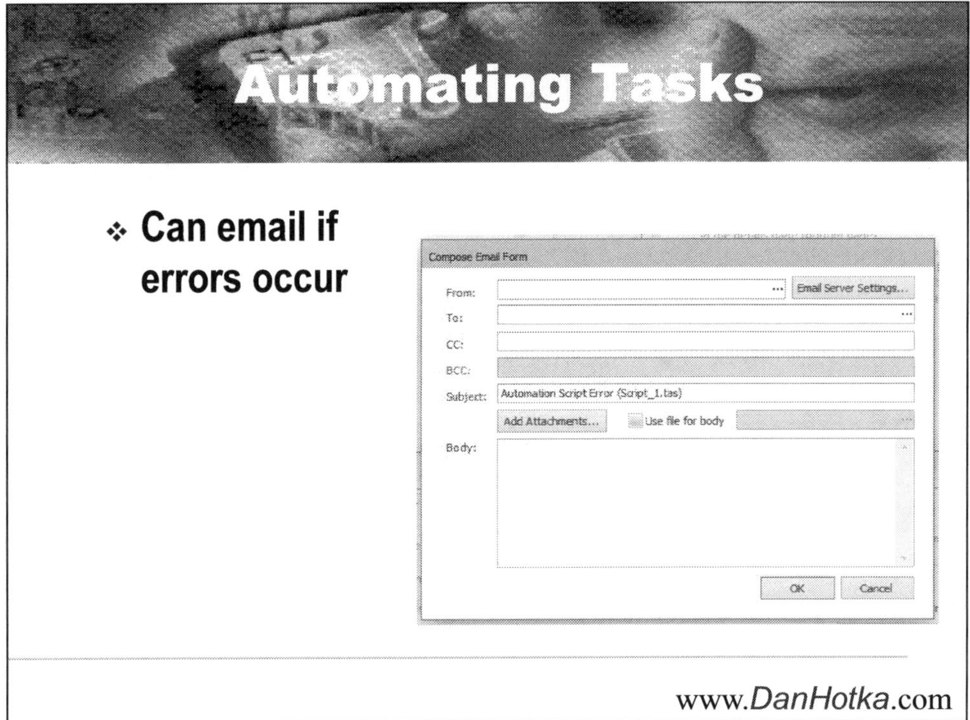

## Automation Tasks

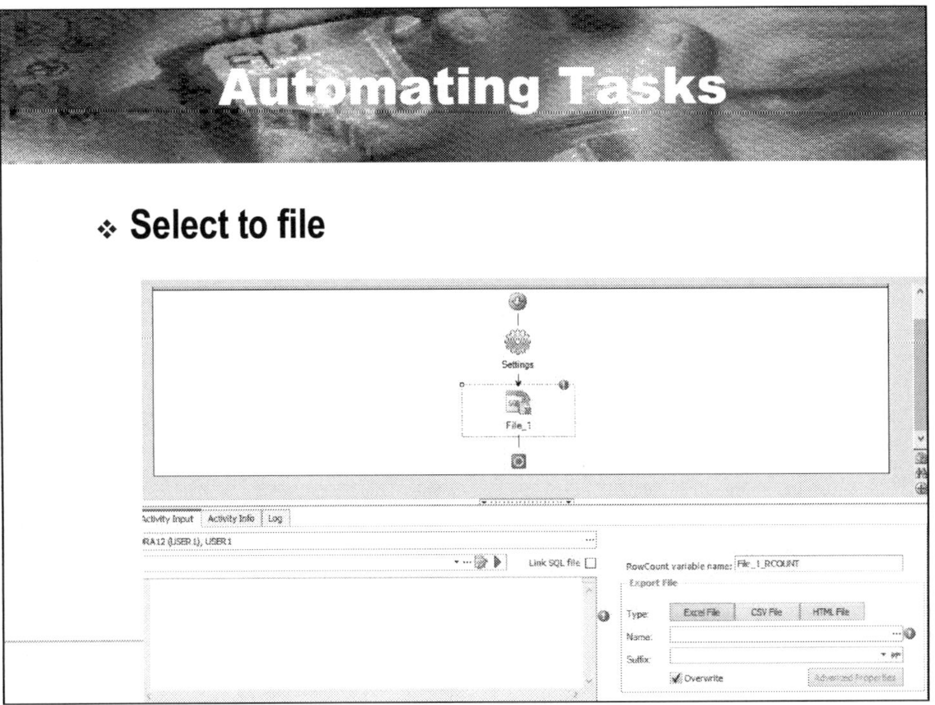
Automating Tasks
Select to file
Settings
File_1
Activity Input
Activity Info
Log
Link SQL file
RowCount variable name:
File_1_RCOUNT
Export File
Type:
Excel File
CSV File
HTML File
Name:
Suffix:
Overwrite

Runs a SQL statement and exports the result

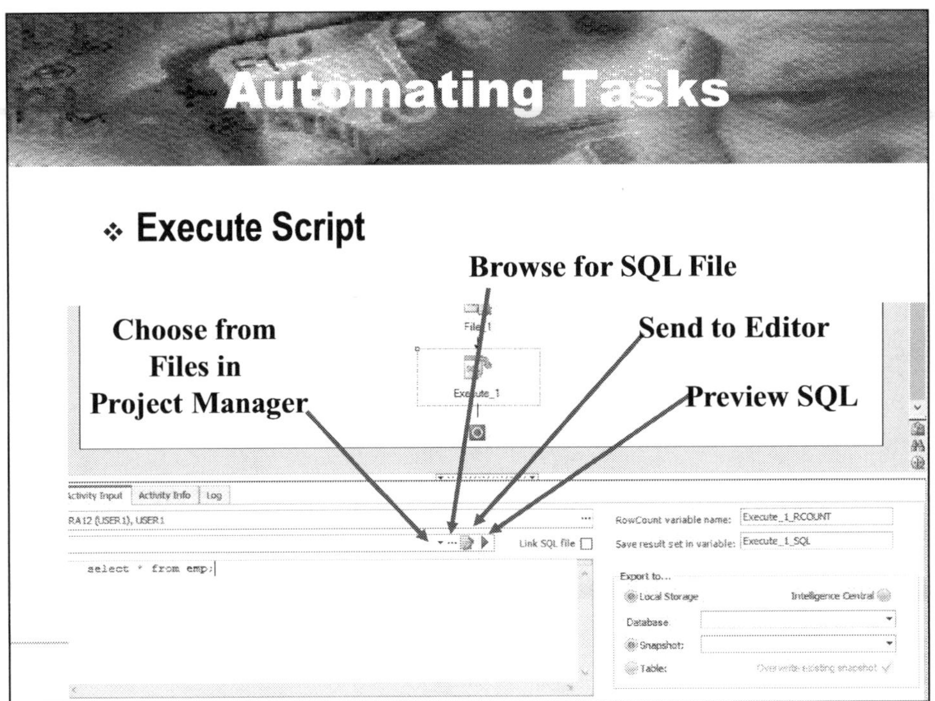
Automating Tasks
Execute Script
Browse for SQL File
Choose from Files in Project Manager
Send to Editor
Preview SQL
Execute_1
Activity Input
Activity Info
Log
Link SQL file
select * from emp;
RowCount variable name:
Execute_1_RCOUNT
Save result set in variable:
Execute_1_SQL
Export to...
Local Storage
Intelligence Central
Database
Snapshot:
Table:

This option runs a SQL then can do various things with the output including populating variables, saving, and publishing. Notice the various buttons and what they do. You can also adhoc enter a SQL statement. These windows have a lightweight editor that does include the code completion.

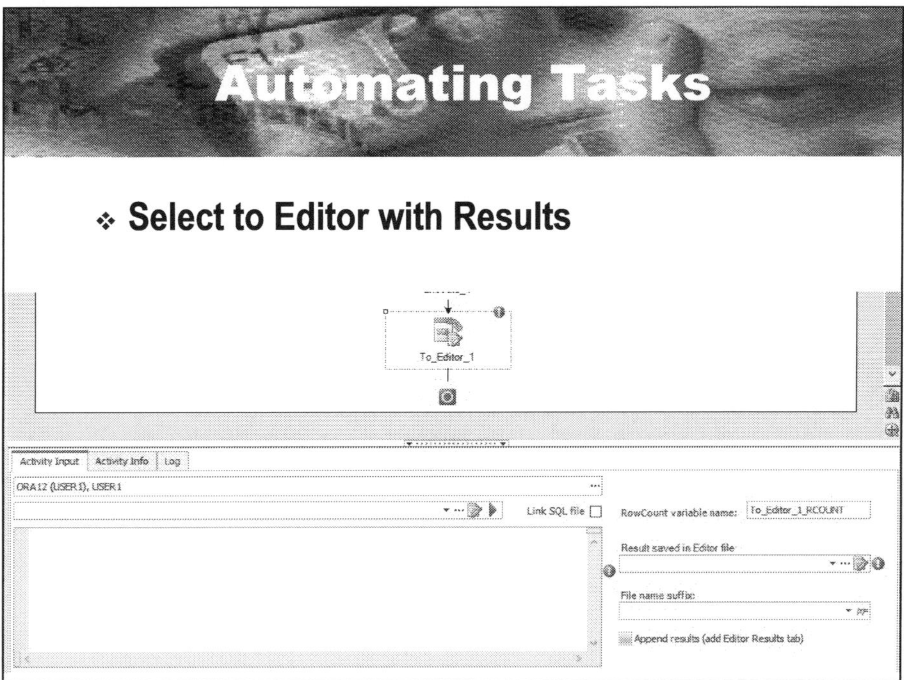


This option saves the output from the SQL as a Toad Editor file.

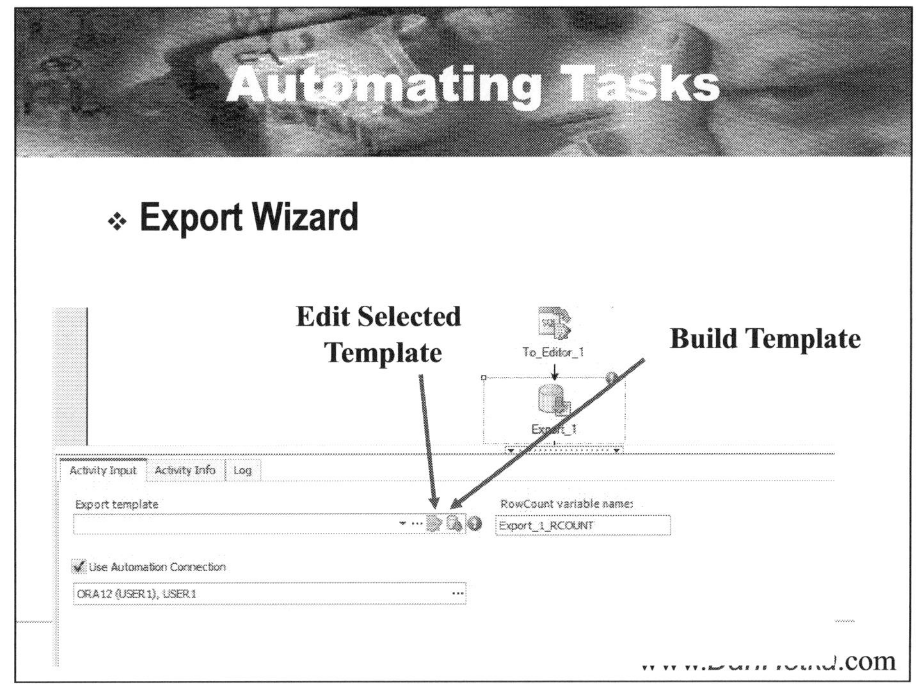

This option allows you to automate an export wizard file. You can also build the template from here as well.

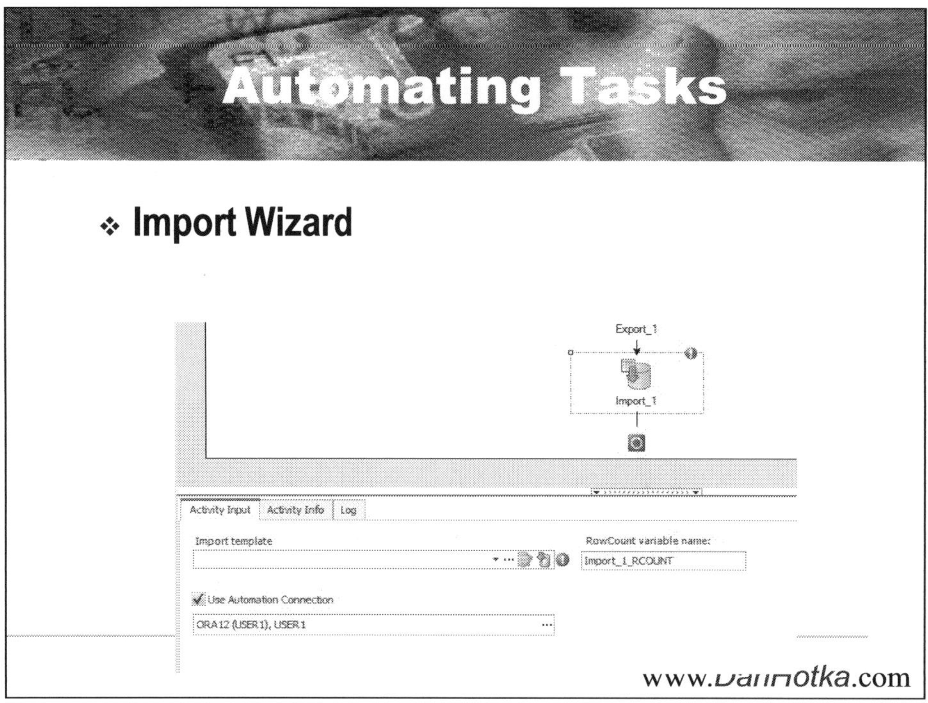


Same thing here with the import wizard. You can automate populating tables or your local storage from files/spreadsheets.

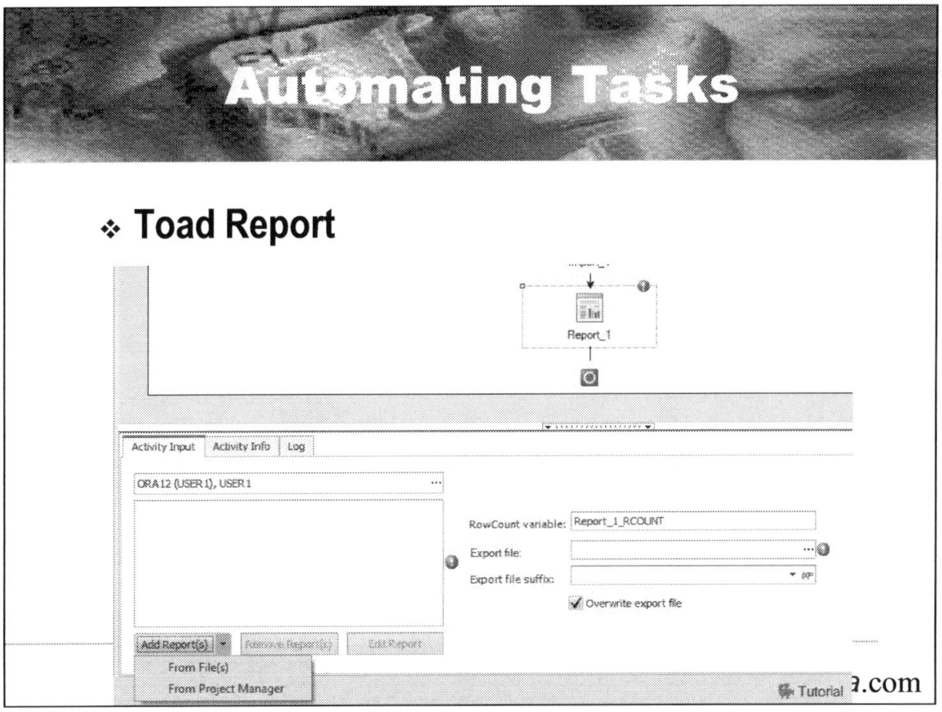

Automating Tasks
Toad Report
Report_1
Activity Input
Activity Info
Log
ORA12 (USER1), USER1
RowCount variable:
Report_1_RCOUNT
Export file:
Export file suffix:
Overwrite export file
Add Report(s)
Remove Report(s)
Edit Report
From File(s)
From Project Manager
Tutorial

You can run existing Toad reports.

Automating Tasks
Toad Pivot Grid
Pivot_1
Edit Toad Pivot File
Activity Input
Activity Info
Log
Connection:
ORA12 (USER1), USER1
Pivot file:
Export file:
File name suffix:
Overwrite export file
RowCount variable name:
Pivot_1_RCOUNT
www.DanHotka.com

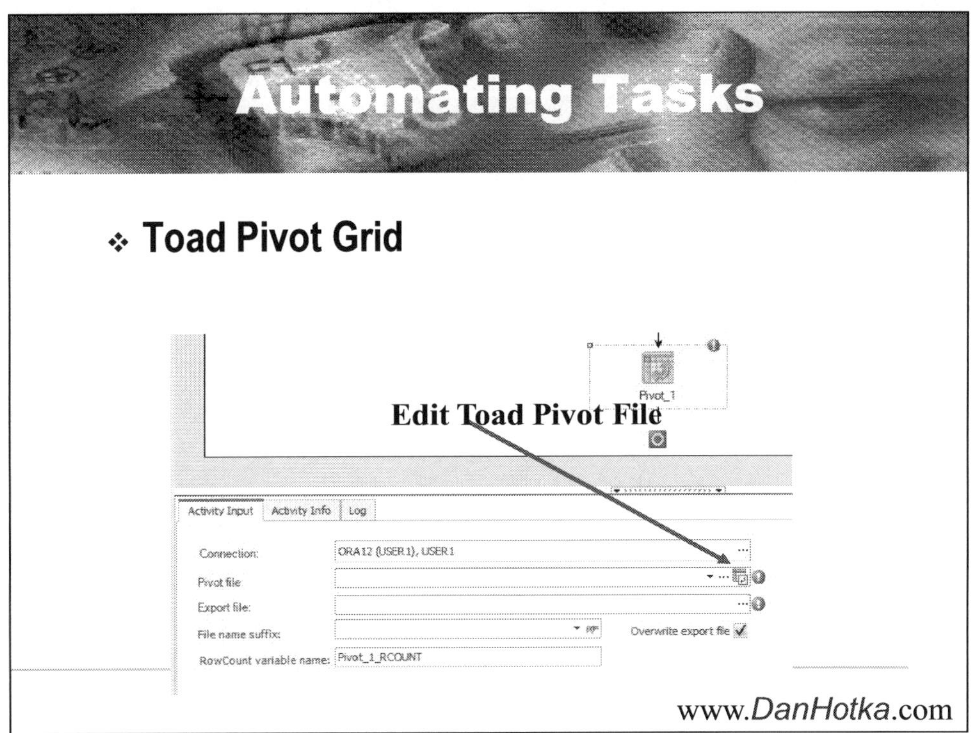

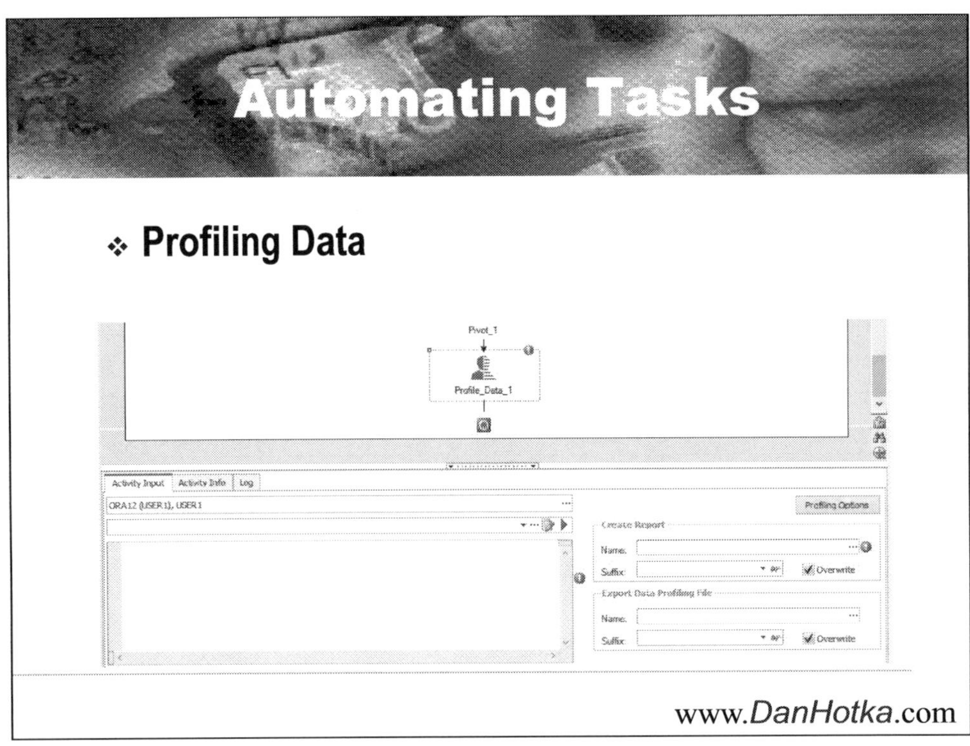
Automating Tasks
Profiling Data
Pivot_1
Profile_Data_1
Activity Input
Activity Info
Log
ORA12 (USER1), USER1
Profiling Options
Create Report
Name:
Suffix:
Overwrite
Export Data Profiling File
Name:
Suffix:
Overwrite
www.DanHotka.com

Automating Tasks
Profiling Data Options
Profiling Options
Options
Query
Columns
Sampling
All Rows
First
1000
rows
Random
10
% sample of rows
Data Options
Basic Analysis
Distinct Analysis (Required for several related measurements)
Pattern & String Analysis
Domain Analysis
Enable Drill Down of Actual Values
www.DanHotka.com

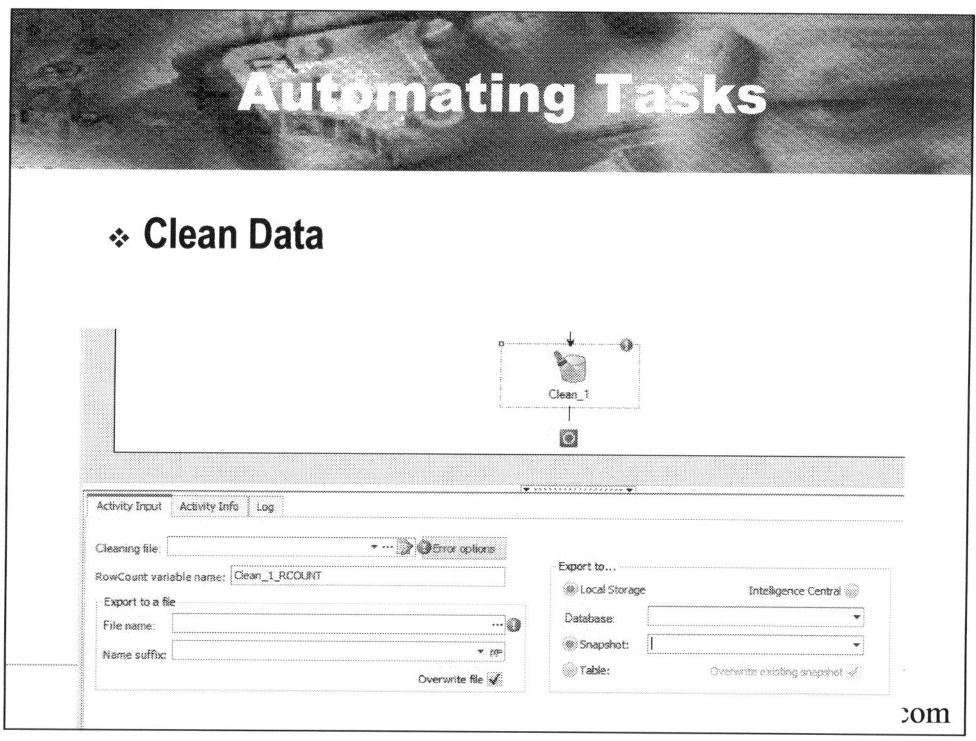
Automating Tasks
Clean Data
Clean_1
Activity Input
Activity Info
Log
Cleaning file:
Error options
RowCount variable name:
Clean_1_RCOUNT
Export to a file
File name:
Name suffix:
Overwrite file
Export to...
Local Storage
Intelligence Central
Database:
Snapshot:
Table:
Overwrite existing snapshot

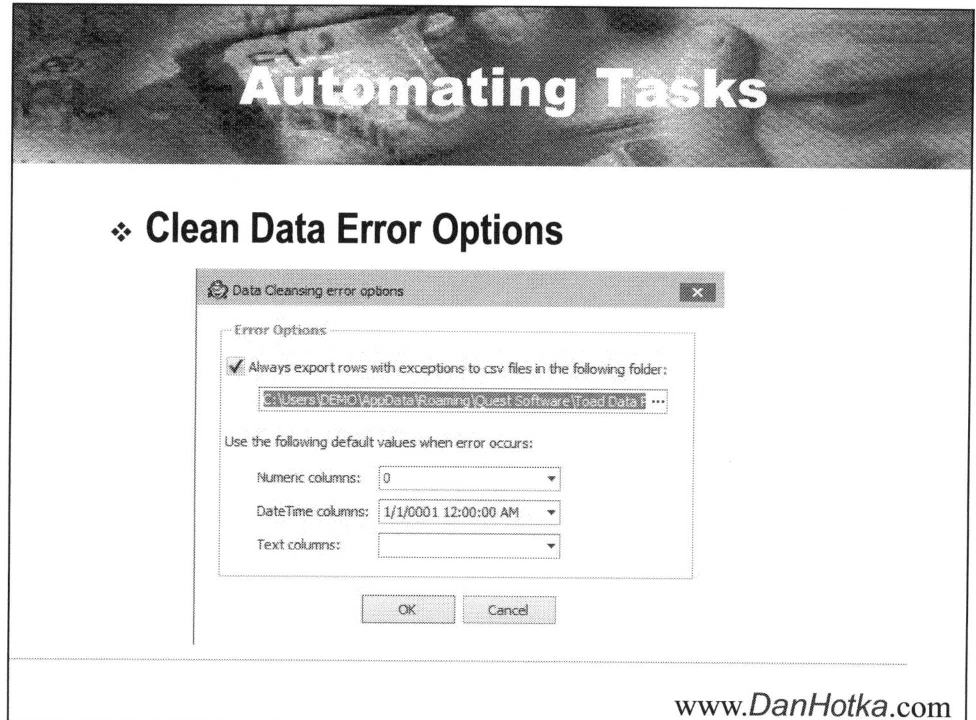
Automating Tasks
Clean Data Error Options
Data Cleansing error options
Error Options
Always export rows with exceptions to csv files in the following folder:
Use the following default values when error occurs:
Numeric columns:
0
DateTime columns:
1/1/0001 12:00:00 AM
Text columns:
OK
Cancel
www.DanHotka.com

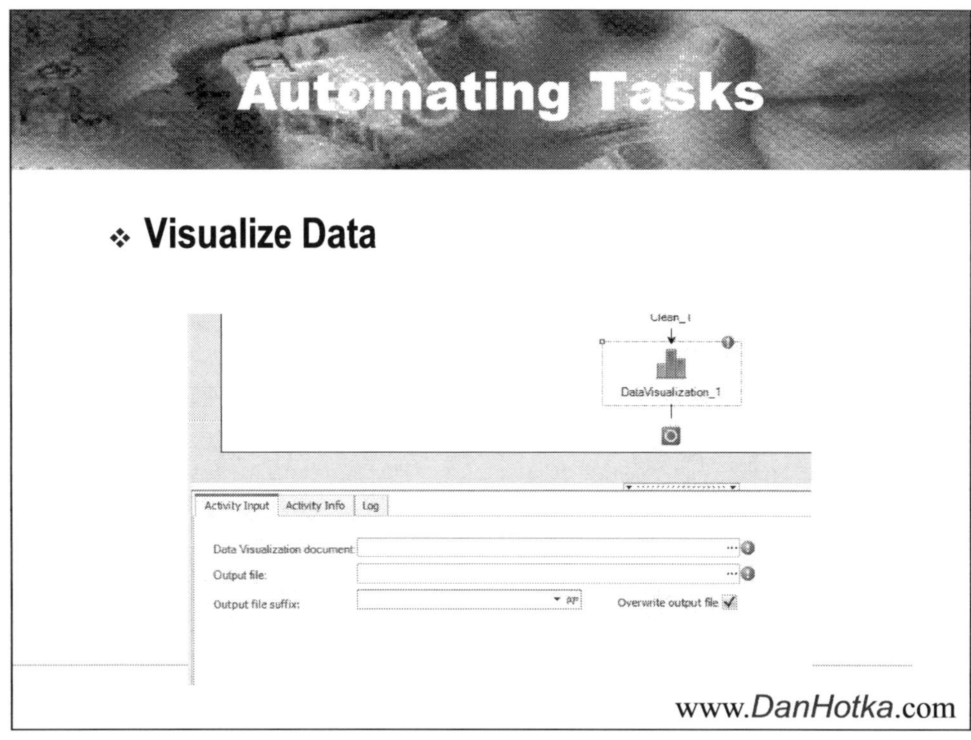

Automating Tasks
Visualize Data
Clean_1
DataVisualization_1
Activity Input
Activity Info
Log
Data Visualization document:
Output file:
Output file suffix:
Overwrite output file
www.DanHotka.com


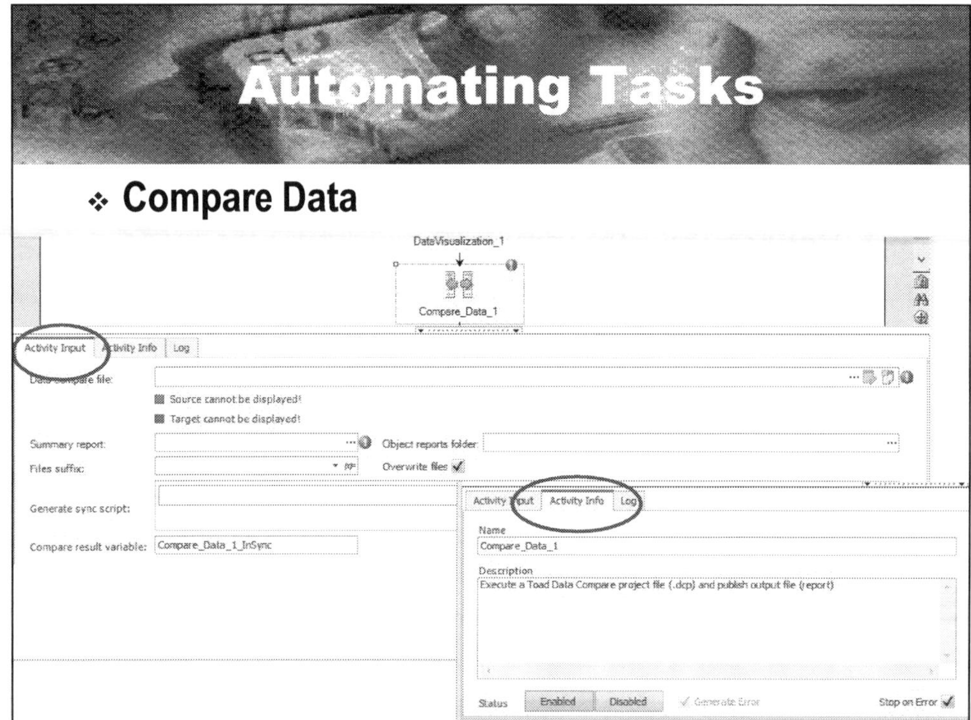

Automating Tasks
Compare Data
DataVisualization_1
Compare_Data_1
Activity Input
Activity Info
Log
Data compare file:
Source cannot be displayed!
Target cannot be displayed!
Summary report:
Object reports folder:
Files suffix:
Overwrite files
Generate sync script:
Compare result variable:
Compare_Data_1_InSync
Name
Compare_Data_1
Description
Execute a Toad Data Compare project file (.dcp) and publish output file (report)
Status
Enabled
Disabled
Generate Error
Stop on Error

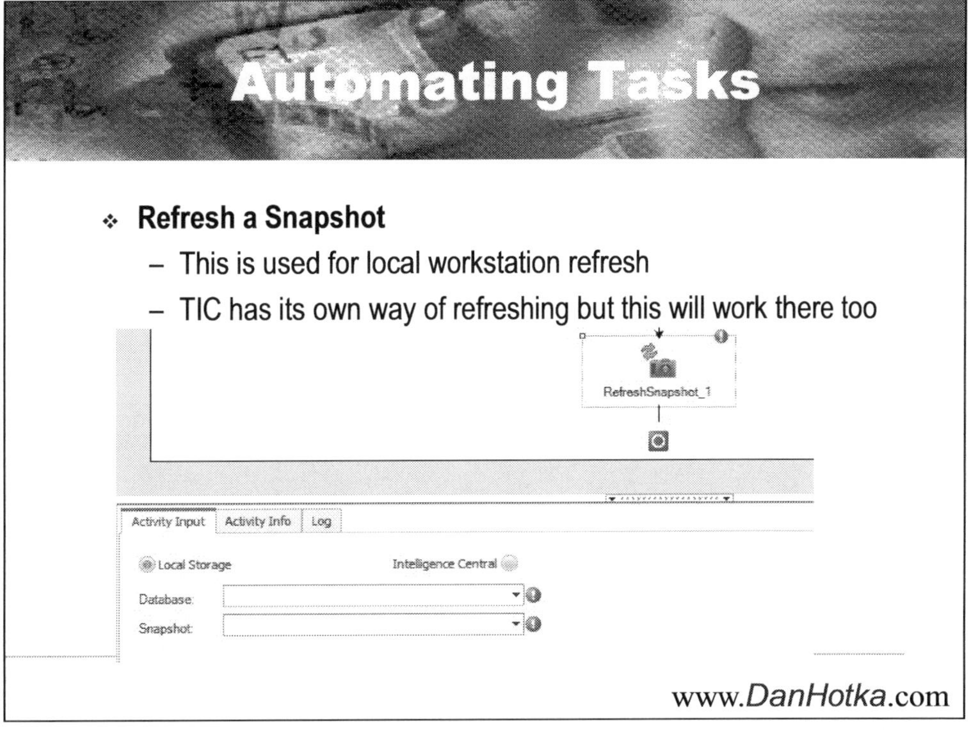
Automating Tasks
Refresh a Snapshot
– This is used for local workstation refresh
– TIC has its own way of refreshing but this will work there too
RefreshSnapshot_1
Activity Input
Activity Info
Log
Local Storage
Intelligence Central
Database:
Snapshot:
www.DanHotka.com

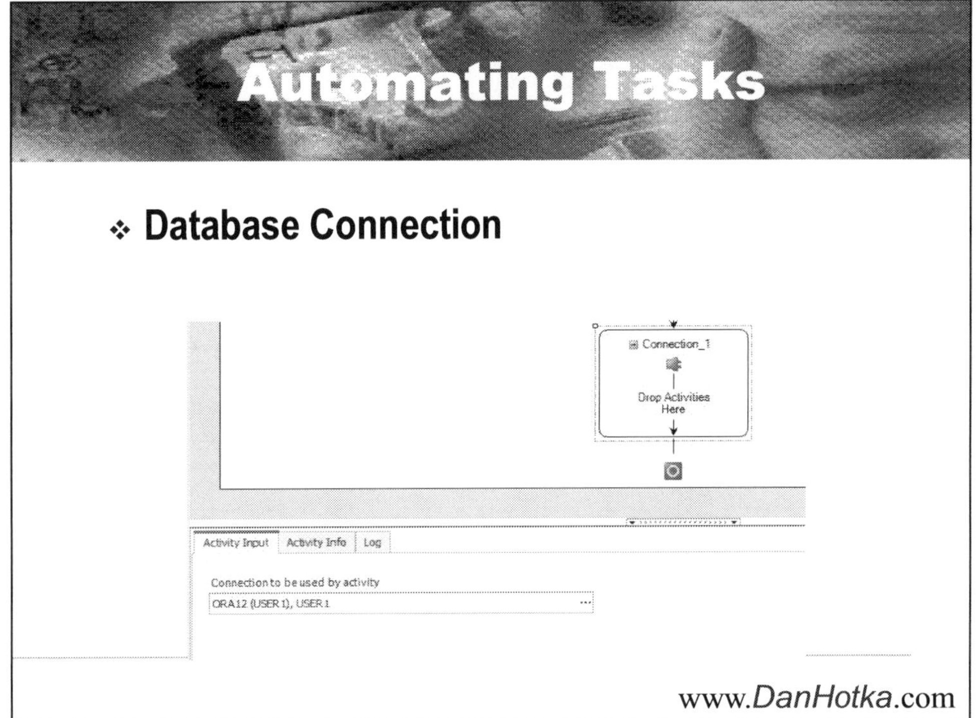
Automating Tasks
Database Connection
Connection_1
Drop Activities Here
Activity Input
Activity Info
Log
Connection to be used by activity
ORA12 (USER1), USER1
www.DanHotka.com

This one is useful if you need to switch connections during the course of your script. Also requires saved passwords.

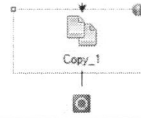

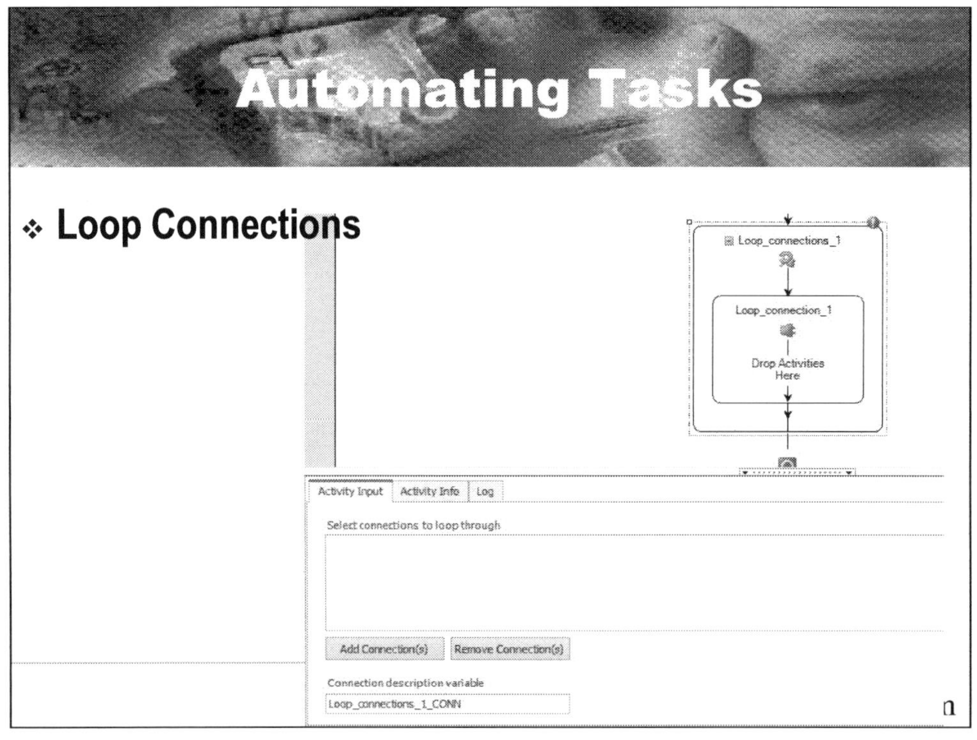


# Automating Tasks

- Copy File

Activity Input | Activity Info | Log

Source file:

Copy to folder:

Copy name:

Copy file suffix:

Overwrite file

Delete source file

Copy_1

www.*DanHotka*.com

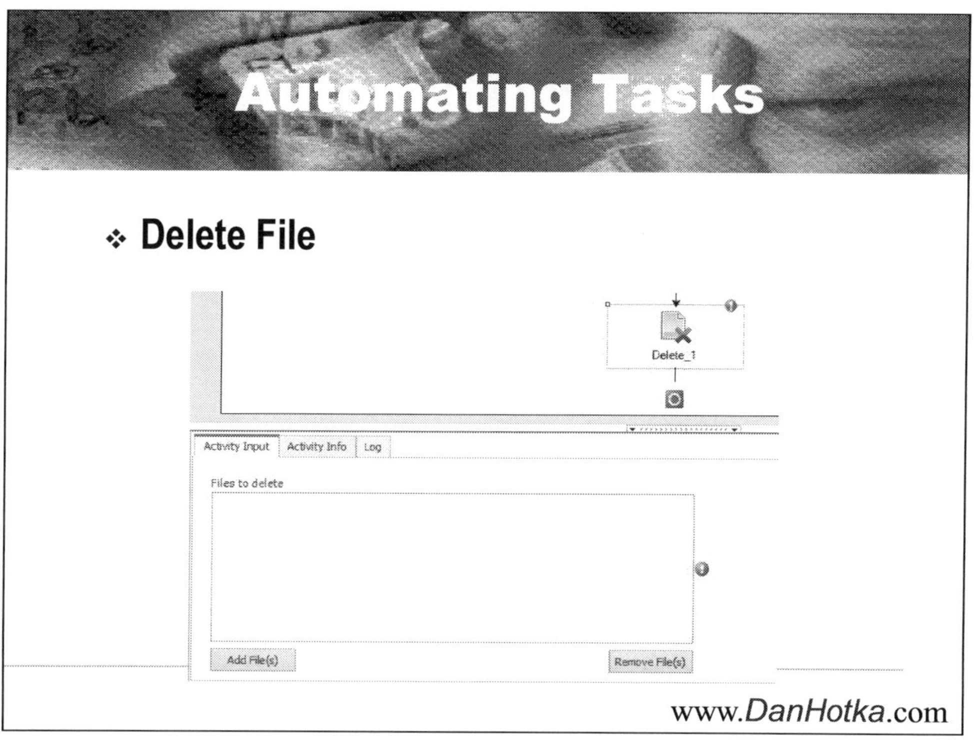
Automating Tasks
Delete File
Delete_1
Activity Input
Activity Info
Log
Files to delete
Add File(s)
Remove File(s)
www.DanHotka.com

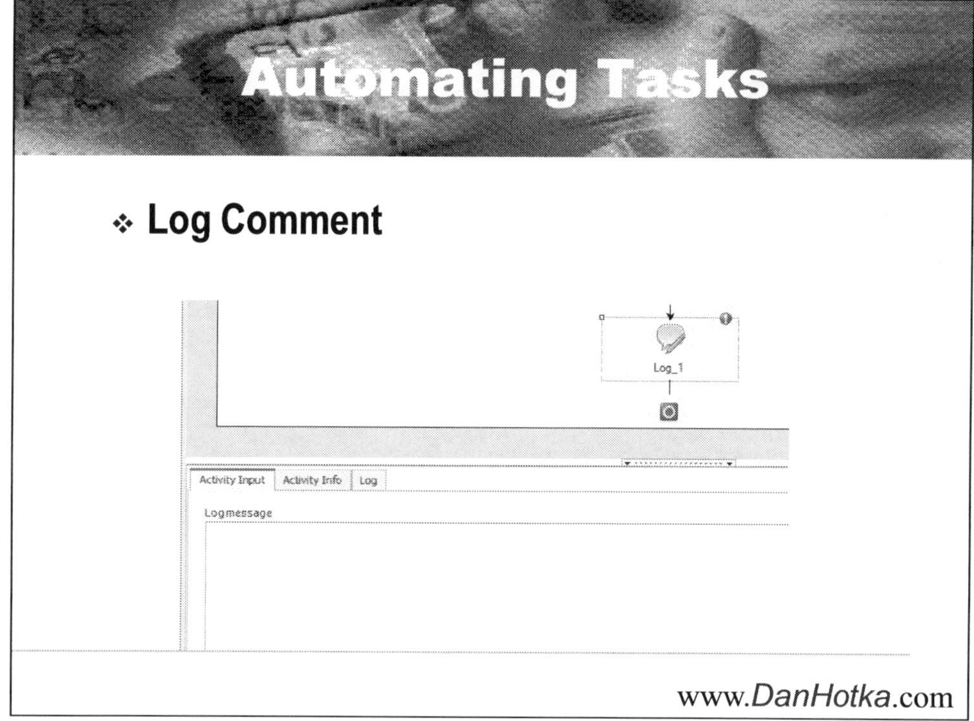
Automating Tasks
Log Comment
Log_1
Activity Input
Activity Info
Log
Logmessage
www.DanHotka.com

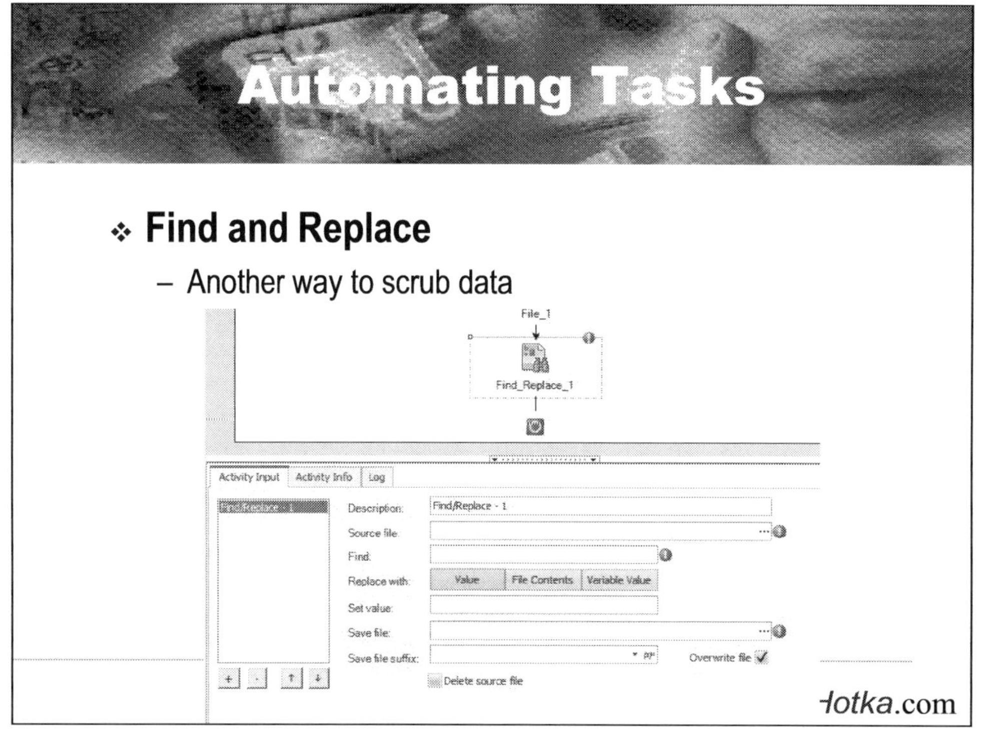


# Automating Tasks

- **FTP**

FTP_1

Activity Input | Activity Info | Log

Select an FTP connection

Define Operations...

Transfer ONLY if

www.DanHotka.com

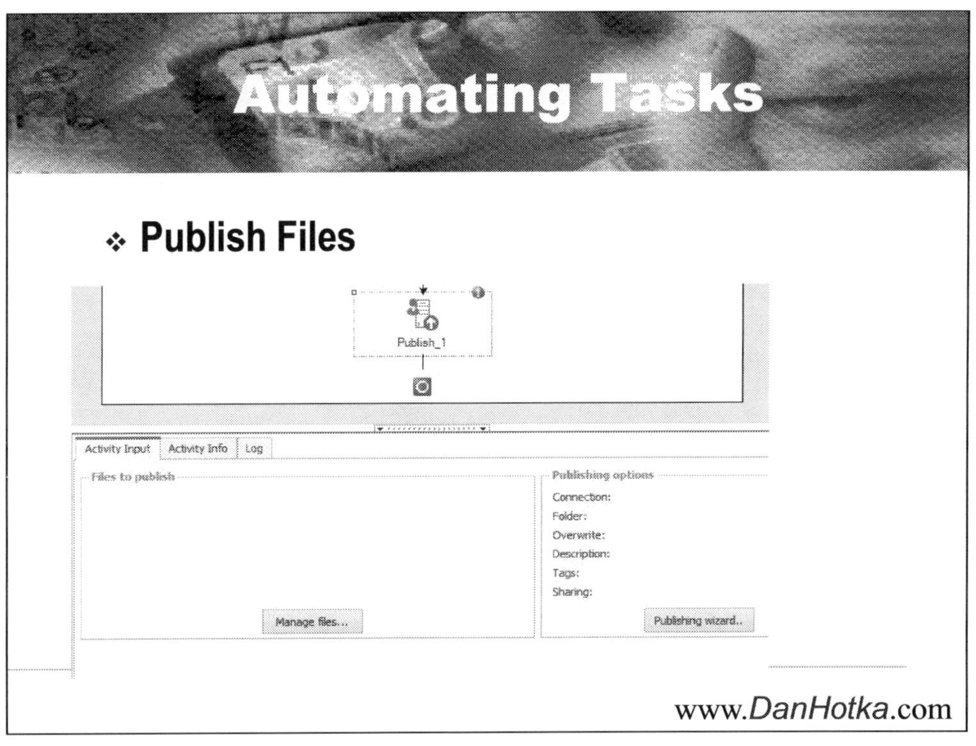
Automating Tasks
Publish Files
Publish_1
Activity Input
Activity Info
Log
Files to publish
Manage files...
Publishing options
Connection:
Folder:
Overwrite:
Description:
Tags:
Sharing:
Publishing wizard..
www.DanHotka.com

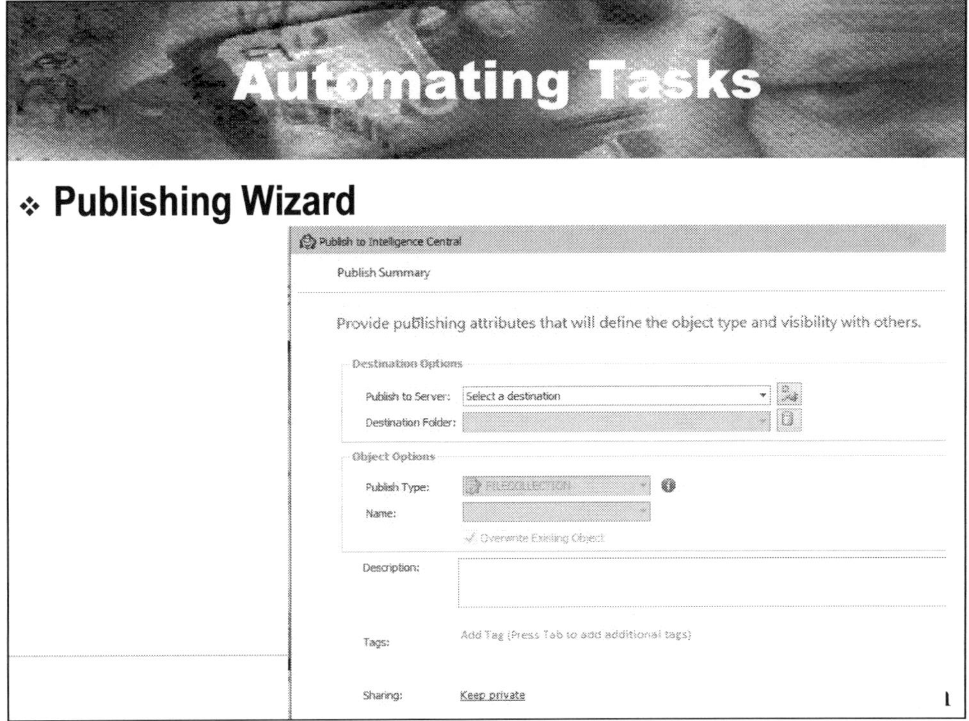
Automating Tasks
Publishing Wizard
Publish to Intelligence Central
Publish Summary
Provide publishing attributes that will define the object type and visibility with others.
Destination Options
Publish to Server:
Select a destination
Destination Folder:
Object Options
Publish Type:
Name:
Overwrite Existing Object
Description:
Tags:
Add Tag (Press Tab to add additional tags)
Sharing:
Keep private

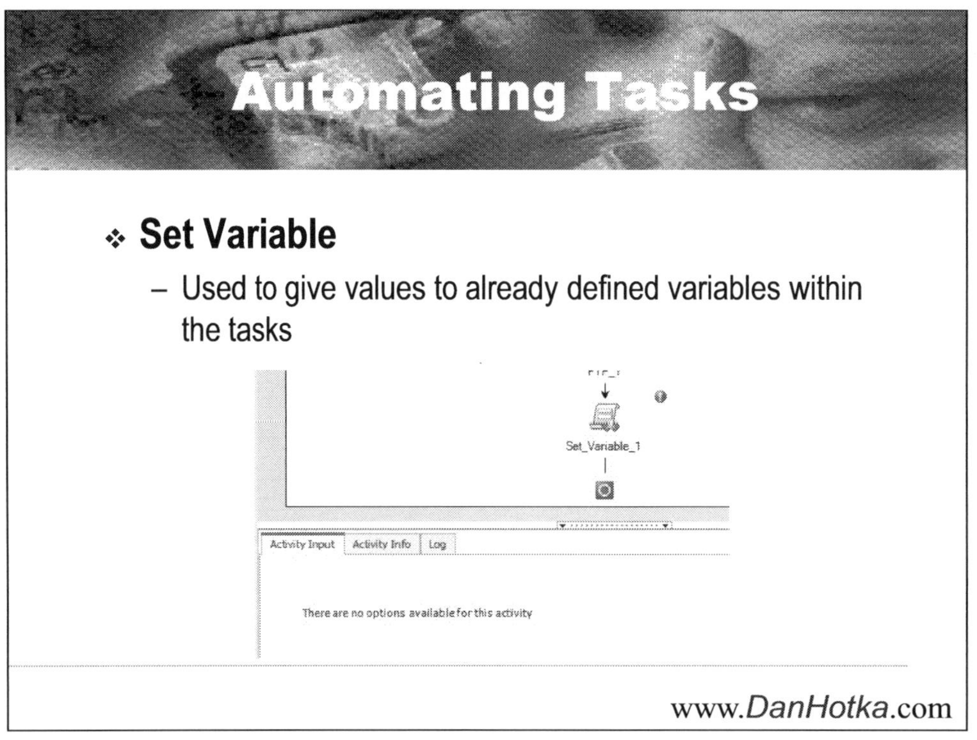
Automating Tasks
Set Variable
– Used to give values to already defined variables within the tasks
Set_Variable_1
Activity Input
Activity Info
Log
There are no options available for this activity
www.DanHotka.com

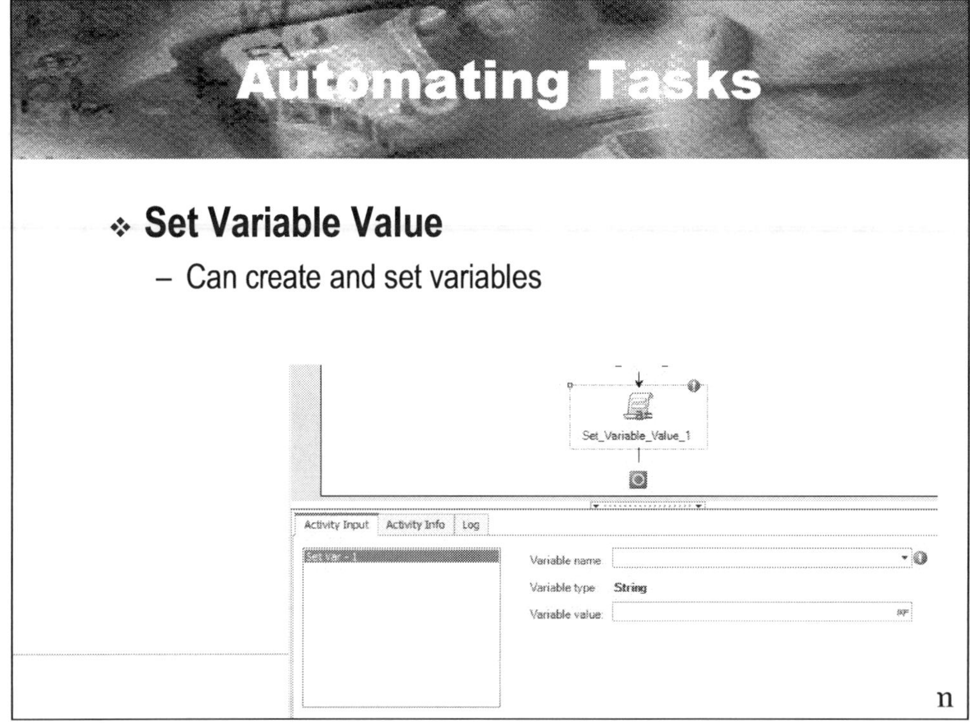
Automating Tasks
Set Variable Value
– Can create and set variables
Set_Variable_Value_1
Activity Input
Activity Info
Log
Variable name
Variable type
String
Variable value

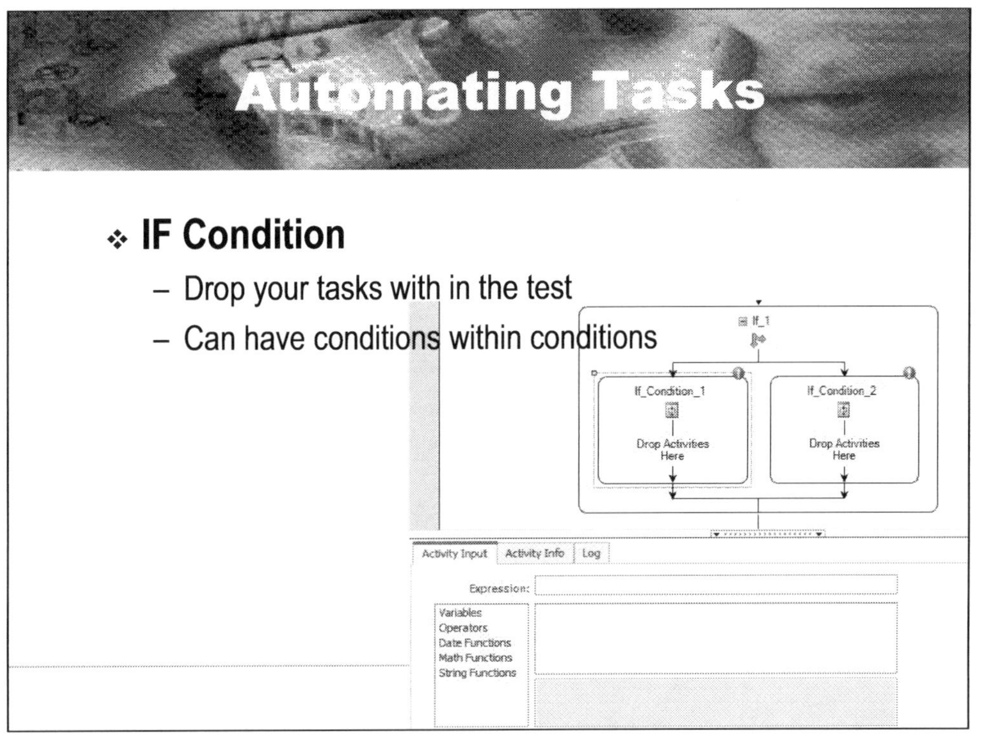
Automating Tasks
IF Condition
– Drop your tasks with in the test
– Can have conditions within conditions
If_1
If_Condition_1
Drop Activities Here
If_Condition_2
Drop Activities Here
Activity Input
Activity Info
Log
Expression:
Variables
Operators
Date Functions
Math Functions
String Functions

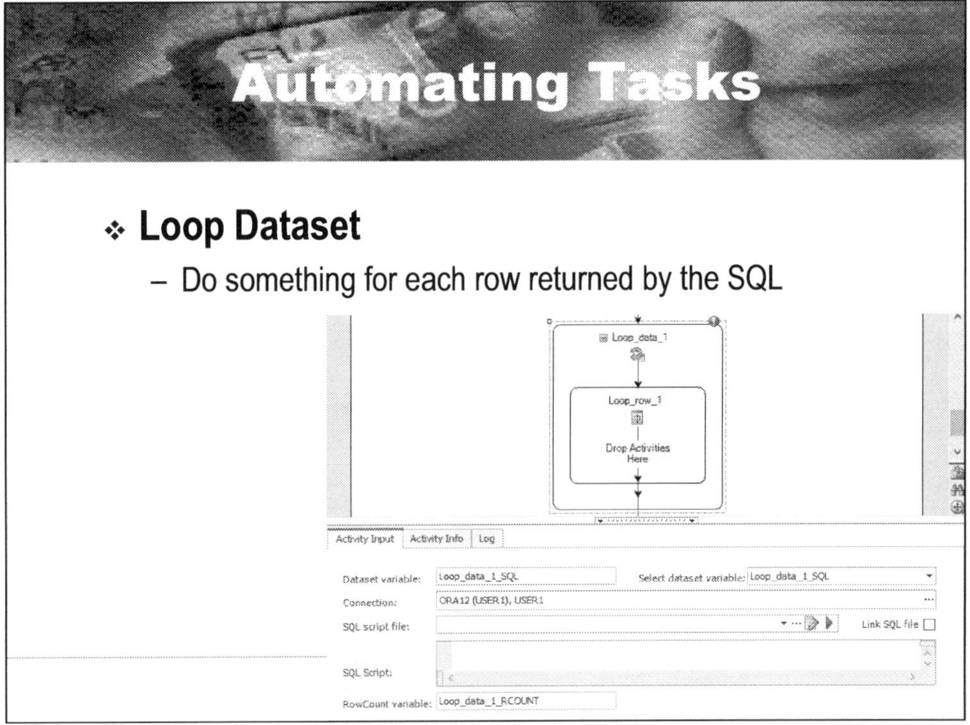
Automating Tasks
Loop Dataset
– Do something for each row returned by the SQL
Loop_data_1
Loop_row_1
Drop Activities Here
Activity Input
Activity Info
Log
Dataset variable: Loop_data_1_SQL
Select dataset variable: Loop_data_1_SQL
Connection: ORA12 (USER1), USER1
SQL script file:
Link SQL file
SQL Script:
RowCount variable: Loop_data_1_RCOUNT

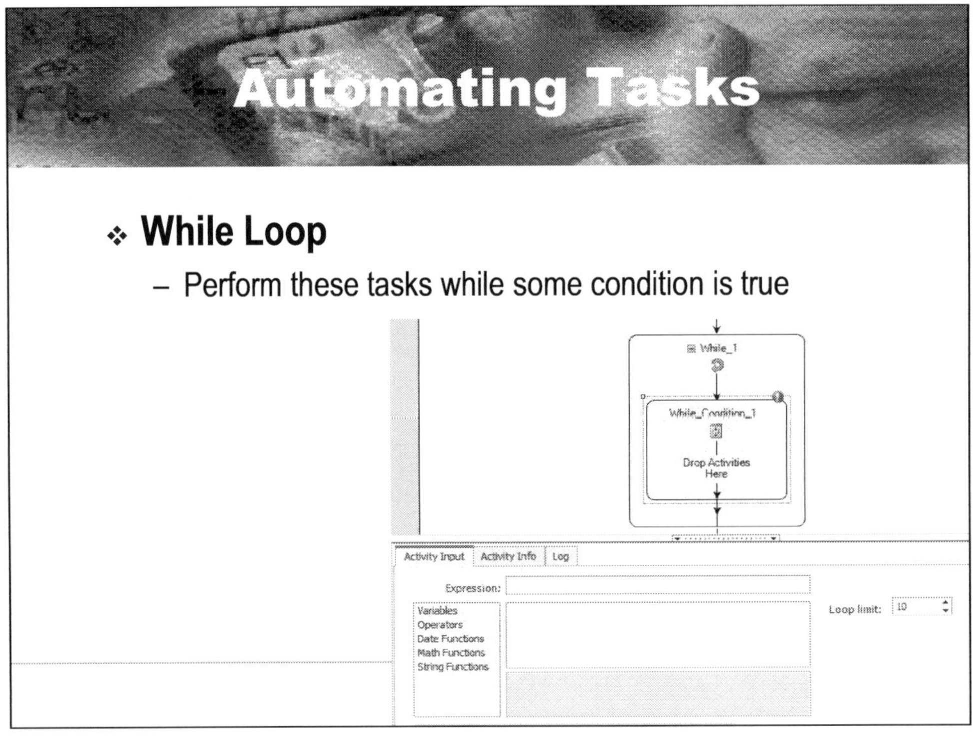
Automating Tasks
While Loop
– Perform these tasks while some condition is true
While_1
Drop Activities Here
Activity Input
Activity Info
Log
Expression:
Variables
Operators
Date Functions
Math Functions
String Functions
Loop limit:
10

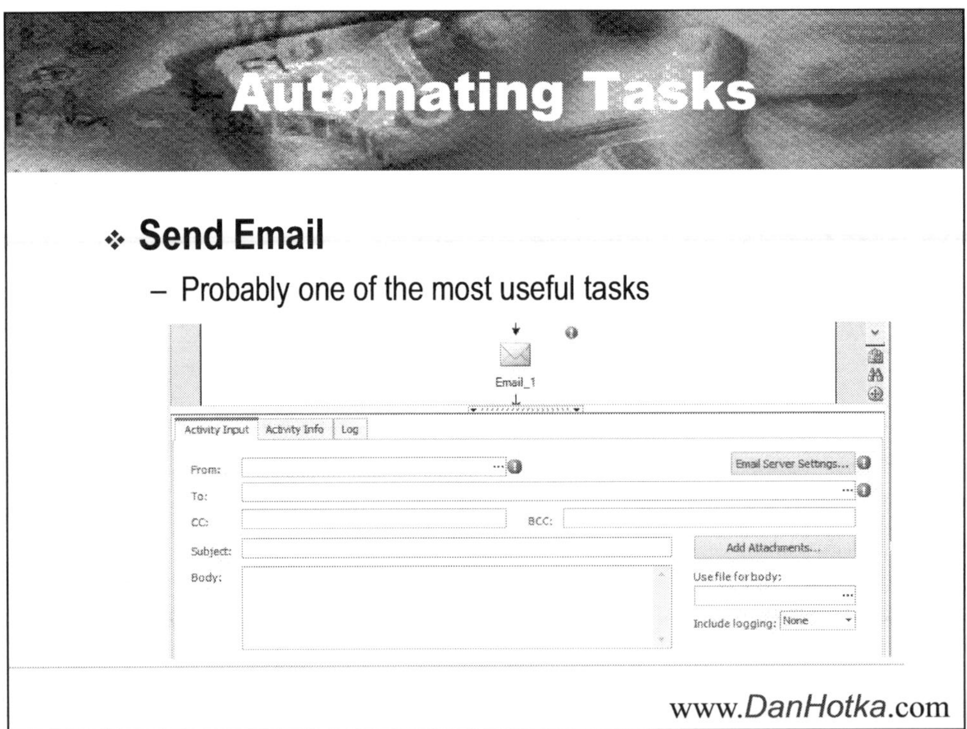
Automating Tasks
Send Email
– Probably one of the most useful tasks
Email_1
Activity Input
Activity Info
Log
From:
Email Server Settings...
To:
CC:
BCC:
Subject:
Add Attachments...
Body:
Use file for body:
Include logging:
None
www.DanHotka.com

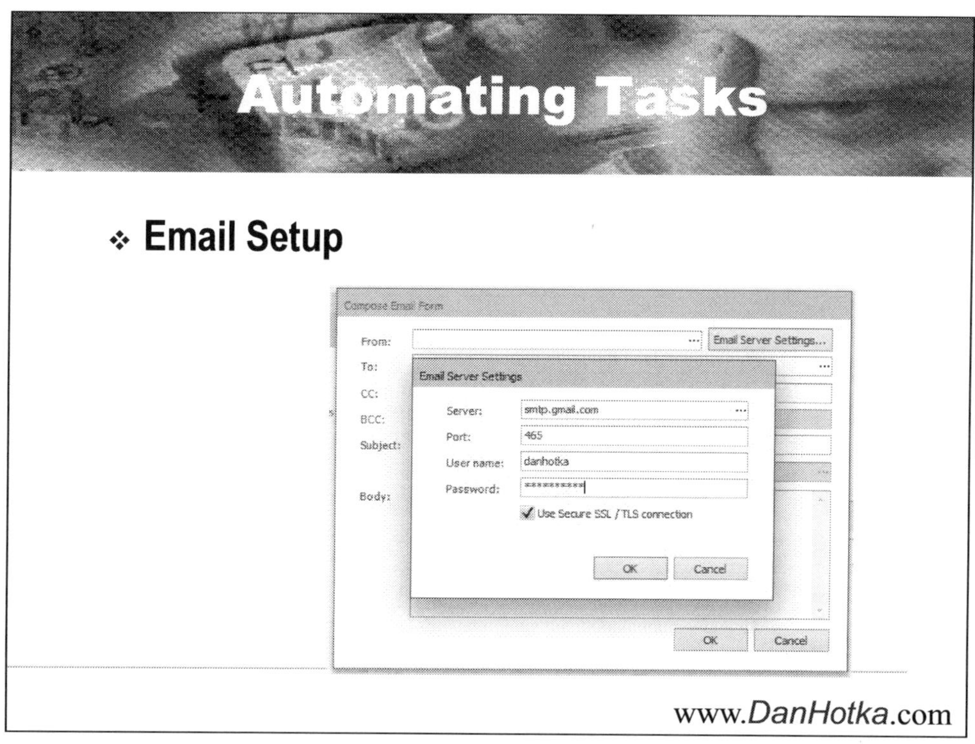
Automating Tasks
Email Setup
Compose Email Form
From:
Email Server Settings...
To:
CC:
BCC:
Subject:
Body:
Email Server Settings
Server: smtp.gmail.com
Port: 465
User name: danhotka
Password:
Use Secure SSL / TLS connection
OK
Cancel
OK
Cancel
www.DanHotka.com

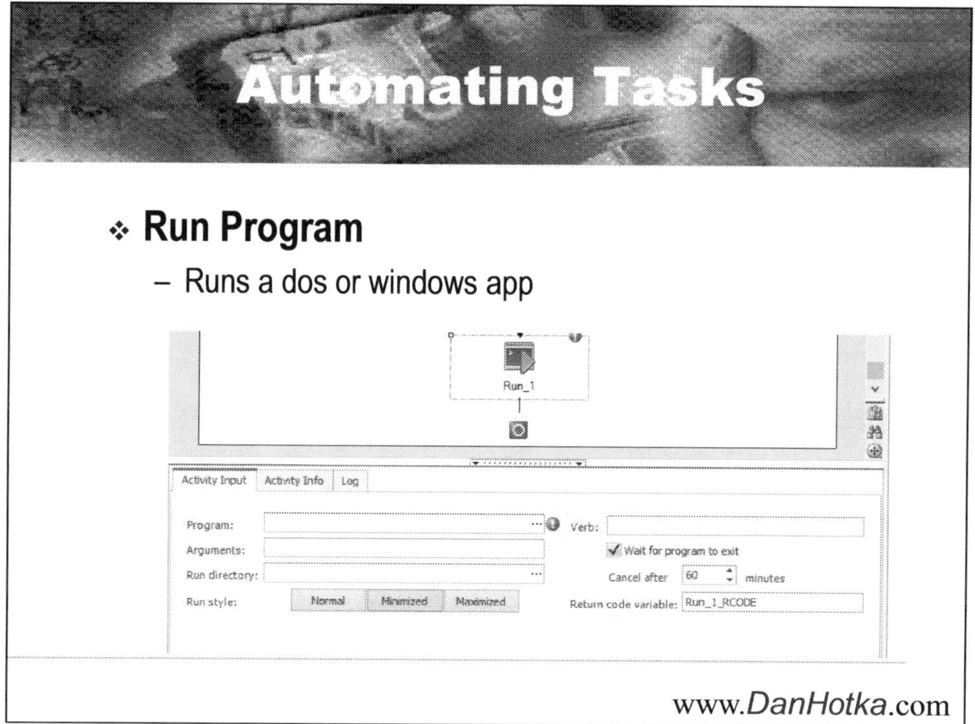
Automating Tasks
Run Program
– Runs a dos or windows app
Run_1
Activity Input
Activity Info
Log
Program:
Verb:
Arguments:
Wait for program to exit
Run directory:
Cancel after 60 minutes
Run style:
Normal
Minimized
Maximized
Return code variable: Run_1_RCODE
www.DanHotka.com

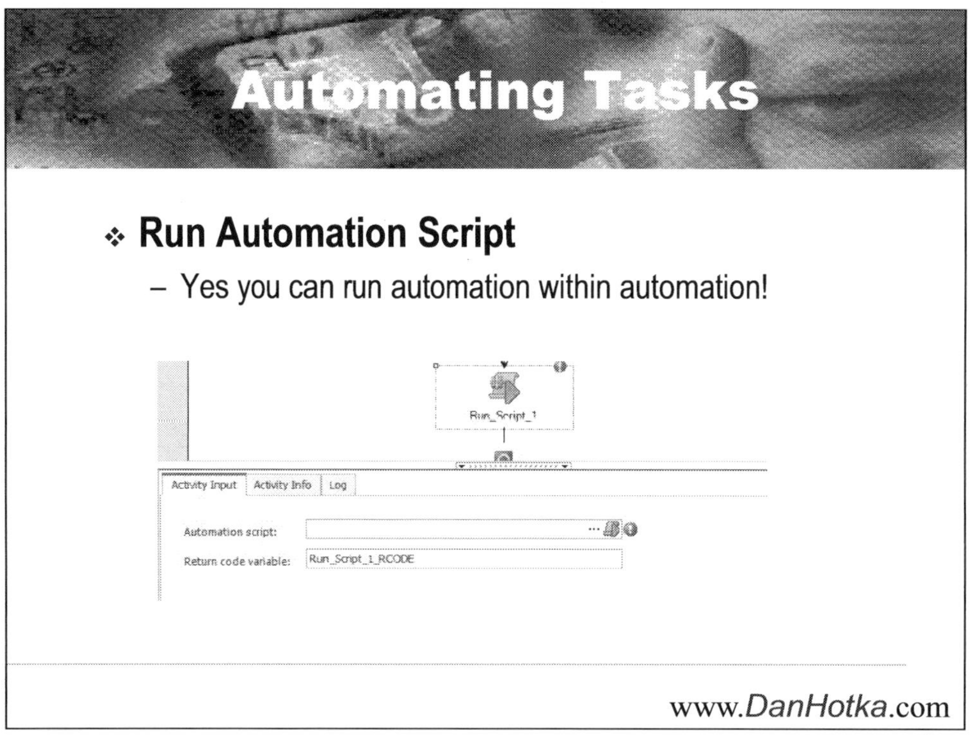
Automating Tasks
Run Automation Script
– Yes you can run automation within automation!
Run_Script_1
Activity Input
Activity Info
Log
Automation script:
Return code variable:
Run_Script_1_RCODE
www.DanHotka.com

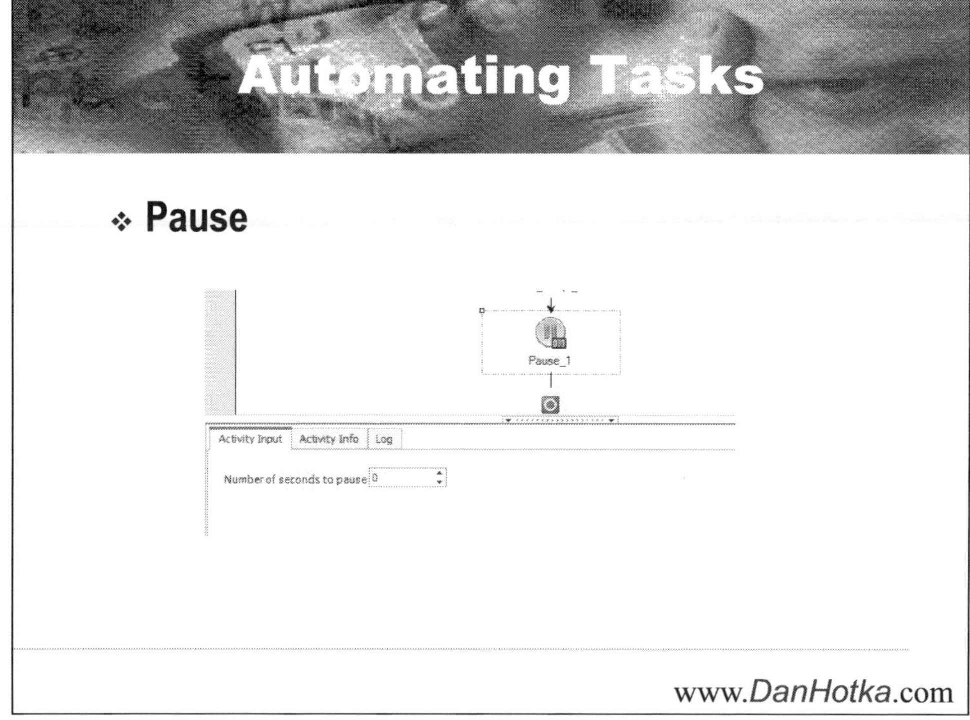
Automating Tasks
Pause
Pause_1
Activity Input
Activity Info
Log
Number of seconds to pause
0
www.DanHotka.com

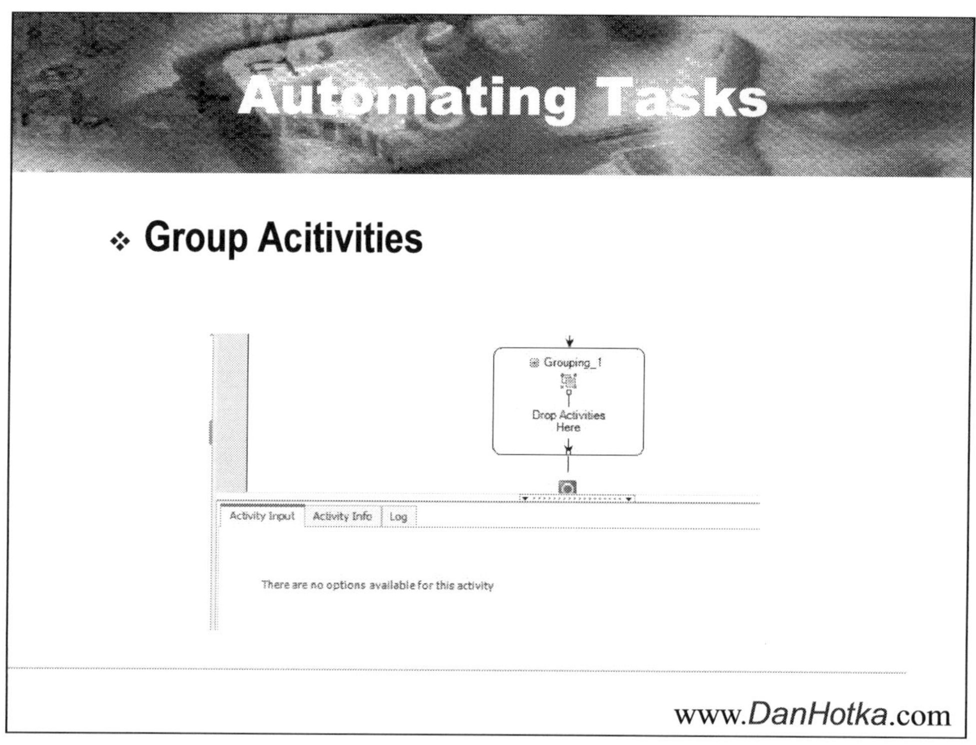
Automating Tasks
Group Acitivities
Grouping_1
Drop Activities Here
Activity Input
Activity Info
Log
There are no options available for this activity
www.DanHotka.com

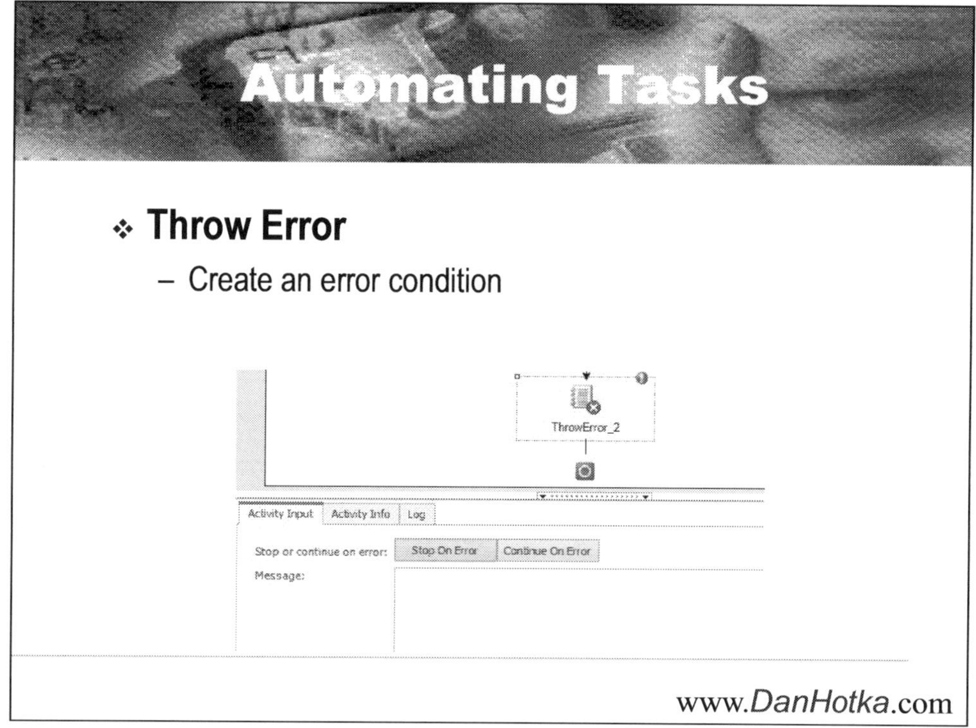
Automating Tasks
Throw Error
– Create an error condition
ThrowError_2
Activity Input
Activity Info
Log
Stop or continue on error:
Stop On Error
Continue On Error
Message:
www.DanHotka.com

# Automating Tasks

- **Parallel**
  - Run tasks at the same time

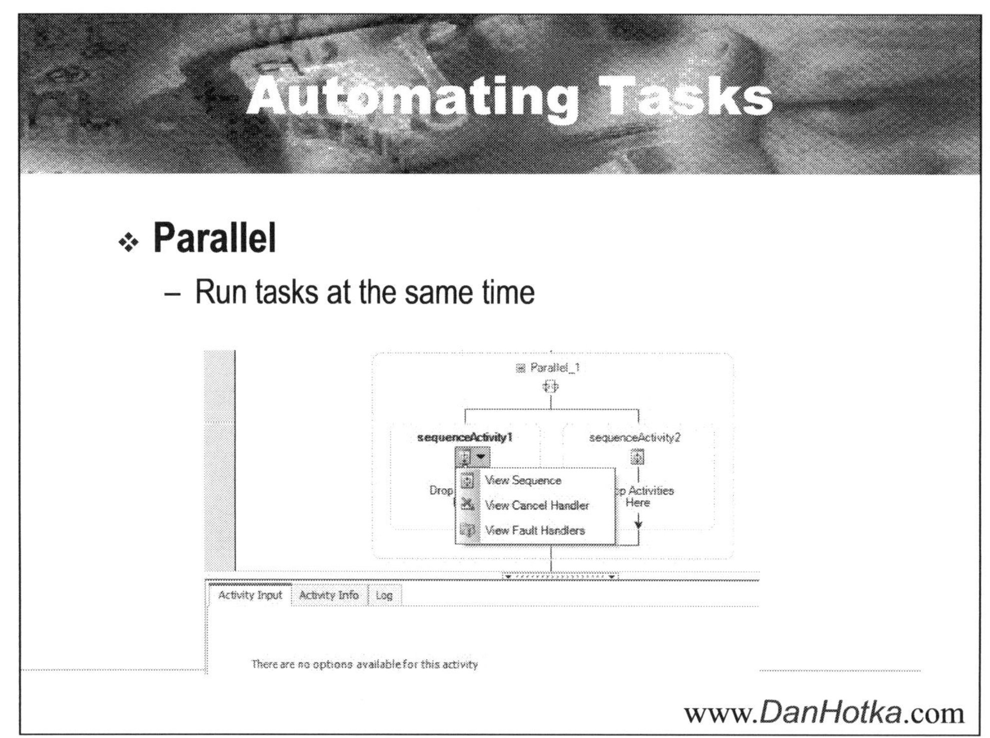


www.DanHotka.com

## Using Automation Designer

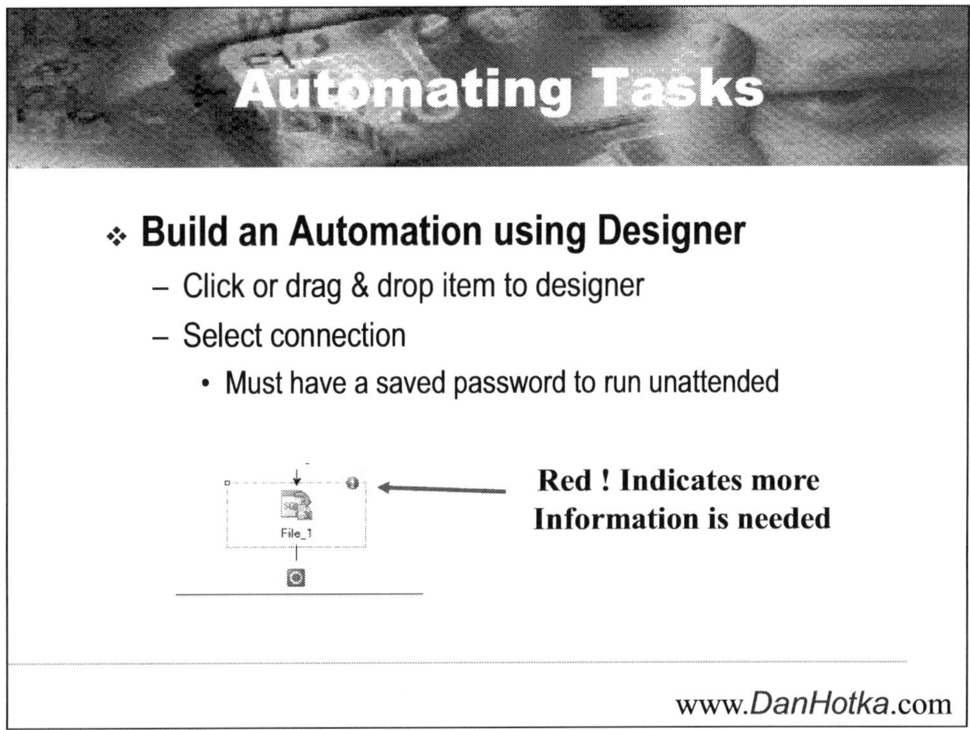
Automating Tasks
Build an Automation using Designer
– Click or drag & drop item to designer
– Select connection
• Must have a saved password to run unattended
File_1
Red ! Indicates more
Information is needed
www.DanHotka.com

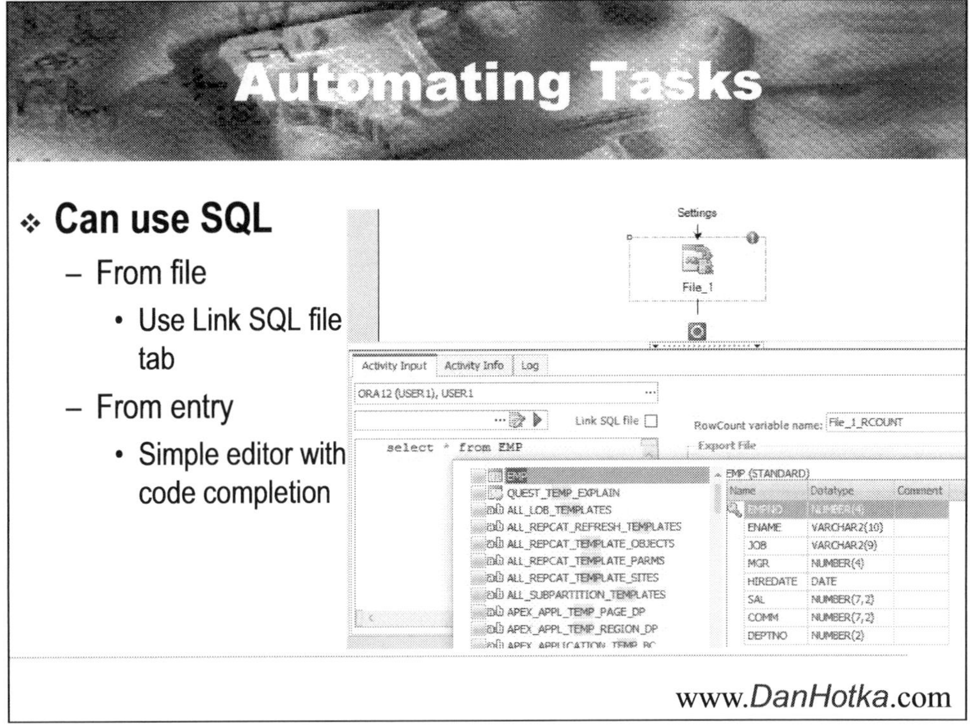
Automating Tasks
Can use SQL
– From file
• Use Link SQL file tab
– From entry
• Simple editor with code completion
Settings
File_1
Activity Input
Activity Info
Log
ORA12 (USER1), USER1
Link SQL file
RowCount variable name:
File_1_RCOUNT
select * from EMP
www.DanHotka.com

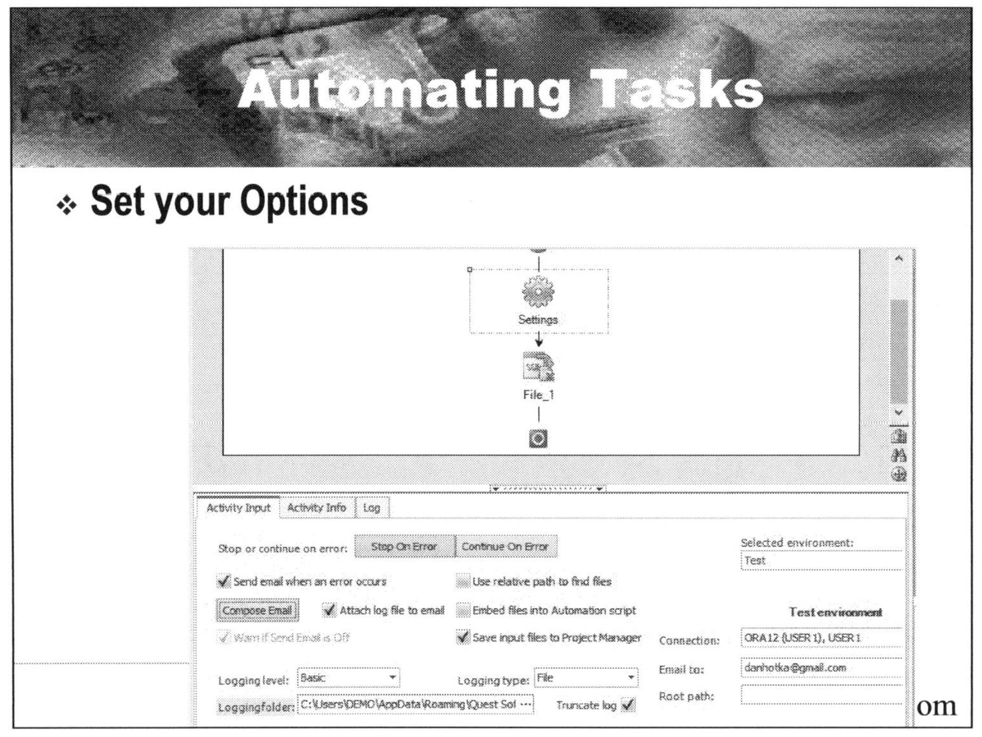
Automating Tasks
Set your Options
Settings
File_1
Activity Input
Activity Info
Log
Stop or continue on error:
Stop On Error
Continue On Error
Selected environment:
Test
Send email when an error occurs
Use relative path to find files
Compose Email
Attach log file to email
Embed files into Automation script
Test environment
Warn if Send Email is Off
Save input files to Project Manager
Connection:
ORA12 (USER1), USER1
Email to:
danhotka@gmail.com
Logging level:
Basic
Logging type:
File
Root path:
Loggingfolder:
C:\Users\DEMO\AppData\Roaming\Quest Sof
Truncate log
om

Automating Tasks
Setup the error notification email
Compose Email Form
From:
danhotka@gmail.com
Email Server Settings...
To:
danhotka@gmail.com
CC:
BCC:
Subject:
Automation Script Error (Script_1.tas)
Add Attachments...
Use file for body
Body:
errors in my Emp to Excel automation script
OK
Cancel
www.DanHotka.com

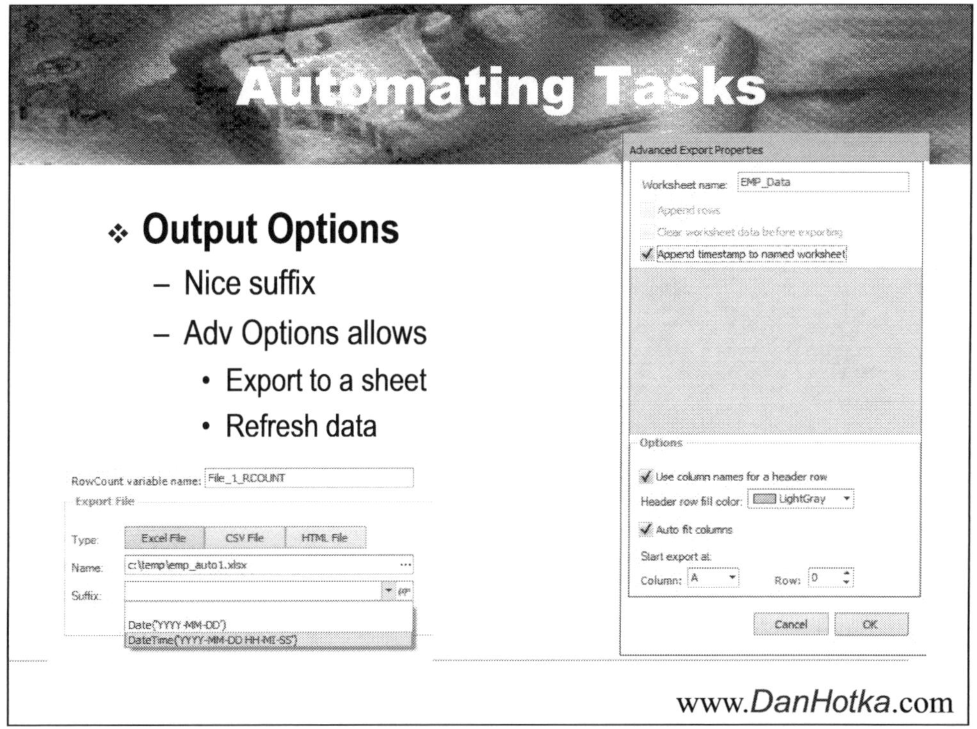
Automating Tasks
Output Options
– Nice suffix
– Adv Options allows
• Export to a sheet
• Refresh data
Advanced Export Properties
Worksheet name: EMP_Data
Append rows
Clear worksheet data before exporting
Append timestamp to named worksheet
Options
Use column names for a header row
Header row fill color: LightGray
Auto fit columns
Start export at:
Column: A
Row: 0
Cancel
OK
RowCount variable name: File_1_RCOUNT
Export File
Type:
Excel File
CSV File
HTML File
Name: c:\temp\emp_auto1.xlsx
Suffix:
Date('YYYY-MM-DD')
DateTime('YYYY-MM-DD HH-MI-SS')
www.DanHotka.com

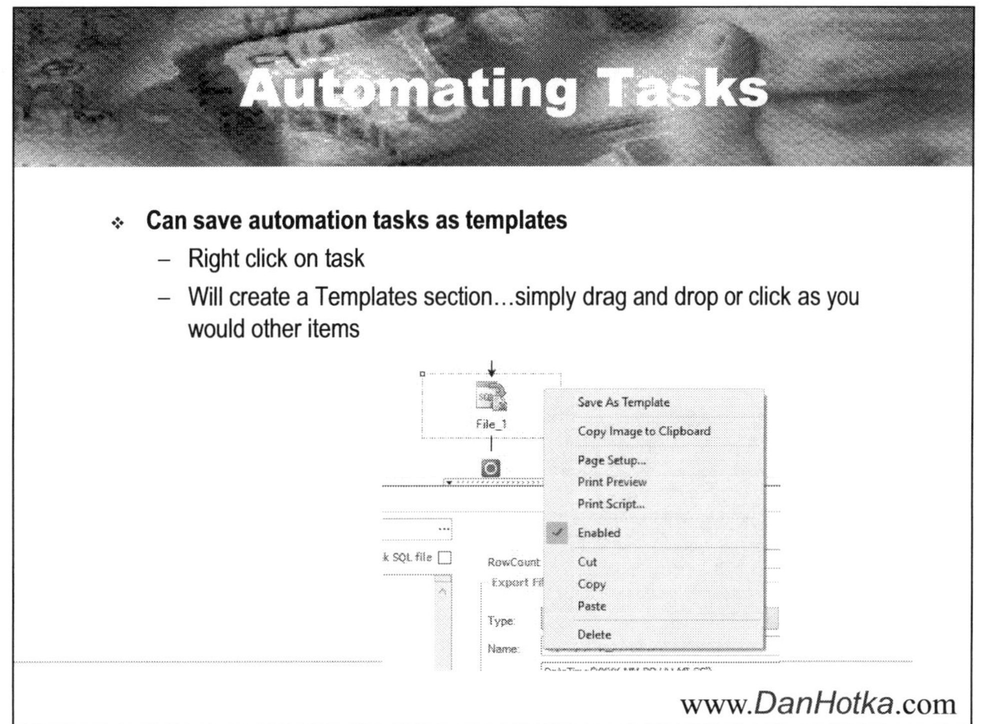
Automating Tasks
Can save automation tasks as templates
– Right click on task
– Will create a Templates section…simply drag and drop or click as you would other items
File_1
Save As Template
Copy Image to Clipboard
Page Setup...
Print Preview
Print Script...
Enabled
Cut
Copy
Paste
Delete
RowCount
Export Fi
Type:
Name:
www.DanHotka.com

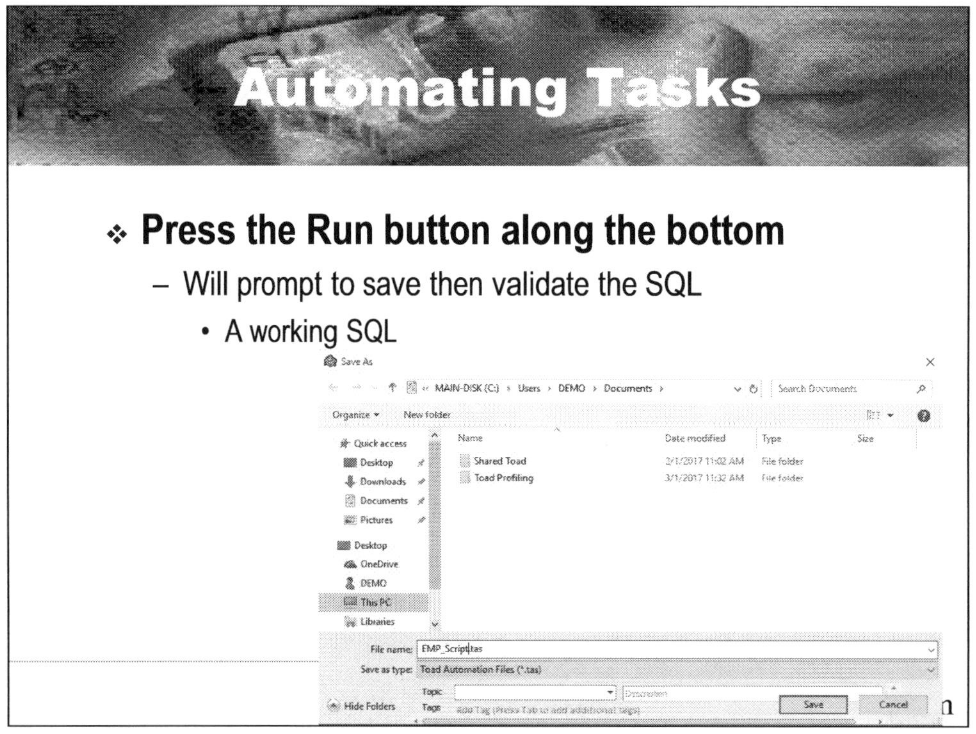
Automating Tasks
Press the Run button along the bottom
Will prompt to save then validate the SQL
A working SQL
Save As
MAIN-DISK (C:) › Users › DEMO › Documents ›
Organize ▾
New folder
Name
Date modified
Type
Size
Shared Toad
Toad Profiling
File folder
Quick access
Desktop
Downloads
Documents
Pictures
OneDrive
DEMO
This PC
Libraries
File name: EMP_Script.tas
Save as type: Toad Automation Files (*.tas)
Hide Folders
Save
Cancel

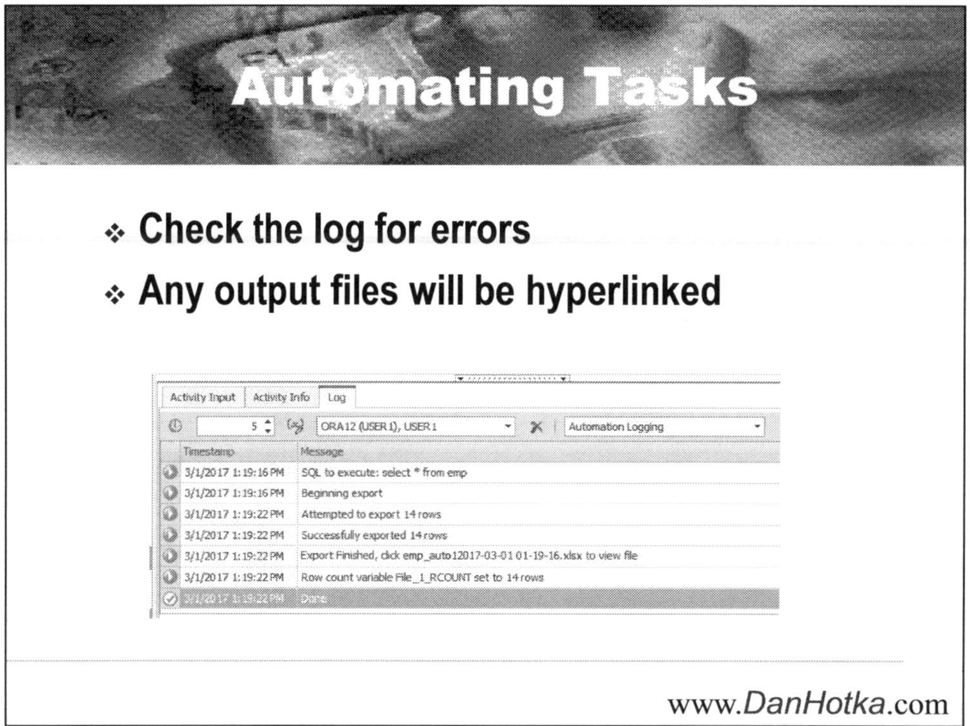
Automating Tasks
Check the log for errors
Any output files will be hyperlinked
Activity Input
Activity Info
Log
ORA12 (USER1), USER1
Automation Logging
Timestamp
Message
3/1/2017 1:19:16 PM
SQL to execute: select * from emp
3/1/2017 1:19:16 PM
Beginning export
3/1/2017 1:19:22 PM
Attempted to export 14 rows
3/1/2017 1:19:22 PM
Successfully exported 14 rows
3/1/2017 1:19:22 PM
Export Finished, click emp_auto12017-03-01 01-19-16.xlsx to view file
3/1/2017 1:19:22 PM
Row count variable File_1_RCOUNT set to 14 rows
3/1/2017 1:19:22 PM
Done
www.DanHotka.com

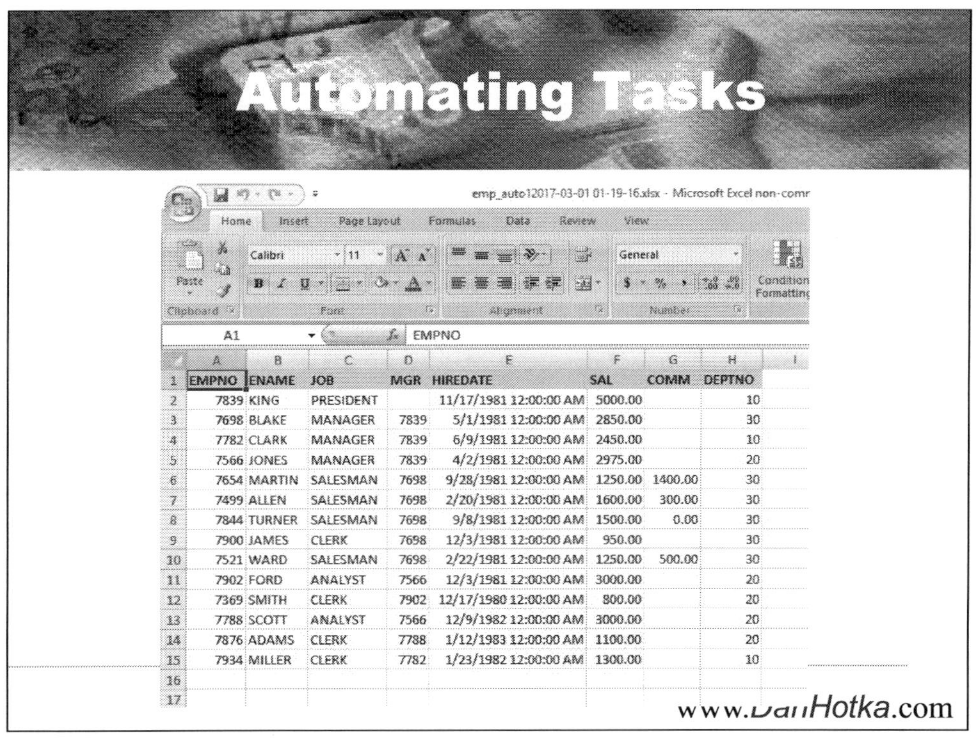

Automating Tasks

emp_auto12017-03-01 01-19-16.xlsx - Microsoft Excel non-comm

| EMPNO | ENAME | JOB | MGR | HIREDATE | SAL | COMM | DEPTNO |
|---|---|---|---|---|---|---|---|
| 7839 | KING | PRESIDENT | | 11/17/1981 12:00:00 AM | 5000.00 | | 10 |
| 7698 | BLAKE | MANAGER | 7839 | 5/1/1981 12:00:00 AM | 2850.00 | | 30 |
| 7782 | CLARK | MANAGER | 7839 | 6/9/1981 12:00:00 AM | 2450.00 | | 10 |
| 7566 | JONES | MANAGER | 7839 | 4/2/1981 12:00:00 AM | 2975.00 | | 20 |
| 7654 | MARTIN | SALESMAN | 7698 | 9/28/1981 12:00:00 AM | 1250.00 | 1400.00 | 30 |
| 7499 | ALLEN | SALESMAN | 7698 | 2/20/1981 12:00:00 AM | 1600.00 | 300.00 | 30 |
| 7844 | TURNER | SALESMAN | 7698 | 9/8/1981 12:00:00 AM | 1500.00 | 0.00 | 30 |
| 7900 | JAMES | CLERK | 7698 | 12/3/1981 12:00:00 AM | 950.00 | | 30 |
| 7521 | WARD | SALESMAN | 7698 | 2/22/1981 12:00:00 AM | 1250.00 | 500.00 | 30 |
| 7902 | FORD | ANALYST | 7566 | 12/3/1981 12:00:00 AM | 3000.00 | | 20 |
| 7369 | SMITH | CLERK | 7902 | 12/17/1980 12:00:00 AM | 800.00 | | 20 |
| 7788 | SCOTT | ANALYST | 7566 | 12/9/1982 12:00:00 AM | 3000.00 | | 20 |
| 7876 | ADAMS | CLERK | 7788 | 1/12/1983 12:00:00 AM | 1100.00 | | 20 |
| 7934 | MILLER | CLERK | 7782 | 1/23/1982 12:00:00 AM | 1300.00 | | 10 |

www.DanHotka.com

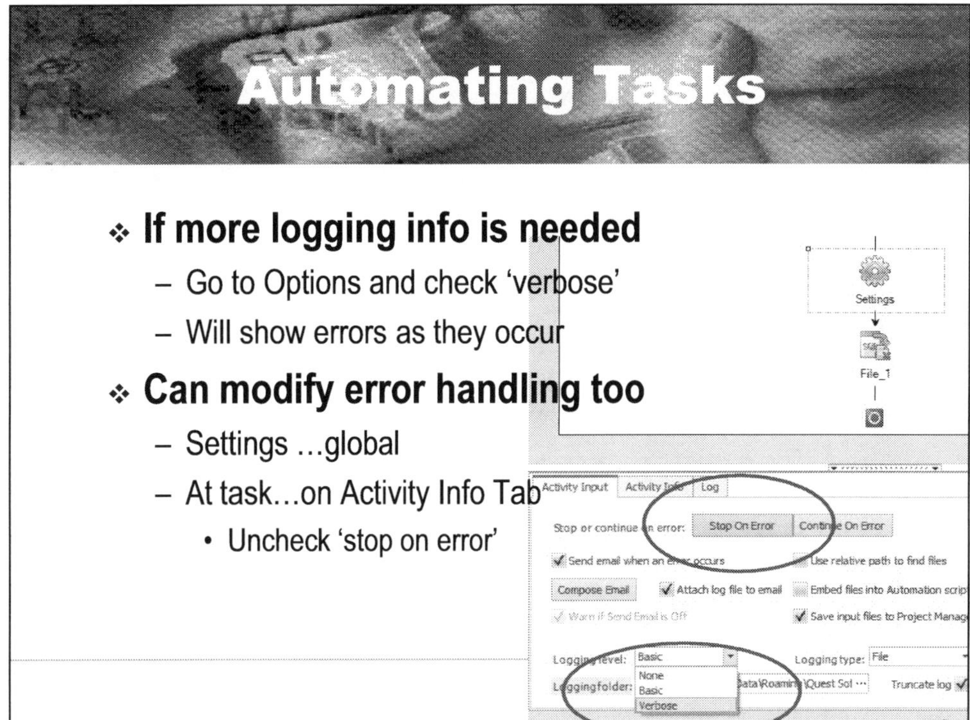

## Scheduling Automations

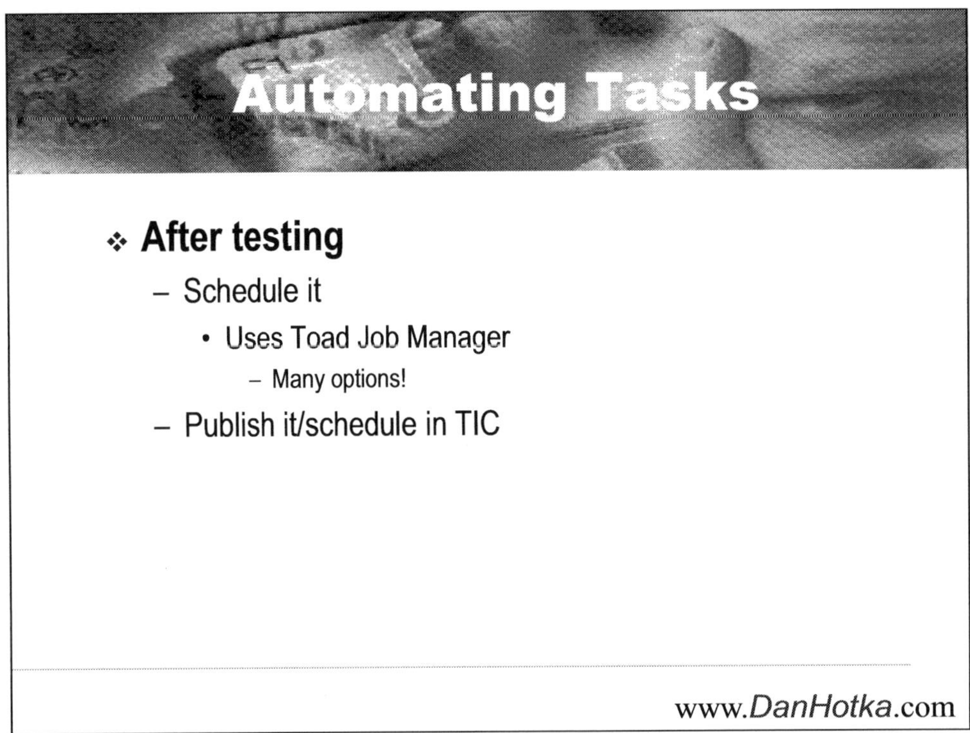
Automating Tasks
After testing
– Schedule it
• Uses Toad Job Manager
– Many options!
– Publish it/schedule in TIC
www.DanHotka.com

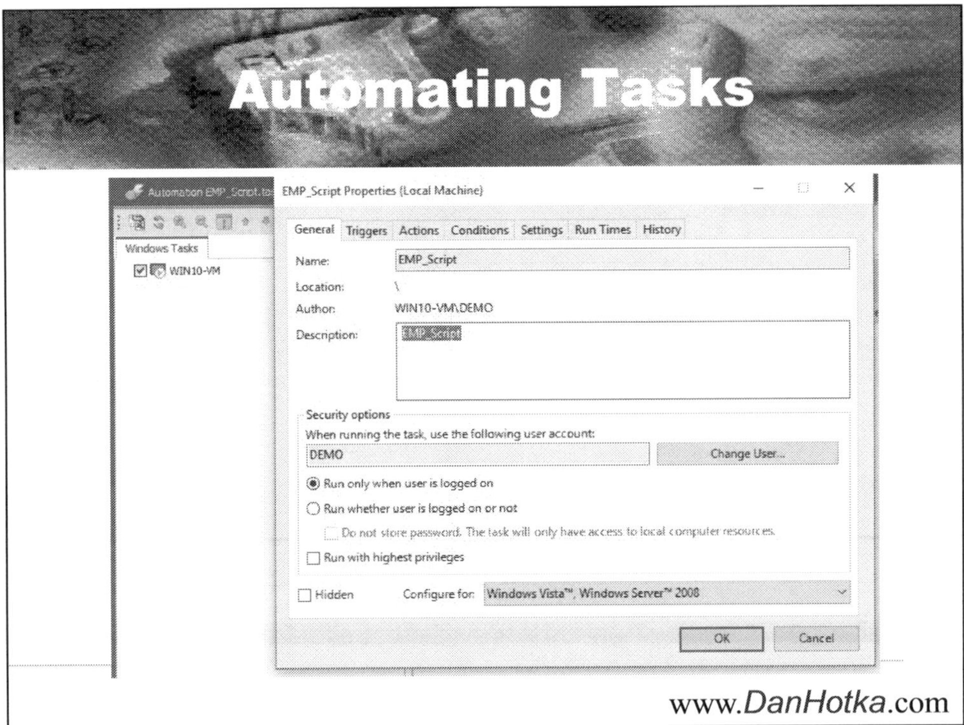
Automating Tasks
EMP_Script Properties (Local Machine)
General
Triggers
Actions
Conditions
Settings
Run Times
History
Name:
EMP_Script
Location:
Author:
WIN10-VM\DEMO
Description:
Security options
When running the task, use the following user account:
DEMO
Change User...
Run only when user is logged on
Run whether user is logged on or not
Do not store password. The task will only have access to local computer resources.
Run with highest privileges
Hidden
Configure for:
Windows Vista™, Windows Server™ 2008
OK
Cancel
Windows Tasks
WIN10-VM
www.DanHotka.com

## Automating Tasks

- ❖ **We can email the spreadsheet to anyone...**
  - Add Send Email
  - In Attachments…files generated by the script will appear
    - Simply add them to attachments
    - Can include file in email body
  - When the task is done, the email will send the file just created

www.*DanHotka*.com

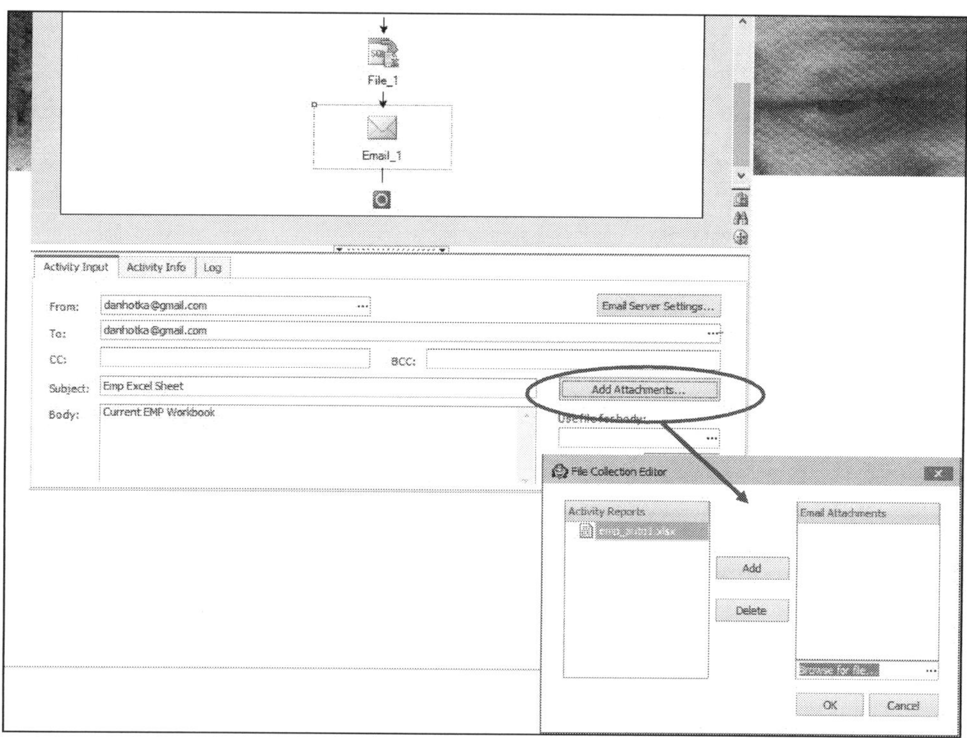

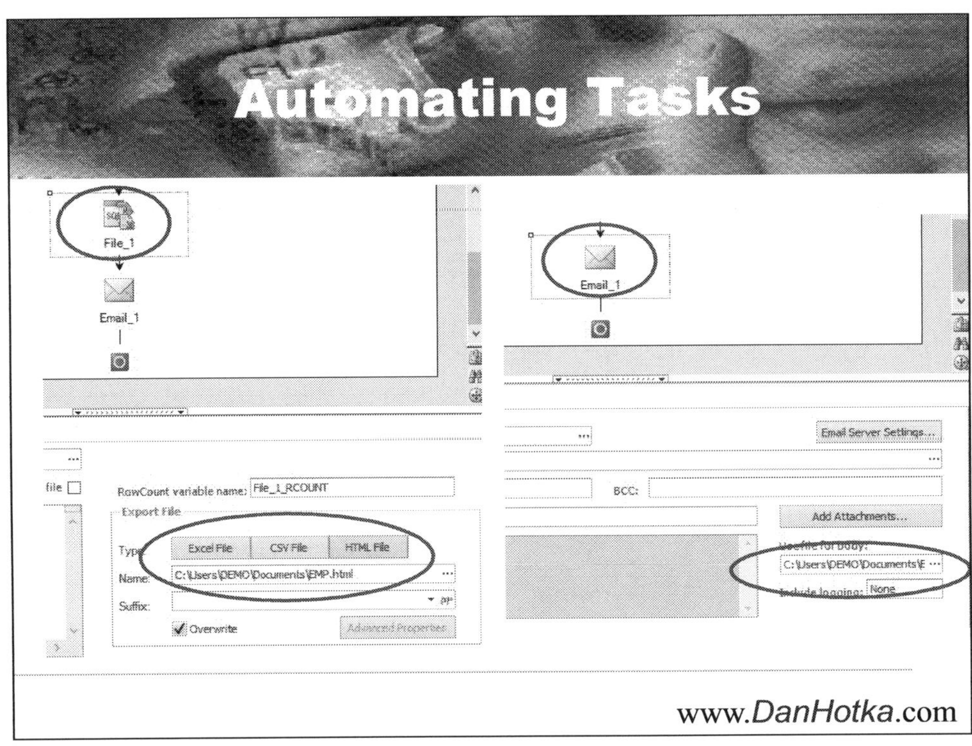
Automating Tasks
File_1
Email_1
RowCount variable name: File_1_RCOUNT
Export File
Type:
Excel File
CSV File
HTML File
Name:
C:\Users\DEMO\Documents\EMP.html
Suffix:
Overwrite
Advanced Properties
Email Server Settings...
BCC:
Add Attachments...
Include logging:
None
www.DanHotka.com

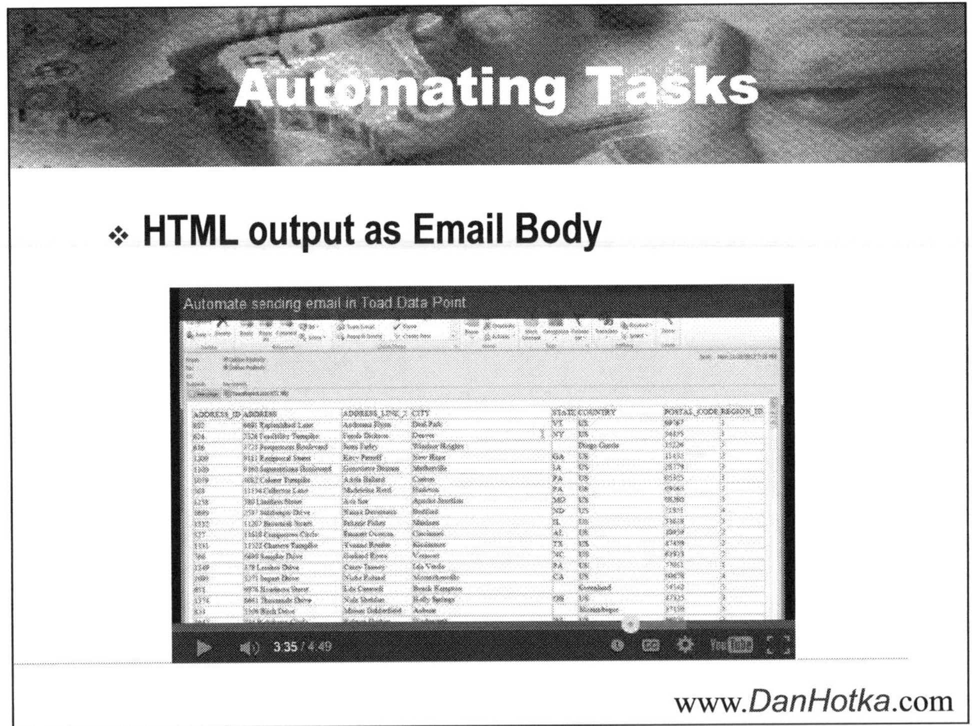
Automating Tasks
❖ HTML output as Email Body
Automate sending email in Toad Data Point
3:35 / 4:49
www.DanHotka.com

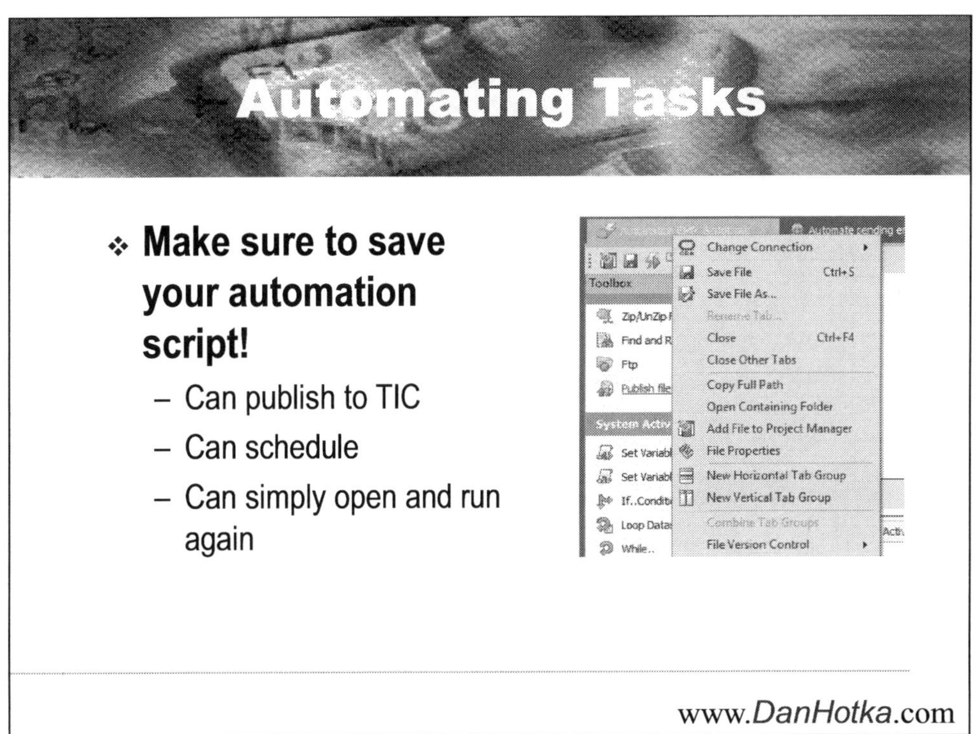


## Automation from Editor/Wizard

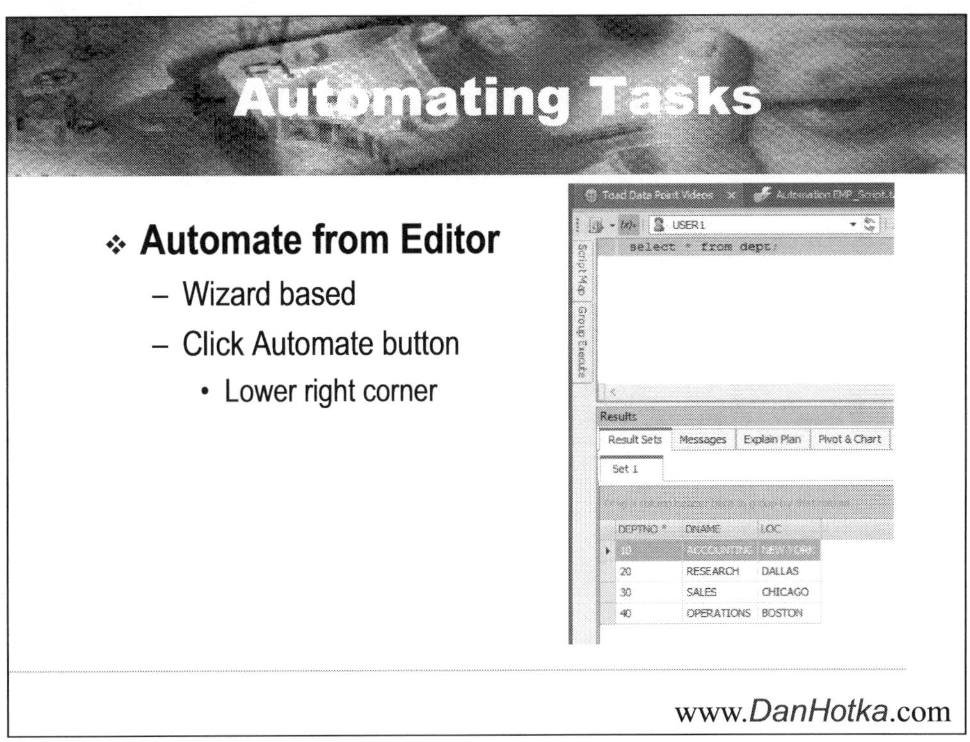

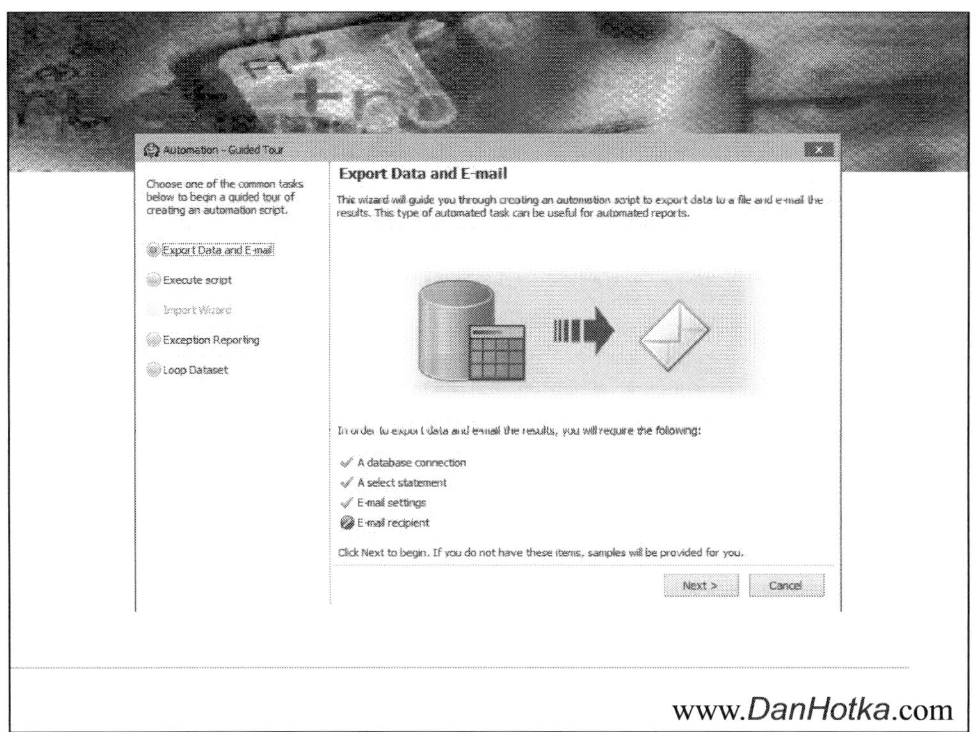
Automation - Guided Tour
Choose one of the common tasks below to begin a guided tour of creating an automation script.
Export Data and E-mail
Execute script
Import Wizard
Exception Reporting
Loop Dataset
Export Data and E-mail
This wizard will guide you through creating an automation script to export data to a file and e-mail the results. This type of automated task can be useful for automated reports.
In order to export data and e-mail the results, you will require the following:
A database connection
A select statement
E-mail settings
E-mail recipient
Click Next to begin. If you do not have these items, samples will be provided for you.
Next >
Cancel
www.DanHotka.com

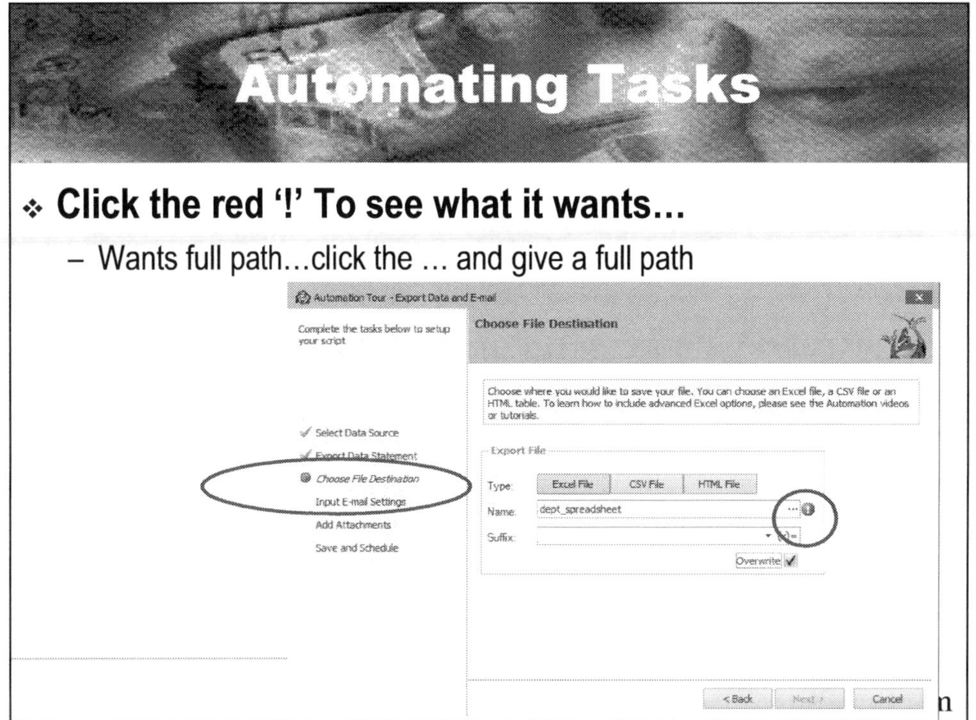
Automating Tasks
Click the red '!' To see what it wants…
– Wants full path…click the … and give a full path
Automation Tour - Export Data and E-mail
Complete the tasks below to setup your script
Select Data Source
Export Data Statement
Choose File Destination
Input E-mail Settings
Add Attachments
Save and Schedule
Choose File Destination
Choose where you would like to save your file. You can choose an Excel file, a CSV file or an HTML table. To learn how to include advanced Excel options, please see the Automation videos or tutorials.
Export File
Type:
Excel File
CSV File
HTML File
Name:
dept_spreadsheet
Suffix:
Overwrite
< Back
Next >
Cancel

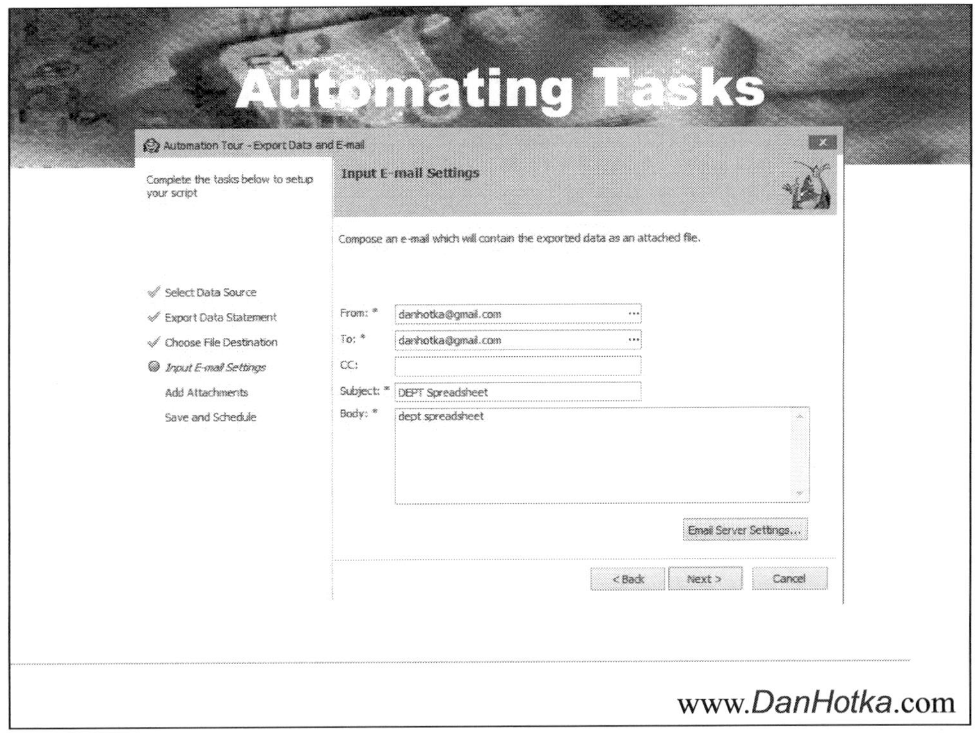
Automating Tasks
Automation Tour - Export Data and E-mail
Complete the tasks below to setup your script
Input E-mail Settings
Compose an e-mail which will contain the exported data as an attached file.
Select Data Source
Export Data Statement
Choose File Destination
Input E-mail Settings
Add Attachments
Save and Schedule
From: *
danhotka@gmail.com
To: *
danhotka@gmail.com
CC:
Subject: *
DEPT Spreadsheet
Body: *
dept spreadsheet
Email Server Settings...
< Back
Next >
Cancel
www.DanHotka.com

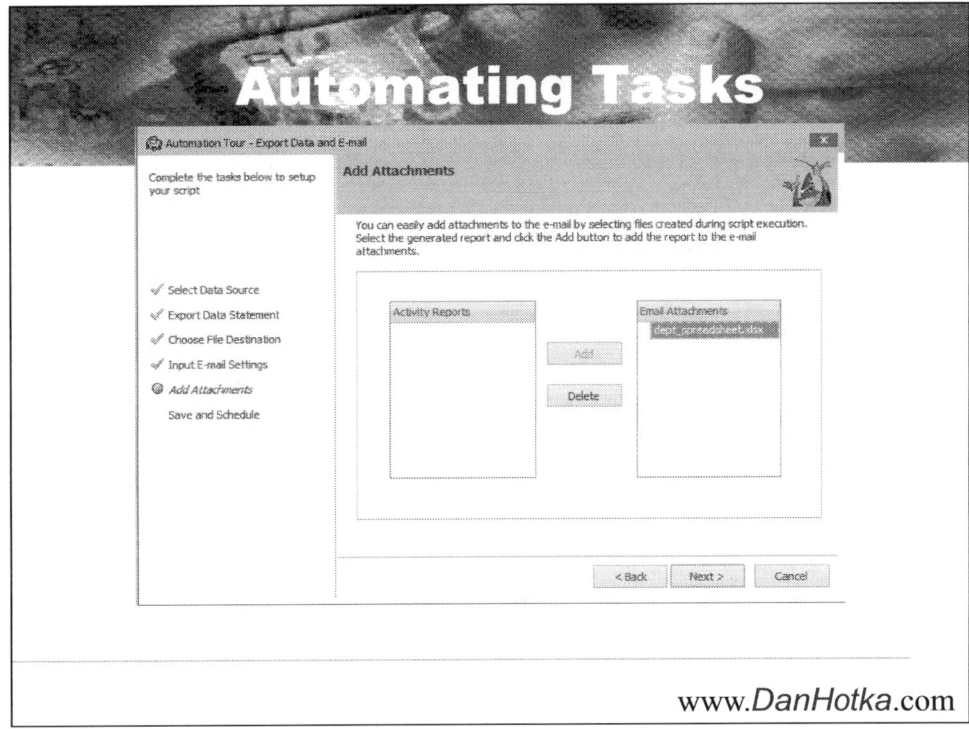
Automating Tasks
Automation Tour - Export Data and E-mail
Complete the tasks below to setup your script
Add Attachments
You can easily add attachments to the e-mail by selecting files created during script execution. Select the generated report and click the Add button to add the report to the e-mail attachments.
Select Data Source
Export Data Statement
Choose File Destination
Input E-mail Settings
Add Attachments
Save and Schedule
Activity Reports
Add
Delete
Email Attachments
dept_spreadsheet.xlsx
< Back
Next >
Cancel
www.DanHotka.com

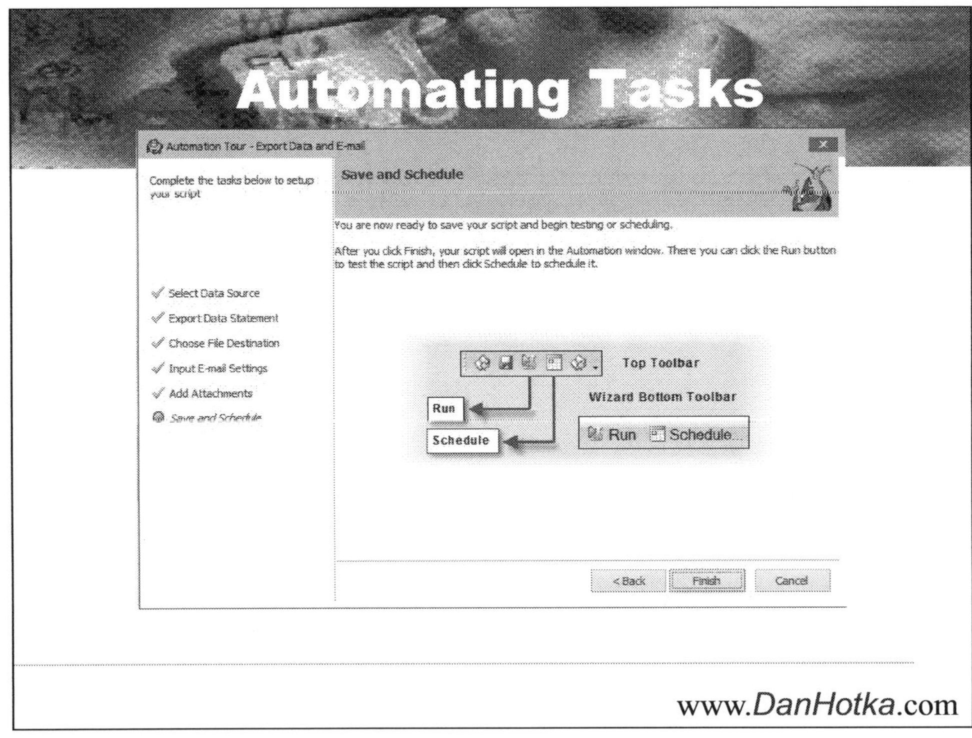
Automating Tasks
Automation Tour - Export Data and E-mail
Complete the tasks below to setup your script
Save and Schedule
You are now ready to save your script and begin testing or scheduling.
After you click Finish, your script will open in the Automation window. There you can click the Run button to test the script and then click Schedule to schedule it.
Select Data Source
Export Data Statement
Choose File Destination
Input E-mail Settings
Add Attachments
Save and Schedule
Top Toolbar
Wizard Bottom Toolbar
Run
Schedule
Run
Schedule...
< Back
Finish
Cancel
www.DanHotka.com

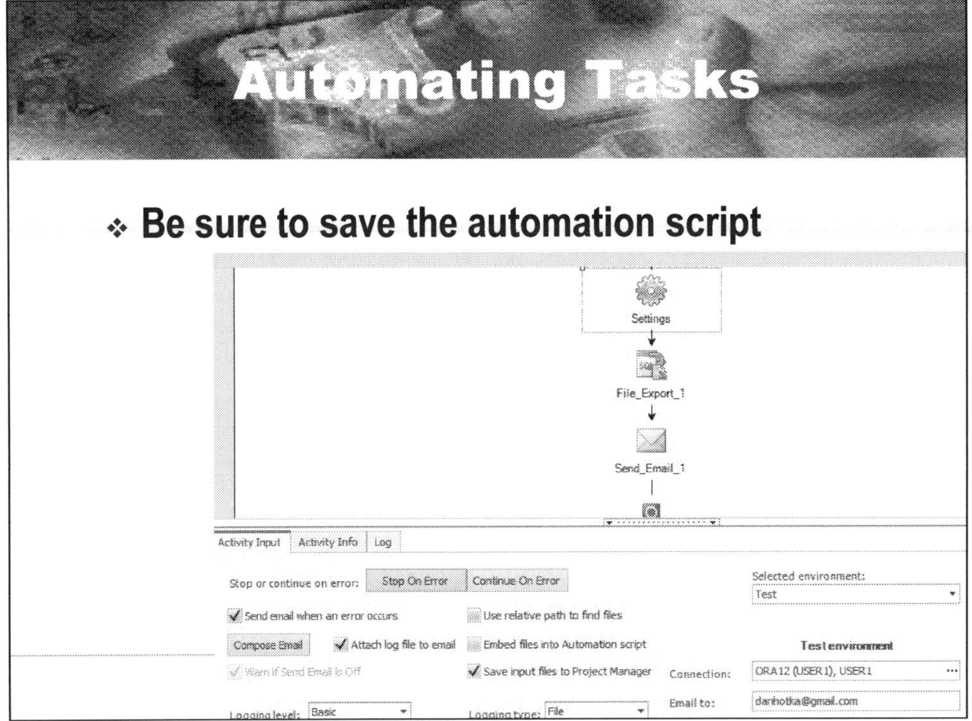
Automating Tasks
Be sure to save the automation script
Settings
File_Export_1
Send_Email_1
Activity Input
Activity Info
Log
Stop or continue on error:
Stop On Error
Continue On Error
Selected environment:
Test
Send email when an error occurs
Use relative path to find files
Compose Email
Attach log file to email
Embed files into Automation script
Test environment
Warn if Send Email is Off
Save input files to Project Manager
Connection:
ORA12 (USER1), USER1
Email to:
danhotka@gmail.com
Basic
File

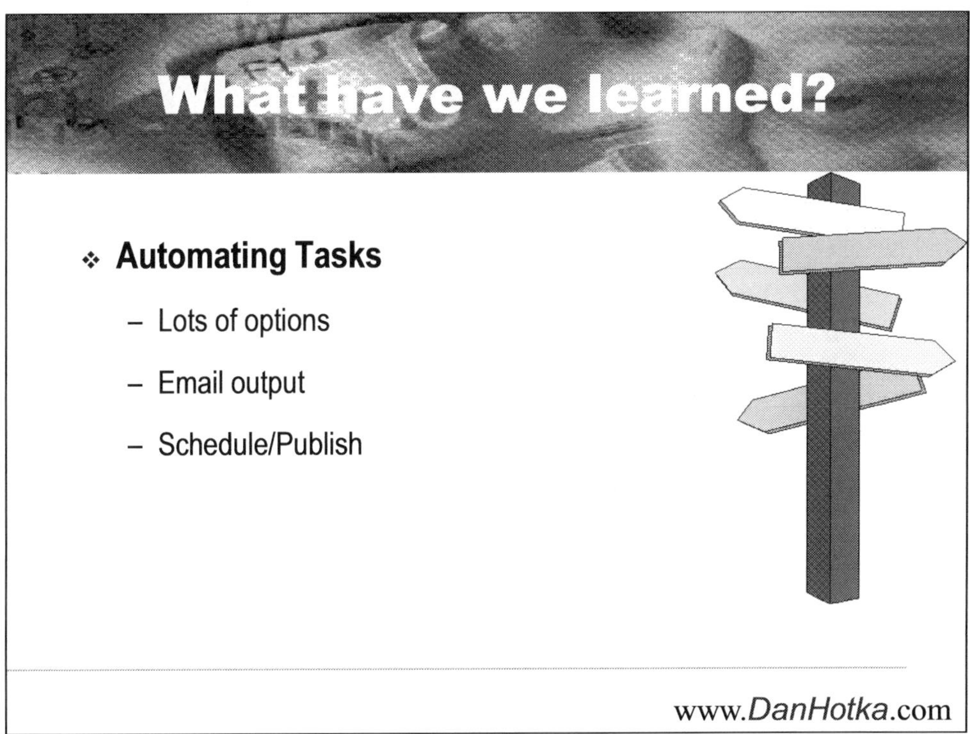
What have we learned?
Automating Tasks
– Lots of options
– Email output
– Schedule/Publish
www.DanHotka.com

## Automating Tasks Lab

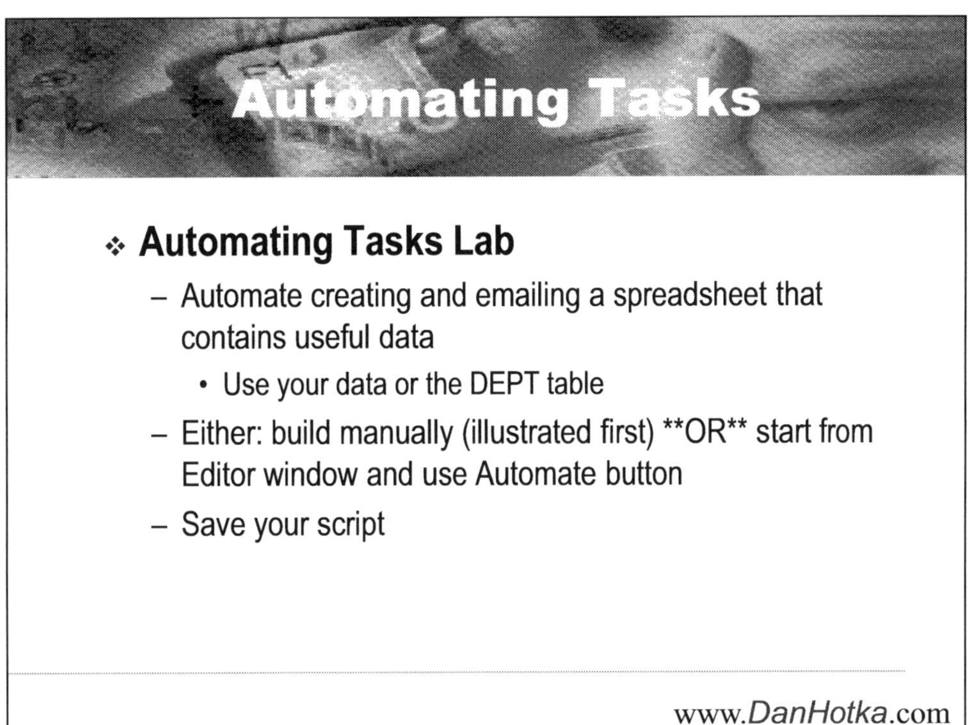
Automating Tasks
Automating Tasks Lab
– Automate creating and emailing a spreadsheet that contains useful data
• Use your data or the DEPT table
– Either: build manually (illustrated first) **OR** start from Editor window and use Automate button
– Save your script
www.DanHotka.com

## Automating Tasks Lab Answers

Automate creating and emailing a spreadsheet that contains useful data
- Use your data or the DEPT table

Save your script

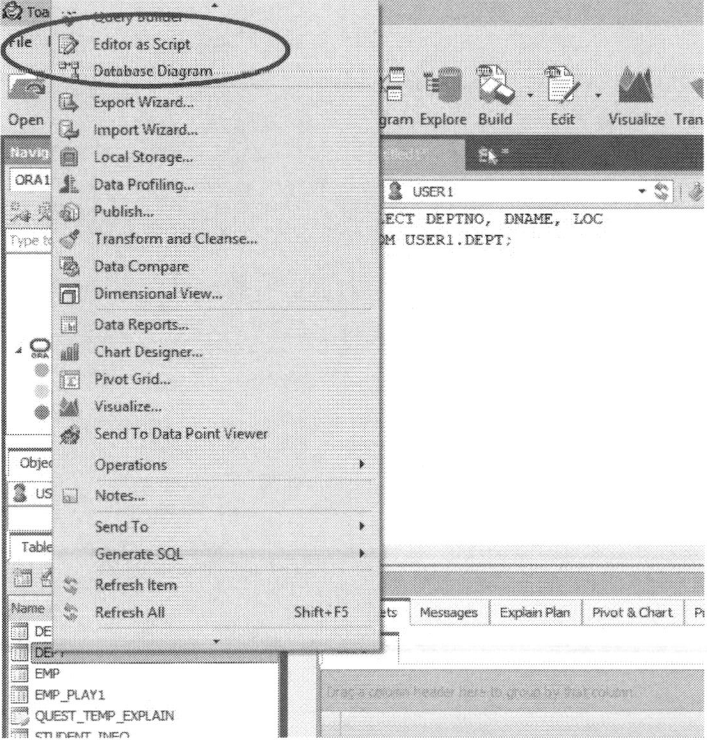


Yet another way to get a script complete with all the columns is to right click on the table object and select 'Editor as Script'.

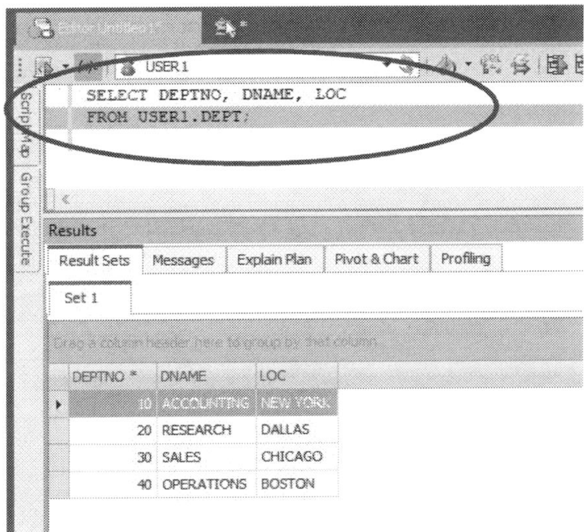


Press the 'Automate' button on the tool bar or in the lower right corner of this panel.

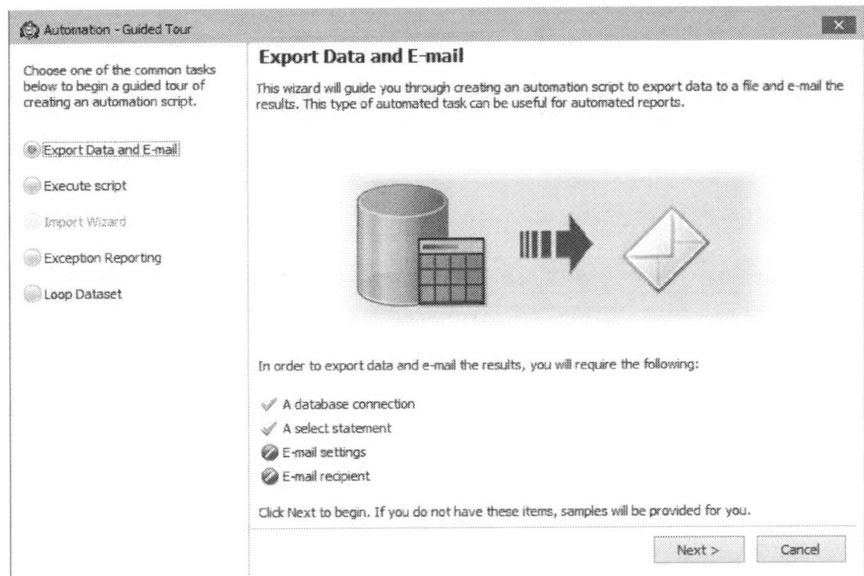


When ever there is a red button, that means the automation needs more information. Click 'Next'.

*****Note***** Notice the option to Export and E-mail! This option is your friend and will set most of this up for you…check the lecture notes to review this option.

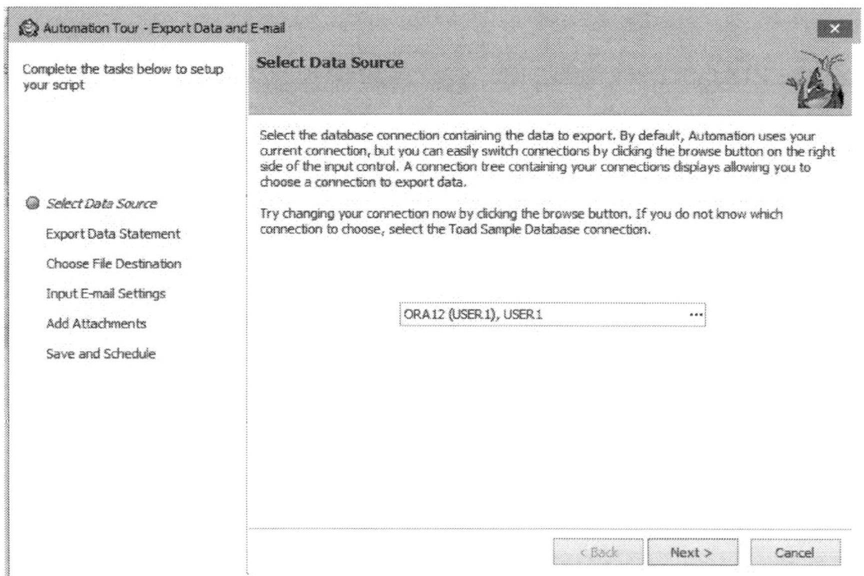


Select the database account associated with the data…click 'Next'

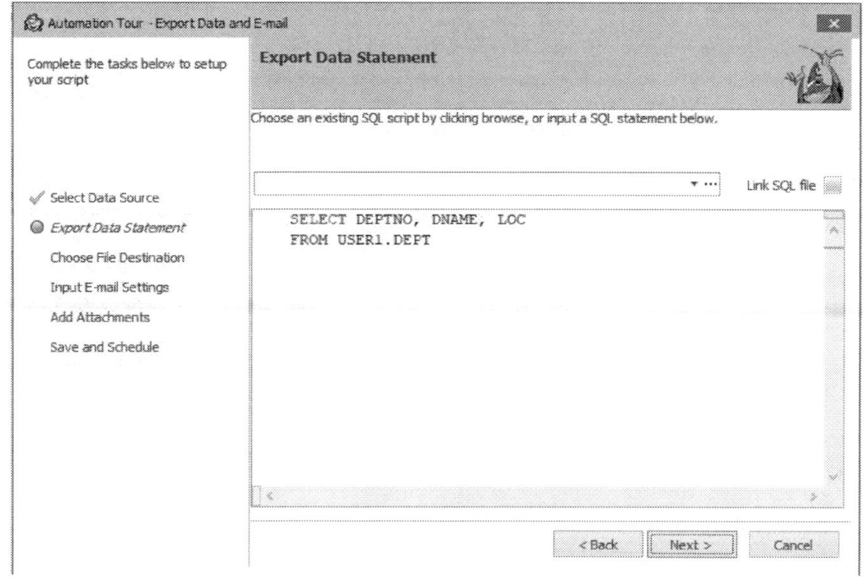


Review the SQL and click 'Next'

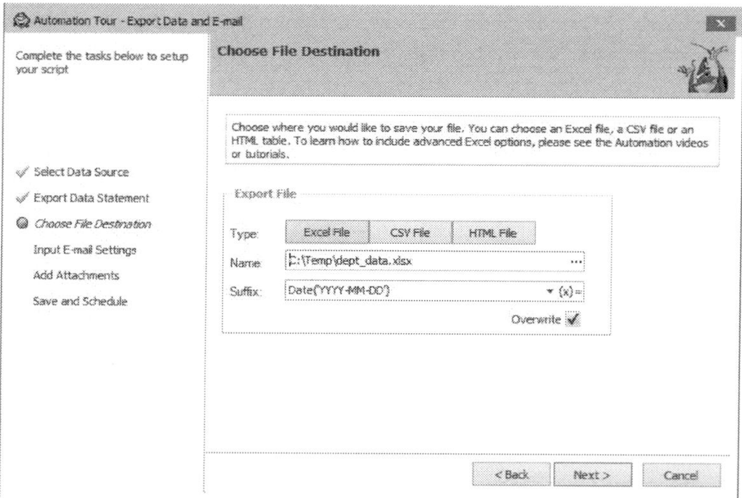


Here you decide the type of spreadsheet you want and give it a name. Notice, I added the date suffix. Click the down arrow indicator to provide the options for the suffix. I also chose to overwrite the file if it is already there. Solve the red warning issues then click 'Next'.

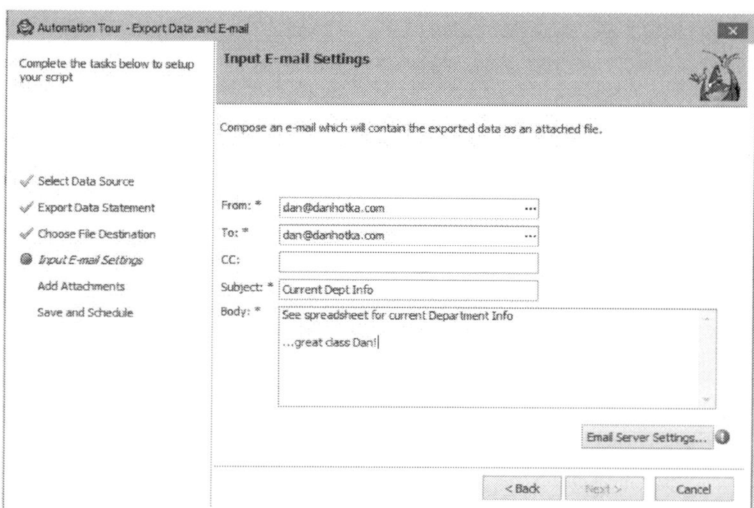


Fill out the email information with info that will work for you. Fix the warning by clcking on Email Server Settings…

Email Server Settings
Server:
danhotka.com
Port:
25
User name:
user1
Password:
*****
Use Secure connection
OK
Cancel

I do not have an email server on this computer, so, the sending of an email will result in an error when we run the script…will show you! Fill this out the best you can, back at your desk…as someone for help or your help desk…more than likely, this is already setup for you.

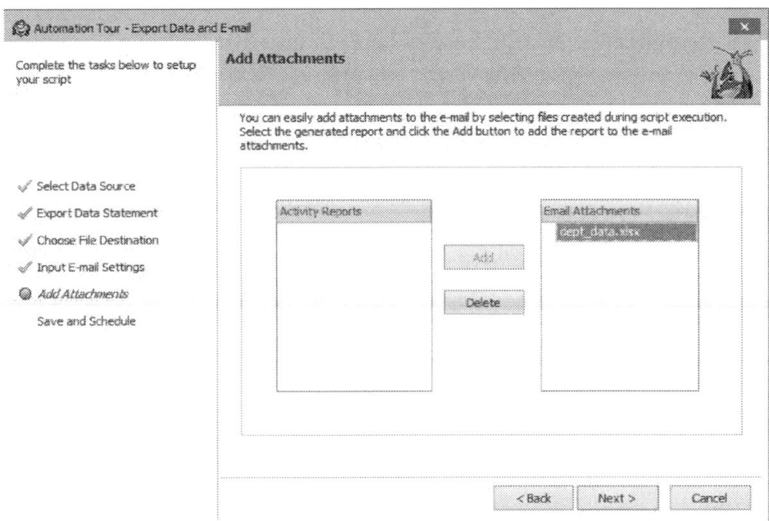
Automation Tour - Export Data and E-mail
Complete the tasks below to setup your script
Add Attachments
You can easily add attachments to the e-mail by selecting files created during script execution. Select the generated report and click the Add button to add the report to the e-mail attachments.
Select Data Source
Export Data Statement
Choose File Destination
Input E-mail Settings
Add Attachments
Save and Schedule
Activity Reports
Email Attachments
dept_data.xlsx
Add
Delete
< Back
Next >
Cancel

Click 'Add' to add the spreadsheet as an attachment. Click 'Next'.

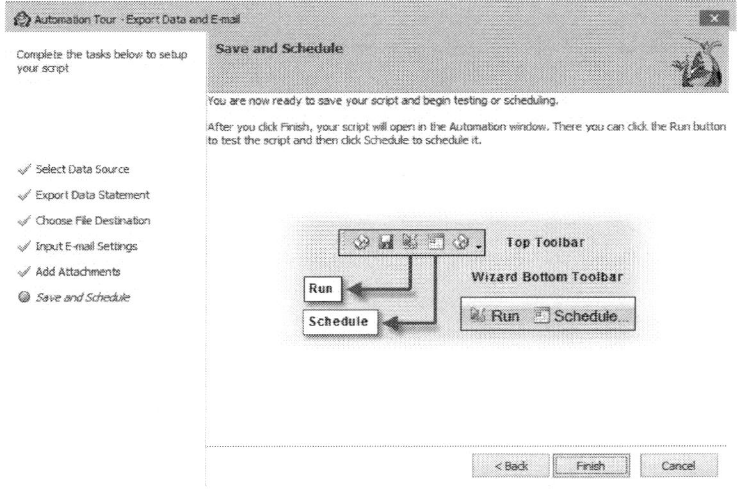


Click 'Finish' to create the automation stream.

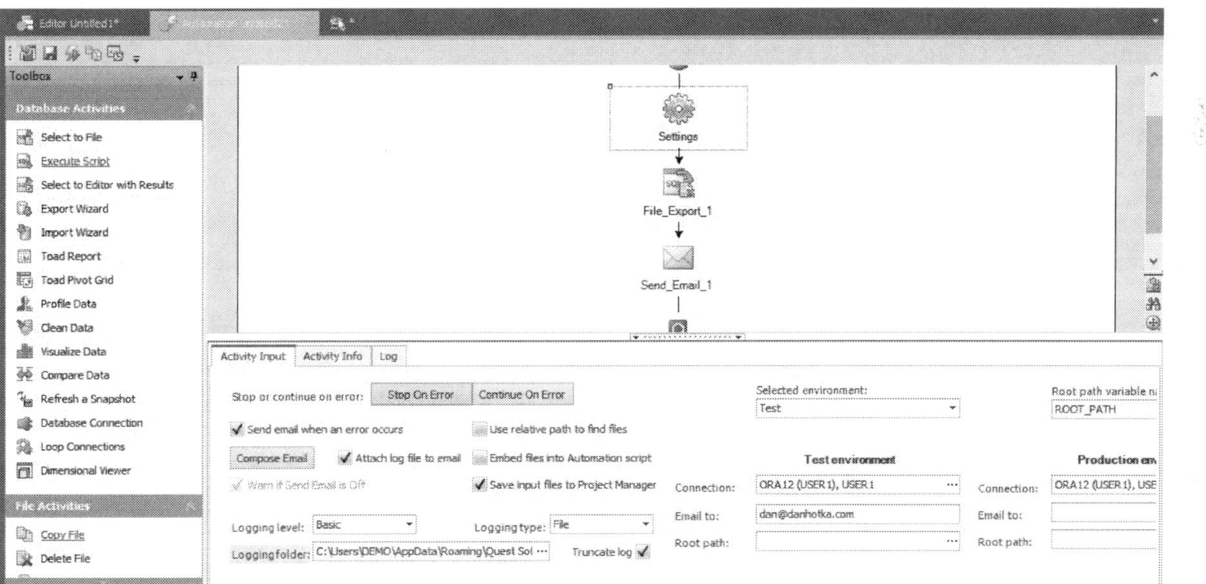


Lots of options here to consider. You can change almost anything. You can click on any of these steps to change any of the information. You can save this for future executions…both locally and to be scheduled using TIC.

This wizard builds a great template to start from. To add other tasks, simply drag and drop them into the location of where they should execute and fill out the panel associated with it.

Run it/save it!

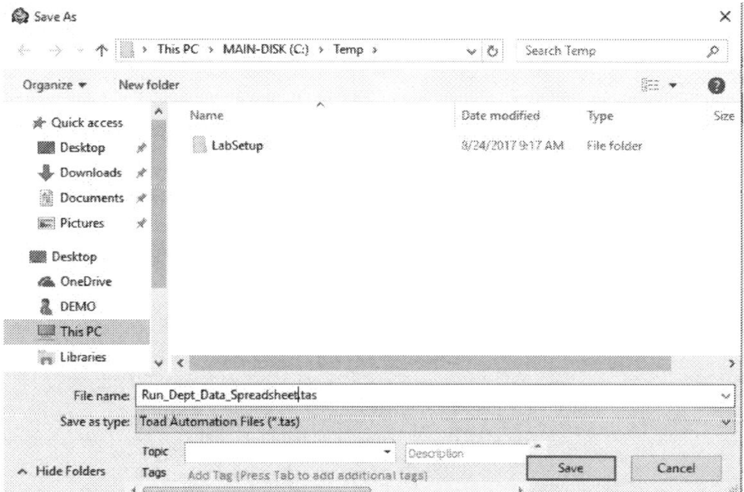
Save As
This PC › MAIN-DISK (C:) › Temp ›
Search Temp
Organize ▾
New folder
Quick access
Desktop
Downloads
Documents
Pictures
Desktop
OneDrive
DEMO
This PC
Libraries
Name
Date modified
Type
Size
LabSetup
8/24/2017 9:17 AM
File folder
File name: Run_Dept_Data_Spreadsheet.tas
Save as type: Toad Automation Files (*.tas)
Topic
Description
Tags
Add Tag (Press Tab to add additional tags)
Hide Folders
Save
Cancel

Run it from here by clicking on the Run Automation Script button on the tool bar. You can also double click on it from the library.

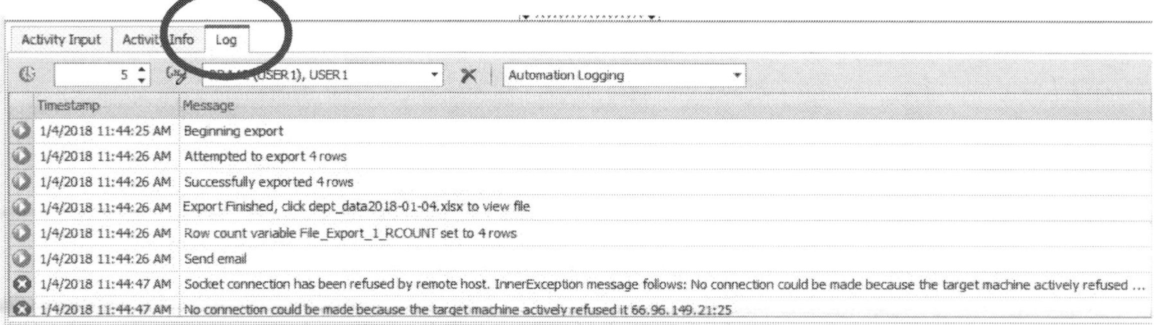
Activity Input
Activity Info
Log
Automation Logging
Timestamp
Message
1/4/2018 11:44:25 AM Beginning export
1/4/2018 11:44:26 AM Attempted to export 4 rows
1/4/2018 11:44:26 AM Successfully exported 4 rows
1/4/2018 11:44:26 AM Export Finished, click dept_data2018-01-04.xlsx to view file
1/4/2018 11:44:26 AM Row count variable File_Export_1_RCOUNT set to 4 rows
1/4/2018 11:44:26 AM Send email
1/4/2018 11:44:47 AM Socket connection has been refused by remote host. InnerException message follows: No connection could be made because the target machine actively refused ...
1/4/2018 11:44:47 AM No connection could be made because the target machine actively refused it 66.96.149.21:25

I love the running log. This automation script did indeed create the spreadsheet and did return some errors because I don't have email setup here…

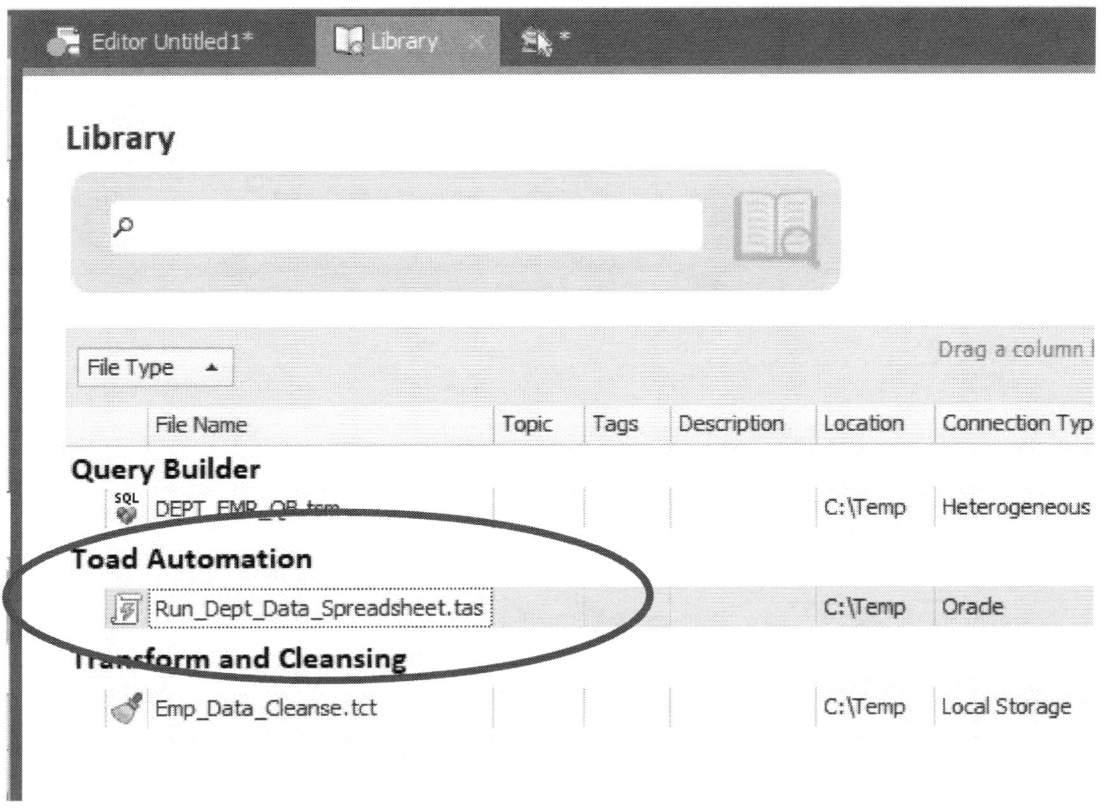


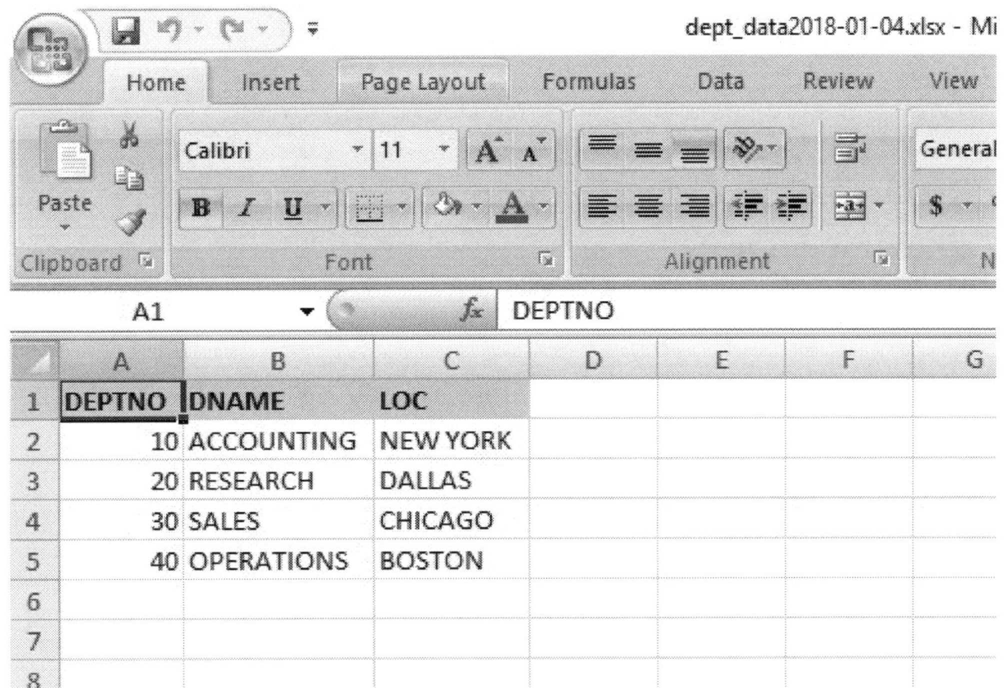


| | A | B | C |
|---|---|---|---|
| 1 | DEPTNO | DNAME | LOC |
| 2 | 10 | ACCOUNTING | NEW YORK |
| 3 | 20 | RESEARCH | DALLAS |
| 4 | 30 | SALES | CHICAGO |
| 5 | 40 | OPERATIONS | BOSTON |

## Working with Excel

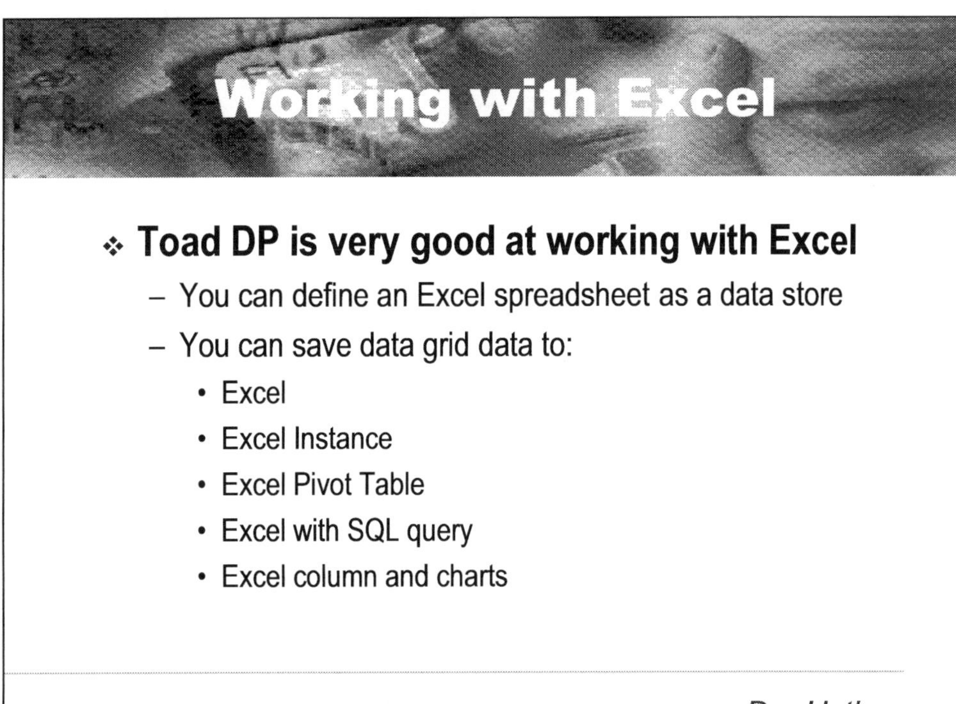

Working with Excel
Toad DP is very good at working with Excel
– You can define an Excel spreadsheet as a data store
– You can save data grid data to:
• Excel
• Excel Instance
• Excel Pivot Table
• Excel with SQL query
• Excel column and charts
www.DanHotka.com


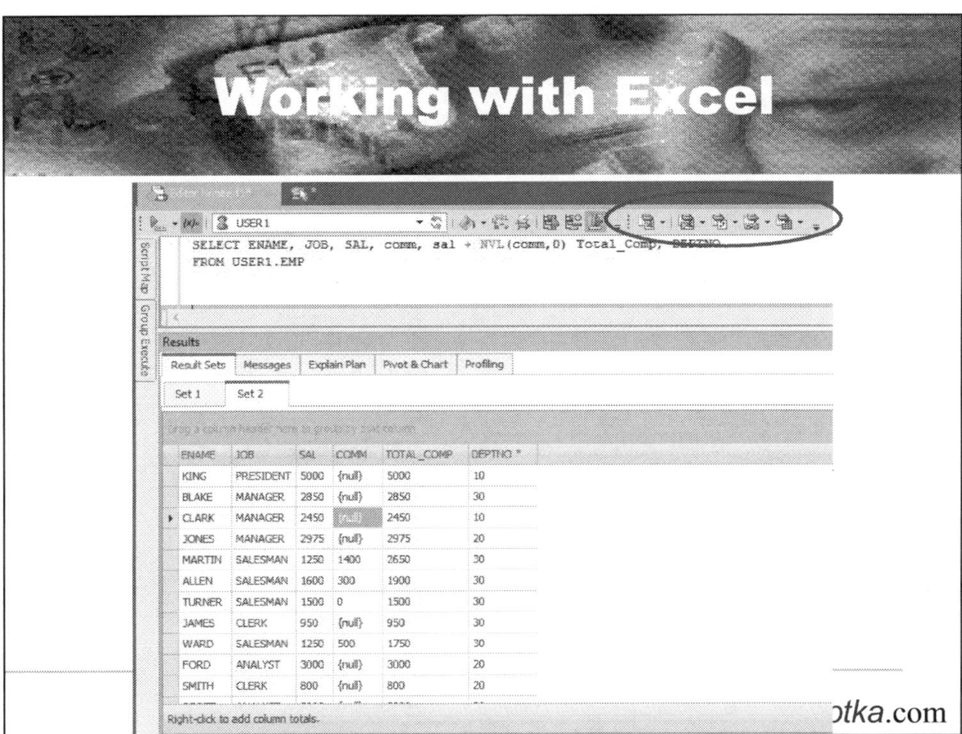

Working with Excel
USER1
SELECT ENAME, JOB, SAL, comm, sal + NVL(comm,0) Total_Comp, DEPTNO
FROM USER1.EMP
Results
Result Sets
Messages
Explain Plan
Pivot & Chart
Profiling
Set 1
Set 2
ENAME JOB SAL COMM TOTAL_COMP DEPTNO
KING PRESIDENT 5000 {null} 5000 10
BLAKE MANAGER 2850 {null} 2850 30
CLARK MANAGER 2450 {null} 2450 10
JONES MANAGER 2975 {null} 2975 20
MARTIN SALESMAN 1250 1400 2650 30
ALLEN SALESMAN 1600 300 1900 30
TURNER SALESMAN 1500 0 1500 30
JAMES CLERK 950 {null} 950 30
WARD SALESMAN 1250 500 1750 30
FORD ANALYST 3000 {null} 3000 20
SMITH CLERK 800 {null} 800 20
Right-click to add column totals.

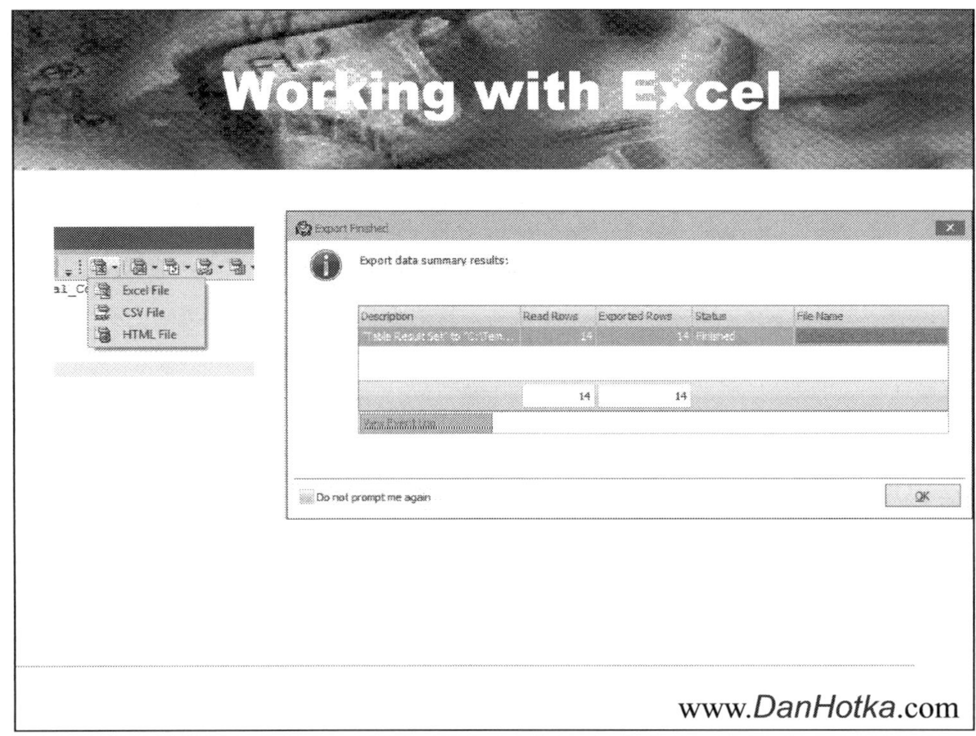


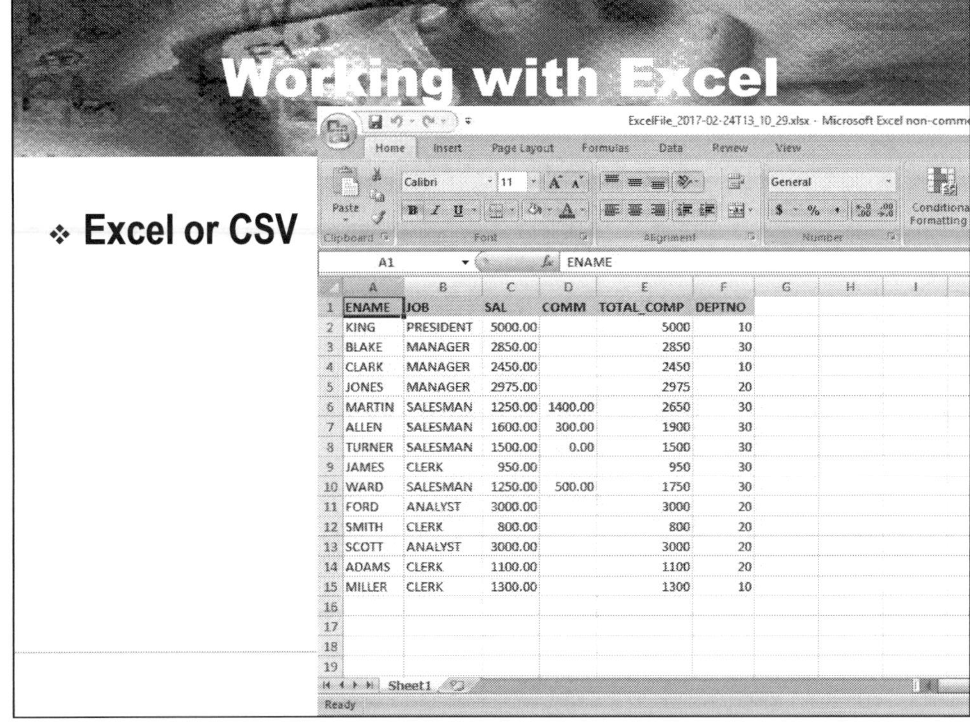


| ENAME | JOB | SAL | COMM | TOTAL_COMP | DEPTNO |
|---|---|---|---|---|---|
| KING | PRESIDENT | 5000.00 | | 5000 | 10 |
| BLAKE | MANAGER | 2850.00 | | 2850 | 30 |
| CLARK | MANAGER | 2450.00 | | 2450 | 10 |
| JONES | MANAGER | 2975.00 | | 2975 | 20 |
| MARTIN | SALESMAN | 1250.00 | 1400.00 | 2650 | 30 |
| ALLEN | SALESMAN | 1600.00 | 300.00 | 1900 | 30 |
| TURNER | SALESMAN | 1500.00 | 0.00 | 1500 | 30 |
| JAMES | CLERK | 950.00 | | 950 | 30 |
| WARD | SALESMAN | 1250.00 | 500.00 | 1750 | 30 |
| FORD | ANALYST | 3000.00 | | 3000 | 20 |
| SMITH | CLERK | 800.00 | | 800 | 20 |
| SCOTT | ANALYST | 3000.00 | | 3000 | 20 |
| ADAMS | CLERK | 1100.00 | | 1100 | 20 |
| MILLER | CLERK | 1300.00 | | 1300 | 10 |

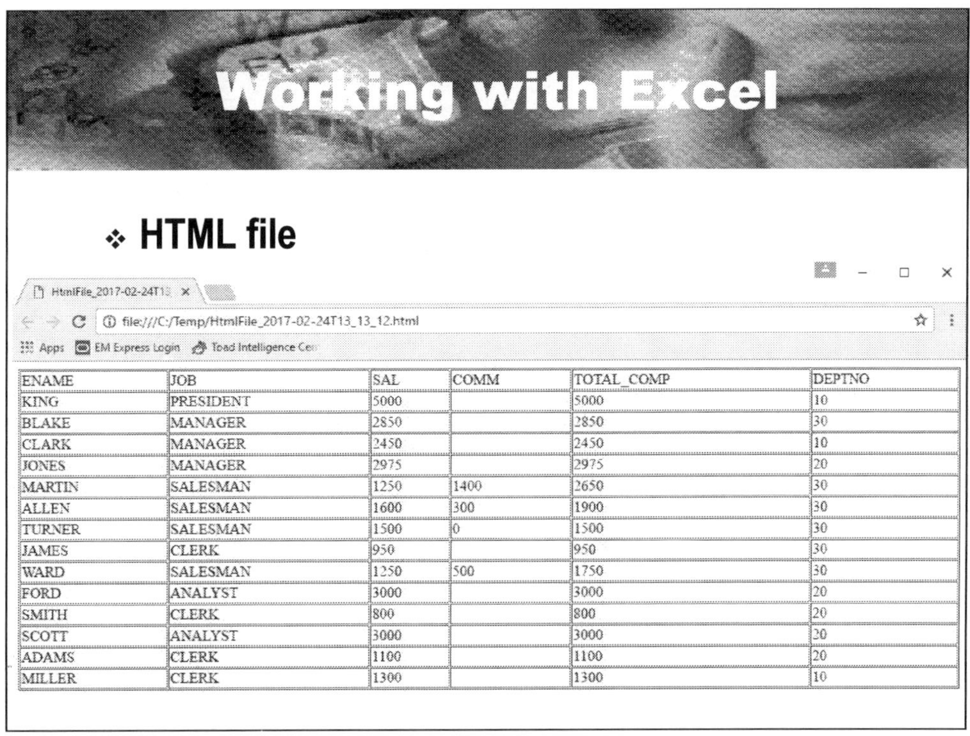


| ENAME | JOB | SAL | COMM | TOTAL_COMP | DEPTNO |
|---|---|---|---|---|---|
| KING | PRESIDENT | 5000 | | 5000 | 10 |
| BLAKE | MANAGER | 2850 | | 2850 | 30 |
| CLARK | MANAGER | 2450 | | 2450 | 10 |
| JONES | MANAGER | 2975 | | 2975 | 20 |
| MARTIN | SALESMAN | 1250 | 1400 | 2650 | 30 |
| ALLEN | SALESMAN | 1600 | 300 | 1900 | 30 |
| TURNER | SALESMAN | 1500 | 0 | 1500 | 30 |
| JAMES | CLERK | 950 | | 950 | 30 |
| WARD | SALESMAN | 1250 | 500 | 1750 | 30 |
| FORD | ANALYST | 3000 | | 3000 | 20 |
| SMITH | CLERK | 800 | | 800 | 20 |
| SCOTT | ANALYST | 3000 | | 3000 | 20 |
| ADAMS | CLERK | 1100 | | 1100 | 20 |
| MILLER | CLERK | 1300 | | 1300 | 10 |

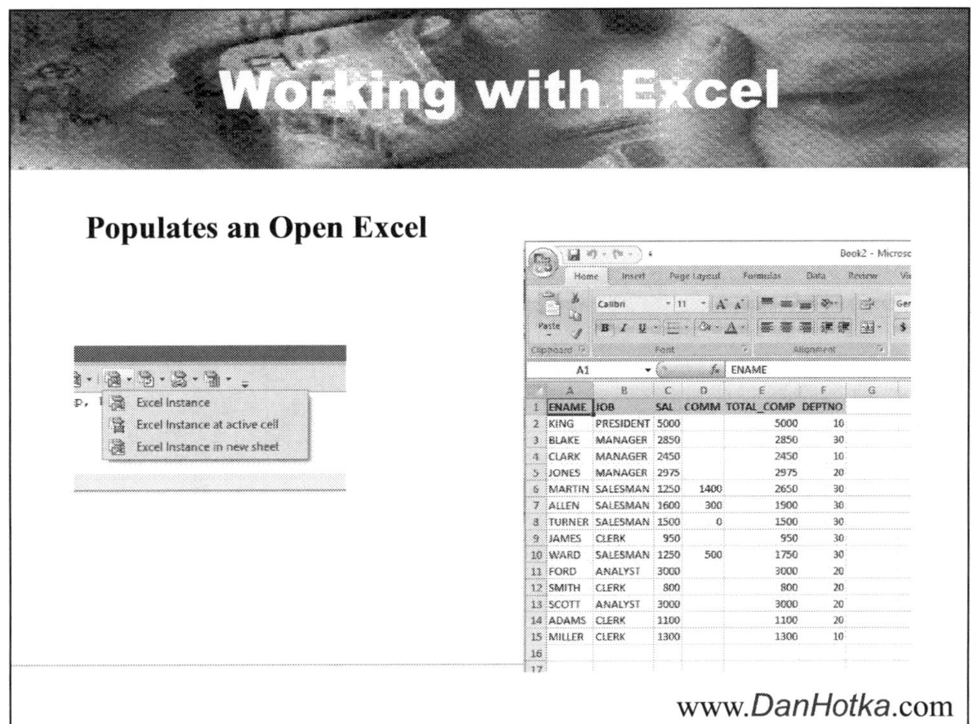


| | A | B | C | D | E | F |
|---|---|---|---|---|---|---|
| 1 | ENAME | JOB | SAL | COMM | TOTAL_COMP | DEPTNO |
| 2 | KING | PRESIDENT | 5000 | | 5000 | 10 |
| 3 | BLAKE | MANAGER | 2850 | | 2850 | 30 |
| 4 | CLARK | MANAGER | 2450 | | 2450 | 10 |
| 5 | JONES | MANAGER | 2975 | | 2975 | 20 |
| 6 | MARTIN | SALESMAN | 1250 | 1400 | 2650 | 30 |
| 7 | ALLEN | SALESMAN | 1600 | 300 | 1900 | 30 |
| 8 | TURNER | SALESMAN | 1500 | 0 | 1500 | 30 |
| 9 | JAMES | CLERK | 950 | | 950 | 30 |
| 10 | WARD | SALESMAN | 1250 | 500 | 1750 | 30 |
| 11 | FORD | ANALYST | 3000 | | 3000 | 20 |
| 12 | SMITH | CLERK | 800 | | 800 | 20 |
| 13 | SCOTT | ANALYST | 3000 | | 3000 | 20 |
| 14 | ADAMS | CLERK | 1100 | | 1100 | 20 |
| 15 | MILLER | CLERK | 1300 | | 1300 | 10 |

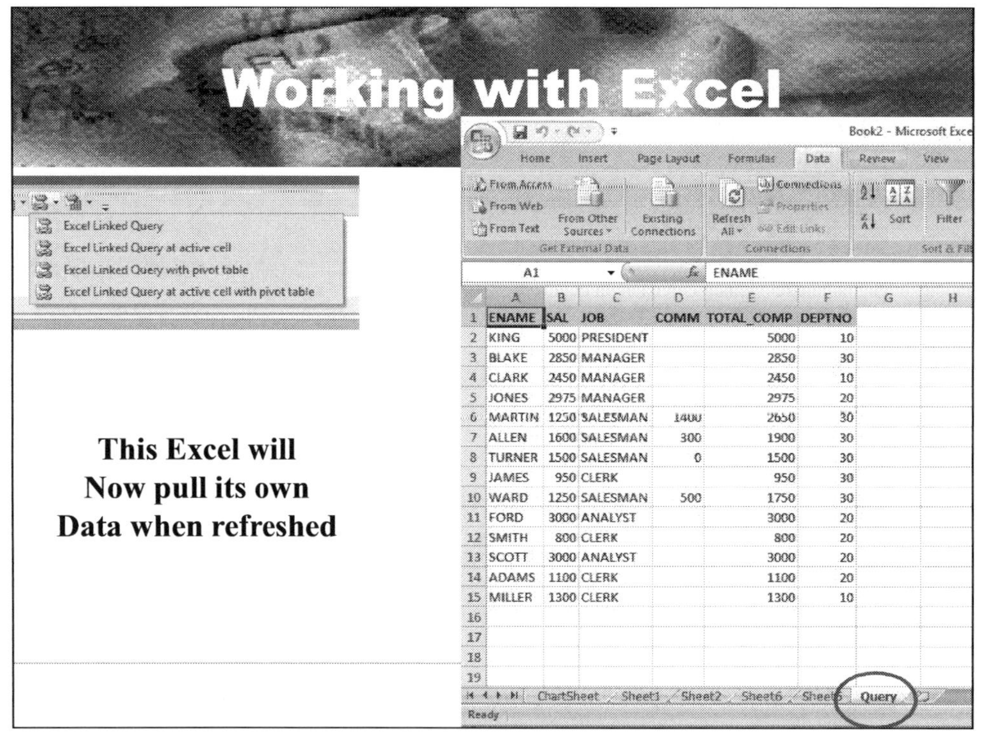
Working with Excel
Excel Linked Query
Excel Linked Query at active cell
Excel Linked Query with pivot table
Excel Linked Query at active cell with pivot table
This Excel will
Now pull its own
Data when refreshed
Query

| ENAME | SAL | JOB | COMM | TOTAL_COMP | DEPTNO |
|---|---|---|---|---|---|
| KING | 5000 | PRESIDENT | | 5000 | 10 |
| BLAKE | 2850 | MANAGER | | 2850 | 30 |
| CLARK | 2450 | MANAGER | | 2450 | 10 |
| JONES | 2975 | MANAGER | | 2975 | 20 |
| MARTIN | 1250 | SALESMAN | 1400 | 2650 | 30 |
| ALLEN | 1600 | SALESMAN | 300 | 1900 | 30 |
| TURNER | 1500 | SALESMAN | 0 | 1500 | 30 |
| JAMES | 950 | CLERK | | 950 | 30 |
| WARD | 1250 | SALESMAN | 500 | 1750 | 30 |
| FORD | 3000 | ANALYST | | 3000 | 20 |
| SMITH | 800 | CLERK | | 800 | 20 |
| SCOTT | 3000 | ANALYST | | 3000 | 20 |
| ADAMS | 1100 | CLERK | | 1100 | 20 |
| MILLER | 1300 | CLERK | | 1300 | 10 |

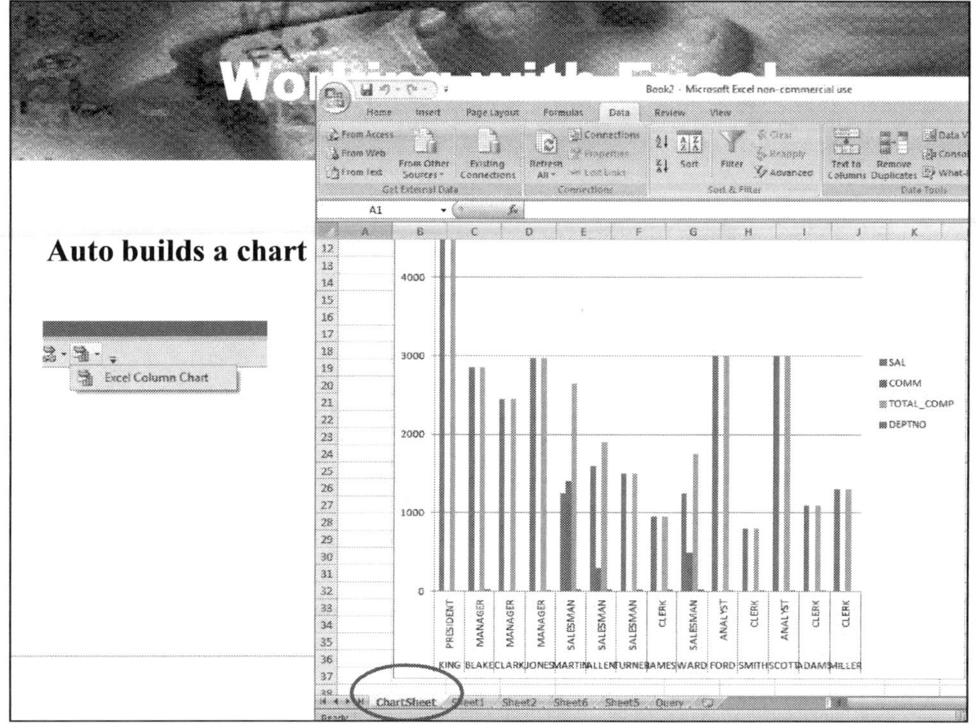
Auto builds a chart
Excel Column Chart
SAL
COMM
TOTAL_COMP
DEPTNO
ChartSheet

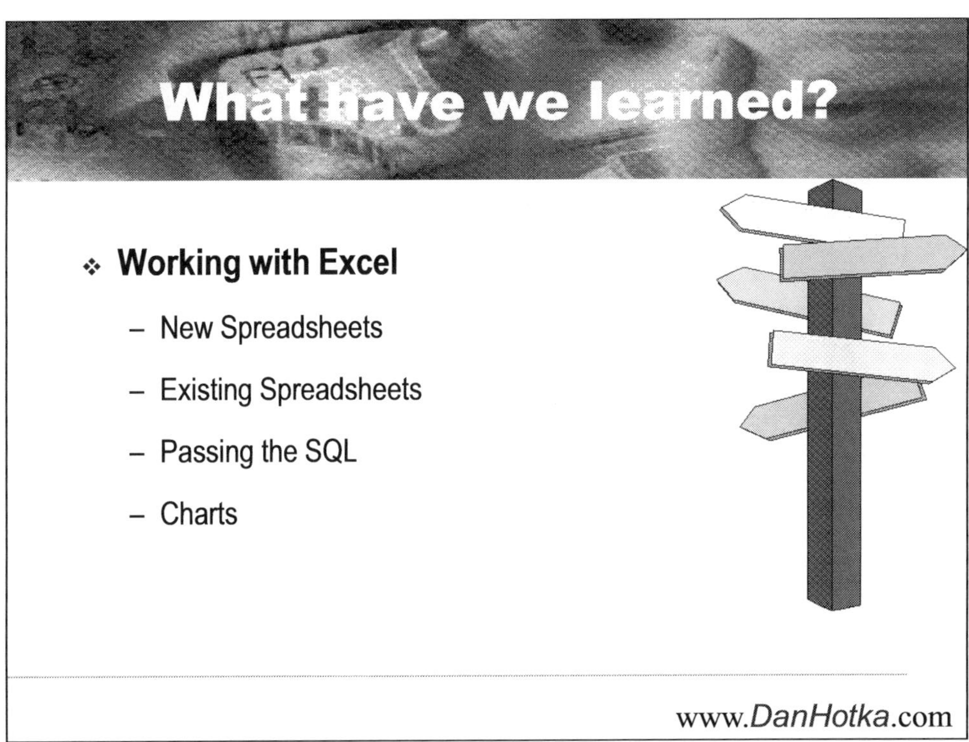
What have we learned?
Working with Excel
– New Spreadsheets
– Existing Spreadsheets
– Passing the SQL
– Charts
www.DanHotka.com

## Working with Excel Lab

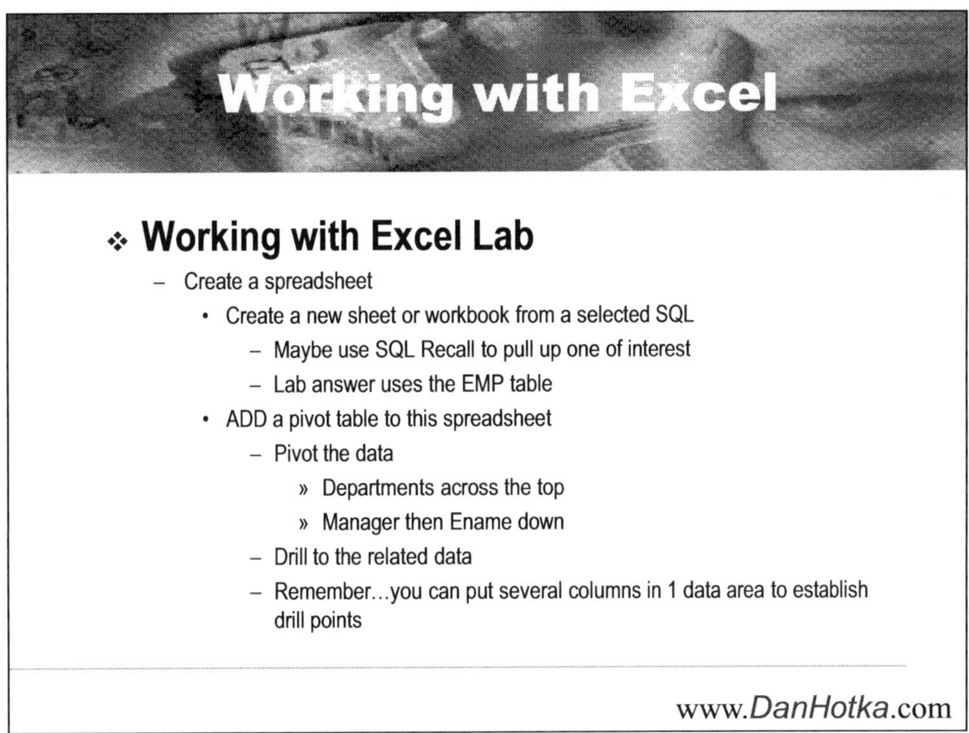
Working with Excel
Working with Excel Lab
– Create a spreadsheet
• Create a new sheet or workbook from a selected SQL
– Maybe use SQL Recall to pull up one of interest
– Lab answer uses the EMP table
• ADD a pivot table to this spreadsheet
– Pivot the data
» Departments across the top
» Manager then Ename down
– Drill to the related data
– Remember...you can put several columns in 1 data area to establish drill points
www.DanHotka.com

## Working with Excel Lab Answers

Create a spreadsheet

- Create a new sheet or workbook from a selected SQL
  - Maybe use SQL Recall to pull up one of interest
  - Lab answer uses the EMP table

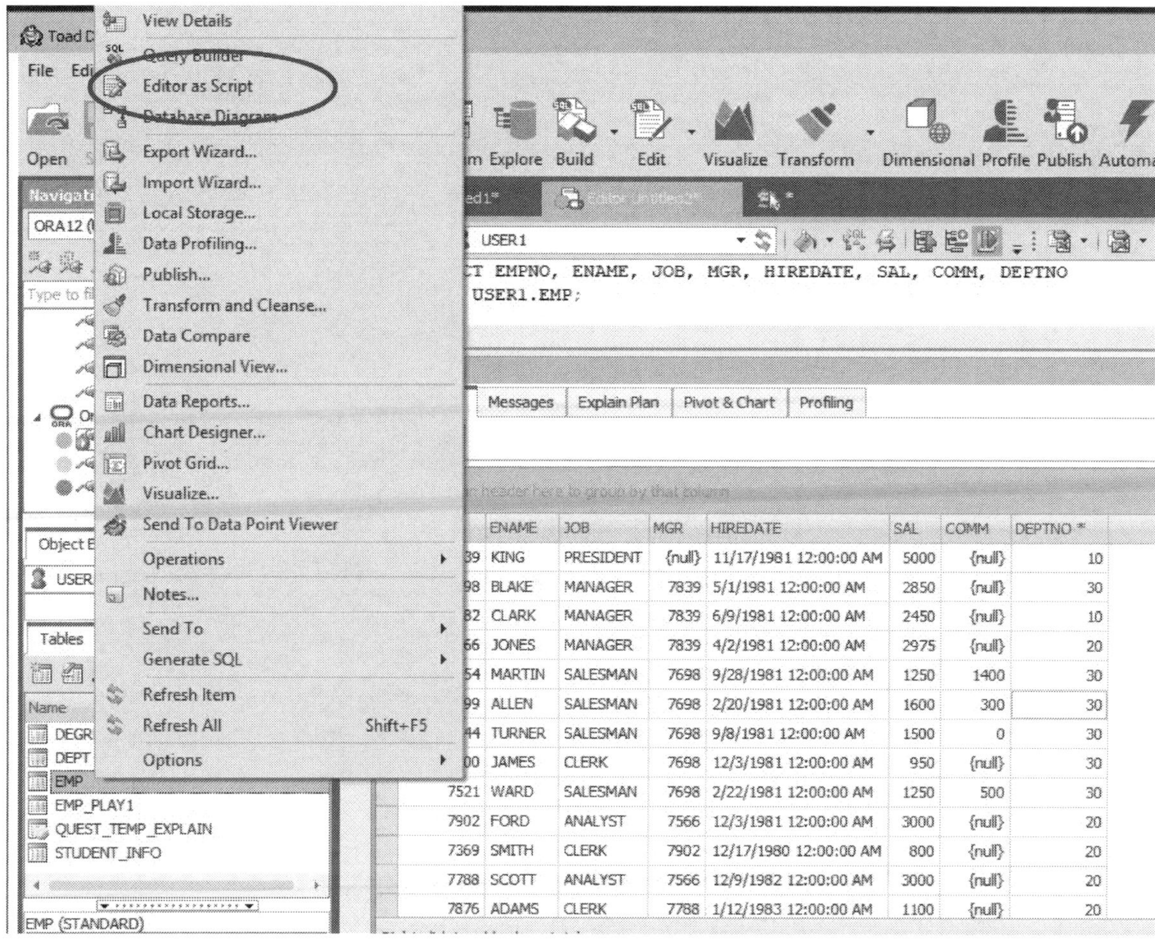


I start with the EMP table from the Navigation Panel, right click and select 'Editor as Script'. I executed the SQL as well.

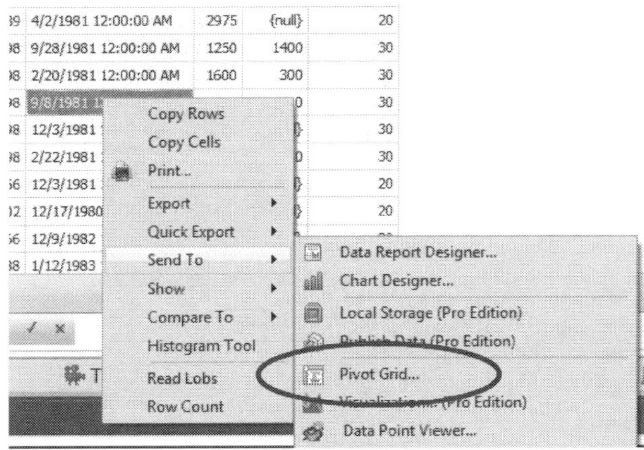

From the data grid, right click and select 'Pivot Grid…'.

ADD a pivot table to this spreadsheet

- Pivot the data
    - Departments across the top
    - Manager then Ename down

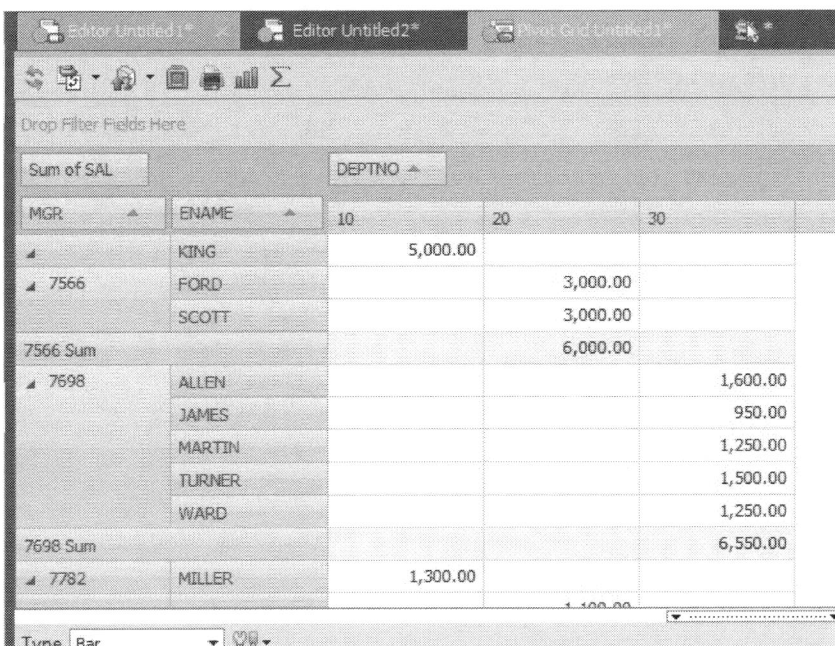

Drag and drop the fields to the locations indicated above. Notice you can expand and condense the ENAME data!

Click the Export Pivot button

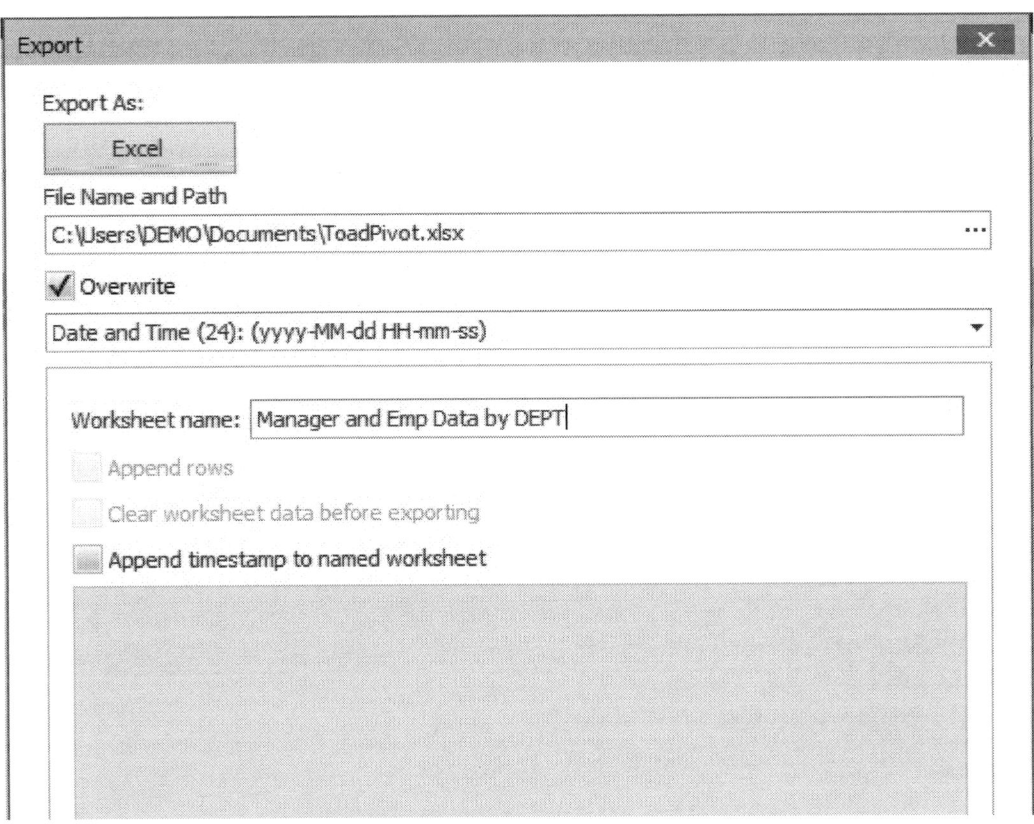


Fill out the name and worksheet name if desired…

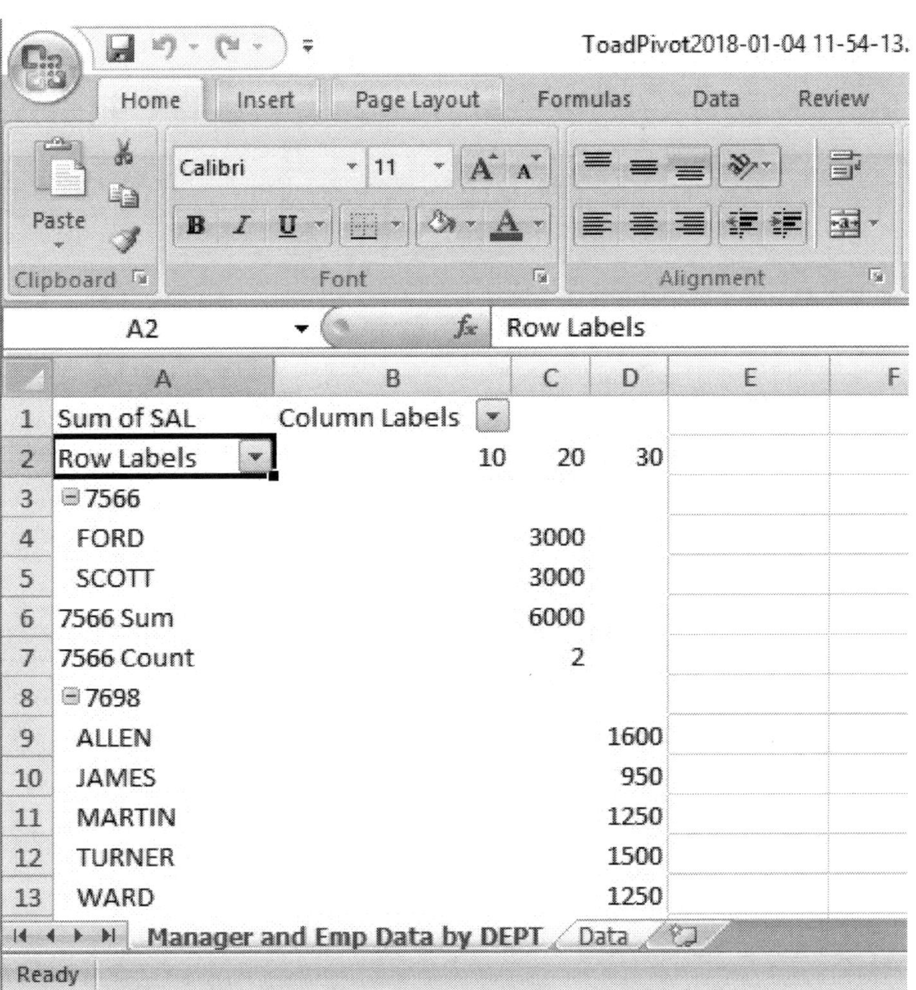


The drilling (expanding/contracting) seems to work better from Toad but the instructor is not an Excel expert…

# Features not previously discussed

This section will cover some additional features of Toad Data Point/Intelligence Central. and beyond.

## Additional Toad DP Features

- **Features not previously discussed**
  - Working with Snapshots
    - What are they
    - Saving to TIC
    - Saving to Local Storage
  - Using Local Storage
  - Toad Views
  - Project Manager
  - Data Compare and Sync
  - Dimensional Views

www.DanHotka.com

# Working with Snapshots

- **Working with Snapshots**
  - Stored data from any data grid
  - Can be published to TIC
  - Can be saved in Local Storage
  - Can be scheduled for automatic refresh
  - VERY useful to subset then use the data for reporting
  - Pushing to TIC allows this data to be shared with the team

www.DanHotka.com

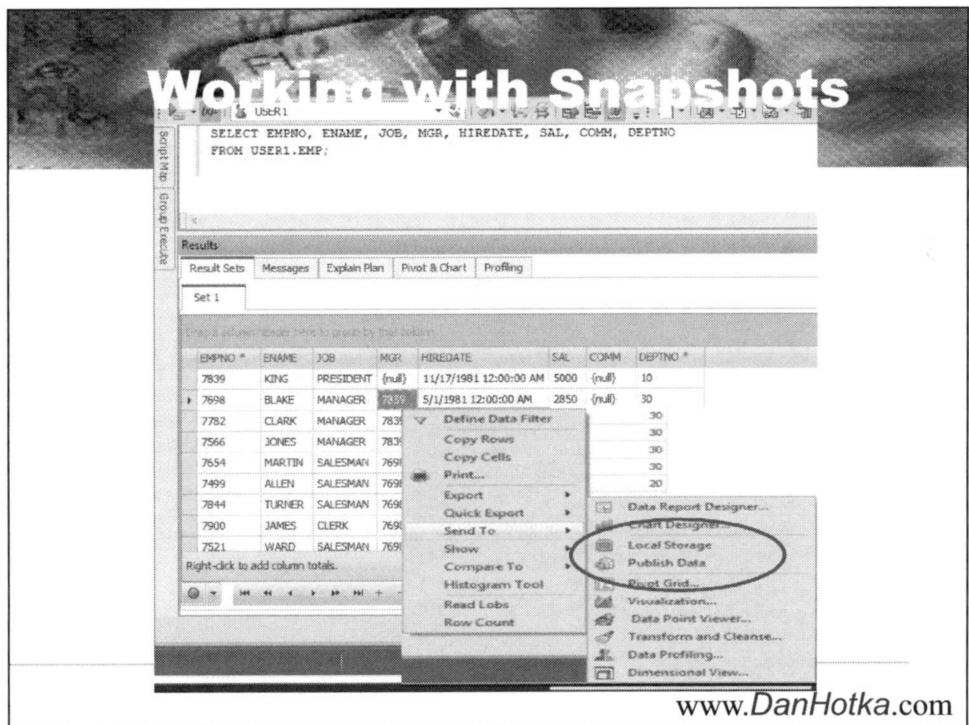

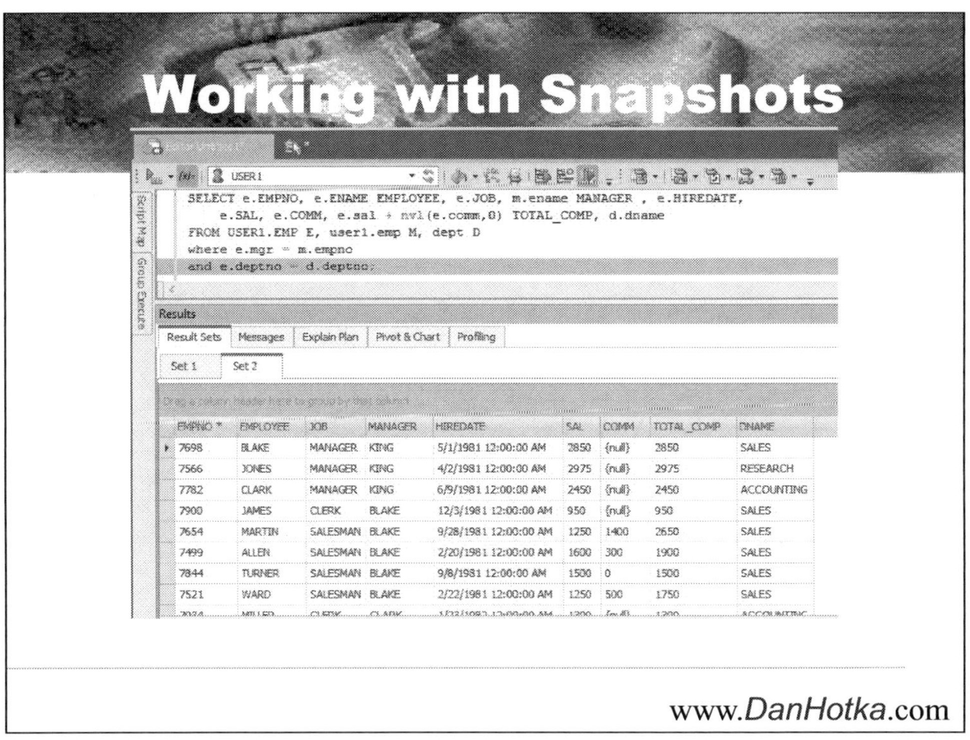
Working with Snapshots
USER1
SELECT e.EMPNO, e.ENAME EMPLOYEE, e.JOB, m.ename MANAGER , e.HIREDATE,
e.SAL, e.COMM, e.sal + nvl(e.comm,0) TOTAL_COMP, d.dname
FROM USER1.EMP E, user1.emp M, dept D
where e.mgr = m.empno
and e.deptno = d.deptno;
Results
Result Sets
Messages
Explain Plan
Pivot & Chart
Profiling
Set 1
Set 2
EMPNO EMPLOYEE JOB MANAGER HIREDATE SAL COMM TOTAL_COMP DNAME
7698 BLAKE MANAGER KING 5/1/1981 12:00:00 AM 2850 {null} 2850 SALES
7566 JONES MANAGER KING 4/2/1981 12:00:00 AM 2975 {null} 2975 RESEARCH
7782 CLARK MANAGER KING 6/9/1981 12:00:00 AM 2450 {null} 2450 ACCOUNTING
7900 JAMES CLERK BLAKE 12/3/1981 12:00:00 AM 950 {null} 950 SALES
7654 MARTIN SALESMAN BLAKE 9/28/1981 12:00:00 AM 1250 1400 2650 SALES
7499 ALLEN SALESMAN BLAKE 2/20/1981 12:00:00 AM 1600 300 1900 SALES
7844 TURNER SALESMAN BLAKE 9/8/1981 12:00:00 AM 1500 0 1500 SALES
7521 WARD SALESMAN BLAKE 2/22/1981 12:00:00 AM 1250 500 1750 SALES
www.DanHotka.com

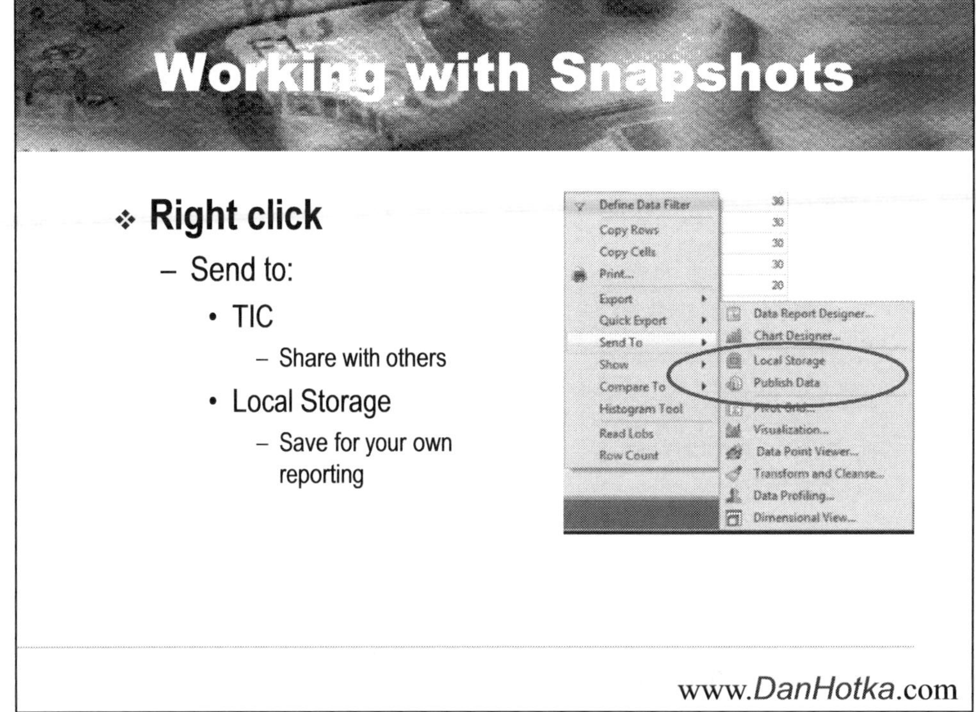
Working with Snapshots
Right click
Send to:
TIC
Share with others
Local Storage
Save for your own reporting
Define Data Filter
Copy Rows
Copy Cells
Print...
Export
Quick Export
Send To
Show
Compare To
Histogram Tool
Read Lobs
Row Count
Data Report Designer...
Chart Designer...
Local Storage
Publish Data
Visualization...
Data Point Viewer...
Transform and Cleanse...
Data Profiling...
Dimensional View...
www.DanHotka.com

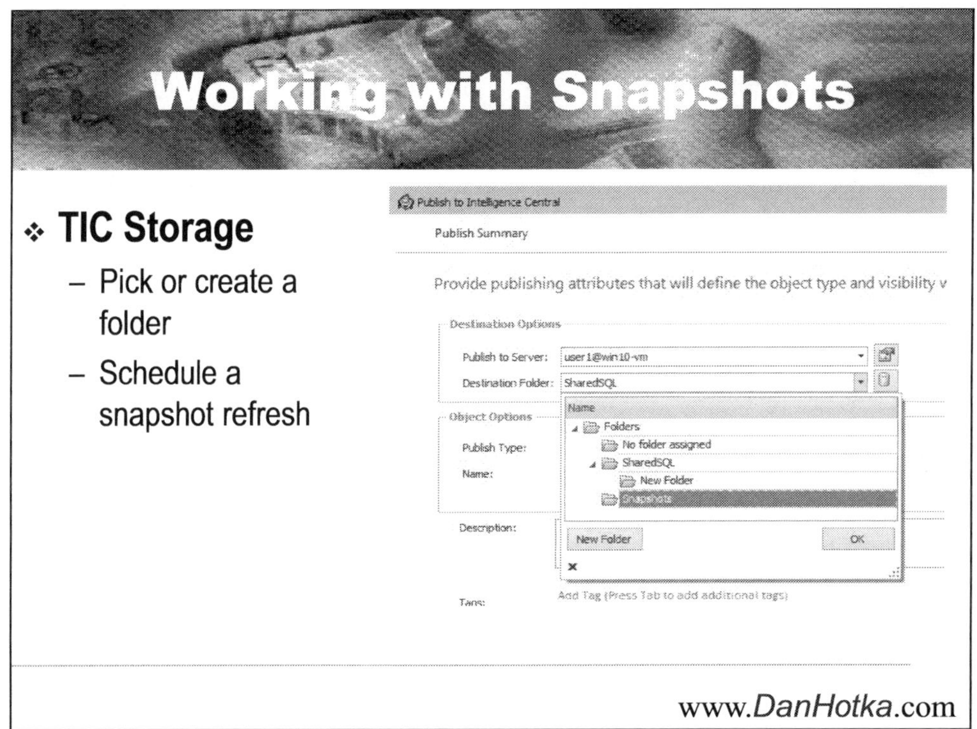
Working with Snapshots
TIC Storage
– Pick or create a folder
– Schedule a snapshot refresh
Publish to Intelligence Central
Publish Summary
Provide publishing attributes that will define the object type and visibility
Destination Options
Publish to Server: user1@win10-vm
Destination Folder: SharedSQL
Object Options
Publish Type:
Name:
Description:
Tags:
Name
Folders
No folder assigned
SharedSQL
New Folder
Snapshots
New Folder
OK
Add Tag (Press Tab to add additional tags)
www.DanHotka.com

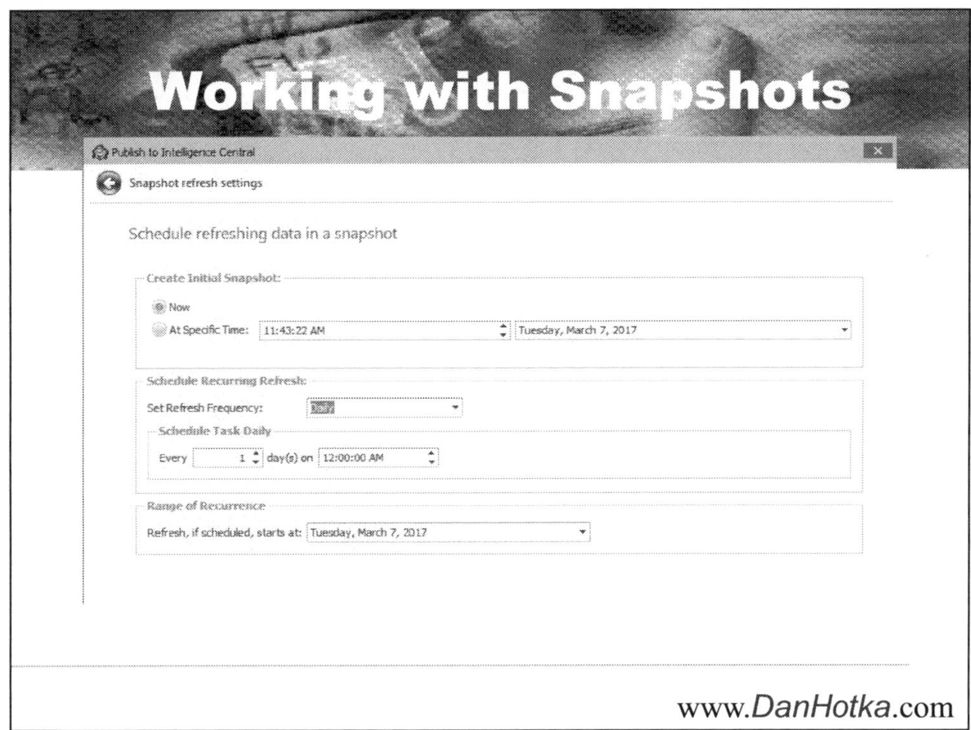
Working with Snapshots
Publish to Intelligence Central
Snapshot refresh settings
Schedule refreshing data in a snapshot
Create Initial Snapshot:
Now
At Specific Time: 11:43:22 AM
Tuesday, March 7, 2017
Schedule Recurring Refresh:
Set Refresh Frequency: Daily
Schedule Task Daily
Every 1 day(s) on 12:00:00 AM
Range of Recurrence
Refresh, if scheduled, starts at: Tuesday, March 7, 2017
www.DanHotka.com

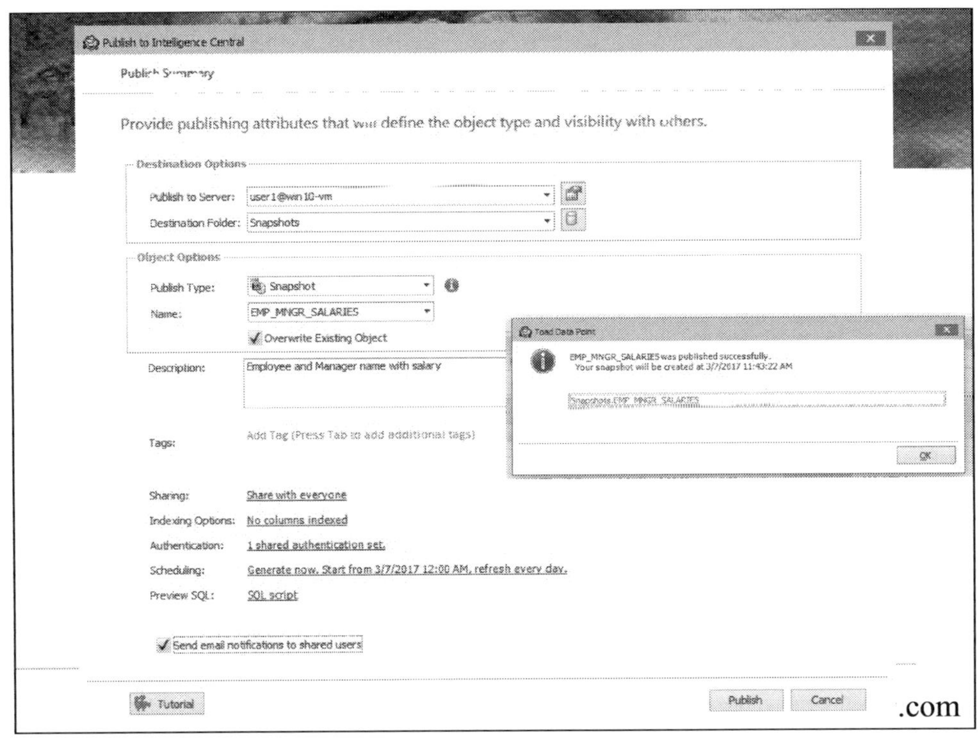
Publish to Intelligence Central
Publish Summary
Provide publishing attributes that will define the object type and visibility with others.
Destination Options
Publish to Server: user1@win10-vm
Destination Folder: Snapshots
Object Options
Publish Type: Snapshot
Name: EMP_MNGR_SALARIES
Overwrite Existing Object
Description: Employee and Manager name with salary
Tags: Add Tag (Press Tab to add additional tags)
Sharing: Share with everyone
Indexing Options: No columns indexed
Authentication: 1 shared authentication set.
Scheduling: Generate now. Start from 3/7/2017 12:00 AM, refresh every day.
Preview SQL: SQL script
Send email notifications to shared users
Tutorial
Publish
Cancel
.com

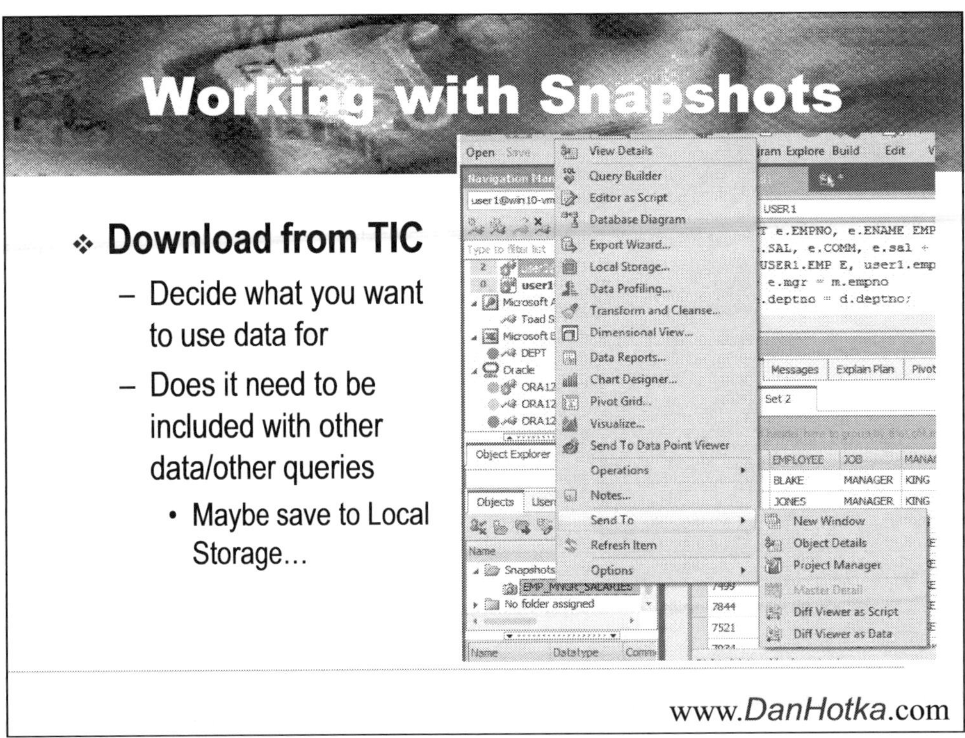
Working with Snapshots
Download from TIC
– Decide what you want to use data for
– Does it need to be included with other data/other queries
• Maybe save to Local Storage…
View Details
Query Builder
Editor as Script
Database Diagram
Export Wizard...
Local Storage...
Data Profiling...
Transform and Cleanse...
Dimensional View...
Data Reports...
Chart Designer...
Pivot Grid...
Visualize...
Send To Data Point Viewer
Operations
Notes...
Send To
Refresh Item
Options
New Window
Object Details
Project Manager
Master Detail
Diff Viewer as Script
Diff Viewer as Data
www.DanHotka.com

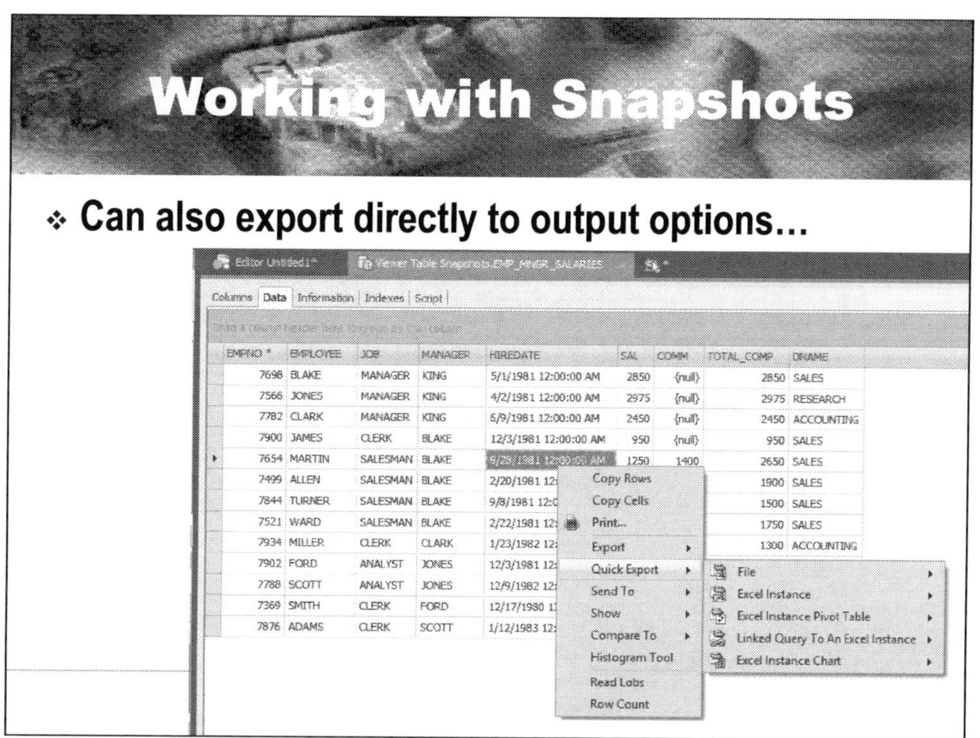
Working with Snapshots
Can also export directly to output options…
Columns
Data
Information
Indexes
Script
EMPNO
EMPLOYEE
JOB
MANAGER
HIREDATE
SAL
COMM
TOTAL_COMP
DNAME
Copy Rows
Copy Cells
Print…
Export
Quick Export
Send To
Show
Compare To
Histogram Tool
Read Lobs
Row Count
File
Excel Instance
Excel Instance Pivot Table
Linked Query To An Excel Instance
Excel Instance Chart

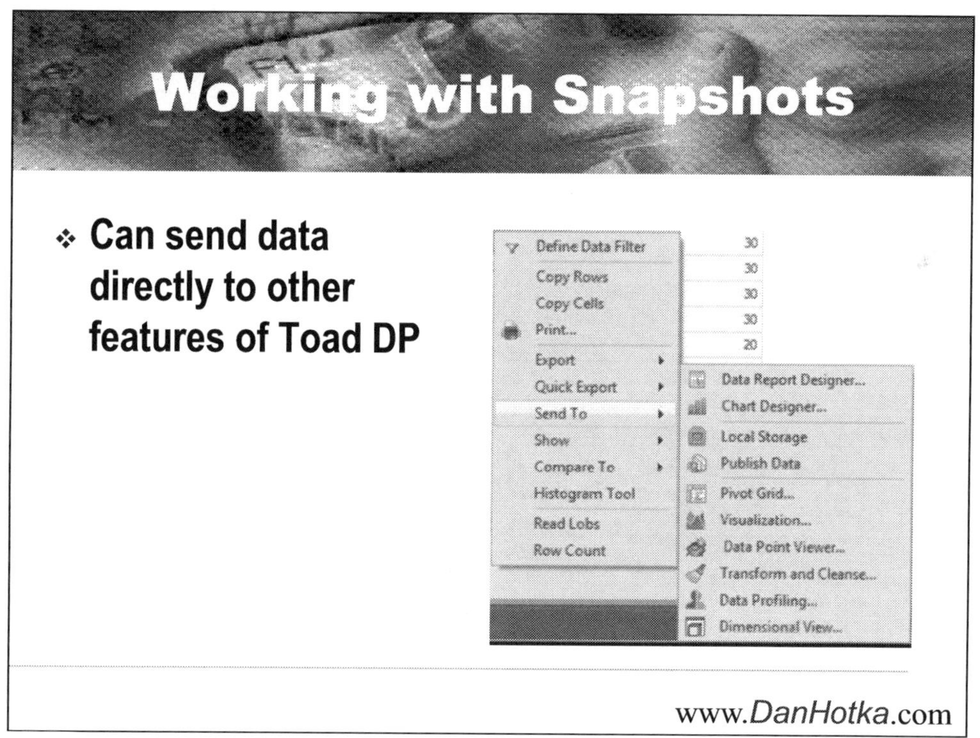
Working with Snapshots
Can send data directly to other features of Toad DP
Define Data Filter
Copy Rows
Copy Cells
Print…
Export
Quick Export
Send To
Show
Compare To
Histogram Tool
Read Lobs
Row Count
Data Report Designer…
Chart Designer…
Local Storage
Publish Data
Pivot Grid…
Visualization…
Data Point Viewer…
Transform and Cleanse…
Data Profiling…
Dimensional View…
www.DanHotka.com

# Working with Snapshots

- **Saving to Local Storage**
  - Does store as a table
    - Instructor PC has Oracle, its stored there using Toad DP credentials
    - No DB installed…uses MySQL with Toad DP credentials
  - IF saved as SnapShot…
    - User manually refreshes
      - Can use Automation to automatically refresh
  - Acts like any other table data store
    - Send to Editor, Send to Query Builder

www.DanHotka.com

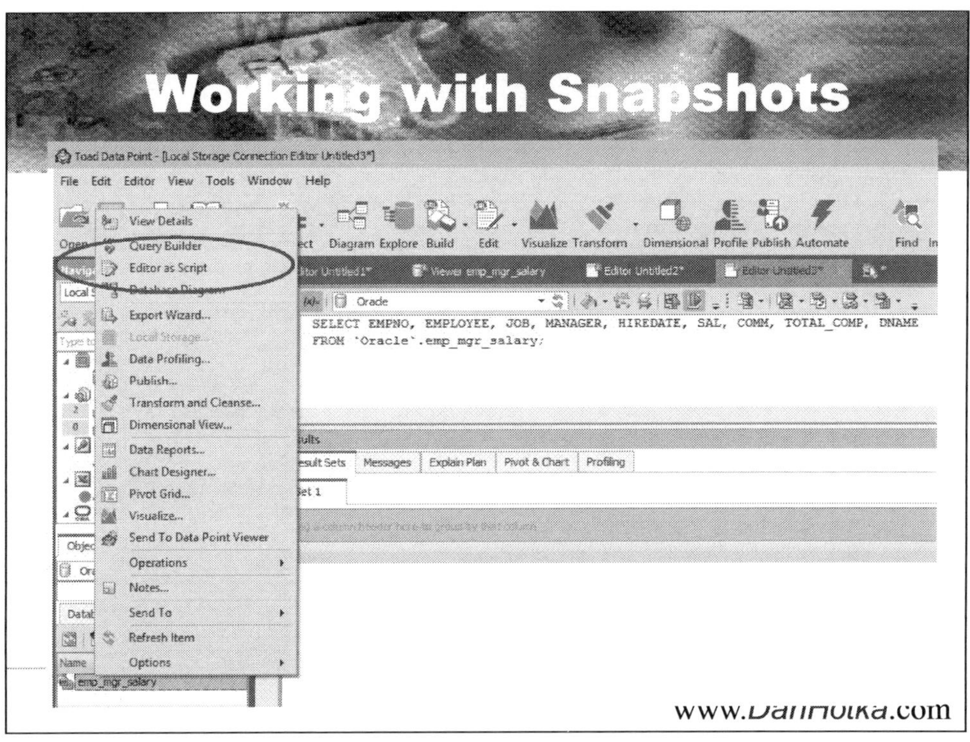
Working with Snapshots
Toad Data Point - [Local Storage Connection Editor Untitled3*]
File Edit Editor View Tools Window Help
View Details
Query Builder
Editor as Script
Export Wizard...
Local Storage...
Data Profiling...
Publish...
Transform and Cleanse...
Dimensional View...
Data Reports...
Chart Designer...
Pivot Grid...
Visualize...
Send To Data Point Viewer
Operations
Notes...
Send To
Refresh Item
Options
Diagram Explore Build Edit Visualize Transform Dimensional Profile Publish Automate Find
SELECT EMPNO, EMPLOYEE, JOB, MANAGER, HIREDATE, SAL, COMM, TOTAL_COMP, DNAME
FROM `Oracle`.emp_mgr_salary;
Messages Explain Plan Pivot & Chart Profiling
emp_mgr_salary
www.DanHotka.com

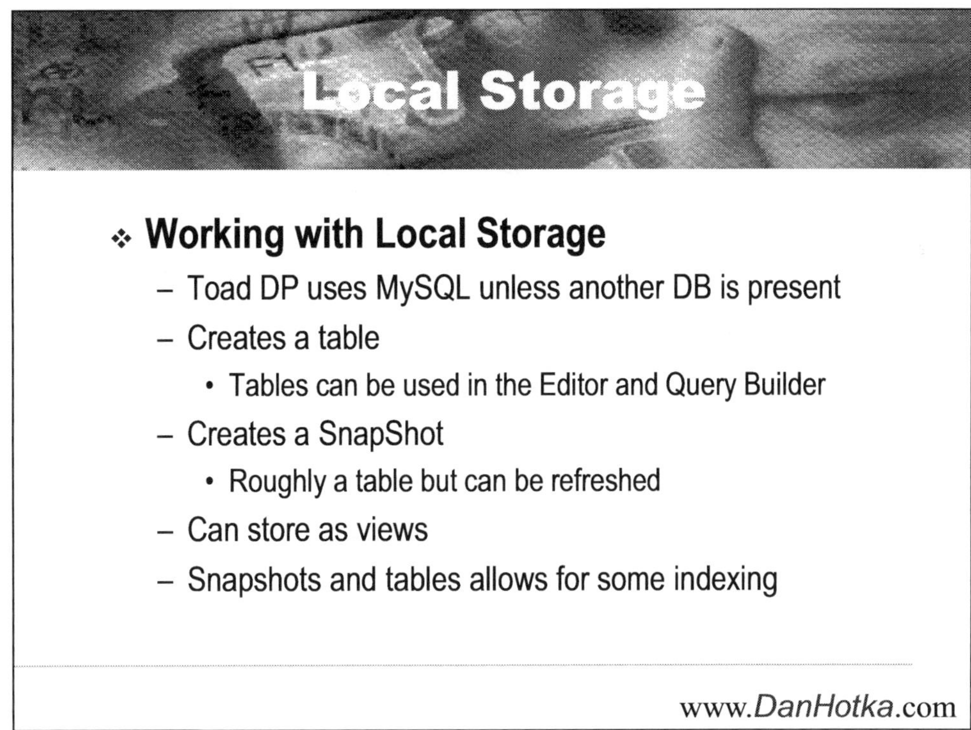
Local Storage
Working with Local Storage
– Toad DP uses MySQL unless another DB is present
– Creates a table
• Tables can be used in the Editor and Query Builder
– Creates a SnapShot
• Roughly a table but can be refreshed
– Can store as views
– Snapshots and tables allows for some indexing
www.DanHotka.com

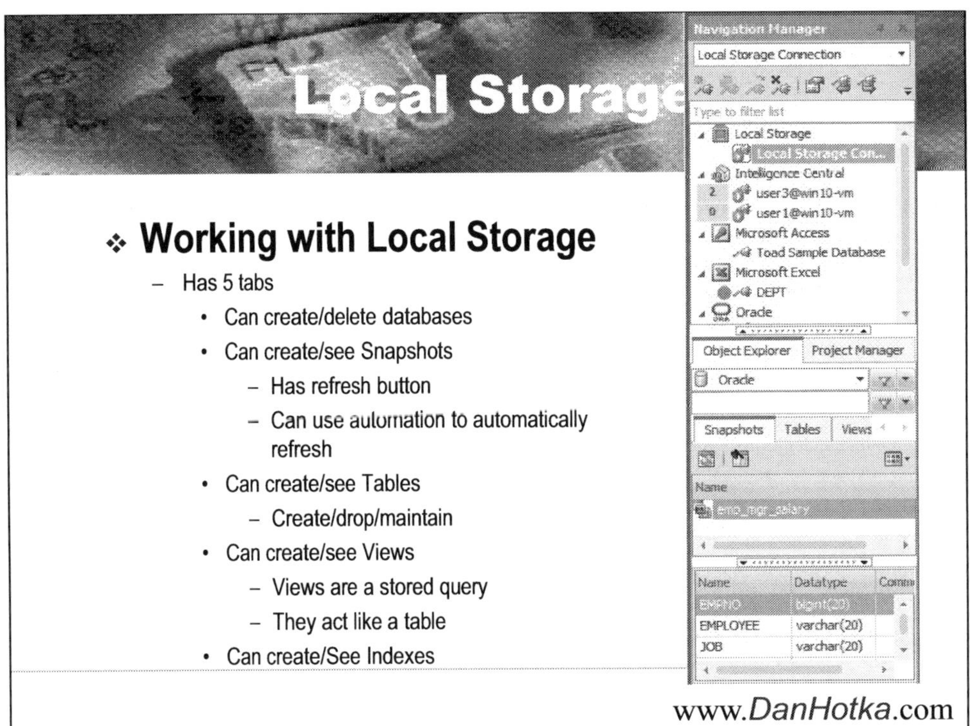
Local Storage
Working with Local Storage
– Has 5 tabs
• Can create/delete databases
• Can create/see Snapshots
– Has refresh button
– Can use automation to automatically refresh
• Can create/see Tables
– Create/drop/maintain
• Can create/see Views
– Views are a stored query
– They act like a table
• Can create/See Indexes
Navigation Manager
Local Storage Connection
Type to filter list
Local Storage
Intelligence Central
user3@win10-vm
user1@win10-vm
Microsoft Access
Toad Sample Database
Microsoft Excel
DEPT
Oracle
Object Explorer
Project Manager
Snapshots
Tables
Views
Name
Datatype
EMPLOYEE
varchar(20)
JOB
varchar(20)
www.DanHotka.com

## Toad Views

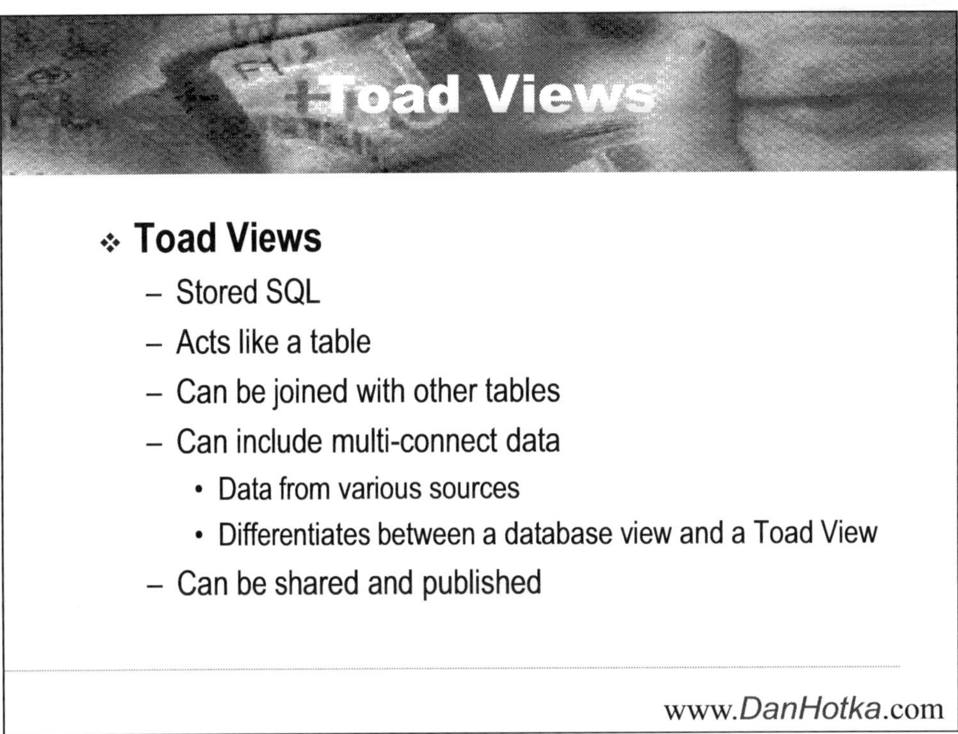
Toad Views
Toad Views
– Stored SQL
– Acts like a table
– Can be joined with other tables
– Can include multi-connect data
• Data from various sources
• Differentiates between a database view and a Toad View
– Can be shared and published
www.DanHotka.com

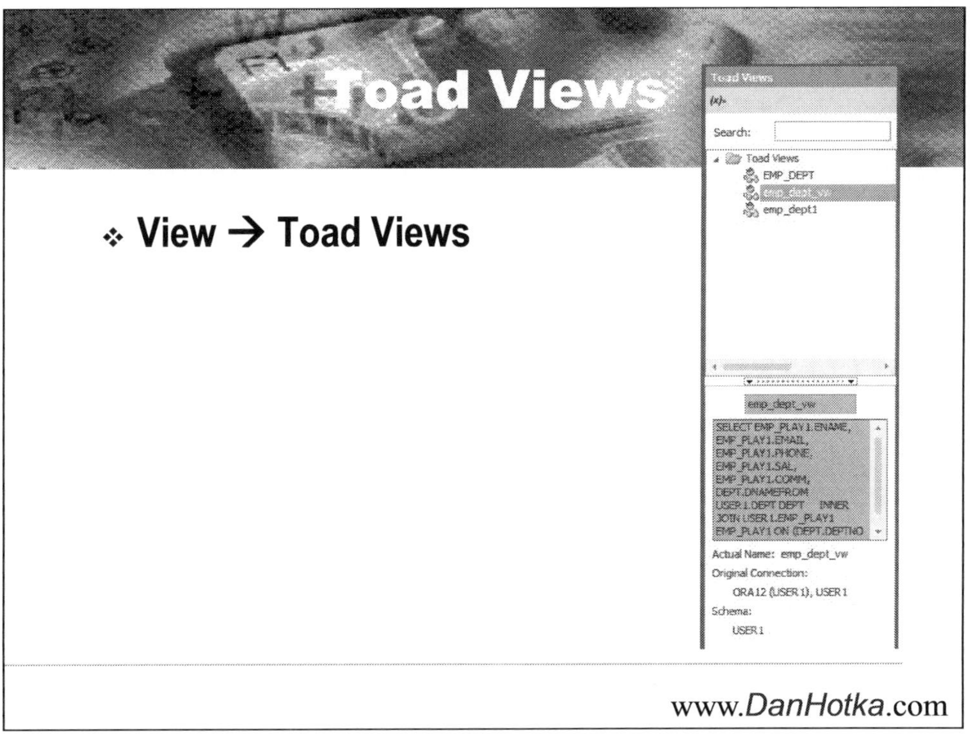
Toad Views
❖ View → Toad Views
Toad Views
Search:
Toad Views
EMP_DEPT
emp_dept_vw
emp_dept1
emp_dept_vw
SELECT EMP_PLAY1.ENAME, EMP_PLAY1.EMAIL, EMP_PLAY1.PHONE, EMP_PLAY1.SAL, EMP_PLAY1.COMM, DEPT.DNAMEFROM USER1.DEPT DEPT INNER JOIN USER1.EMP_PLAY1 EMP_PLAY1 ON (DEPT.DEPTNO
Actual Name: emp_dept_vw
Original Connection:
ORA12 (USER1), USER1
Schema:
USER1
www.DanHotka.com

Toad Views
USER1
SELECT * FROM ((emp_dept_vw))
Results
Result Sets
Messages
Explain Plan
Pivot & Chart
Profiling
Set 1
Set 2
ENAME EMAIL PHONE SAL COMM DNAME
KING King@Acme.com (202) 444-1212 5000 (null) ACCOUNTING
CLARK "Clark"@Acme.com (202) 444-7782 2450 (null) ACCOUNTING
MILLER Miller@Acme.com (202) 444-7934 1300 (null) ACCOUNTING
ADAMS Adams@Acme.com (512) 444-7876 1100 (null) RESEARCH
SCOTT Scott@Acme.com (512) 444-7788 3000 (null) RESEARCH
SMITH Smith@Acme.com (512) 444-7369 800 (null) RESEARCH
FORD Ford@Acme.com (512) 444-7902 3000 (null) RESEARCH
JONES Jones@Acme (512) 444-7566 2975 (null) RESEARCH
WARD Ward@Acme.com (312) 444-7521 1250 500 SALES
JAMES James@Acme (312) 444-7900 950 (null) SALES
ALLEN Allen@Acme.com (302) 444-7499 1600 300 SALES
Right-click to add column totals.
Record 1 of 14
Tutorial
Open SQL
Save as Toad View
Run SQL
Run Script
Publish File
Add to Project
www.DanHotka.com

## Project Manager

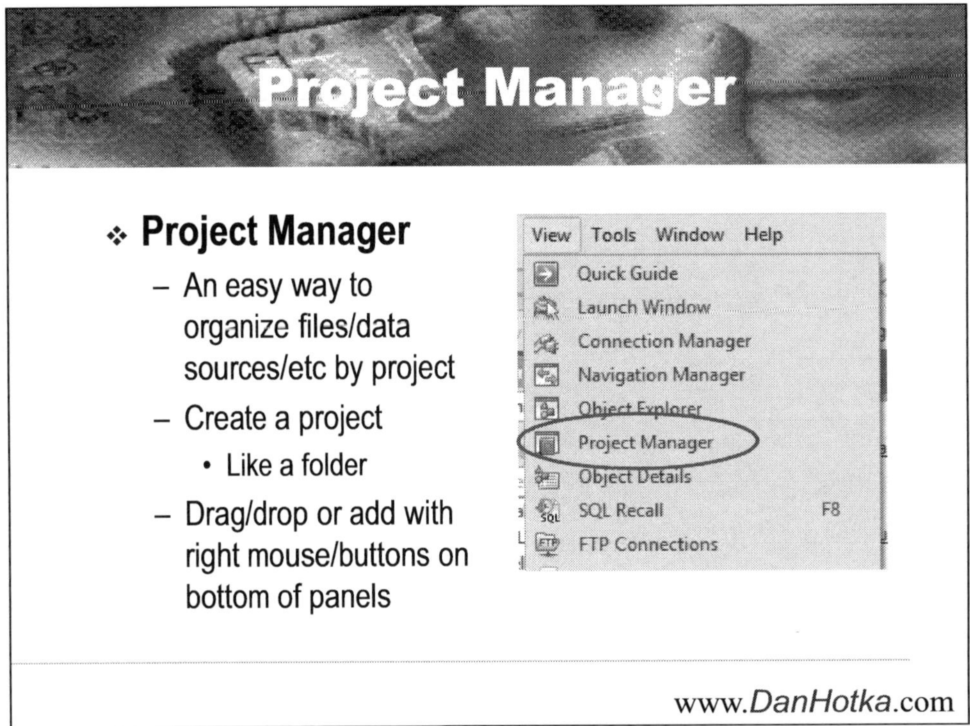
Project Manager
Project Manager
– An easy way to organize files/data sources/etc by project
– Create a project
• Like a folder
– Drag/drop or add with right mouse/buttons on bottom of panels
View Tools Window Help
Quick Guide
Launch Window
Connection Manager
Navigation Manager
Object Explorer
Project Manager
Object Details
SQL Recall F8
FTP Connections
www.DanHotka.com

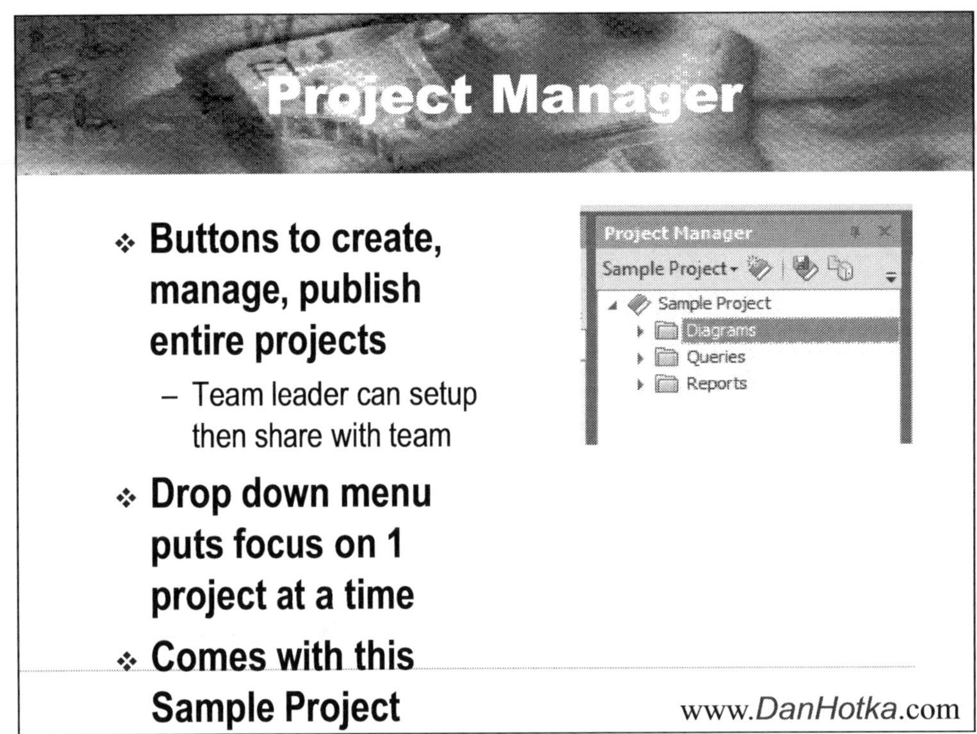
Project Manager
Buttons to create, manage, publish entire projects
– Team leader can setup then share with team
Drop down menu puts focus on 1 project at a time
Comes with this Sample Project
Project Manager
Sample Project
Sample Project
Diagrams
Queries
Reports
www.DanHotka.com

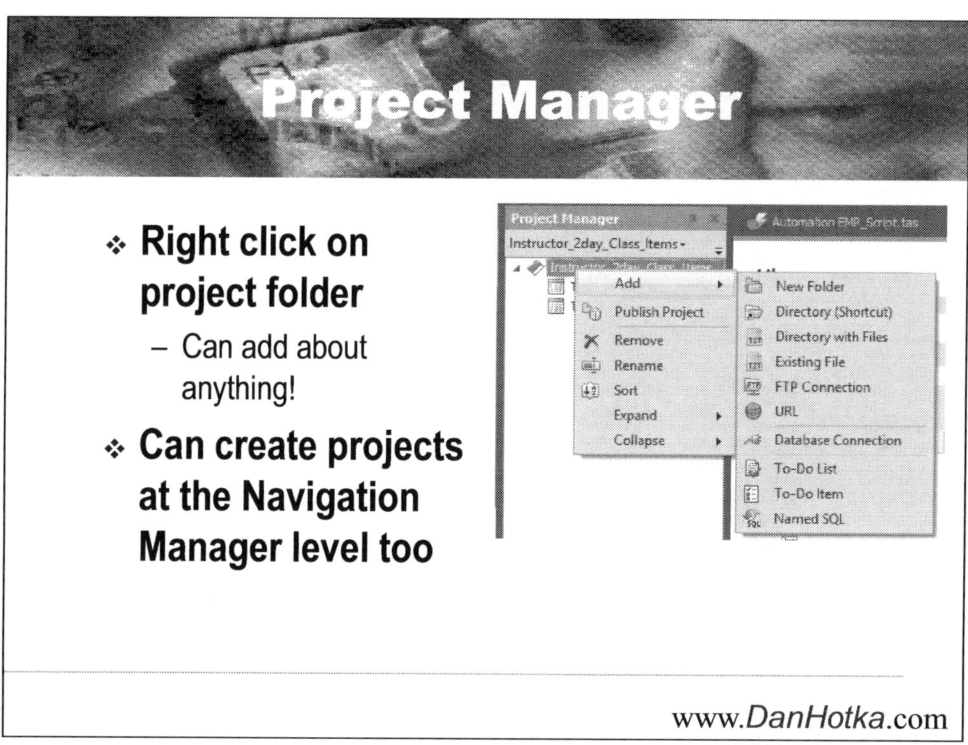
Project Manager
Right click on project folder
– Can add about anything!
Can create projects at the Navigation Manager level too
Project Manager
Instructor_2day_Class_Items
Add
Publish Project
Remove
Rename
Sort
Expand
Collapse
New Folder
Directory (Shortcut)
Directory with Files
Existing File
FTP Connection
URL
Database Connection
To-Do List
To-Do Item
Named SQL
www.DanHotka.com

## Library

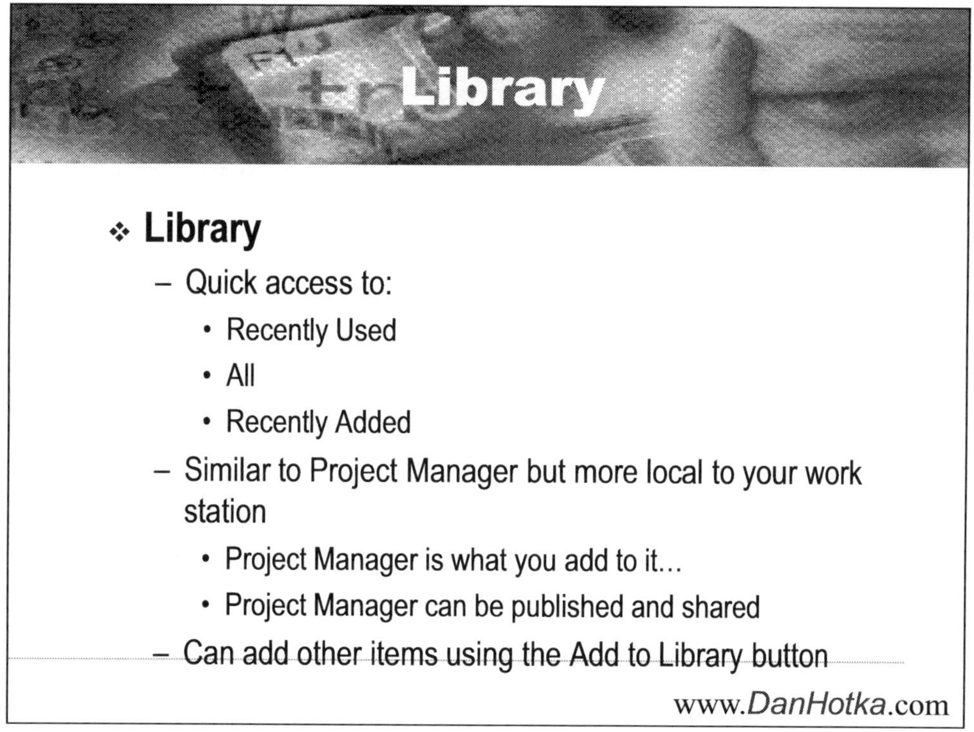
Library
Library
– Quick access to:
• Recently Used
• All
• Recently Added
– Similar to Project Manager but more local to your work station
• Project Manager is what you add to it…
• Project Manager can be published and shared
– Can add other items using the Add to Library button
www.DanHotka.com

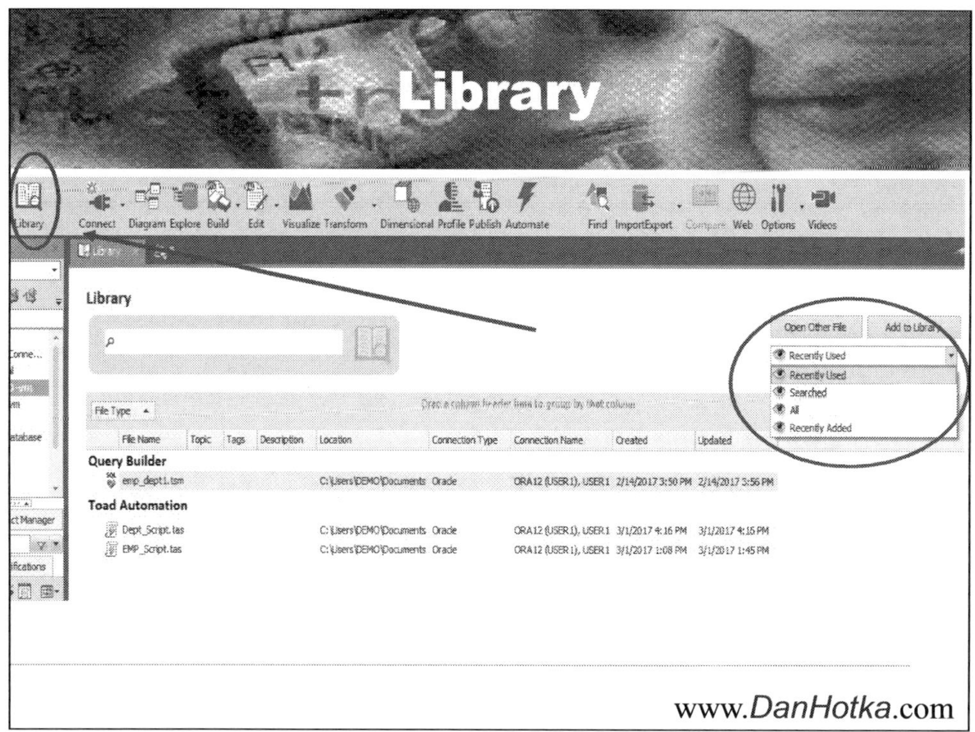


## Data Compare and Sync

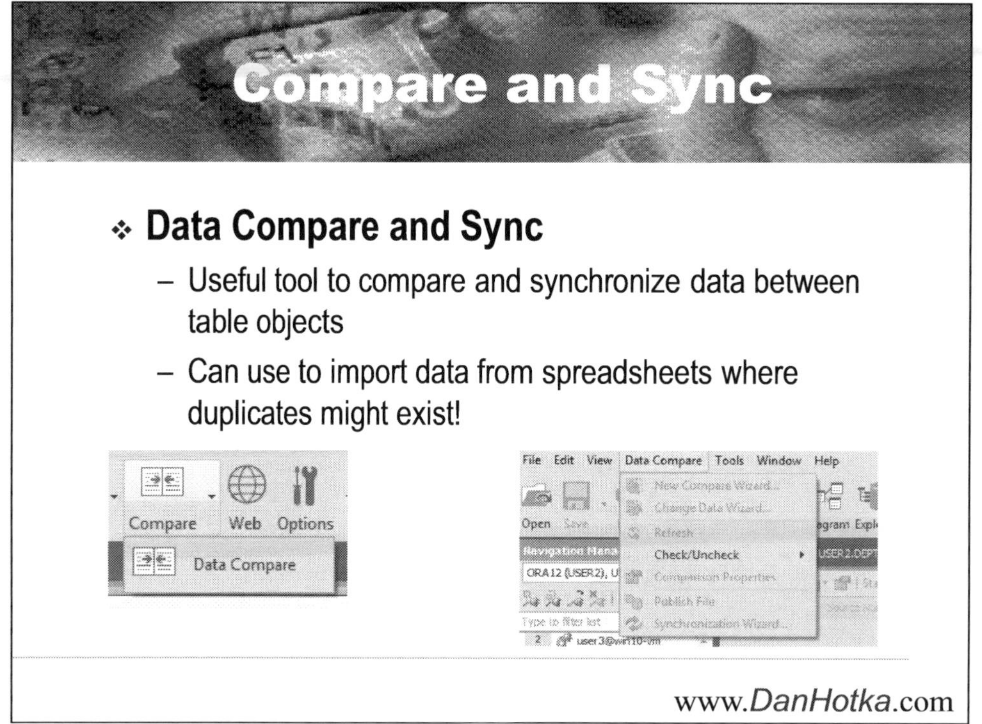

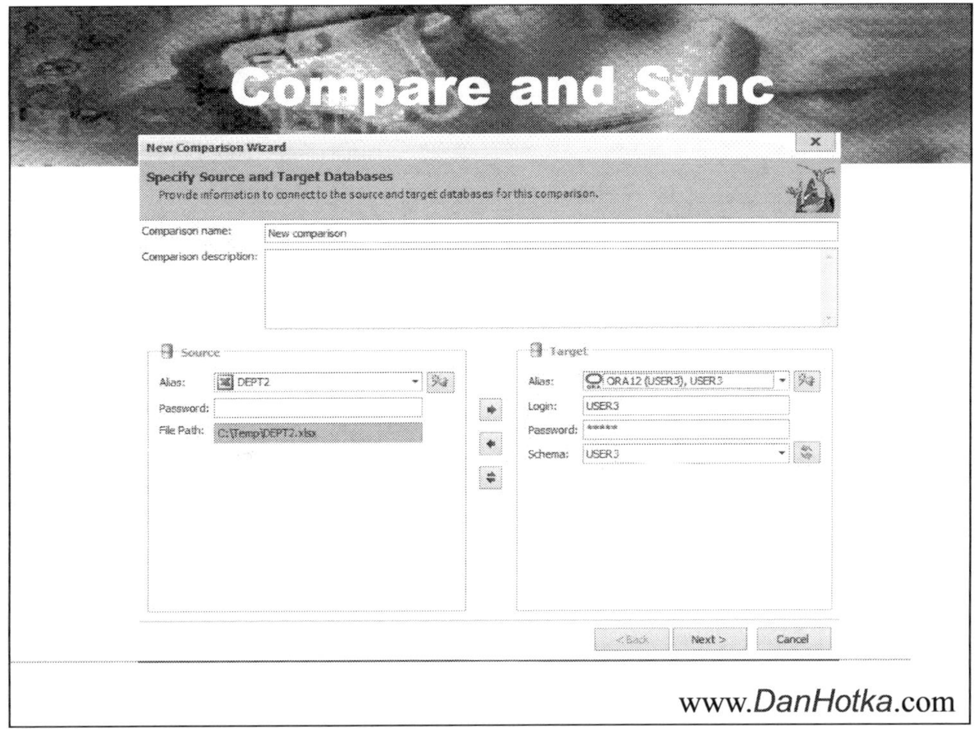


# Compare and Sync

**New Comparison Wizard**

**Select a Range of Cells for Source File**

Select a range of cells you want to compare

Source: DEPT2 — Reset selection to default for all sheets

Sheet1

☑ Include this sheet in comparison — Select columns from A to C — Reset selection to default

Select rows from 1 to 6 (first row must contain columns names)

| # | A | B | C |
|---|---|---|---|
| 1 | DEPTNO | DNAME | LOC |
| 2 | 10 | ACCOUNTING | NEW YORK |
| 3 | 20 | RESEARCH | DALLAS |
| 4 | 30 | SALES | ATLANTA |
| 5 | 40 | OPERATIONS | BOSTON |
| 6 | 50 | HR | DES MOINES |

< Back | Next > | Cancel

www.DanHotka.com

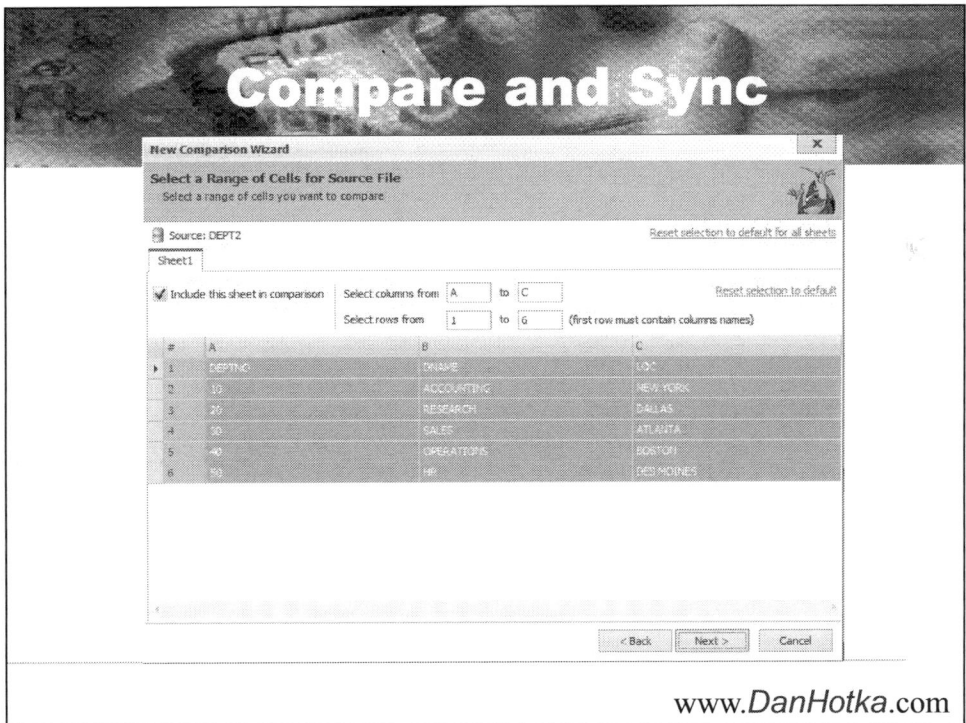

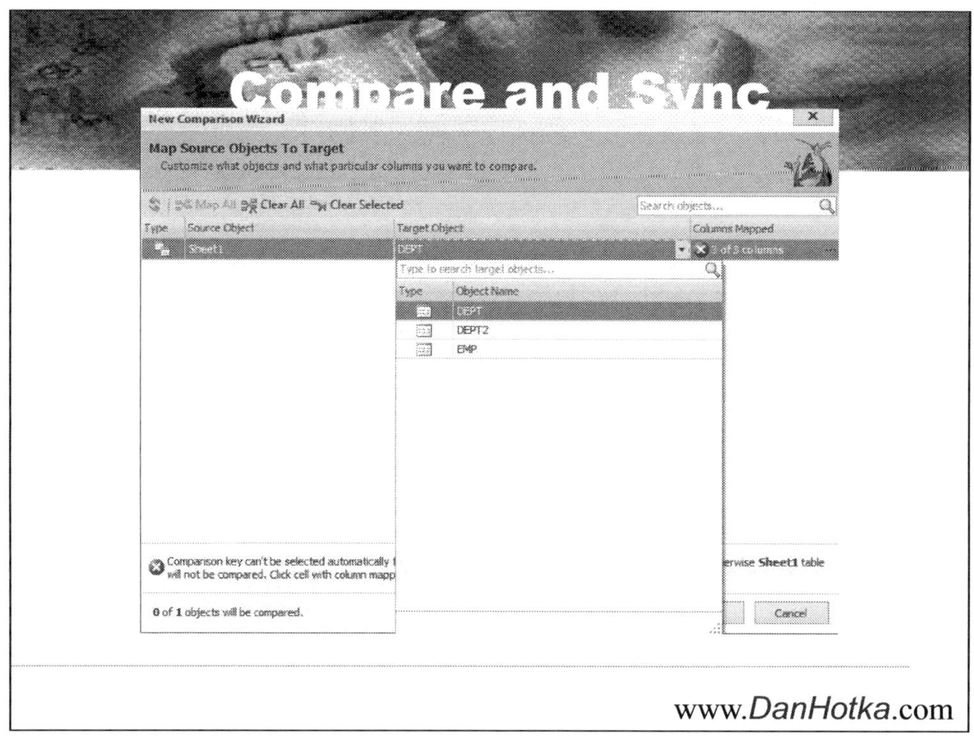
Compare and Sync
New Comparison Wizard
Map Source Objects To Target
Customize what objects and what particular columns you want to compare.
Map All
Clear All
Clear Selected
Search objects...
Type
Source Object
Target Object
Columns Mapped
Sheet1
DEPT
3 of 3 columns
Type to search target objects...
Type
Object Name
DEPT
DEPT2
EMP
Comparison key can't be selected automatically
will not be compared. Click cell with column mapp
erwise Sheet1 table
0 of 1 objects will be compared.
Cancel
www.DanHotka.com

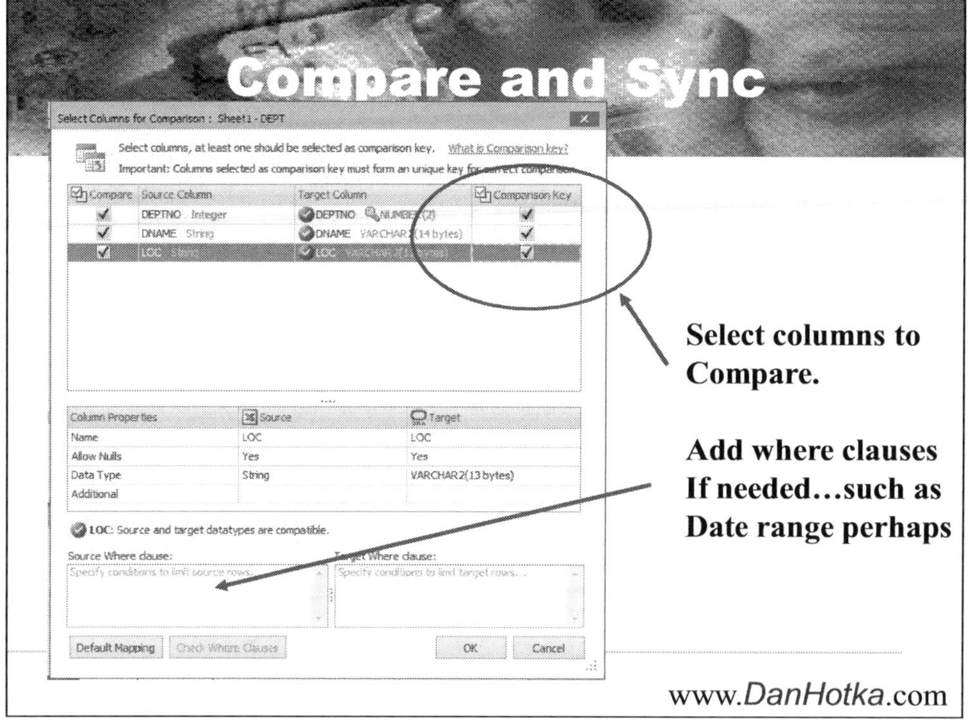
Compare and Sync
Select Columns for Comparison : Sheet1 - DEPT
Select columns, at least one should be selected as comparison key.
What is Comparison key?
Important: Columns selected as comparison key must form an unique key
Compare
Source Column
Target Column
Comparison Key
DEPTNO Integer
DEPTNO
DNAME String
DNAME
LOC
Column Properties
Source
Target
Name
LOC
LOC
Allow Nulls
Yes
Yes
Data Type
String
VARCHAR2(13 bytes)
Additional
LOC: Source and target datatypes are compatible.
Source Where clause:
Target Where clause:
Default Mapping
Check Where Clauses
OK
Cancel
Select columns to Compare.
Add where clauses If needed…such as Date range perhaps
www.DanHotka.com

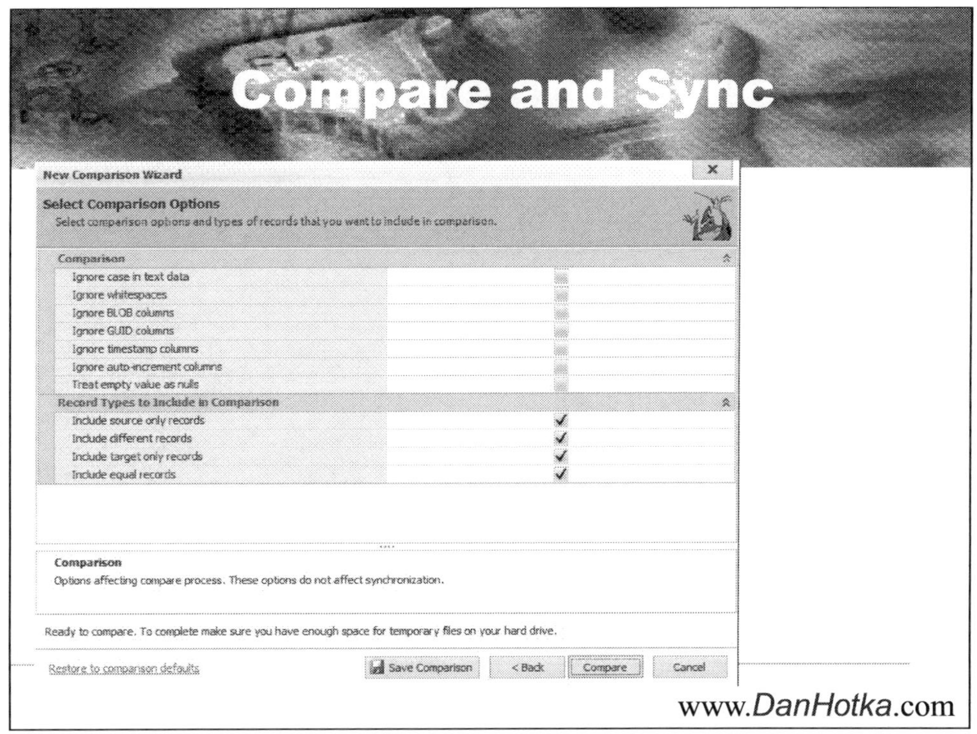
Compare and Sync
New Comparison Wizard
Select Comparison Options
Select comparison options and types of records that you want to include in comparison.
Comparison
Ignore case in text data
Ignore whitespaces
Ignore BLOB columns
Ignore GUID columns
Ignore timestamp columns
Ignore auto-increment columns
Treat empty value as nulls
Record Types to Include in Comparison
Include source only records
Include different records
Include target only records
Include equal records
Comparison
Options affecting compare process. These options do not affect synchronization.
Ready to compare. To complete make sure you have enough space for temporary files on your hard drive.
Restore to comparison defaults
Save Comparison
< Back
Compare
Cancel
www.DanHotka.com

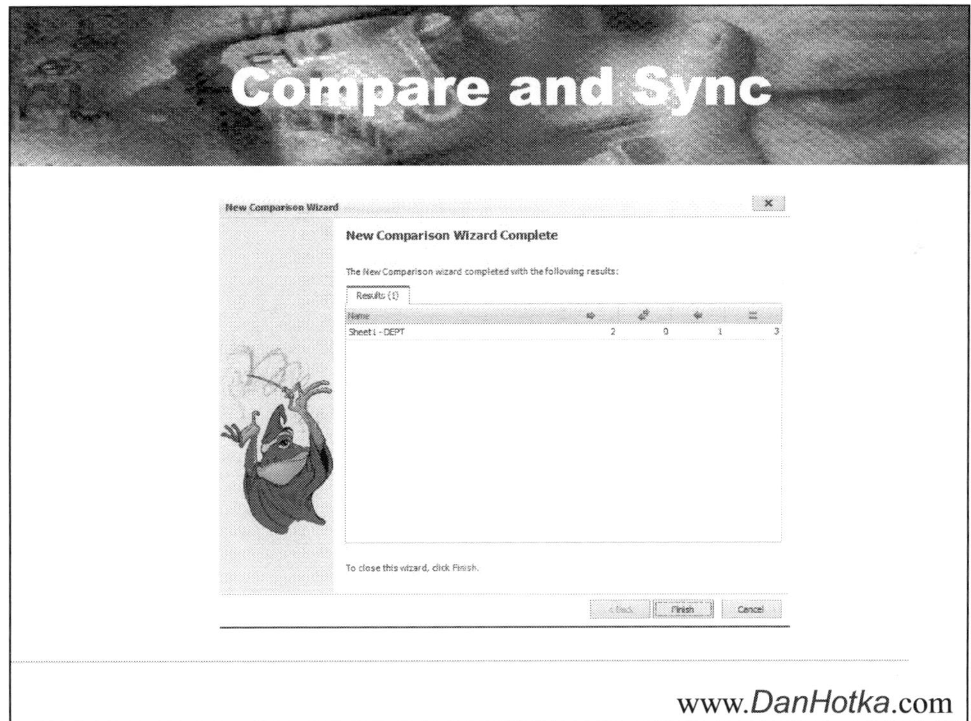
Compare and Sync
New Comparison Wizard
New Comparison Wizard Complete
The New Comparison wizard completed with the following results:
Results (1)
Name
Sheet1 - DEPT 2 0 1 3
To close this wizard, click Finish.
< Back
Finish
Cancel
www.DanHotka.com

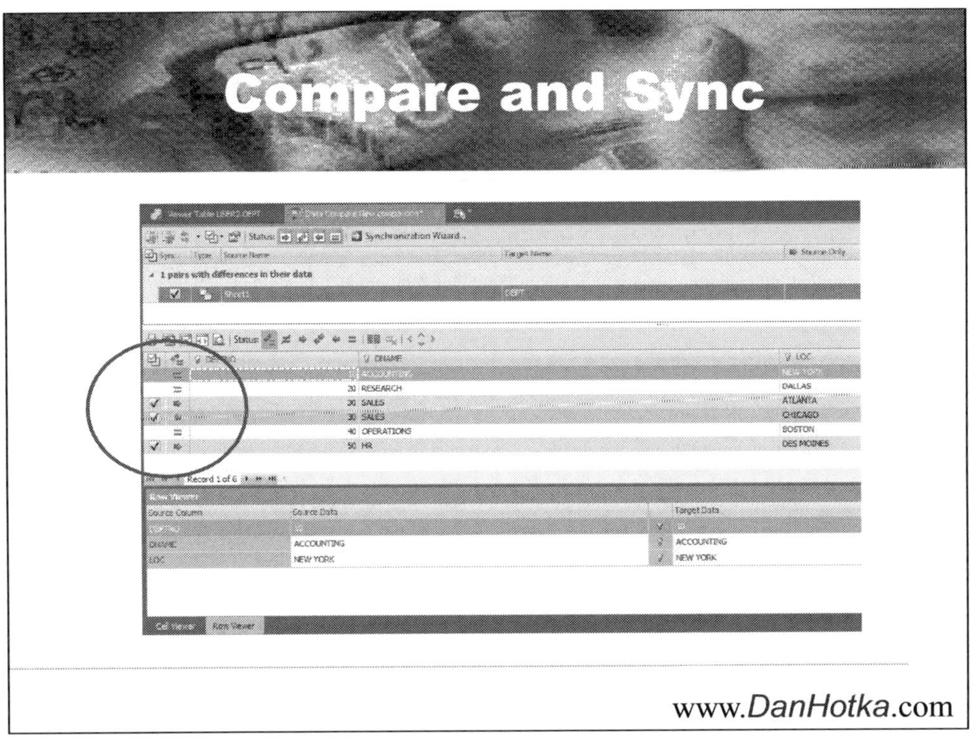
Compare and Sync
Synchronization Wizard...
1 pairs with differences in their data
20 RESEARCH
30 SALES
30 SALES
40 OPERATIONS
50 HR
DALLAS
ATLANTA
CHICAGO
BOSTON
DES MOINES
Record 1 of 6
ACCOUNTING
NEW YORK
ACCOUNTING
NEW YORK
www.DanHotka.com

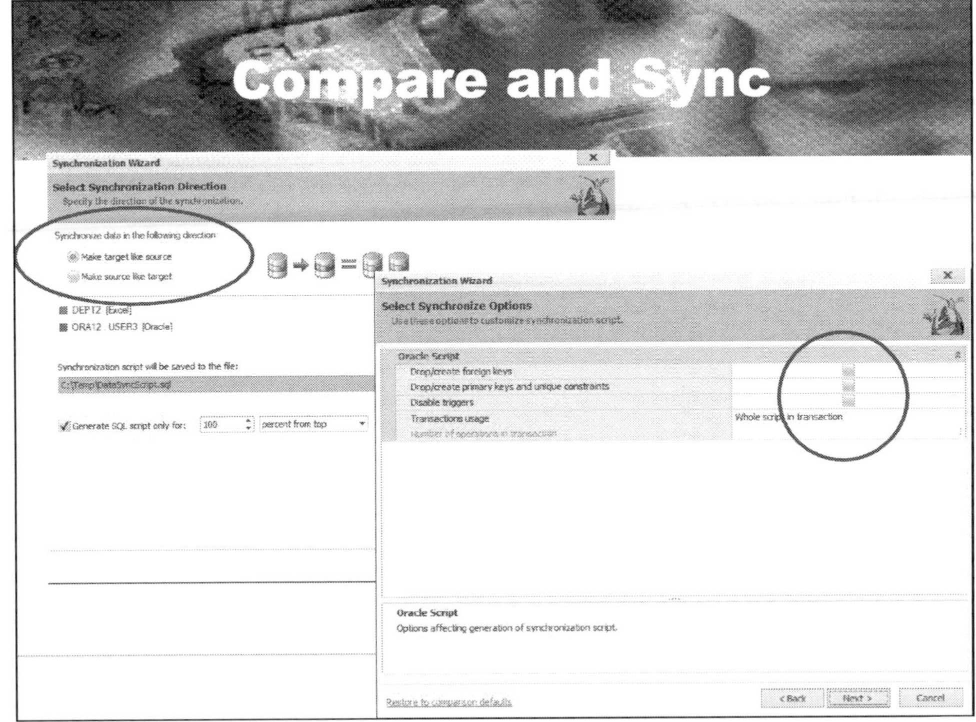
Compare and Sync
Synchronization Wizard
Select Synchronization Direction
Synchronize data in the following direction
Make target like source
Make source like target
Synchronization script will be saved to the file:
Generate SQL script only for:
Synchronization Wizard
Select Synchronize Options
Oracle Script
Drop/create foreign keys
Drop/create primary keys and unique constraints
Disable triggers
Transactions usage
Whole script in transaction
Oracle Script
Options affecting generation of synchronization script.
< Back
Next >
Cancel

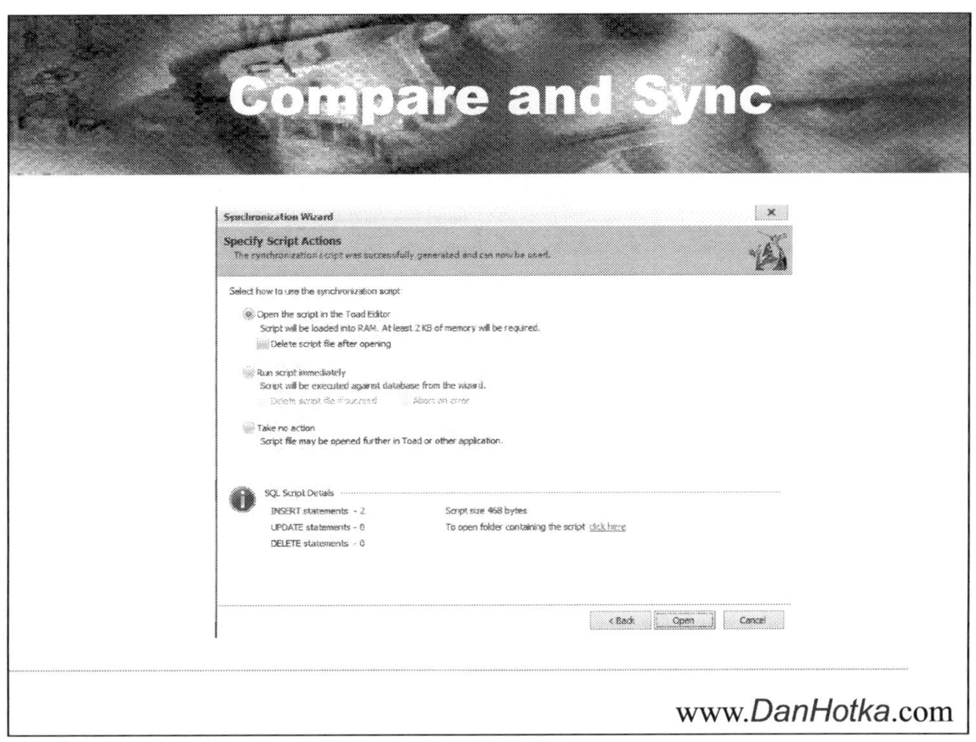
Compare and Sync
Synchronization Wizard
Specify Script Actions
Select how to use the synchronization script
Open the script in the Toad Editor
Run script immediately
Take no action
SQL Script Details
INSERT statements - 2
UPDATE statements - 0
DELETE statements - 0
Script size 468 bytes
< Back
Open
Cancel
www.DanHotka.com

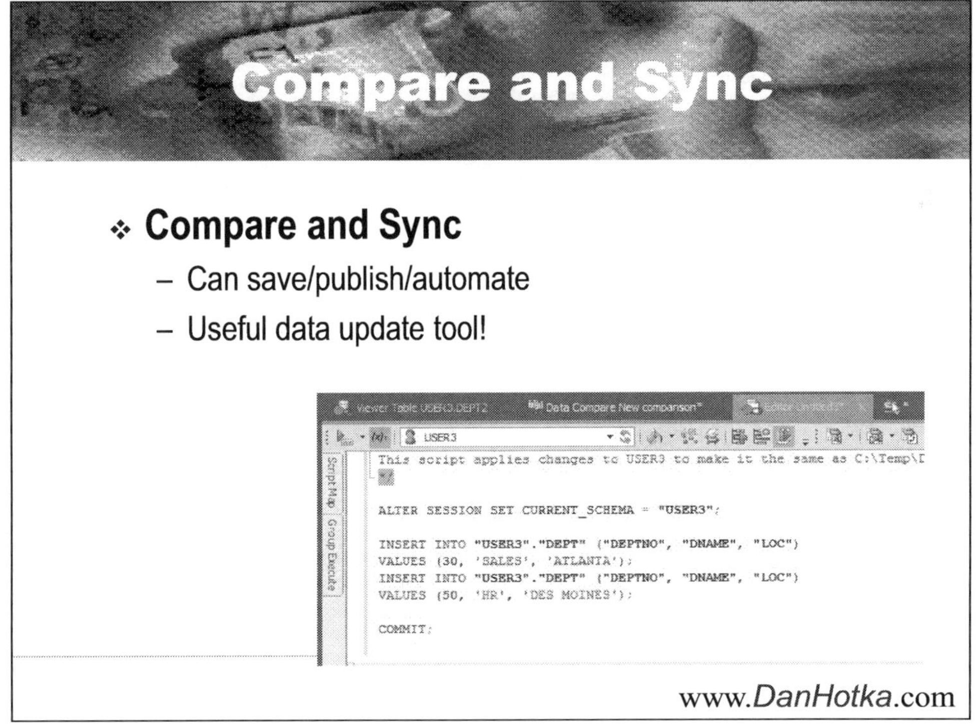
Compare and Sync
Compare and Sync
– Can save/publish/automate
– Useful data update tool!
This script applies changes to USER3 to make it the same as C:\Temp\D
ALTER SESSION SET CURRENT_SCHEMA = "USER3";
INSERT INTO "USER3"."DEPT" ("DEPTNO", "DNAME", "LOC")
VALUES (30, 'SALES', 'ATLANTA');
INSERT INTO "USER3"."DEPT" ("DEPTNO", "DNAME", "LOC")
VALUES (50, 'HR', 'DES MOINES');
COMMIT;
www.DanHotka.com

## Dimensional Views

### Dimensional Views

- **Dimensional Views**
  - Quick/Easy Data Grouping for analysis
    - Can use as a digital dashboard
    - Can use as a digital dashboard in Excel
    - A hidden gem for sure!

www.*DanHotka*.com

### Dimensional Views

- **Dimensional Views**
  - Can use any Table, View, SQL, Toad View, QB, any data grid
  - Can easily get summary data with counts/totals/other aggregate functions
  - Can save as tables/Toad Views
    - For joins/use later in other queries/reports
  - Can save as multi-tabbed spreadsheets
  - Can be published and refreshed

www.*DanHotka*.com

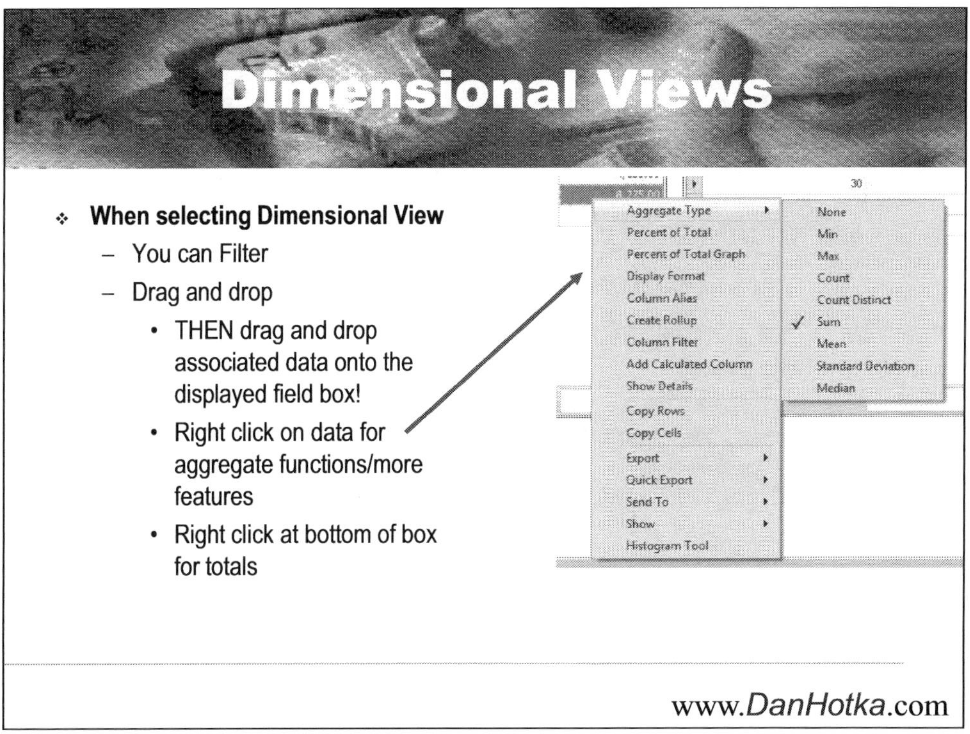
Dimensional Views
When selecting Dimensional View
You can Filter
Drag and drop
THEN drag and drop associated data onto the displayed field box!
Right click on data for aggregate functions/more features
Right click at bottom of box for totals
Aggregate Type
Percent of Total
Percent of Total Graph
Display Format
Column Alias
Create Rollup
Column Filter
Add Calculated Column
Show Details
Copy Rows
Copy Cells
Export
Quick Export
Send To
Show
Histogram Tool
None
Min
Max
Count
Count Distinct
Sum
Mean
Standard Deviation
Median
www.DanHotka.com

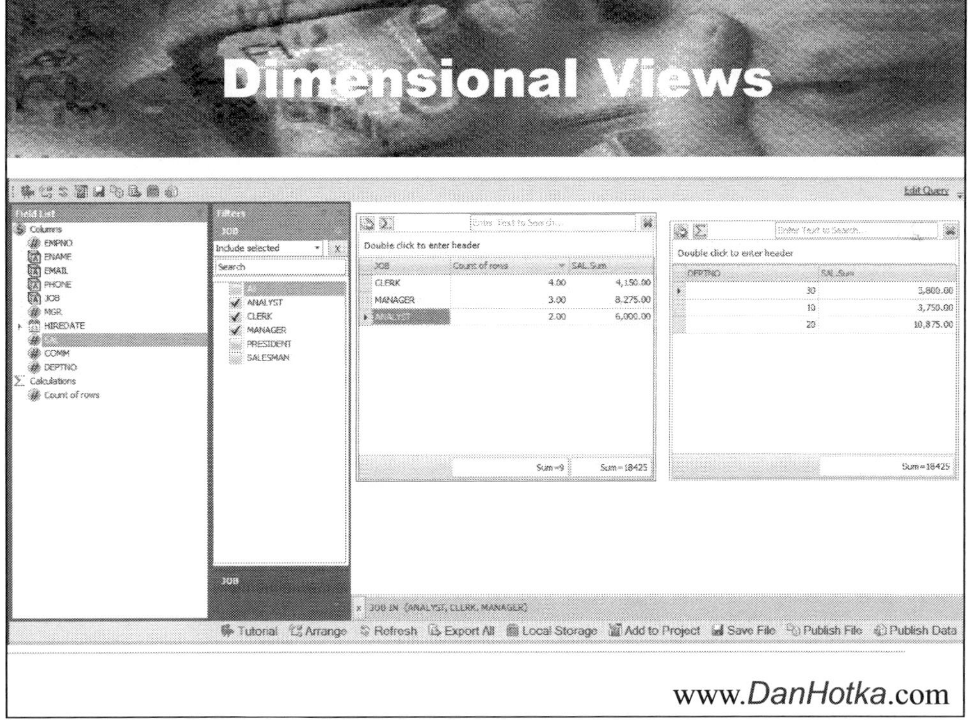
Dimensional Views
Tutorial
Arrange
Refresh
Export All
Local Storage
Add to Project
Save File
Publish File
Publish Data
www.DanHotka.com

# Dimensional Views

- **Dimensional Views**
  - Allows for precise data analysis
  - Results can be saved and re-used in a variety of formats

www.*DanHotka*.com

## Summary

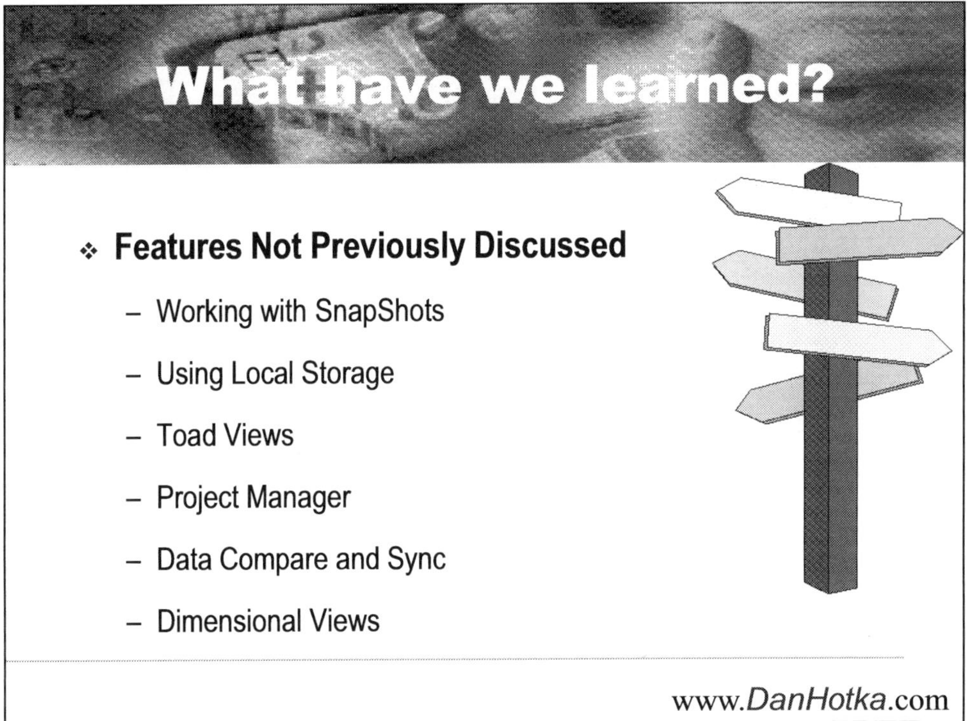
What have we learned?
Features Not Previously Discussed
– Working with SnapShots
– Using Local Storage
– Toad Views
– Project Manager
– Data Compare and Sync
– Dimensional Views
www.DanHotka.com

## Features Not Previously Discussed Lab

### Additional Toad DP Features

- Features Not Previously Discussed Lab
  - Access an EMP table and save it to local storage
    - You can use one of your supplied tables if you like
  - Synchronize the spreadsheet DEPT2 with the DEPT in your schema
    - Go ahead and let it do the update if you like
    - If some of your data was prepared for this task…you can use it

www.DanHotka.com

### Additional Toad DP Features

- Features Not Previously Discussed Lab – Part 2
  - Using Query Builder
    - Quickly create a view of EMP and DEPT
      - Using ENAME, JOB, SAL, DNAME
    - Make sure it works
    - Save as a Toad View
    - Select from the Toad View

www.DanHotka.com

## Additional Toad DP Features

- **Features Not Previously Discussed Lab – Part 3**
  - Using the Toad View just created (or using your data, follow instructors advise)
    - Make a Dimensional Comparison
    - Create a department salary summary with totals at the bottom
    - Create a job and salary summary with totals at the bottom for everyone but the PRESIDENT
    - Organize into a dashboard
    - Save to a spreadsheet

www.DanHotka.com

## Features Not Previously Discussed Lab Answers

- Access an EMP table and save it to local storage
    - You can use one of your supplied tables if you like

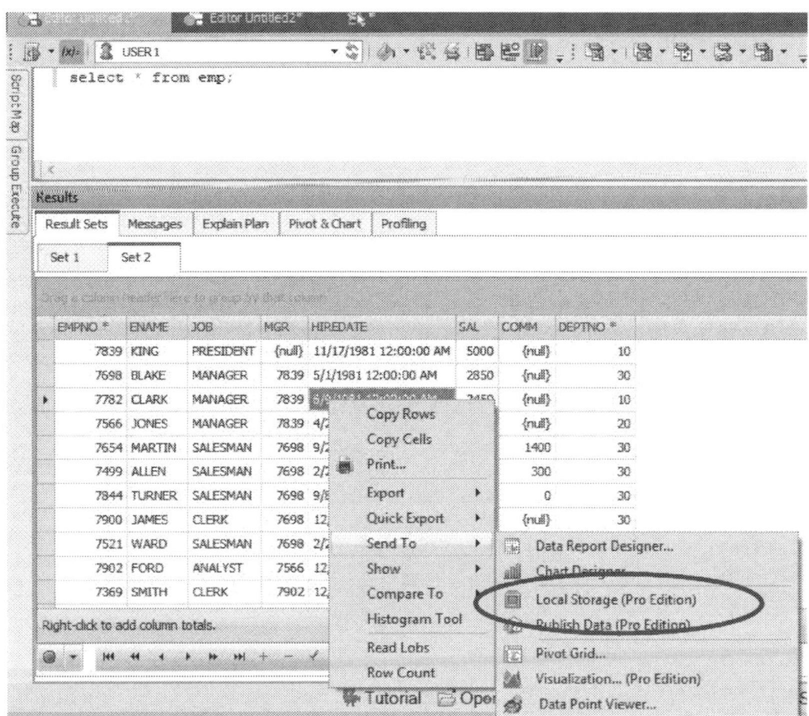

Select your data, from the data grid, right click on the data grid and select Local Storage…

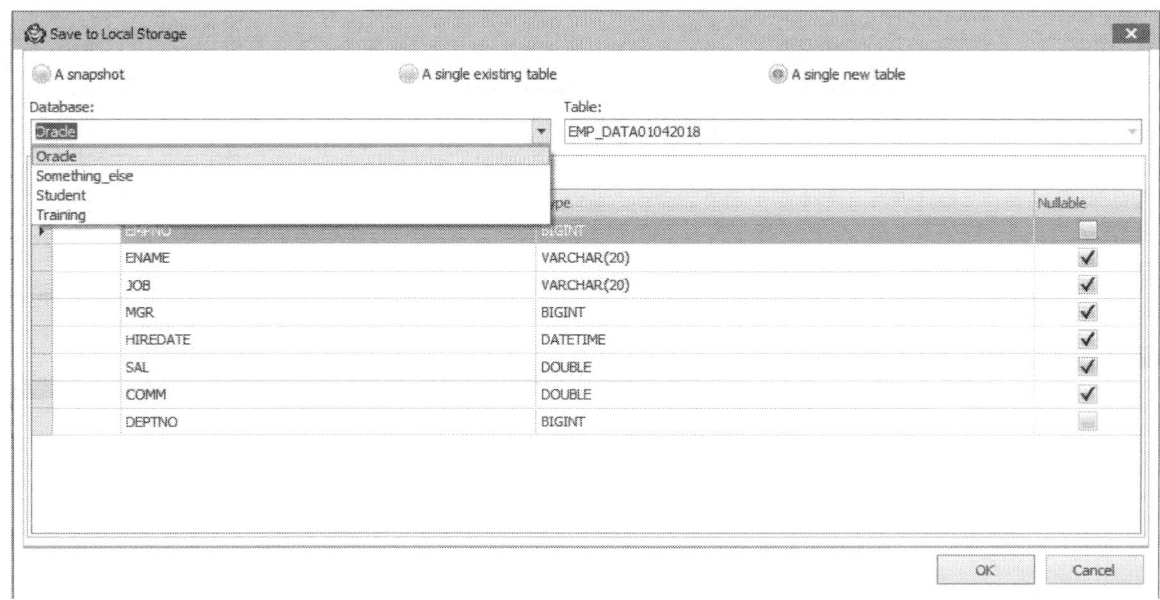

Select a database and pick your option on the top. Remember that these Local Storage Databases are like folders. If you need a new database name (folder), create this from the Navigation Manager.

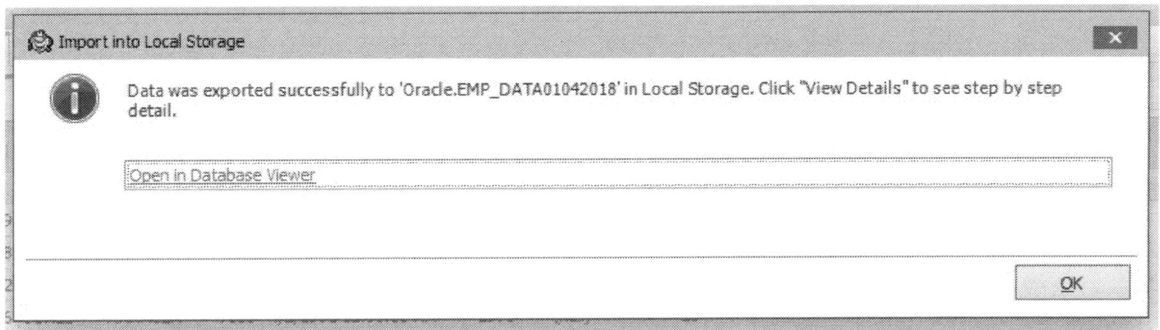


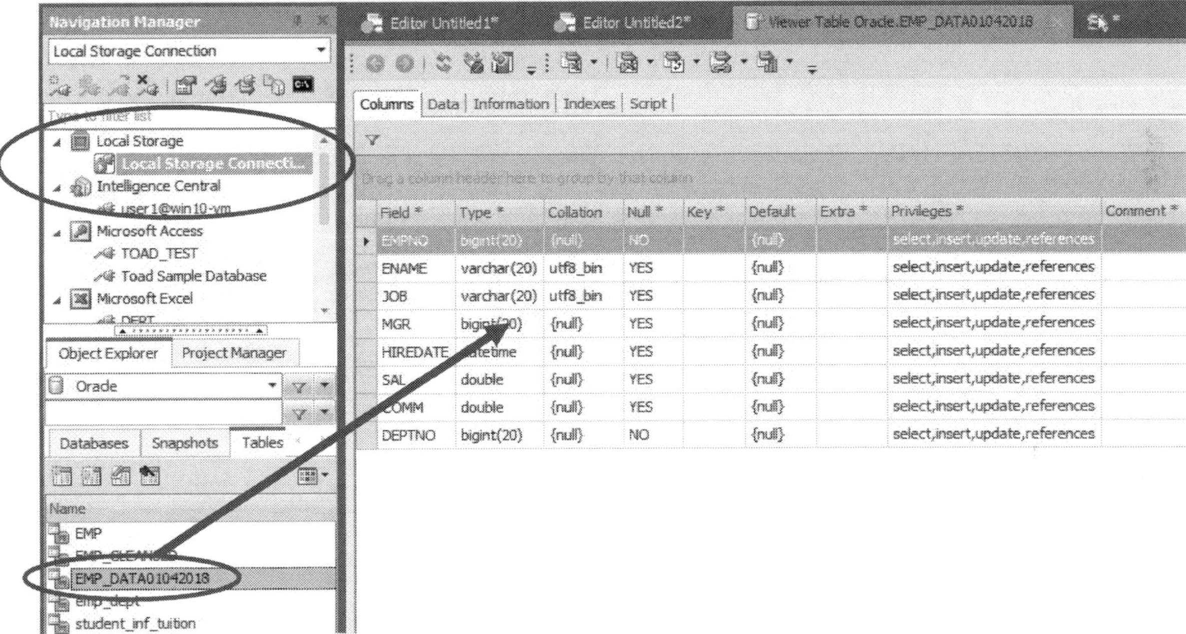


– Synchronize the spreadsheet DEPT2 with the DEPT in your schema
  - Go ahead and let it do the update if you like
  - If some of your data was prepared for this task…you can use it

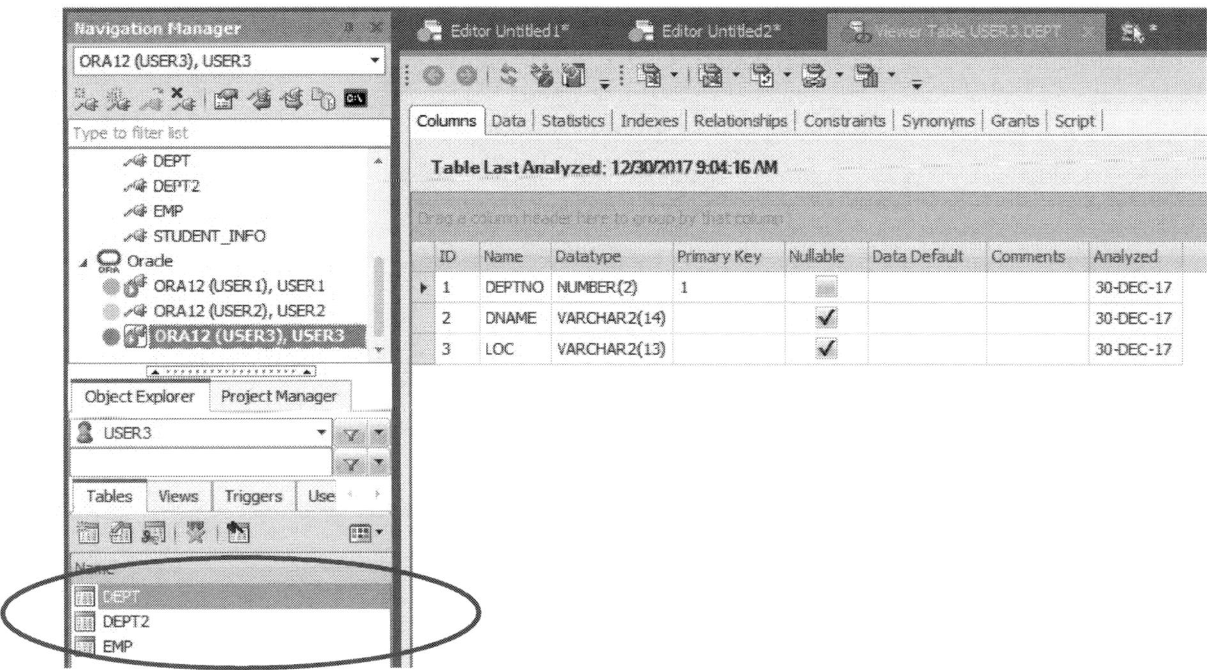


I imported both DEPT and DEPT2 spreadsheets into this database connection USER3.

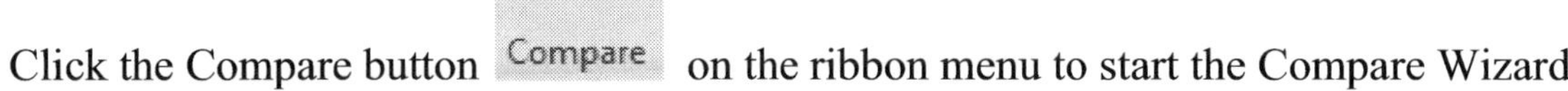

Click the Compare button Compare on the ribbon menu to start the Compare Wizard.

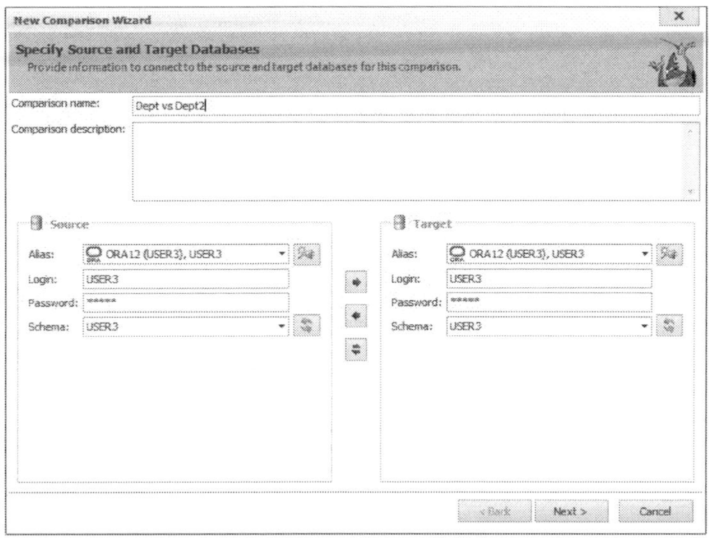


Toad DP fills out the connections based on your current ‘focus’ (ie: highlighted connection in the Navigation Manager). Click ‘Next’.

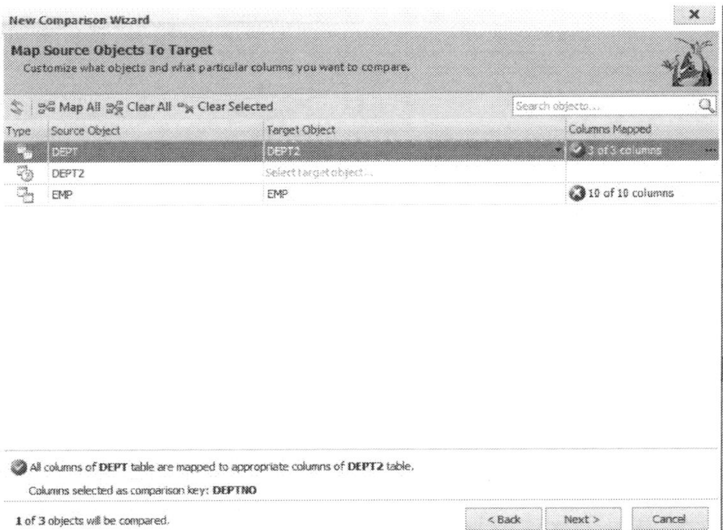


Click in the Target Object and change the Target Object to DEPT2, as seen in this illustration…click 'Next'

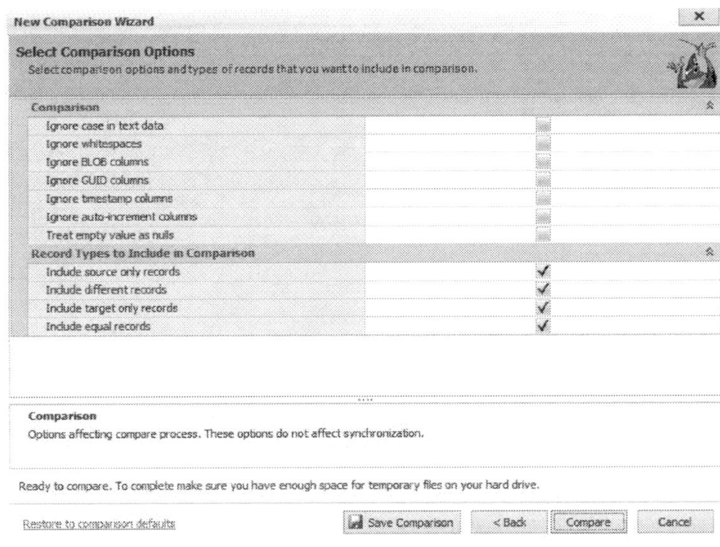


I only want to know about the differences…check the correct boxes then click 'Compare'. IF you will be automating this, make sure to save it.

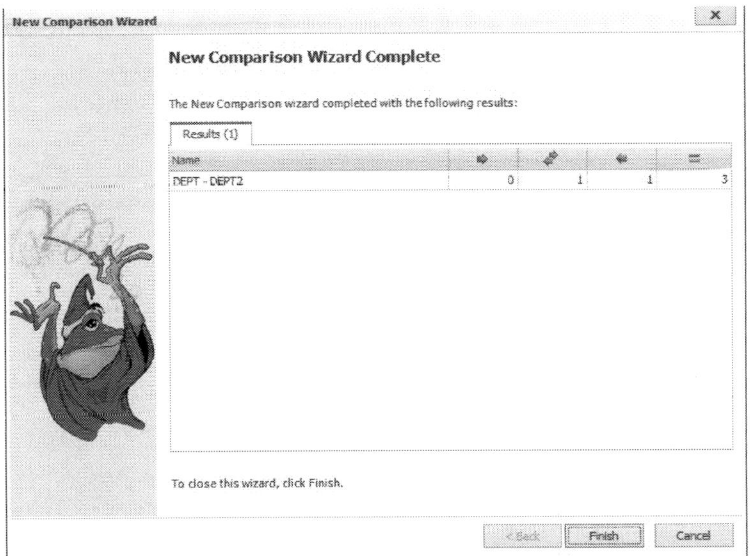


Yes…we have differences…click 'Finish'…

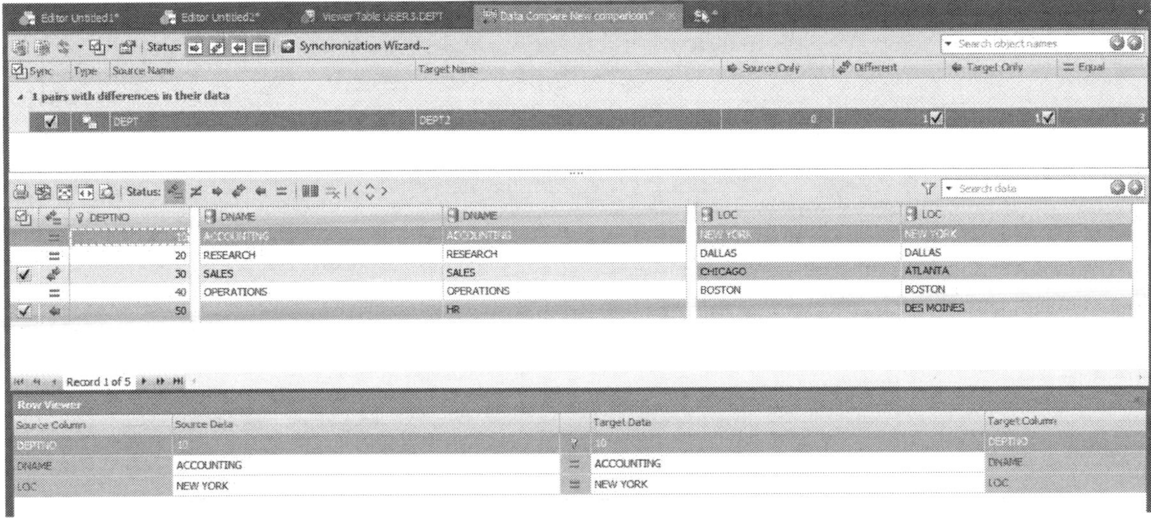


From here, you can create a script to sync them up, using the Synchronization Wizard.

- Using Query Builder
    - Quickly create a view of EMP and DEPT
        - Using ENAME, JOB, SAL, DNAME
    - Make sure it works
    - Save as a Toad View
    - Select from the Toad View

Start with the Build button  on the ribbon menu and pull in your EMP and DEPT tables:

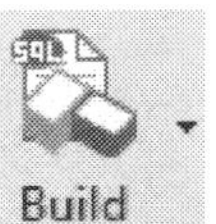

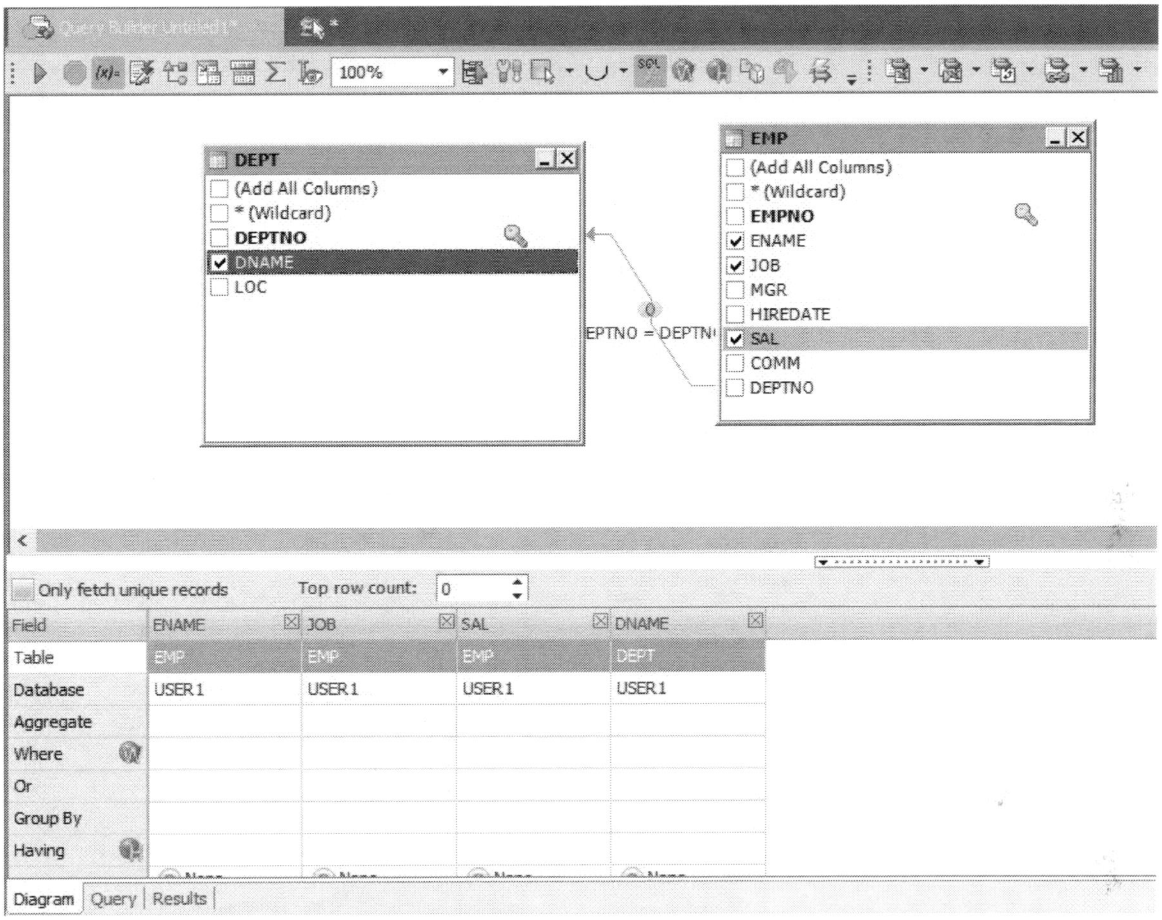

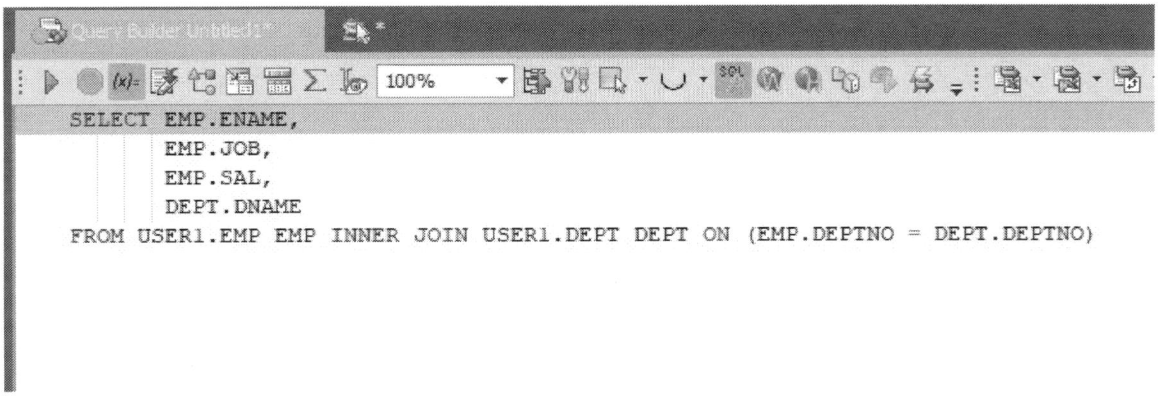

Query Builder Untitled1*
100%
DEPT
(Add All Columns)
* (Wildcard)
DEPTNO
DNAME
LOC
EMP
(Add All Columns)
* (Wildcard)
EMPNO
ENAME
JOB
MGR
HIREDATE
SAL
COMM
DEPTNO
EPTNO = DEPTN
Only fetch unique records
Top row count: 0
Field
ENAME
JOB
SAL
DNAME
Table
EMP
EMP
EMP
DEPT
Database
USER1
USER1
USER1
USER1
Aggregate
Where
Or
Group By
Having
Diagram
Query
Results

Query Builder Untitled1*
100%
SELECT EMP.ENAME,
EMP.JOB,
EMP.SAL,
DEPT.DNAME
FROM USER1.EMP EMP INNER JOIN USER1.DEPT DEPT ON (EMP.DEPTNO = DEPT.DEPTNO)

Review the results then click on Save as Toad View along the bottom of this panel…

Save as Toad View

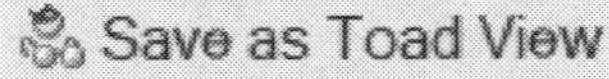

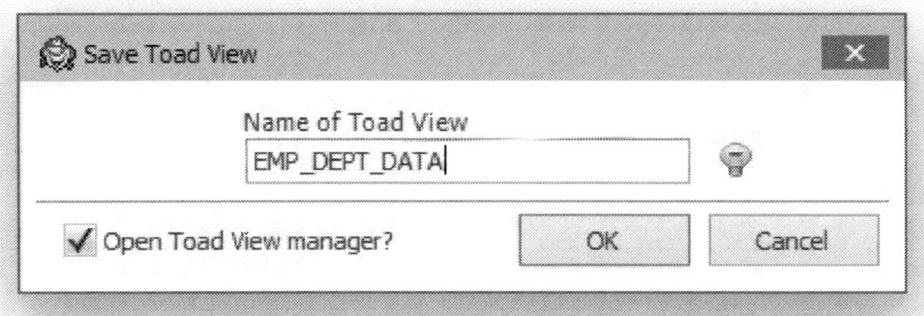


Sure…open the Toad View Manager. This manager is also accessible from the 'Views' menu item. These also appear in the library…

These views make it easy to save your fancy cross-database queries for future use, use in automation, use in future reports and spreadsheets. They do not save data, they merely save the query.

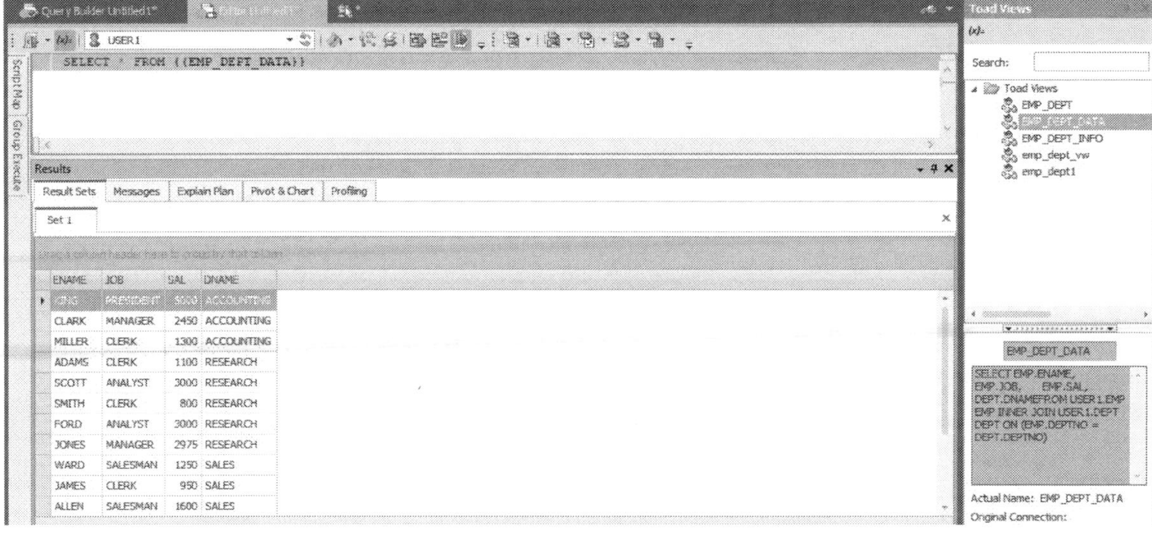


– Using the Toad View just created (or using your data, follow instructors advise)
    - Make a Dimensional Comparison
    - Create a department salary summary with totals at the bottom
    - Create a job and salary summary with totals at the bottom for everyone but the PRESIDENT
    - Organize into a dashboard

Save to a spreadsheet

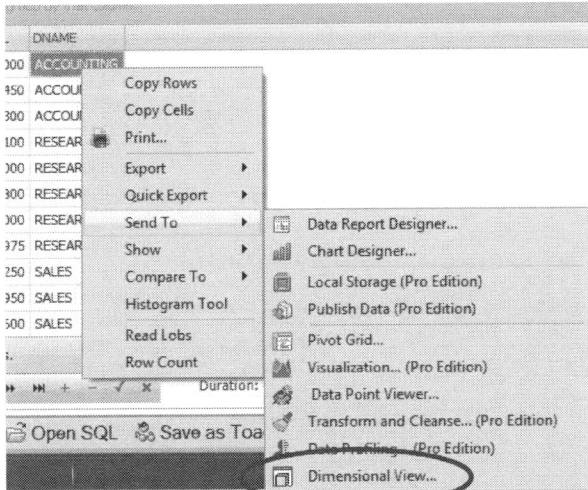

Right click on the data grid and select 'Dimensional View…'

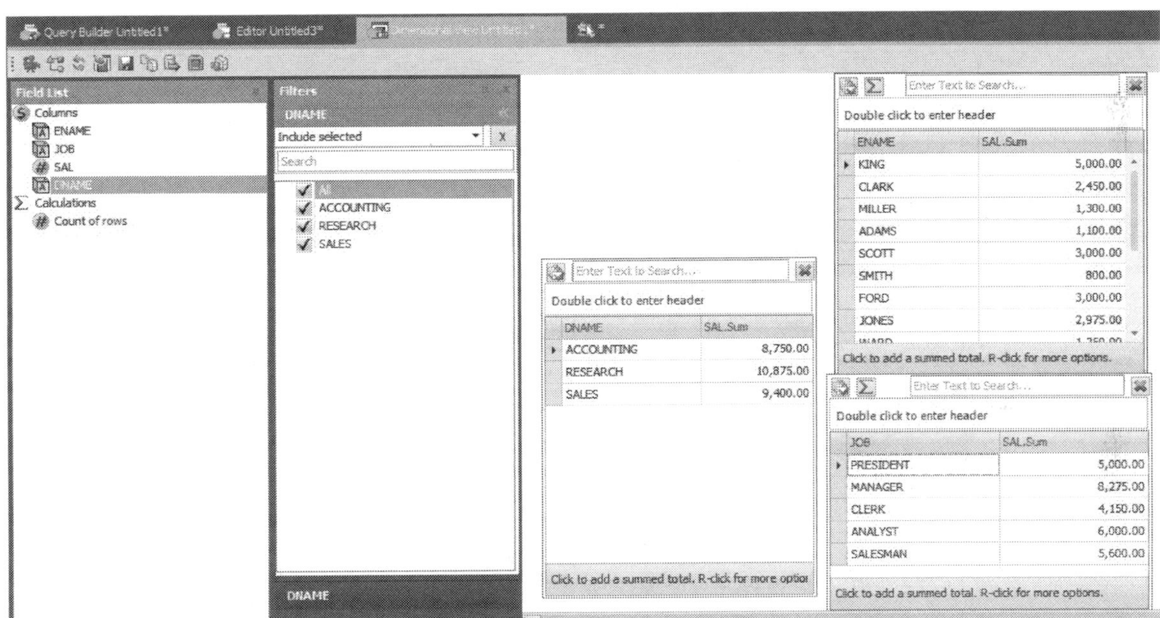


Drag and drop ENAME to the open area of the canvas. Drag and drop SAL into the same box. Do this for DNAME and JOB…

Drag DNAME into the Filter box…now…you can deselect some of the departments or just select 1 department and all the frames will show just that data!

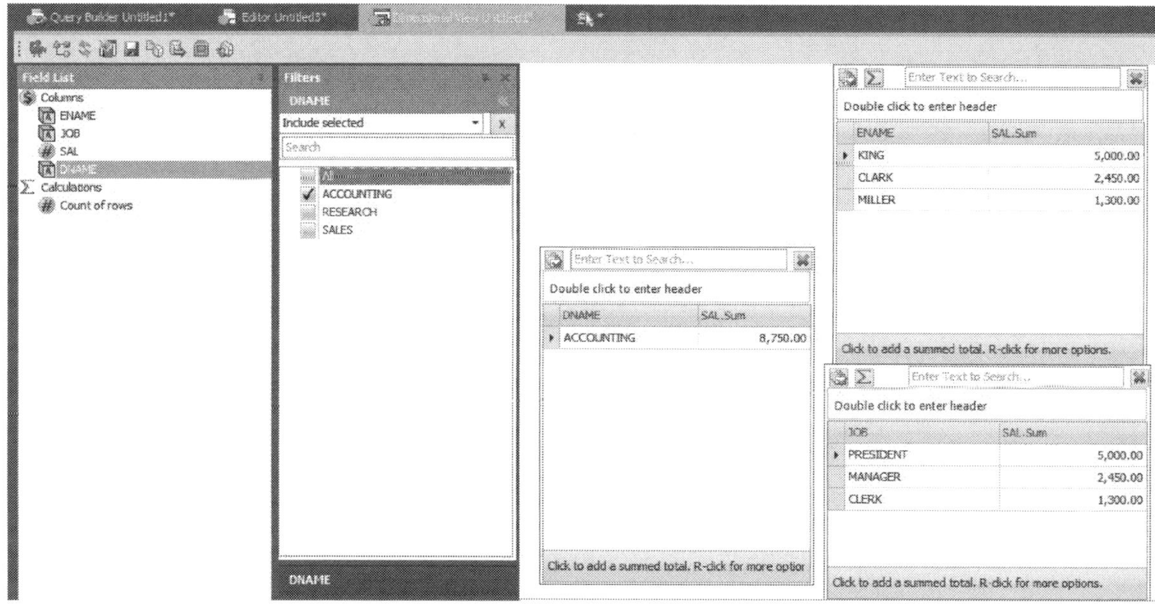

This is a true hidden gem of analytical tools! Easy to do too.

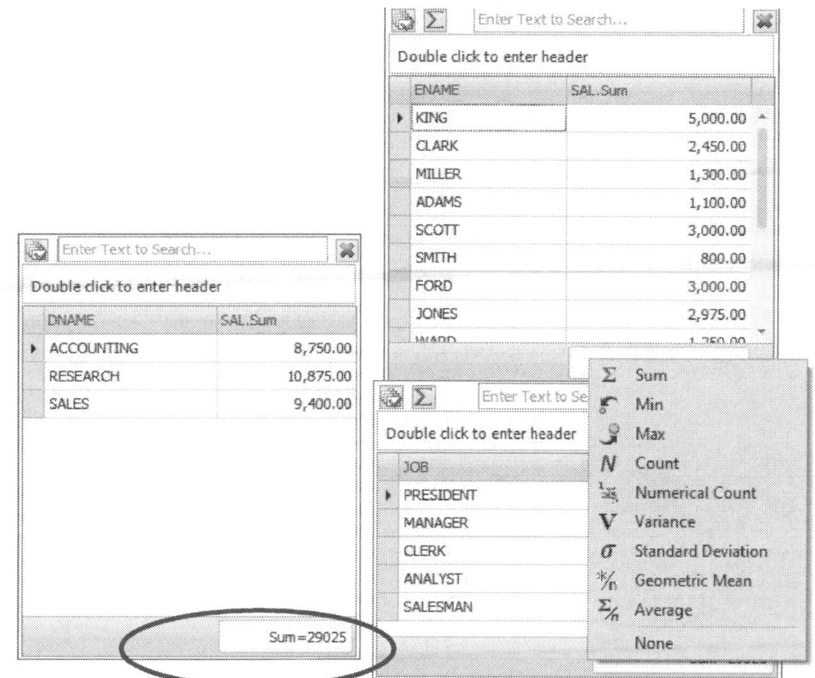

To add totals, like any other data grid, right click on the bottom of the grid under the column you wish to total and select 'Sum' in this case. Notice the totals above.

Yes…you can drag in more than one filter item…drag JOB into the filter box…and select just CLERK perhaps…

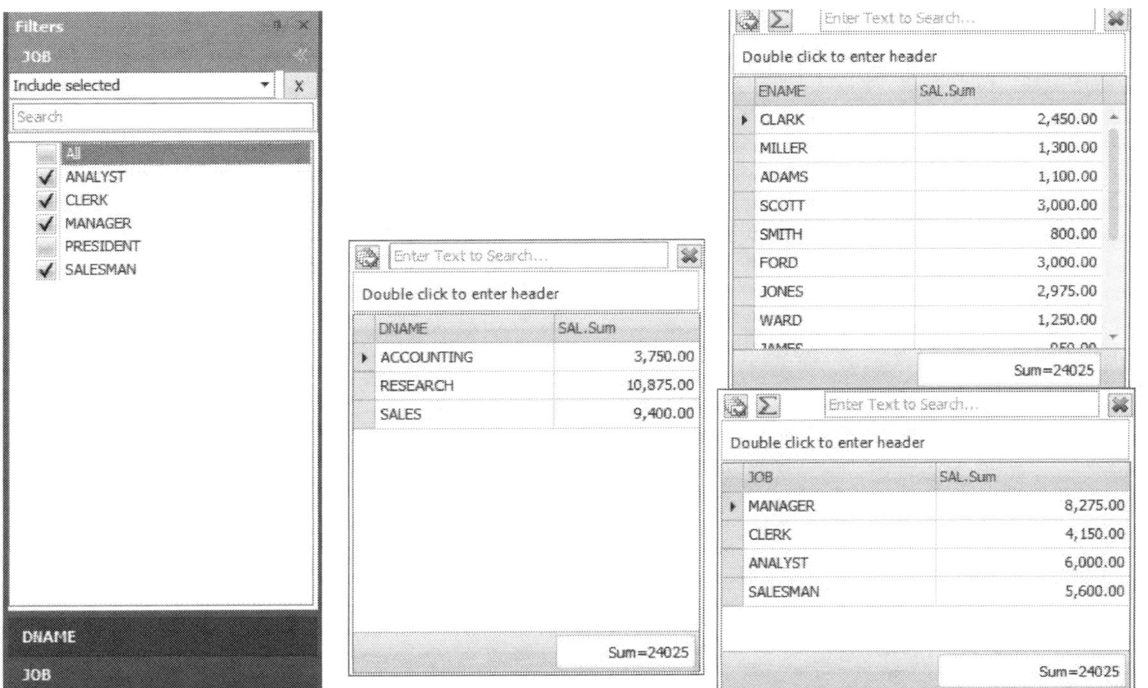
Filters
JOB
Include selected
X
Search
All
ANALYST
CLERK
MANAGER
PRESIDENT
SALESMAN
DNAME
JOB
Enter Text to Search...
Double click to enter header
DNAME SAL.Sum
ACCOUNTING 3,750.00
RESEARCH 10,875.00
SALES 9,400.00
Sum=24025
Enter Text to Search...
Double click to enter header
ENAME SAL.Sum
CLARK 2,450.00
MILLER 1,300.00
ADAMS 1,100.00
SCOTT 3,000.00
SMITH 800.00
FORD 3,000.00
JONES 2,975.00
WARD 1,250.00
Sum=24025
Enter Text to Search...
Double click to enter header
JOB SAL.Sum
MANAGER 8,275.00
CLERK 4,150.00
ANALYST 6,000.00
SALESMAN 5,600.00
Sum=24025

Now we have a nice bit of knowledge about just the everyone but the PRESIDENT.

Click the 'Export All' button on the tool bar or along the bottom Export All

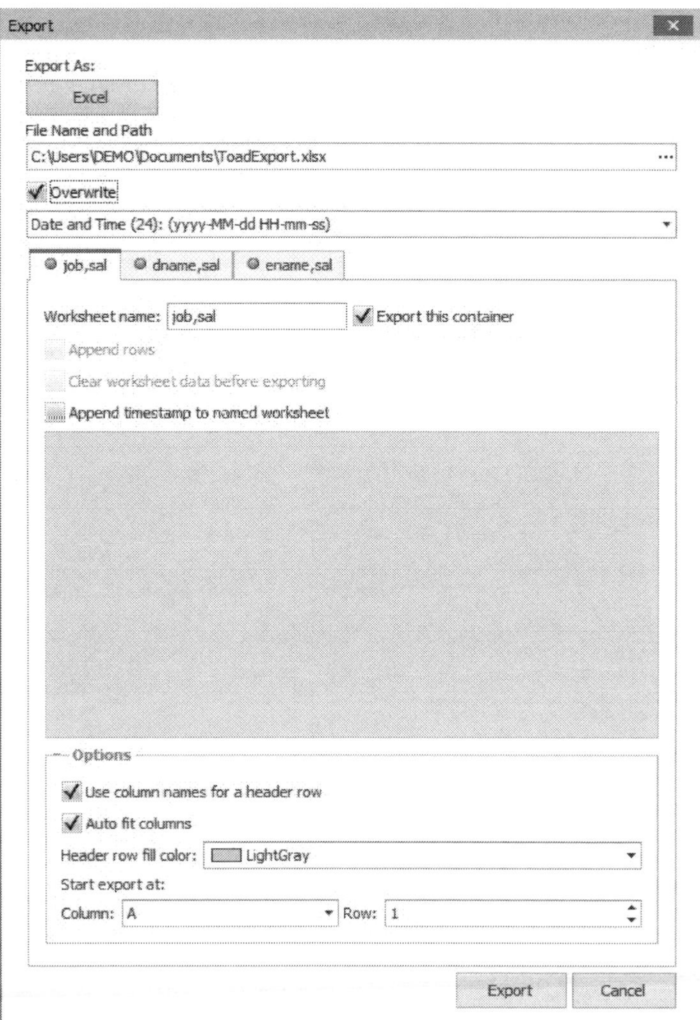


Notice that there will be a sheet made for each dimensional view…

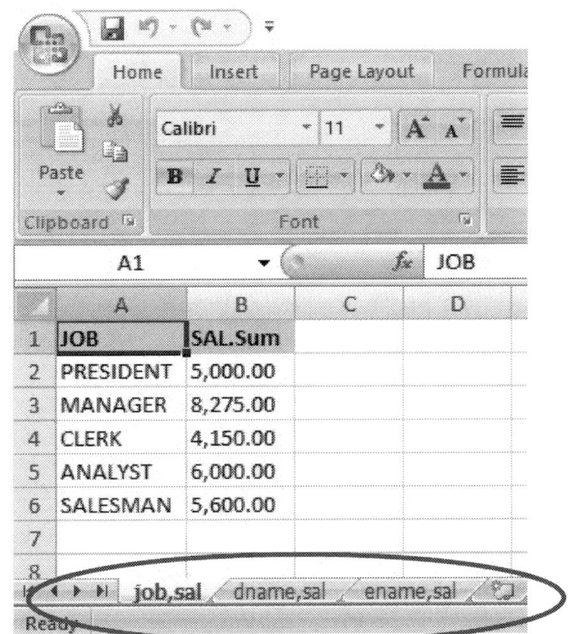

Home
Insert
Page Layout
Formula
Calibri
11
Paste
Clipboard
Font
A1
JOB
A
B
C
D
JOB
SAL.Sum
PRESIDENT
5,000.00
MANAGER
8,275.00
CLERK
4,150.00
ANALYST
6,000.00
SALESMAN
5,600.00
job,sal
dname,sal
ename,sal
Ready

# Help!

Toad DP has a robust Help facility. The contents and index can really help with about any related topic. The User Guide is another useful resource. Release Notes are always good to read, especially upon a new release of the software. All the new features will be listed in this document.

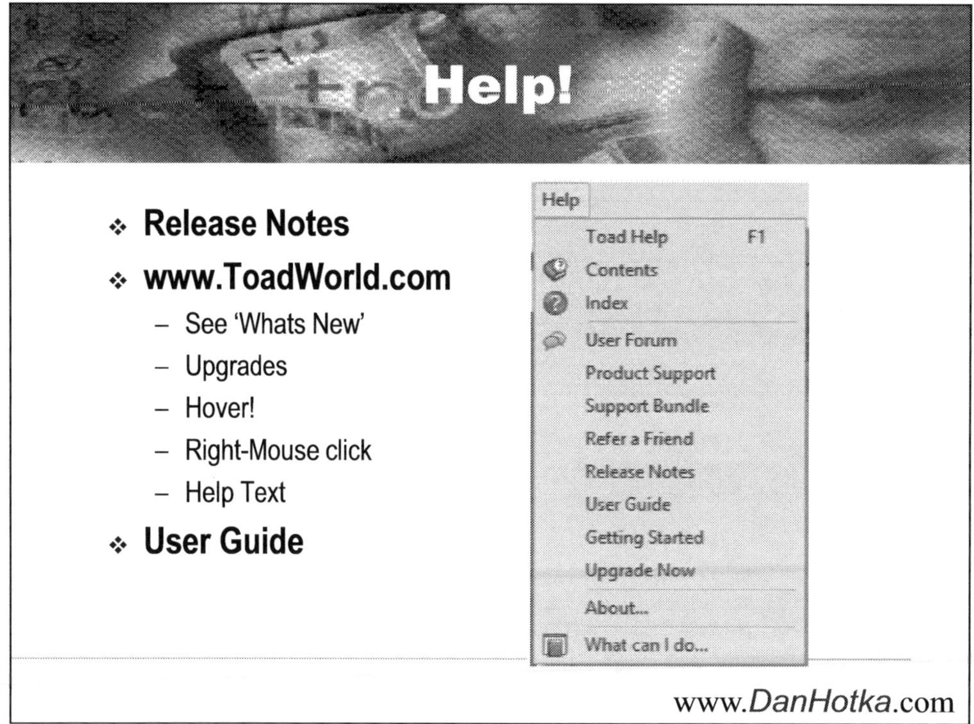


Toad DP has quite the following. You can join the User Forum where others and even the Quest development team monitor the traffic as it comes in.

Hover the mouse pointer over most anything. You can right-mouse click in most any entry area.

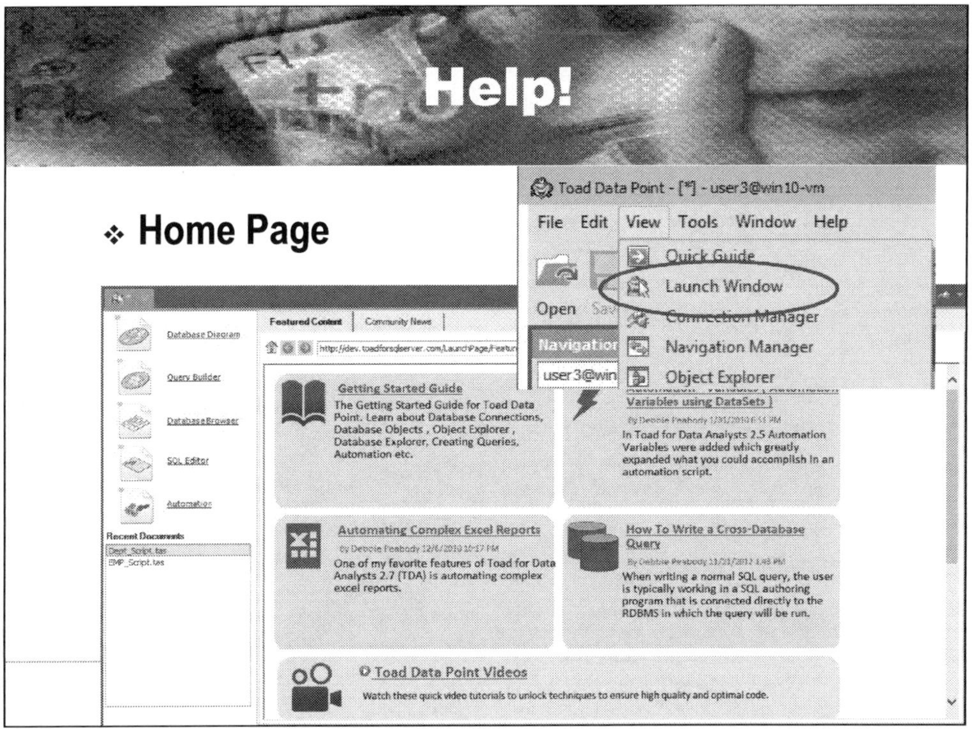
Help!
Home Page
Toad Data Point - [*] - user3@win10-vm
File Edit View Tools Window Help
Quick Guide
Launch Window
Connection Manager
Navigation Manager
Object Explorer
Open
Database Diagram
Query Builder
Database Browser
SQL Editor
Automation
Recent Documents
Featured Content
Community News
Getting Started Guide
The Getting Started Guide for Toad Data Point. Learn about Database Connections, Database Objects , Object Explorer , Database Explorer, Creating Queries, Automation etc.
Variables using DataSets )
In Toad for Data Analysts 2.5 Automation Variables were added which greatly expanded what you could accomplish in an automation script.
Automating Complex Excel Reports
One of my favorite features of Toad for Data Analysts 2.7 (TDA) is automating complex excel reports.
How To Write a Cross-Database Query
When writing a normal SQL query, the user is typically working in a SQL authoring program that is connected directly to the RDBMS in which the query will be run.
Toad Data Point Videos
Watch these quick video tutorials to unlock techniques to ensure high quality and optimal code.

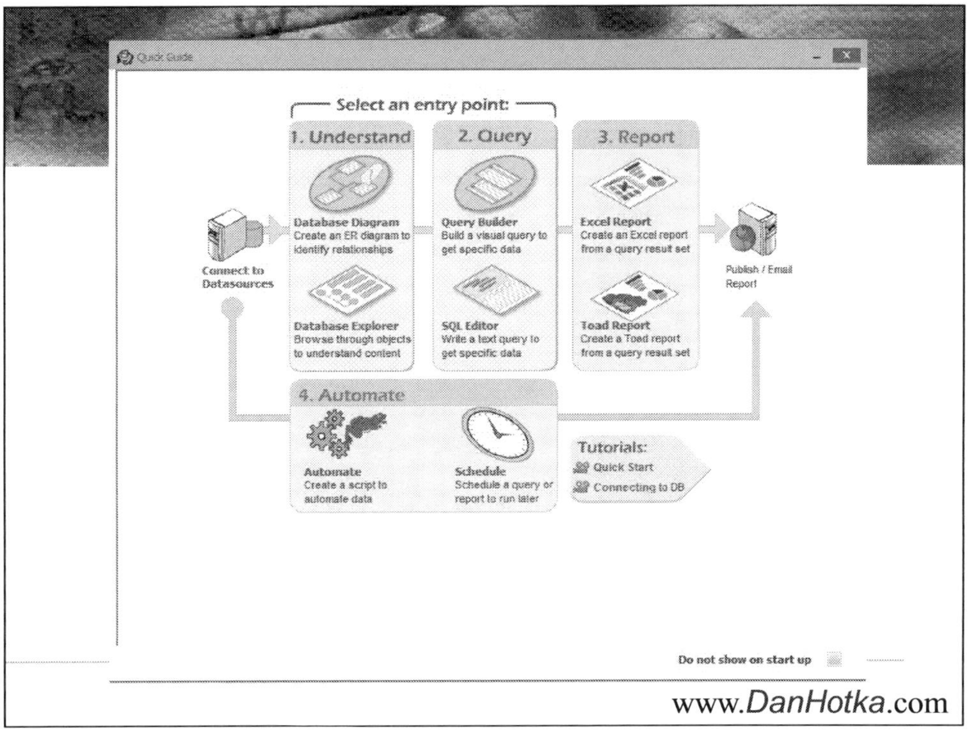
Quick Guide
Select an entry point:
1. Understand
2. Query
3. Report
Connect to Datasources
Database Diagram
Create an ER diagram to identify relationships
Database Explorer
Browse through objects to understand content
Query Builder
Build a visual query to get specific data
SQL Editor
Write a text query to get specific data
Excel Report
Create an Excel report from a query result set
Toad Report
Create a Toad report from a query result set
Publish / Email Report
4. Automate
Automate
Create a script to automate data
Schedule
Schedule a query or report to run later
Tutorials:
Quick Start
Connecting to DB
Do not show on start up
www.DanHotka.com

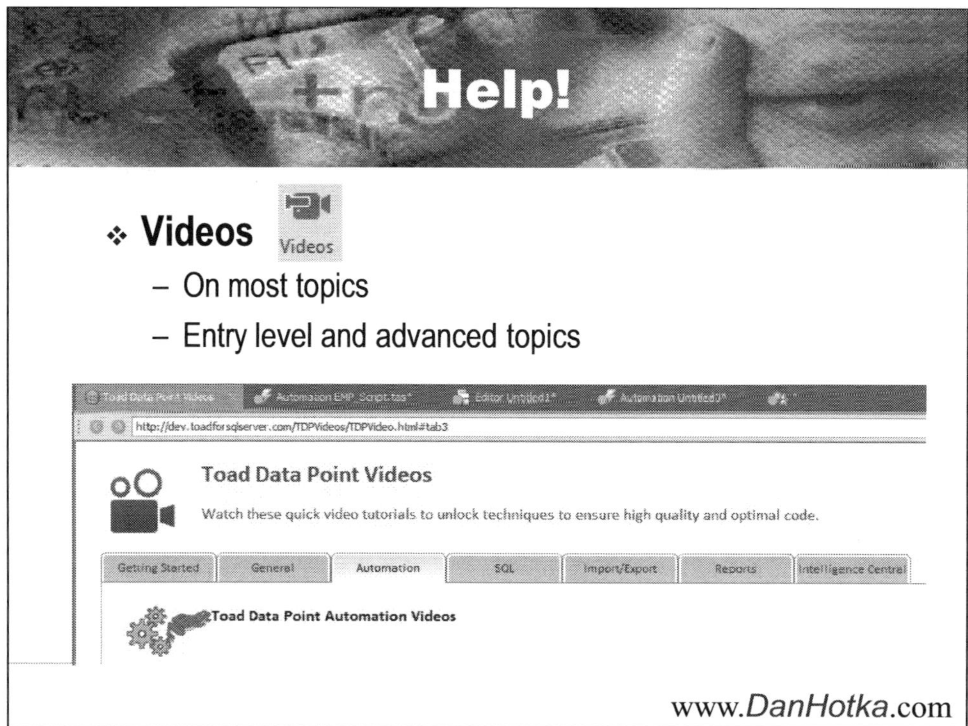
Help!
Videos
Videos
– On most topics
– Entry level and advanced topics
Toad Data Point Videos
Watch these quick video tutorials to unlock techniques to ensure high quality and optimal code.
Getting Started
General
Automation
SQL
Import/Export
Reports
Intelligence Central
Toad Data Point Automation Videos
www.DanHotka.com

## TOAD for Oracle Unleashed

Bert Scalzo and I updated this book together. It is most of the information is TOAD generic and you will find the examples of use in your day-to-day use of TOAD. This book will help you with Query Builder, SQL, templates, and short cuts.

This book is available on Amazon and discount codes are available via www.DanHotka.com .

New Book
Bert Scalzo
Dan Hotka
Toad
for Oracle
UNLEASHED
SAMS
ISBN: 978-0-13-413185-6
Great Chapter on SQL Tuning
Useful Tips for Toad DP
www.DanHotka.com

## Course Summary

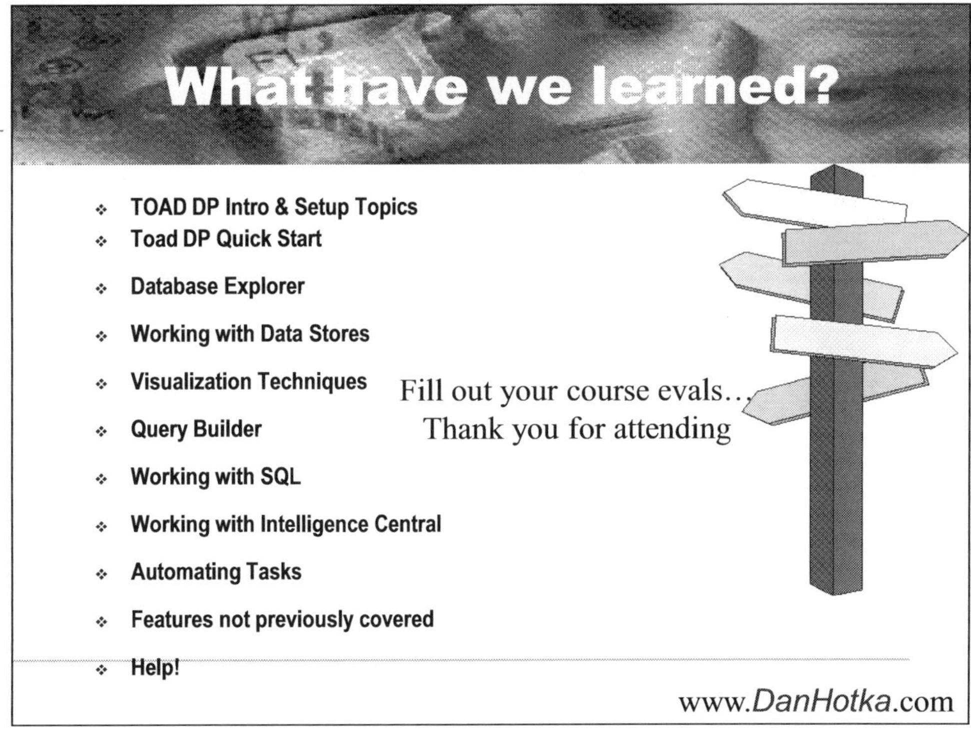
What have we learned?
TOAD DP Intro & Setup Topics
Toad DP Quick Start
Database Explorer
Working with Data Stores
Visualization Techniques
Query Builder
Working with SQL
Working with Intelligence Central
Automating Tasks
Features not previously covered
Help!
Fill out your course evals…
Thank you for attending
www.DanHotka.com

Made in the USA
Middletown, DE
17 July 2019